# MAKING SCIENTIFIC INSTRUMENTS IN THE INDUSTRIAL REVOLUTION

At the start of the Industrial Revolution, it appeared that most scientific instruments were made and sold in London, but by the time of the Great Exhibition in 1851, a number of provincial firms had the self-confidence to exhibit their products in London to an international audience. How had this change come about, and why?

This book looks at the four main, and two lesser, English centres known for instrument production outside the capital: Birmingham, Liverpool, Manchester and Sheffield, along with the older population centres in Bristol and York. Making wide use of new sources, Dr Morrison-Low, curator of history of science at the National Museums of Scotland, charts the growth of these centres and provides a characterisation of their products. New information is provided on aspects of the trade, especially marketing techniques, sources of materials, tools and customer relationships. From contemporary evidence, she argues that the principal output of the provincial trade (with some notable exceptions) must have been into the London marketplace, anonymously, and at the cheaper end of the market. She also discusses the structure and organization of the provincial trade, and looks at the impact of new technology imported from other closely-allied trades.

By virtue of its approach and subject matter the book considers aspects of economic and business history, gender and the family, the history of science and technology, material culture, and patterns of migration. It contains a myriad of stories of families and firms, of entrepreneurs and customers, and of organizations and arms of government. In bringing together this wide range of interests, Dr Morrison-Low enables us to appreciate how central the making, selling and distribution of scientific instruments was for the Industrial Revolution.

**About the Author**

**A.D. Morrison-Low** is Principal Curator in the Science Section, National Museums of Scotland, UK.

# Science, Technology and Culture, 1700–1945

Series Editors

**David M. Knight**
University of Durham

and

**Trevor Levere**
University of Toronto

*Science, Technology and Culture, 1700–1945* focuses on the social, cultural, industrial and economic contexts of science and technology from the 'scientific revolution' up to the Second world War. It explores the agricultural and industrial revolutions of the eighteenth century, the coffee-house culture of the Enlightenment, the spread of museums, botanic gardens and expositions in the nineteenth century, to the Franco-Prussian war of 1870, seen as a victory for German science. It also addresses the dependence of society on science and technology in the twentieth century.

*Science, Technology and Culture, 1700–1945* addresses issues of the interaction of science, technology and culture in the period from 1700 to 1945, at the same time as including new research within the field of the history of science.

Also in the series

# Making Scientific Instruments in the Industrial Revolution

A.D. MORRISON-LOW

ASHGATE

Published by
Ashgate Publishing Limited
Gower House
Croft Road
Aldershot
Hampshire GU11 3HR
England

Ashgate Publishing Company
Suite 420
101 Cherry Street
Burlington, VT 05401-4405
USA

Ashgate website: http://www.ashgate.com

**British Library Cataloguing in Publication Data**
Morrison-Low, A. D.
  Making Scientific Instruments in the Industrial Revolution. – (Science, Technology and Culture, 1700–1945)
  1.Scientific apparatus and instruments – England – History – 19th century. 2.Scientific apparatus and instruments – England – Design and construction – History – 19th century
  I.Title.
  681.2'0942'09034

**Library of Congress Cataloging-in-Publication Data**
Morrison-Low, A. D.
  Making Scientific Instruments in the Industrial Revolution / by A.D. Morrison-Low.
     p.    cm. – (Science, Technology and Culture, 1700–1945)
  Includes bibliographical references and index.
  1. Scientific apparatus and instruments industry – England – History. I. Title.
  HD9706.6.E62M67 2007
  338.4'768175094209034–dc22                                              2006018488

ISBN 978-0-7546-5758-3

This book is printed on acid-free paper.

Printed and bound in Great Britain by MPG Books Ltd, Bodmin, Cornwall.

# Contents

# List of Figures

# List of Graphs and Tables

## Graphs

## Tables

# Acknowledgements

This book is the result of a thesis, and that thesis took many years to put together. So many friends, colleagues, relatives have been involved, offering me help, advice, support and kindness over many years, that it seems invidious to single out individuals: so if your name is not here, it is not because your assistance has been forgotten or underrated. My thanks go again to my institution, the National Museums of Scotland, which has put collections care at the centre of its activities, and the research and scholarship of material culture at the top of its list of priorities: long may this continue to be the case. To my colleagues on the curatorial and conservation staff, the photographers and the efficient library staff, my renewed thanks. Thanks once again to my supervisors at the University of York, Jim Matthew and Ron Weir, who must have wondered whether anything at all was ever going to emerge from all that effort. Further thanks to my mentors of many years, Anita McConnell and Allen Simpson, without whom this would never have got under way, let alone been seen by an audience. Additional gratitude goes to Morag Lyall for reading the thesis with an editor's eye, and being so encouraging.

I would also like to thank the curators and librarians of all the collections that I used to put this book together. For extra advice and assistance, additional thanks go to Jim Bennett, Anthony Turner, Jonathan Barry, Gloria Clifton, Gill Cookson, Ludmilla Jordanova; also to Molly Freeman for the use of the Harriet Wynter Archive; to Alma Howarth-Loomes for the use of the Howarth-Loomes Collection; to Leslie Florence for her photography and for keeping me cheerful.

And to my family and friends, who put up with me moaning about doing something that they and I know that I actively enjoy, thank you.

# Foreword

Specialization is a curious phenomenon. I refer not to historical processes, such as the 'industrial revolution', which certainly involved, among many other phenomena, changes we might well call 'specialization'. Rather I am thinking of our own times, of the elaborate division of labour among scholars, that involve a certain narrowness of vision, which permits phrases like, 'that's not my period' or 'this is not in my field' to be bandied about. And I am thankful for notable exceptions to the rule, such as this book, which, by virtue of both its approach and subject matter, considers economic history, gender and family, the history of science and technology, material culture, business history, patterns of migration, and much more besides. It has a notably generous compass and spirit.

As the author points out, work on scientific instruments has been, and has been perceived to be a specialized domain in which practitioners all too often talk to each other, but not to those even in closely related fields. All that has been changing recently and it is this most welcome shift that allows readers to appreciate just how central the making, selling and distribution of scientific instruments has been for that most complex of historical phenomena, 'the Industrial Revolution'.

In this book a strong case is made for the integration of different types of history, for the use of a wide range of evidence, for thinking about shifts over long periods of time, for taking material culture seriously and for seeing instruments as important historical phenomena in their own right. We might say that this is an integrative form of history, one that brings apparently disparate phenomena together. I note that many historians now crave forms of research and writing that take this more satisfying, holistic form, even as other professional pressures encourage the production of more tightly focused and narrow accounts.

Many commentators have noted with concern the decline of interest in economic history among students, who seem drawn to parts of the discipline that are apparently more relevant, more fashionable, more exciting. Let us hope that it is possible to buck this trend. One possible way of doing so is to show, vividly and convincingly how the economic past is integral to all other aspects of the past, and hence is not to be lightly put aside. Writing the history of businesses that made scientific instruments, which in turn played, as Morrison-Low insists, such a central role in the development of the British empire, must involve a grasp of major economic issues, but it also demands an ability to interpret advertisements, to appreciate the instruments themselves, which were often meticulously crafted works of art, as well as all the skills of a detective.

Anyone reading this book will be struck by the myriad of stories of families and firms, of entrepreneurs and customers, of organizations and arms of government that are assembled here. Nor could they fail to appreciate the geographical spread of instrument making. It is important and enthralling to realize the roles of Bristol and Liverpool, York and Sheffield, Manchester and Birmingham, as well as of many other places, in the intricate story of instrument making. London, too, receives it due, but rightly as part of a much larger, richer picture than had hitherto been appreciated.

My hope is that this work will draw attention to the broad importance of the history of scientific instrument making and in the process generate fresh audiences not only for this field but for the instruments themselves, which can be seen and appreciated in many museums and galleries not only in Britain, but across the world. This is another kind of integration, where scholars and museum professionals, sometimes but not always the same people, enjoy closer collaborations. This particular integration should then stimulate new museum audiences, who will be able to see, quite literally, the importance of scientific instruments. To enable them to do so, much painstaking research is required in order to continue to piece together both the bigger picture and its constituent stories that are presented here. It is to be hoped that work in the style of this book is continued and disseminated in order that the historical vitality of scientific instruments is not primarily a matter for specialists but for all those who possess a passion for the past.

*Ludmilla Jordanova*
*King's College, London*

# Introduction

The Introduction is where the author justifies herself, and produces the reasons for having put this book, which grew out of a doctoral thesis, into publishable form. There are two main reasons for my having done this, the first of which perhaps has no immediate further justification. The second, I hope, is justified by the rest of this book. First, all my working life I have been surrounded by the debate: what are science museums for? Why do we collect the material culture of science? This debate has become more pressing as life and work have become more politicized, and the public sector (in which museums are placed) becomes increasingly more answerable to its multiplying political masters.

And if we are worried about why we collect scientific artefacts, why on earth do we collect any historical scientific material? For, despite history becoming increasingly popular with an ageing population, whose leisure time is spent on pastimes such as genealogy, visiting stately homes, reading history books, or watching history on television, some museums (certainly in the United Kingdom, although I must emphasize not the National Museums of Scotland) seem to be putting their history of science collections into their storerooms, and replacing historic displays with action-packed interactives. This actively undermines one of the core functions of the curator, which is to research the collections, in order to provide information, understanding and contextualization of what is already there, and to work out strategies and collecting policies for what else might be acquired.[1]

Research into surviving scientific apparatus (of whatever age) used to be the prerogative solely of curators and a few discerning collectors, but more recently the fashion in history of science has moved away from ideas, theories and philosophies towards the instrument, workshop and laboratory.[2] Never have the two disciplines, instrument history and the history of science, seemed so close. As J.A. Bennett has commented, 'We [that is, museum curators and instrument historians] must continue to demonstrate that actively managed collections of scientific hardware are essential primary sources for a full account of the past practice of science, and "managed" here means collected, researched, preserved, included in published catalogues, and used in teaching and in historically-informed displays and special exhibitions'.[3] Yet despite these oft-expressed hopes, academic historians now rarely consult collections of historic instruments, and their

---

[1]   Anderson (1993), 2.
[2]   The book that exemplifies this is the award-winning study by Shapin and Schaffer (1985).
[3]   Bennett (1993), 17.

custodians, torn between many conflicting and multiplying duties, apparently devote less time to the study and publication of the material culture in their care than did their predecessors.[4]

This brings me to my second justification. This book developed as a logical extension of earlier projects in instrument history undertaken with colleagues in the course of my work as a museum curator. It became apparent, in the course of my research into the history of Scottish and Irish instruments, that the trade in these localities was bound up closely with that of England, and in particular, during the early modern period, with that of London.[5] Nonetheless, it appeared that the powerful influence of London waned during the Industrial Revolution, and some new locations in the English provinces – in particular, four: Birmingham, Liverpool, Manchester and Sheffield – became important in providing instruments on an international scale. Why should this have been, and how did it happen? Yet there was a paradox. The survival rates of instruments with a provincial signature from this period seemed far too small to support this theory that the English provinces were manufacturing instruments on an international scale by the mid-nineteenth century. Why did the material evidence apparently contradict the written sources?

When I began this work, there was no survey covering the entire country of this once particularly successful English industry. This was partly because of the difficulty, diffusion and scarcity of source material, but also because the instrument-making workforce was never very large. This has meant that the industry had not been perceived as particularly important, either in economic or social terms. It had its beginnings in England in late Tudor times, reached an international standing during the eighteenth century, and encountered growing foreign competition from the mid-nineteenth century. In its older industrialized form – perhaps epitomized by the traditional staple of optical instruments – it declined steeply after the Second World War, although British manufacturers continued to produce instruments for the experimental, usually state-subsidized, part of the market: in vacuum science, mass spectrometry and MRI (magnetic resonance imaging), for example.[6] Today most of the instrument types covered in this book have either been technically superseded, or are manufactured largely by German or Japanese firms.

Apparently only of antiquarian interest, it would yet seem that the earlier English trade and manufacture of scientific instruments was important for the economic upheaval which historians call the Industrial Revolution. Instrument

---

4    Anderson (2005). In the early 2000s there appears to be less published than the late 1980s: see SIC website, www.sic.iuhps.org.

5    Burnett and Morrison-Low (1989); Clarke et al. (1989).

6    Much of the chronology of the British instrument industry for the twentieth century can be traced through the *Journal of Scientific Instruments*, published by the Institute of Physics from 1922–67, subsequently continued as the *Journal of Physics E: Scientific Instruments*.

making brought varied skills together into a single trade, one which produced items that assisted change in many economic activities. The trade was a small, albeit significant, section of the skilled metal trades, in which specialist craftsmen produced relatively expensive commodities, initially in the sixteenth century for the luxury end of the market. In due course, however, it was the more practical and useful items that formed the bulk of the trade's production.

For example, increasing numbers of surveying instruments were needed to expand and develop the transport system of late eighteenth century England, beginning with the canals, but extending to the road system and eventually helping to create the railway network. A large demand for navigational instruments was created by the increasing overseas trade connected with imperial expansion, and with the growth of a merchant navy to carry goods and the Royal Navy to defend them. Technological change in the making of instrumentation, such as the introduction of the dividing engine,[7] may have ensured that this growing demand was largely met. Considerable numbers of scientific instruments, across a broad spectrum, from very cheaply produced pieces to bespoke individual items, appear to have been exported, while the London shops were also able to supply a healthy home market. A closer examination of this business, using some of the methods of social and economic history, could lead to a better understanding of this specialist trade, its networks and its more general effects, and perhaps enable us to better gauge its significance. Using the recent literature of these disciplines might also provide some further clues as to how it evolved.

It had also struck me that using the emphasis of different histories could shed new light on this somewhat obscure corner of material culture. Historians of science have, since their relatively new discipline found a legitimate footing inside the universities just after the Second World War, only recently become interested in the tools of science, and what these might tell them about how that science was performed. Here we have one of those maddening problems of terminology: 'scientific instruments', as we shall discover, were really not particularly 'scientific'. Many were luxury items intended to impart cultural prestige, others were everyday tools of particular trades, which themselves at this time were undergoing radical transformation into professions. Further items could be classified as domestic: only a few, it appears, were used for what we would describe today as 'science'. It might therefore be of some use to examine how some other historical disciplines, outside instrument history itself, characterized the production and manufacture of these instruments, and both the histories and their definitions are examined later in this Introduction.[8]

Not only is there a problem with the definition of a 'scientific instrument' at the time of the Industrial Revolution, but also museums currently seem to be worried about why they collect them. The interpretation of material culture can

---

[7]   A device which marks out circular or linear scales into degrees or measured intervals: see Chapman (1995).

[8]   Fox (1993), 20–21.

provide evidence not available elsewhere to support or counter theories about historic events: a recent project in which I had been involved has done just that.[9] I became eager to see whether surviving instruments could support my theory for their significance in industrializing England, as early modern weights and measures had done for the medieval and later economy of Scotland.

It seemed important when I embarked on this project to stand back from all the recent detailed publications to try to work out if there was a 'bigger picture'. I was able to find an agenda to drive this in a work of focused criticism by the late John Millburn, which discussed an exhibition (which I had greatly admired) concerning instrument making in eighteenth-century London. This asked the questions that might provide a framework which I could work towards, and this is discussed in Chapter 1.

Chapters 2 to 5 examine such evidence as I could uncover in provincial centres in England for the period of the Industrial Revolution, grouping them by similarity of geographical location but emphasizing how more local aspects of each affected the development of their trade. Thus, I contrast the ports of Bristol and Liverpool (Chapter 2), the Yorkshire towns of York and Sheffield (Chapter 3), the very different later new population centres of Birmingham and Manchester (Chapter 4), and then examine the other locations where instrument making apparently flourished at this time (Chapter 5). These all provide some sort of external backdrop to the contemporary London trade, which is described in Chapter 6. So much effort has been concentrated on investigating the London trade by instrument historians in the past that this can only represent a summary context for the London trade. Of course, London never ceased producing instruments and instrument parts during this entire period, and indeed, became pre-eminent internationally; reasons for this will be outlined in Chapter 6.

There is evidence of instrument production in all four main new provincial centres – Birmingham, Liverpool, Manchester and Sheffield – throughout the period of the Industrial Revolution, and the size of the trade in each location will be estimated and compared with that of London, together with some identification (where possible) of the nature of provincial input to the London trade.

Not every new industrial population centre became a base for instrument making: particular conditions had to be in place before a provincial centre could flourish. Was this because the instrument trade of that time fulfilled the conditions of what economic historians have defined as a 'proto-industrial' trade? As economic historians have come to an appreciation of the slower rates of economic growth at this time, it has led to discussions about the period and conditions before industrialization, through the concept of 'proto-industrialization'. Although this term was first coined as long ago as 1972 to connect areas of rural manufacture with growing populations that could not be sustained solely by local agriculture, it has proved a useful theoretical tool, which has been able to show that there was a more evolutionary form of capital accumulation and technological change, with

---

[9]     Connor and Simpson (2004).

emphasis as much on cultural changes and labour organization as on mechanical innovation.[10]

The symbiosis of agriculture and industry across the seasons, the co-ordination of rural industries by urban merchants, and the dependence of those industries on distant markets – these have all been supported by evidence in some geographical regions, most especially in metal-working trades.[11] However, the concept of proto-industrialization is not always appropriate, for as D.C. Coleman has found, of the ten English regions which experienced it, six did not move on to experience the Industrial Revolution proper.[12] Coleman also stressed the precondition of local coal reserves as an important factor in industrialization; Pat Hudson has demonstrated that other quite unrelated factors, such as the gender division of labour and the complexity of the development of industrial capitalization – which varied in each specific instance – were crucial in the industrialization of the textile industries.[13]

Unfortunately, the model does not work for instrument manufacture in the case of Birmingham, since the trade – as a component of the metal trades based there – was so nationally and externally oriented for the marketing of its products, that it had clearly developed along lines of its own.[14] Even in the case of Sheffield, which appears superficially to have some of the characteristics of proto-industrialization – in that makers of instruments appeared to support themselves with seasonal agricultural work – its products were also sent to distant markets, and there was no accompanying population explosion. In both cases, the manufacture of instruments or their components remained within small-scale, family-run enterprises, in which aspects of production were farmed out to subcontractors.

Chapter 7 looks at the industrial organization and production of instrument making outside London: where the brass and glass came from, and how the finished goods were taken to market. The following two chapters examine the economic historian's double-sided mechanism for the rise of a consumer society: supply (Chapter 8) and demand (Chapter 9). These look at how new and existing markets were encouraged, and put some sort of definition on what these were, and how they might have affected instrument production more generally in England. Finally, Chapter 10 provides some conclusions from the overall picture sketched in the book, which may be different from what might initially have been expected, since the literary evidence and the surviving material artefacts tell somewhat contradictory stories. The remainder of this Introduction outlines the differing historiographies of instrument historians and those of related histories, noting how this divergence of disciplines presents barriers.

---

[10]  Berg et al. (1983), 1–32.
[11]  Hey (1972); Rowlands (1975); Crafts (1985); Berg (1991), 3–26; Berg (1994).
[12]  Coleman (1983).
[13]  Hudson (1992), 111–20.
[14]  Berg (1991), 173–201.

## A Survey of the History of British Instruments 1760–1850

The literature produced in the last fifty years or so concerning the instrument trade in England during the Industrial Revolution has been mostly descriptive and self-contained in its nature, and predominantly consulted within the museum profession or antique collectors' marketplace. It has been produced, in the main, by curators, working backwards from specific end products in their care. Much ground has been covered, but it has been characterized by the discovery of facts, flavoured with connoisseurship, and has lacked contact with other relevant historical disciplines, which might have helped it become more reflective and self-critical.

Until recently, issues important to instrument historians were not embraced by historians of science, whose post-war work focused on issues more closely akin to those studied by philosophers and historians of ideas. The methodology of the study of the history of scientific instruments has therefore hardly moved since the war; hence the eminent instrument historian John Millburn's dissatisfaction with it as 'altogether too complacent and uncritical'.[15] Some facts, in the form of detailed information, have been added, of which more could be made if different methodologies or interpretations were applied, especially those used by economic historians, a plea put forward specifically by the historian of science Robert Fox.[16]

The starting point for any discussion of post-war literature about the instrument trade (as opposed to the development of particular instruments over time) has to be E.G.R. Taylor's two monographs, and for this period in particular, her 1966 book, *The Mathematical Practitioners of Hanoverian England 1714–1840*, which has an excellent and under-valued introduction, followed by an alphabetical directory of short biographies of individual 'mathematical practitioners'.[17]

These biographies, often just a line or two, are given with minimal references, and unfortunately this work has been used heavily in a manner which the author had not intended. Until recently, Taylor has been over-relied upon for accuracy and veracity, especially where dating is concerned.[18] Taylor's treatment tends to trail off by the end of the eighteenth century, and her coverage of provincial makers is scanty: there are biographies of 36 Birmingham makers, 43 from Liverpool, 15 from Manchester, 27 from Sheffield and 99 from other provincial centres (220, or about 10 per cent, out of a total of 2282 numbered individual biographies). As a biographical study, Taylor chose the date 1840 as her terminal point, linked loosely with the ascent to the throne of Victoria. The depersonalization and fragmentation of the subject through changed circumstances forced her to conclude that:

---

[15]   Millburn (1986c), 84.
[16]   Fox (1993), 20–22.
[17]   Taylor (1966); the timespan of Taylor's excellent earlier monograph, Taylor (1954), rests largely outside the period of this book.
[18]   See Crawforth (1987a) for a corrective of Taylor.

as the years passed the [British] Association [for the Advancement of Science] tended to promote sectionalism, and to treat applied science as the poor relation of pure science. Such changes were fostered inevitably by the transformation of the craftsman into the factory-hand, of the instrument-maker into the retailer, of the man of science into the salaried professor. The old personal links and the identifications of inventor, maker and user were lost.[19]

One of the limitations of her biographical approach is that it precludes an elaboration of the impacts of these fundamental changes on the making and marketing of instruments.

The work of Maurice Daumas, a curator at the Conservatoire National des Arts et Métiers in Paris during the 1950s and 1960s, concerns an earlier period and emphasizes the French input, although he included a short chapter on late eighteenth-century English (meaning London) workshops. His important contribution to Charles Singer's multi-volume *Oxford History of Technology* concerns innovations in tools which enabled instrument makers to create late eighteenth-century instruments, and the subject has only recently been reassessed by Randall Brooks, John Brooks and Allan Chapman: more will be said about this in Chapter 7.[20]

G. L'E. Turner, also a museum curator, has provided two useful bibliographies on instrumentation, and these include items that examine aspects of the trade during the period of the Industrial Revolution.[21] A further bibliography compiled by Turner in conjunction with D.J. Bryden, also with a museum background, covers articles and monographs produced internationally between 1983 and 1995, capturing particularly exhibition catalogues, those most ephemeral pieces of literature which often contain new information or ideas.[22] However, the majority of the contributions are what one would expect: scholarly but often minutely focused contributions, lacking a broader perspective.

More extended business histories of a number of individual London firms have appeared during the last forty years, among them works about Benjamin Martin;[23] Troughton & Simms; R.B. Bate and Jesse Ramsden;[24] James Short;[25] and the George Adamses, senior and junior.[26] Each of these provides a different success story, or one of ultimate economic failure. Martin was a successful self-publicist: some of his advertising methods will be examined in Chapter 8. However, he died bankrupt, a probable suicide, and his business went not to his son, but to

---

19  Taylor (1966), 105.
20  Daumas (1972); Daumas (1958); Brooks (1989); Brooks (1992); Chapman (1995).
21  Turner (1969a); Turner (1983b).
22  Turner and Bryden (1997). This has now been continued with regular updates on the website of the Scientific Instrument Commission: www.iuhps.org.
23  Millburn (1976); Millburn (1986a) and Millburn (1986b).
24  McConnell (1992); McConnell (1993a); McConnell (forthcoming).
25  Bryden (1968); Turner (1969b).
26  Millburn (2000).

his rivals, W. & S. Jones. Troughton & Simms managed to align themselves with a government institution and weather a change of direction, but in the end were forced into a convenient business partnership with a provincial manufacturer, Thomas Cooke of York. James Short's business lasted until his death, when his heirs proved to be unbusinesslike failures. Bate coped by pushing his business out on a number of different fronts, and won government contracts (through family contacts) with a number of government agencies, subcontracting on a grand scale, perhaps the grandest seen to date. Yet his business did not survive his death either.

Lacking English eyewitness accounts, G. L'E. Turner has provided an overview of the eighteenth-century London trade described by suitably impressed contemporary visiting foreigners,[27] whereas Anthony Turner has provided another view, placing the London trade into its European context, showing that the local guild structure in Paris failed to enable Parisian makers to flourish on an international scale.[28] Dan Christensen has looked at the problems encountered by a Danish instrument maker who came to London at the end of the eighteenth century in order to learn the trade and transfer it to his native land, which he attempted with only limited success.[29]

G. L'E. Turner, who has published a number of monographs on instruments, in particular on the development of the microscope, produced his *Nineteenth Century Scientific Instruments* in 1983. This surveyed a century of instrument development and is very much an artefact-based study, with some new contributions made to the area under discussion.[30] For instance, he drew out new areas of instrumentation that developed during the nineteenth century, in the fields of electricity, acoustics, photography and telegraphy. Turner considered that the Great Exhibition of 1851 was 'an international occasion [that] was the peak of the Industrial Revolution, the triumph of steam-power technology and machine-tool engineering', and extracted the names of all instrument makers who had exhibited there.[31] Turner highlighted material hitherto considered 'too modern' as being worthy of consideration by instrument historians, and generally led the way to an awareness of a period which had been neglected.

More recently, Anita McConnell has studied some of the main late eighteenth-century London makers' problems in meeting market demands, and the resulting effects this had on the size of their premises. It appears to have implied a decision to specialize either as retail suppliers of small off-the-peg instruments, or as precision engineers of large bespoke items. This resulted in the latter moving to larger premises; however, none moved out of London at this time.[32]

---

27   Turner (1979a).
28   Turner (1987), especially chapter 5; Turner (1989) and (1998).
29   Christensen (1993).
30   Turner (1983a).
31   Ibid., 24, 309–10.
32   McConnell (1994b).

Guild structure, always stronger in London than in the English provinces, has been closely scrutinized. Originally the means by which a craft ensured its skills was protected from infringements by outsiders of any sort, in London it became a feature of trade succession, in which skills were passed down through a codified series of rituals: indenture, apprenticeship, and freedom. More will be said about the transfer of skills in Chapter 7. The trade of mathematical instrument making developed too late to have a guild formed around it, and instead its practitioners emerged from or were obliged to join other guilds.

Instrument historians realized during the 1970s that instrument makers had not only joined the most likely guilds, such as the Clockmakers' or Spectaclemakers', but all other guilds, including such unlikely companies as the Broderers' (embroiderers) and the Joiners'. Joyce Brown has examined the Grocers' and the Clockmakers' Companies; Allen Simpson has described an important craft succession in the Turners' guild; Michael Crawforth of Project SIMON has published with particular reference to the Broderers' and Joiners' guilds, while Gloria Clifton, continuing with Project SIMON, has produced an essay about the Spectaclemakers' Company.[33] Clifton's completed work on the British trade between 1550 and 1851, published in 1995, attempts to provide some correctives to Taylor's earlier work, has comprehensively mined London guild sources, and is strongest on the London instrument trade.[34]

By the early nineteenth century, the power of the London guilds was terminally on the wane; and no guild structure appears to have encompassed instrument making in the provinces, apparently because most English centres were located in areas where the population grew for the first time during the Industrial Revolution, rather than in established medieval centres where guilds were already present. There were, however, formal apprenticeship systems in place in Bristol and York at this time, whose records give some idea of trade succession and continuity in those cities.

Very little instrument history had been produced specifically on the nineteenth-century trade, nationally or internationally, until a symposium held in Amsterdam in 1984. The papers included a number that looked at aspects of the London trade: R.G.W. Anderson discussed the problems; J.A. Bennett looked at institutional change, its effects on the makers and their corresponding change in status; Willem Hackmann examined the trade in natural philosophy instruments.[35]

Anderson, indeed, took issue with Taylor's work by asking 'What, then, led to change in the 19th century?'[36] Qualifying his remarks by saying that a definitive answer was currently unavailable due to a lack of underpinning research, he suggested that Taylor's characterization of depersonalisation of production was correct, and that it was owing to the concomitant massive and comprehensive

---

[33] Brown (1978); Brown (1979); Simpson (1985); Crawforth (1987b); Clifton (1993a).
[34] Clifton (1995).
[35] Anderson (1985); Bennett (1985) and Hackmann (1985).
[36] Anderson (1985), 2.

reorganization of science during the nineteenth century. Anderson suggested that the nature of this scientific reorganization 'might be crudely categorized under six headings: education, research, scientific institutions and societies, industrialisation, colonial expansion and public health,' but there has been little response to his agenda.

Subsequent work on the nineteenth-century trade has focused on the business history-type studies mentioned above, with similar publications for Scotland and Ireland, and a single discursive look at the role of women within the trade.[37] Indeed, more substantive work has been carried out on the later nineteenth-century trade, for instance by Mari Williams and Ilaria Meliconi.[38] There have also been a number of short articles about individual firms, which add factual details to the overall picture of London's nineteenth-century trade, amongst them pieces about the Elliotts, Newtons, Bardins, Janet Taylor and W. & S. Jones.[39] These have outlined the dates, addresses, types of output (although not volumes, for which there appears to be no source, reliable or otherwise) of these firms, and demonstrated that they remained family businesses throughout this period.

Three theses have added to our understanding of the London trade at this period.[40] Brian Gee looked at the contribution to scientific development by a particular group of instrument makers, centred on electrical/magnetic science and its instrumentation for the years between 1820 and 1850. Alice Walters examined the links between the book trade and instrument making at the end of the eighteenth century, and William Ginn focused on the relationships of a number of individual scientific customers with their chosen specialist suppliers.[41]

On the marketing side, which will be discussed in Chapter 8, there has been interest in the ephemera that were associated with the retailing of instruments. A wealthy collector, Ambrose Heal, produced a pioneering general work on tradesmen's cards in 1925, followed only in 1971 by the London Science Museum, which published an illustrated catalogue of their instrument makers' trade card collection.[42] Heal described a trade card as follows:

> the engraving giving the Trader's name, his sign and his address, and the setting forth of the list of his wares occupies the whole of the face of the Bill, except for the well-proportioned margins which are an integral part of the design of all carefully planned pages. This announcement, then, of his shop is the first and principal use of the Tradesman's Card, and much skill has gone into the making of it.[43]

---

[37]   Clarke et al. (1989); Burnett and Morrison-Low (1989); Morrison-Low (1990).

[38]   Williams (1994); Cattermole and Wolfe (1987); Meliconi (2000).

[39]   Clifton (1993b); Bristow (1993); Holland (1993); Gee (1992) and (1993); Millburn (1992d); Millburn and Rossaak (1993); Alger (1982); Simpson (1993); de Clercq (2005a).

[40]   Gee (1989); Walters (1992); Ginn (1993).

[41]   Ibid.

[42]   Heal (1925); Calvert (1971).

[43]   Heal (1925), 2.

Perhaps the most thoughtful discussion of trade cards, and how they can be used to reveal information about the trade, is to be found in Michael Crawforth's work on the subject.[44] Outside the period under discussion, D.J. Bryden has written several papers that look at advertising at an earlier date, linking booksellers and printers closely to instrument production and distribution.[45] Trade catalogues, or lists of retailed items with their prices, appear to have evolved during the late seventeenth century, and there have been a number of discussions about these, but only one work devoted exclusively to the instrument trade.[46] However, this latter has done little more than try to locate copies these ephemeral items internationally, and some interesting work could yet be done with the material assembled there, such as price statistics, availability of particular instruments over time, or change within the repertoire of a single workshop, as has been undertaken by Peter de Clercq for the Dutch firm, Musschenbroek, between 1694 and 1748.[47] New technology has allowed a number of web-sites to give access to collections of trade literature, and perhaps this will allow consultations to go beyond mere identification of items to the abstraction of characteristics of a changing trade.[48]

Finally, let us turn to the literature covering the English provincial trade during this period. One of the main reasons for producing this book was that no framework or synthesis of the subject has been provided by instrument historians, and very little has been produced in the way of business histories of individual firms or personalities beyond the slight biographies by Taylor, and the necessarily factual information given by Clifton.[49]

Some work, however, has been carried out on the Manchester trade, particularly by Jenny Wetton, a curator at the Museum of Science and Industry in Manchester.[50] She has also written about Manchester's most prominent nineteenth-century maker, John Benjamin Dancer, as have others.[51] The Liverpool trade was outlined by Paul Dearden for a visit of the Scientific Instrument Society, and briefly summarized by Ron Bristow.[52] Another paper by Terry Bryant has sketched possible connections between the trade in Bristol and Birmingham,

---

[44]  Crawforth (1985).

[45]  Bryden (1992) and (1993), and a series on 'Early Printed Ephemera' in the *Bulletin of the Scientific Instrument Society*.

[46]  Jones and Taylor (1984); Davis and Dreyfuss (1986); Crom (1989); Anderson et al. (1990).

[47]  De Clercq (1997), 65–72.

[48]  For instance the web-site at the Smithsonian Institution Library, Washington DC at www.sil.si.edu/DigitalCollections/Trade-Literature/Scientific-Instruments/. The Scientific Instrument Commission provides a link page to a number of such web-sites at www.sic.iuhps.org/refertxt/catalogs.htm.

[49]  Taylor (1966); Clifton (1995).

[50]  Wetton (1990–91); (1994) and (1996).

[51]  Wetton (1991); Hallett (1979); Hallett (1986); Nuttall (1980); Butler (1987); Logan (1989); Luther (1992); Bracegirdle and McCormick (1993).

[52]  Bristow (1992).

and a further publication by him examined the possible Irish origins of a Bristol maker.[53] In 1984 D.J. Bryden, in a short paper entitled 'Provincial Scientific Instrument Making', proposed that:

> ... by the nineteenth century, whilst London retained its technical supremacy, provincial centres like Birmingham and Sheffield were responsible for the mass production of many common instruments – Birmingham part-making folding rules to be finished in London, Sheffield cheap optical instruments for retail in London and elsewhere.[54]

At the time this was written, there was almost no supporting evidence for such a view, based as it was on inference from provincial production at a later period.[55] However, the present study has helped to substantiate it directly, as has an earlier paper discussing Sheffield instrument making.[56] Yet there remains much to be uncovered about the provincial trade: if and how its character altered between localities, the extent to which its nature was changed at all by industrialization, and how it related over time to the London trade.

## The Industrial Revolution and Instrument Production

The Industrial Revolution appears to be something of a battleground amongst economic historians, in which the estimates for economic growth assembled in 1967 by P. Deane and W.A. Cole have been revised, in particular by N.F.R. Crafts.[57] This has produced a less 'revolutionary' model of the period, in which slower rates of growth than had previously been estimated are put forward for the late eighteenth and early nineteenth centuries, the classic period of the Industrial Revolution. Crafts's somewhat pessimistic picture has been countered by a number of writers, notably Julian Hoppit, Maxine Berg and Pat Hudson, and further newly-calculated rates have been put forward by R.V. Jackson.[58] David Cannadine has suggested that the Industrial Revolution is seen by various generations of economic historians in the light of their own experience, but Berg has retorted that there is a missing dimension which Cannadine has overlooked: the component of the 'hidden' workforce, in the form of unrecorded women and children.[59] Certainly, the women and children who must have worked in family-based enterprises like those in the instrument trade have gone virtually unnoticed.

How have economic historians seen the instrument trade, and what significance has it had, for them, as a factor for change in the Industrial Revolution? As I have

---

[53]  Bryant (1994); Bryant (1999).
[54]  Bryden (1984).
[55]  J. Rabone, 'Measuring Rules', in Timmins (1866), 628–32; Hallam (1984).
[56]  Morrison-Low (1994b).
[57]  Deane and Cole (1967); Crafts (1985).
[58]  Hoppit (1990); Berg and Hudson (1992); Jackson (1992).
[59]  Cannadine (1984); Berg (1993).

adopted J.R. Millburn's agenda as my *modus operandi* for this book (as we shall see in Chapter 1), I should also examine the publication that prompted his critique. The essay written by Roy Porter for the book to accompany the 1985 exhibition 'Science and Profit in 18th-Century London' was entitled 'The Economic Context', and it offers some explanations for the growth in the London instrument trade at the end of the eighteenth century.[60] In it, he credits as authorities, for his contention that 'no-one ... doubted that high craft skills were indissolubly linked with economic transformation', the economic historians Peter Mathias and T.S. Ashton.[61] These skills, brought in at an earlier date by foreigners, were by the mid-eighteenth century to be found indigenously: Porter quotes David Landes's example of the English invention of jewelled bearings for timepieces, and goes on to remark upon the contemporary awareness of the importance of good design to industry.[62] He notes that in England, unlike in her European neighbours, the trade flourished 'in economic opportunity, in market openings'.[63]

The patenting of mechanical improvements appears to have been of minor importance at this date, writes Porter (quoting H.I. Dutton), and 'foreigners were staggered by the strength of consumer demand'.[64] Much of Porter's argument is the one of the 'consumer revolution' of Neil McKendrick, John Brewer and J.H. Plumb, and he draws upon their thesis to support his claim for mid-market growth. Porter stresses that this was a London-centred phenomenon, for after 'a through training in basic skills ... almost all [instrument makers] gravitated to London, for only there did a specialist market exist'.[65] Also, there was no guild of instrument makers that might have stifled individualism, although as we have seen there was a guild structure that had operated in the City of London since medieval times. Trading as a freeman within the City required membership of a guild, and hence many settled outside the City in Westminster.

However, Porter admits that prices were high, and makers feared having too much capital tied up in a large precision piece; those makers who found institutional or government contracts were fortunate. He rounds off his essay with a thumbnail sketch of the career of the London retailer Benjamin Martin (1704–82), characterizing him as a 'dealer ... [who] grasped the importance of catalogue selling'.[66] He mentions Martin's large, but relatively cheap ready-made stock, tempting the impulse buyer, and his promotion of wares through books and lectures. Porter does not mention that Martin died a bankrupt – as Millburn (author of several monographs on Martin) does in his essay review of

---

[60]  Porter et al. (1985), 1–4.
[61]  Ibid., 1, quoting Ashton (1968) and Mathias (1983).
[62]  Ibid. 2, quoting Landes (1983).
[63]  Ibid.
[64]  Ibid., 3, quoting Dutton (1984).
[65]  Ibid., 3, quoting McKendrick (1982).
[66]  Ibid., 4.

this publication – but does suggest that 'in an increasingly competitive market, business enterprise became no less vital than technical skill'.[67]

This is instrument making seen as helping to create its own demand: nurturing a new middle-class market, which grew as increasingly wealthy customers, dazzled by entertaining displays presented as education, or desiring to emulate their betters, provoked increasing public demand. Porter's answer to the economic question of why there was considerable and successful expansion of London instrument trade during the Industrial Revolution is 'consumption'. However, his four pages scarcely allow him to address some of the more intricate problems, for which he and his co-authors were taken to task by Millburn.[68] The rise of consumption is clearly part of the economic equation, but not all of it, as we shall see in Chapters 8 and 9. A recent general survey of the history of technology by Donald Cardwell mentions in its introduction that encyclopaedic studies on the subject, such as the seven volumes of the *Oxford History of Technology,* consisted of many contributions by subject specialists, and thus miss the importance of links between technologies:

> Habbakuk, Landes, Musson, Robinson, Rosenberg and other economic historians have made penetrating studies of the circumstances that have favoured particular innovations and the economic and social consequences of those innovations. Usually, and understandably, economic historians have been rather less interested in the technology than in the economic and social factors associated with it.[69]

He goes on to point out the huge rift between historians of science and historians of technology, and the failures of continuing line of studies which 'tend to inflict division rather than encourage unification, with the added disincentive that those who elect to study history may well have deliberately rejected science, and vice versa'.[70] What hope is there of any reasonable synthesis, with such disparate historiographies?

Cardwell's *History of Technology* tries to comprehend elements of both economic history and history of science, and concludes that for the Industrial Revolution

> textiles and steam engines combined to stimulate new technologies. One of the most important of these was the design and manufacture of machine tools, or machines to make machines ... 'Mathematical instruments', such as telescopes and sextants, were commonly of brass, a soft metal, and were made in large numbers by the skilled instrument makers of the eighteenth century using small lathes, screw-cutting lathes and drills ... But the industrial machine tool working on hard iron or steel was very much a product of the demands of the textile and the steam engine industries.[71]

---

[67]  Millburn (1986c), 85; Porter et al. (1985), 4.
[68]  Millburn (1986c), 84.
[69]  Cardwell (1994), 5.
[70]  Ibid., 7.
[71]  Ibid. (1994), 216.

For Cardwell, as an historian of technology, the instrument trade's importance in these years was its role in the creation of machine tools that were later transferred and applied to engineering.

Economic historians, as opposed to historians of science, such as Porter, or of technology, such as Cardwell, have looked at other causes and effects of the Industrial Revolution, and the instrument trade scarcely figures in their accounts. However, to examine the specific role of instrumentation, I would like to look at those economic histories that stress technological change as a means of industrial development I shall look in particular at the work of T.S. Ashton, D.S. Landes, Peter Mathias, Joel Mokyr, Nathan Rosenberg and Maxine Berg.

T.S. Ashton's contribution to the historiography of the Industrial Revolution is of primary importance, validated by the fact that his succinct classic essay *The Industrial Revolution* has been in print since it was first published in 1948. In it he shows how in the late eighteenth century, the composition of the membership of the Royal Society – including as it did instrument-makers – demonstrated how closely allied were theoretical science and its practice at this time.[72] In the provinces:

> ... the [nonconformist] academies ... at Bristol, Manchester, Northampton, Daventry, Warrington and elsewhere – did for England in the eighteenth century something of what the universities did for Scotland. ... they were nurseries of scientific thought. Several of them were well-equipped with 'philosophical instruments' and offered facilities for experiment: their teachers included men of the quality of Joseph Priestley and John Dalton ...[73]

Ashton, as did so many historians of his generation and the next, brings in the complex and heroic figure of James Watt (1736–1819), 'mathematical instrument-maker' at Glasgow University, whose scientific conversations with the great chemist Joseph Black (1728–99) enabled him to understand how to repair the university's steam-engine model and make it more efficient, thus leading to the road south to Birmingham, and the wealth that lay in successfully synthesizing the works of others and bringing together 'the varied skills required for the creation of a complex mechanism'.[74] Indeed, Ashton goes on to trace the origins of the engineering industry, and shows that the ancestry of the modern fitter can be found in elements of the repairing millwright, 'clock-makers, instrument-makers, ironfounders and cotton spinners, who, during the industrial revolution, turned

---

[72]  Ashton (1968), 13.

[73]  Ibid., 15.

[74]  Ibid., 55–8. Recent work, especially by Macleod (1998), on the personality of James Watt, has concluded that his importance has been over-emphasized in the past, through a careful selection of manuscript evidence engineered by his heirs; nonetheless he remains a significant figure, whose apprenticeship in instrument making lay with the London trade.

from using to making the appliances of their trades'.[75] For Ashton, the skills of the instrument trade provided part of a pool of skill which was available for new techniques, although he admits that the bottleneck, particularly in engineering, was the time spent training even skilled hands.[76]

No less a classic is David S. Landes's *The Unbound Prometheus*. This, too, has remained in print since its first publication in 1969. Despite Landes's emphasis on technological change, instrumentation does not figure in his work at all. He does discuss the crucial importance of machine tools, but stresses the anonymity of the authors of small incremental improvements, and shows that interchangeability of parts took longer to arrive than might be thought: 'Every screw had its individual thread'.[77] For Landes, technological change was an integral part of the economic background and England was especially ripe for technological change, thanks to cultural institutions which allowed the development of an individualistic, and ultimately, capitalist, society.[78]

In later essays, Landes's interest in the 'nuts and bolts' aspect of history, in particular the hair springs and escapements of the horologist, becomes more evident, particularly in his *Revolution in Time*, first published in 1983. In the preface to this, he explains how an economic historian was seduced by material culture: 'I was smitten – caught by the combination of mechanical ingenuity, craftsmanship, artistry, and elegance'.[79] The whole book, which proposes the thesis set out in the subtitle – *Clocks and the Making of the Modern World* – discusses the evolution of an industry which lent much of its technology and organizational change to the instrument trade. Instruments themselves, however, are mentioned only once, in connection with the Portuguese voyages of discovery in the fifteenth and sixteenth centuries, followed by the scientific revolution of the seventeenth century, which 'was linked closely to the availability of new instruments – telescope, microscope, thermometer, barometer, pendulum – that made possible observations finer than any before and posed issues never suspected'.[80]

In 1993, Landes revisited the territory of *The Unbound Prometheus* with an incisive review of the preceding and intervening historiographies, especially those concerning rates of change: 'in the Industrial Revolution debate, as in most ... others, both sides are right: History, of its nature is a constant interplay of continuity and change'.[81] He sees the change as 'essentially technology – the way of doing and making things – with substantial and ramifying effects on productivity,

---

[75]   Ibid., 71.
[76]   Ibid., 96.
[77]   Landes (1969), 105–7, quote 107.
[78]   Ibid.
[79]   Landes (1983), xiii.
[80]   Ibid., 160.
[81]   Landes (1993), 153.

prices, and size of market'.[82] His most recent 'magisterial work' is a discussion of the causes of wealth through examples of world history, where his thesis is that 'human action and human organization seem to be more likely explanations of wealth and poverty than any other variables'.[83] Among the technological changes in the Industrial Revolution in Britain: steam-power, waterpower, improvements in iron-smelting, the introduction of powered machinery (particularly in textiles), Landes stresses that in metallurgy:

> most important was the growing recourse to precision gauging and fixed settings. Here the clock and watchmakers and instrument makers gave the lead. They were working smaller pieces and could more easily shape them to the high standards required for accuracy with special-purpose tools such as wheel dividers and tooth-cutters. These devices in turn, along with similar tools devised by machinists, could then be adapted to work in larger format ... [suggesting] in turn the first experiments in mass production based on interchangeable parts (clocks, guns, gun carriages, pulley blocks, locks, hardware, furniture).[84]

At the same date as the publication of Landes's *The Unbound Prometheus*, in 1969, Peter Mathias had voiced similar opinions in the first edition of his *The First Industrial Nation*, characterizing the precision instrument trade as 'partly the world of the Royal Society; partly that of the Admiralty; partly that of the luxury market for watches and performing dolls'.[85] In relation to technological innovation, Mathias found the high standards of mechanical precision, the complicated division of labour, and the production of specialist tools problematic, in that they had all pre-dated the Industrial Revolution. His answer to the problem of this 'time lag' – their delayed adoption by the textile-machinery builders – is that instrument making was small-scale, at the luxury end of the market, did not use mass production of parts by automatic machinery, and relied for the most part upon human muscle power and was thus extremely expensive, with low productivity per head.

Brass was unsuitable for textile machinery, which was large scale, required a massive power source and the skills of the blacksmith, miller and carpenter welded to the accuracy of the precision instrument maker. 'But this did not begin to take place', Mathias states, 'until the development of momentum in strategic industries, such as iron and textiles, created the inducements for businessmen to demand these skills in producing iron machinery and new forms of power'.[86] His subsequent mention of the trade is in 1900, by which time it was clear that the

---

[82]   Ibid., 157.
[83]   Oliver Letwin, review of Landes (1998), in *The Times Literary Supplement*, 14 August 1998.
[84]   Landes (1998), 191.
[85]   Mathias (1983), 126.
[86]   Ibid., 127.

British instrument industry had lost all hope of a European lead to the Germans.[87] For Mathias, the scientific instrument trade was not of front-rank significance for the course of the Industrial Revolution.

However, Mathias's interest in the relationships between science and technology during the eighteenth century resulted in his writing a number of essays on this theme. In one, first published in 1972, entitled 'Who Unbound Prometheus?' he discusses the linkages between the two:

> The state actively sought to press scientists into utilitarian endeavour. A long list of instances can be drawn up. Typical examples are ballistics and navigation (improvements in cartography, scientific instruments, astronomy, mathematical tables, accurate time-keeping lay behind this). ... Standardization in production, in dockyards, of interchangeable parts, exact measurement techniques, were much encouraged. Industrial and scientific skills likely to be useful in war received particular attention.[88]

He points out that 'state patronage' after the Stuart Restoration meant the Royal Society. Although this body had virtually no resources, in fact it proved a fertile breeding ground for innovation. And he makes the point that innovation moved 'to the many provincial societies linking amateur scientists with gentlemen-manufacturers', in, for instance, the Lunar Society of Birmingham, and others.[89] These links between English amateur science and its practice in industry, which were emphasized by the historians of science A.E. Musson and Eric Robinson in the 1960s, are acknowledged by Mathias to be unique in Europe at this time. However, he also states that:

> mathematics may well have played a wider role in these relationships than science until the end of the eighteenth century. Navigation techniques and improvements at sea (not only sponsored by the navy), land surveying techniques for estates, accountancy for business, assaying, architectural drawing, spectacle making are examples of practical skills that gained and were seen to gain, from mathematical knowledge. ... The utility of such mathematical expertise, coupled with precision measurement by new instruments, for a trading, industrial, sea-faring nation was sufficient for it to become institutionalized on a fairly wide scale in eighteenth-century England.[90]

Joel Mokyr's 1990 work, subtitled *Technological Creativity and Economic Progress*, has four indexed references to 'instruments and instrument making', which is unusual in an economic history.[91] His first mention of these, in a Renaissance context, makes the claim that:

---

87   Ibid., 383.
88   Mathias (1979), 50–51.
89   Ibid., 52; for the Lunar Society see Schofield (1963); Uglow (2002); for other societies, see Averley (1989).
90   Mathias (1979), 52–3; Musson and Robinson (1969).
91   Mokyr (1990), 338.

instrument making in the sixteenth and seventeenth centuries was an art, not a standardized technique ... the Industrial Revolution became possible when mechanics and machine tools could translate ideas and blueprints into accurate and reliable prototypes. Until then, instruments and tools were handmade, expensive to make and repair, and limited in their uses.[92]

Although mass-production, or the 'so-called American system of manufacturing assembled complex products from mass-produced individual components' took place in the instrument industry towards the end of the nineteenth century, Mokyr, like Landes, demonstrates that the idea had occurred to Europeans in the eighteenth century, and was in some instances realized. He temporizes this by observing that 'although in the long run, interchangeability of parts was inexorable, its diffusion in Europe was slowed down by two factors: its inability to produce distinctive high-quality goods, which long kept consumers faithful to skilled artisans, and the resistance of labor, which realized that mass-production would make its skills obsolete'.[93]

In an investigation into the factors responsible for technological creativity, Mokyr demonstrates that many of the micro-inventions developed during the Industrial Revolution in Britain were inspired by original inventions from the Continent. Despite a lack of formal education, 'as long as technological advances did not require a fundamental understanding of the laws of physics or chemistry on which they were based and as long as advances could be achieved by brilliant but intuitive tinkerers and persistent experimenters, Britain's ability to create or adapt new production technologies was supreme'.[94]

The causes of technological change have concerned the economist-turned-historian Nathan Rosenberg. In one essay, after remarking on the frequency of individual mechanics taking their 'know-how' (or skills) with them, he examines the transfer of technology between industries producing 'convergent' products, demonstrating that American consumers were happy to accept

> a homogeneous final product [which] was a decisive factor in the transition from a highly labor-intensive handicraft technology to one involving a sequence of highly specialized machines. Across the whole range of commodities we find evidence that British consumers imposed their tastes on the producer in a manner which seriously constrained him with respect to the exploitation of machine technology.[95]

Resistance to mass-production in a craft industry, such as the instrument trade in Britain was, meant problems in subcontracting components, or even the construction of compatible machine tools: 'users of capital equipment such

---

[92]  Ibid., 72–3.
[93]  Ibid., 136–7.
[94]  Mokyr (1993), 34–5.
[95]  Rosenberg (1982), 158.

as machine tools', Rosenberg observes, 'often made the tools themselves'.[96] Thomas Cooke of York's earliest surviving trade catalogue lists four pages of 'lathes and tools for ornamental and general purposes, planing and wheel-cutting machines'.[97]

In his essay entitled 'How Exogenous is Science?', Rosenberg stresses the human input into technological development:

> another fundamental way in which technology shapes the scientific enterprise that I can only mention because it is, by itself, an extremely big subject. I refer to the development of techniques of observation, testing, and measurement – in short, instrumentation … [however,] different instruments may differ enormously in the specificity of their impact upon fields of science. Therefore, any attempt to establish tight links between progress in specific subfields of science and an associated field of instrumentation is doomed to failure.[98]

Rosenberg's understanding of 'scientific instruments' is clearly as instruments-for-science, in a late-twentieth century 'Black Box' way. It is not the broader, wider-ranging definition of the Industrial Revolution, where practical everyday scientific tools were much less frightening. By 1994, 'instrumentation' has half a column in the index to his work, mostly concerning late twentieth-century technological devices such as electron microscopes, lasers or particle accelerators. Rosenberg writes that 'the economics of technological change is a subject that is still seriously befuddled by the failure to come to grips with the diversity of the contents of the black box'.[99] His essay on 'Scientific Instrumentation and University Research' gives a very late-twentieth century, American viewpoint: for instance, the first computer described is the 1946 ENIAC, and nothing is said about the wartime conditions that produced Bletchley Park's earlier Colossus.[100]

Maxine Berg has shown that the factory and large-scale firm have dominated considerations of the Industrial Revolution, but that on closer inspection many of the units of production were small scale, especially in the Birmingham and Sheffield metal trades, parts of which were formed by the provincial instrument-making trade.[101] 'The specialisation of labour and subdivision of trades in both Birmingham and Sheffield created a niche for the development of the workshop economy … there appears to be a strong case on the basis of descriptive evidence … for a workshop economy built on specialisation and the division of labour, on dispersed units concentrated in specific locations and on close networking among these units.'[102] She envisages a stage of 'small producer capitalism', subsequently

---

[96]   Ibid., 161.
[97]   Cooke [1863], 13–16.
[98]   Rosenberg (1982), 158.
[99]   Rosenberg (1994), 269 and ix.
[100]  Ibid., 259.
[101]  Berg (1993), 20–21.
[102]  Ibid., 25.

forgotten, which came before the traumatic introduction of the factory system to the metal trades in Birmingham and Sheffield during the nineteenth century.[103]

In her book *The Age of Manufactures 1700–1820*, Berg notes that the Birmingham and Sheffield metal trades 'really were the locus of Nathan Rosenberg's "continuum of small improvements", or anonymous technical change'.[104] She observes the growth of metal tool making trades alongside the smithing trades by the seventeenth century, in London, the Midlands and South-West Lancashire, and argues that with this development came division of labour and specialization of function:

> The manufacture of watch movements and tools was 'put out' as early as the seventeenth century to rural workers in South-West Lancashire by all the big watch firms in London, Coventry and Liverpool [subsequently these were sent back for 'finishing'].[105]

Berg stresses the importance of skill, which determined the location of the brass and copper trades: 'by the early eighteenth century many towns carried on the manufacture of brass, with no other special advantage than a resident class of artisans already skilled in working in metals'.[106] However, she demonstrates that the perceived 'independence' of metal-working artisans was an illusion: 'capitalist expansion and industrialization in the metal trades found their context not in the factory but in the garret master and other forms of sweating'.[107] Berg found that evidence for industrial growth could be found throughout the eighteenth century, and not just in its final quarter; there was extensive technical change, but this was not devoted exclusively to mechanisation. She found that the organization of work was one of the keys to understanding industrialization: 'decentralization, extended workshops, and sweating were equally new departures in the organization of production'.[108] She also found that the impact of technical and industrial change was variable, and did not always lead to growth.

To a considerable extent, professional historians work in their own particular areas without much reference to what others in closely related disciplines are concluding about the same period. Since the Second World War, economic historians have allowed a considerable amount of technological history to have a bearing on their own work; of necessity, since technological change is seen as one of the 'causes' of the Industrial Revolution, and the reverse can be seen also.

Historians of science have become more interested in instrument history, realizing that science is not just an abstract, pure mind-game but one that has applications. Yet, their interest in instrumentation has centred on the instrument

---

[103]  Ibid., 36–7.
[104]  Berg (1994), 256, quoting Rosenberg.
[105]  Ibid., 260.
[106]  Ibid., 262.
[107]  Ibid., 274.
[108]  Ibid., 281.

itself, or where it impinges on philosophy or scientific thought.[109] On the other side, sadly, instrument historians have, if anything, become more antiquarian in their approach than before. This is possibly because their numbers have risen sufficiently internationally, enabling them to become a self-supporting community, so that they no longer need to confer with 'outsiders'. It is to be hoped that this will change in the future, as instrument history has become part of the curriculum at the universities of Oxford and Cambridge, and is placed in its scientific, technological and economic context: most importantly, it is taught within the discipline of history.

Instrument historians have not specifically asked whether the instrument trade had an economic effect on the Industrial Revolution, although some technological and economic historians have come close to it. In this book I shall look at the main headings under which this question has appeared – technological change; the transfer of skill, within and without Britain; the rise of new markets through consumerism and education – and try to find some economic and social explanations for the growth of the trade outside London.

I shall try to assess whether the English instrument trade contributed at all to the emergence of Britain as the 'first industrial nation', and if so, how it was driven. My approach is through the investigation of the structure of the trade in the four newer and two longer-established towns that by 1851, according to entries in local directories, had noticeable and growing communities of instrument producers. In most cases where I can find evidence, I shall look at the unit of production, which, as with Berg's investigation into provincial metalworking, has proved also to be a family affair.

---

[109] See, for instance, Shapin (1996).

# Chapter 1

# Making Scientific Instruments in the Industrial Revolution

**The Scientific Instruments of the Industrial Revolution**

Instrument historians have discussed definitions of the term 'scientific instrument' extensively.[1] However, contemporaries classified instruments by their use, as 'mathematical', 'optical' and 'philosophical' instruments, and examples of each variety can be identified illustrated in the trade-card advertising the business of J.M. Hyde of Bristol, between 1841 and 1855 (Figure 1.1).

Historically, mathematical instruments were the first to be developed, and included such items as sundials, logarithmic scales and sighting instruments. Any device that had a graduated scale that was used to measure angles or distance, or perform calculations, could be regarded as a mathematical instrument. This level of complexity meant that both maker and user had to be numerate and literate (Figure 1.2).

Optical instruments were developed after the discovery, probably in the Netherlands at the end of the sixteenth century, that two or more lenses could enlarge distant or very small objects: it led to the construction of the telescope and the microscope (Figure 1.3). There is still great controversy about who, and of what nationality, actually invented the telescope and the microscope.[2] It would seem that improvements in glass production enabled spectacles to be made from about 1300, but the idea of combining of lenses for magnification did not occur to anyone until much later. In fact, glass quality remained poor, inhibiting the performance of both telescopes and microscopes until the nineteenth century – so much so that for much of the eighteenth century the larger aperture telescopes had polished metal mirrors rather than glass optics. Optical components began to replace open sights on various mathematical instruments, such as the octants and sextants used in navigation, and the theodolites and levels used in surveying, to improve pointing accuracy.

---

[1]    For example, Field (1988); Warner (1990); Van Helden and Hankins (1994), 1–6.

[2]    Discussed by van Helden (1977). More recently, see the meeting report 'Was there an Elizabethan Telescope?' with further references and contributions from Ronan et al. (1993). For the microscope, see Wilson (1995); Ruestow (1996); Fournier (1996). The general consensus appears to be that the telescope first appeared in Middleburg, in the Netherlands, in 1608: the microscope was rapidly derived from it.

**Figure 1.1    Trade card of J.M. Hyde, Bristol, 1841–55**

*Source*: Reece Winstone Archive & Publishing

**Figure 1.2    Circular protractor signed by W.C. Cox, Devonport, *c.*1830**

*Source*: National Museums of Scotland, NMS.T.1911.120

The third grouping, 'philosophical' instruments, dates from the mid-seventeenth century, coinciding with what is often described as the Scientific Revolution, or the New Science, which was characterized by a spirit of enquiry into the natural and physical world. In England, this occurred politically with the Stuart Restoration and the founding of the Royal Society, which had as its patron the King, Charles II. Although he showed little sustained interest in science, as royal patron Charles gave this spirit of enquiry validation of the highest social order. New instruments were developed to investigate or demonstrate naturally occurring phenomena. For example, magnetism, although long used at sea in the mariner's compass, was newly investigated when it was realized that the Earth itself behaved like a giant lodestone, and that its magnetic field had changing vertical and horizontal components. The barometer, invented in Italy, was used to measure air pressure and predict changes in the weather (Figure 1.4), whereas the air pump demonstrated to those willing to observe – and there were many – how a guinea and a feather fell at the same rate in a vacuum; or, as dramatically portrayed by the artist, Joseph Wright of Derby, how life itself could be extinguished without God's great gift of air (Figure 1.5).

Other apparatus illustrated the action of static and dynamic forces and electrical phenomena – the latter being among the most popular of eighteenth-century demonstrations, believed to have beneficial medical properties.

This variety of instrumentation resulted in a correspondingly wide range of customer types. The eighteenth-century market for instruments was identified in

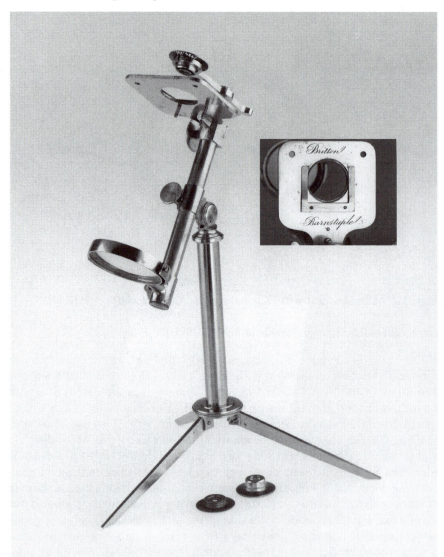

**Figure 1.3    Simple microscope signed by William Britton of Barnstaple, Devon,**
**                        *c.*1840**

*Source*: National Museums of Scotland, NMS.T.1984.141

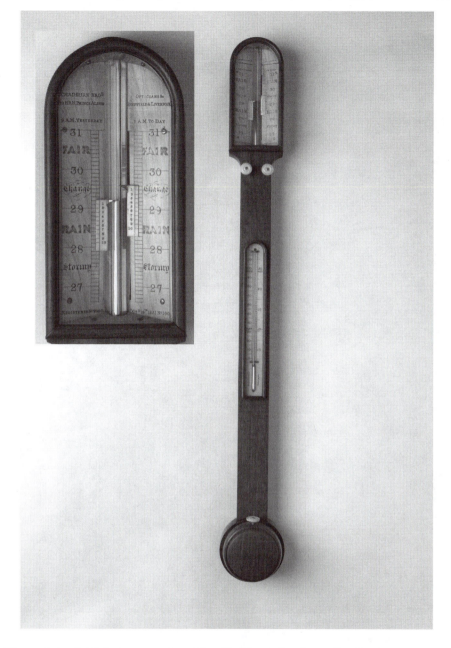

**Figure 1.4    Stick barometer signed by Chadburn Brothers, Sheffield and Liverpool, *c*.1855**

*Source*: National Museums of Scotland, NMS.T.1984.83

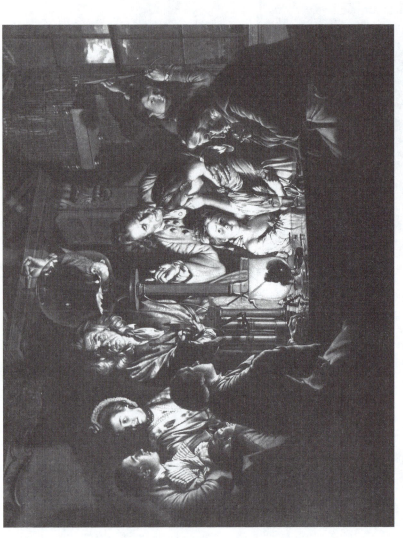

**Figure 1.5** Joseph Wright, *A Philosopher shewing an Experiment on the Airpump*, engraving by Valentine Green, 1769

*Source:* © National Museum of Science and Industry

the 1960s by the American instrument historian Silvio Bedini as threefold: first, there were the men of science – the philosophers who performed experiments, and who needed new apparatus to help them in their investigations. Although a proportionally small part of the market, this important relationship between maker and user was on a one-to-one basis, and the technology thus developed helped to increase scientific understanding, while the scientific ideas brought technological improvements. It helped develop the instrument-maker's skill, and if the user published the device, thus stimulating interest in the demonstration, then the maker could produce it in larger numbers. A second and somewhat larger group of customers were the dilettanti; that is, the gentlemen with sufficient disposable income to be able to buy the latest fashionable microscope (for instance), either as an amusement or to entertain and impress friends. Bedini's third and largest group can be identified as the so-called 'mathematical practitioners' – those who required instruments for practical use in everyday life.[3]

Substantial collections of all these categories of complex items have survived as material evidence, some of it accessible for study in public museums.[4] It is worth stressing that this material can be used as a three-dimensional archive, because careful examination of individual items often reveals information about its manufacture or subsequent history. Objects can be used as historical evidence in the same way that material culture is used in archaeology. There is, therefore, scope for analysis of its manufacture, the workshop organization of the trade, and the development of the market during this period. For example, during manufacture, individual surveying instruments were assembled in small groups or batches, but because the parts were only approximately interchangeable, each was identified by a number within the batch, so that all components with a particular number could be finely-adjusted to fit that individual instrument. Only by dismantling such instruments do these numbers come to light, but they give an idea of the size of the batches produced in an individual workshop.[5]

---

[3]   Bedini (1964), 3–13. The term 'mathematical practitioner' was popularized by E.G.R. Taylor's two books containing the expression in the title: Taylor (1954) and Taylor (1966).

[4]   In the United Kingdom, the major collections of such material are held at the Science Museum, London; the National Maritime Museum, Greenwich; the National Museums of Scotland; and the university museums at Oxford and Cambridge, respectively, the Museum of the History of Science and the Whipple Museum of the History of Science. Much of the material is published in catalogue form, and currently more of it is being made accessible on-line; however, there are no substantial collections of English provincial instruments. The local authority museums in Bristol and Manchester hold representative collections of locally-made instruments. Abroad, the principal collections are to be found in the Deutsches Museum, Munich; Musée des Arts et Métiers, Paris; Museum Boerhaave, Leiden; Museo di Storia della Scienza, Florence; and the National Museum of American History, Washington DC.

[5]   Clarke et al. (1989), xi.

The nature of the instrumentation being produced had changed somewhat by the mid-nineteenth century from what it had been in the early-eighteenth century. There was certainly a wider variety to choose from, demonstrated by the contents of catalogues advertising items on offer from individual firms, and there were entirely new classes of instrument, for example, in telegraphy and photography. However, the markets appear to have remained substantially the same. Willem Hackmann has stressed (as has J.A. Bennett) that the market in precision instruments (which were principally astronomical) was stimulated in the late eighteenth century by three London institutions (of which two were arms of the state): the Royal Society, the Board of Longitude and the Royal Observatory.[6]

In time, the powerful influence of these bodies waned. The Royal Society became more of a gentlemen's club and less of a focus for scientific work, until reformed during the 1830s.[7] Once the clock-maker John Harrison (1693–1776) had effectively 'solved' the problem of longitude, the Board's purpose changed, and it was finally wound up in 1828.[8] During the nineteenth century, the long incumbency of the seventh Astronomer Royal, George Biddell Airy (1801–92), saw the pre-eminent London firm of Troughton & Simms regarded 'as his personal mechanics for any small task, from repairing spectacles to making up some gadget from his scribbled sketch'.[9]

Indeed, by the early decades of the nineteenth century, the scientific input into the British Industrial Revolution was perceived by some contemporaries to be 'running out of steam'.[10] The mathematician Charles Babbage (1791–1892) was one of the most vocal of this point of view, publishing in 1830 a famous essay on 'The Decline of Science in England', arguing that this trend could be reversed only if the State rewarded scientists properly for their endeavours, instituted research grants, and provided an effective system of scientific education.[11] Hackmann goes on to demonstrate that in some ways, the Great Exhibition of 1851 vindicated Babbage's point of view: 'the organizers who were keen to show the triumph of British industrial power, in the end demonstrated that Britain might be eclipsed by the technical capabilities of her faster-growing European rivals'.[12]

Hackmann has analysed the contents of the Great Exhibition's Class X, Philosophical Instruments, together with relevant Jury reports: the English entries took the majority of the prizes, as might have been expected. However, on closer inspection, this was less impressive: 'it is difficult to identify national trends in

---

[6]   Hackmann (1985), 58; Bennett (1985), 14.
[7]   Hall (1984).
[8]   Landes (1983), 143–57; Andrewes (1996).
[9]   McConnell (1992), 39.
[10]   Hackmann (1985), 61.
[11]   Ibid., 65–6, quoting Charles Babbage, *Reflections on the Decline of Science in England, and on Some of its Causes* (London, 1830).
[12]   Ibid., 65.

these awards, except that a great deal of energy was devoted in England to the new field of electric telegraphy which had much trade potential, while French makers developed their market for well-made optical instruments'.[13] It was felt, by Babbage and others, that the trade itself required better rewards, together with some form of technical education for skilled workmen, as by this time the apprenticeship system in the London craft guilds was clearly inadequate. Attempts to move in such a direction – by the London-based Society of Arts, founded in 1754 (as the Society for the Encouragement of Arts, Manufactures and Commerce), by the Mechanics' Institutes movement, dating from the 1820s, or by the British Association for the Advancement of Science, founded in 1831 – proved to be insufficient for the demands of industry. State-organized scientific and technical education did not come to England until the 1870s.[14] This was to prove a growth area in the latter part of the nineteenth century, and large numbers of provincial instrument firms were to benefit from the captive markets in schools, both at home and in the colonies.[15]

## Methodology and Sources

An agenda for an analysis of the instrument trade during this period was set indirectly in 1985 by an exhibition in Cambridge entitled 'Science and Profit in 18th-Century London'. This was accompanied by a published collection of essays under the same title on aspects of the eighteenth century London trade: 'The Economic Context', by Roy Porter, 'The Scientific Context', by J.A. Bennett, 'Scientific Instruments and their Public', by Simon Schaffer, and 'The Instrument-Making Trade' by Olivia Brown.[16] Generally, curators and historians of science received this more or less favourably, but there was some sharp criticism from the respected instrument historian, John Millburn, who took the monograph to task for being

> altogether too complacent and uncritical. Reading this, one would never guess that little is in fact currently known about the detailed structure of the instrument-making trade in the eighteenth century, or about the lives of the individuals around whom the whole fabric of the exhibition is constructed ... Detailed studies of individual instrument-makers – their finances (this exercise is supposed to be about profit as well as science), their marketing techniques, their sources of materials and components, their tools, their relationships with their workmen, subcontractors and each other – are, with very few exceptions, non-existent. For example, almost nothing is known for certain about the size of the individual instrument makers' workshops, or how many specialist craftsmen were involved in the construction of different types of instrument, apart from what can be deduced from numbers of apprentices bound and a few isolated 'facts' such

---

[13]  Ibid., 64.
[14]  Ibid., 66–7.
[15]  Meliconi (2000), 258–63.
[16]  Porter et al. (1985).

as the claim that Ramsden employed 50 men. Economic historians resort frequently to citing two major business archives that happen to have survived, the Wedgwood papers and the Boulton/Watt papers, though in the absence of similar material on their competitors it is debatable whether the conclusions drawn are reliable. Historians of scientific instruments in the eighteenth century have no such convenient stores to draw upon. The relevant information must be painstakingly extracted piece by piece from a variety of sources ... a daunting task but one which nevertheless must be undertaken before a reliable and comprehensive synthesis of the trade in the 18th century can be constructed.[17]

Since this 1986 review, the access to historical records has improved considerably with the recent and increasing availability of all sorts of records and information on-line. This has enabled historians to pull together hitherto remote and scattered material of just the type that Millburn was bewailing as 'a daunting task'. Primary sources of many types are becoming much more readily available, and increasingly so, and instrument historians are taking advantage of these developments.[18] However, the number of pertinent sources has not significantly increased.

A few definitions should be clarified here. The terms 'precision instruments' and 'scientific instruments' were not used during the Industrial Revolution: these are late nineteenth-century descriptions, and are terms that have come to denote specific categories for instrument historians. 'Precision instrument' now means a finely divided, usually London-made, probably large astronomical or first-order surveying item, or a metrology standard, made by a front-ranking craftsman working near the limits of what was technologically possible. It would probably have proved expensive in time and materials, and might well have been specially commissioned. 'Scientific instruments' are understood to have also been made in London, and provided the everyday trade that allowed the 'precision' items to be made in terms of expertise and cash flow.

But whereas 'scientific' instruments began to be made in increasingly large numbers in the provinces, it was only by the mid-nineteenth century that 'precision' instruments could be produced there. The instrument 'trade' is used as a term that embraces both named manufacturers and retailers, and should be extended to encompass all who participated in the making or selling of 'scientific' instruments. In view of the recent historiography among professional economic historians debating the parameters of the Industrial Revolution, this phrase should certainly be extended to look at the roles of women and children. Due consideration should also be given as to what extent this particular business was a family enterprise.

---

[17]  Millburn (1986c), 84. Posthumous tributes to Millburn in 2005 suggested that this review encouraged more rigorousness in subsequent instrument history: see *Bulletin of the Scientific Instrument Society*, No. 86 (2005), esp. p. 9.
[18]  For example, McConnell (forthcoming), where she uses 'The Proceedings of the Old Bailey 1674 to 1834' (www.oldbaileyonline.org) to uncover the names of Jesse Ramsden's workmen.

The expression 'Provincial England', or 'the provinces', may appear on the surface to be a pejorative term, but in the context of this book it merely means outside the capital. However, there is a problem with including Scottish or Irish instrument making in this provincial England category, as some have done, because their centres of patronage were to be found locally.[19] Yet it has been claimed that:

> ... instrument making in the British Isles outside London was a provincial activity at least until the latter years of the 19th century. It was provincial in that London was the centre of activity, with manufacture in other towns and centres largely a peripheral activity.[20]

Nevertheless, no instrument historian appears to have asked why this was so, or even if it was not merely apparently so, nor described how it had come to have changed by the late nineteenth century.

Traditionally, the most obvious source for uncovering the numbers of instrument-making firms has been the local street directories that started to appear as increased commercial activity spread throughout the English provinces. Often, the information found in these has been taken at face value, despite the knowledge that there are a number of inherent problems.[21] Among these, there is a lack of knowledge concerning the motives of the contributors, the topicality and veracity of the information, and whether entries had to be paid for. Directories, often produced intermittently, are a flawed source – yet they remain the most important starting point for uncovering the names and probable longevity of businesses, and have been used as such here.

Even so, the first extensive directory-based listing of the instrument trade was published only as recently as 1995, and although the last twenty years have seen individual lists published for Scotland, Ireland and Victorian London, nothing has been produced for provincial England.[22] This *Directory of British Scientific Instrument Makers 1550–1851*, completed by Gloria Clifton, was the culmination of over a decade of research by Project SIMON (Scientific Instrument Makers, Observations and Notes), set up in 1984 by Professor G.L'E. Turner, to create a national database of instrument makers and sellers. Signed instruments, particularly those signed by the 'best' makers, survive in reasonably large numbers, because they are usually beautifully designed and finished, and because collectors

---

[19]  Clarke et al. (1989); Burnett and Morrison-Low (1989); Morrison-Low (2002).

[20]  Bryden (1984).

[21]  These are discussed in Goss (1932); Norton (1950); Shaw and Tipper (1988). See also Shaw (1982).

[22]  Bryden (1972) (revised as Clarke et al. (1989)); Burnett and Morrison-Low (1989) and Downing (1984). Clifton (1995) looks in particular at London instrument makers within the London guilds, but takes provincial instrument-making only partially into account, using some provincial directories. The SIMON database has been continued, and there is to be a revised and extended publication at some future date.

have traditionally considered the signature as indicating the maker's pride in the quality of the piece. Yet the signature indicates only the point of retail, usually in London (for reasons that will be discussed in Chapter 7), and parts (or the entire instrument) may have been made by local or distant sub-contractors.

Early items with provincial signatures are most unusual; yet it is apparent from contemporary street directories and other archival sources that instruments were being produced in the provinces, especially in what were later to become the major provincial centres, from a reasonably early date. Trawling through London guild records, Corporation of London records, trade directories, parish records, wills, insurance registers, advertisements, trade cards and inscriptions on instruments, Project SIMON compiled these different fields in a database, currently held at the National Maritime Museum. The emphasis of this whole work – correctly – has been on the centre of the trade: London.

Much of the data on Scottish and Irish makers has been supplied by earlier publications produced by the National Museums of Scotland, and some raw data from research for this book has also been fed in for Birmingham, Sheffield, Manchester and Liverpool makers. One of the aims of this present work has been to supplement the Project SIMON database. On this basis, broadly similar comparisons can be made between the London trade and that in the provinces. However, the principal difference between the figures obtained by Project SIMON and those in this book is that SIMON contains all named individuals (including apprentices and otherwise unrecorded signatories of instruments), whereas here I look at the numbers of businesses operating in each of my target areas (as a starting point).

In attempting to respond to Millburn's 1986 agenda of criticisms, a range of quantitative and qualitative questions emerges: what was the size, scale, and structure of the trade? Conventionally, the economic historian would turn to relevant business archives to answer these questions. However, few business archives of this type of enterprise, particularly for this time, have survived. For England, a handful can be named: the archive from the businesses of the telescope maker Thomas Cooke of York, and the associated London firm of Troughton & Simms (now in the Vickers Collection, University of York Library, York); some early records associated with the London firm of William Elliott (now at the Museum of the History of Science, Oxford); and later the stockbooks, from 1866–1944, of J.H. Dallmeyer. There are otherwise no substantial business records known to survive from this type of firm for this period.[23] In their absence, other methods have to be used.

Even looking at the rates of success or failure is complicated: surviving English bankruptcy proceedings are hard to find, as the official papers relating to these were destroyed earlier last century.[24] Bankruptcy papers from only two English

---

[23]  McConnell (1992) made extensive use of the Vickers Archive; early Elliott records were used by Holland (1993). The Dallmeyer stockbooks were consulted by Williams (1994).
[24]  Marriner (1980).

instrument-making concerns have survived, both London-based, and one of these has recently been scrutinized in some depth.[25] Other sources – probate, insurance records, wills, bank accounts and rate books – can be used to fill out the details of business biography necessary to provide a picture capable of the synthesis required by Millburn.[26] Millburn made a start by looking at the records of the Board of Ordnance at the Public Record Office, to work out how lucrative the royal appointment holders found their contracts during the French and Napoleonic Wars.[27]

The very nature of the business undertaken was technologically sensitive, in that the major London workshops were producing the most highly sought-after precision instruments, at the industry's leading edge, and there was a government embargo on information about production until the 1820s. The men who ran these firms in any case wished to keep their competitors, whether foreign or provincial, in the dark about their innovations. Unsurprisingly, no English descriptions of workshop floors appear to have been made, apart from George Adams's brief and general description of subcontracting in the London trade of the 1740s, which was really a personal reassurance of quality control to prospective customers:

> In the construction of all the Machines I have ever made, my first and greatest Care hath been to produce good Models and Drawings, several of them I have imitated from the best Authors, as well as Foreigners, as those of our own Country. I have altered and improved others, and have added many new ones of my own Invention ... That their Exactness may be particularly attended to, I always inspect and direct the several Pieces myself, see them all combined in my own House, and finish the most curious Parts thereof with my own Hands.[28]

Other accounts of the English trade come from travellers from abroad: the eighteenth-century London trade as seen through the eyes of impressed visiting foreigners was examined by G. L'E. Turner.[29] Given the dearth of contemporary descriptive documentation by its own practitioners, the diaries and letters of foreign visitors can shed fresh insights into what was then seen as a reasonably 'secret' activity; for example, the career of the Dane, Jesper Bidstrup (1763–1802) has recently been outlined to throw new light on technology transfer from London to Europe, but it also supplies badly-needed details of London trade organization.[30]

---

[25] McConnell (1993b); McConnell (1994a); an overview of the instrument trade and bankruptcy is given by Morrison-Low (1994a).

[26] Westall (1984).

[27] Millburn (1988a); Millburn (1992a); Millburn (1992b); Millburn (1992c).

[28] Adams (1746), 224, quoted by Brown in Porter et al. (1985).

[29] Turner (1979).

[30] For a general overview of foreign espionage and British industry, see Woolrich (1988), Harris (1998), McConnell (2004) and more specifically for the instrument trade, Christensen (1993).

**The Nature of the Scientific Instrument Trade: 1760 and 1851**

Recent publications seem to suggest that we have some idea about the organization, structure and external pressures upon the English instrument trade at the dates generally taken to mark the start and end of the Industrial Revolution in England. In addition, there are some similarities with other trades – in particular those that shared some of the characteristics evident earlier, such as clock-making, printing and the book trade. These included methods of passing on craft skills through formal apprenticeship in the older centres of population, where such structures could be enforced. Also similar were the long-established lines of communication and delivery into the provinces, where the products could be sold.

Initially, the instrument trade catered largely for the luxury end of the market: it was primarily based in London, where the richest people were located. It was largely a hand-crafted industry, in which an apprenticeship had to be served in order to be initiated into its particular skills. These included brasswork, glasswork, precision engraving and more generally, the uses of numeracy and literacy. There is not much evidence of mechanization of processes, or of power being applied to tools – although foot-operated lathes and grinding machines were available, these simple devices were driven by human muscle power.

Skills were learned 'on the job', and attempts to codify experience and disseminate it, along the lines of the French *Encyclopédie*, were doomed to failure as the 'know how', or skills, had to be taught by one-to-one transmission. Hence the recurring attempts by foreigners to bribe workmen to learn about current shop floor practice, and the sad comment from the young James Watt in 1755 on finding that the London instrument trade was a closed shop to outsiders: 'I have not yet got a master', he wrote despondently to his father in Greenock, 'we have tried several, but they all made some objection or other. I find that, if any of them agree with me at all, it will not be for less than a year; and even for that time they will be expecting some money'.[31]

The trade appears to have been very much an enclosed family enterprise in which women and children participated, although there are no figures that show to what extent this was the case, as might be expected during this period. (Even by the time of the first Census to record occupations in 1841, this information was not necessarily recorded.) As Alice Clark and Ivy Pinchbeck make clear, this characteristic of family enterprise, including women and children in the instrument trade, was common to most craft-based industries.[32]

During the period covered by this book, the workforce was transformed from one that was competent in a series of craft-based skills, to one becoming more reliant on some of the machine tools that were then being developed. With the addition of steam power, these tools came to be used with great effect in heavy

---

[31]   Quoted in Smiles (1865), 102.
[32]   Clark (1982); Pinchbeck (1981).

engineering.[33] However, their early application and initial development within precision instrument making was important for the development of the trade. These 'tools to make tools' included the lathe, the dividing engine and the precision screw. Not only did their use speed up many time-consuming operations, it also improved the inherent accuracy of the instruments produced. It is also important to remember that, as Raphael Samuel has demonstrated, hand technology existed successfully side-by-side with mechanization well into the mid-Victorian period, and it is clear that instrument production remained mainly a hand technology manufacture until the late nineteenth century.[34]

Other questions remain more opaque. For instance, did the instrument trade, especially in the provinces, move into 'factories', as did the textile industry at this period? David Landes has defined the factory as a 'concentration of production and maintenance of discipline'.[35] The answer appears to be 'only partially', as examples can be discovered, in particular in Sheffield, where water power could be supplied to individual buildings to shape the wood for telescope barrels, or to grind the glass for optical components; and clearly some form of discipline was in place to keep the workforce to task.[36] Nevertheless, the pattern in Birmingham, Manchester and Liverpool appears to have remained that of small workshops, in which – particularly in Birmingham – entrepreneurs managing such small-scale metal workshops were able to produce other commodities, and not solely instruments. There is a parallel here with the division of labour in watch manufacturing, where parts were passed between small workshops.

Gloria Clifton remarked in the Introduction to her 1995 *Directory* that the numbers of individuals involved in the instrument trade outside London were larger than previously thought. She notes that 'although London remained the principal centre of production ... provincial instrument making was more significant than has generally been assumed'.[37] Her figures for those individuals show increases from 71 outside London (161 within) in 1751, to 287 outside London (297 within) in 1801, to 339 outside London (498 within) in 1851.[38] Clifton's figures are for the whole British Isles, including Scotland and Ireland. It should be noted, though, that the distinctive nature of public administration in Scotland and Ireland provided different opportunities for trade to develop. Thus, these markets cannot be considered as equivalent to English provincial centres (Graph 1.1). Instead, this present book looks at numbers of firms – rather than of individuals – in specific centres, and tries to match Millburn's agenda by providing further detail about such businesses.

---

[33]  Rolt (1965), 33–9.
[34]  Samuel (1977).
[35]  Landes (1969), 121.
[36]  Morrison-Low (1994b).
[37]  Clifton (1995), xiv.
[38]  Ibid., xv.

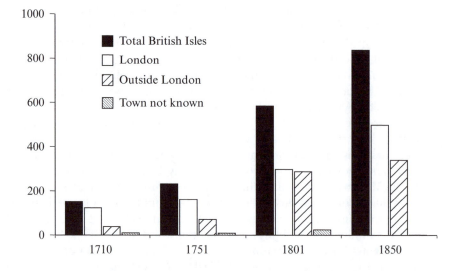

**Graph 1.1    Numbers of individual scientific instrument makers working in the British Isles, including Scotland and Ireland, whose names have been traced (from Gloria Clifton, *Directory of British Scientific Instrument Makers 1550–1851* (London, 1995), xv)**

There were four new major places where instruments, or parts of instruments, were produced in England, outside London, during the period between 1760 and 1851. These were Birmingham, Manchester, Liverpool, and Sheffield, all new centres of population whose growth coincided with the change of pace in the economy at this time. Population growth was not, however, the sole reason for these becoming the specific locations for the provincial instrument trade, which quite clearly did not take root in a number of other expanding cities. It would seem that the growth of the trade in these specific locations was in some measure due to the gradual emergence of an integrated and specialized economy, which gradually spread throughout England during this period.

As the economic historian Martin Daunton put it: 'Far from producing homogeneity, the emergence of an increasingly integrated economy led to a greater degree of specialisation between regions which were tied together by more efficient transport, marketing and financial systems.' [39] Either – as in the case of Birmingham – the trade reached what Pat Hudson has termed 'the achievement of critical mass' by close association with other similar industries, or – as in the case of Liverpool – the trade relied on a hinterland of expertise from which it

---

[39]   Daunton (1995), 279.

drew 'a nucleus of labour for the developing engineering trades', as described by – among others – Sheila Marriner.[40]

The following four chapters will provide an outline of these four centres, together with some discussion of smaller clusters of (usually specialist) provincial makers, which, by the time of the Great Exhibition, were clearly supplying substantial quantities of instruments in their own right, and trace their newly-found self-confidence from small beginnings. This mapping exercise is based on extracting the names – and thus the numbers – of firms describing themselves as instrument-makers from local street directories, and supplementing this bare skeleton, as Millburn suggested, with other information 'painstakingly extracted piece by piece from a variety of sources'.[41] This produces a local picture that shows whether firms clustered together in a particular district of a town centre, or whether some other pattern prevailed. It also gives some indication of the longevity of businesses, and entry/exit rates.

There were a variety of reasons that the instrument industry took root in particular localities. It would appear that certain conditions had to be met before an ambitious entrepreneur might move to what seemed to him to be an auspicious place. In the abstract, these might include: aristocratic or state patronage; the existence of a pool of skilled labour; nearby sources of essential raw materials of construction; local learned societies; a ready-made, sympathetic financial infrastructure; an accessible market; handy transport methods; comparatively low costs of workshop premises; comparative lack of guild control; and possibly an already-existing group of friendly co-religionists or immigrants who would act as a support group should the enterprise fail. These have been listed in Table 1.1.

Of course, not all these possible conditions necessarily applied in a single place simultaneously, and there were individuals who began in one location and subsequently moved to another more promising location (for example, the Davis family, who initially settled in Leeds from Continental Europe, but whose younger members moved subsequently to Derby).[42] Some locations, such as Bristol, appear to have prospered with the growth of local trade but waned with its decline, since Liverpool replaced Bristol as England's most prosperous Atlantic port during this period. Most of these elements appear in various guises in the provincial centres under discussion at one time or another.

These centres were selected by working backwards from an examination of the contents of Class X, philosophical, musical, horological and surgical instruments, of the 1851 Great Exhibition, as presented in the *Illustrated Catalogue of the Exhibition of all Nations* ... (London, 1851). A total of 751 businesses had displays there. The 'Introduction' described 'this Class as representing the culminating point of mechanical skill'; they were thus seen to be the makers (rather than

---

[40] Hudson (1992), 114; Marriner (1982), 55; see also Bailey and Barker (1969).
[41] Millburn (1986c), 84.
[42] Anon. (1979).

**Table 1.1     Possible factors influencing locations of the instrument trade, and where these might apply between 1760 and 1851**

| Possible location factors | Where found |
| --- | --- |
| 1  Aristocratic patronage | London; Bath; Cheltenham |
| 2  State patronage | London, but still unknown to what extent subcontracting reached provincial trade before 1851 |
| 3  Local learned societies | London (Royal Society 1660); lecturing spreading to all provincial centres from early 18th century |
| 4  Skilled labour pools in related trades | London (particularly Clerkenwell); Sheffield (cutlery); Birmingham (brass); Liverpool (watchmaking hinterland); Manchester (textile machinery) |
| 5  Accessible raw materials | |
|    (a) brass | Bristol; imported into London from an early date; available cheaply in Birmingham and Sheffield from about 1750. |
|    (b) glass | London glass houses from medieval times; activity centred on Lancashire coalfields from mid-eighteenth century, but not produced in industrial quantities until after 1848 |
| 6  Financial infrastructure | Banking well-developed throughout the period, but small family businesses still reliant upon family capitalisation |
| 7  Accessible markets | Items either sold locally e.g. navigation instruments in ports (Bristol, Liverpool, and Hull) or small and robust enough to parcel up and send to more distant markets e.g. telescopes to London (from Birmingham or Sheffield) |
| 8  Transport | All provincial centres connected to London by carrier, subsequently by canal, then railway systems |
| 9  Low cost of workshop premises | Unknown |
| 10 Guild control | Ineffective guild control in long-established provincial centres (York, Bristol); none in new centres |
| 11 Co-religionists or immigrants | Possibly in larger new population centres (with other stronger location factors taken into consideration) |

retailers) of their wares.[43] G.L'E. Turner has identified 108 of these businesses as instrument makers; of those, 53 firms were located in the United Kingdom, but a mere fifteen came from outside London.[44]

Leaving aside George Yeates of Dublin, Thomas Dunn and James Liddell of Edinburgh, Paul Cameron and Gardner & Co., of Glasgow, this leaves ten instrument-making firms in England outside the metropolis. These were: Abraham Abraham and Gray & Keen of Liverpool, John Braham and Thomas King of Bristol, Chadburn Brothers of Liverpool and Sheffield, Samuel Sharp of Sheffield; Robert Field & Son and J. Parkes & Son of Birmingham, J.N. Hearden of Plymouth and William Wilton of St Day, Cornwall.[45] These were not the names of first-ranking, international businesses, and we do not even know if the firms were a fairly representative cross-section of provincial English instrument making at this time. All we know is that they were prepared to display their wares in an international forum, and be judged on their own merits.

It was also clear from surviving instruments that – although numerically far fewer than those with a London address – instrument makers from outside London were by this time confident enough to engrave addresses such as 'Sheffield' and 'Birmingham' on their wares. The contribution of these newcomers to the industry should be assessed, the impact of their arrival appraised, and the sizes of their different centres gauged. Characterisation of the differences between the products of new, yet geographically close, instrument-producing centres such as Liverpool and Manchester should also be undertaken.

The four towns thus selected were also, of course, major new centres of industrial population and thus contained pools of skilled and semi-skilled labour, an important prerequisite for any manufacturing undertaking. Marriner has underlined the existence of skilled metal workers in Warrington, making tools: 'watch- and clock-making were extremely important craft industries in Liverpool, Prescot and Warrington, and they spread to other parts of south-west Lancashire such as Ormskirk.'[46] She points out that these skills could be applied to 'making other precision products such as chronometers, sextants and other navigational aids for ships'.[47]

Both Liverpool and Manchester, as Hudson outlines, were built on cotton, which brought in 'considerable external economies [which] accrued because of the specialist services of the regional infrastructure'.[48] Instrument making was

---

[43]   *Catalogue …* (1851), 405.
[44]   Turner (1983), 309–10.
[45]   None of these firms has been the subject of a business history, although Elizabeth Cavicchi is working on the activities of J.N. Hearden (1809–76): 'Blind Experimenting in a Sighted World: the Electrical Innovations of Jonathan Nash Hearden', unpublished paper presented to the History of Science Society, Minneapolis, November 2005.
[46]   Marriner (1982), 55.
[47]   Ibid.
[48]   Hudson (1992), 121.

able to flourish in these centres because there were supplies of raw materials, a skilled workforce, legal, financial and credit facilities, and a readily available transport system. In Sheffield and Birmingham, which did not follow the 'factory textile' model, the appearance of an instrument-making industry during this period is perhaps less surprising. The work of Maxine Berg has demonstrated that in Birmingham, where small metal workshops were the norm, the trades had been nationally and externally oriented since at least the seventeenth century; the instrument trade appears to have become a part of this already existing structure.[49]

In Sheffield, although the metal workers were cutlers and thus working in steel rather than brass, David Hey has asserted that the 'structure of the local economy was little affected by new crafts, for they were largely organized on traditional lines'.[50] As a contrast to these 'successful' new centres, instrument activities in two earlier towns with comparatively large populations, York and Bristol, will be outlined as illustrative of the pre-industrial norm. As in London, both York and Bristol retained their guild structures, which although weakening by the end of the eighteenth century, nevertheless were used as a means of transmitting specialist trade skills. York will be contrasted with Sheffield, to show two very different developments within the same region; and Bristol will be contrasted with Liverpool, both as ports clearly supplying a navigational market, yet displaying diverging characteristics with the passage of time.

It could be said that instrument making was 'provincial' when it first arrived in Tudor London, because for a period this new industry was still dominated by the workshops of Flanders.[51] In due course, men with mathematical and engraving skills moved out of London to find new and local markets during the more stable later Stuart period: in the late seventeenth century, they moved to established and growing population centres. Thus, Thomas Moone was making instruments in Bristol in 1669 when his fellow Bristolian Samuel Sturmy described him as 'an ingenious smith', and there had been Philip Staynred preceding them both;[52] the brothers John and Robert Roscoe were active in Liverpool from around 1696;[53] and an hour glass-maker, Nicholas Cosens, obtained his freedom in York in 1638.[54]

At the start of the period of the Industrial Revolution, by about 1760, these centres of instrumental activity – and there were few communities of more than a handful of specialist instrument makers to be found anywhere outside London – were located in the major centres of population, because that is where people would buy or use instruments. Even where there were no actual instrument

---

[49]   Ibid., 122; Berg (1993).
[50]   Hey (1991), 136.
[51]   Harkness (2002), especially 147–51.
[52]   Taylor (1954), 260.
[53]   Clifton (1995), 237.
[54]   Ibid., 66, quoting Loomes (1981), 166.

makers resident, the mathematical practitioners – as described by E.G.R. Taylor: the teachers, writers, inventors, surveyors, architects, mapmakers, both amateurs and professionals – were to be found in provincial England from a fairly early date. They would have bought their instruments in London, or made them for themselves.

This can be illustrated with the example of two surviving instruments, which date from before 1760. One, a brass rule (Figure 1.6), marked with various useful scales and with the name of its one-time owner Robert Trollap of York (an architect and builder), is dated 1655 – the year in which Trollap designed and built the Exchange and Guildhall, Newcastle. The second item is a boxwood sector or joynt rule (Figure 1.7), again marked with the owner's name and address 'Robert Hudson, Leeds, 1686', and it includes a perpetual almanac, dialling and trigonometrical scales, as well as timber measures useful for carpenters.[55] Both items were probably – but not irrefutably – London-made, but demonstrate that demand existed outside the metropolis from about the mid-seventeenth century, a demand that came to attract makers away from the south-east to nascent markets in the provinces.

This gradual growth in local market demand led to instrument manufacture – as distinct from importing and repairing – in some areas only. For instance, the practical users – that is, the surveyors, the architects, the carpenters, the masons and other wrights – who were building new towns well away from London, encouraged those with the right skills to move out into the provinces, or, if already there, to diversify into these areas of manufacturing expertise. Repairing was, and remained, an important function of these new enterprises, however, as the cost and delay, as well as the risk and uncertainty of sending an item back to its London manufacturer often proved unrealistic.

Yet it remains very difficult to gauge who was actually 'making' or manufacturing entire instruments in the provinces at all: advertised claims in newspapers and street directories often masked the amount of material bought-in for re-sale, either from London or from other local manufacturers. Despite this, it is clear from a closer examination of the artefacts that the ability to make instruments outside London was there from at least the early eighteenth century. Leaving aside the examples of Scotland and Ireland, which to some extent developed their own indigenous trades (and although outside London, cannot be regarded as 'provincial England'), these pockets of instrumental activity initially remained close to their markets, and these tended to be where there were new population centres.

Graph 1.2 shows the numbers of instrument-making firms to be found in local directories,[56] which give an idea of trends over much of the period. Unlike the earlier figures in Graph 1.1, from Clifton, these figures show the numbers of

---

[55]  National Museums of Scotland, inventory numbers NMS T.1978.92 and T.1990.88. For Trollap, see Colvin (1995), 989–90.

[56]  Despite the problems with these discussed earlier in this chapter.

**Figure 1.6    Brass calculating rule, owned by Robert Trollap of York, 1655**

*Source*: National Museums of Scotland, NMS T.1972.92

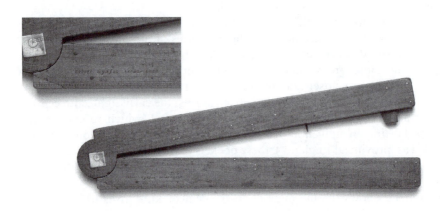

**Figure 1.7    Boxwood sector, owned by Robert Hudson, Leeds, 1686**

*Source*: National Museums of Scotland, NMS T.1990.88

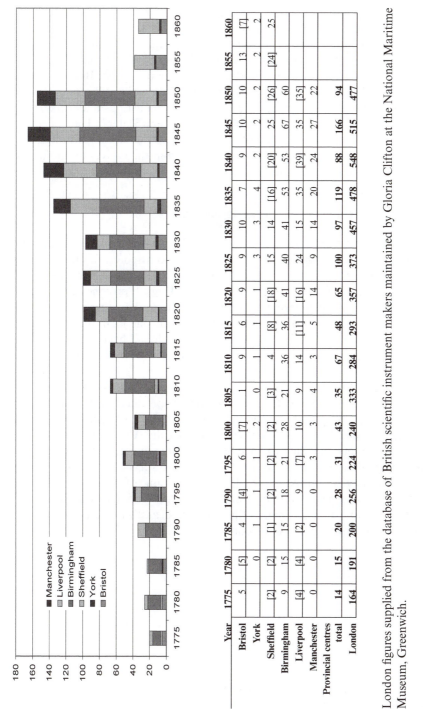

| Year | 1775 | 1780 | 1785 | 1790 | 1795 | 1800 | 1805 | 1810 | 1815 | 1820 | 1825 | 1830 | 1835 | 1840 | 1845 | 1850 | 1855 | 1860 |
|---|---|---|---|---|---|---|---|---|---|---|---|---|---|---|---|---|---|---|
| Bristol | 5 | [5] | 4 | [4] | 6 | [7] | 1 | 9 | 6 | 9 | 9 | 10 | 7 | 9 | 10 | 10 | 13 | [7] |
| York | 0 | 0 | 1 | 1 | 1 | 2 | 0 | 1 | 1 | 1 | 3 | 3 | 4 | 2 | 2 | 2 | 2 | 2 |
| Sheffield | [2] | [2] | [1] | [2] | [2] | [2] | [3] | 4 | [8] | [18] | 15 | 14 | [16] | [20] | 25 | [26] | [24] | 25 |
| Birmingham | 9 | 15 | 15 | 18 | 21 | 28 | 21 | 36 | 36 | 41 | 40 | 41 | 53 | 53 | 67 | 60 | | |
| Liverpool | [4] | [4] | [2] | 9 | [7] | 10 | 9 | 14 | [11] | [16] | 24 | 15 | 35 | [39] | 35 | [35] | | |
| Manchester | 0 | 0 | 0 | 0 | 3 | 3 | 4 | 3 | 5 | 14 | 9 | 14 | 20 | 24 | 27 | 22 | | |
| Provincial centres total | 14 | 15 | 20 | 28 | 31 | 43 | 35 | 67 | 48 | 65 | 100 | 97 | 119 | 88 | 166 | 94 | | |
| London | 164 | 191 | 200 | 256 | 224 | 240 | 333 | 284 | 293 | 357 | 373 | 457 | 478 | 548 | 515 | 477 | | |

London figures supplied from the database of British scientific instrument makers maintained by Gloria Clifton at the National Maritime Museum, Greenwich.

**Graph 1.2   Number of instrument making firms in six provincial centres (figures from local street directories, square brackets indicate inferred numbers for years where no directory exists).  See Graph 6.1 for London figures**

enterprises, rather than individuals. Local directories were only being introduced from somewhat after the mid-eighteenth century, and a 'start-date' of 1760 for these places is not possible: Birmingham's first directory was published in 1767; Liverpool's in 1766; Manchester's in 1772 and Sheffield's in 1774. Other substantial provincial cities soon had their own directories, too: Bristol, almost annually from 1775, Newcastle-upon-Tyne from 1778, while still others – York, Hull, Leeds – were encompassed in the huge provincial listings undertaken first by Bailey in 1781, and subsequently by Holden, Pigot and Slater.[57] The directories were produced to satisfy the demands of the rise of commerce, and although they remain a flawed source, the information gleaned from them gives an indication of trends within the provincial instrument trade.

**Instruments, Utility, and the Industrial Revolution**

The instrument trade changed greatly during the period of the Industrial Revolution. It moved from being a small, London-centred craft, commanding international markets, to one which (as Clifton has indicated, and this book will confirm) trebled in size,[58] with strong roots in the English provinces, feeding its products into the London market but also prepared to look further afield. Clouds were, however, gathering on the economic horizon, in the form of the strongly commercial industries in France and Germany, which had been supported with more state backing, through technical education for workmen, from an earlier date.

The instrument trade has previously been studied almost entirely from the perspective of its end products. These can often be appreciated as items of beauty as well as of utility. Nonetheless, their creators were making them for utilitarian reasons: they needed to be successful at what they did, they had to reach and expand their markets, they had to have business acumen, and they had to make a profit and pay their workmen. In short, they had to survive. This book will try to explain how they attempted to do all of this, in a time of great economic and technological change, population flux, and a prolonged period of war. It will also look at the larger question of whether the trade, small as it was, had any influence on the Industrial Revolution and its course.

---

[57]   For more detail, see Norton (1950) and Shaw (1982).
[58]   Clifton (1995), xiii, citing nineteenth-century Census figures.

# Chapter 2

# Bristol and Liverpool

## Bristol

Recent work has confirmed that instrument-making skills were transferred from the workshops of Flanders to new ones in London sometime towards the end of the sixteenth century.[1] From the capital, these skills were, in due course, transmitted to a few places outside London, usually where the population was fairly substantial, and where there was some local demand for instrument production or repair. Bristol was probably among the first of these English centres, as it was an important port from early times, and navigators – as they left the coasts behind them – clearly had a need of instrumentation to find their destinations, and perhaps more importantly, to find their way home.

Bristol's economic position was based on maritime trade and commerce. Unlike many other West Country towns, it was not an administrative centre. Before the discoveries in the New World, its growth and prosperity depended on its geography: the safety of its natural river harbour and the steepness of its surrounding hills ensured the security of shipping from bad weather and other hazards. In early modern times, Bristol exported finished cloth and soap from its immediate hinterland, importing sweet Spanish wines, and trading with the Canary Islands, through which dyes, drugs, sugar and kidskins were imported from further afield. From the mid-sixteenth century, its trade with the Mediterranean, privateering, and the beginnings of its traffic with Africa were all established. By the end of the seventeenth century, its main imports were sugar and tobacco from the West Indies, and together with the supply of slaves from West Africa to those colonies in the Caribbean, this formed the core of Bristol's wealth.

Navigation seems to have been the real driver for any early instrument production in Bristol. Indeed, if we start at the beginning of E.G.R. Taylor's magisterial work on the *Mathematical Practitioners of Tudor and Stuart England* – bearing in mind that her focus is not upon instrument making – her third and tenth biographies are the Bristolians Roger Barlow (fl.1526–54) and James Alday (1516–76).[2] Both were practical navigators, associated with Sebastian Cabot (c.1481–1557). Cabot, the son of a Venetian, may have been born in Bristol in about 1481 (both date and place are uncertain), and although he might be classified as an adventurer, his activities so chimed with the new Tudor dynasty's aspirations

---

[1]   Turner (2000); Harkness (2002); and Ackermann (1998).
[2]   Taylor (1954), 166 and 168.

to become a European power through exploration and empire-building that he was employed by both Henry VII and Henry VIII on voyages of discovery. He made maps and investigated the variation of the compass-needle, but was not himself an instrument maker.[3]

Roger Barlow of Bristol presented Henry VIII with a manuscript containing the earliest nautical tables in English. His friend Nicholas Thorne, who died in 1546, left a collection of nautical books, maps, charts, globes and instruments – including an astrolabe – to found a sailors' library in Bristol.[4] Another Bristol-born mariner who was specially trained in the art of navigation was Richard Chancellor (c.1525–56). Chancellor became a close friend of John Dee (1527–1608), who was about the same age. Dee, having spent his formative years from 1547 to 1550 in Louvain, Brussels and Paris, had become acquainted with the foremost Continental mathematicians, 'among whom', wrote Taylor, 'the designing, description and use of instruments in the service of geodesy, cartography, dialling, gunnery, etc., was taken for granted in their work'.[5] On his return to London, Dee was introduced into court circles, and 'for the next thirty years he gave advice and instruction to pilots and navigators and collected a great mathematical and scientific library, besides a variety of mathematical instruments'.[6] Dee's pupil and friend Thomas Digges (c.1543–95), as well as Dee himself, wrote of Richard Chancellor's ingenuity as an instrument maker. Dee possessed 'an excellent, strong and fair quadrant of five foot semidiameter' made by his friend.[7]

The political impulse of the English Tudor court for economic expansion led to a search for a North-East passage, through which spices could be imported and new markets in cold lands be found for exporting English woollen cloth. Detailed instructions for this expedition were drawn up by Cabot, and these included the specification of the post of Chief Pilot, for which Richard Chancellor was specially trained. In this Chancellor sought the help of John Dee, writes Taylor, and 'the two young men made observations together of the height of the noon sun, and Chancellor proved to have not only mathematical ability but real mechanical genius; he was able to redesign and improve the instruments it was proposed he should use and actually invented independently the diagonal scale'.[8] Chancellor's voyage successfully opened the White Sea route to Muscovy, but he drowned at sea off the north coast of Scotland in 1556.[9] With the death of Cabot a year or so later (incidentally, confiding on his deathbed that he had solved the problem of longitude), there was something of a lull in Bristol-grown instrument-makers.[10]

---

3　　Pope (1997), 16–18, 43–68; Taylor (1954), 10–11.
4　　Ibid., 166. This legacy was left to Bristol Grammar School.
5　　Ibid., 170. See also Turner (2003).
6　　Taylor (1954), 170.
7　　Quoted by Taylor, ibid.
8　　Ibid., 18–20.
9　　Hakluyt (1886), 137.
10　　Taylor (1954), 21.

Just over a century later, another group of Bristolians who were linked to the publisher of the *Mariner's Magazine*, Samuel Sturmy (1633–69), became active in instrument studies. Sturmy, again according to Taylor, made observations of the local magnetic compass variations in 1666 and 1667 together with Philip Staynred (fl.*c*.1621–69), sending their results to the Royal Society. Staynred was older than Sturmy, and had published an almanack for Bristol in 1635, finding its latitude at 51° 28'. He was a quantity surveyor and gauger, and had devised and made his own measuring rulers and gauging rods, besides selling other mathematical instruments.[11] Sturmy also mentioned Thomas Moone as 'an ingenious smith' who would make mathematical instruments to order in Bristol at this period. 'Professional instrument makers were rarely to be found outside London at this date', comments Taylor, 'although a quadrant signed by Ann Shepard of Bristol in 1676 points to one such establishment'.[12]

Fragmentary evidence and information about instrument making in Bristol survives from the end of the seventeenth century. For instance, Anselm Jenner (fl.1685–92) advertised together with the London instrument maker Walter Hayes in Matthew Norwood's 1685 *System of Navigation*, and both men's names were on the engraving of a form of circular slide-rule illustrated in this work, suggesting some sort of business arrangement between them.[13]

In an unpublished analysis of Bristol probate inventories between 1640 and 1775, Jonathan Barry has found that seafarers were those most likely to be found in possession of scientific instruments: 'The well-equipped mariner possessed plots and charts, as well as books for the sea, with compasses and dials, a prospecting or spy glass, and a range of such things as cross staffs, fore staffs, scales and quadrants'. Barry located two inventories which contained all these items, both dating from 1684, but instruments other than these essential navigation tools were only occasionally mentioned in the inventories. Unfortunately, no inventories for any of the scientific instrument makers known to have been active in the city at this period were found.[14] Three navigation instruments signed by Robert Yeff survive, with dates from 1693 to 1721, and Yeff's certificate of his Freedom of Bristol is dated 1697.[15]

---

[11]  Ibid., 208 and 242.

[12]  Ibid., 260 and 272; in fact, this ivory Gunter's quadrant is the only piece known from her workshop, and it may have been retailed: National Maritime Museum inv. no. NAV 1036.

[13]  Taylor (1954), 281 and 401.

[14]  Barry (1983), 11–12.

[15]  A nocturnal by Yeff in the National Maritime Museum is dated 1693, inv. no.AST0141, see Higton (2002), 400; another in the Science Museum is dated 1702, NMSI inv. no. 1903–80. Nocturnals are time-telling devices, used in conjunction with tide tables, which, as their name suggests, are used at night. Robert Yeff's Certificate of the Freedom of Bristol, 1697, is Science Museum NMSI inv. no. 1987–61; also a 24-inch Gunter's scale dated 1721 at the Whipple Museum of the History of Science, Cambridge, inv. no. 2823; see Clifton (1995), 308.

**Figure 2.1    Nocturnal by Robert Yeff of Bristol dated 1702**

*Source*: © National Museum of Science and Industry, NMSI inv. no. 1903–80

By 1726, the English spy and man of letters, Daniel Defoe (1661?–1731), was able to stress the continuing importance of Bristol as England's second major port after London: ' … the greatest, the richest and the best port of trade in Great Britain, London only excepted … It is supposed they have an hundred thousand inhabitants in the city, and within three miles of its circumference; and they say above three thousand sail of ships belong to that port'.[16] Local legend has it that Defoe met the Scots mariner, Alexander Selkirk (1676–1720), in a Bristol tavern and subsequently turned his story into *Robinson Crusoe*. However, the instrument making and activities associated with navigation from Tudor times had not apparently proved sufficient for a community of specialist practitioners to sustain itself, with skills passed on from one generation to the next, even by the mid-eighteenth century in Bristol. Jonathan Barry notes that there were few optical or other instrument makers recorded in Bristol between 1700 and 1750. However, we have the names of some earlier instrument-makers, who like Yeff, became burgesses: J. Willis (June 1662), T. Wells (July 1678), Thomas Plummer (November 1718) (Figure 2.2) and E. Woolfe (January 1700).[17]

**Figure 2.2    Backstaff with the signature of Thomas Plumer (*sic*)**

*Source*: Sotheby's London

By the beginning of the eighteenth century, the cloth manufacture around Bristol had declined because of competition from elsewhere, and new industries of iron, tin, copper and brass were established. The Bristol Brass Wire Company began manufacture of brass in 1702. Copper ore was supplied from Cornwall, while calamine was found to occur more locally. Coal for smelting was mined in the area, and waterpower could be harnessed from the Avon and the Frome. There were extensive markets for brass products in the western colonies and particularly on the west coast of Africa, where slaves were exchanged for brass 'toys', and also more locally in Birmingham where those 'toys' were manufactured.

---

[16]    Defoe (1971), 361, 363.
[17]    These early Bristol makers are mentioned by Barry (1985), 258. A backstaff by Thomas Plumer (*sic*) was offered by Sotheby's, 20 May 1992, lot 388.

Initially, brass-making skills had to be imported by bringing workmen from the Netherlands and Germany.[18]

Bristol's shipping volume had increased: the vessels were built in the port and manned from the city. Taking home-produced items from England they sailed for West Africa, where these cargoes were exchanged for slaves; the ships then proceeded to the West Indies, where the slaves were sold and sugar, tobacco, indigo, cotton and ginger bought with the proceeds. These were either returned to Bristol, or were taken to other European ports for sale. Defoe commented that

> the Bristol merchants as they have a very great trade abroad, so they have always buyers at home, for their returns, and that such buyers that no cargo is too big for them. To this purpose, the shopkeepers in Bristol who in general are all wholesale men, have so great an inland trade among all the western counties, that they maintain carriers just as the London tradesmen do, to all the principal counties and towns from Southampton in the south, even to the banks of the Trent north.[19]

Yet a proportion of the goods, especially luxury items, sold in Bristol were associated with London manufacturers, and the cachet of London manufacture can be seen in 1756 (see Figure 8.10), when advertisements were appearing in the Bristol press for

> John Wright (From LONDON) ... [and at the foot] Gentlemen may depend upon being served with the above, and all other Instruments, made according to the latest Discoveries, JOHN WRIGHT being late an Apprentice to Mr COLE, Successor to Mr THOMAS WRIGHT, Instrument Maker to his Majesty.[20]

Although threatened by competition on at least one occasion, when the London instrument makers James Ayscough and Henry Gregory appointed a local bookseller as an agent for their wares, John Wright appears to have supplanted them. He subsequently advertised himself as 'the ONLY MATHEMATICAL, PHILOSOPHICAL and OPTICAL Instrument-Maker in BRISTOL', and he may briefly have been survived by his wife, Susanna, as a backstaff with her signature has been recorded.[21]

By 1759, his shop 'At Hadly's [sic] Quadrant ... Lately the SHOP of Mr JOHN WRIGHT' was being run by Joshua Springer, implying a firm trade succession: Springer may well have learned his trade in Wright's workshop.[22] Springer is known to have sold a variety of instruments, among them octants and mariner's

---

[18]  Hamilton (1967), 108–9.
[19]  Defoe (1971), 362.
[20]  *Felix Farley's Bristol Journal*, 13 March 1756.
[21]  Ibid., 20 November 1756; *Bristol Weekly Intelligencer*, 1 January 1757; Sotheby's, 20 September 1983, Lot 104: 'Made at Sus$^a$ Wright$^s$ in Briftol'.
[22]  *Felix Farley's Bristol Journal*, 29 September 1759.

compasses (Figure 2.3).[23] By 1774, Springer was to be found in premises at no 2 Clare Street – an address which was to be used in turn by R. & C. Beilby from 1808.[24] The Beilbys retailed a range of instruments, including David Brewster's kaleidoscope in 1818; this last was manufactured in Sheffield.[25] Subsequently the same premises in Clare Street were occupied by John King, who advertised as 'late foreman to C. Beilby' – in a direct line, begun by John Wright in 1756 that continued until well after the Great Exhibition of 1851.[26] Where a family succession failed through death, lack of inclination or provision of heirs, it seems that a trade succession was the preferred option. This pattern is most clearly seen in Bristol, where a much more modest expansion in the trade occurred than in other English provincial towns at this time.

Joshua Springer may have inherited Wright's premises and commercial goodwill, but in 1774 he also found himself with competition in the person of Henry Edgeworth, who described himself as 'The only Person in this City, who served a regular Apprenticeship' in instrument making.[27] Edgeworth (Figure 2.4) appears to have arrived in Bristol from Dublin, where he may have served an apprenticeship with John Margas, a London instrument maker forced by bankruptcy in 1758 to move to the Irish capital.[28] In 1790, Richard Rowland advertised that he had 'succeeded to the business of the late Mr HENRY EDGEWORTH, which he intends carrying on in all its branches', and his signature is known on a number of navigation instruments.[29] Again, in partnership with his sons Edward and Thomas Rowland, and long after his death, the firm also survived to just beyond the Great Exhibition, going bankrupt under Richard's grandson Edward, in 1851. In 1792, William Watson, son of a

---

[23] Items recorded with Springer's signature include: an octant in Hamburg Museum; another dated 1795 in a private collection; a barometer at Gloucester Museum, and a mariner's compass at Hull Museums and Galleries: see Holbrook et al. (1992), 135, 139; another mariner's compass at the National Museums of Scotland: NMS.T.1969.33; a Cuff-type microscope at the Science Museum, inv. no. NMSI 1938–698, and an equinoctial ring dial in the Museum of the History of Science, Oxford, inv. no. 54552.

[24] *Felix Farley's Bristol Journal*, 10 September 1774 and 9 July, 20 August 1808.

[25] A Culpeper-type microscope is in the Wellcome Collection, inv. no. A601179; and a kaleidoscope is in the Museum of the History of Science, Oxford, inv. no. 76530: Beilby's advertisement for the kaleidoscope appeared in ibid., 4, 11 and 25 July 1818.

[26] Undated trade card, Blaise Castle Museum, Bristol, inv. no. TA 5109.

[27] *Felix Farley's Bristol Journal*, 25 June 1774.

[28] Burnett and Morrison-Low (1989), 39; Clifton (1995), 92, 178. Two octants with Edgeworth's signature have been recorded, one in the National Maritime Museum, inv. no. NAV1281, the other in South Carolina: see Bryant (1999).

[29] *Felix Farley's Bristol Journal*, 6 February 1790; Edgeworth's death was announced in Ibid., 23 January 1790. Rowland's signature is known from an octant offered at Christie's South Kensington, 14 March 1985, Lot 240; a mariner's compass offered at Sotheby's, 21 June 1983, Lot 266. Rowland also held English Patent no. 3525 of 1812, for 'ships' steering wheels, compasses and binnacles'.

**Figure 2.3   Mariner's compass, card signed by Joshua Springer, Bristol, 1790**

*Source*: National Museums of Scotland, NMS.T.1969.33

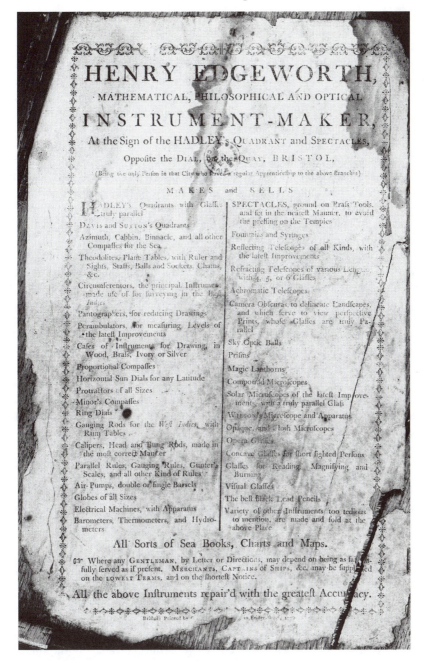

**Figure 2.4    Trade card for Henry Edgeworth, Bristol**

*Source*: © National Maritime Museum

Gloucestershire yeoman, was apprenticed for seven years to Richard Rowland and Ann, his wife, and was made free in July 1801. He subsequently appeared in the directory for 1805 as an independent mathematical instrument maker in St Michael's Hill, where he evidently prospered. He married in 1811, and a few years later described himself as a manufacturer of mathematical, philosophical, optical and nautical instruments, 'At the Lord Nelson', 16 St Augustine's Back. The business survived until 1832, and there is anecdotal evidence that he may have emigrated to the United States.[30]

The numbers of firms of instrument makers or retailers in Bristol remained small and relatively static during this period: at around five in 1775, rising to seven or eight in 1800, and to nine in 1810, at which figure it remained until after 1850 (see Graph 2.1). The longevity of these firms, provided they survived the first two or three years, appears to have been relatively stable, extending over a number of generations or trade successors.[31] Among contributing factors – other than the obvious one of supplying and repairing navigational instruments – must have been the long-established large houses and estates around Bristol, and a steady market for the supply of quality items: the fashionable spa of Bath was merely a few miles away, while larger landowners with their surveying and building requirements were to be found in the surrounding countryside.[32] Unsurprisingly, early Bristol instrument makers had their premises close to the quays, where their marine customers could find them without too much trouble (see Graph 2.1).

By the mid-nineteenth century, however, there had been a distinct move of these premises into the centre of town, where the main shopping area was to be found. Nor was the production of instruments by now exclusively for a maritime market. By the beginning of the nineteenth century, the slave trade had effectively transferred to Liverpool (later to be abolished in Britain, in 1833). Sugar continued to be a main industry (upon which depended a vast cooperage business), along with import and export of rum and molasses, but despite these and other activities, Bristol was in a period of relative commercial decline. Partly this was due to Bristol's political structure, which had allowed only freemen to trade within the city boundaries, and as Defoe remarked: 'were it not for this, the city of Bristol, would before now, have swelled and increased in buildings and inhabitants, perhaps

---

[30] Bristol directories, *passim*; information supplied by the late T.J. Bryant. Watkins' signature has been recorded on three items in Bristol Museums and Art Galleries: a portable sundial (inv. no. J. 1537), a waywiser (inv. no. J. 2760) and a telescope (inv. no. J. 3942); a pocket horizontal dial and compass is in the Museum of the History of Science, Oxford (inv. no. 52880).

[31] Numbers gleaned from Bristol directories, which run almost annually from 1772.

[32] Bath managed to support a handful of resident instrument retailers during this period including, at different times, Jacob Abraham (who also had a shop in Cheltenham), Lyon and Thomas Davis, James Field, Henry Oakley, John Orchard, Peter Salmoni, Benjamin Smith and Henry Tulley: for whom, see Clifton (1995). William Herschel was of a different stature: see Chapter 5.

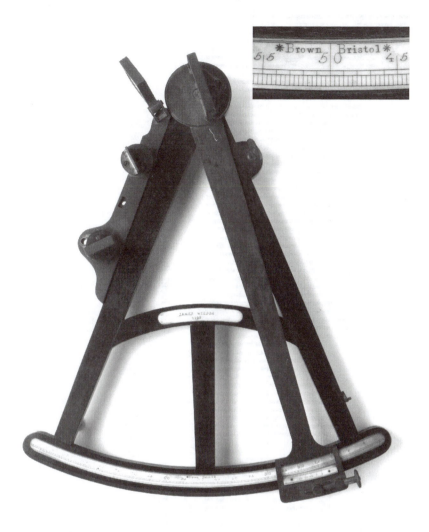

**Figure 2.5    Octant by Brown of Bristol, 1792**

*Source*: National Museums of Scotland, NMS.T.1967.87

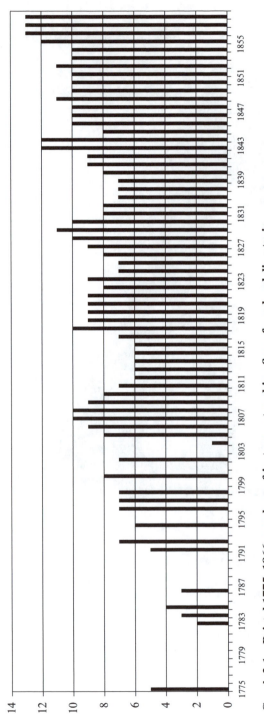

**Graph 2.1  Bristol 1775–1866: numbers of instrument making firms from local directories**

to double the magnitude it was formerly of'.[33] Partly it was due to geography: the port's location was seven miles upriver and it was subject to strong tidal variations, which meant that much of the western maritime trade was attracted to Liverpool, which had no such disadvantage. Harbour improvements, such as the building of the New Cut in the early nineteenth century, were put into the hands of a private company, which further exacerbated the situation by levying crippling rates to the detriment of harbour traffic. Finally, the sugar trade with the West Indies was effectively killed off by central government's free trade policy.[34]

There was some interest in scientific culture in Bristol from the late eighteenth century: for instance, the instrument maker Joshua Springer, together with John Weeks of the Bush Tavern, proposed a scientific ascent in a three-man balloon, provided that £300 could be raised by public subscription. However, this funding was not forthcoming and the project never left the ground.[35] From about 1809, there was a Literary and Philosophical Society, and the Bristol Institution was founded in 1823, but Michael Neve makes the point that 'a notable aspect of the history of Bristol, and its neighbouring town of Bath, was the absence in the heyday of the eighteenth century "Enlightenment" of organized scientific culture'.[36] This, together with Bristol's period of economic decline, perhaps explains the lack of growth of the instrument trade there in the early nineteenth century.

Two Bristol instrument makers exhibited at the Great Exhibition. John Braham first announced his 'mathematical instrument warehouse' in Clare Street in 1828, but by the following year he was in the more fashionable College Green. In the early 1830s his premises moved to St Augustine's Parade, where he managed to acquire the agency for selling Admiralty charts. However, he was clearly finding that optical material was the most lucrative, and his display at the Great Exhibition was almost entirely composed of spectacles. The Jury was most unimpressed: 'It is with regret that we observe that the exhibitors of spectacles in the British portion of the Exhibition have done nothing more than exhibit a collection of shop goods, and have regarded the improvement of the glasses themselves as a matter of little moment'.[37] An octant in the Bristol Museum was evidently retailed rather than made by Braham, as its scale is marked as having been divided by the London wholesalers and dividers to the trade, Spencer, Browning and Rust.[38] In the Census

---

[33] Defoe (1971), 362.
[34] Reasons for Bristol's economic decline are given by Neve (1983), 182–3.
[35] *Felix Farley's Bristol Journal,* 23, 30 April, 14 and 21 May 1785.
[36] Neve (1983).
[37] *Catalogue ...* (1851), 439; *Reports...* (1852), 272–3.
[38] Holbrook et al. (1992), 101. Other instruments recorded with Braham's signature include a Cary-type microscope in the Wellcome Collection (inv. no A645010); proportional compasses, and a hygrometer in the Science Museum (inv. no. NMSI 1916–300 and 1917–103); a simple microscope in the Whipple Museum of the History of Science (inv. no. 985); a plotting scale in the Museum of the History of Science, Oxford (inv. no.45461); and a telescope offered by Sotheby's, 21 October 1975, Lot 53.

of 1851, John Braham, aged fifty, described himself as a 'manufacturing optician', employing two men. He had been born in Plymouth, and was Jewish, probably with European family origins. The business was taken over by another ocular specialist, M.W. Dunscombe in 1874, according to the street directories.

John King, as we have seen, began as foreman to Charles and Richard Beilby, and took over their premises on their retirement in 1821, but he was probably born in London, as was his son John, according to the 1861 Census. This was plainly a family firm, although the family appears not to have been as cohesive as some: members splintered into individual businesses, and some acrimonious correspondence survives between John King the elder and his son John, who had abandoned his wife and children, apparently for another woman, in 1831.[39] Thomas Davis King was a son of the younger John King, but left the business in 1857, and is mentioned in his father's will 20 years later as a journalist living in Montreal, Canada. Their display at the Great Exhibition consisted of microscopes of which T.D. King was 'designer and manufacturer'; and the Jury thought that 'the workmanship ... is of the first order ... The Jury considered Mr King as well deserving Honourable Mention'.[40] Unusually, the Kings developed their own microscope model (Figure 2.6), based on a London design by the eminent specialist microscope makers Powell & Lealand, and these were numbered: the lowest number recorded is 81, dating sometime between 1846 and 1850; the highest is numbered 223, and is inscribed with the date 1857.[41] Unfortunately, no information has surfaced to provide a price for these instruments, but this implies a total sale of about 140 microscopes over a period of seven to 11 years. By the 1851 Census, Thomas Davis King, aged 32, was employing five journeymen, all working on the premises at 2 Clare Street.

During the mid-century, the main Bristol instrument-making business was probably that of John Moor Hyde, and it flourished between 1841 and 1854 (he also ran a nautical academy from 1844 to 1851). The instrument side of his business was subsequently run by Hill & Price, at Hyde's Broad Quay address. Husbands & Clarke – from whose workshops many items survive – began their business at 1 Denmark Street in 1858, and appear to have been the main suppliers of instruments locally in the latter part of the nineteenth century.

---

[39]  Bristol Record Office, Accession N. 4966 (36).
[40]  *Catalogue...* (1851), 439; *Reports...* (1852), 266–7.
[41]  J.B. Dancer of Manchester, and R. Field of Birmingham also numbered their microscopes: for which, see chapters 4 and 8. The King instrument 81 (now in the Pompidou Centre, Paris) is discussed in Nuttall (1979), 49; no. 113 was offered by Phillips, 11 November 1981, lot 100; no. 133 (by King & Coombs) was offered by Christie's South Kensington, 23 November 1977, Lot 12; no. 165 (also by King & Coombs) by Phillips, 16 May 1978, lot 102; no. 171 is in Bristol Museums; no. 192 was offered by Tesseract, Catalogue 21, Summer 1988, item 17; no. 221, also by Tesseract, Catalogue 17, Summer 1987, item 22; and no. 223 is in Bristol Museums: see Holbrook et al. (1992), 100.

**Figure 2.6    Microscope signed by Thomas Davis King, dated 1857**

*Source*: Bristol Museums Galleries and Archives, inv. no. J.445

The striking characteristics of the Bristol instrument-making community during the period of the Industrial Revolution up to the Great Exhibition are how small, yet stable, it appears to have been, and also how few early instruments (even with a maritime purpose) have survived with a Bristol signature. Unlike the newer centres of population, such as Manchester and Liverpool, there seems to have been no large influx of immigrants who tended towards the instrument trade. There were one or two: John Braham, as we have seen; the Levy family (presumably also with Jewish origins), whose optical glass warehouse expanded to become Levy's Bristol Bazaar; and P. Tarone, weather glass and thermometer maker, whose name implies Italian roots, and who settled in Bristol between 1806 and 1812. He may have been related to the Anthony Tarone based in Dundee at a slightly later date, or others with similar names recorded subsequently in Hull, Leeds and London. For a port, and for one that was for much of this time England's second largest maritime settlement, where immigrants would disembark, Bristol clearly held few attractions for newcomers with instrumental skills. The trade appears to have reached equilibrium early in the nineteenth century.

## Liverpool

It is perhaps illuminating to contrast Bristol's instrument activities with those of another port: Liverpool. In 1726, Daniel Defoe commented: "'tis probable it will in a little time be as big as the city of Dublin ... 'Tis already the next town to Bristol, and in a little time may probably exceed it, both in commerce, and in number of people'.[42] During the period of the Industrial Revolution, for a number of reasons, Liverpool overtook both Bristol and Dublin in size. A centre for the slave trade and for imports of cotton, tobacco and sugar, Liverpool was a dynamic, chaotic and growing mass of seething humanity. Unlike Bristol, whose street plan remained recognisably the same throughout this period, Liverpool's population grew enormously, with the town reconstructing its docks and waterside as the port expanded. As a result, instrument makers did not remain in the same premises; nor indeed did their trade successions appear to be so smooth.

The earliest instrument makers recorded in the Liverpool area appear to be the brothers John and Robert Roscoe, whose business is recorded from about 1696 until John's death in 1713, with Robert continuing until he died ten years later. Roger Wild became Robert Roscoe's apprentice in 1714.[43] Although there were a few other instrument makers in Liverpool in the first half of the eighteenth century, besides Roger Wild – Thomas Kendal, James Dykes, Henry Roberts, Thomas Woodside and William Skegg – all these individuals' histories are very obscure, known only from the description of their occupation in parish registers.[44]

Perhaps the most significant figure in eighteenth-century Liverpool was the clock and watchmaker Joseph Finney (*c.*1708–72). Oliver Fairclough has suggested that as instrument making was usually a distinctly separate craft from that of clock-making, Finney should be compared with individuals such as George Graham and John Ellicott of London, and a very select group of provincial figures including Henry Hindley of York, John Whitehurst of Derby and John Hallifax of Barnsley. This comparison may be more informative, even though there had been 'a small and unadventurous instrument making industry in Liverpool since the reign of William III'.[45] Few instruments signed by Finney survive, and most of these are in the collection formed by George III.[46] 'Yet despite his august patronage', writes Fairclough, 'Finney is a peripheral figure

---

[42]    Defoe (1971), 392.
[43]    Fairclough (1975), 407. No instruments have been recorded with their signatures.
[44]    Listed in ibid., 225, 405–8.
[45]    Ibid., p.xix.
[46]    These are a barometer, NMSI inv. no. 1927–1911; an elliptical trammel, NMSI inv. no. 1927–1210; a dial micrometer (a form of pyrometer) NMSI inv. no.1927–1663: Morton and Wess (1993), 226, 377 390–91; another pyrometer is in the cabinet at Burton Constable,

in the history of the Liverpool instrument-making industry which had turned largely to the manufacture of navigational instruments by 1800'.[47]

By the time the first Liverpool street directory was published in 1766 there were already two mathematical instrument firms listed, one proving very short-lived.[48] At the turn of the century there were ten firms, and these numbers increased gradually over the next 50 years to 36 in the year of the Great Exhibition (see Graph 2.2). Initially some, such as John Grindrod, listed in the 1766 directory, and Thomas Howard, who appeared the following year, may well have been locals (judging by their names).[49] Others, for example John Leverton, were trained in and had migrated from London. Advertisements appeared in the local paper *Gore's Liverpool General Advertiser* in 1766 and 1767, in which Leverton claimed that he was 'from London'.[50] Clifton's *Directory* confirms that his father was Lancelott Leverton, bricklayer of Waltham Abbey, Essex, and that he was apprenticed to William Parsons of the Goldsmiths Company in 1749 and freed in 1761.[51] William Drury, active in Liverpool between 1769 and 1773 (Figure 2.7), may have been an apprentice of the London ship chandler and instrument maker, John Urings.[52] A Richard Urings, mathematical instrument maker, is recorded in a Liverpool marriage register in 1766.[53]

There do seem to be strong links between the specialist provincial trade in Liverpool and the navigational instrument makers and suppliers from the docks of London at the end of the eighteenth century, and these persisted well into the

---

near Hull: Holbrook et al. (1992), 105; a number of clocks and watches by Finney are known and these are discussed in Fairclough (1976–78).

[47] Fairclough (1975), xix.

[48] John Grindrod, mathematical instrument maker, appeared in directories for 1766 and 1767 only; John Leverton first appeared in 1766, succeeded by S. (Susannah) in 1787; she made her last appearance in the 1790 directory.

[49] Grindrod is a location name: 'Greneroade' was a locality in Rochdale parish, Lancashire, which became 'Greenroad': Grindrod Family Index 1584–1837 (in which John Grindrod, Liverpool mathematical instrument maker, does not appear). See www.grindrodlr.freeserve.co.uk/. Thomas Howard may have been related to two others with the same surname and occupation, Henry and William, recorded in the parish registers: Fairclough (1975), 406. An octant '.Made. by. Thos. Howard. Liverpool.. / .For Mr. Joseph. Hunter. March. 30. 1769' is in the Museum of the History of Science, Oxford, inv. no. 33700.

[50] *Gore's Liverpool General Advertiser*, 14 May 1766, quoted by Fairclough (1975), 226.

[51] Clifton (1995), 166–7. Instruments with Leverton's signature include dated octants at the National Maritime Museum (1777), inv. no. NAV1295; and Sotheby's, 4 December 1961, Lot 35, now at Harvard University (1783), inv. no. CHSI WP 884 and a Cuff type microscope, Phillips, 14 May 1974, Lot 93.

[52] Ibid., 89. A telescope with Drury's signature was sold at Christie's South Kensington, 29 September 1994, Lot 212.

[53] St. Nicholas Parish Register, 27 February 1766, marriage of Robert Urings to Alice Pills, quoted by Fairclough (1975), 407.

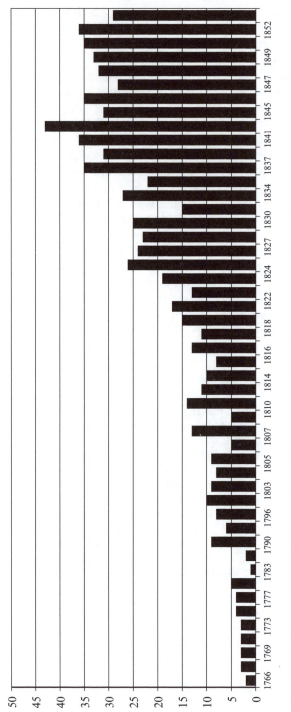

**Graph 2.2  Liverpool 1766–1853: numbers of instrument making firms from local directories**

**Figure 2.7    Refracting telescope signed by W. Drury, Liverpool, c.1770**

*Source*: Christie's South Kensington

nineteenth. This is demonstrated by a number of surviving nautical instruments, recorded with a Liverpool signature, which appear to have London connections. For example, one late-eighteenth century ebony octant, signed on the ivory plate, 'Thomas Holliwell, Liverpool' has the ivory scale marked with the dividing engine symbol of a foul anchor, implying that it had had its scale divided by Jesse Ramsden's dividing engine, in London.[54]

An unsigned octant with the dividing mark on the scale for the London wholesalers and scale dividers Spencer, Browning and Rust, and with several trade labels, some now loose within the case, may provide further links between Liverpool and London.[55] The label still attached inside the lid is for 'Charles Jones, real manufacturer of sextants and quadrants …' at a Liverpool address occupied by Jones between 1823 and 1827 (Figure 2.8). Jones clearly felt the need to emphasize his 'real' instrument making skills. The label also reveals that 'C.J. [was] Step-son & late Apprentice to I. Gray', who was at that Liverpool address between 1814 and 1822. One of the loose trade labels is for 'John Gray, manufacturer of sextants, quadrants, compasses telescopes &c., No 13, Little

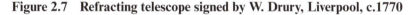

[54]   Noted at the Scientific Instrument Fair, London, May 1994: for the use of such marks, see Stimson (1985).
[55]   Museum of the History of Science, Oxford, inv. no. 52728.

Hermitage Street, Wapping, London'.[56] This must imply not only the stated relationship by marriage between John Gray of Liverpool and Charles Jones, but also a family relationship between the two John Grays, who may even have been one and the same. However, not every octant with a Liverpool signature has a dividing engine stamp, and so not all Liverpool octants – or even just their scales – can be assumed to have been divided in London.

Yet the question remains: did any instrument maker in Liverpool possess a dividing engine, and if so, at what date was it obtained?[57] At the least, this shows that the wholesale prices asked by volume manufacturers of specialist instrument types undercut smaller-scale construction elsewhere and led to complex supply arrangements, in which both London and provincial manufacturers were undoubtedly active.

The navigational element of Liverpool's instrument trade, located in or near the docks, remained its backbone well into the latter part of the nineteenth century. 'Navigational warehouses' were run, for instance, by John Bywater's firm between 1814 and 1835, by Dawson & Melling and Melling & Payne (latterly Melling & Co.) from 1837 to beyond 1852, by Palmer, Steele & Co., which began in 1814 and continued as John Steele, and by John & Alexander Walker's business, which combined the selling of navigation instruments and charts.[58] It would appear that most of the navigation instruments sold in these premises were retailed.

The most long-lived, and possibly also the most diverse of these businesses was run by the Egerton Smiths, father and son, between about 1770 and 1820. The elder Egerton Smith had started to run the Red-Cross Street School from 1759, and from at least 1765 gave annual public lectures on geography, astronomy and navigation. By 1773, he had obtained his 'Mathematical, Philosophical and Optical Shop' in Pool Lane, and electricity became an important component of his lectures thereafter.[59] Smith was described in the local directories as 'schoolmaster and printer' between 1766 and 1773, and for the remainder of the 1770s as 'mathematical instrument maker and lecturer on philosophy'.

Smith died in 1788, following which the firm was taken over and run by his widow, Ann Prescot, whom he had married in 1766; she took her son, the younger Egerton Smith (1774–1841) into partnership in 1800, and left him to run the business with his brother William in 1803.[60] E.G.R. Taylor wrote: 'Although

---

[56]   Clifton (1995), 118.
[57]   The Edinburgh instrument maker John Miller had apparently obtained or built a circular dividing engine by 1793: see Clarke et al. (1989), 30, quoting the *Caledonian Mercury*, 31 December 1793.
[58]   Liverpool directories, *passim.*
[59]   Inkster (1977), 318, quoting *Williamson's Liverpool Advertiser*, 4 October 1765; 518, quoting ibid., 12 November 1773.
[60]   Liverpool directories, *passim;* Clifton (1995), 255; *Liverpool Mercury*, 26 November 1841. Two octants signed 'Egerton Smith Liverpool' and dated *c.*1780, are in the National Maritime Museum, inv. nos. NAV1256 and NAV1309.

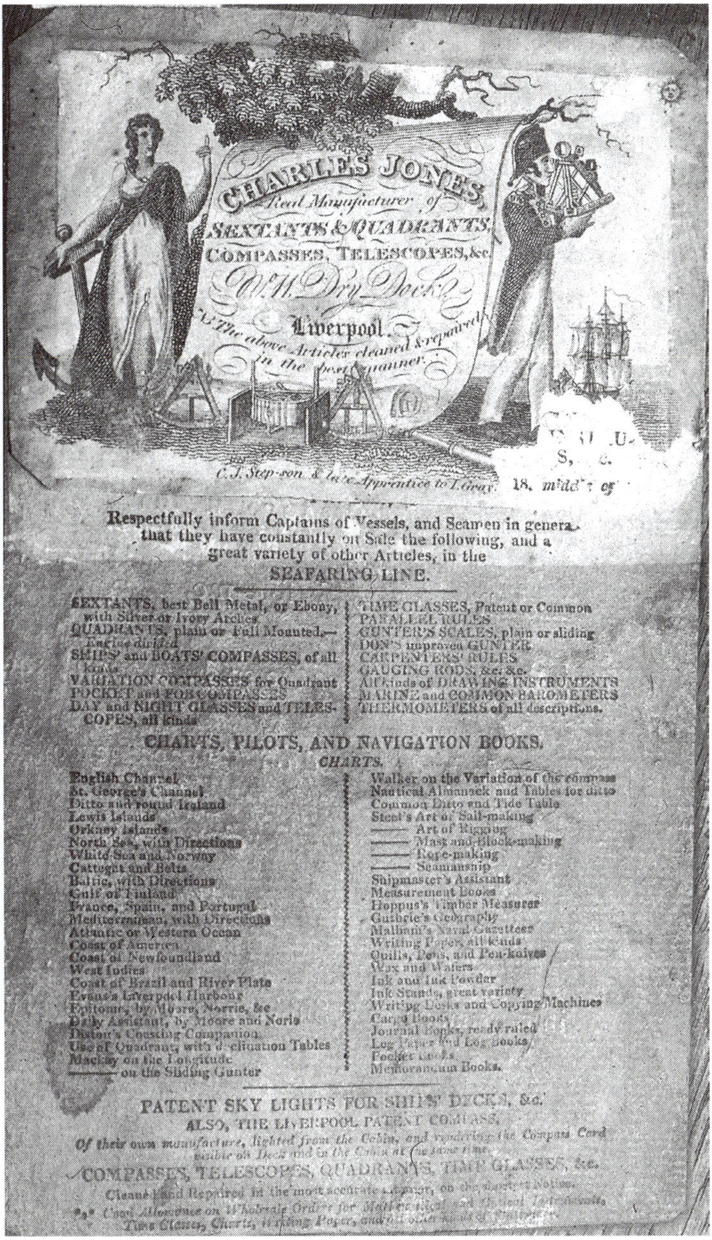

**Figure 2.8    Trade card for Charles Jones, Liverpool, 1823–27**

*Source*: Museum of the History of Science, Oxford, inv. no. 52728

by profession a stationer, [the younger] Smith employed skilled workmen, and with his mechanic Michael Harris took out a patent for improvements in ships' binnacles and compasses (1809)'.[61] This was repeatedly advertised in one of the local papers, the *Liverpool Mercury*, which had been founded by Smith in 1811. Its early numbers stated: '[this newspaper] Printed and Published by Egerton Smith, Pool-Lane ... [sells the] NEW INVENTED PATENT LIFE PRESERVER'.[62] The younger Smith also founded and ran a periodical named *The Kaleidoscope* during the 1820s, eventually devoting most of his time to the press and leaving the navigation shop to be run by his brother William. In later life, he was a noted philanthropist and anti-slavery campaigner, also founding a 'night asylum' for the homeless which had over one hundred beds.[63]

Smith acted as Liverpool agent (and was one of the financial backers) for the Newcastle-under-Lyme clockmaker Edward Massey (1768–1852), who took out his first patent for a ship's log (water speed indicator) and sounding machine in 1802, followed by a second in 1806.[64] Sales were initially slow, and Smith tried to boost them with advertisements in his newspaper and by writing and publishing a pamphlet, *Observations on the Principle and Use of the New Patent Sea Log and Sounding machine invented by Edward Massey* (Liverpool, 1805). By 1811 the Navy Board had purchased 1750 of Massey's sounding machines.[65] In a lengthy (but presumably free) advertisement placed in Smith's paper in 1815, Massey extolled the virtues of his improved chronometers, and then went on to discuss the 'superiority' of his sounding machine and the 'unrivalled accuracy' of his patent perpetual log:

> E.M. trusts that it will not be looked on as presumption in him to say, that, after the Compass and Quadrant, the SOUNDING MACHINE, the CHRONOMETER, and the PERPETUAL LOG are the most important Inventions ever introduced into navigation; whether they are viewed as giving the means of traversing the ocean, or as ensuring the safety of the Ship, and the lives of the Crew: and he firmly believes, that the time is not far distant, when Underwriters will deem it a necessary security that no Ship in which they are concerned, shall leave a Port, without being provided with a Sounding machine, and Log; and when the Chronometers can be supplied in proper numbers, that no Commander of a Ship shall ever undertake a long voyage, or a voyage of discovery, without having one on board.[66]

---

[61]  Taylor (1966), 297; Michael Harris and Egerton Smith, patent no 3265, 26 September 1809, for 'Ships' binnacles and compasses; and mode of lighting the same'.

[62]  For example, 2 July 1813; advertisements for the patent binnacle and compass, as well as the wide range of instruments on offer appeared 27 August 1813, 21 January 1814.

[63]  See Perkin (1990), and Smith's obituary, *Liverpool Mercury*, 26 November 1841.

[64]  Treherne (1977), 7–8; patent no. 2601, 24 March 1802, for 'Instrument for taking soundings at sea', and no. 2938, 6 June 1806, for the same.

[65]  Ibid., 8.

[66]  *Liverpool Mercury*, 19 and 26 May 1815.

The advertisement ends by stating that Massey's chronometers can be obtained from Aaron Arrowsmith of Soho Square, London, and Messrs Norie & Co., at 157 Leadenhall Street, London; and that the latter also supply the sounding machine and log. Evidently, these devices were not produced for a local market.[67] Treherne explains that by the 1830s, after some initial technical problems were overcome, the device began to sell well, when Massey and his descendants took out a series of further patents covering the development of the device. 'This indicates', writes Treherne, 'a lively trade throughout the nineteenth century, with the Masseys (running small workshops employing only members of the family and a few journeymen) attempting to keep the initiative and the production in their own hands'.[68]

Keeping the business in the family seems also to have been one of the driving forces behind the production of an improved spirits hydrometer in late eighteenth-century Liverpool. John Dicas (*c*.1741–97) appeared in the local directories first as a liquor merchant between 1774 and 1787, then as a 'mathematical instrument maker and navigation shop[keeper]' in 1790, and finally as a 'patent hydrometer and mathematical instrument maker' in 1796. He had patented his form of hydrometer, a device used for measuring the alcohol content of liquids, in 1780 (see Figure 7.2), and it was adopted in 1790 by the United States government for estimating the strength of imported spirits.[69] After his death in 1797, the business was carried on by his daughter Mary, and she presented herself and her father's hydrometer to a Board of Inquiry set up in 1802 by the Royal Society to investigate the merits of the many rival designs of the instrument then in use across the country.[70]

The Dicas hydrometer was unsuccessful in being chosen as the standard for the United Kingdom, but continued in production, presumably for the United States, first by Mary Dicas. She married a scale-beam and mathematical instrument maker named George Arstall in 1806, and the firm became Dicas & Arstall, with the Dicas manufactory on the north side of the Old Dock, while Arstall maintained his own business separately in Temple Court. George and Mary Arstall had four children, and the eldest, Frederick Dicas Arstall, in due course became a scale maker, working in Manchester from 1838 and returning to Liverpool in 1851. With the redevelopment of the Old Dock from about 1812, hydrometer manufacture moved to Temple Court. It is difficult to estimate the numbers that were made, but by the time that the firm was being run by Mary's sister Ann Dicas, from 1818, serial numbers had reached 5600. From 1833,

---

[67] See Clifton (1995), 183, for the Massey firm's range of addresses in different towns. Also Fisher (2001), 78 and 91.

[68] Treherne (1977), 8–9.

[69] Liverpool directories, *passim*; patent 1259, 27 June 1780 for 'constructing hydrometers with sliding rules, to ascertain the strength of spirituous-liquors, malt worts and wash for fermentation'. See also Warner (1991), 33.

[70] Ashworth (2001) and (2003), 275.

Ann's husband Benjamin Gamage, ran the business, and the hydrometers were marked 'Gamage late Dicas'. Benjamin Gamage continued to be listed in the local directories as a 'hydrometer maker (Dicas' patent)' until 1851.[71]

Liverpool is a geographically close neighbour of Prescot, which by the early nineteenth century was the centre of watch-part construction and machine-tools for watch making in England. Thus, close to the growing community was a great pool of men with mechanical ability and skilful craftsmanship, from which individuals no doubt moved to the flourishing port.[72] It is apparent that the rising number of chronometer makers in the Liverpool area – among them the businesses of the Frodshams,[73] Gray & Keen, and Edward Massey[74] – drew upon this expertise. From a relatively early stage, too, there was an apparent demand for domestic barometers initially tied in with mirror supply, and weatherglass makers with experience in glass working were able to survive – the earliest of these, Henry Roberts, was active between about 1746 and 1756.[75]

Amongst them were peripatetic Italians (appearing in almost every town of any size from the late eighteenth century onwards), who made this part of the trade very much their own, starting in Liverpool with one Antonio Beptsy, who married a local woman in 1771.[76] Incoming Italians who stayed longer included the later arrivals of the Casartellis (whose Liverpool base was first established in 1821, and continued until the end of the century; see Chapter 4 for their Manchester relatives), and the Pastorellis, whose links with the London firm of the same name have yet to be established.[77] Anthony Introvino, whose main business was in Manchester, had a shop in Liverpool for a few years during the 1820s. The Gallettis, William and Anthony, settled in Liverpool in the 1820s, and may have been related to their namesakes who became established as carvers, gilders, and opticians in Glasgow from 1805.[78]

Other itinerant newcomers to the growing town at this date who were involved with instrument making were Jewish. Bill Williams has described how the first Jewish traders in both Manchester and Liverpool were mainly hawkers, peddling their wares on the newly built streets. As time went by, some became settled and

---

[71] For details of the family connections, see Morrison-Low (1990), 94 and 113–4; and Morrison-Low (1996).
[72] Bailey and Barker (1969); Smith (1977).
[73] Mercer (1981), Chapter VI 'The Liverpool Frodshams', 56–61.
[74] Treherne (1977).
[75] Fairclough (1975), 407, quoting parish registers.
[76] Antonio Beptsy, instrument maker, married Elizabeth Merryjohn, 2 March 1771. Liverpool: St Nicholas's Parish Registers: Marriages.
[77] For the links between the Manchester and Liverpool Casartellis, see Wetton (1990–91), 63–6; for the Pastorellis, see Clifton (1995), 211. Although John Pastorelli first appears in the Liverpool directory for 1834, Joseph Pastorelli & Co. advertised quitting their business, selling (among other merchandise) 'weatherglasses and barometers' at 43 Atherton Street, Liverpool, some considerable period earlier: *Gore's General Advertiser*, 8 May 1800.
[78] Clarke et al. (1989), 205–7.

found themselves premises; by mid-century, they were becoming integrated with the new middle classes of both cities. 'By the early 1840s most of the travelling opticians, dentists, and chiropodists of an earlier age had either proved their worth and settled down as shopkeepers and surgeons or else had sunk, with their hawker companions, into an underworld of petty crime, itinerant quackery and dingy boarding houses.'[79] In Liverpool, one of the longest surviving of these firms was that of Joseph Sewill & Co., which, although it turned to nautical instrument supply in 1837, had been in the locality in various guises since the turn of the century; it continues today.[80]

But perhaps the most prominent of these successful businessmen was Abraham Abraham, who first appeared in the local directory in 1818. Williams remarks: 'Abraham Abraham, the son of a Bath optician, who moved to Liverpool during the war years, and paid regular visits to Manchester in the 1820s, in the following decade was the president of the Liverpool [Jewish] congregation responsible for the introduction of sermons in English. In 1841 he established a branch of his Liverpool business in Cross Street, Manchester, in partnership with the well-known instrument maker, John Dancer'.[81] Curiously, Dancer says almost nothing about Abraham in his autobiography, except to mention the partnership briefly, but giving no clues as to how they met, or why they parted.[82]

Jacob Abraham, Abraham Abraham's father, had premises that lasted long enough to be noted in local street directories in Bath, and subsequently in Cheltenham.[83] Abraham's advertisement announced the reasons for opening the new branch in Manchester in 1841: 'at the solicitation of many scientific gentlemen, and upon the conviction that Manchester imperatively requires an establishment to which the manufacture of philosophical and chemical instruments is immediately directed'.[84] This advertisement mentioned, besides a broad range of instruments, 'a large collection of Pictures from the Daguerreotype', and it appears that, as in Dancer's case in Manchester, Abraham was involved with some early experiments with daguerreotype photography in Liverpool.[85]

An indication of his business acumen was revealed in a letter published in 1868 by his former business partner George S. Wood, in which he describes how his 'late partner and friend, Mr A. Abraham' was amongst the first opticians to sell cheap achromatic microscopes outside London. As early as 1841 he sold large numbers complete in a case with two lenses made by Nachet of Paris, for only

---

[79] Williams (1985), 122. Advertisements in the *Manchester Guardian*, 17 July 1841, and the *Manchester Courier*, 12 June 1841.
[80] Wolfman (1995).
[81] Williams (1985), 123.
[82] Hallett (1979), 13 and 18.
[83] Clifton (1995), 1.
[84] *Manchester Courier,* 12 June 1841.
[85] *Liverpool Mercury*, 25 October 1839.

£8 per set, capitalizing on the popularity of the new instrument and reaching new markets by forcing the price down.[86] Earlier, in 1838, he had opened his first retailing branch in Glasgow, run by Simeon Phineas Cohen, who took this over on his own account in 1843; however, Cohen was declared bankrupt in 1853, mostly through debts to his former partner.[87] In 1851, Abraham was joined in Liverpool by two new partners, both of whom had previously been in business as opticians on their own account, Charles West and George Smart Wood. They continued the firm as Abraham Abraham & Co. for many years after the original proprietor had retired.[88]

By 1851, only three firms based in Liverpool – Chadburn Brothers (as part of their main Sheffield enterprise), Gray & Keen, and Abraham Abraham – were prepared to exhibit at the Great Exhibition. The description of the Chadburn display did not distinguish between its Liverpool and Sheffield elements, and included optical glass in various stages of preparation before being made 'ready for fitting into spectacles. The exhibitors grind 750 dozen per week, on the average'. Gray & Keen put themselves forward as 'manufacturers and designers' of 'wheel barometers mounted according to various designs', while Abraham Abraham & Co., describing themselves as 'manufacturers' displayed a large and impressive triple magic lantern, and a 'compound microscope, exhibited for workmanship', none of which the Jury saw fit to comment upon.[89]

Nonetheless, Liverpool instrument making in the second half of the nineteenth century remained what it had been earlier. It consisted of a core of relatively small numbers of businesses, catering for a predominantly maritime clientele, with only the firm of Abraham Abraham & Co. apparently attempting to reach a larger customer base with their new designs of microscope and trade catalogues offering a wide range of 'optical, mathematical and philosophical instruments'.[90]

---

[86]  Quoted in ibid. Also confirmed by an advertisement in *The Times*, 6 October 1841, page 7, where 'Achromatic microscopes ... price £7 15s. Manufactured and sold by A. Abraham', at branches in Liverpool, Manchester and Glasgow are offered: my thanks to the late J.R. Millburn for this reference. Instruments sold by A. Abraham include: an achromatic microscope [NMS.T.1980.43] and an improved compound microscope [NMS. T.1979.45]: see Nuttall (1979), 32.

[87]  Clarke et al. (1989), 298–300.

[88]  Bracegirdle (1996), 1.

[89]  *Catalogue ...* (1851), 422, 436; *Reports ...* (1852), 301, 273.

[90]  In 1853 and 1855.

# Chapter 3

# York and Sheffield

## York

Across the Pennines from Liverpool were to be found another two centres of instrument making, which provide contrasts since one was older than the other; and, as neither Sheffield nor York were great ports, they in turn should illustrate characteristics different from those shown by Bristol and Liverpool. 'York,' wrote Daniel Defoe,

> is a spacious city, it stands upon a great deal of ground, perhaps more than any city in England out of Middlesex, except Norwich; but then the buildings are not close and thronged as at Bristol, or as at Durham, nor is York so populous as either Bristol or Norwich. But as York is full of gentry and persons of distinction, so they live at large, and have houses proportioned to their quality; and this makes the city lie so far extended on both sides of the river.[1]

The see of one of England's two archbishops, the centre of the northern medieval wool trade, and one of the country's richest and most settled communities, York had known instrument making for some time:

> No city in England [Defoe wrote] is better furnished with provisions of every kind, nor any so cheap, in proportion to the goodness of things; the river being so navigable, and so near the sea, the merchants here trade directly to what part of the world they will ....[2]

However, during the eighteenth century, York's importance as a port went into decline. Gloria Clifton's *Directory* mentions the group of men centred around the eminent early eighteenth-century clockmaker Henry Hindley (*c*.1701–71), which included John Stancliffe and John Smeaton, both of whom migrated in due course to London, and subsequently became more involved in engineering.[3] All of them appear to have been involved in instrument manufacture at some stage in their careers – Stancliffe and Smeaton soon after they arrived in London. Hindley's significant contribution was that he made the first circle-dividing engine,

---

[1]  Defoe (1971), 523.
[2]  Ibid., 521.
[3]  Clifton (1995), 137; see also Setchell (1971), which formed the basis of Setchell (1973); Setchell (1970a) and (1970b); see also Law (1971).

and this will be discussed further in Chapter 7. A Roman Catholic, he had moved from Manchester to York by 1730 apparently because of religious persecution. He made at least two refracting telescopes, one of which has survived, and it has been suggested that he was supplied with glass of a suitable character by a local spectacle maker, Richard Eggleston, whose shop in Minster Yard was only a few yards from Hindley's workshop; both men were mentioned in the same advertisement (for an auction) in December 1734.[4]

Because of York's relative decline, the city had far fewer firms of instrument makers in the late eighteenth century than Bristol. Indeed, a more telling contrast can be seen by comparing York with Bath at this period. Both contained shops and amusements catering to the wealthy, and thus provided wares at the luxury end of the market rather than the tools of industrialisation or scientific endeavour (the exception being the case of Bath-based William Herschel, for whom, see Chapter 5). In York, however, 'RICHARD EGGLESTON, Spectacle-Maker from London ...' advertised his 'new Improved Dioptrical Telescope' in a local newspaper in October 1740.[5] He had served his apprenticeship with the London optician Richard Roak, but it is not clear why he chose to move to York.[6] In 1768, his son Nathaniel, who had served his apprenticeship with 'Mary Eggleston, optician' (presumably his widowed mother) also advertised himself as a spectacle maker in York, making and selling 'all Sorts of Spectacles, Telescopes, Microscopes ...'.[7]

In March 1774, shortly after Nathaniel Eggleston's death, his brother-in-law John Berry announced that 'he [Berry] continues to make and sell all sorts of reflecting and refracting Telescopes, single and compound Microscopes', and so on.[8] Berry himself died the following year, and his widow (born Elizabeth Eggleston) then remarried someone outside the trade.[9] Until this happened, the business had remained tightly within the family, with the involvement of at least two women. Now, one 'Matthias Wisker, glassgrinder and spectacle maker at the

---

[4]    *Yorkshire Courant*, 24 December 1734, quoted in Setchell (1971), 10. Hindley supplied his first equatorial telescope to Burton Constable in 1773, but this has disappeared: Hall (1991), 28; the second was supplied to the Duke of Norfolk, and is now in the Science Museum: inv. no. NMSI 1948–153. There is also a signed sundial at the Castle Museum, York, see Holbrook et al. (1992), 220; an azimuth theodolite attributed to Hindley, or John Smith who worked with him, is in the Science Museum, inv. no. NMSI 1927–1920; and a pyrometer, inv. no. NMSI 1927–1184: Morton and Wess (1993), 396, 158–9.
[5]    *Yorkshire Courant*, 28 October 1740.
[6]    Clifton (1995), 93.
[7]    York City Archives: Register of Freemen, 1680–1986; *Yorkshire Courant*, 23 February 1768.
[8]    Ibid., 22 March 1774.
[9]    *York Chronicle*, 4 August 1775 and 12 April 1776. She married John Prince, senior. No instruments with an Eggleston or Berry signature have been recorded.

Golden Spectacles, Spurriergate, successor to the late Mr Berry' continued this trade succession, presumably having purchased the business.[10]

Unlike some of the examples at Bristol, the business did not remain in the same premises, but appears to have moved around within York, although remaining in the fashionable centre. Matthias (or Matthew) Wisker had served his apprenticeship with George Cowley, a York glass grinder, and was made free in 1774; he was succeeded by his son John in August 1804, when the goods supplied took a more definite turn away from the scientific towards those of the general store – candles, spermaceti oil and lamps becoming the wares in preference to telescopes and microscopes, although spectacles were still on offer.[11] John's widow, Elizabeth, continued in business after his death at the age of 48 in 1822, with her son Matthias's assistance,[12] giving up in his favour in 1827.[13] She died, at the age of 78, in 1854.[14]

This second Matthias Wisker retired in favour of his son, John Thomas Rigg Wisker in 1859, meaning that this was another business which lasted beyond the date of the Great Exhibition, by which time their publicity was claiming that it had been established in 1762.[15] This was a relatively common theme in advertisements, with the longevity of a firm implying its reliability. Besides the Wiskers, there were the barometer-makers, Joshua Croce and his son, Joseph, who were in business in Grape Lane from 1823, and a handful of short-lived optical businesses that flourished for a year or two.[16] In York, the Wiskers had no real competition in the instrument line until Thomas Cooke (1807–68) founded his business in Stonegate in 1837.

Cooke's business broke the mould of the typical provincial enterprise described so far: the small family-run workshop, focusing on the supply of mainly retailed instruments to a fairly conservative local market, with most of the income coming from repairs and retailing, and supplemented by other ventures outside this narrow market when necessity demanded. By managing to produce a winning product (refracting telescopes), successfully finding and wooing local patrons (in particular

---

[10] Ibid., 7 November 1777.

[11] York City Archives: Register of Freemen, 1680–1986; *Yorkshire Courant*, 20 August 1804. Most instruments recorded with the Wisker signature have been barometers; for example, Figure 3.1, offered by Bonham's, London, 13 December 2005, Lot 1.

[12] *Yorkshire Gazette*, 9 and 16 March 1822.

[13] Ibid., 9 June 1827.

[14] Ibid., 21 October 1854.

[15] Ibid., 11 June 1859; the firm first appeared in *Bailey's British Directory … for the year 1784* in 4 vols. Vol III, first edition (London, 1784).

[16] Joshua Croce first appeared in the local directory in 1823, and advertised in the *Yorkshire Gazette*, 23 September 1837; his death was announced ibid., 10 July 1841; his son, Joseph, announced his marriage to Miss Elizabeth Bayldon in ibid., 29 May 1847; and his death on 13 October 1874, ibid., 24 October 1874; her death at the age of 71 on 28 November 1886, ibid., 4 December 1886.

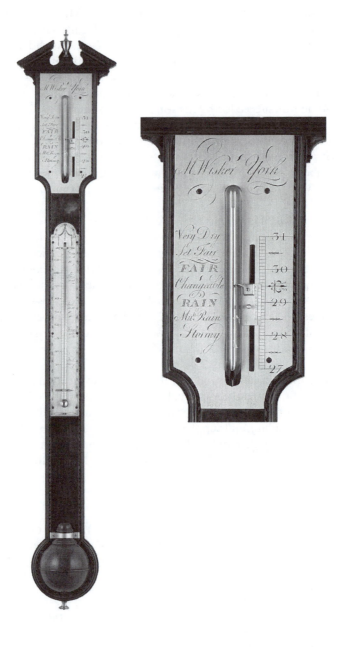

**Figure 3.1    Barometer signed by Matthew Wisker, York, *c*.1800**

*Source*: By kind permission of Bonhams Auctioneers

those in the Yorkshire Philosophical Society),[17] Cooke was then able to expose his narrowly concentrated skills to a wider audience – initially through the British Association for the Advancement of Science (which had first met in York in 1831), and subsequently through patrons with wider influential networks. This he did by embracing such figures as the seventh Astronomer Royal, G.B. Airy (1801–92) and the eminent astronomer Norman Lockyer (1836–1920), and through exposure of his products at the well-attended international trade exhibitions. Although no York instrument firm exhibited at the Great Exhibition in 1851, Cooke managed to put on a display at the Paris Exhibition of 1855, with some success.[18] As Anita McConnell has written:

> Cooke's business did not suffer from being based in York rather than in London. Like his contemporary Thomas Grubb of Dublin, Cooke found that the astronomical market for large telescopes was so dispersed that any location with good transport links would serve as a base.[19]

By this time Thomas Cooke's business was able to take advantage of the railways. As one of Samuel Smiles's self-help heroes, slightly more is known about Cooke than most other provincial instrument makers.[20] Reputedly inspired by the circumnavigational voyages of another Yorkshireman, Captain James Cook (1728–79), Cooke (no relation) taught himself practical mathematics and navigation. The son of a shoemaker, he was determined to go to sea, but was persuaded against this course by his mother, and, instead became a village schoolteacher, pursuing practical optics in his spare time. Legend has it that he constructed a lens from the bottom of a glass tumbler, fabricating a rudimentary telescope which deeply impressed the curator of the Yorkshire Museum, John Phillips, who subsequently became a leading light in the British Association.

Cooke's wife's uncle provided a loan of £100 for him to set up in business, with his wife looking after the shop premises:

> Cooke set up his workshop in the rear and prepared to make, repair or retail instruments to order. One of his first tasks was to build his own screw-cutting machine … Thus equipped, he was ready to undertake his first substantial commission, an equatorial telescope of 4½ inches aperture, for William Gray. The Gray family had an established legal practice in the city of York, and their financial advice and support, again on the basis of family friendship, gave Cooke the practical assistance that he needed to get his business under way.[21]

The reasons for Cooke's success may be seen as fourfold. First, his skills as an engineer enabled him to design and build sophisticated mounts for his large

---

[17]  Brech and Matthew (1997).
[18]  *Catalogue* … (1855), 23.
[19]  McConnell (1992), 51.
[20]  Ibid., 106, gives a bibliography; Smiles (1884), 336–48.
[21]  McConnell (1992), 50.

instruments. Second, the quality of his objectives was very good, and here the writings of his patron Norman Lockyer were to help in promoting them. Third, this period marked the start of a new astronomical field, one in which Lockyer was deeply involved: astronomical spectroscopy, and Cooke manufactured apparatus for this. Finally, his timing was also propitious: the effective demise of the long-lived telescope-producing London house of Dollond with the death of George Dollond (1774–1852) possibly allowed Cooke to fill a gap in the market.

Cooke's business flourished, and grew. His stock became more varied, and in 1849 he advertised a drainage level (Figure 3.2) of his own design, for use by farmers.[22] By 1843, he had moved to larger shop premises at 12 Coney Street, and according to McConnell, the 1851 Census 'shows him employing four men and an apprentice – one Lewis Angell, from Clerkenwell'.[23] In 1855, with Gray's financial support, Cooke purchased land at Bishopshill, within the York city boundary, where he erected his Buckingham Works (Figure 3.3). His orderbook, dating between 1856–68, a rare survival, gives a flavour of the range and cost of items that it was possible to supply from these new purpose-built premises (Graph 3.1). Approximately half of the orders recorded from this period were for items under £10; yet a substantial fraction, mostly turret clocks, which would have to have been installed by skilled workmen, cost over £100 per order. As McConnell writes:

> This must have been one of the earliest scientific instrument manufactories; Cooke made most of his own machine tools and lens-grinding equipment, driven by steam power. There were workshops for brass, glass and wood, and a foundry where all but the largest castings were made.[24]

In fact, there had been an earlier factory at Sheffield at the turn of the nineteenth century, but, as we shall see, this was run along different lines. As noted earlier, David Landes defined a factory as having two critical criteria: 'concentration of production and maintenance of discipline'.[25] Clearly, Cooke's workmen were employed on this basis, and a printed sheet of the Buckingham Works' 'Rules and Regulations' survives from 1865 (Figure 3.4). At the time of the 1861 Census, the workforce consisted of 26 men and 14 boys.

Unfortunately, the very success of Cooke's enterprise almost led to its destruction. He underestimated the cost and time required to work an extremely large achromatic telescope for a wealthy Newcastle industrialist and amateur astronomer, Robert Newall (1812–89), while at the same time winning a contract for a new venture. This was for supplying the India Office with large quantities of surveying equipment, which required the designing and building of new precision machinery in the factory for their construction. Aged 62, Cooke died in 1868;

---

[22]  *Yorkshire Gazette*, 27 January 1849.
[23]  McConnell (1992), 51.
[24]  Ibid.
[25]  Landes (1969), 121.

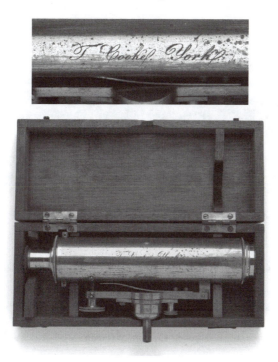

**Figure 3.2 Drainage level by Thomas Cooke, York, *c.*1850**

*Source*: National Museums of Scotland, NMS.T.1980.46

as McConnell recounts, Newall tried to force his heirs – his widow and two sons – into liquidation for non-delivery of his telescope. Once again, wealthy family friends stepped in and rescued the firm.[26]

## Sheffield

Contrast York's settled, regular existence with the explosion of activity, particularly of heavy industry, which occurred at the same time slightly further south, at Sheffield. The reputation of Sheffield-made knives and edge tools goes back long before the Industrial Revolution. Hallamshire (an area including the parishes of Sheffield and Ecclesfield) was famous for the quality of its metalwares as long ago as the Middle Ages, but by the sixteenth century local iron was considered to be of inferior quality for tools requiring a sharp edge: iron was

---

[26]   McConnell (1992), 53–7.

**Figure 3.3    Cooke's Buckingham Works, York, *c.*1860**

*Source*: Vickers Collection, Borthwick Institute, University of York, VI/TC/5/8/1

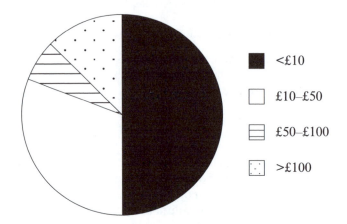

**Graph 3.1    Thomas Cooke's Orderbook 1856–68**

*Source*: Vickers Collection, Borthwick Institute, University of York

Much of the material is unpriced: orders estimated from Cooke (1863) and Cooke (1868). For a description of the orderbook and its problems and shortcomings, see McConnell (1993c).

# BUCKINGHAM WORKS.

## RULES AND REGULATIONS.

### FINES.

| | s. | d. |
|---|---|---|
| 1. For smoking in the Works | 1 | 0 |
| 2. For bringing in malt liquors or spirits during the working hours | 1 | 0 |
| 3. For introducing a stranger into the Works without leave | 2 | 6 |
| 4. Any workman taking chips, tools, or any other thing belonging to his employers, from the premises, otherwise than for the purpose of the business, will be regarded as guilty of felony. | | |
| 5. For taking another person's tools without his permission | 0 | 6 |
| 6. For altering any model, pattern, standard tool or measure, without leave | 2 | 6 |
| 7. For tearing or defacing drawings | 1 | 0 |
| 8. For neglecting to return to their proper places within a quarter of an hour from the time of having used them, any taps, screw stocks, arbors, or other tools, considered as general tools | 0 | 6 |
| 9. For injuring a machine or valuable tool, through wantonness or neglect, the cost of repairing it. | | |
| 10. For striking any person in the Works | 2 | 6 |
| 11. For ordering any tool, smith's work, or castings, without being duly authorized | 1 | 0 |
| 12. For reading a book or newspaper in the working hours, wasting time in unnecessary conversation or otherwise, or whistling | 0 | 6 |
| 13. For washing, putting on his coat, or making any other preparation of a similar kind for leaving work before the appointed time | 0 | 6 |
| 14. For neglecting after his day's work is done to note down correctly on his time slate the various jobs he may have been engaged upon during the day, with the time for each job | 0 | 6 |

| | s. | d. |
|---|---|---|
| 15. For leaving work without having carefully extinguished his light | 0 | 6 |
| 16. For using any stores, such as wood, iron, steel, oil, paint, tallow, candles, or waste improperly, or cutting and using large wood where small would do, or wasting brass turnings | 1 | 0 |
| 17. For being in any other than his own workship without leave, or sufficient cause | 1 | 0 |
| 18. For handling work not his own | 0 | 6 |
| 19. For picking or breaking any drawer or box lock | 2 | 6 |
| 20. For swearing or using indecent language | 1 | 0 |
| 21. Any apprentice absenting himself without leave from Messrs. Cooke or the Clerk, be fined | 1 | 6 |
| 22. For writing or sketching anything indecent upon, or defacing any part of the Works, or the Rules, Regulations, or Notices therein fixed up | 2 | 6 |
| 23. For neglecting to hang up his cheque when leaving work, or for losing it | 0 | 6 |
| 24. Windows broken will be charged to the parties working in the same room, unless the person who did the damage be ascertained. | | |
| 25. Boys' fines to be only one half, except the Rule which applies to the breaking of windows; in which case the full amount will be levied. | | |
| 26. That every man sweep and make tidy his bench or lathe every Saturday commencing not before ten minutes to One. | | |

☞ The above Fines and Regulations are intended solely for the purpose of maintaining better order in the Works, preventing wasteful and unnecessary expense, and for promoting the good conduct and respectability of the workmen.

*August*, 1865.     T. COOKE & SONS.

LANCASTER, PRINTER, YORK.

**Figure 3.4   Buckingham Works' 'Rules and Regulations', 1865**

*Source*: Vickers Collection, Borthwick Institute, University of York, VI/TC/5/5/141

therefore imported for such steel manufactures, while local iron was used in nail making and goods without cutting edges, such as cooking pots.[27]

Sheffield had one great natural advantage over other provincial cutlery centres, namely an abundance of local waterpower. At least 90 water mills were in operation in 1740, and two out of every three were used for the grinding of cutlery and edge tools. Another fortunate geological feature was the sandstone found alongside local coal. This was ideal for the manufacture of grinding wheels, and these were of such quality that they were sold all over England from an early date.[28]

When Daniel Defoe visited Sheffield in 1726 he wrote that:

> The town of Sheffield is very populous and large, the streets narrow, and the houses dark and black, occasioned by the continued smoke of the forges, which are always at work ... The manufacture of hard ware, which has been so antient in this town is not only continued but much increased.[29]

Some time after 1750, the cutlers diversified into a huge range of products: those in the town centre made the high quality goods, while specific geographical areas were devoted to sickle makers, or nailmakers or scythemakers. In rural districts, metalwares were a part-time occupation, often combined with the farming of smallholdings. By the seventeenth century, further specializations had developed – filemaking, buttonmaking and metal box construction.[30] The small workshops or forges were run by the so-called 'little mesters' (or masters), and well into the nineteenth century hand technology and craft skills dominated the Sheffield metal trades with their small units of construction, marked by the division of labour.[31] Despite Sheffield's landlocked position, there was no difficulty getting its sought-after goods to market: there was a weekly carrier service to London from at least 1637, but most manufactures went by inland waterways, which were being constantly improved.[32] Although bespoke precision instruments required extra-careful packing for transport – which added to their expense – the items being produced in Sheffield were not in this category, as we shall see.[33]

---

[27]  Pollard (1959), 54–9 and David Hey, 'Introduction' to Barnes (1992), 9–12.

[28]  Ibid.; Crossley et al. (1989), viii–xv; Hey (1991), 8–9.

[29]  Defoe (1971), 482.

[30]  Hey (1991), 93–144; Barnes (1992), 9–12.

[31]  Hey (1991), 287.

[32]  Ibid., 145–96.

[33]  An instance of items being sent from London on long sea voyages is provided by the lading bill for new demonstration apparatus ordered from W. & S. Jones by Harvard University in 1797: 16 items costing £53.5s.6d, packing cases an extra 10s 6d: Harvard University College Papers IV HUA I.5.100* vol 4. Also an acrimonious exchange between the Colonial Office, the Transport Board and the London instrument makers Watkins & Hill, where despite the 'strong packing case' costing £1.3s, an item was damaged in transit: TNA CO 201/81, dated 3 April 1816.

The first optical business in Sheffield, according to an apparently reliable local historian, was founded by

> Mr Samuel Froggatt ... although the exact year is uncertain. He was the inventor of the process of grinding the perspective glasses, concave or convex, though of course many improvements have been made since his day. He had his grinding wheel near the Twelve o'Clock public house, and there he carried on business many years. His trade was chiefly in common acromatic [sic] telescopes, microscopes, spectacles, reading glasses, &c. Mr Froggatt died in the year 1797.[34]

The first local directory was published in 1774, and it records the names of two other instrument makers: John Handcock, or Hancock, a ring sun-dial and buckle-maker (Figure 3.5); and Joseph Wilson, an optician, mathematical instrument maker and spectacle maker.[35] Proctor & Beilby, the largest of the late eighteenth-century Sheffield instrument manufacturers, appeared first in the directory of 1781: according to a contemporary account they ran a 'little mesters' system in their purpose-built premises in Market Street, in the centre of town.[36] This system, borrowed from the cutlery trades, allowed self-employed men to rent space within their factory under contract to carry out specific work. Each 'little mester' would employ and pay his own workmen, providing them with both tools and equipment; materials were either bought from the factory proprietor or elsewhere, and the finished items sold back to the factory proprietor: this allowed enormous flexibility in times of economic hardship, although few great fortunes were made.

The diversification of Sheffield-made goods can be seen in the advertisements of the Chadburn firm, whose close-knit family enterprise ensured that the business survived and expanded over a number of generations. The partnership of Chadburn & Wright was formed in 1818 between William Chadburn and David Wright and, as an advertisement from 1825 [Figure 3.6] shows, they manufactured optical goods as well as dealing in 'all kinds of hardware'.[37] William Chadburn, who had begun as an optician in 1816, was by 1828 advertising a greater versatility as a 'brass and iron founder, optician, cutler and general dealer'.[38] In turn the firm became Chadburn Brothers, who were Alfred and Francis Wright Chadburn

---

[34] Unsigned article [Robert Leader], 'A Chapter on Old Sheffield Trades', *Sheffield & Rotherham Independent*, 12 April 1873; and Leader (1875), 94–7: much of this material was garnered through oral tradition from eye-witnesses and descendants.

[35] No instruments signed by either Froggatt or Wilson appear to have been recorded; Hancock is known from the dial illustrated here.

[36] [John Holland], 'Reminiscences of an Old Sheffield Workshop', *Sheffield Telegraph*, 23, 24, 26 and 27 December 1867; republished in Morrison-Low (1994b).

[37] *A new general and commercial Directory of Sheffield and its vicinity ... Compiled by R Gell.* (Manchester, 1825).

[38] *Sheffield Directory and Guide ...* (Sheffield, 1828).

**Figure 3.5   Ring dial signed by John Hancock, *c.*1775**

Source: Museum of the History of Science, Oxford, inv. no. 35440

from 1837, joined by a third brother, Charles Henry, in 1841.[39] 'The sycamore and mahogany outsides of the telescopes were made at a [water] wheel on the Rivelin by William Chadburn, grandfather of Chadburn Brothers, the well-known opticians, of Nursery street', wrote the local poet and journalist John Holland, 'and it seems probable that his father had been there before him'.[40]

Charles Henry Chadburn started up a branch in Liverpool in 1845, and by 1851 the Sheffield firm was awarded an honourable mention for the items which they displayed in the Great Exhibition: '... everything exhibited by Messrs. Chadburn are remarkable for extreme cheapness, and in this respect they deserve Honourable Mention'.[41] They were granted Prince Albert's Royal Warrant, and continued well beyond 1851. An account of the firm published in 1893 stated that:

> This is one of the oldest businesses of the kind in the kingdom, having been founded over a century ago. For many years it has been carried on under the ... title [Chadburn

---

[39]   Chesworth (1984), 14–15.
[40]   Holland (1867), reprinted in Morrison-Low (1994b), 13.
[41]   *Catalogue...* (1851), 436; *Reports...* (1852), 273.

Brothers], the present proprietor, Mr W.T. Morgan, a nephew of Chadburn Brothers, having been connected with the establishment over forty years. The premises comprise a spacious and well-appointed shop and show-room, to the rear of which is a long three-storey block of buildings used as work-rooms, and fitted with elaborate and especially-constructed machinery and appliances suitable to the various requirements of the manufacturing optician ....[42]

Alfred Chadburn appears to have been the member of the firm who was the most concerned with practical optics – although a commonplace book belonging to his brother Francis, dated 1855, also survives, filled with tabulations of sizes, curvatures and distances of lenses – 'The 3$^{rd}$ glass always a Crown' – and descriptions and recipes for lacquers. Alfred published a pamphlet on spectacles which ran to many editions, and he was also involved in early experiments in photography in Sheffield.[43] He was also the artist responsible for the famous engraving of their showroom (Figure 8.8). Survival of instruments with the Chadburn name coupled with a Sheffield address is extensive, but one suspects that most of these post-date the Great Exhibition.[44]

The other Sheffield firm to exhibit at the Great Exhibition was that of Samuel Sharp, who displayed a set of ten lenses of differing powers for a simple microscope, but the Jury did not comment on the quality of these.[45] Sharp was first mentioned in local directories as a journeyman optician in 1845, but this may have been the Samuel Charles Sharp recorded in London directories as an optician between 1827 and 1848.[46] Nothing has been recorded with Sharp's signature.

The numbers of such businesses in Sheffield appear to be initially few, two or so from 1775 until 1800. We are fortunate that a contemporary description of early eighteenth-century Sheffield instrument making survives. As John Holland's

---

[42]  Anon (1893), 141.

[43]  For the commonplace book, see Sheffield City Archives: Records of Chadburn Brothers, opticians; SYCAS ref: 231/B reversed microfilm. Unfortunately, no accounts survive; Alfred Chadburn, *Observations on the Choice of Spectacles: how to use them; and on the preservation of sight*, 11th edition (Sheffield, 1894): in this, Chadburn claims to have sold 5000 spectacles with each edition. See Smith (1987), which discusses Alfred Chadburn's role in Sheffield photography. One of his early daguerreotypes is reproduced in the *Weekly Independent*, 18 May 1918; agreement to take out a license with Richard Beard, *Sheffield Independent*, 20 August 1842; advertisement for photographic portraits, ibid., 21 January 1843.

[44]  For instance, in the Whipple Museum of the History of Science, Cambridge, a refracting telescope (inv. no. Wh: 2858), a compound microscope (inv. no Wh: 16) and a drum microscope (inv. no. Wh: 1806); in the National Museums of Scotland, a Cary Gould microscope (NMS.T.1979.71) and a barometer (NMS.T.1984.83); a brass circular protractor was offered at Christie's South Kensington, 6 May 1993, lot 137. The Liverpool branch turned to the manufacture of ships' telegraphs in 1898, and has survived into the twenty-first century after a series of name changes.

[45]  *Catalogue...* (1851), 442; *Reports...* (1852), 267.

[46]  Sheffield directories, *passim*. Clifton (1995), 249.

**Figure 3.6    Advertisement of Chadburn & Wright, Sheffield, 1825**

*Source*: Sheffield Archives

account makes clear, Proctor & Beilby acted as a 'manufactory' in the sense that completed parts of instruments were brought into their premises for assembly and passed on to the point of sale by the firm; unlike Thomas Cooke's later Buckingham Works, however, the men were not 'employed' by Proctor & Beilby. They were contracted to do piece work, although there was considerable division of labour. That this was indeed a large factory can be corroborated by a surviving instrument trade catalogue or pattern book dating from 1815, which reveals an extensive range of items made there. It also shows the printed wholesale prices against the manuscript piecework costs.[47]

The manufacturing work, the casting of the brass or glass components, which was skilled work, appears to have been done exclusively by men. Various parts of the work – such as the boring of wooden telescope tubes and the grinding of optical glass components – were done in water-powered mills on the rivers Don and Rivelin: Proctors was also the first Sheffield firm to acquire a steam

---

[47]    Holland, 1867, reprinted in Morrison-Low (1994b); Sheffield City Libraries, Special Collections no. 33237: Bradbury Record 293.

engine, used in the grinding of optical glass.[48] Holland's account also mentions the methods used by the firm to tie the workforce to their particular business through what Holland describes as 'stuffing', elsewhere called 'trucking'. In order to keep the workers completely bound to their employers, they were obliged to buy their food, clothes, tools and any other commodities from a shop owned by the firm, and 'the prices charged were usually exorbitant'.[49] He comments on other general social aspects, deploring the drunkenness, the lack of godliness and education. He also stresses the rural aspects of life, which kept employees aware of the seasons, similar to the rural metal-workers or hand-loom weavers, whose work on their small-holdings appears to have been a seasonal but vital part of their overall earning capacity.

Family enterprise was clearly behind what Holland characterised elsewhere as the 'largest optical manufactory in the world'.[50] The Sheffield venture of Proctor & Beilby was begun by the brothers Charles and Luke Proctor, who initially made 'lancets' or fleams, devices used as surgical or veterinary blades, and they subsequently moved into making other items of brass.[51] Luke left the firm but Charles, a widower when John Holland knew him, was committed to the business. It first appeared in the Sheffield directories in 1781, and by the turn of the century had become George & William Proctor, sons of Charles. There was also a large shop in Birmingham, where, as Proctors & Beilby, the firm first appeared in the directories in 1788 (Miss Deborah Proctor married Thomas Beilby). The Sheffield business became Proctor & Beilby in 1800, Proctor Beilby & Co. in 1809, George & William Proctor in 1815, and finally George Proctor in 1818, with the firm disappearing by 1821.

Unfortunately, in the second generation, the spirit of entrepreneurship failed, and William Proctor went bankrupt and subsequently sold up the remains of the business. The advertisement for this, given below, illustrates what was necessary to run this sort of enterprise. In 1818 his plant consisted of:

---

[48] The involvement of Proctor & Beilby in two watermills is noted in Crossley et al. (1989), 40 and 65. One, on the Loxley at Wisewood, was leased by G. Proctor from 1813 to 1816; the other, on the Rivelin at Rivelin Bridge Wheel, was leased to Charles Proctor and Thomas Beilby for 63 years. By 1814, glass-grinding troughs there were let to a lens-maker by the name of Chadburn. Proctor & Beilby erected the first steam-engine in Sheffield, in 1786: see Leader (1875), 97. This is confirmed by a letter from Proctor & Beilby enquiring about application of the steam engine to rotary motion, dated 22 November 1776 in Birmingham Reference Library, Archives Department: letter to Boulton & Fothergill, steam engine manufacturers, B&W: Box 26/1/2.

[49] Holland (1867); reprinted in Morrison-Low (1994b), 19.

[50] Holland (1834), 261.

[51] Examples noted are in the Wellcome Museum, Science Museum, London, inv. no. A626565; and a four-bladed fleam offered for sale by Tesseract, Summer 1988, Catalogue 21, item 57.

The Working Tools and Fixtures AT SHEFFIELD, comprising sixteen valuable turning engines, a boring engine, a powerful fly, two brushing engines, two glazing engines, a hearth of tools, two grindstones in frames, draw bench with all the valuable tools, large shears, pair of rollers, two glass cutting machines, a globe grinder, a water engine, twenty-five capital vices, a quantity of glazers, mandrills, guages [sic], files, and other tools, beam and scales, metal weights, work benches, five cwt. of brass tools, and cwt. of metal tools, writing desks, two iron bookcases, shelving, counters, cupboards, tables, nests of drawers, work benches, stools &c.

At the Wheels, near Sheffield, all the machinery for glass grinding, lot of telescope wood, lot of timber, a quantity of old iron and old metal, a turning engine, a joiner's bench, vice and quantity of tools.[52]

William Proctor managed to struggle back into business in Sheffield by 1825, and only disappeared from the directories there in 1834. A number of simple ring dials are known with the signature 'Proctor', but often without their place of origin; and later items, which must have been manufactured in Sheffield, are known with a London address (for which, see Chapter 8).[53]

Although this instrument trade was tiny compared with the extent of the cutlery trade in the eighteenth century (when it was estimated at one point that half the male population of Sheffield was engaged in the cutlery industry), and vanishingly small compared with the subsequent late nineteenth-century heavy engineering industries, instrument making in this locality survived and grew during this period. By 1815 there were about eight instrument businesses in Sheffield, rising to 18 in 1820, with a slight diminution in numbers over the next 15 years or so, but rising to 20 in 1840 and 26 in 1850 (Graph 3.2).

It is clear from the directory descriptions that Chadburn's ran a number of powered premises by 1850: for example, the 'Steam wheel, Johnson street', the 'Shilo Wheel, 44 Stanley street' of 1841, and their subsequent 'Nursery Wheel', named after the rural days when the land was a market garden, or 'nursery', belonging to the dukes of Norfolk.[54] Eight years later, a description of the firm mentioned that 'a curious and peculiar branch of Messrs. Chadburn's business is the manufacture of models of locomotive and other engines, which they carry on to a surprising extent. They also make ingenious steam guages [sic], on principles

---

[52] *Sheffield Mercury*, 21 and 28 February 1818. The announcement of Proctor's bankruptcy had appeared in ibid., 14 February 1818; see also Sheffield City Archives: Parker Collection 859: Petition for Bankruptcy of William Proctor, 1818, 'Petition for bankruptcy of William Proctor of Sheffield, Optician, Dealer & Chapman ... by James Deakin & Thomas Deakin of Sheffield, dated 27 January 1818'. The Deakins were Proctor's brothers-in-law.

[53] The Whipple Museum of the History of Science has a ring dial marked 'PROCTOR' (inv. no. 1179); the National Maritime Museum has another marked 'L. PROCTOR SHEFFIELD' (inv. ASTO 435): see Higton (2002), 241; the Museum of the History of Science has three examples: one marked 'PROCTOR' (inv. no. 33544), a second 'CHA PROCTOR' (inv. no. 46125), and the third 'L. PROCTOR' (inv. no. 48396).

[54] Sheffield directories, *passim*.

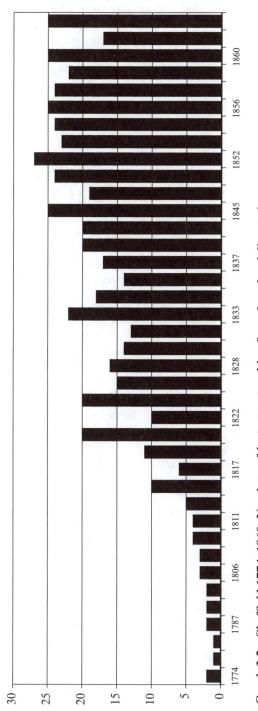

**Graph 3.2　Sheffield 1774–1860: Numbers of instrument making firms from local directories**

peculiar to themselves; and have introduced numerous improvements in the manufacture of philosophical instruments, stereoscopes, microscopes, &c'.[55]

Much less is known about the three other principal firms in this line that were apparently successful and long-established – the Froggatts, the Friths and J.P. Cutts, Sutton & Son. Although Samuel Froggatt first appeared in the directory at Walk Mill as an optical glass grinder in 1814, the business had begun at an earlier date. The 1873 newspaper reference to Froggatt's early optical business, already quoted, drew the following more informative response from his grandson:

EARLY SHEFFIELD OPTICIANS

TO THE EDITOR – In your impression of Saturday, April 12th, relating to Sheffield trades, you say – 'Mr Samuel Froggatt was the first person who introduced the optical trade into the town and invented the machinery for grinding glass. He died in the year 1797'. I beg to correct this. It was the year 1787 when he died. It is added that 'he had his grinding wheel near the Twelve o'Clock Public-house'. It was my father who occupied the room at Walk Mills, now the Albion Works, opposite the '12 o'clock'. My grandfather (Samuel Froggatt, the subject of your notice) had his works at Royds Mill, adjoining Marrian's Brewery; and in conclusion I may say I am the only representative of the name in the trade (which is the oldest established in Sheffield), and that, along with my son, I still carry on the business in the same neighbourhood, viz., near the 'Twelve o'clock', Attercliffe Road. – Yours respectfully, T. FROGGATT.[56]

The first Samuel Froggatt (d.1787) was succeeded in business by his son, also Samuel. His brother, Thomas Froggatt (1777–1853) ran the firm from 1821 until at least 1860, with his own son Thomas (1817–83), the writer of the letter above, joining and then succeeding him. The elder Thomas Froggatt ran a concurrent business for at least part of this time at the New Inn Beerhouse, a pairing of occupations that Maxine Berg comments was not at all unusual in the metal trades.[57] John Holland's account mentions that one of the Froggatts left for London and set up in business there, using water and subsequently steam power to establish 'at Hackney-Wick one of the largest glass-grinding works in the world'.[58] More shall be said about this in Chapter 7.

Peter Frith & Co. appeared in the Sheffield street directories in 1814 based in Arundel Street, and was in business beyond 1860; indeed, it may have had its roots in the earlier firm of Frith & Robinson, of West Bar. Initially described as an optician, between 1817 and 1833 the firm is listed as 'optician and powder

---

[55]  Billing (1858), 30. Model steam locomotives have been offered for sale, for example, at Christie's South Kensington, 17 August 1995, lot 52; in the two surviving trade catalogues dating from about 1850, 'Various Historical Models to Order' are priced from £1 5s to £52 10s.

[56]  *Sheffield and Rotherham Independent*, 15 April 1873.

[57]  Froggatt (1991); Berg (1994), 54.

[58]  *Sheffield Telegraph*, 23, 24, 26 and 27 December 1867. See also Clifton (1995), 107. No instruments with a Froggatt signature appear to have been noted.

flask manufacturers'. It appears to have had a London agency or branch for some time, from at least 1829, and this will be discussed further in Chapter 8.[59] Between 1818 and 1825, Peter Frith also advertised a branch in the Birmingham directories, although judging from the entries there, this appears to have been the powder flask end of the business only.[60] Confusingly, Peter Frith was not the only one of that name to work in Sheffield: James and Henry Frith, also opticians and powder flask makers, received separate entries, in addition to joint entries as 'Frith Brothers' in the directories between 1839 and 1860. They are listed as working in different premises to Peter Frith, but also in Arundel Street. They, too, had a London base during the 1840s.[61]

Two advertisements dating from the 1860s appear to give some idea of the size and scope of Peter Frith's activities, together with the claim that the firm was 'established 1790' (Figure 8.3). Despite these claims, and because the firm appeared only rarely to sign its instruments, it is difficult to tell just how large or successful it was.[62] However, Scottish sequestrations (the official papers for bankruptcy) record that when the instrument makers M. Gardner of Glasgow petitioned for sequestration in 1832, one of their creditors was Peter Frith & Co., mathematical instrument makers of Sheffield, who were owed £302 16s 3d.[63] When James White, later instrument maker to William Thomson, Lord Kelvin, went broke in 1861, he owed £11 10s 7d to J.P. Cutts, Sutton & Son and £12 14s 11d to Peter Frith & Co., both of Sheffield.[64] From this, it may be deduced that Peter Frith's output – and possibly that of other Sheffield manufacturers – was mostly sold on to other retailers, and that the firm acted largely as a subcontractor to the trade.

The long-established firm of I. [sic] P. Cutts, Sutton & Sons claimed in an advertisement of 1880 that they had been established in 1804. However, 'J.P. Cutts' first appeared in the Sheffield directories in 1825, moving to Division Street as 'I.P. Cutts' in 1828. From 1839, the firm advertised as 'opticians to Her Majesty', and various permutations of the firm's name – I.P. Cutts, Sons & Sutton; J.P. Cutts, Sutton & Co.; I.P. Cutts & Co; I.P. Cutts & Sons – appeared over the years. Their final appearance was in 1895. The firm also had a London branch for a few years after 1851, and in 1854, one at Pearl Street, New York.[65] This may have been as a result of the Great Exhibition, although they did not

---

[59] London directories, 1829–74. See Clifton (1995), 106.

[60] Birmingham directories, *passim.*

[61] London and Sheffield directories, *passim.*

[62] A telescope signed 'Frith, London' is in the National Museums of Scotland, NMS. T.1993.119. A spring-loaded drum microscope signed 'P. Frith, London' was offered by Tesseract, Catalogue 13, Spring 1986, item 15.

[63] National Archives of Scotland (NAS), CS 96/4215, Sederunt Book, 7; quoted in Clarke et al. (1989), 167.

[64] NAS CS 318/6/362, Sederunt Book, 11, quoted in Clarke et al. (1989), 253.

[65] Sheffield directories, *passim.*

exhibit there. A number of instruments with variations of their signatures have been preserved in public collections.[66]

John Preston Cutts was born in Leeds in 1787, dying at the age of seventy-one in 1858; his partner John Sutton's death was recorded in 1859.[67] An account of Proctor & Beilby's workshop included the statement that 'The late Mr I.P. Cutts served his time with them, and my impression of the issue of the firm is different from Mr Holland's; for I have understood that he was taken into partnership, and ultimately had the trade in his sole possession'.[68] However, no evidence has been found to support this remark. The firm was described in 1858 as being

> amongst the oldest and largest manufacturers of philosophical and optical instruments in the kingdom, and enjoys a high reputation for the excellence of their goods. A reference to their advertisement will show the immense variety of this trade, the minute subdivision and extensive ramifications of which will astonish any person accustomed to use only the customary phrase of "philosophical and optical instruments," without reflecting the vast number of wonderful inventions comprehended under that term, and the incalculable value of such appliances to every branch of scientific investigation, the development of the useful arts, and the extension of commerce. It is no small credit to Sheffield that it should command and retain, in the face of keen opposition, so important a branch of manufacture.[69]

The specialist surveyor's tape measure maker, James Chesterman (1792–1867), first listed alone in the directories in 1833, was the following year 'at Mr Cutts' Division Street', and incorporated into the business between 1849 and 1852, before in 1859 becoming James Chesterman & Co., at Bow Works, Nursery Street in 1859.[70] However, a business history of the firm explains that in the slump following the Napoleonic Wars, many skilled craftsmen were attracted to the relative prosperity of Sheffield, and one of these was the 25 year old James Chesterman, who arrived, probably on foot, from London. He obtained employment initially

---

[66]  Signed 'J.P. Cutts': a telescope at Dundee Art Galleries and Museums; a botanical microscope at Maidstone Museum and Art Gallery; a four-draw telescope at Sheffield City Museum (inv. no. 1970.624); a drum microscope in the Wellcome Collection (inv. no. A140128); signed 'J.P. Cutts & Sons': two 10-inch octants at Dundee Art Galleries and Museums (inv. nos 70–306–2 and 1973–1003); a compound microscope in the Wellcome Collection (inv. no. A129600). Signed 'J.P. Cutts, Sutton & Sons': a microscope at the National Museums of Scotland (NMS.T.1979.72); and at the Science Museum, a lithograph (by M. Billing) advertisement for I.P. Cutts, Sutton & Sons, opticians to Her Majesty, Sheffield, undated, *c.*1858–60, NMSI inv. no. 1988–5050. See also Morrison-Low and Nuttall (2003).

[67]  International Genealogical Index; *Sheffield Daily Telegraph*, 11 September 1858 and 25 April 1859.

[68]  Leader (1875), 97.

[69]  Billing (1858), 30.

[70]  Sheffield directories, *passim*.

from James Dixon & Sons, silversmiths.[71] Intrigued by the properties of crucible steel, first devised in the mid-eighteenth century by Benjamin Huntsman, a Doncaster clockmaker, for producing reliable watch springs, Chesterman applied steel springs to produce automatically rewinding linen measuring tapes.[72]

Chesterman apparently attempted to patent his invention, and went into partnership with a Bartholomew Hounsfield (who presumably provided the business capital), producing a number of other items from a workshop in Nursery Street. Chesterman was in partnership with various people during the next few years, co-operating over specific products: for instance, in 1842 he and one John Bottom took out a joint patent for 'Improvement of Tapes for Measures', the first woven tape which incorporated copper wires, still known as 'metallic woven tape'. Demand for this increased so much that he formed a new partnership in 1849 with James Cutts and James Bedington. Almost immediately, Bedington left the business and moved to Birmingham, where he started a rule-making business that continued until 1890. In 1853, Chesterman developed and patented the process for heat-treating continuous lengths of steel strip for use in tape measures. The firm has continued to prosper until the present day.[73]

Other specialist makers in Sheffield seem to have been few: one rule maker, Zachariah Belcher, seems to have flourished from at least 1792, when the following advertisement appeared in the local press:

A Manufactory of Rules.
ZACHARIAH BELCHER,
Box & Ivory Rule Maker,
Wishes respectfully to inform the Merchants, Factors, Hardwaremen, and the Public in general, in Sheffield and its Vicinity, that he has taken a Shop in the New-Market, opposite the Gaol, where he makes RULES of all Sorts, in the best and neatest Manner, which he sells on the lowest Terms, Wholesale or Retail, and shall be particularly thankful to receive their Orders, which they may depend upon being executed with the greatest Punctuality and Dispatch. Rules mended in the neatest Manner.[74]

Belcher first appeared in the directory in 1797; by 1879, as Zachariah Belcher & Sons, the firm had moved to Mary Street, apparently making a final directory appearance in Napier Street in 1909. Yet no items with their signature have been recorded, suggesting that other firms retailed their products, perhaps on the

---

[71]  Hallam (1984), 57–8.

[72]  For crucible steel see Barraclough (1976), 12–13; Hallam (1984), 58. For Huntsman and patents, see Macleod (1988), 94.

[73]  Ibid., 58–64; Barnes (1992), 87. Chesterman's patents were: 5817, dated 14 July 1829: Apparatus for measuring land, and for other purposes; 9214 (with John Bottom), dated 11 January 1842: Tapes for measuring and boxes for containing the same; 11962, dated 13 November 1847: Tape-measures and cases for containing the same; also machinery for making such measures and cases, or parts thereof. Seventeen price lists, dating between 1849 and 1921 are in Sheffield Archives, LD 11 24/1–17.

[74]  *Sheffield Register*, 16 March 1792.

model which was to be found in Birmingham, as explained in Chapter 4.[75] A few barometer makers, most of whom appear to have been Italian immigrants, seem to have stayed long in Sheffield: the Stopanis, Nicholas and John, were resident longest, recorded between 1822 and 1852; Francis Prandi, a maker of barometers, thermometers and hydrometers appeared only in the directory for 1825, but was advertising in the local press in 1821 and 1822.[76] Others included Angelo Alberti, recorded between 1817 and 1828, Charles Guggiari from 1828 to 1830 and Ferdinand Riva in 1833 and 1834.[77]

William Warris took out a patent for opera glasses in 1804; he and his father Thomas had been in business together since 1797 as opticians, but by 1814 Thomas Warris was on his own. In April 1815, he advertised that 'being desirous, on account of the Infirmities of Age, to retire from the Business' he intended selling up his stock and tools, and the good-will that he had developed over many years in business. In August of that year, there was a death notice, 'of a gradual decay, Mr Thomas Warris, of this place, optician, aged 76'.[78]

Staying successfully in business was as difficult in Sheffield as anywhere else; these examples show that bankruptcy and ill health could terminate a vulnerable small firm rapidly at this time. However, the fact that several instrument-making businesses managed to survive for long periods, and that the numbers of firms joining the trade grew, must strongly suggest that they were able to sell their wares successfully. That few instruments survive with a Sheffield signature and address dating before about 1850 must point to markets elsewhere; because Sheffield's other industries had relied on long-standing transport networks to carry manufactured goods out of its land-locked position, it is more than probable that instruments went this way too. Other infrastructures, such as banking and the supply of raw materials and skills, had also been in place for some time: where other metal-working industries flourished, instrument making could successfully grow alongside.

---

[75]  Sheffield directories, *passim.*; Barnes (1992), 65.

[76]  *The Iris, or Sheffield Advertiser,* 30 October 1821, 2 April, 7 and 14 May 1822.

[77]  Sheffield directories, *passim.* A wheel barometer signed by Alberti was offered by Phillips London, 3 June 1987, Lot 66.

[78]  Patent 2779, 4 August 1804, 'Mounting opera glasses'. An example of a silver thirteen-draw monocular, with 2-inch lens, and crest stamped 'WARRIS'S PATENT' was offered for sale at Phillips London, 15 September 1998, Lot 55. Sheffield directories, *passim; Sheffield Mercury,* 22 April and 19 August 1815.

# Chapter 4

# Manchester and Birmingham

## Manchester

On the opposite side of the country from Yorkshire, the unprecedented growth of Manchester into an industrial city produced entirely different circumstances from those to be found in either York or Sheffield. There was early industrial growth in the traditional textiles of woollen cloths and linen, and this was followed by the introduction of fustians (which was dependent on cotton imports) and silks (also dependent on importation of the raw material).[1] Manchester's proximity to the Lancashire coalfields meant a variety of new industries emerged from the mid-Tudor period onwards. Geoffrey Timmins indicates that these, together with other extractive industries – iron, lead, copper, alum and limestone – all added to the local economy.[2] 'We came on to Manchester', wrote Daniel Defoe in about 1725, 'one of the greatest, if not really the greatest mere village in England'. He was struck by its size and the recent rapidity of its growth, but deplored its lack of formal governance and political muscle.[3] Defoe did not need to spell out why Manchester was famous: 'the Manchester trade we all know; and all that are concerned in it know that it is, as all our other manufactures are, very much increased within these thirty or forty years especially beyond what it was before'.[4] Demand grew for cotton goods; these were lighter to wear and easier to clean than woollen goods, and although initially these were supplied by the East India Company, legislation passed in 1721 (and later reinforced in 1736) banned these foreign imports while encouraging the sale of home-made products.[5]

Manchester's growth and prosperity during the Industrial Revolution was based on the importing of raw cotton and turning it into something that could be sold for many times the cost of the raw materials. Timmins has described this, stressing the rise of an all-cotton cloth production, and its dominant position in the Lancashire economy; however, he sees this against a background of long-established smaller industrial concerns, including coal mining and glass making, together with newer enterprises, such as chemical manufacturing, engineering and textile printing. On the supply side he examines technical innovations, such

---

[1]  Timmins (1998), 11–19.
[2]  Ibid., 19–23.
[3]  Defoe (1971), 544–5.
[4]  Ibid., 545.
[5]  Timmins (1998), 51.

as the introduction of new types of powered machinery into the textile industry, while there was considerable new impact from rising demand from markets both at home and abroad. Yet Timmins concludes that there was less economic discontinuity than might have been thought; for instance, even in textiles, there were strong continuities, especially a reliance on hand technology. As he points out, the shift away from an agricultural economy had occurred long before this period.[6] Much of what he has to say has a bearing on the small but apparently strongly rooted group of businesses connected with supplying instrumentation of one sort or another at this time.

From the seventeenth century, Lancashire and especially Merseyside had seen the continuation of crafts, such as the making of watch-parts in Liverpool, Wigan and Prescot, and glass production – both of which are closely allied to instrument production. Apparently, these had never taken root in Manchester itself; the engineering workshops which emerged instead were of the large or heavy engineering sort, with which the Industrial Revolution is often identified: 'steam engines, weigh-bridges, boilers, general millwork, wrought-iron boats, and parts for bridges'.[7] Nonetheless, having instrument-making parts and skills available in Manchester's hinterland must have made the trade more viable.

This description perhaps begs the question why there should be any successful instrument-making community in a town that had no real tradition of brassware skills, nor any apparent wealthy clientele for luxury goods. There was, however, a small but growing public demand for scientific discussion, which led to the founding, in 1781, of the Manchester Literary and Philosophical Society, which continues to this day.[8] In the spirit of the Enlightenment, many such societies were formed throughout England; and, as we shall see in Chapter 9, this development was one of the factors influencing the rise in demand for instrumentation outside London.

Although they were never numerically substantial, an unexpectedly high proportion of instrument makers was apparently offering barometers for sale in Manchester throughout the period from about 1760; among the earliest instruments known to have been retailed there were barometers signed by the mid-eighteenth century clockmakers, John Berry and Peter Clare.[9] Two of the first three instrument makers recorded in the local 1794 directory, John Gally and Baptist Ronchetti, were 'weather-glass makers'. Jenny Wetton, who has done extensive work on Manchester instrument making, explains that many of these were Italians who had made similar instruments in the Lake Como and Lake Maggiore areas, but had been forced by local taxation and population growth to emigrate. 'Barometer makers' reached a maximum of 13 in the directory for

6     Ibid., 83–172.
7     Ibid., 25–7; 102–7.
8     Makepeace (1984).
9     Goodison (1977), 302 and 312; Wetton (1994), 71. Clare's signature is also known on a sundial: Clifton (1995), 56.

1843, but this line 'may never have been very profitable and those who could do so supplemented their trade with other business'.[10]

Judging by their names, most of the instrument makers who started up in Manchester towards the end of the eighteenth century were foreigners, and much of Wetton's further research has verified this: many were indeed immigrant Italians, and there were also a number of Jewish opticians.[11] This is not to say that Italian or Jewish instrument makers were not to be found in other provincial centres, but that there seemed to be a higher proportion of instrument-making immigrants in Manchester than elsewhere. Manchester's population was expanding rapidly at this point, and the newcomers came from all parts of the United Kingdom as well as from abroad. As with the Italians, the Jews were initially peripatetic, peddling their goods in the streets.

Bill Williams explains how these incomers, mostly from Europe, settled into Manchester, and by the mid-nineteenth century their second generation could be found being absorbed in the professional classes as medical men: 'The "Jewish trades" were also sufficiently flexible to absorb immigrants at any level of capital and experience, since each represented, in effect, a continuum from the pedlar's tray to the substantial shop or warehouse'.[12] Among the new Jewish arrivals who joined the instrument trade was the Franks family, originally from the Netherlands, who became opticians. Isaac Franks appeared in the Liverpool directory in 1787 as a butcher to the Jewish synagogue there, but was travelling to Manchester as a hawker by 1808. His son Jacob obtained shop premises in the Oldham Road from 1819.

Jacob Franks was in business with his son Abraham, in whose name the firm continued from 1848, with Abraham's half-brother Joseph. There are two receipts in the family archives for items purchased by Jacob Franks from Birmingham makers: from William Parkes, Sand Pits, Birmingham, for spectacles and frames, dated 25 April 1846; and from Robert Field & Son, 113 New Street, Birmingham, for three compound microscopes, dated 14 August 1846.[13] Elias Nathan was noted in the local directory as an optician from 1834 until beyond 1850, but had set up in business in 1829. He was the son of Jacob Nathan, who, with his brother Lemon, had migrated from Liverpool during the 1780s, although they had been born in

---

[10]   Wetton (1990–91), 37–8.
[11]   Wetton (1994) and (1996).
[12]   Williams (1985), 122–4.
[13]   Copies of family records held at Museum of Science and Industry in Manchester. Instruments held there with a Franks signature include: a drum microscope by Joseph Franks, *c*.1845 (inv. no. 1971.51); a microscope by A. & J. Franks, *c*.1869 (inv. no. 1976.26); a six-draw refracting telescope by J. Franks, *c*.1820 (inv. no. 1987.148) and a boxwood slide-rule (inv. no. 1994.147.2); also a three-draw refracting telescope signed 'J. Franks Manchester', Tesseract catalogue H, Fall 1984, item 4; and a hand-held 'Engels'-type microscope, 'A. Franks 95 Deansgate Manchester' at the National Museums of Scotland (NMS. T.1979.131).

Bavaria.[14] Abraham Levi was described as an optician between 1794 and 1799, and was also Jewish. Members of the Franklin family were listed as mathematical instrument makers between 1832 and 1846; the family had originated in Prague, coming to London from Breslau in about 1763. Abraham Franklin moved to Liverpool in about 1815, before moving to Manchester in 1823.[15]

The Italian immigrants to England have been studied in some detail.[16] Their arrival in Manchester was commented on, as early as 1884: 'for some reason there was a remarkable influx of Italians into Manchester about 1810, including Zanettis, Bolongaros, Casartellis, Ronchettis, Peduzzis, Bianchis and others who were carvers, gilders, picture dealers, makers of barometers and thermometers and of plaster casts'.[17] John Baptist Ronchetti came from Tavernerio in 1785, and set up in business as a weather-glass maker, retiring to Italy in 1805. That same year his son, Charles Joshua came to Manchester, and began to work with the Zanettis – the brothers Vittore and Vincente Zanetti had emigrated from Lake Garda in about 1795 – and Ronchetti set up in business himself in about 1817. Evidence suggests that he went on to run a waterproofing factory at Clayton, leaving his sons John Baptist and Joshua to manage the instrument business at 43 Market Street from about 1840.[18]

The Casartellis also came from Tavernerio, and married into the Ronchetti family.[19] Dominic Bolongaro was born in 1780 in Stresa, Piedmont, and emigrated to Manchester in about 1805, and worked for some time with Vittore Zanetti until about 1817, when he set up on his own account. He took on Joseph Gale as an apprentice in about 1820; Gale started his own business in 1829, but it failed in 1843. Bolongaro took over Gale's premises at 32 Market Street in 1836, and took his son Peter, aged 31, as a business partner, in 1848. Dominic married an Englishwoman, Ellen Tucker, and they had four children including Peter, who went into the business and married Mary Gale, who may well have been the daughter of his father's apprentice. Peter ran the firm after his father's death in 1856 until his own death in 1892.[20] From these and other examples, it can be seen that, just like other new arrivals, Italian immigrants felt happier clustering together in a new country, thereby enjoying common religious, language and cultural affinities, and reinforcing these characteristics by intermarriage, and by working alongside their fellow countrymen.[21]

---

[14]   Williams (1985), 11, 66.

[15]   Ibid., 35–8, 65.

[16]   Banfield (1993) appears full of useful information, but its lack of references renders it effectively useless.

[17]   *Manchester Guardian*, 1 September 1884, quoted in Ronchetti (1990), 51.

[18]   Ronchetti (1990), 54; Manchester directories, *passim*.

[19]   Ronchetti (1990), 54.

[20]   Records held at the Museum of Science and Industry in Manchester; Ronchetti (1990), 54.

[21]   Sponza (1988), 267–71.

Unlike many of the other centres discussed in this book, it does not appear that many London-trained instrument makers came to Manchester thinking it a likely new market for their skills. Exceptions were Stephen Norris Cooper (Figure 4.1), a rule maker in Holborn between 1809 and 1811,[22] who appeared in the 1817 Manchester directory (after his final appearance in 1843, the business was continued beyond 1851 by Sarah Cooper, presumably his widow); and possibly the Thomas Gregory, optician, who appeared in the 1834 directory only, and may have been the same Thomas Gregory, optician, previously listed in London between 1824 and 1834.[23]

More noticeable is the movement of businesses between Manchester and nearby Liverpool, perhaps the most famous example being that of J.B. Dancer (1812–78), whose grandfather Michael was based in London between 1766 and his death in 1817. One of Michael's apprentices had been Benjamin Jasper Wood, who appears to have moved to Liverpool and started an instrument business there in 1810 (Figure 4.2). Michael Dancer's son, Josiah, upon inheriting his father's business in 1817, moved from London to Liverpool, with his son, John Benjamin, who ultimately took over his father's business after his death in 1835, and in 1841 went into partnership with another reasonably long-established Liverpool optician, Abraham Abraham. Dancer moved to Manchester, and started a branch in Cross Street when his partnership with Abraham ended after only four years in 1845. Dancer remained in Manchester, working there on his own account from 1845 until he died in 1878.

As already noted in Chapter 1, there is a considerable instrument history literature about Dancer and his ventures into photography, microscopy and microphotography, and he has been described as 'the most important provincial instrument maker of his time'.[24] Like Thomas King of Bristol, Dancer numbered his microscopes (Figure 4.3); however, these numbers are more difficult than King's to interpret, especially as Dancer did not number all his microscopes, and thus their rate of production is unclear.[25] Dancer supplied

---

[22]  Clifton (1995), 65: a mileage indicator signed by Cooper, dating between 1847 and 1850 is in the collection of the Science Museum, London, NMSI inv. no. 1988–7509. This simple rule is made for the East Anglian Railway's lines from Ely north to King's Lynn, from King's Lynn east to Dereham, and a spur westward from Ely to the King's Lynn line from Magdalen Road (then called Watlington) to Wisbech. My thanks to David Wright, National Railway Museum, York.

[23]  Ibid., 119.

[24]  Ibid., 75–6; Wetton (1990–91), 59–63; Nuttall (2004a).

[25]  Bracegirdle (1996), 27 states that 'serial numbers from 9 to 407' have been recorded. Other examples with the low numbers of 26 and 38 are in private collections, the second dated to after 1855; number 317 has been dated to after 1861: the Museum of Science and Industry in Manchester, inv. no. 1997.6.3 (this has a design register mark of 1861 on the binocular tube, which may, however, be a later addition to the instrument); numbers 302, 346, 354, 358, 360 and 362 have been noted; number 370 is also in the collection at Manchester (inv. no. 1972.26.1); that numbered 385 has been dated from a trade catalogue,

**Figure 4.1   Mileage indicator signed by S. Cooper, Manchester, c.1850**

*Source:* © National Railway Museum, York, NMSI inv. no. 1988–7509

**Figure 4.2    Trade card for Benjamin Jasper Wood, Liverpool, c.1820**

*Source*: Courtesy of the Collection of Historical Scientific Instruments, Harvard
University

customized apparatus to the Mancunian scientists J.P. Joule and John Dalton;
he was a considerable experimenter himself, and developed a process for making
microscopic photographs (an ancestor of the microfilm). He also patented a
stereoscopic camera in 1856.[26] 'By 1871, he was employing eight men and about
four apprentices,' Wetton recounts, and 'His workshop was powered by steam
and was equipped with machinery for the manufacture of instruments'.[27] It is
not clear at what date the steam power was introduced, and Wetton admits that

---

itself dated at *c*.1855, and costing £18 0s 0d new (now in the National Museums of
Scotland, NMS.T.1979.73: see Nuttall (1979), 49); another example with the binocular
tube dated 1861 is in the collection of the Science Museum, numbered 400 (NMSI inv.
no. 1929–1963); while the highest recorded number of 407 has no clear date (Christie's
South Kensington, 26 September 1991 and 2 April 1992). My thanks to Jenny Wetton for
her help with this.

[26]    English patent no. 2064 of 1852.

[27]    Wetton (1990–91), 63. Evidence for workshop numbers came from the 1871 Census;
that for steam power from Dancer's 1873 trade catalogue: 'JOHN B. DANCER Is enabled
by the aid of STEAM POWER and suitable MACHINERY, to produce Instruments of
the greatest perfection …'.

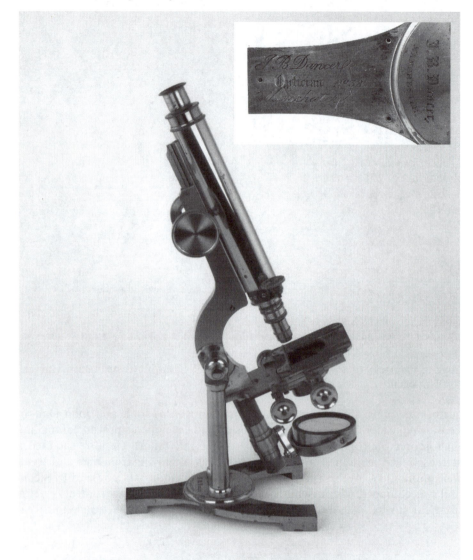

**Figure 4.3    Microscope by John Benjamin Dancer, no. 385, c.1855**

*Source*: National Museums of Scotland, NMS.T.1979.73

for Manchester, 'little evidence remains as to the type of workshop used by instrument makers'.[28]

Other businesses which made the move between Liverpool and Manchester include that of Thomas Underhill, recorded as a mathematical instrument maker and rule maker in the Liverpool directories between 1824 and 1827. He reappeared in the Manchester directories as a 'mathematical rule maker' in 1828, and continued in business there until 1881.[29] William Chadwick, an optician based in Liverpool between 1827 and 1830 may be the same person as William Henry Chadwick, a barometer maker who first made an appearance in the 1836 Manchester directory. The Casartellis of Liverpool, already related to the Ronchettis of Manchester, took over the latter business in 1852 when Charles Joshua Ronchetti retired to Italy.[30] The brothers Antonio and Gaspar Introvino ran their firm in Manchester from 1816 to 1852, but Antonio also had a shop in Liverpool's Duke Street between 1821 and 1825.[31]

No instrument-making or retailing activity was recorded in the Manchester directories until 1794, and then the number of businesses remained at three or four until 1820, when there was a sudden rise to 14 (see Graph 4.1). By 1835, there were twenty firms and the numbers continued to rise until 1845, dropping slightly to twenty-two in 1850. Jenny Wetton divides these into two categories. First there were 'barometer makers', who had to include other lines of business to survive (such as the traditional 'carving and gilding' – that is, providing picture frames and looking-glasses – or venturing into the fine art and the print trade, the most successful example being that of Thomas Agnew, one-time apprentice to the firm of Vittore Zanetti of Manchester).[32] Her second category is 'opticians', who were initially itinerant, and had by the 1820s located in premises close to the main shopping areas. Subsequently, as demand grew, the opticians and barometer makers began to produce 'scientific instruments' – surveying instruments for the growth of the railways; hydrometers for brewers, dyers and excisemen; and microscopes for 'rational recreation'.

The growth of the educational market meant an increased demand for philosophical or demonstration apparatus. As Wetton points out, 'Manchester already had several medical schools, two Mechanics' Institutes, and two other institutions which taught science: the Royal Manchester Institution and the Royal Victoria Gallery. In 1851, Owens College (the forerunner of Manchester University) opened offering courses in science subjects'.[33] However, no instrument makers based in Manchester exhibited their wares at the Great Exhibition. Despite

---

[28]   Ibid., 45.
[29]   Clifton (1995), 284–5. A large boxwood sector, signed 'Underhill, 1 St Mary's Gate, Manchester' was offered by Tesseract, Catalogue 47, winter 1994, item 54.
[30]   Wetton (2004).
[31]   Manchester directories, *passim;* Liverpool directories, *passim.*
[32]   For Agnew as an art dealer, see Kingzett (1998).
[33]   Wetton (1990–91), 43.

this, considerable numbers of instruments signed by the Dancer, Casartelli and Ronchetti workshops and marked with a Manchester address, can be noted in public collections or otherwise recorded. Some of these date from before the Great Exhibition, and must demonstrate a growing self-confidence within the firms in the quality of their products.


## Birmingham

The ninth edition of the *Encyclopaedia Britannica* characterized Birmingham as having long been 'a seat of manufacture in metal' and quoted Leland's 1538 *Itinerary*, explaining that its cutlers had migrated to Sheffield, but its smiths had remained. 'The well-ascertained importance of Birmingham as a centre of manufactures began towards the close of the seventeenth century, one great source of it being the absolute freedom of the town, there being no guilds, companies, or restrictions of any kind; besides which the easy access to cheap coal and iron indirectly helped the development'.[34] Metalworking was Birmingham's main staple, in particular 'the chief variety is the brass-working trade, which employs several hundred masters, and about 10,000 work-people, and consumes probably 50,000 tons of metal annually, which is worked up into an infinity of articles of ornament and utility'.[35]

Daniel Defoe mentioned 'all sorts of wrought iron, and brassware from Birmingham; edged tools, knives, &c. from Sheffield' being brought to be sold at Stourbridge Fair in the 1720s.[36] A recent economic history of the town bewails the paucity of surviving primary sources, but characterizes Birmingham's industrial activity as taking place in small workshops, with a considerable division of labour even by 1760, so that output was relatively high in terms of labour productivity. As Eric Hopkins has written:

> The essential point is that the great economic achievements of the successive decades were based not on massive technological breakthroughs, as in the cotton industry, but on existing modes of production, and principally on the small workshop with its hand machinery. Only in the 1830s did steam power begin to be used on any significant scale, and only then were larger work units becoming more common and more prominent. There was thus a gradual and undramatic change to more modern means of production, in a town which was already industrialized by 1760. By 1840 the larger workplace and the traditional small workshop existed side by side, but with the latter predominating numerically.[37]

---

[34] J.T.B., 'Birmingham', *Encyclopaedia Britannica* ninth edition (Edinburgh, 1874), III, 784.

[35] Ibid.

[36] Defoe (1971), 105.

[37] Hopkins (1989), xii.

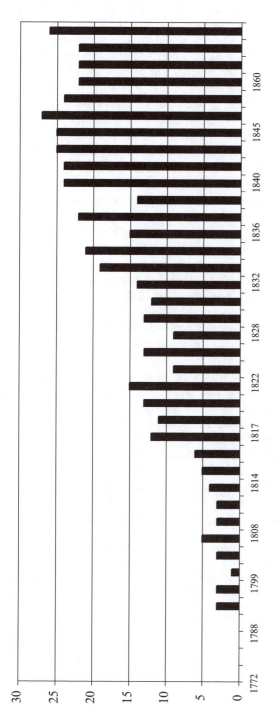

**Graph 4.1   Manchester 1772–1852: numbers of instrument making firms from local directories**

Although it has been difficult to uncover much evidence about the operation of any of Birmingham's instrument makers, it does appear that the small workshop, relying on hand technology, remained the norm, employing family members and perhaps one or two journeymen. Links to London improved throughout the eighteenth century, with a weekly carrier service in place from 1731; roads were improved, and the town became the centre of a hub of canals. There was an increased use of middlemen, or factors, also sometimes known as agents. The factors would sell the workshop goods on to merchants and shopkeepers, and they helped to promote Birmingham's wares nationwide, especially in the main marketplace, London.[38] Although brass was not made in Birmingham until 1740, the variety of the metal trades and the large numbers of small masters meant that craftsmen were able to change from producing one commodity to another with some ease, as economic conditions warranted.[39] This makes following a particular business through the street directories problematic.

There is no evidence of an early development of the factory system in Birmingham, with the exception of Boulton & Watt's factory at Soho, which was not producing instruments; steam power came late to the small workshops, not being introduced until the 1830s.[40] The rule-maker John Rabone brought steam power into his workshop in 1834, and it is claimed that he 'was probably the first in the rule-making business to do so'.[41] Although his workmen were still producing rules by hand, the steam power was probably used for preparing the rules before they were divided. Attempts to mechanize the division of wooden rules in the 1850s proved impracticable.[42]

The Birmingham trade in scientific instruments appears to have had its beginnings in the decisions of some optical workers to migrate there from London (as was also the case at Bristol, York and Liverpool), presumably in the hope of finding and opening up new local markets. In 1758, Joseph Oakley, a 'SPECTACLE MAKER from LONDON' advertised that he 'Makes Temples and all other sorts of spectacles, Reading Glasses, Telescopes, Microscopes, and all other Optical Instruments … Any Person may be supplied with any Apparatus for the above Instruments, by enquiring for him at Mr John Hazeldine's, or at his Workshop near the Dog in Mount-Pleasant, Birmingham'.[43] By 1770, the range of his wares had expanded, presumably in part as a response to local demand:

he hath now ready for Sale an Assortment of Optical Instruments … Reflecting Telescopes, completely mounted in Brass and neat Mahogany Cases, Refracting Telescopes, Prospects and Opera Glasses, either covered with Nourskin and Brass, or Black in imitation of Shagreen, and some Mahogany Tubes mounted with Brass,

---

[38]  Ibid., 11–13.
[39]  Ibid., 17.
[40]  Ibid., 21, 26.
[41]  Hallam (1984), 22.
[42]  Ibid., 25.
[43]  *Aris's Gazette*, 3 July 1758.

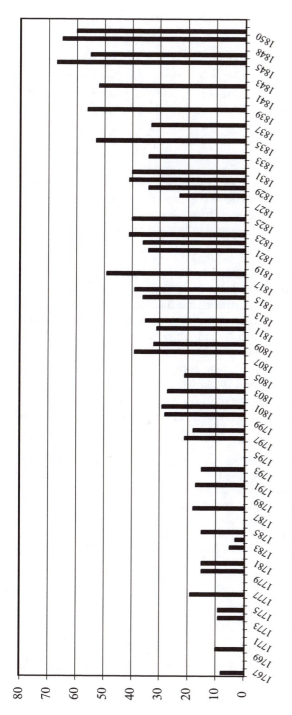

**Graph 4.2  Birmingham 1767–1850: numbers of instrument making firms from local directories**

Microscopes of Different Constructions, Magic Lanthorns and Figures, Diagonal Mirrours [sic], Concaves, Glasses for Short Sight, Convex Glasses of every different Size and Focus &c.[44]

Magic lantern manufacture in Birmingham was reckoned in the late nineteenth century to have begun with Philip Carpenter in 1808; but in this advertisement, we see evidence of the retail, at any rate, of the device some time before.[45] However, chiming with David Landes's observation about retaining a workforce's hard-earned expertise, it is apparent from the remainder of the advertisement that Oakley's bread-and-butter business came from producing spectacles for Birmingham's ageing population:

He will do his utmost Endeavours to suit those who please to favour him with their custom for Spectacles &c. not only with the best of their Kind, but such as peculiarly adapted to their particular Sight, and may depend on having such as will give the Necessary help, and not in the least prejudicial, which is the sure Consequence of an injudicious Choice.[46]

Oakley cannot have been alone in having to find another aspect of his work to make a living wage. In fact, this appears to have been the main characteristic of the Birmingham trade during the period under discussion: those engaged in instrument production – or possibly in the production of parts of instruments – also produced other metal goods to which they could switch as demand dictated (Graph 4.2). For instance, one of the longest-surviving businesses, that of Richard Bakewell (Figure 4.4) and his successor Isaac Trow, continued for over 61 years and was described in the 1791 street directory as a 'mathematical instrument, dog-collar and watch key maker'.[47] A contemporary advertisement, announcing Bakewell's venture into business on his own account, demonstrated this versatility:

RICHARD BAKEWELL, late Partner with Messrs Inshaw and Hinksman, respectfully informs Merchants, Factors and the Public in general, that he carries on the Mathematical Instruments, Brass Compasses, and Brass Dog-collar Businesses, on his own Account, at his Manufactory in Loveday-street, at the bottom of St Mary's-Row, Birmingham; where all Orders will be executed with the greatest Punctuality upon the lowest Terms, and every Favour gratefully acknowledged by
Their humble Servant
R. BAKEWELL.[48]

---

[44]   Ibid., 28 May 1770.
[45]   *Birmingham Weekly Post*, 15 December 1894, quoting the *Engineer*, 23 November 1894, 439.
[46]   Landes (1998), 47; *Aris's Gazette*, 28 May 1770.
[47]   Charles Pye, *The Birmingham Directory for the Year 1791* (Birmingham, n.d. [1791]).
[48]   *Aris's Gazette*, 19 April 1790.

**Figure 4.4** Trade card for Richard Bakewell, Birmingham, c.1820

*Source:* © National Museum of Science and Industry inv. no. 1986–360

Richard Bakewell senior had married Ann Newell in 1763.[49] After his 1783 partnership with Inshaw and Hinksman had ended, his business continued from 1791 until 1825 in Loveday Street, although Richard Bakewell senior died in 1803.[50] His place at the head of the firm was taken by his son Richard, who had probably worked with him for some time: born in about 1781, he died in May 1826.[51] He had married Isabella Burchell in November 1807, and they had ten children, although only one of these – the eldest son, also named Richard – is known to have gone into the firm.[52] Within a month of her husband's death, his widow Isabella had placed an advertisement stating that she would continue her late husband's business, 'having retained the former workmen under the superintendence of a competent person [so that] her goods will be manufactured in the same superior manner as heretofore'.[53]

Isabella Bakewell managed to keep the business running for a few years, perhaps in the unfulfilled hope that one of her children would be able to take over from her (the eldest, Richard, born in 1808, would have been aged 18 at the time of his father's death: he was probably the Richard Bakewell, aged 73, 'retired mathematical tool maker' who was recorded in the 1881 Census, as an inmate in the Birmingham workhouse).[54] Bakewell's trade successor, Isaac Trow, was as versatile as his predecessor judging from the range of his wares more than forty years later, being described as a 'manufacturer of mathematical instruments, surveyors' measuring tapes, dog collars, mariners' and miners' compasses' in 1831.[55] However, Trow's relationship with the Bakewells can only be surmised: he ran the business under his own name from 1829 until 1858 and beyond. Indeed, there may have been no relationship, judging by the evidence of an advertisement in August 1828 which announced:

TO MERCHANTS AND FACTORS.
ISAAC TROW begs to inform the Merchants, Factors and Public in general, that he has purchased the trade (comprising Mathematical Instruments, Surveyors' Measuring tapes, Brass and Plated Dog Collars, Miners' and Mariners' Compasses', &c. &c.) carried on by the late Mr RICHARD BAKEWELL, and subsequently by his widow.
    I. T. having engaged Mr R. Bakewell, son of his predecessor, and also the whole of the workmen, intends carrying on the same in all its branches on the premises as

---

49   Register of St Philip's the Cathedral Church of Birmingham, Marriages 1715–1800, transcribed by P. Shellis (n.p., n.d.). Also the International Genealogical Index [IGI].
50   *Aris's Gazette*, 1 March 1803.
51   Ibid., 5 June 1826.
52   IGI: the ten were Richard, John, William, Henry, Isabella, Catherine, Abigail, Ebenezer, Theophilus and Frances Ann.
53   *Birmingham Journal*, 1 July 1826.
54   IGI: what had brought him there, one wonders.
55   [Wrightson's], *The Directory of Birmingham* ... (Birmingham, 1833).

heretofore, and flatters himself, by strict adherence to quality as well as by punctual attention, to merit their future favours.[56]

Trow had three children who died in infancy, and his wife Sarah (who was not a Bakewell daughter) died in 1860.[57] Here we see evidence of two successive family enterprises, manufacturing a variety of hardware, and able to change production to suit market demands.[58]

In a city renowned for the variety of its brass metal manufactures, it is not surprising to find directory listings for instrument makers coupled with such descriptions as 'manufacturer of plated and brass telescopes, fancy hearth brushes, toasting forks, plated and brass tubes for umbrellas &c plated and brass tubes of every description, umbrella and parasol frames complete &c', or 'compass and pincer maker', or 'military feather and barometer maker', or 'gilt toy, mathematical instrument maker and bell founder', or the more macabre 'coffin furniture and measuring tape manufacturers'.[59] It is apparent that over time various manufacturers would slip in and out of instrument making as markets increased or dwindled. Individual businesses (if they survived) could then switch their goods to suit the economic climate. With this flexibility came survival, but it makes it more difficult to characterize individual businesses or their products as a result.

Few instruments survive with a Birmingham signature. Often all that is known is a single product, which can be tentatively linked with a name that appears in the directories. This is the case with a handsome early nineteenth century theodolite signed by Hart, Birmingham (Figure 4.5), which passed through the antiques trade and may be identified with Joseph Hart, optician and spectacle maker in Digbeth between 1788 and 1801: he became an optical, mathematical and philosophical instrument maker in 1803 on his removal to Dale End, vanishing from the directories by 1815. Yet the theodolite's existence begs a number of questions: as it has Hart's name on it, this indicates the point of sale, which was Birmingham. Who was the initial, presumably local, customer? Doubtless, he was a surveyor. Was the piece actually made by Hart, or bought-in from elsewhere? With the currently available evidence, these questions are unanswerable.

---

[56]   *Aris's Gazette*, 30 June 1828.

[57]   Ibid., 8 May 1826, 27 September 1830, 20 May 1833, 12 March 1860.

[58]   Instruments recorded with Bakewell's signature are a protractor and a slide rule: Clifton (1995), 15; a set of drawing instruments offered at Sotheby's 6 and 7 March 1997, Lot 597; and another in the Museum of the History of Science, Oxford, inv. no. 55342; Trow's signature, 'I Trow late R. Bakewell' appeared on a boxwood rule and ivory sector, Sotheby's 15 October 1973, Lot 3.

[59]   *Wrightson's New Triennial Directory of Birmingham* ... (Birmingham, 1818); [Pigot's] *Commercial Directory for 1818–19–20* ... (Manchester, 1818); *New Triennial Directory of Birmingham* ... (Birmingham, 1812); *The Directory of Birmingham;* ... (Birmingham, n.d. [1847]).

**Figure 4.5    Theodolite signed 'Hart Fecit BIRMING$^H$', c.1800**

*Source*: Harriet Wynter Archive, National Museums of Scotland

Later prominent Birmingham instrument manufacturers – Philip Carpenter, and the two local firms which exhibited at the Crystal Palace Great Exhibition, Robert Field & Son, and James Parkes – will be discussed in more detail in Chapter 8, but the pattern of their workshops is similar to those already discussed. However, perhaps the major eighteenth-century figure associated both with Birmingham and with instrument making (although not simultaneously) is the hero of the Industrial Revolution himself, James Watt (1736–1819). The young Watt's abilities as an instrument maker attracted the attention of the professor of natural philosophy at Glasgow University, Robert Dick the younger, and, under his patronage, Watt was persuaded to go to London with a letter of introduction to the famous Scots-born maker of telescopes, James Short (1710–68).[60] This was to give him the breadth of experience in the trade that he could not have hoped to gain in Glasgow at that time.

---

[60]    Hills (2002), 46–9.

The young Watt spent the year 1755–56 working with John Neale, a watch and globe maker, and John Morgan, a mathematical instrument maker, and returned to Glasgow having 'attained reasonable competence'.[61] Watt's work as a Glasgow instrument maker and retailer is outside the scope of this work, but he bought-in for resale instruments from the London makers Nathaniel Hill, Thomas Jarmain, Charles Lincoln, James Tomlinson, Richard Rust and Christopher Stedman; and supplies for his shop came from across the country, with barometer tubes and sheet brass coming from Bristol, and boxwood from London.[62] There is no reason to believe that this pattern was unusual for an instrument-making workshop, wherever it was located. However, Watt himself was unusual, and in about 1770 he abandoned the scientific instrument business and moved into civil and mechanical engineering; his wife died in 1773 and he left Glasgow for Birmingham and a partnership in steam engine development with the thrusting entrepreneur Matthew Boulton (1728–1809) the following year.

As with so many other areas in England, Birmingham became home to a number of itinerant barometer makers, some of whom stayed long enough to be noted in the directories; others, less settled, engraved the place of manufacture on their instruments along with their names (or had it engraved for them by a supplier), but have left little other trace. One of the former was Peter Borini, who took the opportunity of his removal from Bull Street, Birmingham, to 'more extensive premises [at] No 18 Snow Hill' in 1818, to advertise his 'manufacture of every Description of Looking Glasses, Picture Frames, Barometers, Thermometers, hour, Half hour, three Minutes, fourteen Seconds, and twenty-eight Second Glasses'.[63] His first wife Mary Ann Henley died in 1829, his second wife Sarah Holt in 1836, while he himself died at the age of fifty-six in 1844.[64] Surviving instruments made by Borini include a number of barometers.[65] Other less settled Italian glass-workers include Charles Guggiari in 1846 (a man of the same name was recorded in Sheffield in 1828; and ten years later barometers signed by Guggiari & Anzani of Nottingham have been recorded).[66] The English career of Peter Rabalio, who settled in Birmingham for about a year, is discussed in Chapter 8.[67]

All over England, different trades required devices to help with calculation, measurement and gauging, and a large proportion of instrument-making businesses in the Birmingham area was devoted to producing boxwood and ivory rules for a variety of purposes. This was done by hand, with a high degree of skill

---

[61]  Ibid., 55–8.

[62]  Clifton (1995), 292; Hills (2002), 108.

[63]  *Aris's Gazette*, 30 March 1818.

[64]  Ibid., 30 November 1829, 26 September 1836 and 5 August 1844.

[65]  For instance, an example sold at Christie's New York, 30 April 1997, Lot 15.

[66]  *I. Slater's National Commercial Directory* ... (Manchester and London, 1846); *Sheffield Directory and Guide* ... (Sheffield, 1828); Clifton (1995), 121.

[67]  Charles Pye, *The Birmingham Directory for the Year 1788* (Birmingham, [1788]).

and accuracy: 'straight scales and rules are usually divided by placing the article to be divided and the original pattern side by side, then passing a straight-edge with a shoulder fixed at right angles to serve as a guide along the original, and pausing at each division; then a corresponding line is made on the copy by the dividing knife,' runs a mid-nineteenth-century description. 'Segments of circles are also graduated in the same way, by making a straight-edge revolve on the centre of the circle, and marking off the divisions on the straight scale'.[68]

This specialist area of instrument manufacture had apparently had its beginnings in London, but by the mid-eighteenth century there was a strong and varied production being carried out in and around Wolverhampton, a town about ten miles north-west of Birmingham. In 1767, for instance, there were three rule makers in Birmingham, and three in Wolverhampton; by 1770 this had risen to four in Birmingham, and six in Wolverhampton; ten years later, there were still four in Birmingham, but numbers had dropped to five in Wolverhampton. Christopher Jacob advertised more frequently than his colleagues, so we have more of an idea of the extent of his wares, as well as other aspects of his business, than those of others:

> New Improved SLIDING RULES
> WHICH, for their Utility and Accuracy,
> are much superior to any other Joint Rule whatever; by which may easily be measured Superficies or Solids of all Denominations, by an entire new Method; made by the Improver, Christopher Jacob, in Bilstone-street, Wolverhampton, Staffordshire, or may be had at his Shop on Snow Hill, Birmingham; likewise makes all other Sorts of Sliding Rules, and all sorts of Rules for Gauging, with Rules of all Sorts, and for the Use of all Trades; Also Parallel Rules, T. Squares and bevels, with Drawing Boards for Architecture, Bricklayer's Bevels and Squares, Shipwright's Drawing Bows, sectors, with or without French Joints; either in Brass, Wood, or Ivory, or Silver; Scales of all Sorts, such as Gunter's Scales, Navigation Scales, Plotting Scales, Setting-off Scales, Feather-Edg'd for Surveying, Stationer's Lined Rulers, Station Staves, and Protractors of all sorts; all made after the newest Improvements, and neatest Manner.[69]

This 1761 advertisement shows that Jacob was prepared to produce almost any permutation that a customer might demand, and also that his workshop was in Wolverhampton, with his main shop or retail premises in Birmingham. Other rule makers in the area may have followed this pattern, for instance, Thomas and Benjamin Onions. Further advertisements by Jacob reveal runaway apprentices – three ran away in July 1761, and a further two in September 1767.[70] Whether this was because Jacob was a difficult master, or because times were tense in the workshop – Jacob went bankrupt in 1763 – is unclear.[71] He was not alone. At least

---

68    J. Rabone, jun., 'Measuring Rules', in Timmins (1866), 631.
69    *Aris's Gazette*, 23 November 1761.
70    Ibid., 20 July 1761 and 14 September 1767.
71    Ibid., 11 April 1763; 17 September 1764; 27 July 1767.

two other rule makers, Joseph Edwards and John Mansell, advertised absconding apprentices, in an effort to prevent them from getting employment elsewhere.[72] Mansell's apprentice was named Samuel Haycox, and he may have grown up to become the respectable Samuel Haycock whose mathematical instrument and brass compass-making business began in Birmingham's Lench Street in 1808. His son – also Samuel – continued this until 1852, and died after ten years' retirement at Boulogne-sur-Mer at the age of seventy.[73]

Jacob attempted to sell his wares across the English Midlands. Claiming to have improved the slide rule, he advertised that:

> The Improved Sliding Rule (with Books) may also be had of Mr Joseph [illegible] of the Saracen's head, Birmingham; at Mr John Gilson's in Nottingham; [at Mr] Richard Morgan's in Shrewsbury; and Mr George Whately's in Litchfield.[74]

Evidently there must have been a local market here for solving 'Questions in Superficies or Solids of all Denominations', at a time when Englishmen struggled with calculations in all walks of life. Jacob also advertised for workmen:

> Wanted Three Journeymen in the common burnished Snuffer Way, any man that can use a File well, may have constant Employment and [illegible] Wages, by enquiring of Christopher Jacob, in Wolverhampton; [any] Journeyman in the Steel Snuffer way, that can begin and end his Work may meet with good Encouragement, by applying as above.[75]

It is not clear when Jacob made the move entirely into Birmingham. From the first Birmingham directory in 1767 there is no hint that he might have had premises in Wolverhampton; this information comes entirely from newspaper sources.

Even as early as 1761, this specialized trade was moving into Birmingham. From there it appears that rules of all sorts were sent to London, some for finishing, others for retail to the London market and for export. Indeed, by 1845 one of the longer-surviving firms, F.B. (Francis Blakemore) Cox, was described as an 'ivory, box & foreign rule manufacturer, wholesale and for exportation' (Figure 4.6).[76] An account of the trade written in 1865 by a prominent rule

---

[72]  Ibid., 14 May, 21 May and 3 June 1770. No rules with either Edwards' or Mansell's signatures have been recorded.
[73]  Ibid., 25 January 1862; Birmingham directories, *passim*.
[74]  *Aris's Gazette*, 17 May 1762.
[75]  Ibid. No rules with Jacob's signature have been recorded.
[76]  [Kelly's] *Post Office Directory of Birmingham, Warwickshire and part of Staffordshire* (London, n.d. [1845]). The Coxes were something of a rule making dynasty: Thomas Cox was in business from 1777 until 1798, dying in 1800 (*Aris's Gazette*, 6 January 1800); his son, also Thomas, had died the previous year in Kingston, West Indies (ibid., 29 April 1799); the firm was then run by Ann and George Cox, and from 1822 by Francis Blakemore Cox, who died 5 November 1853, aged 71 (ibid., 7 November 1853).

maker, John Rabone, whose family had also been in this line since the turn of the century, states that:

> At the latter part of the past century only three or four rule masters, each employing a few apprentices and men, were to be found in Birmingham, and one at Harborne adjacent; but now the trade has almost deserted Wolverhampton, which numbers only four or five persons employed in it, while Birmingham affords employment to as many hundreds.
>
>   With the exception of three or four makers scattered throughout the country the trade is now entirely confined to Birmingham and London. Many of the rules sold as London-made are produced in Birmingham, and many are framed in Birmingham and sold to the London makers, who mark or finish them themselves.[77]

**Figure 4.6    Foot rule by F.B. Cox, Birmingham, c.1830**

*Source*: National Museums of Scotland, NMS.T.1973.111

One unusual survival is a sample book from Sampson Aston's Birmingham rule-making business, which operated between 1833 and 1870. There are 14 different types of two-foot two-fold boxwood and brass rules, scales and slide-rules, showing a range of hinges and markings, and short lengths (about three inches) of each have been fastened down on a sheet of cardboard, with their prices marked beneath. Presumably sample sets like this were carried by Sampson Aston

---

[77]   J. Rabone, jun., 'Measuring Rules', in Timmins (1866), 629. A history of the firm of John Rabone can be found in Hallam (1984), 14–56.

and his salesmen or agents to customers and middlemen in London, so that they could see the range, quality and costs of the goods that they might order.[78]

As in Sheffield, a number of instrument makers were connected with pubs or with food supply as a secondary part to their business. Thus Samuel Ault, 'victualler and compass maker', had become solely a 'victualler' by 1788; William Hodges was a 'victualler, compass and pincher maker' in 1801, but by 1805 had moved into the metalware end of the business; and Joseph Lunt both ran 'The Golden Cup' inn and was a 'box [wood] and ivory rule maker' between 1842 and 1852.[79] Sampson Aston, who has been mentioned above, ran a line as a 'dealer in home-cured bacon and hams' between 1833 and 1849; in 1850 he was characterized in one directory as a 'cheesemonger' alongside his regular job producing rules.[80]

At the Great Exhibition, the firms of Robert Field & Son and J. Parkes & Son both exhibited instruments; in the case of Field, these were microscopes and photographic lenses, whereas Parkes displayed mathematical drawing instruments, compasses and slide rules. The Jury thought Field's microscopes 'not as such to demand especial notice', and merely noted Parkes's compasses.[81] The other major Birmingham exhibit in this Class came from Chance Brothers & Co., manufacturers of glass, who displayed a large dioptric apparatus for lighthouse illumination (Figure 4.7), but they won a Council medal in Class XXIV, 'Glass', for their 29-inch diameter disc of flint glass, suitable for grinding into an enormous objective lens.[82] This however, failed to find a buyer, despite some lobbying of the British government. It was again displayed at the Paris Exhibition in 1855, along with a correspondingly large disc of crown glass. Mortifyingly for English instrument makers, both were acquired by the French government.[83]

Glass production was one of Birmingham's staple trades, but it was not until 1845, at the end of the period under examination, that crippling excise taxation (especially on optical glass) was relieved and the business in its widest applications could be undertaken without restriction.[84] So although small glass workers connected with the instrument trade can be identified from earlier street directories, these were never more than suppliers on a workshop scale. For instance, Asher Barnet is described in 1770 as a spectacle grinder, but by 1780 he had become an optician; Samuel Phillips, a glass grinder, was noted in 1777;

---

[78]  David Stanley Auctions, Leicester, 24 September 2005, Lot 966; there is another example, by Rabone, illustrated in Hallam (1984), 12.
[79]  Charles Pye, *The Birmingham Directory for the Year 1788* (Birmingham, [1788]); Chapman's *Birmingham Directory* ... (Birmingham, 1801); *Pigot and Co'.s ... Directory of Birmingham and its Environs* ... (Birmingham and London, n.d. [1842]); *Slater's ... Royal National Commercial Directory* ...(Manchester and London, 1852).
[80]  Birmingham directories, *passim.*
[81]  *Catalogue* ... (1851), 435, 467*; *Reports* ... (1852), 267, 281.
[82]  *Catalogue* ... (1851), 477*; *Reports* ... (1852), 529–30.
[83]  Chance (1919), 176–7.
[84]  Turner (2000); Ashworth (2003), 254–7.

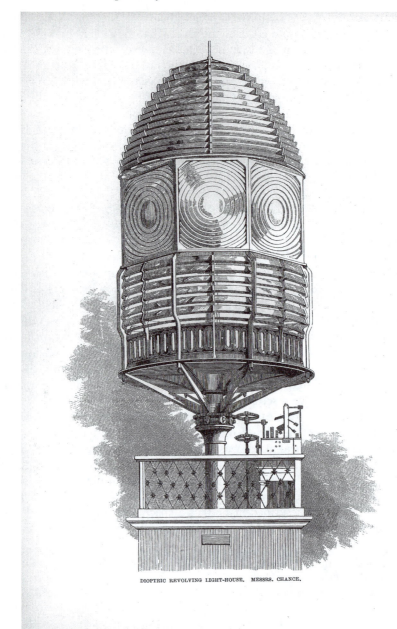

DIOPTRIC REVOLVING LIGHT-HOUSE.  MESSRS. CHANCE.

**Figure 4.7    Dioptric apparatus by Chance Brothers & Co., Birmingham, from the** *Catalogue of the Great Exhibition*, **1851**

*Source*: National Museums of Scotland

and John Pursall, a 'glass grinder and victualler', worked between 1785 and 1788. Richard Dickins, another glass grinder, survived from 1803 until 1815; Benjamin Mucklow described himself on at least two occasions as an 'optical glass grinder' between 1835 and 1839; and Charles and George Macklow began as optical glass manufacturers in 1842, and were still in business a decade later as wholesale opticians.[85]

The existence of these small businesses implies that the supply was adequate for optical instrumentation – telescopes, microscopes, the optics for surveying instruments, and spectacles. But clearly, excellent quality glass-work was also required for thermometer and barometer tubes, to ensure that the bore was uniform, and it was also necessary for the large glass components of electrostatic machines. The first glasshouse recorded in Birmingham was located at Snow Hill in 1762, and there were at least two others established before 1800, but this application never became as important for Birmingham as for the glass industry at Stourbridge. Nevertheless, by 1851, over a thousand Birmingham workers were involved in aspects of glassmaking.[86]

One of the Birmingham firms involved in glassmaking was that of Chance Brothers & Co., where a visiting journalist was all but overwhelmed by the scale of production in 1864:

> … the enormous works at Spon Lane … There, intersected by the canal which we are about to cross, and divided by lines of railways, the stupendous range of workshops, forges, and ovens extends over an area of twenty-four acres; while from amidst the separate piles of building there rise a score of shafts and chimneys – the steeples of this great temple devoted to labour and to art. It will be some indication of the extent of the business carried on at the Spon Lane works to remember that the glass which covered the Great Exhibition of 1851 was supplied by Messrs. Chance, that this occupied only the 'sheet-glass' department, and that 300 000 of the panes, 49 in. by 10 in., were supplied in the course of a few weeks without in any way interfering with the ordinary business.[87]

Optical glass was, by 1864, one of Chance Brothers' most important operations, and one for which they had gained a high reputation, chiefly through their displays at international exhibitions from 1851. The melt took five days: 'rough discs only are manufactured by Messrs Chance. These are afterwards ground and polished by the opticians, and vary in value from a few shillings to £1000 each'.[88] Lighthouse optics were even more complicated, requiring casting of the glass in iron moulds, which had been 'mathematically determined'.[89]

---

85  Birmingham directories, *passim.*
86  Hopkins (1989), 51.
87  Strauss et al. (1864), 186.
88  Ibid., 192.
89  Ibid., 193.

The production of instruments, or instrument parts, in Birmingham during the Industrial Revolution can thus be seen as an industry where the materials available and products required determined the scope of the individual workshop. With such a predominance in brass goods of a wide variety, workshop masters were not forced to remain with instrument making, but could turn their hand to other seemingly unrelated wares: all would be marketed by the factor and find a sale, probably in the London market. Thus, few Birmingham brass workers signed their pieces, making their identification today difficult for the historian. The trade was also divided between the 'brass and glass' form of instrumentation, and the equally large production of brass, wooden and ivory rules. Although there were rule makers based in other towns, as we have seen, Birmingham was clearly the centre of this important trade for much of the time under discussion.

# Chapter 5

# Smaller Centres and Individuals

Besides the four main new areas and two slightly longer-established centres of provincial instrument production described in the previous chapters, there were other small clusters of activity which developed outside London during this period. In an essay pertinent to the issues under discussion here, the English local historian Alan Everitt sketched out an analysis of the English county town during the eighteenth century. Using the examples of Exeter, Shrewsbury, Canterbury, Maidstone and Northampton, he stresses six features common to each: the town's range and growing variety of occupations, its role as an inland entrepôt, its position as a centre for professional and entrepreneurial activity, and its leisured gentry life, culture, and craftsmanship.

Everitt points out that the hinterlands of individual country towns gave each a special characteristic. Taking a long view, the duration of human settlement in each also 'meant that very different types of economy and rural society developed in the various parts of the county'.[1] He demonstrates that the skills in these towns were evolving and diversifying: 'Take the metal trades ... None of the five towns under review was particularly notable as a metal-working centre; they were not miniature Sheffields or Birminghams, yet they contained at least 350 master metal-craftsmen, and the real total was probably nearer 500'.[2] Most of these were of course blacksmiths, but Everitt notes a wide range of specialisms, including mathematical instrument makers and makers of surveyors' equipment, emphasizing that although producing on a small scale, they were serving an extensive regional agricultural hinterland.

The third major pre-industrial English population centre after London was Norwich; but Norwich's instrument-making base was negligible, possibly as small as those in Everitt's five exemplars. As a town in the centre of a large agricultural hinterland, Norwich's local demands for instrumentation were not great: once obtained, surveying instruments would have been owned by the surveyors themselves (as we shall see in Chapter 9), and only towards the mid- to late-nineteenth century were retailers of barometers to be found there, usually combining this occupation with selling jewellery or spectacles, and other optical goods (Figure 5.1). Barometers, as Nicholas Goodison has shown, appealed to a largely domestic market, and perhaps should more properly be considered as furniture rather than as professional mathematical tools; yet they appealed to

---

[1]    Everitt (1979), 88.
[2]    Ibid., 106–7.

the luxury end of the market, and judging by the rate of survivals, they were a popular purchase with the growing wealth of the consumer.[3] In particular, with the growth of amateur interest in meteorology, makers and retailers were able to sell barometers and thermometers in increasing numbers to farmers and horticulturalists: it is possible that their fashion-conscious wives influenced this.

This chapter will sketch other areas in which there is evidence of growth of a scientific trade during this period. Although only a very few of these individuals or firms are known to have been makers, and most must have been retailers, their presence contributes to the larger English framework, just as those noted in Norwich played some valid part in the networks of supply and demand. 'The craft economy of these county towns or regional markets,' states Everitt, 'found a new role for itself in adapting its skill to the needs of an increasing population, a changing countryside, and an expanding leisured class'.[4] Here we will look briefly at instrument supply in the English ports and spa towns, including the activities of some specialist mining equipment manufacturers and a handful of remarkable individuals.

As with York and Bristol, the more recently established ports of Newcastle-upon-Tyne, Hull and those on the south coast, such as Portsmouth, Southampton and Plymouth, all attracted ships' chandlers who could supply necessary equipment and repair navigation instruments in response to a local market. In the north-east of England, Newcastle's first 'mathematical instrument maker', William Bowie, advertised in a local newspaper in 1795.[5] Numbers of businesses there grew to six or so by the mid-1830s. These had increased to eight by 1840, and 12 by 1850:[6] as with Manchester, there was a mixture of 'opticians', Italian barometer-makers, and figures such as John Cail (Figure 5.2), who supplied a whole range of nautical and surveying instruments, and who is known to have bought in examples of Thomas Cooke of York's agricultural level for resale, engraved with his own name.[7] By 1837, Kingston-upon-Hull, on the Humber Estuary on the east coast, had eight instrument suppliers giving varying descriptions to summarize their occupations (Figure 5.3), such as 'ship's chandler'

---

[3]    Goodison (1969); Goodison (1977); for Norwich firms, Clifton (1995) notes the following: Henry Banyon, optician, 1847; John Dixey, optician (previously worked with G. & C. Dixey of London), 1834–41; Thomas Hawkes, mathematical instrument maker, 1750–83; William Thomas Hunter, rule maker, 1830; James Jones, optician, 1847; Michael and Abraham Keyzor, opticians, 1847–54; Francis Molton, optician and barometer-maker, 1822–30; Myers & Wiseman, opticians, 1830; Thomas Page, barometer seller, 1750–84; Baptista Pedralio, barometer seller, 1790–1820; George Rossi, barometer seller, 1822–30; Samuel Sly, optician etc., 1830; Charles Trombetta, barometer seller, c.1800–20.

[4]    Everitt (1979), 109.

[5]    *Newcastle Chronicle*, 31 January 1795: Clifton (1995), 16.

[6]    Newcastle-upon-Tyne directories, *passim*.

[7]    McConnell (1993c), 440; an example made by Cooke but with a trade card for Cail was offered for sale at Christie's South Kensington, 4 June 1987, lot 256: Cooke first advertised his drainage level in the *Yorkshire Gazette*, 27 January 1849, and it appeared unchanged in Cooke's catalogues between 1862–91.

**Figure 5.1    Culpeper-type microscope signed by F. Molton, Norwich, *c*.1825**

*Source*:Whipple Museum of the History of Science, University of Cambridge, inv. no.
1811

or 'nautical instrument seller'.[8] Barnard Cooke, brother of Thomas Cooke of York, worked in his brother's enterprise for many years before moving to Hull and setting up in business there on his own account.[9] By 1851 there were still eight businesses that could be classified as supplying instruments.[10]

**Figure 5.2    Trade card for John Cail, Newcastle-upon-Tyne, c.1825**

*Source*:National Museums of Scotland, NMS.T.1968.125

On the south coast, the neighbouring ports of Portsmouth and Southampton saw the Stebbing family produce nautical instruments on both quaysides from the early nineteenth century; Joseph Rankin Stebbing, who ran their Southampton business from 1845, became Mayor of Southampton in 1867.[11] Clifton lists a handful of Portsmouth opticians, among them Samuel John Browning, who took over the business of George Stebbing & Son in 1847, had been apprenticed to his father, William Browning, one of the London partners of the wholesalers Spencer, Browning & Rust. Another fairly long-lived concern, which similarly had close links

---

[8]    William White, *History, Gazetteer and Directory of the West-Riding of Yorkshire … in two volumes* (Sheffield, 1837 and 1838).

[9]    A binocular microscope, probably retailed by B. Cooke & Son, Hull was offered by Christie's South Kensington, 13 December 1996, Lot 664; a sextant with a similar signature was offered by the same saleroom, 29 January 1995, Lot 85.

[10]    Francis White & Co., *General Directory and Topography of Kingston-upon-Hull and the City of York …* (Sheffield, 1851), 344.

[11]    Clifton (1995), 263–4.

**Figure 5.3   Octant signed by A. Ross, Hull, mid 19th century**

*Source*:National Museums of Scotland, NMS.T.1967.3

with the London trade, was that of George Lee, who had at one time been employed by George Whitbread's business close to the London docks. Lee set up in Portsea in 1847, and in business with his son also maintained premises in Portsmouth until beyond the turn of the century.[12] The long-established naval bases at Portsmouth and Plymouth attracted makers and suppliers who were proud to boast 'by appointment to the Admiralty', including William Charles Cox of Devonport and Plymouth, who had premises in both towns from the early 1820s.[13]

Derby became the eventual home of the Davis firm, for which there is evidence in Leeds from the early 1820s, although it later claimed to have been established as

---

[12]   Ibid., 41, 165 and 293.
[13]   Ibid., 69.

early as 1779.[14] It appears to have originated with Gabriel Davis (d.1851), a Jewish immigrant from Bavaria, who together with two brothers came to England at the turn of the century. Gabriel settled in Leeds, where by 1830 he was in business with his nephew Edward, making and selling instruments. Both Edward and his brother John (1810–73) were born at Thame, in Oxfordshire, and both appear to have worked for their uncle by travelling around the English Midlands selling items from the Leeds Boar Lane workshop. John Davis visited Derby, travelling between there and Liverpool, Cheltenham and Leeds. According to one source, he set up in business in Derby's Iron Gate in about 1826, taking over the instrument workshop of a descendant of John Whitehurst, the renowned clockmaker.[15]

Once settled there, his wares moved from the general to specialist mining equipment, geared towards a local market that developed during the 1840s.[16] More will be said subsequently about this firm and the broadly similar enterprise of William Wilton (1801–60) in the flourishing copper-mining centre at St Day, Cornwall, in Chapter 9. Wilton's business began, according to one account, in 1825, and from the mid 1830s he designed improvements to mining instruments adapted to the local industry. His papers describing these were published in the reports of the Royal Cornwall Polytechnic Society.[17] Through the society, he met other men with an inventive turn of mind, such as Robert Were Fox (1789–1877) and Thomas Brown Jordan (1810–90), both of whom were involved in the development of geomagnetic instruments.[18]

William Wilton exhibited magnetic dip and intensity instruments at the Great Exhibition (Figure 5.4).[19] One of his apprentices was John Teague Letcher, who was subsequently in partnership with his brother T.H. Letcher at Truro, producing a blow pipe analysis apparatus, which won a Society of Arts prize in 1878.[20] Another apprentice, Edward Newton, married Wilton's daughter; and when Wilton died in 1860, 'deservedly esteemed and respected', he and his brother-in-law, William Henry Wilton continued the business.[21] However, the collapse of the copper mining industry brought great distress to the area, and in 1874 the younger Wilton emigrated to Chile, announcing in the press:

> W.H. WILTON OF ST DAY Removed from St Day to A. Jeffrey's, Camborne. W.H. Wilton begs to thank his friends for their liberal support for so many years, and informs

---

[14]  *Leeds Intelligencer*, 1 January, 7 May, 21 May, 10 December 1821; 29 July 1822.
[15]  Craven (1996), 11, 207. Brief histories of the firm are given by Anon. (1979), Hind (1999) and Barnes (2005), but all stress the later period.
[16]  Instruments recorded with Davis of Leeds signature include miner's dials: for which see Holbrook (1992), 120 and 137; for John Davis, see Booth (1963), where a drum microscope and its accompanying literature is discussed.
[17]  Listed by Boase and Courtney (1878), II, 895.
[18]  McConnell (1985).
[19]  *Catalogue ...* (1851), 452–3; *Reports ...* (1852), 254, 281.
[20]  Boase and Courtney (1882), III, 1268.
[21]  Wilton (1989), 71; *West Briton*, 27 April, 1860; *ibid.* 11 May 1860.

them that (having opened business at Valparaiso) he has now declined business in England in favour solely of Mr A. Jeffrey, Mathematical Instrument Maker, Camborne, whom he considers (having been an assistant to his father for several years) is in every way capable of creditably maintaining the good name universally awarded to Wilton's instruments.[22]

**Figure 5.4   Trade card for William Wilton, St Day, Cornwall, 1830–51**

*Source*:© National Museum of Science and Industry inv. no. NMSI 1948–397

In the fashionable spa town of Bath – about 12 miles from Bristol – the opticians Ribright & Smith set up a shop in 1783, which appears to have lasted only a year. Thomas Ribright, a London retailer, was obliged by his father's death in 1783 to return to London and run the business there.[23] Benjamin Smith continued in business on his own account until 1809, and there were a handful of

---

[22]   *West Briton*, 26 March 1874.
[23]   Clifton (1995), 231. The Will of George Ribright, who died March/July 1783, of the parish of St Mary Cole, Poultry, London, stated that all stock in trade, shop fittings, counters, glass cases and the like, both in London and Bath, except working tools, was to be sold. No partnership ever existed between George and his son Thomas, although they traded as George Ribright & Son: if the son wished to set up for himself, he should have first refusal of the shop fittings and stock, but must pay for them or give security. Part of the estate was to be invested in an annuity for George's widow, the remainder to be shared between Thomas and other children. The working tools were bequeathed to Thomas. The National Archives [TNA], PROB 11/1106 f.232r.

retailers over the years that catered for the seasonal visitors and their expensive whims.[24] Michael Neve has made the point that both Bath and Bristol (which also had a hot water spa at the aptly-named 'Hot Wells') looked to London for their culture, especially their scientific culture: 'The cultural development that did take place – assembly rooms, libraries, hospitals, charities, and the visits of itinerant lecturers – display two notable features. They were arranged around a tourist economy, subject to seasonal variation and dominated by visitors, not natives'.[25] This imitative metropolitan culture can be found in the wares of instrument retailers in Cheltenham, and Bath; other spa towns appear not to have had such shops, perhaps because their visitors were not so well heeled. However, Bath supported a good number, the most prominent being Jacob Abraham, who came from Exeter and had settled in Bath by 1809. He remained there for some thirty years, starting a branch in Cheltenham (also a successful early nineteenth century spa town) in about 1830; he retired in 1845.[26] As might be expected, instruments recorded with his signature appear to have been aimed primarily at a dilettante market.

Perhaps the most notable individual provincial firms of the entire period were the telescope-producing businesses, especially those which reached international markets, as did that of Thomas Cooke of York, and the earlier example of William Herschel (1738–1822), based first in Bath and subsequently in Slough. Anthony Turner has made the point that:

> Herschel owed much to Bath. Outside London, the facilities for intellectual exchange were limited, though not completely lacking. The cultural life of the English provinces was buoyant and interesting; but for Herschel, a German outsider, the opportunities were fewer and the isolation from which he suffered in his years in the North was very real. Only in a large town or city could he hope to find men interested in a similar width of philosophical or practical problems as he was himself, and perhaps only in Bath did the conditions exist in which he could amass sufficient wealth as a musician to support a long and expensive series of practical investigations.[27]

William Herschel did most of his work on metal telescope specula in isolation, and spent his time in endless experiments. In 1795, he wrote 'I made not less than 200, 7-feet; 150, 10-feet; and about 80, 20-feet [focal length] mirrors'.[28] In all,

---

[24]   Benjamin Smith is known to have sold a planetarium: Clifton (1995), 255.

[25]   Neve (1983), 182.

[26]   Bath directories, *passim*; Clifton (1995), 1; Rubens (1955–59), 7; Brown and Samuel (1982–86), 135–64; instruments are in the Museum of the History of Science, Oxford: an orrery (inv. no. 44466); and a magnetic dial and thermometer (inv. no. 54028); a telescope is at Snowshill Manor, Broadway; a drum microscope at the Museum of the Pharmaceutical Society of Great Britain; a telescope in the National Army Museum; and a horizontal sundial in York Castle Museum: Holbrook (1992), 104, 162, 220.

[27]   Turner (1977), 115–16.

[28]   Quoted in ibid., 76. Maurer (1998) accounts for 48 of these.

Turner estimates that Herschel sold about one hundred of the 7-feet telescopes which he made: 'although of exceptional quality and widely spread throughout Europe, few of his telescopes seem to have been regularly used by practising astronomers'.[29] The example illustrated should have been an exception, as it was owned by the professor of practical astronomy at the University of Glasgow (Figure 5.5). However, Patrick Wilson (1743–1811) left no records of any astronomical observations. Herschel's reception by King George III, in 1782, and the successful comparison of his telescope design with those of others, together with his international reputation as a practising astronomer – most famous, perhaps, for his discovery of the planet Uranus in March 1781 – eventually led to the award of an annual salary of £200, enabling Herschel to give up music, but compelling him to move close to the court to fulfil his obligation of giving the royal family astronomical entertainment as and when they requested.[30]

During the late eighteenth century, there was a select group of clockmakers who also produced instruments. Oliver Fairclough, in writing about Joseph Finney of Liverpool, also mentions Henry Hindley of York, John Hallifax of Barnsley and John Whitehurst of Derby, and compares them with the pre-eminent London figures George Graham and John Ellicott.[31] John Hallifax (1694–1750) came from a Lincolnshire family, moving to Barnsley in Yorkshire and setting up as a clockmaker there in 1711. In the instrument-making line, he is particularly renowned for the quality of his barometers.[32] John Whitehurst (1713–88) was the son of a Cheshire clockmaker, from whom he learned his craft. Wishing to better himself, he moved to Derby in about 1735, but found he was unable to trade as he was not a freeman. On his completion and donation of a turret clock for the new guildhall, he was made a burgess in 1737. His wide interests, including geology, hydraulics and mechanical devices, led him to investigate the expansion of metals, and he built a pyrometer in 1749 so that he could improve the accuracy of his clocks with temperature-compensated pendulums.

By 1758 Whitehurst had met and joined the group of scientifically minded entrepreneurs and philosophers known as the Lunar Society, which led him to produce elaborate astronomical and tidal clocks for some of its members. For his many powerful patrons he designed and constructed instruments when required, including sundials, chemical balances and, in particular, barometers.[33] He also did

---

[29] Turner (1977), 77.
[30] Ibid., 106.
[31] Fairclough (1975), xix. Finney's instrument making work is considered in Chapter 2; that of Hindley in Chapter 3. For Graham, see Sorrenson (1999).
[32] Goodison (1977), 157–9.
[33] A pyrometer is in the collections at Armagh Observatory; a surveying compass, the indoor dial of a wind vane and a clockmaker's wheel-cutting engine are all in Derby Museum and Art Gallery; and two clocks in the Wedgwood Museum: see Holbrook (1992), 87, 117 and 210; other instruments are discussed by Craven (1996), 100–25; and his barometers by Goodison (1977), 281–6.

important experiments, published in 1787, which had a significant effect on what later became the Imperial system of weights and measures, and his apparatus was subsequently used by Sir George Shuckburgh (1751–1804).[34] His family continued the business in Derby after he removed almost permanently to London in about 1780, but until the arrival of John Davis in the town and their removal to Cherry Street, it was not remarkable for the production of instruments.[35]

To complete this sketch of somewhat isolated members of the trade, and how they plied their wares, I shall choose two nineteenth century figures from the West Country, more or less remote from the metropolis: Alexander Alexander of Exeter and William Britton of Barnstaple. Neither of these is particularly prominent, and their trade was not largely dependent on some local industry such as mining, as those in Cornwall and Derbyshire were. They were perhaps more typical of the skilled craftsman described by Alan Everitt in the essay quoted at the start of this chapter. Alexander, however, is also typical of other members of the instrument trade encountered elsewhere in some respects: he was Jewish, migrating from London and appearing in the local directories from 1830 (he claimed to have begun in business in 1828), and he is noted (if at all) for a single instrument design, in his case a development of Wollaston's camera lucida, a device to assist landscape sketching.[36]

As with the Davis firm of Leeds, Alexander probably survived in business by supplying a selection of instruments to a variety of customers drawn from the town (in his case Exeter) and its hinterland. An advertisement dating from 1835 demonstrates that a relative, a son or possibly a brother, was attempting to find customers as far afield as Cornwall: '... a respectable and scientific Optician, John Alexander of the Establishment of Alexander Alexander, Optician and mathematical Instrument Maker, by Special Warrants to their Majesties, &c. &c. ... solicits the attention of the inhabitants of Falmouth and its vicinity ...'.[37]

My final example is possibly even more obscure. William Britton is listed in a local directory for 1830 as a brazier, tinplate worker and plumber in Barnstaple, North Devon. By 1850 his occupation is given as 'optician &c'. and by 1870, William Britton & Sons are photographers.[38] Britton clearly did not make his living from making microscopes at the cutting edge of instrument technology, although his signature is to be found on at least three such instruments (Figure 1.3). The

---

34   Simpson (1993a), 182.
35   See advertisement dating from 1847 reproduced in Craven (1996), 202.
36   Clifton (1995), 5; Hammond and Austin (1987), 43–4; examples of Alexander's graphic mirror are in collections at the Whipple Museum, Cambridge: inv. no. 498; at the Museum of the History of Science, Oxford, inv. no. 30326; at the Science Museum, London, inv. no. NMSI 1912–206, and the National Museums of Scotland, NMS.T.1994.27. A pantograph with Alexander's signature was offered by Christie's, 12 December 1972, Lot 3.
37   *West Briton*, 16 October 1835.
38   *Pigot & Co'.s Provincial Directory 1830* (London, 1830); White's *Devon Directory 1850* (London, 1850); Morris & Co.'s *Commercial Directory 1870* (London, 1870).

**Figure 5.5    Interior of Jordanhill House, showing a telescope by William
Herschel, once owned by Patrick Wilson (1743–1811), professor of
practical astronomy, University of Glasgow**

*Source*:Photograph by MacClure, Macdonald & Co., Glasgow, *c.*1910. National Museums
of Scotland

prominent London microscope maker Andrew Pritchard (1804–82) designed the
example illustrated in about 1830. Pritchard was consulted from the mid-1820s by
the amateur scientist C.R. Goring (*c.*1792–1840) concerning practical attempts
to improve the image obtained through the compound microscope, and together
they devised a number of new models. However, by about 1830 Goring retired
to South Molton in Devon, not far from Barnstaple, and it seems likely that the
instruments made for Goring which carry Britton's signature were manufactured
in a specialist London workshop and retailed locally.[39] The network of supply
and demand appears clearer here than in many other cases.

---

[39]    Nuttall (1977); *Gentleman's Magazine*, April 1840, 443; instruments with Britton's
signature are a compound microscope in the Science Museum, inv. no. NMSI 1948–329,
and another in the Wellcome Collection, inv. no. A56540; the simple microscope is NMS.
T.1984.141.

A broad characterization of the salient features of each major centre of instrument production during the Industrial Revolution outside London has been outlined in this and the preceding three chapters. Some general statements, supported by regional studies made by economic historians, sustain this overall framework.[40] From the mid-eighteenth century, London provided a pool of skilled labour from which enterprising individuals could make their way to a number of growing and prosperous provincial centres of population, in the reasonable hope of setting up a successful business, initially confined to the local markets. A supporting infrastructure of transport, marketing and banking, often already in place for other growing industries, allowed them to later reach beyond the region to customers further afield, especially in London.

The evidence from local newspaper advertisements shows that in a number of instances the pattern followed was that a London-trained instrument maker would set up in business; if successful, he could maintain a trade succession for several generations, usually through family connections. Often the link was through women: either by marriage or a widow running the business while a son grew to maturity, or else through a trade link with a foreman or former apprentice, when there were no male heirs to inherit a going concern. As Daunton has written, 'most industrial concerns were still family businesses which raised their capital from ploughed-back profits or local contracts through a network of kin and co-religionists', and although there has so far been little direct evidence for this in this trade, presumably this is how the mechanism worked.[41] Immigrants with various skills in metalwork, woodwork and glass manipulation appear to have been attracted to the anonymity of the new industrial centres, matched with the growing opportunities they afforded for expanding markets and prosperity, once the conditions in their place of origin had prompted them to leave behind their native lands.

Between 1760 and 1850, there were several locations outside London which did start to produce instruments in significant numbers: in England, the main centres were Birmingham, Bristol, Liverpool, Manchester and Sheffield. Although their production figures are unknown, they were large enough for the manufacturers to label themselves as 'mathematical instrument makers' or some such permutation, in the local street directories; and many of them remained in business for longer than a year or two. This is not because there were substantial local markets for instruments in the English provinces, although in the cases of the ports of Bristol and Liverpool this may well have been a contributory factor. This period saw the growth of a number of ports which acted as gateways for their own industrial hinterlands, among them, Hull, Newcastle and Liverpool.[42]

Sheffield, home for centuries to the cutlery trade, already had an infrastructure of independent metal workshops, where skills closely allied to those necessary

---

[40]   Hudson (1992), 101–32; Daunton (1995), 279–83; Berg (1993).
[41]   Daunton (1995), 280.
[42]   Corfield (1982), 39–41.

to the manufacture of instruments could be found. It also had regular methods to transport its wares to the London market – carriers, canals, and subsequently the railways.[43] Similarly, Birmingham was the centre for the manufacture of brass goods, and had even fewer restrictions – for instance, there was no guild structure – and metal workers there could make instrument parts as readily as they made dog collars. 'Beginning as a small master,' says an 1866 account, 'often working in his own house, with his wife and children to help him, the Birmingham workman has become a master, his trade has extended, his buildings have increased'.[44] It seems more than likely that most of these anonymous instruments were channelled into the London market for finishing or as their point-of-sale; in fact, to have a Sheffield or Birmingham address engraved on (for example) a telescope in the early part of this period would have proved a distinct disincentive for the purchaser.

The local street directories, despite their problems of lack of continuity and possible inaccuracies, have provided a basic outline upon which further results can be built. Following the model devised from Millburn's criticisms, some details of individual businesses have been provided here for the first time, such as the size of the trade and longevity of particular businesses. Although numerically tiny in comparison with the contemporary London trade, it can be seen that in some instances at least, provincial instrument makers were going to give their metropolitan cousins a run for their money.

---

[43] Barnes (1992), 11.
[44] Timmins (1866), 223.

# Chapter 6

# The London Trade

The instrument-making activity outside London described in the preceding chapters was on a much smaller scale than that which occurred in the capital, and to some extent it has been masked by the apparent pre-eminence of London at this time. It has long been accepted by instrument historians as a given that, during the eighteenth century, London was the world centre for this trade. For example, G. L'E. Turner has observed that 'during this period, the London scientific instrument trade achieved an international reputation';[1] J.A. Bennett has written that 'by the late 18th century, London makers had achieved a position of international pre-eminence in the mathematical instrument trade';[2] and Willem Hackmann, synthesising the earlier authority of E.G.R. Taylor, wrote:

> London emerged as the premier market for scientific instruments in the mid-eighteenth century ... [when] the ... trade consisted of an intricate network of specialist makers and retailers. Workshops congregated in the Clerkenwell region, jostling with makers of clocks, watches and engines, and other craftsmen in wood and metals.[3]

Yet no instrument historian has yet outlined just how and why, in economic terms, this position was attained. In fact, London's pre-eminence was based on its ability to produce 'precision' instrumentation, as opposed to the more general 'scientific' material that could also be made elsewhere; but this more general material helped to underpin the trade and thus assisted in the important work being done by a handful of pioneers on the cutting edges of technical frontiers. These individuals were often of provincial origin, and moved to London in order to reach national and international markets. However, instrument makers who had been trained in London but who migrated to the provinces appear to have served their apprenticeships with masters in the more general 'scientific' instrument trade; the wares they advertised in the provincial press support this thesis.

---

[1]  Turner (1979a), 173.
[2]  Bennett (1985), 13.
[3]  Hackmann (1985), 53–4.

**Bespoke Instruments before about 1750**

Although instrument making had its origins on the continent of Europe, by the mid-eighteenth century London had become the world centre for the precision instrument trade. This has been characterized by Anthony Turner:

> Although special items were still made specially to order, master instrument-makers themselves now routinely invented, developed and improved the standard instruments which made up their stock-in-trade. Although in financial terms instrument-making was still of only minor importance in the national economy, its values in terms of skills and services was far greater, especially with the great trading nations of France and England with large fleets of merchant ships to be navigated ... The changes that had taken place in the structure of the scientific instrument-making trade by the middle of the eighteenth century were the result of changes in attitude towards instruments themselves; the invention of new instruments; a considerable increase in demand; and a greater continuity of workshops and makers.[4]

London makers of precision instruments were able to lead successful careers through having their work promoted by the Royal Society and published in its prestigious *Philosophical Transactions*, a journal which reached an international audience. In particular, the astronomical observatories supplied by the London instrument maker George Graham (1673–1751) and his associates, Jonathan Sisson (d.1747) and John Bird (1709–76), helped to bring the 'Big Science' of its day to Europe with a suite of standard instruments – the mural quadrant, transit instrument, zenith sector and astronomical regulator clock – for the first time (see Table 6.1). This suite of extremely expensive bespoke instruments, in terms of capital investment, was purchased after Edmond Halley (1656–1742), second Astronomer Royal, eventually received a government grant in 1724 to re-equip the largely-empty Royal Observatory in Greenwich, which had been established by Charles II in 1675 specifically to solve the problem of finding longitude at sea.

Although this capital was reluctantly provided by the state, it provides a clear indication of government motivation to invest in expensive plant in order to ensure in the long-term the safety of both its Royal Navy and merchant fleets: improved celestial cartography ensured better navigation in the longer term. It also had longer-term significance for the growth of the nation's trade and imperial ambitions. Nor was this the only way in which state interest manifested itself: a series of maritime disasters, culminating in the loss of a squadron of naval ships under the command of Sir Cloudesley Shovel (1650–1707), wrecked on the Scilly Isles in 1707 with the loss of 800 men, led to a Parliamentary committee of enquiry.[5] This in turn resulted in the setting up of the Board of Longitude by

---

4    Turner (1987), 173.
5    Stimson (1996), 80–81.

Act of Parliament, offering a prize of £20,000 to the discoverer of a method that could determine a ship's longitude to within half a degree.[6]

Perhaps the key breakthrough occurred during the 1730s when the two French longitude expeditions sent to Lapland and Peru to measure a degree in different latitudes bought London-made apparatus. Encouraged by the earlier success of the astronomer James Bradley (1693–1762), who discovered stellar aberration with a zenith sector made by George Graham at a time when Graham had no serious rivals in Paris, it would appear that private and portable observatories may have influenced the ensuing fittings in fixed state observatories.[7] With the provision of a number of technological innovations in the construction and subsequent use of the suite of instruments at Greenwich, their success – publicized through publication and by word of mouth by foreign visitors – led to further orders: a similar suite of instruments was ordered for the Radcliffe Observatory, Oxford, from Graham's successor John Bird in 1771, and subsequently others came from all over Europe.

The next generation of London-based precision instrument makers, Edward Troughton (1756–1835), Jesse Ramsden (1735–1800), the Dollonds (who were optical specialists) and to a lesser extent, Thomas Jones (1775–1852), were able to continue this line, ensuring that where large astronomical instruments were needed, it was the London makers who sprang to the mind of would-be purchasers as being the ones most likely to fulfil the contract: and as these instruments represented a large amount of investment for the purchasers – usually foreign governments – completion as well as quality was important.[8]

Information about the availability and success of these instruments was diffused through the scientific community through its literature, in the form of journals and textbooks that, again, reached an international audience. The size of this scientific community and its composition is difficult to gauge, but it was probably initially very small. In Britain, in the early eighteenth century, Fellows of the Royal Society – amongst whom were numbered these most distinguished instrument makers – were seen as at the forefront of this 'scientific community' (this term is, of course, an anachronism), and the Royal Society's regular publication of its journal, the *Philosophical Transactions*, was central to reaching its members. Each issue would include published correspondence between Fellows on an extremely broad range of subjects; and the journal would have been exchanged abroad with those of similar societies, national observatories and foreign correspondents.

Close contacts, despite political differences, were maintained with, for example, the French Académie des Sciences; for instance, comparisons between the national

---

[6]  12 Anne, *c*.15 (1714): An Act for Providing a Publick Reward for such Person or Persons as shall Discover the Longitude at Sea. This has been dealt with most recently by Andrewes (1996).

[7]  Simpson and Connor (2004), 334–5.

[8]  Gunther (1920–68), II, 311, 319–25, 336, 394–6; Howse (1975); Bennett (1992).

**Table 6.1    Costs for setting up equipment at the Royal Observatory, Greenwich, and at the Radcliffe Observatory, Oxford, in the eighteenth century (figures from Howse (1975), and Gunther (1920–67), vol. 2, 311, 319–25, 336, 394–6)**

| Greenwich | | | | | |
|---|---|---|---|---|---|
| *Primary instruments* | | | £ | s | d |
| 8 foot iron quadrant | 1725 | Graham/Sisson | 322 | 10 | 4 |
| 8 foot brass quadrant (payment included publishing methods of construction and division) | 1750 | Bird | 500 | 0 | 0 |
| 6 foot mural circle | 1810 | Troughton/Dollond | 1816 | 14 | 6 |
| 6 foot mural circle | 1821 | Thomas Jones/?Tully | 411 | 3 | 2.5 |
| 6 foot mural circle | 1822 | Thomas Jones/?Tully | [?] | | |
| 5 foot transit | 1721 | Graham | 61 | 10 | 0 |
| 8 foot transit | 1750 | Bird | 73 | 16 | 6 |
| 10 foot transit | 1816 | Troughton | 315 | 0 | 0 |
| 12 ½ foot zenith sector | 1727 | Graham | [?] | | |
| 2 ½ foot zenith sector | 1735 | Graham | 35 | 0 | 0 |
| 2 × 5 foot equatorial sectors | 1773 | Sisson/Dollond | 642 | 0 | 0 |
| *Smaller instruments* | | | | | |
| 20 foot refractor | 1748 | Bird | 7 | 10 | 0 |
| 6 foot Newtonian reflector | 1748 | Short | 100 | 0 | 0 |
| 46″ focus replacement lens | 1772 | Dollond | 63 | 0 | 0 |
| 62″ focus replacement lens | 1797 | Dollond | 70 | 0 | 0 |
| 10 foot refractor | 1797 | Dollond | 157 | 10 | 0 |
| 7 foot reflector | 1783 | Herschel | 105 | 9 | 0 |
| 10 foot reflector | 1813 | Herschel | 350 | 0 | 0 |
| Clocks | | | | | |
| Plain week clock | 1726 | Graham | 5 | 0 | 0 |
| 2 x month clocks | 1726 | Graham | 24 | 0 | 0 |
| 1st fitted with gridiron pendulum | 1743 | Graham | 15 | 13 | 0 |
| 2nd fitted with gridiron pendulum | 1744 | Graham | 10 | 0 | 0 |
| Month clock | 1750 | Graham | 39 | 0 | 0 |
| Special escapement clock | 1809 | Hardy | 210 | 0 | 0 |
| Oxford | | | | | |
| 2 x mural quadrants, transit instrument, zenith sector and equatorial sector ordered from Bird in 1771: estimate, including optics from Dollond at: | | | 1260 | 0 | 0 |
| Total paid by 1777, for 5 instruments | | | 1392 | 16 | 0 |

weighing systems – enshrined by each state in long-standing legislation – of France and England were undertaken as early as the 1730s through the co-operation of their national scientific societies.[9] However, it is probable that any 'scientific community' in the early eighteenth century was centred around either a capital city, a national observatory or a university town (all of which would have had libraries); whereas a century later this community had spread: there was now a considerably stronger scientific community particularly in the English provinces, thanks to the growth of literacy and a general increase in a desire for knowledge amongst the expanding leisured classes.[10]

The late seventeenth century had seen the creation of cabinets of instruments for wealthy patrons across Europe, but these had only ever been a numerically small part of the market, albeit important for the development of skills and extension of knowledge within the slowly evolving trade. For example, in Amsterdam, the Musschenbroek workshop provided mathematical and philosophical apparatus to a limited market in the Netherlands and to parts of Germany.[11] It was, however, the provision of large good-quality telescopes to wealthy clients that paved the way for English pre-eminence in the European market.[12] These, promoted by influential patrons, particularly the national societies of England and France, were to win this leading position for the London élite makers.

## Breaking into the European market

The first London maker to break into the European market was George Hearne (fl.1725–41), whose reflecting telescopes were sold across Europe from Poland to Lisbon. He learned his skills in a direct line from James Gregory's optician, Richard Reeve, through the towering figure of Isaac Newton, to the Hadley brothers, John, George and Henry.[13] The Hadley brothers' technical information found its way into the standard natural philosophy text book of its day, Robert Smith's *Compleat System of Opticks* (1738), which capitalized on the success of Newton's *Opticks*, and like it, named and recommended specific instrument makers. Smith also spelled out the fact that technical difficulties had inhibited production for some time:

---

[9]   Sorrenson (1993) gives an overview of the importance of the Royal Society to the instrument makers George Graham, Peter and John Dollond, and Jesse Ramsden and, reciprocally, of the instrument makers to the Royal Society; the comparison between French and English weights is discussed by Simpson and Connor (2004).
[10]   Stewart (1992); Golinski (1992); Inkster and Morrell (1983); Elliott (2000).
[11]   For the Musschenbroeks, see De Clercq (1997); for an overview, see Daumas (1972), 136–48. Also Impey and MacGregor (1983) for European cabinets.
[12]   This has been investigated by Simpson (1981), chapter 4.
[13]   Simpson (1985); Clifton (1993a).

The main drift of all our tryals [by Bradley, Hadley and Smith] hath been if possible to reduce the method of making these instruments [i.e. reflecting telescopes] to some degree of certainty and ease; to the intent that the difficulty in making them, and the danger in miscarrying, might no longer discourage any workman from attempting the same for publick sale; which no body but Mr *Hauksbee* in *Crane Court* hath ever ventured upon. He has made a good one of about 3½ foot, and is now about one of 6 foot and another of 12 foot, and deserves very well to be encouraged, being the first person who hath attempted it without the assistance of a fortune, which could well bear the disappointment. About the beginning of the last winter being pretty well satisfied as to most of the circumstances in this performance, and being desirous that these instruments might become cheap and of publick sale, we acquainted Mr *Scarlet* near St *Anne*'s Church, and Mr *Hearne* a Mathematical Instrument-maker in *Dogwel Court, White Friers*, with the whole process of the operation as we had practised the same; and they have since succeeded in making these instruments. However as they are not yet become so common, so cheap and so universally made and used, as one would wish an instrument of this nature to be, we have been encouraged to give this following account, for the general information of all persons who would make the same for their own use or for sale.[14]

Technological obstacles, rather than economics, initially hampered the production of good-quality large telescopes. Anthony Turner has commented that 'Even in the eighteenth century the apparatus of astronomy, although still relatively simple, was expensive'.[15] This was because it was time-consuming and difficult to construct. The section of Smith's work entitled the 'Mechanical Treatise' explains in great detail how to make a number of different optical instruments, including telescopes and microscopes, and the tools necessary to construct them, drawn from earlier authorities such as Christiaan Huygens (1629–95) and Samuel Molyneux (1689–1728). Smith's book was part of the vindication of the optical theories of England's great scientist, Sir Isaac Newton (1642–1727).[16]

The most prolific manufacturer of telescopes during the eighteenth century was Edinburgh-born James Short (1710–68), who constructed a numbered sequence of over 1300 instruments, most of which were of medium size and aimed at the new consumer market of wealthy gentlemen who could afford to dabble in astronomy as a pastime (Figure 6.1).[17] D.J. Bryden estimated that '[telescope] models with focal lengths of 18 inches and below accounted for 90% of this output. The larger and more expensive models were probably made for specific customers, whereas the smaller telescopes could have been purchased off the shelf'.[18] Short was fortunate to have worked at a time when popular interest in astronomy was heightened by two rare celestial events in the 1760s, when the planet Venus twice

---

14   Smith (1738), II, 302–3.
15   Turner (1977), 53.
16   Simpson (1981).
17   Bryden (1968); Turner (1969b); 'James Short', in Clarke et al. (1989), 1–10.
18   Bryden (1968), 23.

passed in front of the Sun's disc. Short was able to meet substantial demands for telescopes to observe the second transit, many of which were used abroad in a co-ordinated programme of observations.

G. L'E. Turner was able to produce a graph showing the serial numbers against the dates of Short's instruments, and using the figures given in Figure 6.1, estimated an approximate annual sales income at about £620. He went on to suggest that Short did not make any of the brasswork associated with his instruments, but focused exclusively upon the manufacture of the reflecting optics:

> Assuming Short's working life was thirty-five years, his total income from sales was at least £21,700. This figure is an underestimate ... Short's outgoings must, unfortunately, be a matter of guesswork. A good-sized house in central London could have been leased for around £50 a year. *A General Description of All Trades* [London, 1747, p.138] records that the cost of setting up a private workshop is £50 for tools, and a mathematical instrument maker is said to earn a guinea a week ... [Short] would have bought wholesale, and without mirrors, perhaps at 60 per cent of retail price, so making the cost to him of the telescopes he sold 30 per cent of their retail price. According to these rough estimates, expenses to be taken away from the gross income are: £6500 for materials (stands), thirty-five years' rental £1750, the same for living expenses (Short had no dependants), for tools £50; a total of some £10 000, which leaves in round figures a profit of £12,000, almost certainly an underestimate... It is not inconceivable that he left an estate worth over £20,000, made chiefly out of polishing speculum metal.[19]

It has been established more recently that Short did indeed buy in the brasswork for his telescopes from a London supplier, and was involved in negotiations for this as early as 1736.[20] Short worked alone, and by keeping the volume of work within his own control, he did not have to share the secrets of his skill with others. His instruments were expensive, but such was his reputation that he was able to command twice the price of his contemporaries. After his death, his tools were acquired by a Swedish instrument maker, Carl Apelquist (*c*.1749–1824), but tools alone could not reproduce Short's superlative telescopes: Apelquist did not have Short's 'know-how'.[21]

Although Short left no description of his mirror-making methods, the Plymouth physician John Mudge (1721–93), an amateur astronomer and telescope maker, visited Short's London workshop and, in 1777, after Short's death, he presented before the Royal Society a detailed investigation into the methods of making speculum metal for reflecting telescopes, and discussed some of the skills which he thought must have been employed by Short. These included particular

---

[19]  Turner (1969b), 100–102.
[20]  Clarke et al. (1989), 3.
[21]  Bryden (1968), 31. According to Pipping (1977), 54–5, Apelquist, originally a gunfounder, had spent time learning about scientific instrument making in Ramsden's workshop.

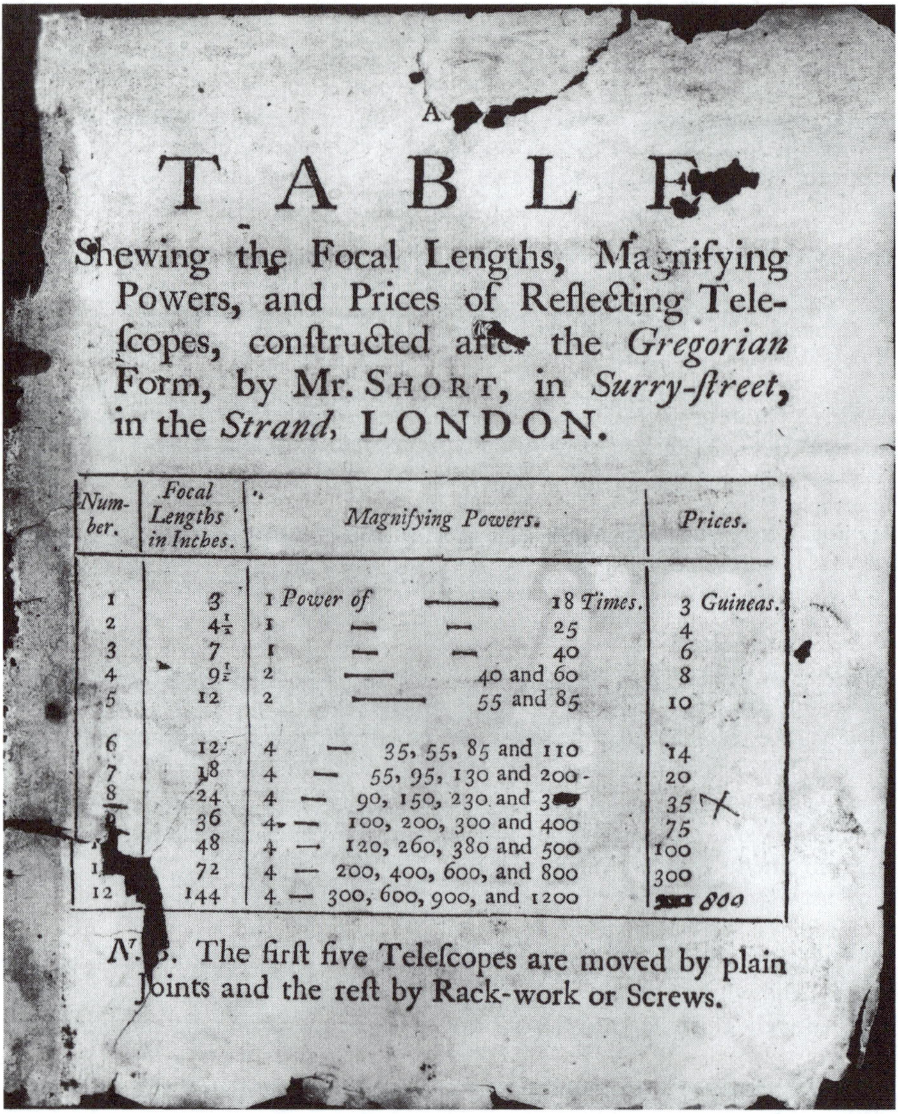

A

# TABLE

Shewing the Focal Lengths, Magnifying Powers, and Prices of Reflecting Telescopes, constructed after the *Gregorian* Form, by Mr. SHORT, in *Surry-street*, in the *Strand*, LONDON.

| Number. | Focal Lengths in Inches. | Magnifying Powers. | | Prices. |
|---|---|---|---|---|
| 1 | 3 | 1 Power of ——— 18 *Times*. | | 3 *Guineas*. |
| 2 | 4½ | 1 — — 25 | | 4 |
| 3 | 7 | 1 — — 40 | | 6 |
| 4 | 9½ | 2 ——— 40 and 60 | | 8 |
| 5 | 12 | 2 ——— 55 and 85 | | 10 |
| 6 | 12 | 4 — 35, 55, 85 and 110 | | 14 |
| 7 | 18 | 4 — 55, 95, 130 and 200 | | 20 |
| 8 | 24 | 4 — 90, 150, 230 and 3— | | 35 |
| 9 | 36 | 4 — 100, 200, 300 and 400 | | 75 |
| 10 | 48 | 4 — 120, 260, 380 and 500 | | 100 |
| 11 | 72 | 4 — 200, 400, 600, and 800 | | 300 |
| 12 | 144 | 4 — 300, 600, 900, and 1200 | | 800 |

*N*. B. The first five Telescopes are moved by plain Joints and the rest by Rack-work or Screws.

**Figure 6.1   Undated price list for James Short's telescopes**

*Source*: Private collection

recipes for specula casting, in order to allow subsequent grinding; polishing directly on pitch, which would leave no minute scratches on the surface; aiming to achieve final parabolic figure for the spherical mirror; and finally, matching and rotating the two mirrors so that their aberrations most nearly cancelled each other.[22] Yet English-made telescope specula did not again reach Short's standards, as we have seen, until William Herschel (1738–1822), based in Bath, had worked them out for himself, through a heroic series of trials, undertaken in isolation from other workers.[23]

Nevertheless, James Short was not alone in adding to London's prestige as the instrument-making centre for large astronomical instrumentation during the latter part of the eighteenth century, as J.A. Bennett has observed:

> Any survey of the observatory instruments in use on the Continent towards the end of the eighteenth century will soon come upon the names of such English makers as Bird, Sisson, Dollond and Ramsden ... There is no doubt that London makers dominated the trade in mathematical instruments in the second half of the century. This is clear from the historical record, but was also well understood at the time. If we look for examples of large fixed instruments at observatories in France, Italy and Germany, we know of mural quadrants by Sisson in Paris, Bologna, Pisa and Berlin; by Bird in Paris (two examples), Göttingen, Mannheim and Berlin; and by Ramsden in Milan and Padua. There were transit instruments by Sisson in Bologna and Florence; by Ramsden in Paris, Mannheim, Gotha, Leipzig and Palermo. There was a zenith sector by Sisson in Florence, and equatorial sectors by Sisson in Milan and Naples, and by Dollond in Kassel. There were altazimuth circles by Sisson in Naples and by Ramsden in Palermo. This list is not exhaustive, but can easily be extended by looking further afield ....[24]

That even French scientists were prepared to turn to London makers can be demonstrated by the price list included in the 1771 second edition of Jerome Lalande's *Astronomie* (Figure 6.2), which lists items by Dollond, Ramsden, Bird and the more expensive and larger items given on Short's price list, with the comment 'Il faut une permission pour les faire entrer dans le Royaume'.[25] J.A. Bennett has contrasted the wider London instrument trade with that of Paris throughout the eighteenth century. He compares the arena of polite shopping for instruments in London by knowledgeable foreign clients with that of Paris, and finds that in the early eighteenth century 'informed observers did not go to Paris to shop for instruments ... it is only toward the end of the eighteenth century that a few visitors to Paris indicate the beginnings of a revival in the French industry'.[26]

---

[22]  Mudge (1777); discussed by Simpson (1981), 314–326.
[23]  Turner (1977), 53–109.
[24]  Bennett (1987), 88.
[25]  Lalande's third edition of 1791 had a variation on this list: see Howse (1989).
[26]  Bennett (2002), 377.

Why did instrument makers in France not dominate this embryonic global – European and North American, at any rate – market? Economic historians interested in 'the key problem of growth' have asked a more broadly focused question, in order to see 'what factors were peculiar to England and might therefore have determined what is a unique phenomenon, the English Industrial Revolution of the eighteenth century'.[27] A.E. Musson, paraphrasing François Crouzet, summed this up:

> ... despite French leadership in many branches of industrial science, the British were able to adopt French advances fairly quickly, as well as making many of their own, and forged ahead in industrial development. Practical scientific knowledge seems to have been more widely and deeply diffused in Britain than in France. Britain also had substantial economic advantages in natural resources (especially coal) and wider overseas trade and empire, as well as institutional advantages such as freedom from tolls and fewer government restrictions, together with social advantages such as a more developed and enterprising middle class and greater social mobility.[28]

These last reasons have been developed by Anthony Turner in a series of essays on the French instrument trade at this period, in one of which he writes as a footnote, citing the work of Maurice Daumas:

> Daumas's exceptional and pioneering study remains the authoritative work on French instrument-making. If it is cited only on this one occasion, it is because I have deliberately sought to re-examine the evidence (and to find some new) independently of Daumas's perspective. That in the end we arrive at somewhat similar conclusions is reassuring.[29]

Turner begins his work on the Parisian instrument maker Etienne Lenoir (1744–1832) by discussing the 1771 price list published by Lalande, which by its inclusion of London-made precision instruments demonstrates for him that 'by the end of the third quarter of the eighteenth century, French (which is to say Paris) instrument-makers could no longer compete with their English counterparts in the production of large-scale, precision, observing instruments'.[30] This was because, as Turner describes, Parisian workshop size was closely controlled by the inflexible Paris guild structure, and was thus dependent on a very small, local, luxury clientele: that of the royal court, a few nobles and colleges. Unlike the London trade, which was able to support investment in large-scale, technically innovative precision instruments, or large-scale production of essential, and thus lucrative, instruments such as octants or sextants, 'no Paris manufacturer had a sufficiently large everyday retail trade to enable him to carry out development,

---

27  Crouzet (1967), 139.
28  Musson (1975), 82.
29  Turner (1998), 84, citing Daumas (1972), first published in Paris in 1953.
30  Turner (1989), 3.

## PRIX DES INSTRUMENS D'ASTRONOMIE en 1771.

*Lunettes,*

UNE LUNETTE de fix pieds avec un tuyau de tôle ou de fer battu, fait de quatre pieces qui fe montent à vis, chez M. Georges, Opticien de M^r de l'Acad. des Sciences, quai de Conty, coûte quatre louis ou ........................... 96 livres.

Les fucceffeurs de M. Paffemant au Louvre, M. Paris à l'Eftrapade, & M. Gonichon, rue des Poftes, font auffi de très-bonnes lunettes de toutes les longueurs.

Pour une lunette de 15 pieds (2284) il faut un objectif de 15 pieds de foyer qui coûte un écu le pied, c'eft-à-dire, 45 liv. un tuyau de fer blanc de 15 liv. (un tuyau de bois ne coûte que 10 liv.); un oculaire de 6 liv. Total, foixante fix livres .... 66 liv.

Les lunettes achromatiques (2298), qui font deftinées à mettre dans la poche, toutes montées coûtent deux guinées & demi, à Londres, ou 60 liv. de France, celles de 3 pieds, 3 guinées; les objectifs achromatiques de 3 pieds, 3 guinées; ceux de 12 pieds, 10 guinées; ceux de 18 pieds, 15 guinées. On en trouve chez M. Dollond dans le Strand, & chez M. Ramfden. Il y a de nouvelles lunettes achromatiques de 3½ pieds qui ont 3½ pouces d'ouverture (2307) & qui coûtent 26 louis à Londres, environ un louis de port; mais il faut une permiffion pour les faire entrer dans le Royaume.

*Quart-de-cercle.*

Un quart-de-cercle mural de 8 pieds Anglois de rayon, fait à Londres par M. Bird; tels que font ceux de Gréenwich, celui de Petersbourg, & celui de M. le Monnier à Paris ...... 8000 liv.

Quart-de-cercle de 18 pouces de rayon, avec deux divifions de Vernier; une lunette fixe, une mobile, & un micromètre extérieur, chez M. Bird ................... 1200 liv.

Quart-de-cercle mural d'un pied, 25 guinées, ou 600 liv. & les autres à proportion du rayon, pourvu qu'ils ne foient pas fort grands.

Un quart-de-cercle mural de 6 pieds de rayon, tel que celui de l'Obfervatoire de Paris, & celui de Milan chez M. Canivet, Ingénieur du Roi & de MM. de l'Académie Royale des Sciences pour les Inftrumens d'Aftronomie. .......... 5000 liv.

*Sextant,*

Un fextant (Fig. 207) de 6 pieds de rayon, à deux lunettes, ................ 3000 liv.

*Tome I.*     g

## 1 PRIX DES INSTRUMENS

Un fextant pareil de 4 pieds de rayon, ........ 2000 liv.
Un fextant de 3 pieds, ............... 1500 liv.
Un petit fextant d'un pied, pour prendre feulement les hauteurs correfpondantes, ................... 600 liv.
Un quart-de-cercle de 2 pieds ½ (Fig. 149), avec une alidade pour mefurer les angles fur le terrein, & un double genou, (Fig. 153) ........................ 240 liv.

*Autres Inftrumens,*

Lunette parallac. en bois avec fon axe (Fig. 176).... 240 liv.
Un micromètre, tel que celui que j'ai décrit (2358).... 300 liv.
Un micromètre fimple de la grandeur de celui qui eft décrit (2366) ........................ 160 liv.
Micromètre fimple, plus petit, fuffifant pour une lunette de 7 à 8 pieds, ........................ 150 liv.
Lunette méridienne, ou inftrument des paffages (2387) avec fes fupports & fon niveau. ............ 600 liv.
Le niveau de 2 pieds feul, avec un tube calibré (2398), 144 liv.
Octant de réflexion de 18 pouces de rayon, en bois, pour obferver en Mer les hauteurs & les diftances (2458) avec une lunette, ........................ 120 liv.
Le même en cuivre, ................... 150 liv.
Le même de 2 pieds de rayon, fait avec un foin particulier par Ramfden à Londres, ............ 300 liv.

*Télescopes.*

Les TÉLESCOPES de Short à Londres, mefure d'Angleterre, ou 11 pouces ½, mefure de France, coûtoient 14 guinées, c'eft-à-dire, 14 louis d'or, ou 336 liv. & groffiffoient jufqu'à 110 fois; on verra les prix des autres grandeurs dans la Table ci-jointe avec les amplifications. Je fuppofe que les artifes qui lui ont fuccédé, ne s'éloigneront pas des prix qu'il avoit fixés; mais je doute qu'ils vouluffent entreprendre le télefcope de 144 pouces de foyer (ou 11½ pieds de Paris), que Short lui-même n'a jamais exécuté qu'une fois.

| Pouces Anglois. | Guinées. | Amplification. |
|---|---|---|
| 12 | 14 | 110 |
| 18 | 20 | 200 |
| 24 | 35 | 300 |
| 36 | 75 | 400 |
| 48 | 100 | 500 |
| 72 | 300 | 800 |
| 144 | 800 | 1200 |

Les télefcopes François fe comptent ordinairement, non pas fur le foyer de leur grand miroir, mais fur leur longueur totale, y compris le petit miroir & les oculaires. Nous allons rapporter les prix de M. Paffemant d'après le catalogue qu'il en avoit donné au public, peu de temps avant fa mort, & qui feront entretenus par fes fucceffeurs.

Les télefcopes de 16 pouces qui équivalent à des lunettes de

**Figure 6.2** Lalande's price list for astronomical instruments, 1771

*Source:* Jerome Lalande, *Astronomie* second edition (Paris, 1771). From the copy in the Crawford Library, Royal Observatory, Edinburgh

innovation and improvement on his own behalf'.[31] Despite attempts to reform this system by the astronomers Lalande and J.D. Cassini, it was the radical social change effected by the 1789 Revolution that finally ended the inextricable straitjacket in which the Paris trade had found itself.

Turner maintains that from the early 1790s, the state saw instrument making as 'essential to French national security', and thus an industry to be encouraged. 'The exigencies of war, the reform of the weights and measures, the introduction of metrication, the installation of Chappe's telegraph system, all produced an immediate governmental need for the skills of not just one or two instrument-makers but of many.'[32] However, these were numerically few, and not particularly skilful. This led to further governmental encouragement in the form of training and education, and a programme of frequent national exhibitions with prizes. Turner shows how the vast governmental order for new weights and measures led to the development of new tools and machines within the workshops of Paris, while one instrument business, the brothers Jecker, pioneered 'the introduction of large-scale mechanized production into Paris instrument-making' along the lines already used in the London workshop of Jesse Ramsden, with whom François-Antoine Jecker (1765–1843) had worked for five years.[33] The Jecker business was to survive for some 40 years.

### The London Trade in the Mid-eighteenth Century

By the mid-eighteenth century, the instrument making business, dominated by firms based in London, would have been a traditionally organized craft. How did it compare with other industries in about 1760? It was quantitatively tiny in size – the figures produced by Project SIMON suggest that in 1751, there were 161 makers in charge of their own businesses in London, compared with a total of 232 in the entire British Isles.[34] More recent figures, produced in Graph 6.1, show the number of London businesses at five year intervals from 1760, compared with those uncovered in the provincial centres in the course of work for this book.[35] Numbers in the London instrument community over this period show that it was always the largest centre nationally for this trade, although there were two periods where numbers declined: during the 1790s, and in the second decade of the nineteenth century.

Apprenticeship was strictly governed (although there was not an exclusive London guild which covered the trade, and theoretically the restrictions applied

---

[31]  Ibid., 8.
[32]  Ibid., 17.
[33]  Ibid., 20.
[34]  Clifton (1995).
[35]  Statistics supplied from the database of British scientific instrument makers maintained by Dr Gloria Clifton at the National Maritime Museum and Old Royal Observatory, Greenwich, London SE10 9NF.

only within the City of London and not in neighbouring Westminster), so that the transfer of skills was through a seven-year training and initiation into trade secrets. Yet, in comparison with the Paris guild-structure, the craft was protected without being suffocated.[36] The markets were largest where the population was greatest and wealthiest, that is, in London. As Gloria Clifton has shown, the external economies created outside the trade in eighteenth-century London gave individual firms a number of advantages deriving from their proximity to each other, where 'clusters of small firms could form a critical mass, creating a pool of skilled labour, exchange of ideas, and support services, which allow the whole industry to advance'.[37]

The markets were also at their most diverse in London, ranging from dilettantes paying for the newest technical toy to impress their contemporaries, to clients at the Royal Society wanting to realize ideas in brass, through to burgeoning custom from mariners, surveyors and teachers; and although the finished products could be any of a growing variety, there were few of the pitfalls inherent in some of the other luxury trades – such as whimsical changes in fashion, as befell the bucklemakers – which would mean that overnight, goods became unsaleable. This is not to say that instrument making was a secure business: bankruptcy, like the other Grim Reaper, was always just around the corner. Between 1774 and 1786, five London-based instrument businesses went bankrupt; however, of these, three businesses apparently recovered and continued.[38] If too much capital was tied up in stock – as in the example of Jeremiah Sisson, who, according to Lalande, began too many projects but completed none, and found himself having to pawn his tools in order to pay his workmen – and if this was compounded with the length of time taken to complete a large order, the creditors would be at the door.[39]

Despite such pitfalls, however, it would have made more economic sense for any aspiring instrument maker setting up in business in the middle decades of the eighteenth century to be located in London rather than in the provinces, as that was where the markets were located, and where the foreign visitors would come. Entry to the trade was secured by paying a fee to become an apprentice, followed by seven years' apprenticeship to gain the necessary skills, under a master. Then, it was necessary to obtain freedom of the company and the City in order to trade, take apprentices and employ journeymen. Finding the necessary capital to set up on one's own after this probably depended critically upon family networks; however, in London, there were large enough workshops to absorb skilled hands, and the sub-contracting networks – although difficult to trace – were clearly run along well-established lines. 'Trained apprentices provided a pool of skilled labour, and the enormous range of individual crafts facilitated subcontracting of

---

[36] See Bennett (2002) for a comparison.
[37] Clifton (1994), 68, quoting M. Porter, *The Competitive Advantage of Nations* (London, 1990), 434, 735–6.
[38] Anon. (1789), discussed in Morrison-Low (1994a).
[39] Quoted in Morrison-Low (1994a).

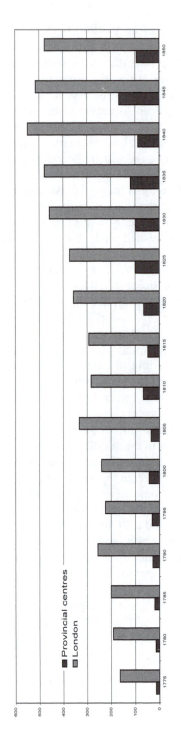

**Graph 6.1 Numbers of London instrument makers compared with six provincial centres, see Graph 1.2 for data**

specialist work, the transfer of skills, and the exchange of ideas,' Clifton has noted. 'The existence of merchant bankers, packers, shippers, insurance companies and agents provided the services needed for those who wished to conduct business beyond London.'[40]

An oblique indication of the nature of his in-house and sub-contracted support of any particular commission is provided in a comment first published in 1746, by the prominent London instrument maker George Adams the Elder:

> I always inspect and direct the several Pieces myself, see them all combined in my own House, and finish the most curious Parts thereof with my own Hands.[41]

In his day, Adams was one of the most prestigious figures in the instrument trade, who held the appointment of Mathematical Instrument Maker to the Board of Ordnance between 1748 and 1753, and later held Royal Appointments to the Prince of Wales and to George III.[42] His statement implies that his business was underpinned by a complex trade structure – hidden to historians, yet probably taken for granted by contemporaries – of outworkers and subcontractors, channelling specialist instrument parts to be assembled for sale or finished in Adams' Fleet Street premises. Just how complex this structure was at this date can be gleaned only from foreign attempts to acquire these skills through espionage.

Other European countries – and their governments – were eager to find out what went on inside individual first-rate workshops. As David Jeremy has pointed out, there was legislation in place to prohibit the export of machinery from before the 1760s, and 'no skilled artisan or manufacturer was legally free to leave Britain or Ireland and enter any foreign country outside the Crown's dominions for the purpose of carrying on his trade'. Although this legislation, up to 1824, was 'comprehensive' with respect to textile machinery, that covering metal-working tools (including so-called 'clock-making' tools) was not.[43] Occasionally, friendly foreign powers would – with greater or lesser success – place men in some of the top-ranking London workshops for a considerable fee. At other times, the manufacturer would refuse to take them on.

In conjunction with Catherine the Great's policy of enticing skilled workers from England to Russia, a series of commercial treaties between the two countries during the eighteenth century allowed some exemptions from the general restrictions on technological exchange. Thus, the Russian instrument maker Nikolai Chizhov worked with George Adams the Elder for eight months during 1759,[44] but towards the end of the century, when Vasilii Sveshnikov and Osip Shishorin came to London, they had to bribe workers to disclose the secrets

---

[40]   Clifton (1994), 68.

[41]   Adams (1746), 224.

[42]   Clifton (1995), 2; Morton and Wess (1993), 243–372; Millburn (2000), 75–106.

[43]   Jeremy (1977), 2. He lists the following acts: 5 Geo. 1, c.27 (1718); 25 Geo. 3, c.67 (1785) and 26 Geo. 3, c.89 (1786), covering the metal trades.

[44]   Boss (1972), 204–5; Cross (1979), 35.

their masters refused to show them.[45] Reciprocally, a number of British-born, London-trained instrument makers were inveigled to go abroad, taking their trade with them: John Bradley worked in Moscow between 1710 and 1716, and then went to St Petersburg, where he died in 1743; Francis Morgan emigrated to St Petersburg in 1772 and died there in 1803 (Figure 6.3); Samuel Whitford went to St Petersburg in 1771, but returned to London and took over Morgan's business. Benjamin Scott emigrated in 1747, and Robert Hynam in about 1775, both to St Petersburg; they were contracted not just to make instruments but also to train young Russian craftsmen in their skills.[46]

Anita McConnell lists a number of foreign workers of various nationalities who were allowed to work with Jesse Ramsden, considered to be the pre-eminent London instrument manufacturer of his generation. Among them were the Frenchmen François-Antoine Jecker and Edmund Nicholas Gabory; the Germans Georg Dreschler of Hamburg and Wilhelm Baumann from Tumlingen in the Duchy of Würtemburg; Jasper J. Marquez and Jose Maria Pedroso – both Portuguese – each paid 150 guineas for the privilege of being taken on in the Ramsden workshop in 1798; while Carl Apelquist, also mentioned above, was sponsored by the Swedish king.[47] How little of Ramsden's secrets could be gleaned from such a position is revealed by the frustrated comments of the Dane, Jesper Bidstrup (1763–1802), to his patron, Thomas Bugge (1740–1815), as we shall see shortly.

**Figure 6.3    Inclining dial by Francis Morgan at St Petersburg, late eighteenth century**

*Source*: Museum of the History of Science, Oxford, inv. no. 55364

---

[45]    Woolrich (1988), 36.
[46]    Cross (1980), 185–9; Chenakal (1972).
[47]    McConnell (1994b), 46; see also McConnell (forthcoming).

## How Foreigners Saw the London Trade

Foreigners from all over Europe came to visit London – and later the English Midlands and subsequently Scotland – and were often allowed, thanks to their contacts, to look around all manner of industrial sites. However, those who came to gather information rather than as innocent sightseers, were usually obliged to make their descriptions and sketch their illustrations of what they had seen, presumably some hours after the event, rather than at the time. David Jeremy has observed that 'we have ... little idea of the extent to which technology transfer occurred through correspondence'.[48] As an example of one country's attempt to bring its knowledge up-to-date, Denmark would appear superficially to be an unlikely place to have (or even desire) a flourishing trade in indigenously-manufactured scientific instruments, but by the late eighteenth century there was evidently a perceived need for this.

Denmark was and remains predominantly rural, its native geology lacking both coal and iron, and its population small. Denmark had, of course, produced earlier scientists of European stature, principally the astronomers Tycho Brahe (1546–1601) and Ole Rømer (1644–1710).[49] Thomas Bugge had studied theology and mathematics at the University of Copenhagen, had worked as an assistant at the Royal Observatory at Copenhagen and subsequently was appointed chief land surveyor of the kingdom of Denmark. He made two visits abroad to see foreign observatories and examine instrument making concerns, the first of these in 1777 shortly after his appointment as professor of astronomy and mathematics at the University for Copenhagen and Danish Astronomer Royal.[50]

The journal recording Bugge's 1777 journey was made as a personal *aide-memoire*, and was not published during his lifetime; he appears to have jotted his daily impressions and sketches later the same day. He visited the Netherlands and England, and was naturally most interested in astronomical material at this point in his career. Evidently, his position had equipped him with suitable introductions to eminent scientific circles: on 2 October 1777 he was introduced to the Royal Society Club, and invited to dine with the president, Sir John Pringle (1707–82), the following night.[51] In turn, this would have furnished him with introductions to places where science was practised: in the observatories, and in the instrument workshops. He first visited mathematical instrument shops in and around the Strand, including that of Addison Smith: 'He is a very polite man. At

---

[48]   Jeremy (1977), 16.
[49]   For Tycho, see most recently Thoren (1990); for Danish astronomy, including Rømer and Tycho, see Thykier (1990).
[50]   Crosland (1969), in his Introduction, gives the background to Bugge's life and times. A transcript of Bugge's diary of his 1777 visit to the Netherlands and England has been translated and edited by Karl Møller Pedersen of Aarhus University, 1997, and is here referred to as Bugge (1777). See also Pedersen (2001) and de Clercq (2005b).
[51]   Bugge (1777), 191.

his shop I bought a ruler with English, French, Dutch and Antwerp standards for 3 sh[illings]'.[52] Subsequently, Bugge visited a Mr Russell who lived nearby, who 'showed me a small scale by [John] Bird … I compared an inch rule, bought at Smith's, and found that 24 inches were $1/_{10}$th too short.[53]

Already Bugge was discovering that retailed instruments were not necessarily of the quality of bespoke items. Bugge went on to describe his 'very beautiful transit instrument by Bird … I also saw one of Graham's astronomical clocks with a Gridiron pendulum; it had a peculiar device for correcting the pendulum if the brass and steel rods did not have the correct ratio, if the pendulum changed with warm and cold'.[54] Again, this is sketched in detail and carefully described. George Graham's gridiron pendulum was an improvement on that of John Harrison, announced in 1728, and by the 1770s was seen as a fundamental part of observatory equipment for accurate timekeeping: it was not, however, new.

Bugge visited other precision clockmakers, notably the eminent chronometer maker John Arnold (*c.*1736–99), who showed him his chronometer improvements using helical instead of spiral springs, his balance movement, and his heat-compensated pendulum for astronomical clocks.[55] He also visited Alexander Cumming (1733–1814), and saw an example of his famous barometer clock on his shop premises.[56] Cumming had a small observatory at the top of his house, with two instruments used for calibrating his clocks made by Jesse Ramsden, which Bugge examined closely and subsequently described and sketched.[57] Bugge went to see Ramsden 'who at once showed me an 8-foot mural quadrant which was in preparation'. There then ensued some technical conversation, with the heading underlined: 'Ramsden's ideas about some new instruments'.[58] However, he clearly learned nothing of any crucial importance on this brief visit.

Foreign visitors interested in astronomy and precision instruments always made a point of seeing Ramsden, considered by contemporaries to be at the pinnacle of the trade. After commenting on the general state of the instrument trade, the eminent geologist and Frenchman Barthélemy Faujas de Saint Fond (1741–1819) stated in 1784 that its practitioners:

> are, in general, men of great information; and spare neither time nor expense to carry their workmanship to a high degree of perfection. A more careful education than is elsewhere is obtainable; the demands of the navy, and the great number of persons whose wealth enables them to appreciate and to pay well for the best-constructed

---

[52]  Ibid., 129. These rules are not uncommon: an example by John Urings of London is illustrated in Connor and Simpson (2004), 40 and 41.
[53]  Ibid., 191–3. John Russell (1745–1806) was a portrait painter, but also known for his maps and globes of the Moon: Ryan (1966).
[54]  Ibid., 199. For Graham, see Sorrenson (1999).
[55]  Ibid., 157–61; 171–7. For Arnold, see Betts (1996).
[56]  Goodison (1977), 315. For Cumming, see Cosh (1969).
[57]  Bugge (1777), 163–71.
[58]  Ibid., 185.

instruments, are causes which have concurred to form artists of high reputation, and who have served as instructors to others... .

I found the skilful and modest Ramsden occupied in making an instrument simple in appearance, but which demanded much care and many combinations to make it perfect ....

I had much pleasure in conversing with Ramsden. I went to see him several times; and I purchased several instruments at his shop. He possesses all the modesty and simplicity of manners of a man of great talents.[59]

The apparent accessibility of Ramsden, together with his 'modesty and simplicity of manners' impressed foreign scientists, and Bugge, a few years before De Saint Fond, had found him happy to discuss theory, and for a few brief hours politely show the visitor instruments under construction. However, this was not to be the case with foreigners who wished to learn his trade and export it back to their native land, as Bugge was subsequently to find.

Bugge listed the books and instruments he bought in London. In total, he paid £34 6s 6d for books, but bought only one – Ramsden's *Description of an Engine for Dividing Mathematical Instruments* (1777) – which was new.[60] Although books would have been available through exchange at the Royal Danish Academy of Sciences and Letters and at the Royal Danish Observatory, Bugge built up his own large personal library. This, containing some seven thousand volumes, together with his collection of mathematical instruments, was destroyed in the bombardment of Copenhagen by the British fleet in September 1807.[61]

For his instruments he paid considerably more: a total of £88 4s. Apart from the substandard rule purchased from Smith, he bought an eight-guinea compound microscope from Peter Dollond in St Paul's Churchyard; then 'I visited the other Mr Dollond who lives in the Hay Market. I bought the new parallel ruler invented by him. None of the Dollond brothers seems to have any theoretical knowledge'.[62] This comment can only be seen as damning, and is corroborated by a comment by the Swiss astronomer Jean Bernoulli (1744–1807), but the firm and its outstanding reputation, particularly with optical instruments, had been established by the father of the two brothers, with the solution of the problem of chromatic aberration and the patenting of the achromatic lens in 1758.[63]

Most of the rest of Bugge's purchases were made to order at Nairne & Blunt's in Cornhill, where on 20 September Bugge had been treated to a demonstration

[59] De Saint Fond (1907), 91–3.

[60] Bugge (1777), 199–205.

[61] Crosland (1969), 17.

[62] Bugge (1777), 155. These would appear to be the sons of John Dollond the elder: John (1733–1804) and Peter (1731–1820). The brothers were in partnership between 1766 and 1804, with Peter running the shop in St. Paul's Churchyard and John that in the Haymarket: see Clifton (1995), 87.

[63] Bernoulli's *Lettres astronomiques* (Berlin, 1771) is quoted by Daumas (1972), 239; see also Bennett (2002).

of 'several experiments with the electrical machine', and subsequently ordered an electrical machine and an airpump.[64] Then he visited the observatories at Oxford, Greenwich and Cambridge, marvelling at their instrumentation and sketching them beside the notes in his journal. By early November, he was back in the capital where: 'On my last day in London I saw the instruments which Mr Nairne and Blunt had made for me, and I found them all very pleasing'.[65] These appear to have been good-quality, standard demonstration instruments of the time, presumably to be used in his university teaching.

Bugge returned to Denmark in late 1777, where it seems that only one instrument maker was then at work: this was a Swedish immigrant, Johannes Ahl (1729–95), who had fled his native land in 1762 to escape personal debt, and was welcomed by the astronomy faculty at the University of Copenhagen. Ahl had learnt his craft through apprenticeship under the pre-eminent eighteenth-century Swedish instrument maker, Daniel Ekström (1711–55).[66] Part of Ekström's own education, with his government's patronage and encouragement, had been a year spent in England, working in George Graham's workshop during 1739–40; he had also visited Greenwich Observatory, and listened to J.T. Desaguliers (1683–1744) lecturing at the Royal Society.[67] Through Bugge's patronage, Ahl supplied major instruments to the Royal Observatory at Copenhagen, and to the national survey carried out by Bugge under the Royal Danish Academy; other clients, such as army engineers involved in the construction of the Ejder Canal, and the Admiralty which required its navy supplied with navigation instruments, had to be supplied by Parisian and London products.[68]

Bugge was determined to establish an indigenous instrument trade, and he encouraged one of Ahl's apprentices, named Jesper Bidstrup (1763–1802), to take up a university grant as well as a supplementary royal grant, and travel to London with letters of recommendation, one addressed to Sir Joseph Banks (1743–1820), president of the Royal Society in succession to Sir John Pringle. This explained that Bidstrup had already had some instruction from Johannes Ahl, and that he came with a government stipend of £100 a year, as 'he has a mind to begin with the beginning and to work as a common workman'. Bugge suggested Ramsden as a possible master, diffidently anticipating that he 'will perhaps not trouble himself with the case of a foreigner', discarded the idea of the bankrupt Jeremiah Sisson, and hoped that a good word from the powerful Banks would persuade 'Mr Nairne and Blunt [who] will not disdain to bring a youth of knowledge and ability to perfection in his favourite art'.[69]

---

[64]   Bugge (1777), 141. For Edward Nairne, see Warner (1998c).
[65]   Ibid., 345.
[66]   Andersen (1995), 12.
[67]   Amelin (1994).
[68]   Ahl and Bidstrup are discussed by Christensen (1993).
[69]   British Library Add Mss. 8097 ff 14–15, Thomas Bugge to Sir Joseph Banks, 9 July 1787.

Bugge also wrote a letter of recommendation to the renowned maker of reflecting telescopes, William Herschel, summarizing his letter to Banks, and after some well-placed flattery concerning Herschel's skills in both astronomy and telescope construction, requested that 'you will give Mr Bidstrup leave to look on your other instruments and your other fine inventions ...'.[70] However, this hopeful approach was not to succeed. As Bidstrup subsequently wrote to Bugge, he was unable to find work with any of the first rank workshops, and in particular, not with Jesse Ramsden, but he was able to report back to Bugge in March 1789 that he had found a position with a 'Mr White':

> ... with whom I work. He is an honest man and has most readily passed on to me all his own learning, and even introduced me to artists, whose acquaintance I have turned to good account and hope moreover to retain in the future, just as I am also pleased with the decision I took and adhered to, for I am now fully convinced that it was not Nairne & Blunt, Adams or Dollond or their peers from whom I would have learnt anything, as their most prestigious instruments are manufactured all around the city, and what men they employ in their houses are either simply put to repairing instruments, or for executing some [...], on the other hand I should not omit to ask for these men's opinions for I dare say it is not from lack of knowledge that they deal with instruments like that, but because it is to their advantage to do so.[71]

'Mr White' was probably Joseph White, identified from insurance records, who had been working off Gray's Inn Lane as a subcontractor until 1786, and subsequently at Hatton Street.[72] It would appear from Bidstrup's description that little of ground-breaking technical importance was constructed on most London shop premises, although he went on to say:

> Ramsden is the only one to have the most important instruments manufactured in his house, he has often got 40 to 50 workers each of them manufacturing various parts of an instrument, some are plane filing, others turning on the lathe, making screws and so forth. Those few who create or sometimes even manufacture an instrument, doing nothing else, must already be well known as a good and experienced craftsman. Had I even entered his workshop as a hired man, this being the only way, yet it would have been of little advantage to me, for they would of course have set me to plane, file, turn on the lathe, and so on, just like everyone else, and being a hired man, I would have had to do what was ordered of me, by which I would have been deprived of increasing my knowledge of other parts of the art, not because Ramsden could not give the best instruction, but because no mortal would make him do that.[73]

[70]  Royal Astronomical Society, Herschel letters, W1/13.B.171, Thomas Bugge to William Herschel, 6 July 1787.

[71]  This correspondence is in Royal Library, Copenhagen: Ny Kongelig Samling 287 ii 4, translated by Claus Thykier and Anita McConnell. Jesper Bidstrup to Thomas Bugge, 6 March 1789.

[72]  Clifton (1995), 30 and 296.

[73]  Royal Library, Copenhagen: NKS, Bidstrup to Bugge, 6 March 1789.

This description of a London 'factory', where an entire instrument appears to be constructed on the premises – instead of going to specialist makers to the trade located all around London – demonstrates at least one example of the specific division of labour in the trade at this time. Anita McConnell sees this as unusual in the instrument trade at this date, commenting that Ramsden, a known associate of the Birmingham engineering entrepreneur Matthew Boulton (1728–1804), may have been influenced by the division of labour practised at Boulton's Soho Works.[74] Yet, Bidstrup also made it clear that Ramsden and others at the top of the trade were masters of all the skills necessary to produce a completed instrument. They were also, evidently, keen to keep strangers out of their workshops, and managed to do so by keeping to a strict division of labour. Bidstrup emphasized the trade secrecy:

> For the most part the artists here are particularly reticent, keeping these secrets among their acquaintances, and the smaller masters keep the secrets of their own people who in turn keep many tricks of work secret from each other, and it is seldom that anyone can be found who is willing to show anything to another man.
>
> So this art perhaps more than any other is richer in intrigues than people imagine, and if you want to search for insight and artifice in it, then you must take your time undeterred by the first difficulties, and not trying to save money as this often clears away secrecy if you want to attain the object of your desires, and hardly anyone unless he has tried can imagine the difficulties with which this is encumbered.
>
> So I have spent the greater part of my time on the art and becoming familiar with the artists, particularly the journeymen, which I soon learned was most useful to me; and as often as I could find time from practical exercises I have frequented the Library of the British Museum, and with Professor Torkelin visited the societies ....[75]

Bidstrup was finding the whole venture expensive and insecure, but hoping that the end results – setting up in Denmark and running a monopoly – would pay off, pleading that it took time to obtain the 'know-how' of the trade. After 18 months he wrote:

> England is beyond question the only place where I can progress to be the best in my trade ... I should be reluctant to leave England, having just gained the confidence of some of the artists, something which is difficult and takes time to achieve. I was nearly 8 months in London before I came to know any artist to my advantage ... my wish is to acquire as much learning as I can, to the benefit of my native country, in compensation for the expense to which it has been put that I might be admitted to the company of artists here ....[76]

---

[74]   McConnell (1994), 46.

[75]   Royal Library Copenhagen, NKS: Bidstrup to Bugge, 6 March 1789. 'Torkelin' was the distinguished Icelandic scholar Grimur Jonsson Thorkelin (1752–1829).

[76]   Ibid.

After a year in London, Bidstrup constructed a sextant, diagrams of which he forwarded to Bugge, so that it might be shown to various powerful Danish patrons, 'for I think that it would recommend me somewhat, especially as there is no-one in Copenhagen manufacturing similar instruments'.[77] He continued:

> Instruments here are no longer divided by hand, unless their radius is 2 feet or more, but everything is done on machines of which there are about 3, namely: Ramsden's, Stancliffe's and Troughton's, this last being here considered to be the best, and my sextant was divided on this machine. Their owners will not permit anyone to see these machines, for fear that others should have any similar, by which they would lose their share of the advantage they have by dividing.
>
> However, there is no witchcraft at all in the establishment of machines like these, which you may clearly see from Ramsden's description, besides I know an artist who has been a foreman with Ramsden and had there the opportunity of acquainting himself with the arrangement of his [machines]. The screw is the principal part, which to begin with you need a machine to cut, I know an artist here has offered another £50 sterling for a pair of screws (for you must have 2, one for cutting grooves in the wheel, and another for the proper screw), but he would not sell them for that ....[78]

Spies were clearly everywhere, and Bidstrup was keen to gain all the knowledge that he could, from whatever source.

Correspondence between Bidstrup and Bugge was infrequent, partly because Bidstrup kept hoping for an improvement in his finances: with his living expenses, 'the acquisition of knowledge', and being obliged 'to provide myself with my own consumable implements like files and tools etc. which become worn and break, which brought me no small expense ...', he was permanently living on the edge of debt.[79] Yet Bidstrup remained sanguine about his future: 'There are many useful things which I might acquire during my stay and acquaintances here in London which on my return would greatly contribute to my speedily becoming useful to my native country, such as patterns for casting the different instruments manufactured here ... when leaving England I should be the owner of a complete set of patterns, tools and machines necessary for an artist contemplating making himself useful in his art, but for this indeed money is required which I have not got ...'.[80]

Bidstrup left White in August 1789 for another workshop, run by a Mr Higgins, who was a subcontractor for both Nairne & Blunt and George Adams, and had formerly been apprenticed to Ramsden.[81] In order to transfer from White to Higgins, Bidstrup had to buy himself out, 'several tools being common to Mr White and myself', but this meant he now had 'a rather good, though incomplete

---

[77]  Ibid.

[78]  Ibid.

[79]  Royal Library Copenhagen, NKS, Bidstrup to Bugge, 29 December 1789.

[80]  Ibid.

[81]  Higgins has not been identified.

collection of tools ... on the other hand, my time is more restricted and I can hardly manufacture anything for myself, for I must spend at least 10 hours a day in the workshop, the common rule being 12 hours ...'.[82]

At this stage, Bidstrup intended to send back the first of the instruments he had made himself to Denmark for sale, through Bugge, the following spring. He felt that he remained ignorant of only two remaining areas of London instrument manufacture, which would cost money to obtain, as he would have to bribe the specialist workmen involved. These were:

> Dr Herschel's way of giving metal mirrors a true parabolic figure, and [John] Bird's practical way of graduating, both are kept very secret and are, as it were, quite separated from the remaining sections of the art, since the artists of these are occupied with nothing else, still I might be informed about it, if only I had got money to offer, since I know 2 men, after Herschel and [Edward] Troughton considered the best in London in these trades; even though I know the theory of both, and by intercourse with these people have elicited a lot, besides knowing and having been practising the Engl. way of grinding glass and that usual with metal mirrors, yet it would be preferable if I could learn and see these performed. I could soon pick up both, having already a fairly good knowledge thereof, and the knack of the art presumably lying in its practice, but alas! I do not know where to obtain or save [money] for this purpose, probably therefore I must do without, and be content with applying the theory and experience I already have in the best way.[83]

This paragraph demonstrates most clearly that despite Bird's 1767 publication of his method of hand division, this skill still had to be practically taught, and mastered by experience: the 'know-how' for precision instruments could only be learned by doing.

A year later, Bidstrup again contacted his patron to say that he had finally left Higgins's workshop: 'finally I have become familiar with the Engl. working method in all parts of the art, only grinding mirrors with a parabolic shape I have not dared to commence because of the accompanying not inconsiderable expense ...'.[84] Bidstrup was by now in such debt that he asked for more money, otherwise he would be obliged to sell the equipment he was hoping to bring back with him to Denmark:

> Since the beginning of last year ... I have over time amassed a not inconsiderable assortment of models, tools and machines which are all specific to the art and which are for the most part not available in Denmark. These and others, up to a complete set, it would be useful for me to send home before leaving England, by which I should save much time and expense, for should I be unable to begin to procure these things until I returned, it would be some time before I could be active, since conveying them here would involve time and expense. Obviously I should need support until I could

---

[82] Royal Library Copenhagen, NKS, Bidstrup to Bugge, 29 December 1789.
[83] Ibid.
[84] Royal Library Copenhagen, NKS, Bidstrup to Bugge, 31 December 1790.

improve my acquired knowledge, for it stands to reason that even the handiest artist cannot accomplish anything without the requisite models, tools, etc.[85]

By 1793, Bidstrup had set up in business just off Leicester Square, and a copy survives of his *Catalogue of Optical, Mathematical & Philosophical Instruments*, running to eight pages.[86] Judging by the difficulty he had had in selling those few instruments which he had made already, those listed must have been instruments which he could buy-in for resale rather than ones he would have made and had in stock. Christensen has recounted how Bidstrup's entire endeavour then went horribly wrong: despite his country's continuing but stinted financial support (partly engendered by suspicion of his motives), Bidstrup was unable to acquire quickly enough what he considered a viable array of basic tools to set up a Danish instrument enterprise. These were: a dividing engine, a tube-drawing machine with steel cylinders, and a glass-grinding machine with steel cups.

Although he finally managed to do this, and to smuggle them successfully out of the country and to safety in Copenhagen in 1798, after years of debt and worry, he became seriously ill. Bidstrup was hugely in debt to the Danish government, which meantime built him workshops, just as his patron Thomas Bugge left for Paris: Jesper Bidstrup died in 1802, without having begun the enterprise to which he had devoted his life. His workshops, tools and all belongings were claimed as state property, and taken over by his more fortunate compatriot Jeppe Smith, who thus acquired ready-made and up-to-date equipment, and was able to produce instruments, but for the Danish domestic market only, up to his death in 1821, after which the firm was continued to 1855 by his nephew. Any hard-won first-hand 'know-how' was lost.[87]

In this instance, technology transfer through industrial espionage for the instrument industry was not particularly successful, partly because of the reluctance of the London trade to part with its secrets, and partly because of the nature of those secrets. Denmark's indigenous instrument industry over the next century helped serve a local market only, but quantities of apparatus continued to be imported. Ian Inkster has pointed out that it was 'not ... the transfer of scientific knowledge, or of machines and skills [which] determined the industrialization of receiver nations in the eighteenth century ... the mere possession of a technology or set of technologies is not a sufficient explanation of the industrialization process'.[88] It was no trivial task to transfer the secrets of the precision instrument trade out of London: an observation as applicable for provincial England as it was for foreign competitors. Yet the manuscripts which

---

[85]  Ibid.

[86]  In the Bodleian Library, Oxford; Anderson et al. (1990), 12. Instruments known with Bidstrup's London signature are: a telescope offered at Sotheby's, 27 April 1964, Lot 140; a mechanical powers apparatus; a Gregorian telescope; a refracting telescope and a Culpeper-type microscope: see Andersen (1995), 20, 35, 27 and 249.

[87]  Christensen (1993), 225–6; for Jeppe Smith, see Andersen (1993).

[88]  Inkster (1991), 59.

describe the attempts of Bugge and Bidstrup highlight aspects of an industry which has left little record of its day-to-day workings, and as such, are invaluable as detailed historical information, unobtainable elsewhere.

Other glimpses into the day-to-day running of a London instrument-maker's workshop at this period are difficult to find. One illustration – an exceptional portrait identified as the eminent optician John Cuff (Figure 6.4), in his working clothes in his workshop, by Johan Zoffany, dated 1772 – quite literally gives an idea of just how small and cramped the workspace of an instrument maker could be.[89] It also demonstrates how very different the working styles of the distinct types of instrument maker were: here the optical worker Cuff constructs lenses, which are small and precious, and are therefore carefully contained, and he assembles instruments individually, matching the optical components. This is very similar to the watchmakers' practice, but necessarily very different from that of the precision instrument makers, such as Ramsden.

A rare manuscript survival is the daily accounts of John Smeaton's instrument-making workshop between September 1751 and February 1752, and these demonstrate the variety of work within such a business, which was more broadly-based than that of Cuff, and its hierarchy – Smeaton employed three, subsequently four workmen, each doing differently-skilled, and therefore differently-paid work, during a six-day week.[90] Smeaton had come from Yorkshire to London, where he studied law before turning to instrument making, and from that to civil engineering.[91]

During this period, the origins of the most skilful of the London instrument-makers were provincial. This can be corroborated by examining the eight names chosen by J.A. Bennett as the élite makers of the 'heroic' period of London instrument making, namely the mid- to late-eighteenth century: Jonathan Sisson came from Lincolnshire, George Graham and Edward Troughton from Cumberland, John Bird from Durham, Jesse Ramsden from Yorkshire, James Short from Edinburgh, Edward Nairne from Kent, and only the Dollonds appear to have been Londoners, and even they were of comparatively recent Huguenot origin. The links – through apprenticeship, through business and in some cases, through family – between these individuals once they reached London, were close, and Bennett has made the point that these makers had similar career patterns,

---

[89] This portrait is in the Royal Collection, and has been reproduced in Porter et al. (1985), 27; Morton and Wess (1993), 98. Discussed in Millar (1969), 152, where an early identification of the subject as Peter Dollond is discussed; Webster (1976), 55–6.

[90] Institute of Civil Engineers: Smeaton MSS., Private Letter Book for 1764: see Skempton (1981), 239.

[91] For Smeaton, see Skempton (1981). Smeaton worked as an instrument maker between 1748 and 1752. Both the Cuff portrait and the Smeaton accounts are discussed by Werner (forthcoming), demonstrating how unusual this sort of evidence is.

**Figure 6.4    Johan Zoffany,** *Portrait of John Cuff and an assistant*, **1772**

*Source*: The Royal Collection © 2005 Her Majesty Queen Elizabeth II

centred around the patronage of three institutions – the Royal Observatory, the Board of Longitude and the Royal Society.[92]

### The Mid-nineteenth Century London Instrument-making Trade

Finding contemporary descriptions of the instrument trade is always difficult for the reasons given previously. For the mid-nineteenth century London trade this is particularly so, because the status of the maker had changed considerably. No longer did foreigners come to marvel at the craftsman's workshop. This was convincingly argued by J.A. Bennett: 'a revised relationship between scientist and instrument maker became more common, in which leading scientists became intimately involved in instrumentation – George Airy and William Thomson [Lord Kelvin] are important examples – and makers were reduced to contributing their technical skills alone'.[93] His discussion of the changes in the structure of the broader scientific community shows that its effects were being felt, and felt in the trade more generally than at the individual interface between scholar and craftsman: the industrialization of society had left the instrument trade behind, as there was a general neglect of the science education necessary to keep it in touch with new requirements. This is reflected in the brave words in the Introduction to Class X in the *Illustrated Catalogue of the Exhibition of all Nations* ... (London, 1851):

> Regarding this Class as representing the culminating point of mechanical skill, it forms an appropriate conclusion to those devoted to machinery generally. Delicacy and precision of workmanship are absolutely requisite in the industry occupied in producing philosophical apparatus. It will be found, on inspection, that the genius of this country, so remarkably developed in mechanics applied to commercial purposes, is not less successful in its application to the higher pursuits of experimental and practical philosophy.[94]

These remarks belied the outcome of the Exhibition, which, as Bennett has commented, showed unexpectedly that for the host country 'a careful look at the awards of Council Medals at least – remembering that these were intended primarily to reward originality – would have suggested that the lead in developing the traditional areas of manufactured scientific instruments might be slipping away from Britain'.[95] In a careful examination of the outcome of Class X, Bennett has shown that Britain put on a proportionally large display, and thus apparently won most of the prizes: 16 out of the 31 Council Medals. However, seven of these were in the newly developed areas of telegraphy and photography, outside

---

[92] Bennett (1985), and Porter (1985).
[93] Bennett (1985), 25.
[94] *Catalogue* ... (1851), 405.
[95] Bennett (1983), 4.

the traditional areas of instrument making, and of the remaining nine medals, 'four were for rather special pieces of apparatus, or "inventions"'.[96] In fact, the remaining five Council Medals were awarded in 'traditional' areas, and all but one of these makers were based in London, the exception being Chance Brothers of Birmingham, for the large disc of optical glass discussed earlier. John Newman won his medal for an air pump and a tide gauge; that of Ludwig Oertling, a recent immigrant from Berlin, was for his balances; Andrew Ross and Smith & Beck won theirs for their microscopes.[97]

Looking again at the London exhibitors, it is clear that individual firms had become more specialized than their counterparts in the mid-eighteenth century. There were distinct 'microscope makers', such as Andrew Pritchard, Andrew Ross and Smith & Beck; but in the area where London had previously excelled, it was clear that the Germans now produced better precision astronomical instrumentation, and the Americans were more innovative in their designs: both nations won Council Medals. The most successful competition was coming from abroad, but the provincial instrument makers were also clearly seeing their way by this time to bypassing the London market on their own account. After the stimulus of the Great Exhibition, makers outside London were prepared to produce catalogues of their products, to advertise to a broader market, and, in the case of at least one Sheffield manufacturer, to engage agents in London and New York.[98]

As Bennett commented, 'the idea that the exhibition in Class X could of itself do much to increase the scientific and technical expertise in manufacturing industry was short lived'. However, it awoke a complacent government to the real state of affairs, by demonstrating, and not just in Class X, 'the fast-growing capabilities of Britain's European rivals and the suggestion that their success was due to the provision of scientific and technical education that Britain lacked'.[99] Although superficially a triumph for British industry, the Great Exhibition provided confirmation of the 'decline of science'; nonetheless, the educational reform necessary for the country to maintain the lead it had acquired by being the first industrial nation was not to be initiated until the 1870s.

---

[96]  Ibid., 3.

[97]  *Reports* ... (1852), 262, 258, 266; Bennett (1983), 4. For John Newman, see Dawes (1996) and Gee (1996); for Ludwig Oertling, a biographical study is underway by Peta Buchanan and Barry Oliver; and for three of the major London microscope manufacturers, see Turner (1969c).

[98]  J.P. Cutts, Sutton & Son of Division Street, Sheffield, advertised an agency at Hatton Garden, London in the 1852 local directory, and one in Pearl Street, New York in 1854. The role of agents will be discussed further in Chapter 8.

[99]  Bennett (1983), 11.

## W. & S. Jones as a 'Representative' London Instrument Making Firm

There was one substantial London firm of instrument makers that survived for much of the period of the Industrial Revolution. This was the business begun in 1759 by John Jones (1737–1808) and subsequently run by his sons, the brothers William (1762–1831) and Samuel Jones (1770–1859). Between about 1780 and 1855, they published many different lists of the goods which could be obtained from them, and, as one would expect, the compilation of these varied over time (Table 6.2).[100] W. & S. Jones were by no means the first instrument suppliers to publicise their wares in this way – John Prujean's *Catalogue of Instruments* dates from 1701,[101] and the example of the arch-publicist Benjamin Martin provided the Jones brothers with contemporary inspiration[102] – but the range and scope of their catalogues provides detailed evidence of how the firm attempted to reach a broad spectrum of customers. The first 'big break' for the Jones business came in 1782, as a result of Benjamin Martin's bankruptcy, death and the subsequent sale of his business. A second, perhaps even more important boost, came in 1795/96 as a result of the death of the younger George Adams, and the subsequent sales of his effects by his widow Hannah.[103] No specific evidence was found by John Millburn to indicate that the Jones brothers purchased any instruments at either the Martin or Adams sales; but, at the very least, their business must have benefited from the reduced competition after the closure of two of the largest and apparently most successful contemporary London instrument suppliers.[104]

The Jones brothers were able to secure the copyright of the influential scientific and mathematical textbooks written by George Adams; from 1797 onwards, each of these popular Adams works had catalogues and price lists of instruments supplied by W. & S. Jones bound in the back of every volume. As a form of advertising, this appears to have had considerable success, since the Joneses sold the instruments that Adams described, and 'puffs' for Adams' books even appeared within the text of the catalogues. All the illustrated plates were now marked 'W. & S. Jones ...' together with the date, while the inscriptions on the advertised objects read 'W. & S. Jones'.[105] It is possible that the copyright of Martin's popular textbooks was also purchased, because a number of these were revised by William Jones, and W. & S. Jones catalogues are bound in with them. There has been, over the centuries, a long and fruitful connection between printing and the instrument trade. The book trade's long-established networks into the provinces enabled London publishers to send their wares to be sold all over

---

[100]  Anderson et al. (1990), 43–4, gives a brief preliminary listing, which is problematic and incomplete.

[101]  Ibid., i, 65; discussed further by Bryden (1993).

[102]  Millburn (1986b) compares three of Martin's listings: 1757, 1765 and *c*.1780.

[103]  Millburn (2000), 263–9.

[104]  Millburn (1976), 178–80; Millburn (1986b), 75; Millburn (2000), 263–9.

[105]  Millburn (2000), 200, 248–9, 268–9 and appendix IV.

**Table 6.2   Analysis of contents of W. & S. Jones trade catalogues, c.1780–1855, showing breakdown of contents by subject**

| | Date | Phil. | Math. | Opt. | Instruments of recreation | Philosophical Chemistry | Ast. | Total |
|---|---|---|---|---|---|---|---|---|
| [John] | 1784 | 27 | 17 | 46 | – | – | – | 90 |
| 1 | [1793] | 112 | 56 | 86 | 29 | – | – | 283 |
| 2 | [1794] | 133 | 60 | 100 | 30 | 19 | – | 342 |
| 3 | [1795] | 109 | 64 | 107 | 25 | 15 | 25 | 345 |
| 4 | [1797] | 109 | 65 | 107 | 25 | 17 | 26 | 349 |
| 5 | [1797] | 110 | 64 | 107 | 22 | 15 | 33 | 351 |
| 6 | [1797] | 110 | 64 | 107 | 22 | 15 | 33 | 351 |
| 7 | [1800] | 112 | 63 | 103 | 22 | 15 | 33 | 348 |
| 8 | [1801] | 116 | 63 | 103 | 20 | 16 | 34 | 352 |
| 9 | 1804 | 117 | 61 | 103 | 20 | 16 | 34 | 351 |
| 10 | 1805 | 117 | 61 | 103 | 20 | 16 | 34 | 351 |
| 11 | 1810 | 117 | 61 | 103 | 19 | 16 | 34 | 350 |
| 12 | 1811 | 117 | 61 | 103 | 19 | 16 | 33 | 349 |
| 13 | 1814 | 141 | 82 | 117 | – | 32 | 38 | 410 |
| 14 | 1814 | 141 | 82 | 117 | – | 32 | 40 | 412 |
| 15 | Nov. 1817 | 145 | 83 | 120 | – | 33 | 42 | 423 |
| 16 | Jan. 1818 | 145 | 83 | 120 | – | 33 | 42 | 423 |
| 17 | Oct. 1825 | 145 | 84 | 118 | – | 33 | 43 | 423 |
| 18 | Aug. 1827 | 150 | 86 | 121 | – | 33 | 43 | 433 |
| 19 | 1830 | 150 | 84 | 123 | – | 34 | 44 | 435 |
| 20 | 1835 | 151 | 84 | 123 | – | 34 | 44 | 436 |
| 21 | 1836 | 150 | 85 | 124 | – | 34 | 44 | 437 |
| 22 | 1838 | 150 | 84 | 124 | – | 34 | 44 | 436 |
| 23 | 1843 | 220 | 92 | 130 | – | 48 | 42 | 532 |
| 24 | 1850 | 223 | 101 | 133 | – | 48 | 42 | 547 |
| 25 | 1855 | 221 | 99 | 131 | – | 48 | 41 | 540 |

England, and instrument makers and sellers had long used these communication lines out from the metropolis.[106]

There is nothing to indicate that the Jones business was in any way special until, through the action of William Jones, it bought itself a form of advertising that laid its products, standardized by the firm, in front of customers it wished to dazzle with the comprehensiveness of its wares. The virtue of this type of marketing was that it enabled educational establishments which were being set up or re-equipped, particularly in the eastern United States, to purchase by mail order, a complete range of apparatus from a single supplier: 'one-stop shopping' it might be called today. The most prestigious of these colleges was Harvard, which had previously purchased apparatus from Martin, and continued to buy new equipment from London.[107] William Jones presented the American Philosophical Society, based in Philadelphia, with a pair of globes in 1799, remarking that: 'I am a sincere friend to all philosophical institutions & from much encouragement received from *Americans* am happy to make them these small but grateful acknowledgements'.[108] This seems to have been in part because of his warm feelings towards 'my friend Dr Priestley', who at this time was resident in New York.[109]

William Jones's high-profile approach through advertising in this manner, together with his private teaching and public lecturing in London 'introduced him to the society of the most eminent mathematical and astronomical professors of the time, Drs. Priestley, Hutton, Maskelyne, Professor Vince and others', as his obituary noted.[110] In turn, W. & S. Jones offered the works of these authors for sale in their catalogues. William Jones's own publications were fairly extensive, even aside from his editions of the work of others. He wrote several pamphlets about instruments, many of which ran to a number of editions, three articles about optics in *Nicholson's Journal*, and contributed to both the *Encyclopaedia Britannica* and Abraham Rees's technical *Cyclopaedia*. All of these opportunities were used to mention and thus promote apparatus that could be supplied by W. & S. Jones.

It is not known how large the Joneses' workshop was at any point, although a number of individual subcontractors have been identified: most dramatically

---

[106] This point has long been understood: see Taylor (1954); and for a more recent assessment of a slightly later period, see Walters (1992), in which she ably demonstrates that instruments followed the same routes as those of the long-established book trade, by quoting examples of sales by such booksellers in Reading, York, Liverpool and Berwick-on-Tweed.

[107] See Wheatland (1968); Schechner (1982); Bedini (1993); Schechner Genuth (1996); and Walters (2002).

[108] Philadelphia, PA: American Philosophical Society Archives: Letter from William Jones to John Vaughan, Secretary, 24 June 1799.

[109] Ibid., 3 November 1795. Joseph Priestley (1733–1804), man of science and nonconformist has an extensive literature: see, for example, Anderson and Lawrence (1987).

[110] Anon (1831).

William Stiles, the workman who concealed his name inside the globe of a specially-commissioned Bohnenburger gyroscope (Figure 6.5), a demonstration device ordered for a wealthy American collector, Charles Nicholl Bancker (1778/9–1869).[111] In his will, William Jones named 'William Russell our Assistant' and 'John Norton, our Under Shopman' as beneficiaries. Other workmen have been identified as William Eden, between 1818 and 1827; William Chitty, perhaps between 1834 and 1835; and John Dillon, probably a first cousin, in 1844.[112] By the time of Samuel Jones's death in 1859, his will showed that between them the brothers had accrued considerable property and capital. Their only named relatives were female cousins, and the effects of the business were sold over four afternoons from 30 April 1860, comprising 714 lots.[113]

Of Bidstrup's three tools essential for precision instrument making, none was mentioned, confirming that W. & S. Jones used the subcontractors scattered around workshops throughout London and possibly beyond. One lot was described as a '5-feet finely divided brass *Standard Scale*, by [John] *Bird*, with vernier and adjustments complete. N.B. In a Committee of the House of Commons upon Weights and Measures, this Instrument was used by them and highly prized, and has since been much desired to be purchased by the late James Bailey, Esq., the President of the Royal Astronomical Society'. Another was given as 'a large quantity of patterns in wood, various', and a third 'expensively made wood patterns for telescopes'. Patterns are used for casting, and would have been sent to a brass-founder, so that the castings would have been finished, and instruments presumably assembled, in their workshops.[114]

The trade catalogues of W. & S. Jones reveal no printer's name until the firm moved to No. 30 Holborn in 1800, and that year they were marked 'Dillon, Printer, Plough Court, Fetter Lane'. Fetter Lane is a street running northwards off Holborn, and the Joneses appear to have had some financial stake in this nearby printing business: the brothers' father John Jones had married an Elizabeth Dillon. However, between 1801 and 1838 (after William's death), all W. & S. Jones catalogues were printed by William Glendenning of 25 Hatton Garden, master printer; but from 1843, these were printed by George Dillon of 77 Hatton Garden, premises mentioned in Samuel Jones's will.

Some 25 different versions of W. & S. Jones's catalogues have been traced, spanning the years 1793 to 1855, and there may well be further variants. The dating of these is difficult, as they were printed separately from the books in which they were bound, and as Millburn has noted 'catalogues dated as late as 1835 have been found in volumes nominally dated 1812/13'.[115] Later catalogues are to be found as separate publications. Comparison of the individual catalogues shows

---

[111] Simpson (1993) and (1995).

[112] TNA PCC PROB/11/1784 Q.222: William Jones's Will; Clifton (1995), 155.

[113] Samuel Jones's Will; Hammond (1860).

[114] Hammond (1860), Lots 90, 667 and 668.

[115] Millburn (2000), 249.

**Figure 6.5    Bohnenburger gyroscope, supplied by W. & S. Jones, London, c.1835**

*Source*: National Museums of Scotland, NMS.T.1990.26

variation of layout and content, and also some price fluctuations. The W. & S. Jones catalogues, by and large, consisted of 14 pages of instrument and book details, with a further two pages advertising books, in particular those by George Adams edited by William Jones. Over the years, the number of instruments in each category varied (as Table 6.2 shows), their total number moving from just under 300 pieces in 1793 to 540 in 1855. Prices of individual items remained relatively stable, despite war and recession (Table 6.3). The cost implications of printing amendment sheets have to be considered, but having a printer in the family must have been useful. Often a new line of type appears to have been squeezed into existing text. The arrangement with Glendenning between 1801 and 1843 is unclear, but it is conjectured that members of the Dillon family worked for Glendenning during this period.

**Table 6.3    Analysis of contents of W. & S. Jones trade catalogues, c.1780–1855, showing breakdown of contents by price**

|         | Date       | <£1 | £1–£5 | £5–£10 | >£10 | Total |
|---------|------------|-----|-------|--------|------|-------|
| [John]  | 1784       | 16  | 36    | 14     | 24   | 90    |
| 1       | [1793]     | 89  | 109   | 35     | 50   | 283   |
| 2       | [1794]     | 107 | 128   | 45     | 62   | 342   |
| 3       | [1795]     | 104 | 129   | 44     | 68   | 345   |
| 4       | [1797]     | 105 | 129   | 44     | 71   | 349   |
| 5       | [1797]     | 106 | 129   | 45     | 71   | 351   |
| 6       | [1797]     | 106 | 130   | 43     | 72   | 351   |
| 7       | [1800]     | 105 | 125   | 46     | 72   | 348   |
| 8       | [1801]     | 107 | 129   | 45     | 71   | 352   |
| 9       | 1804       | 103 | 131   | 45     | 72   | 351   |
| 10      | 1805       | 103 | 131   | 45     | 72   | 351   |
| 11      | 1810       | 104 | 128   | 44     | 74   | 350   |
| 12      | 1811       | 103 | 128   | 45     | 73   | 349   |
| 13      | 1814       | 101 | 155   | 67     | 87   | 410   |
| 14      | 1814       | 101 | 153   | 67     | 91   | 412   |
| 15      | Nov. 1817  | 101 | 162   | 65     | 95   | 423   |
| 16      | Jan. 1818  | 101 | 162   | 65     | 95   | 423   |
| 17      | Oct. 1825  | 100 | 157   | 72     | 94   | 423   |
| 18      | Aug. 1827  | 101 | 165   | 70     | 97   | 433   |
| 19      | 1830       | 101 | 166   | 71     | 97   | 435   |
| 20      | 1835       | 103 | 164   | 69     | 100  | 436   |
| 21      | 1836       | 101 | 165   | 69     | 101  | 437   |
| 22      | 1838       | 104 | 163   | 81     | 88   | 436   |
| 23      | 1843       | 118 | 216   | 81     | 117  | 532   |
| 24      | 1850       | 120 | 226   | 80     | 121  | 547   |
| 25      | 1855       | 119 | 219   | 78     | 124  | 540   |

Briefly, to characterize the contents of the catalogues over time: in 1794, the final two pages of the Jones brothers' catalogue were dedicated to 'second-hand instruments', but of a particularly high quality. This was material bought, after his death, from the collection of John Stuart, third Earl of Bute. In fact, as G.L'E. Turner has pointed out, W. & S. Jones were chosen to draw up the descriptions for the auction catalogue, and they subsequently purchased 13 of the lots, totalling £206 3s 6d.[116] It is evident from the sale of the business in 1860 that good second-hand instruments remained part of their stock. This same 1794 trade catalogue extolled the firm's ability to provide 'a great variety of articles too numerous to be included', following this with the information in French. Indeed, as Allen Simpson has shown, they were able to provide almost anything on demand: the Bohnenburger gyroscope mentioned earlier was one example. Another example was that of William Henry Fox Talbot's colour photometer of about 1826, described briefly by Talbot in an article in 1834, and made for the same American collector in about 1835 (Figure 6.6).[117] However, the Jones brothers did not supply only private collectors: instruments signed by W. & S. Jones could also be found in serious teaching and research collections in institutions across Europe and North America.[118]

As might be expected, some types of instrument advertised by the Jones brothers were modified and improved over time. Other changes in the catalogue record technological advances, such as the introduction of the corrected objective optics in microscopes in 1830; the invention of photography in 1839/1840; and the gradual shift of emphasis in electrical goods from recreation to something much more serious. Other instruments fell from favour: for example, the 'sagacious swan' and the 'sensitive fishes', quaint descriptions of magnetic devices offered for sale at the turn of the century (Figure 6.7), were now to be found only occasionally in collections. The category in which these had first appeared, 'Instruments for Recreation and Amusement' had become 'Instruments of Recreation' by 1805, and the entire class had been dropped from the catalogue by 1814.

Other more serious workaday instruments, which must have formed the bread-and-butter of their trade, are known to have been sold by the firm: a range of pantographs (for copying, enlarging or reducing drawings) varying from £1 16s to £6 16s 6d were offered from 1793; by 1855 their prices varied from £2 10s to £6 16s 6d. The 'new opake and transparent' solar microscope (a form of magic lantern), with 'improved apparatus', was offered in 1793 from between 12 to 16 guineas; by 1855, it was available only in the 12-guinea size. That numbers of these (and other instruments) survive in collections and are seen to pass through the salerooms regularly, is perhaps a testament to the good businessmanship of both the high profile entrepreneur William Jones, and also to his less prominent, yet equally capable, brother Samuel.

Some of the lower-priced optical items in their catalogues can be compared with those offered by the Sheffield firm of G. & W. Proctor, by looking at

---

[116] Turner (1967). See also de Clercq (2005a), who has dated the catalogue to 1795.

[117] NMS.T.1995.31: illustrated in Morrison-Low and Simpson (1995) and discussed in Simpson (1996). See also Schaaf (2004), 132.

[118] See for example, for Sweden, Pipping (1977); Ireland, Mollan (1995), and the North American examples discussed by Bedini (1964), 137, Schechner (1982), Schechner Genuth (1996) and Walters (2002).

**Figure 6.6    Talbot photometer, supplied by W. & S. Jones, London, *c.*1835**

*Source*: National Museums of Scotland, NMS.T.1995.31

the prices listed in the Proctors' 1815 pattern book and matching them with descriptions which W. & S. Jones used in 1814 (Table 6.4). The Sheffield prices are consistently lower than the London ones, and help to sustain the argument that Sheffield instruments were being retailed in London by establishments such as W. & S. Jones.

Although it may not have been typical, the Jones business was demonstrably successful – Samuel Jones left an estate worth about £25,000, equivalent to several millions today – and some of its success was due to its marketing strategy. A huge variety of material was apparently available 'off-the-shelf', and a statement that other exceptional pieces could be provided 'at good terms' implied that the Jones brothers had good contacts, whether formal or informal. With the large pool of skilled labour within London, the Jones brothers knew who could be called upon to provide extraordinary commissions, such as those required for individuals like Charles Nicholl Bancker, or for institutions such as Harvard College. But perhaps the more important trick they had up their sleeves was in the form of good lines into the printing business, both through family and friends, so that their trade

**Figure 6.7    Magnetic cabinet, including the 'sensitive fishes', sold by W. &. S. Jones, London, c.1800**

*Source*: National Museums of Scotland, NMS.T.2001.20

publications, however ephemeral in the longer term, did not cease to be regularly updated for the entire duration of their business.

In assembling a new suite of instruments for the national observatory – as in fact happened, when G.B. Airy ordered new instruments for Greenwich in the 1840s – would an observatory's governors have approached provincial instrument makers? In the case of Greenwich, the answer was emphatically negative: but this was because the long-standing pre-eminent firm of precision instrument makers Troughton & Simms was on its doorstep, or at least not far away, and Airy, as we have seen, treated members of the firm as his personal mechanics, at his beck and call. But by mid-century, Troughton & Simms were no longer the undisputed masters of their field: the more recent, and provincial, firms of Thomas & Howard Grubb of Dublin, and that of Thomas Cooke of York, both of which specialized in observatory kit-outs in the new technology of giant refracting telescopes, had

**Table 6.4   Comparison of prices of optical instruments offered by W. & S. Jones, London (1814a), and G. & W. Proctor, Sheffield (1815)**

**W. & S. Jones (1814)**

|  |  |
|---|---|
| Refracting telescopes of various lengths | 10s 6d–£1 18s 0d |
| Second best two drawer telescope | £1 4s 0d |
| Achromatic stick telescope of various lengths | £1 1s–£5 5s |
| 2' best three drawers [telescope] | £3 13s 6d |
| 5' four draw best [telescope] | £8 8s |
| 2' day and night best telescopes | £3 13s 6d |
| Achromatic perspective glasses … | 12s–£3 3s |
| 2½' achromatic telescope with stand and box | £10 10s |
| 3½' achromatic telescope with two eyepieces | £21 0s 0d |
| Common microscopes | 5s–£1 1s 0d |
| Botanical microscopes | 9s–£1 11s 6d |
| Pocket microscopes | 16s–£2 12s 6d |
| Compound microscope on common construction | £3 3s–£5 15s 6d |
| Camera obscura for the pocket | 12s–£3 3s 0d |
| Optical diagonal machines | £1 5s–£2 2s |
| Perspective views | 1s 9d each |
| Magic lanterns with various mechanical figures for phantasmagoria etc. | £1 4s to £6 6s |

**G. & W. Proctor (1815)**

|  |  |
|---|---|
| Common telescope with four glasses | 5s–12s |
| Best four glass telescopes | 6s–15s |
| Trumpet telescopes with four glasses | 8s 6d–10s 6d |
| Two draw four glass telescope | 9s 6d–11s 6d |
| One draw achromatic telescope | 14s–£1 5s 0d |
| Walking stick achromatic telescope | 12s–£1 5s 0d |
| Most portable achromatic [14"] | 6s–£1 10s 0d |
| Middle size [18"] achromatic telescope | £1–£2 0s 0d |
| Military [28"] achromatic telescope | £1 5s–£1 16s |
| Large four draw achromatic telescope [40"] | £2 12s 6d–£5 5s |
| Night and Day telescopes | £1 16s–£2 8s |
| Achromatic perspective | 12s to £1 11s 6d |
| 18" two draw achromatic telescope with stand and box | £3 13s 6d |
| 3" achromatic telescope with two eyepieces | £8 8s |
| Various common microscopes | 9s per dozen–10s 6d ea. |
| Portable trunk microscopes | £1 0s 0d |
| Pocket microscope | £1 11s 6d |
| Culpeper's pyramidical microscope | £3 13s 6d |
| Camera obscuras | 7s 6d–£2 2s |
| Diagonal mirrors | £1 5s–£1 8s |
| Coloured/uncoloured prints | £1 4s a dozen |
| Magic lanterns | 12s to £1 16s |

good and growing international reputations.[119] By 1851 the markets, which in 1760 had been concentrated in London, around the court, wealthy society and the City, had spread into the provinces: now, there were centres of local wealth which encouraged local markets; itinerant lecturers toured to entertain local philosophical societies; culture, including interest in science and its accoutrements, had broadened. Nevertheless, despite these new and growing provincial markets, London remained the centre of the instrument trade. But the competition was much stronger than it had been at the start of the Industrial Revolution, as we shall see in the following chapters.

---

[119] For a list of the Grubbs' instruments, see Burnett and Morrison-Low (1989), 113–117, and Glass (1997), appendix c; for those of Cooke, see Brech and Matthew (1997) for a list of those sold to members of the Yorkshire Philosophical Society.

# Chapter 7

# The Industrial Organization and Production of the Provincial Trade

There must have been considerable change between about 1760 and 1850 to allow even the ten instrument-making firms based outside London, identified in Chapter 1, to feel confident enough to display their goods in international exhibitions. This chapter will try to characterize these shifts in the industrial organization and production of the provincial trade. For instance, had there been significant alterations in the structure of the workforce, or marked differences in the products? Were there improvements in the tools that made the instruments? Did the changes associated with industrialization – such as removal into the factory and the application of power – so evident in the textile industries at this time, impact at all on instrument making? Returning to John Millburn's agenda for the effective investigation of instrument makers, this chapter will address the questions of the 'sources of materials and components, their tools, their relationships with their workmen, subcontractors … and each other'.[1]

## Source of Raw Materials: Brass and Glass

Instruments have been made of many different materials since medieval times, depending on customer demand, but the important basics for working instruments throughout the period of the Industrial Revolution were brass, glass and, in comparatively tiny quantities, high-quality steel.[2] As John Burnett has written:

> In the three centuries between 1500 and 1800 a wide range of materials was used in the manufacture of physical instruments. Almost all, however, were used to build the structure of the instrument, or to decorate it. Only a few were employed for what we may call the working parts. Examples of the structural and decorative substances were paper, vellum, leather, a variety of woods, ivory, and precious metals, particularly silver. For the working parts two materials had by 1800 become important beyond all others: glass and brass.[3]

---

[1]   Millburn (1986c), 84.

[2]   Wooden instruments, used in the American colonies where there was a scarcity of brass, are discussed by Bedini (1964), 65–79; in more recent times, special new materials, such as aluminium, have been used: see McConnell (1989).

[3]   Burnett (1986), 217.

Brass alone was used in the making of the earliest mathematical instruments, the oldest category of instruments to be developed. This is because brass has a number of useful characteristics, as R.L. Barclay has observed: 'It can be softened by heating, for ease of working in bending, hammering or drawing; it work-hardens producing tough, resistant components; it is free-cutting; it can be cast; it is easy to solder with both hard and soft solders; it accepts a very high polish with little labour; it tarnishes evenly to produce an attractive patina resistant to corrosion; and it is relatively inexpensive to produce'.[4]

The manufacture of brass – an alloy of copper and zinc, the latter usually from an ore known as calamine – was dependent upon the availability of the right sort of minerals. More importantly, however, it needed the right sort of energy to convert the raw materials into useful, workable metal. This required coal, which was found in abundance in the English Midlands, South Wales, North-east England and in the Forth and Clyde valleys. The treated copper and calamine ores needed to be fused at high temperatures, and this was made possible by the development of the reverberatory furnace, first used, as Martin Daunton observes, in 1612 to heat sand and alkali to produce glass: 'a tall, cone-shaped funnel produced a fierce draught when a coal fire was lit at the base; a curved dome deflected heat back on to raw materials contained in covered pots for protection from smuts and soot; and raw materials and coal were not in direct contact, so that impurities did not affect the final product'.[5]

In the 1680s, this process was applied to the smelting of copper and lead at Bristol, which in due course shifted to Swansea, which was closer to fuel sources and had ready access across the Bristol Channel to the Cornish ores that accounted for 80–85 per cent of national output for most of the eighteenth century. Copper ore was discovered in Anglesey in the 1770s, where a local attorney, Thomas Williams, secured control of the largest mines, and, as J.R. Harris has shown, briefly dominated the industry until the source was exhausted.[6] Output of copper, thanks to technological developments in mining and smelting, rose, according to A.E. Musson, from between 500 and 600 tons per annum in the early eighteenth century to about 12,000 tons in 1850, with a corresponding rise in the number of people involved in its production: by 1851, 61,000 workers were involved in the mining and manufacture of copper, lead and tin, and there were 11,000 brassfounders.[7] By the early nineteenth century, the Cornish mine owners were smelting their own ores in competition with the Swansea smelters; during the 1820s copper ore was discovered in abundance in South America and Australia, and could be imported cheaply to be smelted in Swansea.

Copper and brass became increasingly important during the Industrial Revolution: copper sheathing protected ships' hulls from worm penetration in

4   Barclay (1993), 32–3.
5   Daunton (1995), 209.
6   Harris (1964).
7   Musson (1978), 103–4.

the tropics from the late seventeenth century; copper stills brewed and distilled alcohol; and engraved copper plates were used for printing maps and illustrations. Brass was increasingly used in a wide variety of Birmingham trades, ranging from buckles to bedsteads, and was also used in the manufacture of clocks, instruments, guns, tools and aspects of some machinery.[8] As Daunton has noted: 'The development of labour-intensive hand trades in Birmingham and the Black Country, using hand-operated presses, punches, and lathes, and relying on minute subdivision into specialized trades, rested upon the availability of cheap copper and brass from the reverberatory furnaces'.[9]

By the 1860s, a contemporary account could state:

> The total quantity of copper ore raised in the United Kingdom ... amounts now to about 350,000 tons per annum, and the fine copper obtained from this to about 25,000 tons, of an estimated value of from £2,500,000 to £3,000,000 ... The principal places where brass is manufactured on a large scale, in England, are Bristol and Birmingham, brass-founding being, in fact, one of the leading trades of the latter city ...[10]

This account, which looks at a variety of metal workshops, goes on to outline the activities of one particular brassfounder, the 'Brass Foundry and Tube Works of William Tonks and Sons, Moseley Street, Birmingham', who bought-in ingots of various qualities of copper and spelter, 'principally foreign', to combine into brass, for use in different aspects of the trade. Presumably, Tonks was taken by the volume's compiler as representative of his business at that time. 'There is also a large stock of sheets of rolled brass, used for making tubes and for stamped and pressed work, and of brass wire. Both these articles are procured from mills, whose exclusive business it is to roll and draw for the trade'.[11] Good quality sheet brass had long been difficult to obtain for instrument makers: Barclay quotes the example of R.B. Gordon's examination of an astrolabe made in 1537 by the respected instrument maker Georg Hartmann of Nuremburg, from which he concludes that defects in the brass were so common that Hartmann could not afford to reject a sheet. 'It should be kept in mind that pouring ingots of the quality required for making brass sheet with a good surface finish remained a problem for brass makers up through the first part of the present century'.[12]

The quality of sheet brass was not the only problem encountered by instrument makers. Anita McConnell cites two examples of eighteenth-century London makers being unable to obtain brass bars in dimensions large enough for the instrument specified by the customer. In 1772, John Bird was constructing a pair of eight-foot mural quadrants for the Radcliffe Observatory, Oxford, and was

---

[8]   Daunton (1995), 210.
[9]   Ibid., 211.
[10]  Strauss et al. (1864), 50–51.
[11]  Ibid., 52.
[12]  Barclay (1993), 35, quoting R.B. Gordon, 'Metallography of Brass in a 16th Century Astrolabe', *Journal of the Historical Metallurgy Society*, 20 (1986), 93–6.

unable to acquire brass in such lengths from any English foundry, and was forced to import eight-foot bars from the Netherlands. Similarly, Jesse Ramsden wrote to Matthew Boulton in 1786 to ask whether he thought it possible to have English-made brass bars sufficiently long for a nine-foot radius quadrant: the quadrant subsequently delivered to the Brera Observatory in Milan was only eight feet in radius, McConnell suggests, perhaps because of these difficulties.[13]

After their supporting structures, the major component of instruments of this period is the smooth brass 'telescoping' tubes of precise internal and external dimensions that allow microscopes and telescopes to focus while in use, and compact together when not. This method was introduced during the early eighteenth century – by whom, it is not known. Allan Mills, citing Derek Price, states that the eminent London microscope maker, John Cuff, introduced an all-brass microscope in 1742, and that compound microscopes and refracting telescopes were commercially produced from about 1750.[14]

The method used for all constructing all these instruments was similar. Taking sheet metal, and silver-soldering the edges together, this initial shell would be placed on a steel mandrel and drawn, with considerable force, sometimes amounting to several tons, through a steel hole or die. The inside diameter of the tube was set by the size of the mandrel, and the thickness of its wall controlled by successive passages through dies of decreasing diameter. As Mills observes, this technique is related to wire-drawing, an activity which appears to have begun in fourteenth-century Nuremburg and was introduced to England in 1565. When polished, it is impossible to see the seam in well-made tubing; however, it is a weakness that becomes apparent if the tube is exposed to external or internal pressures, and thus 'seamless' tubing was adopted for use in steam boilers. This is made by casting the initial brass shell around the mandrel before drawing it through the die.

That the manufacture of brass tubing was regarded as a crucial component of instrument-production is shown in a specific instance of industrial espionage by the Scandinavian Jøns Matthias Ljungberg (b.1748). Between 1770 and 1780, he made three journeys to Britain, mainly to investigate newly invented textile machinery, and in 1789 he made another visit, this time primarily to investigate the pottery industry, but attracted the attention of the authorities, and his baggage – which included a large quantity of 'clockmakers' tools', a euphemism, according to D.C. Christensen, for precision tools used for scientific instrument making which were not for export by statute – was impounded by Customs. These were auctioned to cover the Customs officer's expenses, but Josiah Wedgwood was

---

[13]   McConnell (1994), 43 n27, citing for Bird: Bodleian Library, DD Radcliffe e 2, 11–14, letter from Hornsby to Wetherell, 24 October 1771; n29, for Ramsden: Birmingham Public Library, Boulton letters, MB 251, 86, letter from Ramsden to Boulton, 6 September 1786.
[14]   Mills (1990).

clearly more concerned about the fate of Ljungberg's meticulous notebooks, as he expressed in a letter to Matthew Boulton dated 24 August 1789:

> What I am now principally anxious for is, the detention of the manuscript Volume of Drawings and Remarks, which it seems has been 13 or 14 years in composing. My opinion is, that the conveyance of information, which has been collected by so sensible a man as Mr Liunberg certainly is, during so many years, may injure our manufacture very materially and irreparably.[15]

Christensen rediscovered one such intercepted volume, and amongst the information within it, is an account of Jesse Ramsden's tube-drawing machinery.[16] Although unpatented, the design was evidently one kept secret from all but the most trusted workmen. Firstly, Ljungberg bribed a worker to describe the machine, but found that this was too imprecise. So he obtained from the mechanic an engineering drawing, together with a detailed technical description of the machine: 'As far as I know,' comments Christensen, 'this drawing and description of a tube-drawing machine is the only existing piece of evidence illuminating a basic technology of production of scientific instruments left to the historian'.[17] Even so, the confiscation of Ljungberg's notebooks meant that this piece of industrial espionage was successfully thwarted.

By the time of the 1864 account of William Tonks's Birmingham brass-foundry and tube works, the national requirement for secrecy had gone (although commercial motives may have meant that individual instrument makers remained concerned to keep production techniques to themselves), made redundant to some extent by political moves towards free trade, as shown by the 1825 Machinery Act. The techniques had also evolved:

> … we proceed to the tube shop. The brass sheets procured from the rolling mills are here cut, by revolving shears, into strips of any required width; the metal is then partially curved in its length by means of a pair of rolls, and after this transferred to the draw-bench. … [It is] passed through a steel hole or a die of the required gauge, a steel plug being inserted in a position to allow the metal to pass between it and the interior of the hole. The curved end is then laid hold of with a pair of huge nippers, attached to an endless chain, drawn by steam power. By this simple contrivance the flat sheet is in a few seconds converted into a tube, which requires only soldering along the seam to be ready for use. The slicing of the sheets to any required width is effected in the same compartment, by a cutting bench or machine, with circular shears, or cutting discs, revolving in opposite directions.[18]

---

[15]  Quoted by Woolrich (1988), 37.

[16]  Christensen (1998). J.M. Ljungberg's notebook is now in Stockholm, Riksarkivet: Kungliga Myntverkets arkiv, Varia I d: Christensen also recounts how it probably came to be there.

[17]  Ibid., 7.

[18]  Strauss (1864), 45, 56.

Here, too, we must surmise, the casting of instrument parts must have been undertaken, before being sent out to the smaller workshops for assembly. Tonks & Sons' casting pattern room 'contains a bewildering number of metal patterns of every description ... there are more than 10,000 regular trade articles made by the firm, besides thousands of articles made to special order, and patterns are kept here of all of them'.[19] The entire foundry was supplied with steam power 'made to do all the work of which it appears capable, the shafting being carried into every workshop in the building ... The engine works also a fan ... supplying the necessary blast to the forges in the smiths' shops and in other departments, and also to the gas-soldering apparatus in nearly every room'.[20] Most tellingly:

> All the tools used in the establishment are made here, in the engineers' fitting room, which contains various machines for working in iron; among these may be mentioned a self-acting compound slide-rest on a screw-cutting lathe, with wheel-cutting and slotting apparatus, and a combined drilling and surfacing machine of a novel construction.[21]

Although Tonks & Sons had a finishing department in which the filing, turning, sanding, dipping, burnishing, polishing or lacquering was carried out, it appears that this firm did not undertake the complete making and assembly of instruments. Rather, it seems that they supplied cast parts or drawn tube to other small workshops, and were thus part of the subcontracting support for the trade. A slightly later description of the production of optical and mathematical instruments in Birmingham, published in 1866, is disappointing in its lack of detail or explanation, although it lists the end products:

> Mathematical instruments – the compasses, pens, sectors, &c. – have long been made in Birmingham in large quantities, but the manufacture of the commonest sorts has been much affected by the importation of cheap French and German goods, which are sold at very low rates. In consequence of the inland situation of Birmingham, nautical instruments are not produced to any great extent.[22]

In Sheffield, an eyewitness account recalling conditions in the first decade of the nineteenth century at the premises of Proctor & Beilby recalled that the brass-casting for their instruments took place there, rather than the parts being bought-in:

> William Padley was the brass caster ... the moulding and casting in 'front sand' was to me the more interesting operation, and at this Padley was an adept. And, boy as I was, I was both surprised and sorry to see him put in the melting pot shovelsfull of the fine, plump pennies of George the Third's reign, which I thought might have been

---

19    Ibid., 52.
20    Ibid., 56.
21    Ibid.
22    [Robert Field], 'Optical and Mathematical Instruments' in Timmins (1866), 534.

so much better used. But I lived to learn that each of these coins weighed nearly an ounce – while copper in the ingot was nearly two shillings a pound! And as 'defacing the coin of the realm' was a penal offence, it were probable, had Mr Caster's offense against the law been witnessed by eyes less innocent than mine, he or his employers would have got 'into a scrape!' [23]

This Sheffield 'workshop' apparently undertook the entire construction of a variety of scientific instruments and other brass items, from the casting of the brass through to finishing. In an effort to keep prices down, instruments, especially the popular telescope (of which they produced 76 variations in their 1815 pattern book) included body tubes made of wood: 'the boring and turning of the sycamore and mahogany outsides of telescopes – "wood tubes" as they were called ... These bodies, which were beautifully French polished, have mostly been superseded by brass or leather-covered tubes'.[24] The most expensive telescope thus produced, according to the (incorrectly added) scribbled costs in the pattern book (Figure 7.1):

| | |
|---|---|
| Mahogany Tube compleate | 1-1-0 |
| Brass for Telescope | 0-10-0 |
| Brass for Stand | 0-15-0 |
| Making Telescope | 1-11-6 |
| Making Rack Stand | 1-11-6 |
| Mahogany Box Wood & Work | <u>1-15-0</u> |
| Unglazed    [sic] £6-4-0 | |
| Make extra eyepiece | <u>0-2-0</u> |
| | £6- 6-0 |
| | |
| Plain mahogany or Sycamore | 0-1-0 |
| mahogany wood tubes, flowered [illeg] | 0-3-0 |
| | |
| Box with Wood & Work | 1-15-0 |

Brass Work  1-11-6
Stand - weighs 10lb - 1/6                                              <u>0-15-6</u>
                                                                           [sic] 2-6-6

The opposite page of the pattern book notes that this 'Four feet Achromatic Coelestial & Terrestrial telescope [sic]', is sold – presumably wholesale to shops such as that of W. & S. Jones in London – at 12 guineas with the terrestrial eyepiece, and 16 guineas with the celestial eyepiece.[25] As we have seen, a three-and-a-half

---

[23]   Holland (1867), reprinted by Morrison-Low (1994b), 13.
[24]   Ibid.
[25]   Sheffield City Archives, Special Collections no. 33237: Bradbury Record 293.

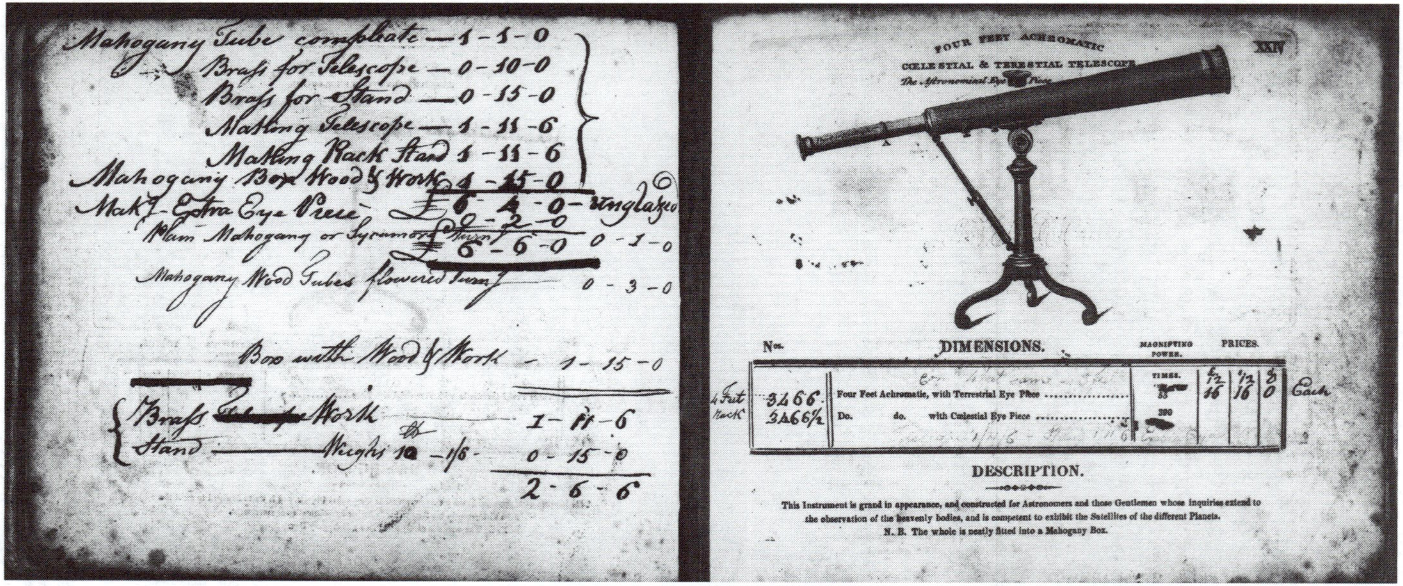

**Figure 7.1** Scribbled costs in Proctor pattern book, 1815

*Source:* Sheffield Archives

foot achromatic telescope with two eyepieces was £21, as retailed by the Joneses at this date. As in the case of Birmingham-made instruments, few Sheffield-made pieces were retailed in the place of construction, and thus few were engraved with their place of origin. The ease with which brass could be cold-engraved is the reason that the most important part of the instrument – the scale for precision measurement – was also constructed of brass and carefully divided, formerly by beam compasses, and subsequently by a dividing engine; methods which will be discussed more fully below. However, to enable such finely engraved scales to be seen clearly, these frequently had been silvered.

The other major component of scientific instruments was optical glass, used extensively in the contemporary instrument category known as 'optical instruments', and those which employed any form of telescopic or microscopic sight. Glass manufacture, like brass smelting, was another fuel-intensive industry requiring specialist plant. In the eighteenth century, the industry moved away from the local markets in London towards the coalfields, centring on St Helens and Warrington. Yet, as Martin Daunton has pointed out, coal was a less significant element in total costs than the skilled, labour-intensive working of the molten glass.[26] The problem with optical glass was not so much the supply of its raw materials as the development of the skills needed to produce it. The above-mentioned general changes in the industry affected all optical instrument makers, and were not resolved on an industrial scale until Chance Brothers imported foreign 'know-how' as late as 1848.

Good optical glass for lenses must be free of the stress features which characterize gathered, spun or rolled domestic glass, and so must be prepared in a different way. It is often described as 'crown' glass to distinguish it from 'flint' glass, which has a higher lead content and different optical characteristics. The demand for optical glass has been always a tiny fraction of the overall glass production, and it was extremely difficult to achieve, as this account dating from 1919 explains:

> The glass from which are fashioned the lenses of telescopes, field-glasses, microscopes, photographic cameras and other scientific instruments is made in a different way from any other. It is neither gathered nor poured, but left, when melted and refined, to solidify in the pot. The block that results, or fragments of it, are moulded by reheating into forms suitable for the completing work of the optician ... Messrs. Chance Brothers & Co. undertook it seventy years since [i.e. 1850], and ... they owed inception of this manufacture to Georges Bontemps.
>
> The function of the finished lenses is to refract the rays of light that traverse them. That they may perform this function perfectly the glass must be free from striae and other defects that may distort the rays in their passage. It cannot, like window glass, be limited to one simple composition; different purposes require glasses of different refractive and dispersive powers.[27]

---

[26]  Daunton (1995), 209.
[27]  Chance (1919), 171.

In proposition III, experiments 7 and 8, in his extremely influential work on *Opticks* (1704), Sir Isaac Newton had demonstrated the apparent impossibility of suppressing chromatic aberration in telescope objectives by using two lenses of different refractive indices. This had resulted in Newton turning to reflecting telescopes and abandoning the refractor. Such was Newton's reputation as a giant in scientific thought that this conclusion went unchallenged for over 30 years.[28] Innovation in telescope optics was channelled into development of the metal specula of reflecting instruments – most successfully by James Short of London, and subsequently by William Herschel of Bath and Slough, as discussed earlier.

However, in 1758, John Dollond, a practical optician, was awarded a patent for the achromatic lenses made of different-density glasses, which he had been constructing over the previous few years: these were made by cementing a convex lens of crown glass to a concave lens of flint glass.[29] In the subsequent trial over the patent, it became clear that Chester Moor Hall (1703–71), an obscure Essex gentleman who dabbled in optical experiments, had stumbled upon this idea before Dollond. In 1733, he had asked two London opticians to grind individual elements, and they had sub-contracted the task to the same jobbing optician, George Bass, who had realised they were for the same person. Yet, as Henry King points out 'news of his [Hall's] lens spread slowly among the London opticians, for none of them grasped its full significance'.[30]

On the Continent, the Swiss Leonhard Euler (1707–83) and the Swede, Samuel Klingenstierna (1698–1765), both worked out mathematical alternatives to Newton's hypothesis, but it was John Dollond's perseverance and skill with grinding and combining lens elements that provided the acknowledged success of the new lens. His telescope and a short report were presented to the Royal Society in June 1758 by his friend, the maker of reflecting telescopes, James Short, and Dollond's European reputation was established. He was admitted to the Royal Society and awarded the Copley Medal, its highest scientific distinction. Encouraged by his astute businessman son, Peter, with whom he was in partnership, John Dollond took out a patent, 'which did not,' as Daumas has observed, 'prevent people from copying him. Since he knew the truth concerning the priority of his discovery John Dollond refrained from using the means the law allowed him'.[31]

Peter Dollond was more hard-nosed, particularly after his father's death in 1761, and by 1764 33 of his business rivals had instituted proceedings to have the patent annulled, on the grounds that they were already selling the results of Hall's invention before Dollond announced it. Dollond's patent was upheld, until

---

[28]  Daumas (1972), 153. There is an extensive literature on this subject, including King (1955), 68; Bechler (1975); see also McConnell (1996).

[29]  Angus-Butterworth (1958); Derry and Williams (1960), 592; Sorrenson (2001).

[30]  King (1955), 145.

[31]  Daumas (1972), 155.

it expired in 1772, but the antecedents of Dollond's discovery – and the huge amount of bad feeling generated – were made public.[32] Yet the real problem appeared to be that optical glass was made in such tiny quantities of such variable quality that, as Anthony Turner noted, 'the best of this, Bernoulli explained, was reserved by the glass-houses for their favourite customers, the rest of the batch being sold to others. However, "... if their maker knows that one orders glass in order to imitate an invention of his country he will not be satisfied with himself unless one takes the worst possible"'.[33]

For optical use, especially for large objectives, the glass had to be perfectly homogeneous; the decomposition of carbonated alkali could produce air bubbles; flint glass, observed Daumas, 'also had the peculiarity that it often presented a gelatinous structure as a result of excess of lead oxide ... the duration of the firing had to be accurately controlled; the difficulty lay in knowing when to stop it in order to avoid the beginning of devitrification. The reaction between the lead oxide and the alumina of the crucibles caused flaws near the side walls'.[34] In addition, the glass within the crucible settled into layers, with only gatherings from the middle portion being suitable for optical purposes; as this was a wasteful method of production, only the largest glassworks could afford to undertake this sort of hit-or-miss production. Perhaps the greatest obstruction to the production of optical glass was the excise duty levied on all glassmaking, severely inhibiting the enterprise until it was repealed in 1845. As the historians of technology Derry and Williams remark: 'the constant supervision practised by the excise officers rankled with the manufacturers, and the effect of the duties themselves was tersely summed up by the economist J.R. McCulloch in 1833: "A man with 125 per cent duty over his head is not very likely to make experiments"'.[35]

In fact, innovation came from the Continent, where Pierre Louis Guinand (1748–1824), a Swiss clock-bell founder applied the technique (suggested by bell-founding) of stirring the molten flint glass in the crucible with a fire-clay stirrer, which distributed the heavy lead oxide more evenly, thus forming a much more homogenous mixture than before. This also helped to disperse the air bubbles, which increased the quality of light transmission and extended the range of flint glass density, and therefore the dispersive power. Most of this activity took place in great secrecy at the Bavarian works of Joseph von Fraunhofer (1787–1826) in the early years of the nineteenth century. After the deaths of both Fraunhofer and Guinand, the secret was purchased by the French glass-maker, Georges Bontemps (1801–82), who in 1837 agreed to share it with the Birmingham firm of Chance Brothers. In 1848, revolution forced Bontemps into exile in Britain,

---

[32]  Daumas (1972), 153–6; King (1955), 144–52; McConnell (1996), 9–1–9–4; Robischon (1983), especially Chapter IX.
[33]  Turner (1987), 222, quoting Jean Bernouilli, *Lettres astronomiques* ... (Berlin, 1777), 68.
[34]  Daumas (1972), 157.
[35]  Derry and Williams (1960), 598. Also discussed by Ashworth (2003), 254–7.

and he set up a new plant for Chance Brothers, which helped to establish them in the forefront of the production of English optical glass.[36] An account, dating from 1864, describes this process:

> One of the most important operations in these works is the manufacture of that optical glass for which the Messrs. Chance have attained a high reputation. A single melting of the material from which this is made lasts five days, during which time the metal is constantly worked in order to clear it and free it from impurities. The whole mass is then allowed to cool, and a large lump of glass is drawn out, varying in weight from 6 cwt. to 12 cwt. This mass is polished and sawn in pieces of pure glass, varying in weight from a few ounces to several hundred pounds. These are again heated in a kiln, where they are moulded into the shape of discs of the required size and thickness. The principal points to be attained are complete freedom from veins, absolute homogeneity of the whole mass, and perfect annealing so as to avoid polarization of the rays of light. Rough discs only are manufactured by Messrs. Chance. These are afterwards ground and polished by the optician and vary in value from few shillings to £1000 each.[37]

As A.E. Musson has commented, by the mid-nineteenth century the growing demand for window, plate and bottle glass, together with the relaxation on heavy excise duty, allowed the firms of Pilkington at St Helens, Chance Brothers in Birmingham, and Cookson on Tyneside, advantageously sited close to sources of chemicals and coal, to develop large glassworks. Yet, in 1851, only ten glass-making firms had a workforce numbering over one hundred, while most had fewer than ten. 'The total labour force was relatively small, only 13,000 being returned in the Census, and these were mainly handicraft workers, for even in 1870 there was only 4000 horse-power of steam in the industry.'[38] Although some developments had taken place in the optical glass industry during the time before the Great Exhibition of 1851, as we have seen output was small, severely inhibited by taxation until 1845.

### Tools and Technological Change

What were the changes in technology and tools in scientific instrument manufacture during this period? Between 1760 and 1850, unlike the textile industry, but like other metalworking industries, the manufacture of instruments was not mechanized to any great extent; rather, there were changes in organization, which will be discussed below. As Raphael Samuel has shown, hand technology continued to exist alongside mechanization well into the mid-Victorian period, where in 'metalwork and engineering ... the production process was discontinuous, and depended on craftsmanly skill. Mechanisation and steampower ... were by

---

[36] Derry and Williams (1960), 593. Also discussed in more detail by Chance (1919), chapter VIII, 'Optical Glass', and Turner (2000).
[37] Strauss (1864), 192.
[38] Musson (1978), 126.

no means inseparably linked, and a vast amount of nineteenth century work was affected by them only at second or third remove'.[39] However, there were a number of improvements to the tools used for constructing instrumentation, and these kept the London makers at the forefront of innovation, earning them a worldwide market. Daumas has discussed these in some detail, and provided some of the reasons why the momentum of improvement was not more rapid:

> ... invention and the putting of invention into effect have been given expression only when there was some chance of a new object being attained by the users. Progress required the work of skilled craftsmen, the use of materials of the best quality, and costly instruments and machinery; in other words, it required relatively considerable human and monetary capital. If the capital thus tied up were not productive – that is to say, if there were no customers – the invention would languish for lack of means. In fact, customers were not numerous; they were not always prepared to use the new invention; and their financial state was variable.[40]

Hand tools, Daumas explains, borrowed from other craft workshops, have not fundamentally varied since the introduction of good manufactured steel, at the start of the seventeenth century. These include the strap drill, the drill with crank and bevel gearing, chisels, gouges, dies, and vices. Mathematical and engraving instruments for the hand-division of circles and rulers have been in use from an early date; however, machinery borrowed directly or derived from clockmakers, was added to the set of standard tools in use. 'New tools and special methods of working were devised; these were not only soon adopted by all clock-makers, but were used in all workshops where precision work was carried out'.[41]

As Nathan Rosenberg has demonstrated, the machine tool industry grew out of the incremental demands of 'a succession of particular industries'.[42] Although made in the context of a later period in a different country, many of his observations are applicable to the tools used for creating scientific instruments during the Industrial Revolution. Rosenberg looks at how the machine tool industry grew out of the requirements for a group of what he calls 'technologically convergent' industries as apparently diverse as 'firearms, sewing machines and bicycles ... if time and space permitted, a more comprehensive account would include also a wide spectrum of machine-tool-using industries ranging from watches and clocks, scientific instruments, hardware, and typewriters to agricultural implements, locomotives, and naval ordnance'.[43] As problems were solved for one industry, it was immediately realized that the solution was applicable in another where there was a close technical relationship; and this was transmitted to them through the machine tool industry, which 'may be looked

---

[39]  Samuel (1977), 19.
[40]  Daumas (1958), 379.
[41]  Ibid., 382.
[42]  Rosenberg (1976), 14.
[43]  Ibid., 16, 18.

upon as constituting a pool or reservoir of skills and technical knowledge which are employed throughout the entire machine-using sectors of the economy'.[44]

Daumas showed that in the period up to and during the Industrial Revolution, new ideas were only slowly adopted in precision mechanics, perhaps because the materials in use were unsuitable for particular techniques, or because there was little demand. However, the instrument maker's workshop became equipped with tools borrowed from 'technologically converging' industries, such as the nascent mechanical engineering trade, and the somewhat older trades of clockmakers, locksmiths and other metalworkers. The lathe was modified in the late seventeenth-century for use by optical workers, and by clockmakers for precision metal work. Clockmakers subsequently began to use mechanically guided tools on lathes at the beginning of the eighteenth century. However, having listed improvements in lathes, screw-cutting machines and drills, Daumas adds that 'all these working methods were adopted by precision-instrument makers during the last quarter of the eighteenth century, but it is not possible to find out to whom the credit for any of these adaptations is due'.[45] It would thus appear that – as in other related industries, such as the manufacture of textile machinery, as discussed by Gillian Cookson – incremental improvements often occurred and were adopted, without either the formality of patenting or the blueprints of written description or drawings, through the expertise of the skilled workman.[46]

One of the most essential operations in the construction of instruments for the measurements of angles' wrote Daumas, 'is the cutting of an accurately threaded screw'.[47] He mentions the two designs, dating from about 1770, credited to Jesse Ramsden; and the screw-cutting lathe of Henry Maudslay, designed in 1797 and subsequently used extensively in the machine tool industry, which had its genesis in Ramsden's published work. Recently, this area of precision mechanics has attracted the attention of a number of instrument historians, who have undertaken extensive fieldwork on surviving examples. Randall Brooks notes that 'there were few makers capable of making screws well above the standard of the day'. He continues:

> Bird's micrometer screws, despite having been hand-made and of coarser pitch, could match or surpass in accuracy those made by Ramsden on his screw lathes during the overlapping periods of their careers. Ultimately, Ramsden's lathes achieved better accuracy. Testing the screws of the dividing engines (*c.*1762) by the Duc de Chaulnes (1714–69) in the Istituto e Museo di Storia della Scienza (Florence) has shown that the skill of Chaulnes surpassed all previous screw makers – including Ramsden. Tests of Maudslay's screws have proved that his reputation as a fine screw-maker was justified. In his experimental screw taps and dies in the Science Museum can be seen the germs

---

44   Ibid., 19.
45   Daumas (1958), 386.
46   Cookson (1994), especially Chapter 4; Cookson (1996).
47   Daumas (1958), 386.

of Joseph Whitworth's (1803–1887) standards, which is not surprising since Whitworth was associated in his early years (1825–3?) with the firm of Maudslay and Field.[48]

Even more complex was the problem of mechanically dividing the graduated silvered-brass (or in the case of earlier nautical instruments, ivory) limbs of instruments or rules. Daumas remarks that previously methods had evolved slowly, over centuries, 'but it took only some forty years for dividing-engines to be adopted in all workshops'.[49] Before this breakthrough, all division had to be done by hand, and could be done to an extremely high standard, perhaps reaching its peak with the mid-eighteenth century London maker, John Bird. The Board of Longitude, 'pursuing its brief to encourage the development of precision instrument-making', as John Brooks remarks, rewarded Bird for the publication in 1767 of his *Method of Dividing Astronomical Instruments*.[50] Within ten years, however, Jesse Ramsden had

> ... despite the limited means available to him for precision machining ... found a precise and elegant means to ratch the teeth of his large wheel so that they matched both the division marks and the screw. In doing so, he constructed one of the first screw-cutting lathes with lead screw and change wheels, although in this he was anticipated by Hindley. Ramsden also introduced many other features, one of the most conspicuous being the ratchet mechanism which enabled the engine to be worked by treadle.[51]

Allan Chapman has traced the history of the mechanized dividing engine back to a machine probably intended for horological gearing, described in Robert Hooke's diary for 1672. Although 'it had been a failure as a method of original division, its basic principle reappeared 70 years later, when Henry Hindley of York used a wormwheel to rotate the denticulated dividing plate of what became the first moderately efficient dividing engine'.[52] Hindley has been mentioned earlier as a clockmaker, but it is apparent from what little is known about his work that he was highly competent in instrument making and precision mechanics. As Chapman states:

> Hindley himself was no failure, being a Freeman of the City of York, a leading provincial clockmaker, and a respected citizen. Though his occasional ventures into instrument making were not crowned with much commercial success, it must be remembered that, within the increasingly specialized world of the eighteenth century, he was not an instrument maker ... Hindley, furthermore, seems to have made no attempt to establish himself as an instrument graduator ... with the exception of enlisting [John] Smeaton in the attempt to sell one of his equatorial telescopes, Hindley made no effort

---

48  Brooks (1989): summary provided in Brooks (1989a), quote 8.
49  Daumas (1958), 388.
50  Brooks (1992); hand division, 106–8.
51  Ibid., 130.
52  Chapman (1995), 124–5.

to break into the London trade. As a maker of fine clocks in Yorkshire, his market was quite different from that of the mathematical instrument makers of Fleet Street.[53]

Both of Jesse Ramsden's dividing engines used endless screws, and were recognised by contemporaries as being of outstanding design: they both won government prizes. Chapman observes that although the designs cannot be linked definitively with Hindley's machine, yet there were connections:

> Though Ramsden was neither apprenticed nor worked in the precision trades whilst resident in Yorkshire, he was nonetheless a native of Halifax and was probably aware of the work of his elder contemporary at York. But a more positive connection can be established through John Stancliffe, who first worked for Hindley in York before entering Ramsden's employ following his migration to London. It was Stancliffe, no less, who is alleged to have revealed to Ramsden the principle of the Hindley cutter and maybe other features as well. In 1788, Stancliffe was said to have built his own engine, though nothing is known of its performance.[54]

This would appear to be a transfer of technology through the practical skills of an intermediary, from Yorkshire to London, rather than the expected movement from the capital to the provinces.

Ramsden's first machine, completed in 1767, did not entirely satisfy its creator; he went on to produce a second dividing engine. This won a prize of £615 from the Board of Longitude, not because it was in itself a method of finding the longitude, but as Chapman explains, it was a way of simplifying a part of the method. With Ramsden's machines, the new nautical sextant could be produced in larger quantities, because it speeded up the method of division, which no longer needed be the highly skilled performance that it had been. As a condition to the reward, Ramsden published a description of his machine in 1777, 'to enable any intelligent workman to construct and use engines of the same kind', and for two years, Ramsden was charged with training ten apprentices in its use, as a condition of the prize.[55]

The development of the dividing engine in the ensuing century, with improvements by the Troughtons, William Simms, James Allen and Andrew Ross, has been discussed in detail and at length by both Chapman and John Brooks. However, the significance of Ramsden's engine was indicated in the *Edinburgh Encyclopaedia* in about 1815, and lay in the fact that 'there may be ten or twelve [dividing engines] in London, generally copies of Ramsden's second engine'.[56] It is not known whether there were any in the provincial centres at this date, and if so, who had them, other than the example announced in Edinburgh in 1793,

---

[53]  Ibid., 127.
[54]  Ibid., 130.
[55]  Ibid., 130; Brooks (1992), 102.
[56]  Quoted in Chapman (1995), 134; Brooks (1992), 102.

as previously noted.[57] It is possible that, on the watch-finishing model, nautical instruments were sent to London to have their scales divided before reaching their point-of-sale, either in the metropolis, or in a port elsewhere.

Other innovations in the manufacture of instruments occurred on the optical glass side. As we have seen, glass was produced in some quantities around the country for use in the building trade, but its status as a luxury commodity attracting increasing taxation also inhibited development of machinery as well as investigation and exploitation of its chemical composition. As A.E. Musson has observed, quoting T.C. Barker, the industry remained heavily dependent on imported skilled craftsmen, and when new methods of production were introduced these were usually of foreign origin. 'But,' remarks Musson, 'although the original processes and skills were mostly French, British glass-makers made significant improvements in their large scale industrial development, especially in coal-fired furnaces, in mechanical grinding and polishing and in the application of steam power'.[58] Such investments in improved plant were made even where there was only a small demand, an example being John Holland's description of the optical glass manufacture in the early nineteenth-century Sheffield premises of Proctor & Beilby:

> ... Thomas Stovin the glass caster ... melted pieces of broken glass – more valuable in those days than now – on a red-hot iron plate; then, with a spotula [sic], transferred the plastic mass to a mould under a screw press, out of which it came ready for grinding as a 'spectacle eye.' ... then there was the still more important and curious operation of glass grinding, comprising the production of lenses of every size and curve, from the hemispherical 'bull's eye' of the magic lantern to the convex or concave 'spectacle eye' ground in or upon 'tools' of a large radius. Surtees, in his History of Durham, claims for the town of Darlington the credit for having invented 'the machinery for grinding optical glasses.' Whatever that may mean, I have always understood that the method of grinding them 'by power' – of water or steam – was first practised on the Rivelin by Samuel Froggatt, who afterwards went to London, and established at Hackney-Wick one of the largest glass-grinding works in the world.[59]

This priority dispute over the introduction of power machinery into grinding optical glass is difficult to resolve: Robert Surtees claimed a Darlington textile machinery patentee, John Kendrew, as the undated inventor, who on this occasion at least did not take out a patent.[60] However, members of the Froggatt family of

---

[57] The Edinburgh instrument maker John Miller had obtained or built a circular dividing engine by 1793: see Clarke et al. (1989), 30, quoting the *Caledonian Mercury,* 31 December 1793.

[58] Musson (1978), 126.

[59] Holland (1867), reprinted in Morrison-Low (1994b), 13.

[60] 'It should be observed, that Mr John Kendrew, an inhabitant of Darlington, was the ingenious inventor and patentee of the machinery for spinning flax, hemp, tow, &c. now of such importance to the manufacturing interest ... Mr John Kendrew was also the inventor of an ingenious machine for grinding and polishing spectacle and other optical glasses, which is now in general use': Surtees (1823), 360.

Sheffield opticians migrated to London, as Holland described, and there was a 'Froggatt's Mill' in Hackney Marshes on maps dated 1831 and 1836.[61] In 1850, Henry Mayhew recorded the following statement in London from a camera obscura maker, which doubtless describes the Proctor & Beilby establishment:

> I have known the camera obscura business for twenty-five years or so; but I can turn my hand to clock-making, or anything. My father was an optician, employing many men, and was burnt out; but the introduction of steam machinery has materially affected the glass grinding – which was my trade at first. In a steam-mill in Sheffield, one man and two boys can now do the work that kept sixty men going.[62]

Unlike the glass-grinding of later years, done to mathematically-devised spherical curvatures, it is apparent from Holland's description that lens-making in provincial England was based on a more empirical approach:

> I need hardly say that the 'glazing' or fitting the higher class of instruments with glasses was in no degree scientifically conducted: of the doctrine of optics, in the abstract, the men and women engaged, of course, knew nothing. They knew that a telescope was called a *chromatic*, which had a compound object glass; and they could measure, in a rude way, the focal length of the lenses used; so that by adhering to a special formula, they succeeded in practically producing a good telescope, the test of which was its revelation of the figure on a watch face fixed on chimney half a mile off. As to microscopes, Beck had not then won his fame as a maker, nor Pritchard his reputation as an observer.[63]

Indeed, even by the mid-nineteenth century, the production of glass lenses – whether for spectacles, telescopes or microscopes – was (at least for the mass-market) left to the hands of unskilled female labour:

> This trade [optical and philosophical instruments] is extensively carried on in Sheffield, and in its various processes affords the visitor opportunities of witnessing highly ingenious applications of machinery to manufacturing purposes. This is especially the case in the grinding of lenses and glasses for telescopes, microscopes, spectacles, &c., many thousands of which are produced every week at the manufactory of Messrs. CHADBURN Brothers, by whom the process was courteously exhibited and explained to us. The glasses are cut out of the required size with a diamond, and the corners

---

[61] 'Plan of the parish of St. John at Hackney … from an actual survey made by order of the Vestry by W.H. Ashpitel' (n.d., *c.* 1831); Greater London Record Office [GLRO]: THCS/P/12, Tower Hamlets Commission of Sewers, large scale atlas of Hackney, surveyed by James Beek, *c.* 1836. A Samuel Froggatt appears in the Hackney Sewer Rate books as early as 1818, and is mentioned in the Census of 1821. My thanks to Dr Anita McConnell for this information.

[62] Thompson and Yeo (1973), 355.

[63] Holland (1867), reprinted in Morrison-Low (1994b), 18. Richard Beck (1827–66) and Andrew Pritchard (1804–82) were pre-eminent makers of achromatic microscopes in mid-nineteenth century London.

are then nipped or broken off with plyers. This branch of the work is performed by females, and an experienced hand will nip or round from sixty to eighty gross per week. The glasses are then taken to the grinding room, where they are placed by women on concave or convex dishes, technically called 'blocks,' which will hold from six to twelve dozen glasses, according to their sizes. The glasses are attached to these dishes by means of pitch, and the dishes so prepared are placed on a machine which causes a number of blocks, constantly supplied with emery and water, to travel over them in regulated curves. The radius and curve of the tool are graduated to the focus of the glass, the magnifying power being increased or diminished by shortening or lengthening the curves or radii. When the glasses have been ground into the required form on the one side, they are smoothed with the finest emery, and polished with a preparation of the oxide of iron. They are next subjected to the same process on the other side, and are then ready to be put into the frames of spectacles. Machine-ground glasses are better polished, and are superior generally to those ground by hand, while the cost of production is reduced by 75 per cent.[64]

The change that has taken place here, and been remarked upon, is one of scale: moving up from a small production unit to a larger one, with initially water-power, and subsequently steam-power, on hand. However, the quality of the finished product – now put together by unskilled female labour to a formula requiring neither literacy nor numeracy – still seems to have been good enough for an uncritical expanding market. Together with the growth in unit sizes of production, there were corresponding changes in the organization of the industry.

**Organization of Workshops and the Development of the Factory**

What happened to the organization of the instrument trade during the Industrial Revolution? There exist a number of accounts dating from after this period of transition, describing provincial premises and what occurred on them, such as the one by John Holland quoted above. In particular, there are two descriptions dating from the 1890s describing the interior of famous and substantial instrument works: one of Grubb in Dublin, and the other of Kelvin & White in Glasgow.[65] It is apparent from both of these that by the end of the nineteenth century, all of the very different processes that went into constructing any of a variety of items which can be described as scientific instruments, were under one roof. How had this happened? What defined a factory at this earlier period? It was not merely a large building in which power was laid on, so that the workforce was compelled to change its earlier work patterns to produce a particular commodity, although for the textile industry in particular this is how it came to appear in the popular imagination.[66]

---

64    Billing (1858), 30.
65    Fitzgerald (1896); Anon. (1898).
66    Tann (1970), 3–7, 27–29.

Even so, the factory building can also serve as the explanation of why this change had occurred. Through technological necessity, innovations in textile manufacture had obliged manufacturers to move from a domestic economy into a more centralized form of production, and this created a workforce which was bound 'by the impersonal forces of wage labour, their pride in old craft skills having been beaten out of them by the relentless march of the machine'. But in fact, as Roderick Floud goes on to demolish his own caricature, by the 1851 Census, half of the 'men' employed by 'masters', were in establishments of fewer than thirty employees.[67] As we have already seen, unskilled female labour was there to undertake the more repetitive tasks by this date, counted or not by the Census enumerators.

Even in the seventeenth century, women were not excluded completely from crafts or trades, and while unmarried women had a measure of independent economic status, the position of married women was that they assisted their husbands, and could assume their positions in business upon widowhood, subject to certain restrictions.[68] Ivy Pinchbeck claimed that by the late eighteenth century 'the craftsman's wife was usually so well acquainted with her husband's business as to be "mistress of the managing part of it," and she could therefore carry on in his absence or after his death, although she herself might lack technical skill'.[69] Indeed, in technical trades, 'a widow usually engaged able workmen to assist her, whilst retaining the management in her own hands'.[70] As Robert Shoemaker and Mary Vincent have pointed out:

> The problem of change and continuity in the history of women's work has much exercised historians, ever since the classic works of Alice Clark and Ivy Pinchbeck introduced the argument that, in England, women's work opportunities were far more equal to men's before fundamental changes in the structure of the economy (the spread of capitalism in the seventeenth century, according to Clark, and the industrial revolution, according to Pinchbeck) pushed them out. While such arguments continue to be influential, they have been rejected by some historians who have stressed the continuities in women's exclusion from the more prestigious jobs, arguing that the so-called 'golden age' of women's work posited by Clark and Pinchbeck never existed.[71]

[67]   Floud (1997), 111.
[68]   Clark (1982), 150–235.
[69]   Pinchbeck (1981), 282–305, especially 284: 'It is only when we come to the skilled artisan and trading classes, however, that we find women still taking a share in their husbands' concerns as a matter of course, and in almost every trade innumerable instances can be cited of widows and single women in business'.
[70]   Ibid., 285.
[71]   Shoemaker and Vincent (1998), 349.

In an important article, Katrina Honeyman and Jordan Goodman suggest that the pattern of women's work is underpinned by two systems, which they define as 'the sex-gender system' and 'the economic':

> historically, these systems have interacted, sometimes in opposition and confrontation, at others in unison to create a specific gender division of labour ... The sex-gender system and its principal component, patriarchy, remain in the background so long as changes within the economic system do not impinge on the operation of the system. But when changes in women's economic position threaten to upset the equilibrium of the sex-gender system, the response of the patriarchal component is to establish a new set of rules defining the acceptable gender division in the workplace.[72]

Only twice between 1500 and 1900 have these two systems come into conflict, say Honeyman and Goodman; one of these protracted occasions being the Industrial Revolution.[73] Maxine Berg and Pat Hudson have demonstrated that the number of women working and the types of jobs they performed expanded during the early years of the Industrial Revolution, contracting after 1850. That this was not previously recognized was owing to the deficiency of the contemporary sources.[74]

As is the case today with many small family businesses, the wife's role was often hidden until she was forced through her husband's death or bankruptcy to assume a more visible role. Perhaps an important part of the work of an instrument maker's wife was to 'keep the books', actually to run or maintain the finances of the business for which her husband made or assembled the stock. Trading could continue with the widow employing journeymen after her husband's death, and certainly in an earlier period when the guild structure in London was more effective, a widow was held responsible for the training of existing and new apprentices. Michael Crawforth has commented that there

> are several implications consequent to the succession of a widow. It suggests that her husband had been running a business in which she had been involved to such an extent that she could continue the business. The training of apprentices infers the employment of at least one journeyman with formal training in the industry, and the approval of the guild officials in binding an apprentice to a widow indicates their confidence that she could reasonably be expected to continue in business for at least seven years.[75]

Widowhood could bring with it privileges not otherwise accessible to single or married women: property rights, the trusteeship of children and apprentices, and responsibilities which would otherwise have been exclusively male.

The reasons why individual women went into business are seldom known, but it would appear from most of the examples found in the provincial directories

---

[72] Honeyman and Goodman (1998), 367.
[73] Ibid.
[74] Berg and Hudson (1992), 35–8; Hudson (1992), 225–30.
[75] Crawforth (1987b), 331.

that widows would carry on their late husband's firm, probably because they were already involved and could offer some form of continuity, sometimes to allow a young son time to grow up and enter the trade. One such example is that of Elizabeth Rabone, née Smith, described as a rule-maker, of Snowhill, Birmingham, widow of Michael Rabone who died about 1803; their son John took over the business in 1817 at the age of 22. During his mother's trusteeship, the firm was called Elizabeth Rabone until 1808, and Elizabeth Rabone & Son from then until 1817. Even so, Mrs Rabone continued to be listed as a rule-maker until 1835, so she must have retained an interest in the firm's affairs after her son assumed his father's position as head of the business.[76]

Other examples show the enterprise of daughters: Mary and Ann Dicas were both daughters of John Dicas, who was a Liverpool liquor merchant and has been mentioned in Chapter 2. His hydrometer (Figure 7.2), a device for measuring the specific gravity of liquids and therefore of interest to the Excise, was patented in England in 1780,[77] and adopted in 1790 by the United States government for estimating the strengths of imported liquors. In London, a Board of Enquiry of the Royal Society was set up in 1802 to investigate the rival merits of a number of different hydrometers then in use throughout the British Isles, with a view to choosing the most effective for revenue use by the Excise. Because her father had died by this time, Mary Dicas submitted his instrument, travelling to London to explain its principles before the Board.[78] She must, therefore, have had some degree of technical understanding. She appears in the street directories as a hydrometer maker in her own right from 1797 to 1806, and the following year with George Arstall, a scale beam maker, whom she married. Ann Dicas, her sister, appears as a patent hydrometer maker between 1818 and 1821, and after her marriage to Benjamin Gamage in May 1821, he became the 'only proprietor of the patent'.[79]

Former apprentices who married their masters' daughters could find themselves inheriting a profitable business; but while it is fair to say that marriage was considered more of an economic contract than it is today, it is not possible to say whether it was entirely mercenary.[80] Two immigrant Italian barometer-making families, that of Casartelli based in Liverpool, and Ronchetti based in Manchester, appear to have intermarried in at least two generations, with

---

[76]   Hallam (1984), 17–20.

[77]   English patent 1259, 27 June 1780, 'Constructing hydrometers with sliding-rules, to ascertain the strength of spirituous liquors, malt worts, and wash for fermentation'.

[78]   Tate and Gabb (1930), 7–8.

[79]   For the trading enterprises of the Dicas, Arstall and Gamage families, and their premises in Liverpool and Manchester, see Morrison-Low (1996).

[80]   See, for example, Davidoff and Hall (1987), 321–9 and the chapter 'Marriage' in Thompson (1988), 85–113.

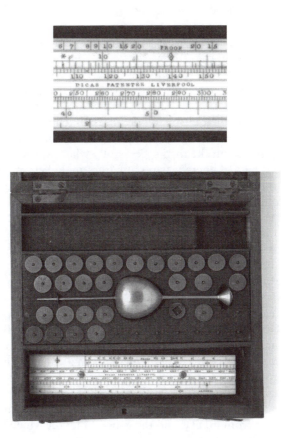

**Figure 7.2    Dicas hydrometer, by Dicas, Liverpool, *c*.1800**

*Source*: National Museums of Scotland, NMS.T.1980.107

implications for the inheritance of their businesses.[81] In this particular instance, and no doubt, with other immigrant Italians, a common religion also played a part in keeping the business within the extended family. Thus through the act of marriage, it is possible that women played a central, but invisible, role in cementing

---

[81]    Wetton (1990–91), 48; ms. copy of 'Brief History of the Firm of Joseph Casartelli & Son', dated August 1915, in Manchester Museum of Science and Industry: 'After some time Baptist Ronchetti Meringio sent to Italy for his son Charles Joshua Ronchetti and also for his nephew Louis Casartelli … In 1851 Jane Harriet Ronchetti marries Joseph Louis Casartelli, of Liverpool, and the latter succeeds Charles Joshua Ronchetti at 43 Market Street [Manchester]'.

and extending a close-knit scientific and business community, thereby ensuring the cultural reproduction of trade knowledge.

Throughout this period, women were evidently much involved in the instrument trade. Their roles, however, varied immensely. The most readily identifiable women were those running a business, since they were listed in trade directories. But often they took over only when widowed, usually whilst a youthful son and heir completed his apprenticeship. The unseen role that they may have played before their husbands' deaths is difficult to assess, but if they had a long-term involvement in the financial side of the business this would certainly have enabled them to run the firm successfully when widowed. The succession of running a business, if there was no apparent male heir, might pass through a female heir to her husband's family. A number of instruments engraved with an apparent woman 'maker's' name survive, but whether the woman in question ever turned at the lathe, or fitted or adjusted the optical parts, is a matter for speculation. Other women, less readily identified by name, drew glass, worked in the cabinet shops, and generally undertook less skilled work.[82]

Apart from being a family enterprise, the other network that might have drawn people into the business was religion. However, this does not appear to have often been the case, although there were Quakers who were also instrument makers – for instance, in the early period, the royal clockmaker Thomas Tompion (1638–1713), his apprentice George Graham (1675–1751) – who married into Tompion's family - and Daniel Quare (1649–1724), maker of royal barometers. Despite being London clockmakers, all are known to have made mathematical instruments, and, given the common ground between the two trades at this date, precision clockmaking can be seen as a specialist subsection of mathematical instrument making. Arthur Raistrick makes the point that the Quaker 'simplicity of living, and moderation in spending, freedom from luxury, and the general literacy which found relaxation and pleasure in learning and pursuit of knowledge … made it easier for them to apply much of their abundant returns to experiments in the processes of their trade, and to promoting the welfare of their employees'.[83]

However, religious persuasion does not appear to have worked as a network in the same way that family connections operated. A later enterprise with Quaker roots was that of the Irish telescope makers, Thomas and Howard Grubb, but it is not clear that they remained non-conformists, and Howard certainly married a member of the established church.[84] The incidental knowledge of an instrument maker's religion does not appear to add significantly to our understanding of other networks which may have had a bearing on the overall operation of the trade: the Dollonds, immigrant Huguenots, did not work within a Huguenot community. Nor did the Birmingham Carpenters, all Unitarians, work exclusively within a Unitarian network, although the entire family clearly took their religion

---

[82]  Morrison-Low (1990).
[83]  Raistrick (1950), 221–42, 339.
[84]  Glass (1997), 10.

seriously.[85] The Roman Catholics appear to have been mostly recently-arrived immigrant Italians, attracted to the new industrial centres as well as London, some of them en route to the United States; again, as with the Jews, most appear to have worked with people culturally like themselves when family ties failed. Yet most provincial instrument makers were apparently nominal members of the established church (they can be found in church registers) and the trade as a whole formed a cross-section of religious convictions.

**Workshop Production**

The changes within the workshop during this period are difficult to quantify. The division of labour has only ever been hinted at by instrument historians, primarily because of lack of evidence. John Holland's account confirms this practice in the Sheffield manufactory of Proctor & Beilby:

> I may remark that the variety of articles manufactured was very great, comprising generally telescopes of all sorts, from the four feet achromatic on brass stand, to the little simple spyglass of a few inches in length; and microscopes … But besides articles which might be called *optical* in a sense more or less strict, the workshop turned out an immense quantity of other things: two may be mentioned, viz., tinder-boxes and inkpots … These articles being made of brass, were all polished by old Daniel Vaughan … Microscopes of all sorts, as well as various optical and other knic-knacs, were mostly made by Dickey Hobson, a Birmingham man, who was accounted an excellent user of a file ….[86]

Particular individuals had specific tasks, although the output of the firm was clearly extremely varied:

> There was a systematic distribution of work throughout the establishment, one man being mostly employed on a special class of articles, in the making of which he acquired great dexterity. Each, too, had his own 'side,' or work-board, and 'engine,' as his lathe was called, about which were arranged 'chucks' of all shapes. Prime, as a workman, was George Hadfield; and not less remarkable as a toper than a turner. I used to wonder at the desperate dash with which, after his weekly drunken fit, his trembling hand applied the tool to a brass-casting, used in the successful production of large 'day and night' telescopes. John Holland [the author's father] was also employed in similar work; and his brother Amos, in making accurate imitations of the 14, 18 and 27 inch telescopes of the celebrated Dolland [sic].[87]

Holland names the workman identified with the production of each particular instrument through the workshop: William Eggington with 'trumpet' telescopes; Johnny Coe with reading glasses, although formerly employed in producing

---

[85]  J. Estlin Carpenter, 'Introductory Memoir' in Carpenter (1888).
[86]  Holland (1867), reprinted in Morrison-Low (1994b), 11–12.
[87]  Ibid.

sundials, while 'of the spectacle makers I remember but little, though they formed a broad feature in "the works" – their "templets," "visuals," "noseys," and "goggles," being produced gross upon gross'.[88] As with W. & S. Jones in London, the large numbers of spectacles sold helped to underpin the cost of constructing other, less profitable optical instruments.

Many of the circumstances of these people's working lives are what one would expect from evidence from other trades, such as the methods used by the employers to tie the men to their particular business through what Holland described as 'stuffing', elsewhere called 'trucking'.[89] Also, the very rural aspects – the bee-keeping, the cows, the bird-fanciers – meant that the employees were kept aware of the seasonal cycle, in a way similar to the better-documented case of the hand-loom weavers, whose work on their small-holdings appears to have been seasonal.[90] All these details seem obvious when stated; but Holland's first-hand account provides direct confirmation to augment what have previously only been scattered clues about the nature of the daily lives of workers in the provincial scientific instrument trade.

Holland's description of the social aspects of workers' lives included their bleaker side. Like all good Victorians, he was by 1867 concerned with the 'excessive drinking' of his colleagues, in his retrospective view. The temperance movement first appeared in the north of England in the early 1830s, initially as an attempt to reform the drinking habits of all classes. It has been commented that during the 1820s: 'it was among the skilled craftsmen, with their exclusive initiation ceremonies, that drink customs had their strongest hold'.[91] Similarly, by 1867, Holland could see with the benefit of hindsight how godless the shop floor had been. He regretted the lack of education and literacy of his co-workers at a time when, as another eminent historian has put it:

> almost the entire skill or 'mystery' of the trade was conveyed by precept and example in the workshop, by the journeyman to his apprentice. The artisans regarded this 'mystery' as their *property*, and asserted their unquestionable right to 'the quiet and exclusive use and enjoyment of their ... arts and trades'.[92]

Education, both for the skilled and the unskilled, was to come only much later.

Although Holland had started life as an optical instrument maker, he subsequently moved into journalism, contributing three volumes to Dr Dionysius Lardner's *Cabinet Cyclopaedia*. This was a cheap and popular work consisting of 133 volumes produced between 1829 and 1849, aimed at those who could not afford the expense of a *Britannica*. Holland's writings for Lardner were on the manufacture of metals – two volumes were concerned with iron and steel, while

---

88  Ibid.
89  The system in Sheffield is discussed by Leader (1905), 109–12.
90  E.P. Thompson (1968), 297–346, discusses the 'myth of the golden age'.
91  Harrison (1971), 40.
92  E.P.Thompson (1968), 279.

the third treated other non-ferrous metals, including brass. These also discussed the uses to which the finished metal might be put. In a chapter discussing the manufacture of 'Optical Instruments', he wrote the following paragraph, which perhaps sums up the essence of his later 1867 articles:

> During the century which followed the invention of telescopes, a proper share of the attention of the philosophic world was directed to the improvement of the instrument. It is, however, little more than within about fifty years since [i.e. since *c.*1785] that the progress of scientific investigation, together with the cheapness of brass, as well as economical and improved methods of fabrication, laid the foundation in this country of an extensive trade in telescopes and microscopes of all descriptions, along with a vast variety of apparatus for philosophical purposes, in which brass is the principal material. Thus, while the more opulent patrons of the science gratified their taste by the purchase of unique instruments at any price from the first makers, the curiosity, and indeed the convenience of the public in general, created a considerable demand, to meet which, *ingenious workmen were set to produce, according to established data, instruments, the theory of which the manufacturer sometimes little understood, and still seldom extended beyond the articles so successfully copied, in vast quantities for the metropolitan houses, and presently, for more direct sale on their own accounts.* [My italics.] Not only in London, but in Birmingham, and particularly in Sheffield, the business of optician has been carried on with success; at the latter place there existed, between thirty and forty years since, the largest optical manufactory in the world; so extensive, indeed, were the operations, that the power of the steam-engine was applied to the grinding of glasses, a process which, as there conducted, is one of the most interesting that a stranger can witness. There are, at present, some extensive works of this description in the last-named town; and there, as well as in other places, instruments, at the sight of which some of the old scientific investigators of this and other countries would have felt no little surprise, are daily produced in a beautiful style at exceedingly low prices. The combination of neatness, efficiency, and cheapness has led to the almost universal possession of some one or more articles of this class.[93]

The italicized passage in the above quotation, describing how Midlands entrepreneurs initially produced, in large numbers, instruments to satisfy the demands of the buoyant London market at the lowest prices, only later selling material on their own account, is central to our understanding of the rise of provincial instrument manufacture. Here, spelled out, is contemporary confirmation of what several instrument historians have long suspected – not everything with a famous London signature was necessarily made in that workshop. Long before the Midlands manufacturers marketed their instruments overtly, they had captured a substantial slice of the London market, and were manufacturing on an industrial scale.

---

[93] Holland (1834), 260–61.

# Chapter 8

# Supply

Manufacturing desirable consumer products in the provinces for good economic reasons was only a first step: somehow these had to be brought to the attention of the would-be customer, who then had to be persuaded to purchase. John Millburn identified 'marketing techniques' as one aspect of instrument making which had barely been studied.[1] At the start of the period under discussion, there were two principal markets for the provincial trade: the local one, which was never large; and the London one, into which the greater part of the provincial output must have anonymously vanished, to reappear inscribed with a 'London' address or signature. In 1851, the London journalist Henry Mayhew (1812–87) wrote:

> An experienced tradesman said to me: 'All these low-price metal things, fancy goods and all, which you see about, are made in Birmingham; in nineteen cases out of twenty at the least. They may be marked London, or Sheffield, or Paris, or any place – you can have them marked North Pole if you will – but they're genuine Birmingham. The carriage is lower from Birmingham than from Sheffield – that's one thing.'[2]

The London market acted as the gateway to the international market. There is some information on the methods of supply to both these markets, but very little about pricing arrangements, particularly wholesale versus retail costs.

Market demand will be examined in greater depth in Chapter 9, but it is not possible to discuss marketing strategies without first defining what that market might be. With industrialization came a number of changes in the economic climate that helped both local and international markets to grow. The revolution in transport meant that, with increasingly improved internal communications, it became possible to move manufactured goods from the growing industrial cities in the Midlands and the North to the marketplace in London, and from there to captive imperial markets overseas.

Not only were instruments a part of that traffic, but they also helped to shape the transport revolution itself: the armies of surveyors who mapped these islands for valuation purposes were succeeded by younger generations who surveyed the landscape with a view to altering it with cuttings and embankments for canals, roads and subsequently, railways.[3] Overseas, parts of the Empire were surveyed

---

[1]   Millburn (1986c), 84. Although this was the case in 1986, more has been produced in this area, especially Crawforth (1985); Anderson et al. (1990); Bryden (1992).

[2]   Mayhew (1861), 333.

[3]   Bendall (1997), 55–8.

and linked together: the growing Royal Navy – Britain was at war for much of the period of the Industrial Revolution – and merchant navy both needed instruments to navigate their ships into safe harbours. There were 12,464 ships registered in the United Kingdom in 1788, rising to 15,734 in 1800, 20 253 in 1810 and 21,869 in 1815; thereafter numbers remained at about 20,000 until the end of the 1830s; then, after a gradual rise, by 1851 there were 26,043 vessels.

Each of these ships would have required at least two sextants or octants, a compass, and a chronometer.[4] Government contracts for the supply of instruments, usually awarded to London instrument makers, were eagerly sought after: for instance, the supply of standardized hydrometers to the Excise. The competition for this was held in 1802, and ten makers from throughout the United Kingdom responded.[5] In order to satisfy this rapidly increasing demand for instruments, the London makers enlarged their local subcontracting circles in Clerkenwell, before turning to metal-workers elsewhere, who were able to turn their production skills from more general manufacture to something more specific; and just such workers and conditions were to be found in the rapidly expanding towns of Sheffield and Birmingham. Demand for nautical instruments, and especially the skills necessary for their repair, generated this type of service in Bristol and Liverpool – it would have taken too long to send an instrument back to London for adjustment.

Public interest in science had grown, reaching new audiences, and permeating down the social scale.[6] The growth in literacy meant that provincial newspapers reports of events in the capital led to the local emulation of cultural events in London. The popularisation of science by travelling lecturers, such as those seen in the vivid paintings of Joseph Wright of Derby, were increasingly noted in the newspapers of the larger market towns.[7] The geographical circuits covered by individuals could be country-wide, while their subjects encompassed much of natural philosophy and were accompanied by lecture demonstrations.[8] Some of these, notably Benjamin Martin (1704–82) and James Ferguson (1710–76), marketed instruments by publishing their lectures in textbooks; catalogues of available instruments would be listed at the end of each volume.[9]

Increasing numbers of provincial literary and philosophical societies were founded, often acquiring their own suite of demonstration apparatus along with

---

4    Numbers from Mitchell (1988), 535–6. For the chronometer, see Davies (1978).
5    Tate and Gabb (1930), 1–13; McConnell (1993a), 9–18; Ashworth (2001) and (2003).
6    There is a considerable literature on this subject: good bibliographies are given in Inkster and Morrell (1983), and Averley (1989).
7    See Schofield (1963); Fraser (1990); Porter (2000).
8    See, for instance, Harrison (1957), who re-creates an Edinburgh-based itinerant lecturer's career covering America, Ireland and the English Midlands, principally traced from provincial newspapers. See also Morrison-Low (1992).
9    For Martin, see Millburn (1976), (1986a) and (1986b); for Ferguson, see Millburn (1988b).

collections of natural history or antiquarian content.[10] With the rise of a consumer society, aspiring members of the middle classes would be happy to acquire the cheaper products of the instrument-makers' workshops: small eyeglasses (too low-powered to be graced with the name 'telescope'), simple magnifying glasses or 'microscopes', or basic box cameras obscura to assist one's clumsy daughters learn the gentle art of sketching.[11] The catalogues of instrument retailers demonstrate that these could be supplied, at prices to suit the new consumer.

After the Napoleonic Wars, public interest in science moved beyond the middle classes to the level of the artisan: the founding of the Mechanics' Institutes in the 1820s provided further lecture circuits on a national scale. This movement was fostered by philanthropic middle-class interests, among them the Society of Useful Arts, founded earlier in 1754, which besides providing premiums for useful inventions, began a series of exhibitions in London from 1760 and in the provinces from the 1840s. The British Association for the Advancement of Science, in its peripatetic annual meetings, held from 1831, soon began to stage displays of 'philosophical instruments, models of invention, products of national industry' from their first exhibition in Newcastle-upon-Tyne in 1838.[12] These were the native precursors of the Great Exhibition of All Nations, held in London in 1851, which reinforced British belief in the success of imperialism, while advertising her commercial expertise to markets overseas.

There was also a series of national exhibitions held by the post-revolutionary French government to encourage manufacturers to improve their products commercially: eleven of these were held between 1798 and 1849, and clearly had some impression, albeit unacknowledged, on the mid-nineteenth century British exhibition movement.[13] During this period, instruments were peddled in the streets, sold in shops, and generally brought to the attention of a wide range of potential customers. To do this, there developed a supply chain of wholesalers, retailers and agents, promoting the methods by which provincial instrument manufacturers managed to attract the attention of customers, so that by the time of the Great Exhibition they were no longer entirely reliant on London middlemen.

---

[10] Brears (1984); Torrens (2003).

[11] Warner (1998b), esp. 48–9, produces a considerable quantity of information about low-cost London-made telescopes, mostly from late eighteenth-century advertisements. Although she appears to take much of this at face value, she does admit that 'it is also likely that some opticians manufactured instruments for the trade – that is, instruments that were sold by, and even with the signature of, another "maker"'.

[12] *Catalogue* ... (1838).

[13] Turner (1989), 24; Beauchamp (1997), 10–11.

**Getting Instruments to the Point-of-Sale**

How were instruments made available to customers during the period of the Industrial Revolution? Changes in retailing during this period helped to open up new markets by stimulating demand, by creating what Martin Daunton has called 'a constant market drawing goods from a wide range of suppliers.'[14] From the late seventeenth century, hawkers and pedlars carried a small number of goods to regularly held markets or fairs, or touted them around the countryside. In a detail of the 1824 painting of 'St. James's Fair, Bristol', by Samuel Colman, an unidentified stallholder offers an hourglass to a woman admiring herself in a mirror, while in the background a pair of globes and two barometers can be seen amongst the items for sale (Figure 8.1).[15] As late as the mid-nineteenth century, hawking remained a method of selling instruments outside the largest cities: in a Scottish example, the Dundonian instrument maker George Lowdon wrote:

> There was when I commenced business [in 1850] no regular manufacturing optician in Dundee. One Balerno, who lived in Yeaman Shore, and another, Antony Tarone, who had his house in Murraygate, gave themselves out as 'barometer and mirror makers'. The former hawked his goods about the street, and usually had a barometer under one arm.[16]

Another earlier example of such a peripatetic hawker was the Italian Peter Rabalio, based in Birmingham for a time, but whose trade card (Figure 8.2), printed in Worcester in about 1790, stated that:

> Mr RABALIO informs the Public, That whoever has bought, or buys a Barometer of him, he will warrant to be good, and will repair them Gratis, at the Sign of the Barometer, in Edgbaston-street, Birmingham; in Coventry, at the Sign of the Dolphin; in Leicester, at the Sign of the Golden Lion, in Hamston Gate; and in Worcester, at Mr Dewce's, in High-street, near the College-Gate.[17]

Rabalio's peregrinations around these Midland towns can be traced in the local press, where he advertised his arrival, and before his departure from Birmingham he offered his stock for sale by lottery.[18] Jenny Wetton comments on the conviction in 1823 of a Manchester man, Jeanno Cocino, servant of the barometer maker Antonio Peduzzi, for hawking Peduzzi's wares without a licence: Peduzzi took no responsibility for his servant's actions, and so Cocino went to

---

[14] Daunton (1995), 270.
[15] Greenacre (1973), 203–6.
[16] Quoted in Clarke et al. (1989), 147.
[17] Trade card at the Whipple Museum of the History of Science, University of Cambridge.
[18] *Aris's Gazette*, 2 June 1788; 9 March 1789; 10 and 17 August 1789; 29 September 1789; he died in Italy at the end of 1790: ibid., 10 January 1791. An angle barometer signed 'No 572 RABALIO Fecit' was offered for sale by Phillips, 18 July 2000, Lot 48.

**Figure 8.1   Samuel Colman,** *St. James's Fair, Bristol,* **1824: detail**

*Source*: Bristol City Museums and Art Gallery/Bridgeman Art Library

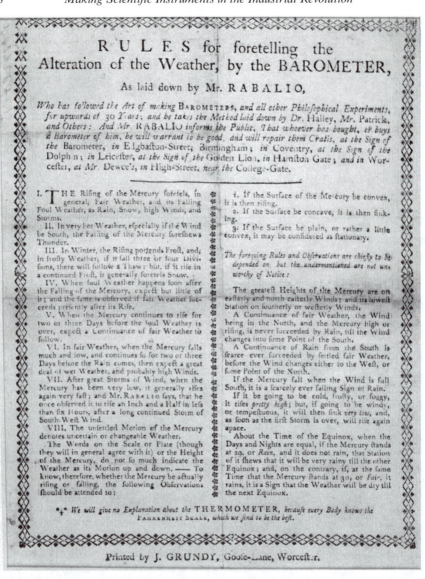

**Figure 8.2    Peter Rabalio's trade card, *c.*1790**

*Source*: Whipple Museum of the History of Science, University of Cambridge

prison for three months.[19] The economic historian Neil McKendrick discusses at some length the 'many other unsung heroes in the spread of [this] fashion to a new market of consumers – the new class of itinerant salesmen and the provincial shopkeepers'.[20] He highlights the obscure figure of the 'Scotch Draper' or 'Scotch Pedlar', who 'specialized in the products of the new industrial centres ... sold on credit ... [and] had his special area in which he called on his customers every week for cash by instalments.' McKendrick concludes that 'without the service of these new itinerant salesmen much of the provincial market would have been stifled for want of opportunity to buy'.[21]

By the mid-nineteenth century, Henry Mayhew reckoned that 'during the last century, and for the first ten years of the present, the hawker's was a profitable calling', and found that the Census return for 1841 gave a total of 17,270 hawkers for Great Britain.[22] He also devoted a section to 'cheap-Johns', or hawkers peddling hardware goods manufactured in Sheffield or Birmingham (not always honestly, as stolen, over-priced and misrepresented wares were common) around the country and on the edge of the capital, and another to the 'swag-shops of the metropolis', or wholesalers. These contained cheap goods to be resold on the street, and amongst 'the useful and the "fancy" goods' included 'Spectacles ..., Telescopes – one, two and three draws [and] Mathematical Instruments'. Mayhew detailed these further: '... dials and clocks, combs, optics, spectacles, eye-glasses, telescopes, opera glasses, each 10d to 10s ...'.[23] He calculated that there were 150 'swag-shops', and that half of these were 'the warehouses described by their owners as "Birmingham and Sheffield" or "English and Foreign", or "English and German". It is in these ... that the street-sellers of metal manufacturers find the commodities of their trade'.[24] Mayhew spoke to an employee of one of the largest and most longstanding of these establishments:

> ... about 200 'hands' are employed, in the various capacities of salesmen, buyers, clerks, travellers, unpackers, packers, porters, &c., &c. ... In one week, when my informant assisted in 'making up the books', the receipts were upwards of £3000.[25]

Mayhew calculated the profit on this £3000 at 35 per cent. Several of the manufacturers based in Sheffield and Birmingham known to have produced instruments, advertised themselves as 'Wholesalers'. For instance, Peter Frith & Co. appeared in the Sheffield directories from 1814, in the Birmingham directories between 1818 to 1825, and in the London directories from 1822. Frith maintained London premises into the 1870s, with a named agent from 1838. In

---

[19]  Wetton (1990–91), 41.
[20]  McKendrick (1982), 86.
[21]  Ibid., 88–9.
[22]  Mayhew (1861), 376.
[23]  Ibid., 335.
[24]  Ibid., 336.
[25]  Ibid., 336.

the Birmingham directory for 1818 the firm was described, not as instrument makers, but as 'manufacturers of bronzed copper, fire proof and other powder flasks, improved shot belts, shot chargers etc. etc. etc. Sheffield, and at No. 6 Cross-street, Hill-street, Birmingham. J. Godfrey agent' J. Godfrey appears in his own right in the Birmingham directory from 1823 until his death in 1842 as a 'manufacturer of all kinds of spectacles etc.' By 1860, 'Peter Frith & Co., wholesale opticians, of 81 Arundel Street, Sheffield and 5, Bartlett's Buildings, Holborn, established 1790', were taking large advertisements in the Birmingham street directories (Figure 8.3).[26]

From these examples, it can be seen that there was a reasonably complex supply chain. One of the difficulties in understanding these advertisements is the language, as there was no legal or enforceable compulsion to tell the truth, especially in advertisements: for instance, Frith's claim, cited above, to have been 'established 1790' when there is no trace of the firm before 1805, is merely made to give the venerability (and by implication, integrity) of age. Firms claimed to be 'real' manufacturers, 'makers', or 'working opticians' in order to try to make the distinction between themselves and retailers; but as Michael Crawforth has pointed out, the name marked on an instrument was a form of free advertisement, and gave the impression, 'not unintentionally', that the owner of the name had made the instrument.[27] It is evident, however, that by the mid-nineteenth century, wholesalers were supplying many retailers who had no making skills themselves. This is a situation which can be traced back in time to the 1760s at least, when a number of the London shops were merely retailing premises.

The role of the agent, based in another city, often London, geographically remote from the manufacturing centre, was important to the firm, although his full purpose remains unclear: was he securing orders, or protecting credit? That such agencies may have acted as retail premises for instruments manufactured in the Midlands is supported by the existence of items with provincial 'names' and London 'addresses' (Figure 8.4).[28]

As T.S. Ashton wrote in his classic account of *The Industrial Revolution*, 'large-scale production required not only division of labour and specialized appliances, but also the support of an organized system of transport, commerce and credit.'[29] Even before the period under discussion, there had been improvements in

---

[26]  Sheffield and Birmingham street directories, *passim*.
[27]  Crawforth (1985), 477–8.
[28]  For example, National Museums of Scotland, inv.no. NMS. T.1993.119: small single draw telescope, signed 'Frith, London'; NMS.T.1993.120: small three draw telescope, signed 'Proctor, Beilby & Co., London'; a Culpeper microscope, signed 'Proctor, Beilby & Co., London', was offered for sale by Christie's South Kensington, 16 September 1982, Lot 81; another microscope, signed 'G. & W. Proctor, London', was offered for sale by Sotheby's, 23 June 1987, Lot 209. Frith had London premises from 1838, but that of Proctors has not been located.
[29]  Ashton (1968), 34.

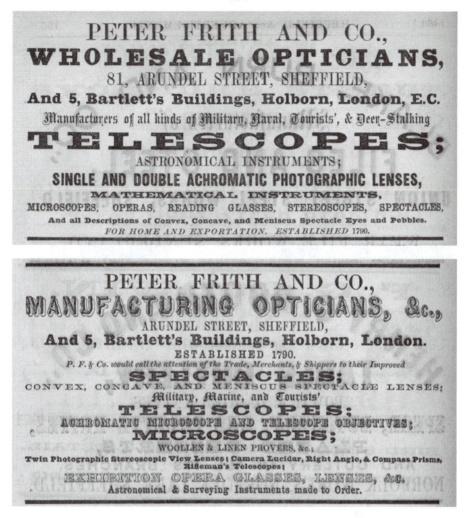

**Figure 8.3    Advertisements for Peter Frith & Co., from Birmingham directories, 1860 and 1865**

*Source*: Birmingham Library Services

**Figure 8.4    Two telescopes with provincial 'names' and London 'addresses',
c.1830**

*Source*: National Museums of Scotland, NMS.T.1993.119 and 120

communications between London and the provinces, producing a more integrated economy: 'investment in roads and the greater efficiency of stagecoach services and road carriers made road transport "a dynamic force in agricultural marketing in the century before 1850"'.[30] Indeed, the idea of a 'transport revolution' as a necessary concomitant to the revolution in industry now rests less on the heroic ages of new canal and railway construction than on general improvements in all forms of transport.

Martin Daunton suggests that 'the crucial point for understanding the chronology of British economic growth [was when] transport costs [fell] sufficiently to make a difference to specialization and competition'.[31] He mentions the piecemeal, unspectacular achievements of the predecessors of the great engineers, who 'devised better road surfaces, altered the design of coaches, modified the rigging or hull design of sailing ships, or improved access to harbours and rivers', and points out that the more modest sums invested in these improvements may

---

[30]  Hudson (1992), 77, quoting J. Chartres, 'The Marketing of Agricultural Produce', in J. Thirsk (ed.), *The Agrarian History of England and Wales* vol. V (Cambridge, 1985), 446.
[31]  Daunton (1995), 285.

well have repaid bigger dividends than the 'investment of large sums in impressive feats of engineering'. The real revolution was not merely in solving the technical problems, but in producing a new infrastructure that could organize investment in change. Thus, investment in the canals, turnpikes and coastal shipping improved these networks, while producing changes in organization and efficiency, and this was continued by the railways: 'above all, investment in transport reduced transaction costs in the economy'.[32]

Yet the 'impressive feats of engineering' mentioned above brought with them armies of the practical users of instruments, and the solution of the 'technical problems' involved produced variations on the types of instrumentation. Both surveying and navigation are intensely practical professional activities. While some of the increased demand for more accurate surveys, or for finding the longitude at sea, or being able to measure the alcohol content of spirits, came from government (and will be discussed more fully in the following chapter), other markets were to be found in the professions themselves, while they were making possible the changes in Britain's internal transport infrastructure.

### Shops, Advertisements and Trade Literature

What methods were used to attract the attention of potential buyers of scientific instruments? As we have seen in Chapter 6, purchases of off-the-shelf items, as reported by visiting foreigners, could be made in shops in London from at least the early eighteenth century. As John Millburn noted, 'Though not such a localized trade as (say) silk-weaving or clockmaking, the instrument makers tended to congregate along the main shopping streets from Cheapside to Charing Cross; Fleet Street in particular was a favourite location'.[33] D.J. Bryden has examined the advertising material concerning mathematical instrument making in London from 1556 to about 1714, and concludes that 'advertising was aimed at informing professional users from whom particular instruments could be purchased, but not on informing customers in specific terms of the range of instruments manufactured ... until the early eighteenth century most mathematical instruments were commissioned. Only [then] ... is there evidence of over-the-counter sales, and advertising aimed at encouraging the growing consumer market to buy mathematical instruments for the practice of science as a social or recreational activity'.[34]

It would appear that buying off-the-peg instruments for pleasure was a part of that 'consumer boom', in which 'those making and selling such consumer goods ... as a result of their earnest commercial endeavours, played a substantial and a

---

[32] Ibid., 285–314.
[33] Millburn (1986c), 82.
[34] Bryden (1992), 301.

positive role in bringing [these changes] about'.[35] The rise of fashion, and other aspects of consumer demands, will be examined in the following chapter; but there were also developments on the supply side, especially in marketing, in particular those pioneered by the master potter, Josiah Wedgwood, and his contemporary in the manufacture of metal goods, Matthew Boulton, as demonstrated by Neil McKendrick.[36]

McKendrick shows that both these entrepreneurs aimed to reach the 'middling' people: 'like Wedgwood, Boulton sought royal and aristocratic patronage to give a lead to the rest of society in the confident knowledge that social emulation would ensure emulative spending in the rest of society'.[37] Some of the greatest figures in the kingdom owned and used scientific instruments: the King himself (unusually for his family) was extremely interested in astronomy and practical mathematics, and owned a large cabinet of them, and he ensured that the royal children were instructed in scientific demonstration by a special tutor.[38] The third Earl of Bute (1713–92), perhaps the most significant politician of his generation and a considerable influence on the young George III, put together an important collection of outstanding instruments, although these were subsequently dispersed at auction in 1793.[39] Patronage of this nature was exploited by the instrument makers, some of whom held royal appointments; perhaps most famously, by the London maker, George Adams the elder, although as John Millburn has shown, these appointments were not always as truthful nor as well regulated as today.[40]

Naturally, this patronage phenomenon occurred first in the capital. However, by the early nineteenth century the advertisements of even relatively obscure provincial instrument makers proclaimed royal and noble customers: for example, Alexander Alexander of Exeter produced an improved drawing device, the 'Graphic Mirror', and in 1834 claimed in advertising the patronage of 'the King, the Duchess of Kent & Princess Victoria' (his brother was a physician in attendance at Kensington Palace); other advertisements for this device and others were more muted (Figure 8.5). By 1851, the Sheffield opticians Chadburn Brothers proclaimed their patronage by H.R.H. Prince Albert, while their rivals, J.P. Cutts, a few streets away stated that they were 'by special appointment optician to Her Majesty' (Figure 8.6). Jacob Abraham, who had shops in the fashionable spa towns of Bath and Cheltenham just before the accession of Victoria, declared on his trade card that he was 'Optician and Mathematical Instrument Maker to His R.H. the Duke of Gloucester and His Grace the Duke of Wellington'.[41] Whether

---

[35]   McKendrick (1982), 2.
[36]   McKendrick (1960); Robinson (1963); McKendrick (1982), 69–78.
[37]   Ibid., 71.
[38]   Morton and Wess (1993); Ackermann and Wess (2003); Anderson (2003).
[39]   Turner (1967); Morrison-Low (1995a).
[40]   Millburn (1991).
[41]   Crawforth (1985), 493, 491 and 500; Calvert (1971).

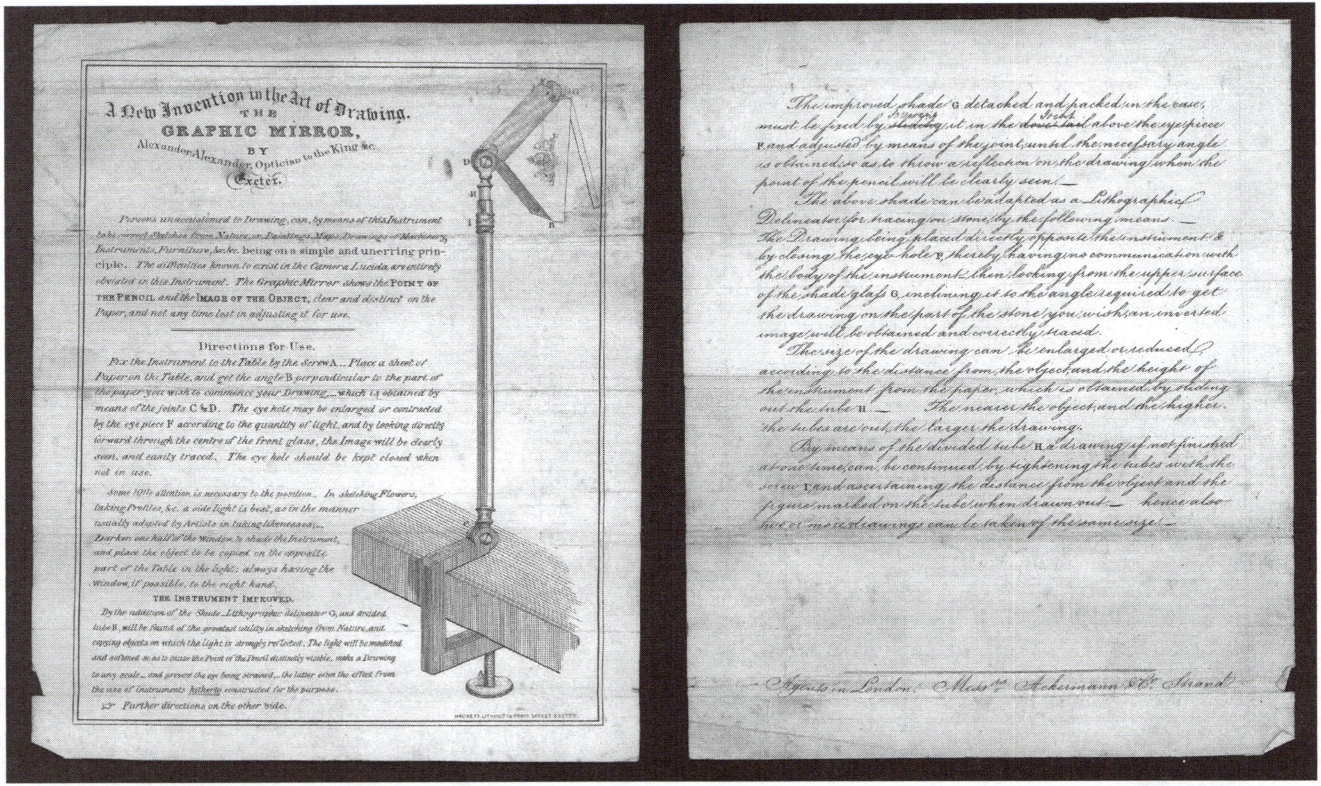

A New Invention in the Art of Drawing.
THE
GRAPHIC MIRROR,
BY
Alexander Alexander, Optician to the King &c.
Exeter.

Persons unaccustomed to Drawing, can, by means of this Instrument take correct Sketches from Nature, or Paintings, Maps, Drawings of Machinery, Instruments, Furniture, &c.&c. being on a simple and unerring principle. The difficulties known to exist in the Camera Lucida are entirely obviated in this Instrument. The Graphic Mirror shows the POINT OF THE PENCIL and the IMAGE OF THE OBJECT, clear and distinct on the Paper, and not any time lost in adjusting it for use.

Directions for Use.

Fix the Instrument to the Table by the Screw A.. Place a Sheet of Paper on the Table, and get the angle B perpendicular to the part of the paper you wish to commence your Drawing,_which is obtained by means of the joints C & D. The eye hole may be enlarged or contracted by the eye piece F according to the quantity of light, and by looking directly forward through the centre of the front glass, the Image will be clearly seen, and easily traced. The eye hole should be kept closed when not in use.

Some little attention is necessary to the position.. In sketching Flowers, taking Profiles, &c. a side light is best, as in the manner usually adopted by Artists in taking likenesses;_ Darken one half of the Window to shade the Instrument, and place the object to be copied on the opposite part of the Table in the light; always having the Window, if possible, to the right hand.

THE INSTRUMENT IMPROVED.

By the addition of the Shade_Lithographic delineator G, and divided tube H, will be found of the greatest utility in sketching from Nature, and copying objects on which the light is strongly reflected. The light will be modified and softened so as to cause the Point of the Pencil distinctly visible, make a Drawing to any scale_and prevent the eye being strained,_the latter often the effect from the use of instruments hitherto constructed for the purpose.

☞ Further directions on the other side.

The improved shade G detached and packed in the case, must be fixed by screwing it in the joint above the eye piece F and adjusted by means of the joint, until the necessary angle is obtained so as to throw a reflection on the drawing when the point of the pencil will be clearly seen.—

The above shade can be adapted as a Lithographic Delineator for tracing on stone, by the following means.— The Drawing being placed directly opposite the instrument & by closing the eye-hole F, thereby having no communication with the body of the instrument_then looking from the upper surface of the shade glass G, inclining it to the angle required to get the drawing on the part of the stone you wish, an inverted image will be obtained and correctly traced.

The size of the drawing can be enlarged or reduced, according to the distance from the object, and the height of the instrument from the paper, which is obtained by sliding out the tube H.— The nearer the object, and the higher the tubes are out, the larger the drawing.

By means of the divided tube H, a drawing if not finished at one time, can be continued by tightening the tubes with the screw I and ascertaining the distance from the object and the figure marked on the tube when drawn out.— hence also two or more drawings can be taken of the same size.—

Agents in London: Mess.rs Ackermann & Co. Strand

**Figure 8.5 Alexander Alexander of Exeter's description of the Graphic Mirror, *c.*1835**

*Source*: National Museums of Scotland, NMS.T.1994.27

this was true or not – the provision of a Royal Warrant was not well controlled at this period – it clearly held immense snob appeal.[42]

**Figure 8.6    Trade card of Charles Henry Chadburn, Liverpool, manufactory Sheffield, *c.*1845**

*Source*: National Museums of Scotland, NMS.T.1979.71

McKendrick demonstrated 'how new methods of display excited not only occasional impulse buying, but more sustained and regular buying than could have possibly occurred without them'.[43] As Dorothy Davis has shown, during the early stages of the industrial revolution, shop premises were to be found mainly in fashionable parts of London and subsequently in the main thoroughfares of growing cities outside.[44] 'They were almost invariably small, independent shops, owned and run by the shopkeeper on the spot … Shopkeepers were regarded as skilled men – skilled, that is, in their particular trade and no other.'[45] The shop premises of the instrument trade contained material made by the shopkeeper,

---

[42]   Millburn (1991), 2.

[43]   McKendrick (1982), 97.

[44]   Davis (1966), 252.

[45]   Ibid., 255–6.

but also by other suppliers: 'where to buy, from wholesalers or manufacturers or individual craftsmen, how to bargain with them for the right purchase and mix ... a stock suitable to their particular custom – these formed, as always the most important and the most difficult part of their skill in any trade'.[46]

Thus, 'shopkeeping' then was as complex a business as it is today. For instance, in Liverpool in 1795, an advertisement by a retailing wholesaler states: 'Robert Preston has on sale at his wholesale commission warehouse in Lower Castle street, Port, Madeira ... Turnery Wares, Brushes, Brass Wares and Furniture, Optical Instruments, Coffin Furniture, Carpenters', Shoemakers', and Smiths' Tools ...',[47] all of which would be bought by eager Liverpudlian consumers. But these wholesale premises were to give way to specialist shops, often, McKendrick asserts, using 'new methods of advertising [which] excited a new eagerness to consume, and made known and desirable goods which would otherwise languish unbought'.[48]

Using trade cards, inventories, plans and contemporary comment as evidence, Claire Walsh has shown how the design of London goldsmiths' shops in the early eighteenth century played an important part in the marketing techniques of the retailer.[49] Unfortunately, few instrument makers' trade cards illustrated their premises, although some are known. One London example illustrates the interior of Thomas Blunt's establishment in about 1800 at 22 Cornhill, and 'shows a shop with two windows displaying an octant, telescope, protractor, spectacles, microscope, and many other items unrecognizable because of their small size', comments Michael Crawforth (Figure 8.7).[50] Walsh explains that goldsmiths put high-value items into 'show-glasses', which were glass display cases which could be either hung in the window or outside the shop where they were placed to attract the attention of passing customers: the glass fronts were an attempt at preventing the expensive, and usually small, contents from being stolen. It would appear that instrument shops also used these to attract passing custom. A paragraph in a Bristol newspaper in 1758 reveals that:

> Last Wednesday, at six o'clock was stolen from the shop window of John Wright, Mathematical instrument Maker, St. Stephen's Lane, a glass case two feet four inches by one foot eight inches, containing about 12 dozen steel bow spectacles, 3 dozen metal ditto, 1 dozen or upward of temple ditto, 7 cases opera glasses, some neat vellum draw'd ditto, 3 hydrostatic instruments, tortoiseshell books, 1 silver name piece, (John Wright, Maker, Bristol) Capt. James McTaggart engraved upon it, with divers other things.[51]

---

[46] Ibid.

[47] *Gore's Liverpool General Advertiser*, 23 July 1795.

[48] McKendrick (1982), 97.

[49] Walsh (1995).

[50] Crawforth (1985), 482. The card is from British Museum, Ambrose Heal Collection, 105.14.

[51] *Bristol Weekly Intelligencer*, 25 February 1758.

**Figure 8.7   Trade card for Thomas Blunt, London, showing interior of the shop, c.1800**

*Source:* © The Trustees of the British Museum: Ambrose Heal Collection, 105.14

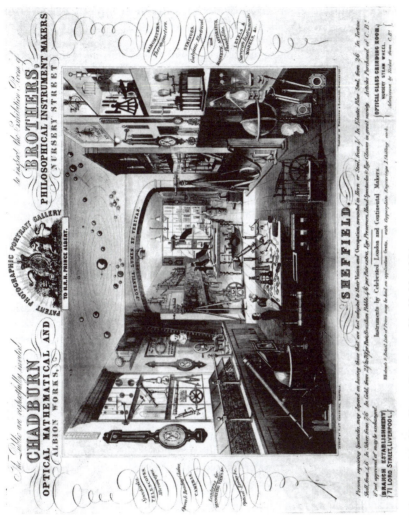

**Figure 8.8   Advertisement for Chadburn Brothers, Sheffield, 1851**

*Source:* © National Museum of Science and Industry

Another interior, produced for the Great Exhibition in 1851 (Figure 8.8), is as Crawforth comments, 'the frequently reproduced interior view of the Chadburn Brothers' shop in Sheffield ... [which] shows a great many instruments in recognizable detail ... it seems justifiable to assume that the firm sold everything that was illustrated'.[52] Although no description of a London instrument maker's shopfloor has been found from the mid-nineteenth century, there is a fictional description of a shop interior, given by perhaps the most famous and prolific novelist of his day, Charles Dickens (1812–70), in 1848:

> Just around the corner [from the premises of Dombey and Son] stood the rich East India House ... Anywhere in the immediate vicinity there might be seen ... little timber midshipmen in obsolete naval uniforms, eternally employed outside the shop doors of nautical Instrument-makers in taking observations of the hackney carriages.
>
> Sole master and proprietor of one of these effigies ... and proud of him too, an elderly gentleman in a Welsh wig ....
>
> The stock-in-trade of this old gentleman comprised chronometers, barometers, telescopes, compasses, charts, maps, sextants, quadrants, and specimens of every kind of instrument used in the working of a ship's course, or the keeping of a ship's reckoning, or in the prosecuting of a ship's discoveries. Objects in brass and glass were in his drawers and on his shelves, which none but the initiated could have found the top of, or having once examined, could have ever got back again into their mahogany nests without assistance ....[53]

Exterior views are more common, although even they number a mere handful. That of Alexander Mackenzie's London premises, dating from about 1822, is dismissed by Crawforth as 'a commonplace shop'.[54] A series of sketches of the exterior of Philip Carpenter's Regent Street shop has survived from the mid-century,[55] while the bill-head of D. Cohen in Newcastle-upon-Tyne shows a corner site on a major thoroughfare.[56] Ambrose Heal comments that in general, for London 'in the nineteenth century illustrations of shop fronts became a much more common feature of the tradesmen's cards, and the transition from the old-fashioned shop fronts, which persisted into early Victorian times (as shown in Tallis's Street Views of 1838) down to the present day [1925], can be traced.'[57] Outside the capital, trade cards of the Gardner business of Glasgow, and of that of Rowland of Bristol, show the exteriors of their respective shop premises.[58] The illustration of the Rowland card shows the pertinent shop sign – the Quadrant – and the windows crammed with a large variety of items, which

---

[52]　Crawforth (1985). The original is in the Science Museum collection.
[53]　Dickens (1970), 88.
[54]　Crawforth (1985), 482; British Museum, Heal Collection, 105.69.
[55]　Delehar (1989).
[56]　Crawforth (1985), 482, British Museum, Banks Collection, 105.11.
[57]　Heal (1925), 29.
[58]　The Gardner image is illustrated in Clarke et al.(1989), 165; the Rowland card is in the collections of the Blaise Castle House Museum, Bristol, inv. no.T8303.

presumably could be bought over the counter; significantly, the penultimate line of the advertisement states that 'old instruments [are] bought, sold or exchanged', and this may have formed a substantial part of the shop business (Figure 8.9). The Rowland business was at this address from 1805.

For provincial producers, the first apparent evidence for commercial activity is the appearance of advertisements in the local press. As with trade directories, the appearance of these has to be treated with some caution: presumably, not everything advertised was instantly available, nor was it necessarily constructed on the premises but could be bought-in, perhaps from London. For instance, John Wright's initial advertisement in the Bristol press in 1756 offered 'in Silver, Brass, Ivory, Wood, &c.' a huge range of devices from demonstration pieces such as orreries, practical instruments such as theodolites and quadrants, mathematical instruments such as rules and sundials, philosophical instruments such as air pumps and barometers, and optical instruments, including telescopes, microscopes and 'Magic Lanthorns'. Wright was, however, insistent on his abilities as a maker, stating that 'Gentlemen, upon signifying the Plate and Figure of any Instrument in *Desaguliers, Gravesand,* or other Authors, may be served therewith, or have any Model or Instrument made according to their own Contrivance' (Figure 8.10).[59] Both J.T. Desaguliers (1683–1744) and W.s'Gravesande (1688–1742) were promoters of Newtonian physics, with richly-illustrated textbooks in many editions to their names.

The growth of the provincial press during this period provides examples of advertisements for instrument makers, such as Wright in Bristol, moving out from London to try to tap into local markets. As seen in earlier chapters, other examples were John Leverton in Liverpool in 1766; Richard Eggleston in York in 1740; and Joseph Oakley in Birmingham in 1758; and the cachet of being 'from London' was used in advertising to denote quality, for instance by William Holliwell of Liverpool, for whom no London connections have been uncovered.[60] However, Sheffield instrument manufacturers in particular rarely bothered to advertise in their local press, and this suggests that their immediate markets were not local.

Other instrument makers remained based in London, but used the time-honoured and fruitful connection between printing and the instrument trade to get their wares out into the country. As seen in Chapter 2, John Wright had set up in his Bristol business for less than a year when the London opticians, James Ayscough and Henry Gregory advertised that 'they have furnished Mr JAMES TEAST, Bookseller in *Cork-street*, with a large assortment of Telescopes, *Hadley's* and *Davis*'s Quadrant and other Instruments for Use at Sea'. John Wright appears to have been warned about this before publication by the newspaper proprietor, and his own advertisement, just below theirs, is over twice as long.[61] John Brewer has noted a bookseller in eighteenth-century Rye, Sussex, selling

---

[59]  *Felix Farley's Bristol Journal*, 13 March 1756.
[60]  Calvert (1971), 26.
[61]  *Felix Farley's Bristol Journal*, 4 December 1756.

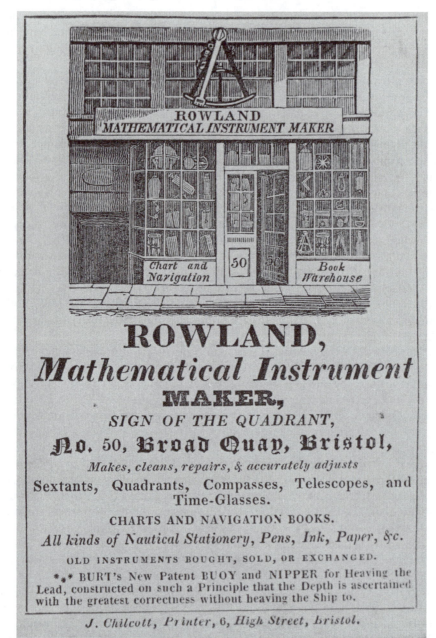

**Figure 8.9    Trade card for Rowland of Bristol, showing exterior of shop, *c.*1830**

*Source*: Bristol Museums Art Galleries and Archives, inv. no. T.8303

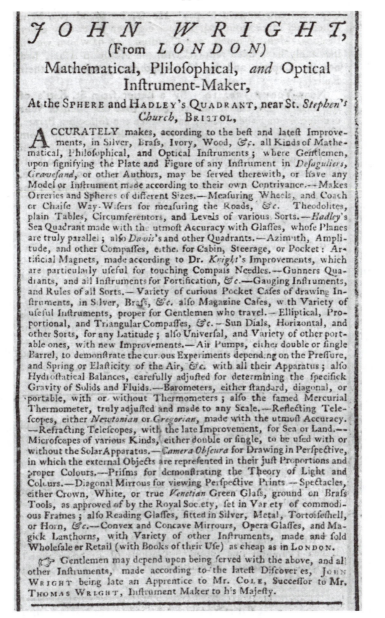

**Figure 8.10  John Wright's advertisement in *Felix Farley's Bristol Journal*, 13 March 1856**

*Source*: Bristol Reference Library

'maps, prints, mathematical instruments, spectacles and globes',[62] and there are instances elsewhere.

Advertisements appearing in the local press in the provinces appear to have been more concerned with points of information for business associates than with attracting retail customers. An example is the notification of a business changing hands, as we have seen in the Bristol press with the successors to John Wright, Joshua Springer, Henry Edgeworth and a number of others. Other advertisements concern changes of address, such as that placed by the Sheffield firm Chadburn & Wright, who 'removed from No 85, Lady's Bridge, Wicker, to the Premises, No 40 Lady's Bridge, Nursery, lately occupied by James Greenwood, Cabinet Case and Razor Strop Manufacturer, where they carry on their Manufactory in all its various branches ...'.[63] Alternatively, it might indicate a change in business circumstances, such as the partnership between Abraham Abraham, optician of Liverpool, and John Benjamin Dancer of Manchester, who 'propose OPENING the above PREMISES [at 13 Cross Street, Manchester] ... and in soliciting public patronage, respectfully state, that all work emanating from their manufactory or sold at their establishment, shall be of guaranteed accuracy, and every instrument combining all recent mechanical and scientific improvements'.[64]

New devices were occasionally promoted at a local level. For example, the invention, and piracy, of Edinburgh scientist David Brewster's patented kaleidoscope in 1817 led to a variety of contradictory advertisements in local newspapers around the country in an attempt to capture new markets while the craze for the device still raged.[65] The Bristol press, for instance, carried an advertisement in April 1818 from a number of businesses not otherwise known to be connected with the instrument trade:

> The *Genuine Kaleidoscope* to be had only *at the Manufactory, No 25 Broadmead*; P. Rose, Broadmead; Mintorn, College Green; Barry & Son, and Rees, High-street; Cookworthy, Corn-street; Prosser and Richardson, Clare-street; Frost, Broad-street; Hillyard & Morgan, and Huntley, John-street, and Wood, Castle-street – *All others are spurious.*[66]

In July, a member of the Bristol instrument trade, Charles Beilby, used the press to state that where the 'Patent Kaleidoscope' was concerned, 'he has extended into an agreement with Dr Brewster the Inventor and Patentee of the above very amusing Instrument, for the Manufacture of them, and that he is the only Person in the West of England who is authorised to make them ...'. In the same newspaper, a Mr J.W. Hall, Broadmead, announced that he 'has this day received a supply of the PATENT KALEIDOSCOPES, with the *new Improvement* as found out by the

[62] Brewer (1997), 174.
[63] *Sheffield Independent*, 18 May 1822.
[64] *Manchester Courier*, 12 June 1841.
[65] Morrison-Low (1984), 60–62.
[66] *Bristol Journal*, 25 April 1818.

*French.*'[67] By early September, despite Brewster's attempts to regulate distribution and make some profit from his design, Edward Bird & Son, Bristol watchmakers and jewellers, advertised that they had been appointed by Philip Carpenter, the Birmingham 'Optician and Sole Maker of the Kaleidoscope, during the term of the patent, his Agent for the sale of these Instruments in this City; they may be had at their Shop, at various prices, from 10s to 6 guineas, accompanied with books of description'.[68] Incensed, Beilby retaliated by advertising his own instruments in the Birmingham press.[69]

By the time Brewster regained some control of the situation by appointing 'approved' makers and retailers in about 1819, the craze for his device was dying away: he estimated that some 200,000 instruments were sold in London and Paris during three months. The more common telescopic instruments (Figure 8.11) appear to have been manufactured in the Midlands by wholesalers such as Philip Carpenter of Birmingham, a firm known to have been providing telescopes to large London firms, such as Dollond. In Birmingham, 'Mr [Philip] Carpenter soon established a large trade, and supplied even Dollond himself with large numbers of telescopes bearing his famous name'.[70] However, Carpenter was able to provide only a part of the unexpectedly substantial overnight demand for kaleidoscopes, as Brewster wrote to his wife from Sheffield about his visit to

Cam & Cutt, who have undertaken to manufacture the kaleidoscope for Mr Ruthven [of Edinburgh.] They have agreed to make and sell the instruments under my patent on the same terms as Mr Carpenter, provided I get his permission to allow them to be employed. This I must do, as he cannot possibly supply the demand.[71]

Examinations of dismantled examples show that the ends of the kaleidoscope, which are stamped pieces of brass, could easily have been produced by, for instance, a button manufacturer: 'the tinmen and the glaziers began to manufacture the detached parts of it, in order to evade the patent', as Brewster growled.[72] The partnership between James Cam and John Cutt or Cutts lasted only one year, that of 1818, and was probably brought about solely to deal with this single lucrative contract.[73] The example of the kaleidoscope demonstrates an instance of an instrument – really no more than a toy – that rapidly captured the public imagination, but did not require enormous skill to make. Brewster had failed to

---

[67]  Ibid., 4 July 1818.

[68]  Ibid., 5 September 1818.

[69]  *Aris's Gazette*, 28 September 1818.

[70]  [Robert Field], 'Optical and Mathematical Instruments' in Timmins (1866), 534.

[71]  Gordon (1869), 96.

[72]  Morrison-Low (1984), 61, quoting [D. Brewster], 'Kaleidoscope' in the *Edinburgh Encyclopaedia* (1830), XII, 410.

[73]  Supported by the entry in [Pigot's] *Commercial Directory for 1818–19–20 ...* (Manchester: James Pigot, 1818) for 'Cam and Cutt opticians Norfolk street'.

**Figure 8.11  Telescopic kaleidoscope, signed by I. Ruthven, Edinburgh, *c.*1820**

*Source*: National Museums of Scotland NMS.T.1985.20

anticipate market demand, understandably, but despite his precaution of a patent there was not yet the means to harness market forces in favour of the inventor.

Instrument historians have studied the trade literature of the scientific instrument industry because it can provide working dates of a firm, or a particular instrument bearing their name. Unfortunately, much of this material is ephemeral, with the bills, catalogues and trade cards appearing less worthy of attention by those who care mainly for the instruments themselves. Trade cards, which appeared as early as the late seventeenth century, were not, as Ambrose Heal notes, strictly speaking 'cards' at all, and their purpose has changed over the years.[74] As we have seen, their illustrations can help to give some idea about the retail premises of a business; and Michael Crawforth used examples to uncover 'many small pieces of information [which will] gradually build a complex picture of an important ... industry'.[75] For instance, some members of the trade were linked with others with the same name in different locations, or indeed, were the same person who had moved. Gloria Clifton's *Directory* cites a number of businesses with the name Abraham, and the trade card of Jacob Abraham, with shops in both Cheltenham and Bath, appears to be separate from his namesake, Abraham Abraham, who appears in the Liverpool street directories in 1818.

---

[74]  Heal (1925), 1–3.
[75]  Crawforth (1985), 453.

However, judging from an advertisement almost ten years later, it would appear that he, too, came from Somerset:

> A. ABRAHAM (from Bath), OPTICIAN and MATHEMATICAL INSTRUMENT-MAKER to the ROYAL FAMILY, *No. 7, Lord-street, Liverpool*, impressed with the gratitude for the liberal encouragement he has received since his establishment in Liverpool, trusts, by adhering to that assiduity and attention which have hitherto been his study, to merit a continuance of public patronage.[76]

In fact, as we have seen, Abraham was Jacob's son.[77]

Another trade card links a business in Liverpool with a shop in Cheltenham, that of the 'Messrs. Davis'. The street directories corroborate this, with Edward Davis running an 'instrument repository' at 65 Bold Street, while his brother John, who had been with him in 1839, was by 1843 at 101 High Street, Cheltenham.[78] John and Alexander Walker, who had a navigation and stationery warehouse at 33 Pool Lane, Liverpool, from 1824, also advertised premises at 47 Bernard Street, London.[79] In Chapter 2, we have already seen business, apprenticeship and family associations between the Liverpool and London firms of John Gray and Charles Jones: this is surely evidence of a distribution network, tying the places of production and point-of-sale of instruments.

A wider market was reached by what are now called 'trade catalogues', priced lists of available instruments, subsequently illustrated. Often bound in the back of illustrated textbooks, the catalogues had considerable novelty appeal: again, the London houses of Benjamin Martin, George Adams and W. & S. Jones led this field in the late eighteenth century. Catalogues advertising products issued by instrument makers outside London appeared much later than those produced in London. A bibliographic listing of 1570 surviving catalogues dated between 1600 and 1914 compiled in 1990 found that 'over three-quarters of the catalogues listed could only be found as single copies',[80] demonstrating their ephemeral nature (catalogues were usually destroyed when superseded by later editions).

But because only one of these – by Parkes of Birmingham, 1848 – was from a pre-1851 English provincial maker, it does not mean that others were not produced. For example, amongst those who exhibited at the Great Exhibition was Chadburn of Sheffield, who stated that their 'Catalogue with prices of optical, mathematical, philosophical, and other instruments, manufactured and sold by them at their exhibition & sale rooms, Albion Works, Nursery Street, Sheffield, 2d each:- with engravings, 1s. each'. As early as 1833, they advertised

---

[76] *The Albion*, 14 May 1827.
[77] Williams (1985), 123.
[78] Calvert (1971), 20; *1841. Gore's Directory for Liverpool and its Environs* (Liverpool: J. Mawdsley, n.d.); *The Cheltenham Annuaire and Directory ... for the year 1843 ...* (Cheltenham: H. Davis [1843]).
[79] Calvert (1971), 44.
[80] Anderson et al. (1990), i.

their illustrated trade literature – 'Chadburn & Co. have published a book, with copperplate engravings, describing the property and use of each article ...'[81] – but none of these have been traced. Their Great Exhibition prospectus covers 24 closely printed pages of items. Another exhibitor, Abraham Abraham & Co. of Liverpool, produced an 81-page *Descriptive and Illustrated Catalogue* in 1853, for the following reasons stated in the preface:

> We have been induced to publish the present Catalogue, from continued enquiries at our Establishment for a description and prices of the various Instruments manufactured by us ... Although we do not profess to manufacture cheap or inferior articles, yet we venture to assert that all Apparatus made by us will be found considerably lower in price than usually charged for goods of best quality. Our aim has hitherto been to obtain the confidence of our friends and patrons, by supplying only articles of superior construction and of guaranteed workmanship, combining all the latest improvements ... Scientific Institutions, Lecturers, and Merchants, favouring us with their orders, will be allowed a very liberal discount from our Catalogue prices ... carriage free, to any part of the United Kingdom.[82]

Although sounding a tentative note – 'we do not profess to manufacture cheap or inferior articles' – perhaps because they were still gaining new confidence in their own abilities, the firm is nonetheless proud of the skill of its workers, as demonstrated by the standards of their 'goods of best quality'. Clearly pitched at a new and growing educational market, by the mid-nineteenth century this Liverpool-based firm was prepared to pay the transport of any sale within the United Kingdom, possibly in order to gain an edge in competing against the large London wholesalers. There is also stress on 'the latest improvements', the advertiser's emphasis on novelty.

McKendrick points out that 'the manipulation of fashion made many consumer goods obsolete long before mere use would have made them so',[83] and this can be observed at the dilettante end of the instrument market, where instruments were acquired for entertainment or as status symbols rather than for practical or scientific use. Taking the example of the microscope, during the period from 1760 until the 1820s there was no technological improvement in the optics – the working parts – and yet, their mechanical characteristics provided an excuse for a proliferation in design, as any illustrated twentieth-century 'history of the microscope' will show.[84] In the only known surviving pattern book from the instrument-making trade, that of G. & W. Proctor, of Sheffield and Birmingham, and dated 1815 (Figure 8.12), there are described and illustrated eleven different

---

[81]   *History and General Directory of the Borough of Sheffield ... By William White* (Sheffield: printed by Robert Leader, Independent Office, for W. White, 1833), advertisement.

[82]   Abraham (1853), 'Preface'.

[83]   McKendrick (1982), 97.

[84]   For instance, Turner (1981).

sorts of microscope, at prices varying from 5s. (for a 'Gardener's microscope in ivory') to £3 13s 6d (for a 'Culpepper's Pyramidical Microscope, with Mahogany Box').[85]

This same pattern book has on its outside cover the remains of a paper manuscript label, 'GENERAL PATTERN and ...', implying that the designs inside were once used as a guide for retailers buying wholesale from the firm. Perhaps of even greater interest are the manuscript notes on the pages opposite the engravings, which appear to be the prices given by the firm for piece work: for instance, the 'Culpepper's Pyramidical Microscope' just mentioned, is annotated 'Box with Wood & Work 0-10-6', whereas the instrument is 'Work 1-1-0 Brass 3-4½' adding in the box, materials and labour came to '£1-14-10½', thus giving G. & W. Proctor £1-18-7½ profit. Naturally, they were supplying considerable overheads, such as their manufactory, tools for their workmen, and presumably also paying the cost of transport to the London market, rates which are so far unknown. The firm prospered under its first owner, Charles Proctor, who was worth just under £12,500 at his death in 1808, but his son, some ten years later, went bankrupt.[86]

Perhaps one of the most effective ways of appealing to the 'middling people' was that pioneered with enormous success by both Wedgwood and Boulton: displaying the latest, and therefore the most fashionable, wares in an exhibition. As Malcolm Baker has shown, this proved an entertaining and popular method of ensuring a wide London audience: he quotes Horace Walpole's remark of 1770, that 'We have at present three exhibitions ... The rage to see these exhibitions is so great that sometimes one cannot pass through the streets where they are.'[87] Exhibitions of instruments were to become an important method of demonstrating that there were skilful workmen in the provinces who could compete with the best London makers; in turn, provincial visitors to London exhibitions returned home, inspired by what they had seen.

## Exhibitions and Prizes

The pre-history of trade exhibitions in the United Kingdom, particularly those with a 'mechanical arts' theme, before the Great Exhibition of 1851 has been

---

[85] Sheffield City Archives, Special Collections no 33237, Bradbury Record 293: pattern book for *G.& W. Proctor, Opticians, No. 11 Market Street, Sheffield and No. 23 New Hall Street, Birmingham ... 1815*. This contains 39 plates of instruments produced by the firm, but has no provenance. The contents have been reproduced, without discussion, by Crom (1989), 357–70.

[86] The National Archives [TNA], IR 26/430 f46v; Sheffield City Archives: Parker Collection 859, 'Petition for bankruptcy of William Proctor of Sheffield, Optician, Dealer & Chapman ... by James Deakin & Thomas Deakin of Sheffield, dated 27 January 1818'. The Deakins were Proctor's brothers-in-law.

[87] Walpole to Horace Mann, 6 May 1770, quoted by Baker (1995), 118.

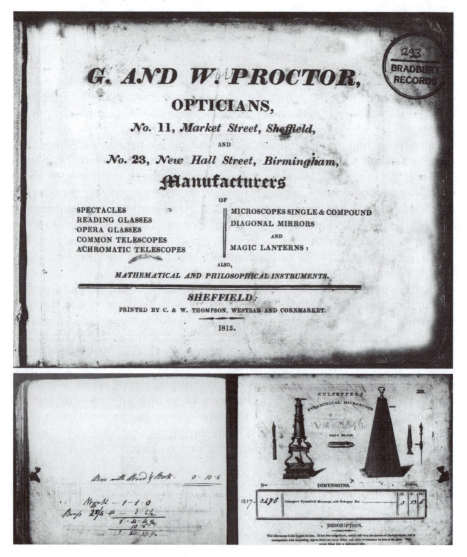

**Figure 8.12　Titlepage and Plate XXIX from G. & W. Proctor's pattern book of 1815, with manuscript annotations of materials and costs**

*Source*: Sheffield City Libraries and Archives

surprisingly poorly served by historians; sometimes the impression is given that the Crystal Palace sprang fully-formed from the head of the Prince Consort, with a little help from a career administrator, Henry Cole (1808–82).[88] In an important article, Toshio Kusamitsu demonstrated that since the late 1820s, several small-scale exhibition galleries had opened in London, the first of them being the National Repository in 1828, and the Royal Adelaide Gallery, which exhibited models of machinery and scientific instruments, in 1832; and visitors from the provinces who saw these brought back the idea of holding similar shows, against a background of 'flourishing bourgeois culture'.[89]

In a revised version of his article, Kusamitsu shows that from the mid-eighteenth century small-scale exhibitions of the industrial arts were fostered by literary and scientific societies, but for visiting by their members only.[90] Kenneth Beauchamp reckoned that the first industrial exhibition in Britain was held in Edinburgh in 1755;[91] while Brian Gee awarded the London-based Society of Arts the honour of holding a 'week-long event in 1761 when machines and models were exhibited'.[92] As with other aspects of this subject, the catalogues of these exhibitions have proved elusive, and specific information, especially about individual exhibits, is hard to find.

The London-based Society of Arts, which became the Royal Society of Arts in 1908, was formed in 1754 (as the Society for the Encouragement of Arts, Manufactures and Commerce) by a body of interested enthusiasts, who attempted to encourage the exploitation of natural resources. By the 1840s, the Society was forced to reassess the emphasis of its aims following the runaway economic success of British industry towards the end of its first century. The award of a premium of a few guineas and publication of an idea in the Society's *Transactions* had become less appealing as industry provided its own rewards. With declining revenues and an unbusinesslike constitution, the Society came close to extinction, but managed to reform itself with a new Council and Charter; it became a forum for the dissemination of information about the industrial arts and sciences. In particular, it organized exhibitions. Henry Cole was Chairman of the Council in 1850 and 1852, and the Society was deeply involved in the Great Exhibition at the Crystal Palace, as well as other international exhibitions later on, besides the lower-key annual exhibitions held by the Society itself.[93] At these last, among other prize-winning instruments, awards had been presented in 1810 for James Allan's dividing engine; in 1830 for another by the specialist microscope-maker Andrew Ross; and in 1831 for Cornelius Varley's microscope for examining pond-

---

[88]  For example, Briggs (1975), 49; Strong et al. (1977).
[89]  Kusamitsu (1980).
[90]  Kusamitsu (1985).
[91]  Beauchamp (1997), 11.
[92]  Gee (1998a), 11.
[93]  For histories of the Society of Arts, see Wood (1913) and Hudson and Luckhurst (1954).

life: however, all these individuals were members of the London trade, and the Society wished to extend its influence into the provinces.

Kusamitsu dates the real English genesis of the 'exhibition movement' – which saw its first international manifestation in the Great Exhibition of 1851 – to December 1837, when the directors of the Manchester Mechanics' Institute advertised in the columns of the *Manchester Guardian* their intention of holding a

> POPULAR EXHIBITION of Models of Machinery, Philosophical Instruments, Works in Fine and useful Arts, Objects in Natural History, and Specimens of British Manufacture, &c. &c. In the Exhibition the Directors are desirous of affording to the working classes a convenient opportunity of inspecting the present state of our arts and manufactures and to present them with a source of rational and agreeable relaxation ....[94]

He goes on to demonstrate that this idea soon spread amongst other mechanics' institutes throughout the country, especially in the Midlands and the North of England. Between 1838 and 1842, he estimates there were at least 35 exhibitions held there and that probably 'several million people visited these exhibitions'.[95]

The Mechanics' Institutes movement began in the early 1820s, although its origins stretched further back into the eighteenth century: the idea was to make education accessible to the working classes, principally through lectures (at a cheaper rate than through the Literary and Philosophical societies), but also through lending libraries and exhibitions.[96] 'The flavour of all Mechanics' Institutes exhibitions,' wrote Paul Greenhalgh, 'was philanthropic rather than economic, the aim being principally to stimulate working class consciousness and to generally advance industrial culture'.[97] Although somewhat politicized through their obvious links with the trades union movement, this was not enough to cause conflict with central government, and 'the achievements of these exhibitions as a whole were to render the urban-industrial environment less despicable in the eyes of the educated classes, and to provoke debate on the nature of working class culture.'[98]

Philosophical instrument makers, especially those involved in the new science of electricity, were amongst those most deeply involved in exhibiting their wares in the permanent London galleries from the 1820s. Amongst them was the Dubliner Edward Marmaduke Clarke, who exhibited at both the National Repository and at the Royal Adelaide Gallery. Brian Gee has shown that he used these exhibitions for publicity in selling his wares, to the extent that his claims on occasion involved

---

[94]  *Manchester Guardian*, 9 December 1837, quoted in Kusamitsu (1985), 34.
[95]  Kusamitsu (1985), 34.
[96]  Inkster (1991), 79–80.
[97]  Greenhalgh (1988), 8.
[98]  Ibid.

him in priority disputes.[99] As these were usually aired in the press, this gave him further exposure.[100] J.A. Bennett reminded his readers that the Great Exhibition 'was very much a competition as well' – the 30 classes were each assigned an international jury, and there was a 'scale of possible awards'.[101]

The distinguished physicist Sir David Brewster chaired the jury for Class X, philosophical instruments, and the Reporter (who wrote the Jury's report) was James Glaisher, superintendent of the magnetic and meteorological department at the Royal Observatory, Greenwich. There were an equal number of foreign and British jurors. The class was well-subscribed, and the United Kingdom won 16 of the 31 Council Medals awarded; but as Bennett has shown, this apparent success masked a lack of investment in technical training, and he quoted Lyon Playfair's contemporary remark that 'our manufacturers were justly astonished at seeing most of the foreign countries rapidly approaching and sometimes excelling us in manufactures, our own by heredity and traditional right'.[102] This may have been a contributory idea behind the 1855 Society of Arts Prize for Microscopes, which usefully illustrates the capabilities of English provincial manufacturers at the close of the period covered by this book.

### The Society of Arts Prize Microscopes, 1855

Although the first award for the design of an instrument cheap enough to be purchased by people previously considered too poor and ignorant to become consumers did not occur until a few years after the Great Exhibition, nevertheless it is included here as a case study: aspects of what happened illuminate the workings of the instrument trade and how it reached – or failed to reach – its customers. It also sheds light on three individual Birmingham firms of instrument makers, and how they responded to changing market conditions. In the *Quarterly Journal of Microscopical Science* for early 1855, there appeared the following statement under the heading 'Cheap Microscopes':

> The President of the Microscopical Society [J.S. Bowerbank] in his late address [published in February 1847] drew attention to the general impression, that in order to make good observations it was necessary to have a high-priced microscope. He denied this .... As the use of the microscope is now becoming a matter of educational importance, and as in order that it may be used by all, it must be sold at a price obtained by all and at the same time a good instrument insured, the Society of Arts has offered two prizes for the best microscopes at stated prices.[103]

---

[99]   Gee (1989), especially Chapters 3 and 4.
[100]  Gee (1998a) and (1998b).
[101]  Bennett (1983), 2.
[102]  Quoted in ibid., 11.
[103]  'Memoranda' (1855).

In effect, the microscope was being driven down-market: it was no longer to be a gadget within the exclusive preserve of wealthy amateurs. In fact, it was those very same 'amateurs' who were attempting to make the instrument more accessible and open up new domestic markets, for philanthropic and possibly other less altruistic reasons. One of these new markets was to be its first professional market: that of medicine, reached through its students.

The Council of the Society of Arts resolved to appoint a committee to discuss 'offering a prize for and promoting the production of a good serviceable microscope for school purposes at a low price' on 22 November 1854.[104] All the eminent members of the Prize Committee were drawn from the membership of the Microscopical Society of London, the forerunner of the Royal Microscopical Society, which received its Royal Charter in 1866, and all but two served as its President. In particular, Dr William Benjamin Carpenter (1813–85) subsequently gave an account of how this had all come about:

> If there be one class more than another, which especially needs to … [be kept] … free from the grovelling sensuality in which it too frequently loses itself, it is our Labouring population …. It was from feeling very strongly how much advantage would accrue from the introduction of a form of Microscope, which should be at once *good* enough for Educational purposes, and *cheap* enough to find its way into every well-supported School in town and country, that the Author suggested to the Society of Arts in the summer of 1854, that it should endeavour to carry-out [this] object.[105]

At its first meeting, this Committee agreed that a simple microscope, costing about £1, was what was required.[106] But subsequently, this was revised by Dr Carpenter,[107] so that the Committee recommended to the Council that the prize should be offered for two microscopes, one to be called the school microscope, priced at 10/6d or less, being mechanically and optically simple; the other to be called the student microscope, costing three guineas or less, and having two eyepieces and objectives and a limited range of stipulated accessories: 'That the medal of the Society be offered, and that the Council should take 100 of the smaller and 50 of the larger microscopes'.[108] Competition entries were to be delivered to the Society before 1 May 1855,[109] and there were 12 submissions, which were referred to the Prize Committee.[110]

The Committee met on 7 May to hear that the following instruments had been received: three simple microscopes (from Parkes & Co. and Field & Co., both of

---

[104] Royal Society of Arts [R.S.A.] MS Minutes of Council, vol. 6, November 1854–January 1856, p.7.
[105] Carpenter (1856), 33–4.
[106] R.S.A. MS Minutes of Committees 1853–1855, 345.
[107] Ibid., 359.
[108] Ibid.
[109] 'Special Prizes' (1855); also noted in 'Memoranda' (1855).
[110] R.S.A. MS Minutes of Council, vol. 6, November 1854–January 1856, 89.

Birmingham, and W. & F. Newton of London); and nine compound instruments (from W.J. Salmon, J.J. Solomon, William Ladd, M.A. Cooper, W. & F. Newton, and Samuel Highley, all of London, the so-far unidentified firm of Bland & Long, and, again, Parkes & Co. and Field & Co. of Birmingham).[111] The Committee met again on 18 May to test the instruments, and the simple microscopes were dealt with first. That offered by Parkes & Co. was deemed 'unfitted'; that by W. & F. Newton 'rejected'; while the example from Field & Co. was 'approved', although suggestions were made for its improvement, and it was observed that 'the mirror does not work either'. Next, the Committee looked at the compound instruments, and 'rejected all except [those by] Salmon, Field & Co. & Ladd', and then tested for the one with the best resolution – with a Nobert's test plate, Field's was best; with a diatom slide, that by Ladd.[112] The Committee 'resolved unanimously to recommend to the Council [that] sent in by Messrs Field & Co. as deserving the prize offered' in the compound category, although with some minor mechanical alterations, which Field agreed to accept.[113]

In June, the Society of Arts heard from Henry Cole, who asked that examples of the winning design be sent to be displayed in the Paris Universal Exhibition (of 1855), where they were shown alongside those of other British makers such as T.D. King of Bristol, William Ladd, Moritz Pillischer, Andrew Pritchard, Joseph Solomon, and Smith & Beck, all of London.[114] This would appear to have been a great commercial success for Field of Birmingham, and this exposure should, if carefully exploited, have led to increased orders and prosperity. Yet, despite winning this prestigious prize, very little is known about Robert Field & Son of Birmingham. According to a local account of 1895:

> Field had been a foreman at Philip Carpenter's factory in Bath Row, and he afterwards started business on his own account in Navigation Street. After Philip Carpenter removed to London, Field bought the business at 111 New Street, which, being a building one storey high only, was taken down to make room for other buildings, and the business removed.[115]

A surviving trade card, dating from between 1826 and 1837 demonstrates that the London and Birmingham businesses were being run by the same people (Figure 8.13). Philip Carpenter was born at Kidderminster on 18 November 1776,

---

[111] R.S.A. MS Minutes of Committees 1853–1855, p.429; identification of the makers has been made from Clifton (1995).

[112] Nobert's test plate and the diatom slide were methods used to test the optical resolution of microscopes. The German, F.A. Nobert (1806–81) mechanically produced micro-ruled lines with a diamond on a glass-plate; diatom slides were made from the naturally-occurring minute plankton found in the sea.

[113] R.S.A. MS Minutes of Committees 1853–1855, pp.433–7.

[114] R.S.A. MS Minutes of Council, vol. 6, November 1854–January 1856, 132; *Catalogue* ... (1855), 23–4.

[115] 'H.B.' (1895).

into a Unitarian family. Although he claimed to have been trained 'in London', it is not clear to whom he was apprenticed, nor why he decided to move back to the Midlands. A later Birmingham account stated that:

> Philip Carpenter was a scientific optician, and had a house and manufactory in Bath Row, and a retail shop at 111 New Street, Birmingham. In July 1826, he removed to 24 Regent Street, London. The Birmingham business in New Street was continued till 1837, when it was transferred to the late Mr R. Field. Philip Carpenter died at Regent Street, April 30, 1833, the business being continued by his sister Mary in partnership with Mr William Westley.[116]

Perhaps the most famous member of the family was Philip's brother, Dr Lant Carpenter (1780–1840), the Unitarian divine, whose own family of six children included the naturalist William Benjamin Carpenter, a great promoter of the microscope, and who apparently saw no conflict of interest in judging a competition where the winner was his uncle's trade successor.[117] Like his nephew, William B. Carpenter, whose text on *The Microscope and its Revelations* was to run to eight editions (six revised by himself) through the nineteenth century, Philip Carpenter was particularly interested in microscopy:

> He paid considerable attention to the manufacture of microscopes ... He opened an exhibition of the solar microscope in the large drawing room (at Regent Street). The images of the objects magnified were projected on a large screen, and great interest was excited by its revelations ... When the novelty wore off the attendance declined, and it was discontinued in 1835.[118]

This exhibition was named the 'Microcosm', and visitors to it were encouraged to buy Carpenter's wares. It is perhaps worth noting that apart from examples of Brewster's kaleidoscopes, all the surviving instruments with Philip Carpenter's signature appear to come from the London end of his business. This must have been a marketing device, given the current understanding that only the best quality goods were manufactured in the metropolis, and that – as Henry Mayhew's 'experienced tradesman' claimed – 'made in Birmingham' had a pejorative ring to it.[119]

Philip Carpenter's other popular line in instrumentation besides the microscope, and the shorter-lived kaleidoscope boom, was in optical projection, which developed from the success of the 'Microcosm'. Solar microscopes, and subsequently magic lanterns, had been used as teaching aids since the late seventeenth century.[120] Indeed, Carpenter produced his own 'improved magic

---

[116] Matthews (1895).

[117] For W.B. Carpenter, see J. Estlin Carpenter, 'Introductory Memoir' in Carpenter (1888), which explains Carpenter's lifelong devotion to the microscope.

[118] Matthews (1895); for Carpenter's solar microscope, see Nuttall (1976).

[119] Mayhew (1861), 333.

[120] Hankins and Silverman (1995), Chapter 3 'The Magic Lantern and the Art of Demonstration', 37–71.

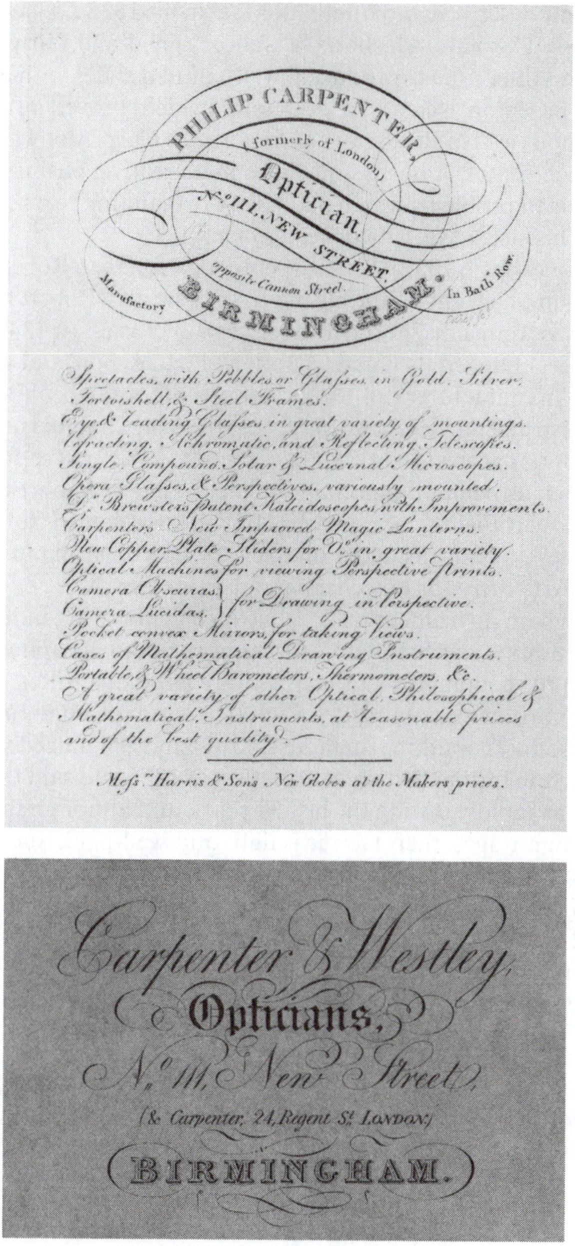

**Figure 8.13  Philip Carpenter's 1833 advertisement; and Carpenter & Westley's
trade card for 1826–1833**

*Source*: Birmingham Library Services; © National Museum of Science and Industry

lantern', which he described and offered for sale in his 1823 *Elements of Zoology*. It is described by Hermann Hecht as 'a well-designed and fairly cheap lantern and – for the first time – mass-produced, well-painted slides with an educational subject matter, based on "scientific" principles [which] proved a turning point in projection methods and in the use of the lantern. ... Carpenter was the first to go about the production of lanterns and slides in a creative, business-like fashion, finding solutions to problems which had been dormant for years'.[121] Both Philip Carpenter and his sister Mary died wealthy people.[122]

For the ten years from 1837 when Carpenter's ex-foreman Robert Field bought and ran the Birmingham end of the business, its name was 'Robert Field', and they were described as 'opticians' in the local street directories. In 1845, the business at 113 New Street changed its name to 'Robert Field & Son' and they advertised themselves as 'manufacturers of every variety of optical, philosophical and mathematical instruments'.[123] As we have seen, the firm exhibited microscopes and photographic optics at the Great Exhibition in 1851, where the Juries dismissed them as 'not such as demand especial notice'.[124] That year, on 14 September, at the age of 64, Robert Field senior died.[125] His son (also named Robert) continued to run the business, and it was under his aegis in 1855 the firm put in for and won the Society of Arts Prize for two cheap microscopes.[126]

The Birmingham instrument trade – like its neighbouring industry, the small arms manufacturers – was made up of a number of small capitalists, who were flexible enough to manufacture, in increasingly large quantities, parts or entire instruments, and had the ability to alter these to suit changing markets by switching the products or taking on more skilled hands, or indeed laying them off. Field himself wrote for the British Association in 1866 and said that 'Few trades have advanced as rapidly during the last 30 years, and although the workmen do not earn very high wages, their labour is light and well-paid, and many of them set up as "small masters", and carry on their business at their own homes ... machinery, although used wherever necessary, is not employed to any great extent; the chief requisites being careful finish and delicate skill ...'.[127] However, even as early as November 1855, when the Society of Arts Microscope Committee met to examine the first batch of the promised one hundred compound microscopes (only fifty had been delivered) they found that:

> the workmanship is generally not so good as it might be & is not equal to the original Instruments furnished, & that in common with respect to the original Instruments

---

[121] Hecht (1993), 77.

[122] TNA, Death Duty Registers, IR 26/1316 Reg. 2 No 229 Philip Carpenter, died 30 April 1833, total £4000.

[123] In Birmingham directories, 1837–1845.

[124] *Catalogue* ... (1851), 435; *Reports* ... (1852), 267.

[125] *Aris's Gazette*, 15 September 1851.

[126] 'Premiums' (1855).

[127] [Robert Field], 'Optical and Mathematical Instruments' in Timmins (1866), 533–5.

furnished [the Committee had passed …] over certain aspects of workmanship on the understanding that they had been finished in a hurry & that subsequent instruments were to be of superior workmanship. That Mr Field also be informed with respect to the smaller microscope the Committee have examined the final twelve & do not find any one properly fitted & they therefore require that Messrs. Field have them all duly examined & fitted before they can recommend the Society to accept them.[128]

Clues to what had happened are to be found in the letters written by Robert Field junior to the Society of Arts: for instance, apologising for the delay in completing the order in July 1855 he wrote: 'We … are sorry they are so long in hand, but some fresh hands are not yet accustomed to our ways of work & do not progress as they should do'.[129] Small batches were sent with further apologies in August and October, and again in early November:

We forwarded the remainder of Microscopes on Saturday … the number sent is 51 large & 101 small as one of each were sent to Mr Barker our Marker the rec[t.] of which we enclose. You do not say if any have been examined & approved. We find the price is very close but still with good demand may pay.[130]

This doubt may be reflected in the 'poor workmanship' that the Committee found. So many short cuts were being taken in the search for economy that the instruments suffered in quality.

Despite this, Field & Son had gained enough self-confidence to advertise the instruments in the 1856 first edition of William Carpenter's *The Microscope: and its Revelations* (Figure 8.14).[131] Field & Son also produced a *Condensed Catalogue of Optical & Philosophical Instruments*, which was bound in the back of a little booklet with a preface written by H. Woodward, of the Geological Department of the British Museum, entitled *The Prize Microscopes of the Society of Arts* in at least two editions, one dated 1859, the second 1863.[132] The 1859 edition lists twenty-one agents throughout the United Kingdom from whom Field's instruments might be procured.[133] The impression given is that in 1859 cheap microscopes with the Society of Arts' stamp of approval were selling rapidly; but the 1863 edition no longer carried the information about the agents, implying that by this date they had stopped retailing Field's microscopes.

By April 1858 at least, one London microscope manufacturer, presumably feeling the competitive pinch, was advertising in the endpapers of the *Quarterly Journal of Microscopical Science* that:

---

[128] R.S.A. MS Minutes of Committees 1853–1855, p.483.
[129] A/RSA/13/F/28: Letter dated 19 July 1855 to the Society from R. Field & Son.
[130] A/RSA/13/F/23: Letter dated 6 November 1855 to the Society from R. Field & Son.
[131] Carpenter (1856), 76 and 81.
[132] Field (1859) and (1863).
[133] Ibid. (1859), 75.

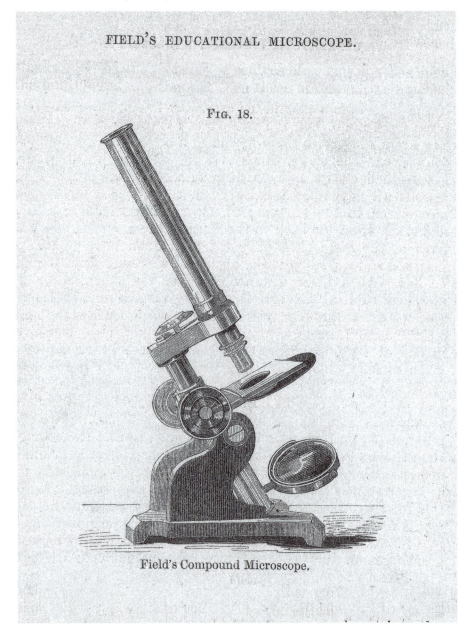

**Figure 8.14  Field's microscope, as engraved for the first edition of William B. Carpenter, *The Microscope: and its Revelations* (London, 1856)**

*Source*: National Museums of Scotland Library

... C. Baker of 243 and 244 High Holborn from the introduction of improved machinery is now able to supply the pattern microscope so much esteemed by the Society of Arts and finished in a very superior manner with three achromatic powers, and apparatus in mahogany case, complete, at the very low price of £3-3-0.[134]

Baker was matching Field's price rather than undercutting him, and evidently using the design devised by Field. Hogg's 1858 third edition of *The Microscope: its History, Construction and Applications* promoted Baker's version of the Society of Arts Prize microscope, with an illustration of it on the title page and Baker's trade catalogue bound in the back, having dropped the advertisement for Field, although continuing to mention his instruments in the text, where it was more difficult and expensive to alter standing print.[135] The following year, the President of the Microscopical Society, Edwin Lankester (another member of the Committee which had chosen Field's instruments as winners) said in his Presidential Address for 1859:

> I am glad to inform you that the sale of cheaper microscopes of powers decidedly available for scientific microscopes has greatly increased .... The makers of the microscope which obtained the medal have sent out 1393 of these instruments, and I find, on enquiry amongst various makers, that, since the appearance of this microscope [presumably the compound instrument], the sale of microscopes at a cost of ten guineas and under has greatly increased. Much is thus evidently done towards making the microscope an instrument of popular use and instruction.[136]

William Carpenter's third edition of his text on *The Microscope* of 1862 noted 'with great satisfaction, that no fewer than 1800 of these Microscopes have been sold up to the end of the year 1861'.[137] These textbooks evidently sold in huge numbers, and were extremely influential in guiding the newcomer to microscopy into his or her first instrument. Indeed, in a small university town in Scotland, the young William Carmichael McIntosh (1838–1931), later to become Professor of Natural History at St Andrews between 1882 and 1916, recalled that:

> hitherto I had depended on the use of Charles Howie's microscope ['a good Nachet's microscope'] but my father resolved to get one for me, & accordingly after an examination of those available in St. Andrews a Field's student's microscope was chosen. This instrument had gained a prize for efficiency & cheapness (£3.3/-), the St. Andrews watchmaker however adding another guinea for expenses. It had 2 eyepieces

---

[134] *Quarterly Journal of Microscopical Science*, endpapers, April 1858: my thanks to Dr R.H. Nuttall for this reference.

[135] Hogg (1858), 67.

[136] Lankester (1859).

[137] Carpenter (1862), 70.

& 2 objectives x250 & 60 respectively. It filled the gap & was useful for some years until a better was obtained.[138]

By the second half of the nineteenth century, there was a large supporting literature for the new markets for microscopy: these audiences now included women, and the industrious mechanic who spent his few leisure hours improving himself.[139] Another was the new and growing market of medical students, for whom a number of textbooks were produced. Carpenter's volume, as already stated, ran to eight editions between 1856 and 1901; although Jabez Hogg had died in 1899, the fifteenth edition of his *The Microscope* appeared in 1911; Lionel S. Beale produced a variety of texts, including *How to Work with the Microscope*, in five editions between 1857 and 1880; and *The Microscope and Clinical* [later *Practical*] *Medicine*, in four editions between 1854 and 1878. In particular, Beale championed the cheap instruments produced by the London makers 'Mr Matthews of Lincoln's Inn', William Salmon, and Samuel Highley (Salmon and Highley had both failed to win the 1855 prize); Highley also published some editions of Beale's books. John Quekett's *Treatise on the Microscope* only went to three editions, probably because of his early death in 1861.

Other influential authors included the Edinburgh university professor of what was to become physiology, John Hughes Bennett (1812–75). He was the first to introduce practical microscopy into the curriculum of any British university, although his first course, given in 1841, was to extra-mural classes at Edinburgh, and made use of microscopes made by the Parisian optician Charles Chevalier. Bennett, who had done some years of postgraduate work in Paris, promoted Continental instruments (especially, latterly, those of Georges Oberhaeuser), and was critical of the brassy splendour and expense of the best London-made instruments. His *Clinical Lectures on the Principles and Practice of Medicine* ran to five editions in Britain between 1856 and 1868; six in the United States; and was also translated into French, Russian and Hindi.[140] Between 1831 and 1859, a period of twenty-eight years, Oberhaeuser's workshop supplied some three thousand microscopes, at the rate of about one hundred a year. Bennett's influential advocacy of the Oberhaeuser microscope probably helped the Parisian instrument maker to sell more student 'drum' models than he might otherwise

---

[138] University of St. Andrews Library: William Carmichael McIntosh Papers, Ms 37113/1, 115.

[139] For women, see Phillips (1990), esp. Part III; the case of the amateur naturalist and coastguard, Charles Peach (1800–86), who was presented with a microscope by W.B. Carpenter, made by Powell & Lealand, and retailed by Carpenter & Westley, is discussed in Smiles (1878), 238–81; the microscope is now in the National Museums of Scotland, inv. no. NMS.T.1999.40: see R.H. Nuttall (2004).

[140] For an assessment of John Hughes Bennett and his influence on the teaching of microscopy, see Jacyna (1997), and Morrison-Low (1997a).

have done: one observer noted that Oberhaeuser exported more of his microscopes to Britain than to any other country.[141]

Field numbered his Society of Arts Prize microscopes. The reasons why a manufacturer would want to do this are not clear, but it may have been a straightforward counting procedure. Other instances of this exist, such as those by the London makers James Short, and Nairne & Blunt, who numbered their reflecting telescopes; the Edinburgh manufacturer Alexander Adie, who numbered his patented 'improved air barometer' called the sympiesometer (admittedly outside the scope of this work); and, as we have seen, microscopes by the provincial instrument makers J.B. Dancer of Manchester and T.D. King of Bristol.[142] The numbering on Field's microscopes has not received much attention from instrument historians, and not many of his instruments have been recorded (Figures 8.15 and 8.16) or appear to have survived, which in turn begs the question, how many were actually made? It is not clear whether there was one series for both types of instrument, or parallel runs for each sort: and there are good marketing reasons why an instrument-maker would not begin his numbering with '1'. The highest number recorded (so far) is 1045 for a school microscope, somewhat short of W.B. Carpenter's 1861 figure of 1800; but if added to the highest known for the compound, 706, the total reaches 1751.[143]

In 1862, another international exhibition was held in London, and again, Field exhibited instruments, but the Jurors took a somewhat critical view of his display:

> Very cheap forms of compound microscope are exhibited by Mr Field, who obtained the Society of Arts' prize some years since, but who does not appear to have in any respect improved his model; and others by Mr Parkes, the cheapest of all, but at the same time it must be added, the least efficient optically; whether the quality is as good as can be procured at the price is a question which none but the manufacturer can determine.[144]

Here it is clear that the Jurors regard the 'manufacturer' as a tradesman, no longer as a part of the 'scientific community', a peculiarly British social change from the earlier, more equable status between craftsman and client, noted by J.A. Bennett.[145]

---

[141] Otto (1970), and Nuttall (1979), 55.

[142] For Short, see Turner (1969b); for Nairne & Blunt, see Turner (1979b); a discussion of the numbered Adie sympiesometers is to be found in Clarke et al. (1989), 37.

[143] See Nuttall (1979), 50: 102 for the compound, now NMS.T.1979.75 and 998 for the school model, now NMS.T.1979.76; two further examples of the 10/6d model are numbered 665 and 827 [inv. nos. Wellcome Museum A645036 and A242702]; while two others are an incomplete school instrument numbered 1045, and a compound 601 [inventory number: York Castle Museum: 105A/36; no inventory number]; another compound is numbered 706 [inv. no. Wh:3191; described and illustrated in Brown (1986), catalogue no. 223].

[144] *Reports* ... (1863), 2*.

[145] Bennett (1985).

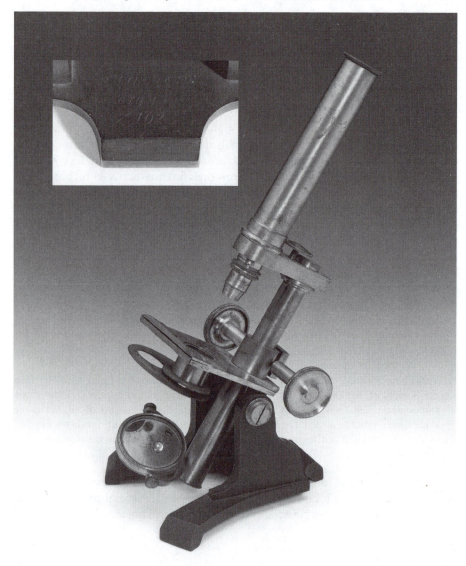

**Figure 8.15  Society of Arts compound microscope, no. 102, by Field & Son,
         Birmingham**

*Source*: National Museums of Scotland, NMS.T.1979.75

**Figure 8.16 Society of Arts school microscope, no.998, by Field & Son, Birmingham**

*Source*: National Museums of Scotland, NMS.T.1979.76

Despite this, Parkes obtained an 'Honourable Mention', although Field was ignored. Parkes, another Birmingham manufacturer, who had participated in the Society of Arts competition in 1855, now produced a trade catalogue after the exhibition results had been announced, and used their success to advertise their microscopes, despite the reservations of the Jurors, which of course they failed to mention: 'Jury Award Class 13, at International Exhibition, 1862: "For economy (*combined with quality*) in the Manufacture of Microscopes and Mathematical Instruments"'. Their 'Compound School Microscope' was available for 11s 6d; their 'Improved School Microscope' (a compound achromatic model) for £1 1s; and their 'Student's Model microscope, – recommended by the Society of Arts' for £3 3s, with the qualification 'N.B. Upwards of One Thousand of these Microscopes have been sold since their introduction'.[146] However, it is not clear whether these figures included those previously sold by Field, or by other makers.

By 1867, a preface to Parkes's *Wholesale Catalogue of Optical, Mathematical and Philosophical Instruments* explained their marketing strategy in a 'mission statement':

> A notion has very generally prevailed (one which formerly had too frequent foundation in fact) that certain articles could only be produced, of first-rate quality, IN CERTAIN LOCALITIES. This, it need scarcely be said, is now very far from the truth.
>
> The improvements which have been made in modern machinery, (especially in the Midland Counties of England,) and the facilities which are afforded by extensive railway intercommunication, have done much to break down such local peculiarities. Manufacturers, therefore, instead of depending on a mere name, or old reputation, have now to study how they may skilfully *combine* the special advantages peculiar to some localities, with those of others; so that, by the aid of machinery improvements, they may obtain a superior total result ....
>
> In some cases, where we have considered our Continental neighbours to excel us in certain *specialities*, (either as to quality or price,) we have combined such portions of their work, with other of our own Manufacture, and have, by such combination obtained advantageous results. Skilled London workmen are also employed by us on certain parts of Instruments used for Optical and Mathematical purposes; so that, with the additional aid of our own special machinery improvements, we have been enabled to produce a really superior article at a far more moderate cost ....

Parkes then illustrated and described two items within their range of stock as 'The Student's Model Microscope, recommended by the Society of Arts ... £3 3s' and the 'Simple Microscope for general use and for dissecting ... 10s 6d. N.B. This instrument is recommended by the Society of Arts.'[147] It would appear that Parkes had taken over producing this cheap but successful model of microscope, while Field withdrew from this particular market.

---

[146] Parkes (1862), 6–7.
[147] Parkes (1867), 43–4.

Correspondence in the archives of the Royal Society of Arts reveals that the main reason Parkes had done badly in the 1855 competition was that the firm had found out about it and the 1 May deadline only in early April; unlike Field, their letters reveal that they continued to develop both microscope models after this deadline. It is perhaps a mark of the proprietor Samuel Hickling Parkes's ability as a businessman that, by 1857, the Parkes catalogue advertised their appointment as 'Instrument makers to the Board of Trade, and Government Schools of Design'; by 1886, they were boasting in their 'Introductory Remarks' that their medical and educational microscopes were being used in all the universities, and in many London and provincial hospitals. The firm of Field & Son appears to have bowed out of the microscope market soon after winning the prestigious Society of Arts competition; possibly because they found it impossible to produce instruments of reasonable quality at such a low retail price. They went on to make larger inroads into the optical projection market, with Robert Field taking out a number of patents before his death in the 1890s.[148] Microscopes on the Society of Arts pattern continued to be advertised by various makers until the end of the nineteenth century: an example dating from 1894 was offered by the London firm John J. Griffin & Sons Ltd. for £2 16s.[149]

Provincial instrument manufacturers appear to have grasped a number of the marketing principles outlined by Neil McKendrick for attracting would-be consumers at the dilettante end of the market. These included more attractive shops, with carefully dressed windows to tempt the passer-by; canny use of advertisement through trade literature in the form of trade cards, press announcements and lists of goods, whether bound in the backs of books, or issued separately. However, Pat Hudson has warned that the theory of a 'consumer revolution' in the late eighteenth century has perhaps been over-emphasised: 'the evidence of change in real incomes for the masses, of poverty levels in the later eighteenth century and of the redistribution of income in society in favour of rent and profit receivers makes it likely that the mass of the population remained below the level at which they could participate in revolutionary fashion-orientated consumption of either domestic manufactures or imported commodities in the period of the industrial revolution itself'.[150] She also feels that Wedgwood, cited by historians as an example of creative salesmanship, is 'perhaps overused: he was not a typical entrepreneur and not even the leading manufacturer in pottery'.[151] Nonetheless, some of his techniques were used by other retailers, even in instrument circles, to great effect.

The example of the Society of Arts microscope, chosen to demonstrate the encouragement of a new market, also shows that the top London microscope makers simply did not, in that instance, bother to compete. Why should this be

---

[148] Hecht (1993), 253 and 296.
[149] Griffin (1894), 302–3.
[150] Hudson (1992), 176.
[151] Ibid., 179.

so? It may show that by 1855, there was already significant market demarcation, and that specialist, top-quality makers of instruments in any field did not need to compete: they already knew what their market parameters were, and were comfortable remaining within them. Of the three pre-eminent London makers, only Smith & Beck produced a 'student microscope' in the latter years of the nineteenth century, priced higher than that of the Society of Arts guideline of three guineas, and clearly did not feel the need to move further downmarket. After mid-century, some firms were able to survive by specializing in a particular line: most provincial firms continued to offer products suitable for needs across a spectrum of potential customers.

Instruments of all sorts – practical, scientific, and educational – were supplied by manufacturers based in the new centres of industry outside London, and transported to their marketplaces. In 1851, ten provincial English firms displayed goods in Class X at the Crystal Palace Great Exhibition, showing that they at least entertained a new-found confidence in selling their wares directly to their customers.[152] The survival of material culture from this period far exceeds that of the preceding century. Even if the majority of the population was unable to participate in a 'consumer culture', the growing middle classes bought their way into 'lifestyles embodying consensus polite culture'.[153] Instruments, representing their owners' intellectual attainments, formed a part of this.

---

[152] Turner (1983a), 309–10; these were: Abraham Abraham & Co., Liverpool; John Braham, Bristol; Chadburn Brothers, Sheffield and Liverpool; Robert Field & Son, Birmingham; Gray & Keen, Liverpool; J.N. Hearder, Plymouth; Thomas D. King, Bristol; James Parkes & Son, Birmingham; Samuel Sharp, Sheffield; William Wilton, St. Day, Truro.

[153] Glennie (1995), 169.

# Chapter 9

# Demand

'Demand' in eighteenth-century England was described by the economic historian Neil McKendrick in 1982 as 'a consumer boom'. For McKendrick, 'the consumer revolution was the necessary analogue to the industrial revolution, the necessary convulsion on the demand side of the equation to match the convulsion on the supply side'.[1] Subsequently, other economic historians have criticized his arguments on two grounds: first, their limited empirical basis – his analysis extended to clothing, pottery, and shaving accessories; and second, that setting 'demand' on an equal footing with 'supply' as an instigator of the Industrial Revolution is at odds with 'the more common theoretical approach which places it in a subordinate position to supply, abetting or constraining it through pressures of overheated, insufficient or fragmented markets. The institution of demand-led growth, let alone revolution seems to follow from the informal extrapolation to the economy as a whole from a particular sector from within it'.[2] Yet, although Joel Mokyr and Deirdre McCloskey convincingly demonstrate that supply conditions are paramount throughout the economy as a whole, there remains a 'demand' side that needs to be explained.[3] In the case of scientific instruments, which range from necessary tools to luxury toys, there would appear to have been a steady and growing demand throughout this period, which led to the establishment and continuing growth of the trade outside London well into the late nineteenth century.

The evidence does not point to the generation of great local provincial demand; rather it suggests a growth of the domestic market and of those abroad. Physically, these markets appear to have been located either in London itself, or (reached through the gateway of London) overseas. The metal industries in general, Ralph Davis has commented, had increased in value almost to match the output of the woollen industries by the 1770s: 'it was growing demand derived largely from the American colonies that pulled the metal industries forward during the first three-quarters of the eighteenth century; and an increasing output made it possible to secure considerable economies from division of labour, and this lowering of costs was able to stimulate demand further.'[4] The success of the business of instrument production outside London, as shown in previous chapters, had much

---

[1]   McKendrick (1982), 9.
[2]   Fine and Leopold (1993), 73.
[3]   Mokyr (1977); McCloskey (1981).
[4]   Davis (1973), 303.

to do with the integration of regional specialized economies – the metal trades of Birmingham or the Sheffield cutlery industry – or an industrializing hinterland providing a ready pool of skilled labour, as in the areas surrounding Liverpool and Manchester. In the capital, as Gareth Stedman Jones has summarized:

> The economic importance of London depended upon three closely-related factors: firstly, it was the major port of the English import and trans-shipment trade; secondly, it was by far the largest single consumer market in England; and thirdly, as a centre of government and the royal court, it was the focal point of conspicuous consumption and its attendant luxury trades.[5]

Stedman Jones went on to show that in the case of 'finished consumer goods', such as scientific instruments, 'proximity to the market could still be a decisive advantage' for the London producer over the provincial manufacturer until well into the 1860s.[6] Although 'some of these trades underwent a gentle decline in the second half of the nineteenth century' – their details are beyond the scope of this study – as long as there was sufficient demand, and as long as 'technological innovators demanded superior handmade, and often new or experimental precision instruments ... there was little chance of real competition from Lancashire, the West Riding, or the Midlands'.[7] I would argue that Stedman Jones has looked only at the small 'precision instrument' fraction of the entire instrument market, and suggest that he has underestimated the diversity of the products of this trade, and thus the range of its customers. So it is important to address what the instruments were, how they changed during this period and who bought them.

Even if the instrument trade was not entirely demand-led, the demands upon it during the Industrial Revolution stimulated its growth, and require further discussion. Maxine Berg comments that historians of consumption have failed to look at the manufacture of luxury products as industries and, conversely, that economic historians have failed to collect output data for industries producing such new consumer wares. In an article demonstrating that product innovation promoted consumerism, Berg has argued that 'scientific instruments were ornaments of consumption as much as they were tools of engineering'.[8] Because of the absence of any meaningful data, especially output or profit figures, this chapter outlines the main types of customer for different sorts of instrument in order to show where and how growth occurred, stimulating new and viable centres for production outside the metropolis. Even without quantitative data, an analysis of demand shows that neither 'ornaments of demand' nor 'tools of engineering' fully describe the products aimed at the various categories within the market.

---

[5]   Stedman Jones (1976), 19.
[6]   Ibid., 20.
[7]   Ibid., 22.
[8]   Berg (1998), 154.

**Consumer Demand: The Customers**

The customers for scientific instruments need to be defined. The market, whether at home or overseas, as briefly discussed in the first chapter to this book, was defined as long ago as 1964 by the instrument historian Silvio Bedini, and was seen as having mainly 'teaching' and 'practical' customers, subdivided into 'scientific', 'professional' and 'dilettante' categories.[9] More recently, Richard Sorrenson, having sketched the supply side of the eighteenth century trade, sums up the demand side as

> domestic, colonial and European consumers purchasing marine, surveying, and household instruments; natural philosophers in Britain and abroad ordering experimental and observational instruments; popular lecturers and schoolteachers buying a whole range of demonstration instruments to explicate the new natural philosophy; and finally ... the British state itself, buying gauging instruments for the customs and excise, marine instruments for the navy, astronomical instruments for the Royal Greenwich Observatory, and surveying instruments for the Board of ordnance, as well as offering prizes for navigational instruments through the Board of Longitude.[10]

Sorrenson has four market categories, merging the 'scientific' with a 'Special Market' that he sees appearing in the eighteenth century, the British state. His contention is that different markets for different types of instruments emerged over time: a 'Natural Philosophical' market appeared in the seventeenth century, absorbing newly-invented instruments such as pendulum clocks, telescopes, air pumps and microscopes as well as older mathematical instruments, such as quadrants and magnetic compasses, used in this new context of demonstration. Two entirely new markets, the 'Natural Philosophical Lecturing' and the 'Household', were created in the late seventeenth and early eighteenth centuries, as applied science moved down the social scale 'into the newly burgeoning commercial market-place of consumers'.[11]

Only his somewhat cumbersome category of 'Marine, Astronomical, Surveying, Weights and Measures' does Sorrensen date as existing from before the scientific revolution, and into it he places most practical instruments (which Bedini characterized as 'practical' or 'professional'), but adds the rider that 'the most important newcomers in the eighteenth century were chronometers, dividing engines, large theodolites, and achromatic lenses, all of which became commonly available only after they had been first developed in response to the demands of the British state'. There are distinct problems with Sorrenson's analysis of the market, especially where he has put scientific demand together with state demand;

---

9   Bedini (1964), 3–13.
10  Sorrenson (1995), 264.
11  Ibid., 265.

however, he appears to be one of the first to articulate in print the role of state demand and intervention.[12]

By building on the analyses offered by Bedini and Sorrenson, and incorporating evidence from the provincial trade, we can create a new characterization of the trade (see Table 9.1). This shows how demand changed over time, and reveals how new markets came into existence. Clearly, the products across all these markets changed with time. For instance, those aimed at the first category, the dilettante market, were generally demand-led luxuries, and in the mid-eighteenth century probably formed a larger proportion of the entire instruments market than in 1851. Their design might have included a certain amount of cultural involution, or change for change's sake, but served the purpose of delighting the fashion sense of the owner and, incidentally, increasing the skills of the maker. The greatest growth was seen in the practical market, especially in the demand for increasing numbers of surveying and navigation instruments. There was not yet an 'industrial' category, as the instruments eventually designed for product control on the factory floor would at this period either have been the 'practical' instruments used in measurement or engineering, or have fallen into the 'state's' market, where standard instruments were required by legislation, from which those in use in the market place were derived.

Not until the late nineteenth century, when university-designed equipment was marketed successfully to industry – examples being the highly-successful business of the Cambridge Scientific Instrument Company, and James White of Glasgow[13] – could an 'industrial' category be said to have come into existence. Driving it were dramatic changes in the applications of science, and in particular the genesis of the electrical industry and its eventual application to the domestic scene. The most significant growth area during the Industrial Revolution was surely the 'teaching' market, which led to new emerging audiences for science and customers for instruments, especially women, younger people and children. This also created a small, but growing 'domestic' market, mostly confined to the upper and middle classes, which would not become widespread throughout society until the late twentieth century. These six broad market categories will be examined in turn, to assess where the demand for instruments grew during this period, even if, as Hudson has remarked, the effects of the consumer revolution have been over-emphasized.[14]

---

[12]   See also Wess (1998).

[13]   For CSI, see Cattermole and Wolfe (1987); for White, see Clarke et al. (1989), 252–75.

[14]   Hudson (1992), 176.

**Table 9.1    Markets for scientific instruments made in England, 1760 to 1851**

| Market | Contents | Examples | Size and Character |
|---|---|---|---|
| 1. Dilettante | Any bespoke item used to demonstrate its owner's virtuosity, cleverness and wealth | Clockwork automata, items constructed in precious metals | Small, metropolitan |
| 2. Practical | Surveying instruments: exploration, mapping, engineering. Navigation instruments: foreign and coastal trade | Compasses, chronometers, tables, telescopes, gunnery and fortification devices, levels, slide rules | Growing with the empire, peripatetic |
| 3. Teaching | Lecture-demonstration material | Orreries, electrical machines, magic lanterns, airpumps, chemical apparatus, magnets, mechanical models | Large growth in late 18th century with the Literary and Philosophical movement, subsequently further down the social scale with the Mechanics' Institutes; metropolitan and provincial |
| 4. Domestic | Items that became 'everyday' | Clocks, spectacles, telescopes, microscopes, opera glasses, cameras obscura, thermometers, barometers, 'toys' | Small, but spreading within the rise of a consumer culture |
| 5. Scientific | Precision pieces, used for specific experiments, or as national standards | Physics apparatus made for J.P. Joule by Manchester instrument maker J.B. Dancer to measure calorific heat. More usually commissioned from London instrument trade than the provinces. Astronomical transit instrument at Greenwich, defining the prime meridian (accepted internationally 1884). | Small, but sometimes expensive; usually London-based or generated, but extremely influential nationally and internationally |
| 6. State | Precision pieces, sometimes made to match legislation | Standard yard for the Royal Society; chronometers and dividing engines for the Board of Longitude; pendulum clocks, quadrants, sectors, telescopes for the Royal Greenwich Observatory; theodolites for the Ordnance Survey; hydrometers and saccharometers for Customs and Excise; navigation instruments for the Royal Navy; surveying instruments for the empire | Extremely large |

## The Dilettante Market

Often scientific instruments were bought for non-scientific purposes.[15] Wealthy customers enjoyed stargazing, or exploring pond-life through a microscope, without necessarily adding to knowledge through their use of these devices, or even understanding fully how the instrument worked. Early twenty-first-century equivalents might be an expensive top-of-the-range camera, or the latest personal computer. As far as the maker was concerned, this did not matter: he had made a sale. This trend can be discerned much earlier on the Continent, where collections of contemporary instruments, often constructed in valuable materials, would be presented to royalty and preserved in cabinets.[16]

These were often given to indicate respect for the recipient's understanding of the knowledge represented by the object – even if this understanding was absent, as very likely for instance, with the gilt astrolabe which may have been presented to Henry Stuart, Prince of Wales (1594–1612).[17] The astrolabe requires an understanding of basic geometry and astronomy in order to be used as either a time-telling, positional-fixing or surveying instrument, and there is no evidence that this example was ever used for the purposes for which it was made. Highly decorated, and usually highly complex instruments – designed to demonstrate the virtuosity of the maker as well as flatter the intellect of the customer or the recipient of his gift – have survived, particularly in princely collections from the Renaissance onwards.

This industry depended on a need for luxury goods, and during the seventeenth century a number of London instrument makers were able to cater for this particular demand, but this luxury end of the market remained tiny, in England as elsewhere. Recent research has shown that instruments have been collected as curiosities or antiquities only in the past 200 years. This means that instruments that found their way into cabinets of curiosities were usually contemporary, for by the eighteenth century it was human curiosity in the natural world which was the driving impetus to forming such a cabinet.[18] These instruments were usually at the forefront of design, and acquired to impress the owner's acquaintances as much as to undertake an occasional scientific programme. Often, the owner would be a member of the Royal Society – based in London – but might undertake his 'research' in the country. More often than not, his instruments would have been made and purchased in London.

---

15 Bryden (1972), 15.
16 For example, those in the Hessian Landgaves' *Kunstkammer* at Kassel, or the Royal Danish *Kunstkammer* at Copenhagen, with items of this nature in both dating from the late sixteenth century: see Impey and MacGregor (1983), 142–4; 182; 301–4.
17 Made by the first native-born English instrument maker, Humphrey Cole: see Ackermann (1998), 32; Turner (2000), 135–9.
18 Turner (1987), 275; Anderson (2003).

During this period, the aristocracy was growing wealthier as land-prices rose. A growing genuine interest in scientific principles led upper-class Englishmen to gather, in their country houses, collections of natural history, rocks and minerals alongside their paintings and antiquities brought back from the Grand Tour. John Stuart, third Earl of Bute (1713–92), had large collections of natural history material, but also a substantial collection of instruments.[19] He had clearly been influenced by the intellectual pursuits and collections formed by his uncle, Archibald Campbell, third Duke of Argyll (1682–1761). Items of conspicuous consumption ordered by the Duke included a grand orrery and a large mechanical equinoctial ring sundial, which incorporated his coat-of-arms.[20] Bute had enormous political power, and was very close to the widowed Augusta, Princess of Wales, and thus in a position to influence her son, who became king in 1760. Bute arranged for the young George III (1738–1820) to attend lectures on natural philosophy, and it has been suggested that the king wished to emulate Bute's example in acquiring an even larger and more complete suite of apparatus: within three months of his accession he had appointed the elder George Adams as his Mathematical Instrument Maker, and commissioned him to make pneumatic and mechanical apparatus.[21]

Part of the theory of the rise of a consumer society is the 'trickle-down' aspect of emulation through society. This model appears to work for England, where society was more open, and where there was comparatively more social mobility than in, for instance, France. There appears to be more evidence in England of the successful emulation of one's betters in the hierarchy, and the possibility of moving upwards through advantageous marriage.[22] This has, however, been dismissed by Ben Fine and Ellen Leopold as 'wishful thinking', in that most contemporary observations deploring emulation of one's superiors were written by upper class observers jealous of their own position.[23] Yet the spread of this sort of collecting of scientific instruments during the late eighteenth century amongst the British upper classes must have been given some stamp of approval by the existence and knowledge of the Royal collection. Also, as we have already seen in Chapter 8, instrument retailers mentioned the patronage of royal or noble customers in their trade literature whenever they could.

These collections were not solely demonstrations of conspicuous consumption. For example, both Bute and Argyll were actively interested in the subjects to which the contents of their collections could be applied. Bute apparently designed a microscope, albeit one subsequently made in extremely limited numbers by George Adams, which sold for £21 (Figure 9.1); and Argyll's patronage of the

[19] Turner (1967), 213–42; Bute's other collections are discussed in Schweizer (1988).

[20] Morrison-Low (1995a); Morrison-Low (2002), 37; Millburn (2000), 94–95 on the fate of Campbell's collection; Emerson (2002).

[21] Morton and Wess (1993), 17–18; Millburn (2000), 94.

[22] Perkin (1969), 17–62.

[23] Fine and Leopold (1993), 138.

youthful watchmaker Alexander Cumming, first at his substantial new house at Inveraray (where he repaired some of the Duke's instruments), and subsequently in London, allowed Cumming access to the wealthiest of customers, including the king.[24] Such patrons had estates all around the country, hence the survival today of significant collections of instruments at Burton Constable, Chatsworth, Kedleston, Longleat and Petworth.

However, none now contain items made outside London: apart from a (no longer extant) pyrometer made by the precision clockmaker Joseph Finney of Liverpool at Burton Constable, the dilettante market was almost exclusively supplied by the London trade.[25] This was because such patrons were spending a good proportion of their year in London, the centre of power, for social as well as political reasons. By the late nineteenth century, however, royal patronage of scientific instrument manufacture had declined, partly because of lack of interest from the reigning monarch.[26]

The significance of wealthy, dilettante collectors, amongst whom the King was the most socially elevated example, is that in order to keep this market supplied with novelties, the instrument makers were forced to re-design and improve existing instruments and to create new ones. For instance, the mechanical parts of the microscope went through a thousand permutations during this period – to the adjustment and control of the instrument, and the range of manipulation of microscopic objects – although very little was done to improve the optical system of the microscope. Significant improvement of the latter had to wait until the early 1830s when mathematical analysis first showed how optical components could be combined to produce distortion-free images with high resolution. Little real scientific work was accomplished with the ordinary compound instruments of this period, and it was with the single lens 'simple microscope', which with

---

[24]   This microscope was first illustrated in Hill (1770), whose patron was Bute, and subsequently described by Adams (1771), 1: 'We owe the construction of the variable microscope to the ingenuity and generosity of a noble person ...'; see also Millburn (2000), 146; for Cumming, see Cosh (1969); Marsden (2004), 298–9.

[25]   Holbrook et al. (1992), 18–19, 105, 113–114, 140–141, 148–149, and 195–196. The George III collection also has pieces made by Finney. For the collection at Burton Constable, see Hall (1991a) and (1991b), 25–32, where it is shown from manuscript sources that some material was provided locally, although most of the items came from Benjamin Cole, or Nairne & Blunt, of London; for that at Chatsworth, see Barker (2003), 226–31; the chemical collections at Petworth are described in McCann (1983). Another collection, still in its country house setting, has been described at Burghley, Lincolnshire, in Baddeley (1986). The founding collections of the British Museum, formed by the London physician Sir Hans Sloane (1660–1753) also contained some instruments, drawn from international sources: see Cherry (1994), 213–15.

[26]   For George III as a collector of instruments and clocks, see Morton and Wess (1993); Millburn (2000), 98–106; and Marsden (2004).

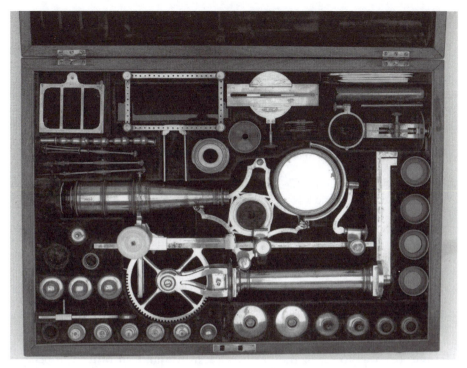

**Figure 9.1    George Adams's 'Variable' microscope, designed by the 3rd Earl of Bute, *c*.1780; this example is made in silver**

*Source*: National Museums of Scotland, NMS.T.1987.344

skill could be used at higher magnifications, that discoveries such as Brownian motion were made.[27]

Even as late as 1862, J. Parkes of Birmingham – a firm clearly in touch with demand, as evidenced by their offering a variety of 'educational' models for newly-expanding markets – was willing to offer a particularly baroque compound instrument in oxidized silver, 'designed specially for the International Exhibition … this magnificent drawing-room instrument is the first successful attempt to combine Science and Art in the construction of a Microscope', at a cost of £150.[28]

---

[27]  For the successful introduction of the achromatic microscope, see Nuttall (1979). Ford (1985) discusses the single-lens instruments used in serious work done by Carl Linneaeus (fungal spores), William Withering (botany), Joseph Hooker (botany), Robert Brown (botany) and Charles Darwin (natural history). Brownian motion is 'the erratic random movement of microscopic particles in suspension, for instance in a liquid or smoke particles in air: caused by the continuous irregular bombardment of the particles by the molecules of the surrounding medium. Named after Robert Brown (1773–1858)': Uvarov et al. (1971), 55.
[28]  Parkes (1862), 12–13.

Whether more were ordered than the single example constructed and shown in London – 'the most magnificent instrument ever produced' – remains to be seen (Figure 9.2).[29] It recalls, in its impracticality, the microscopes made for George III, which, although fit for drawing room entertainment, would accomplish little else. Together with the Bute instrument, these demonstrated little mechanical sophistication, giving the viewer a less-than-steady view of the object under scrutiny.[30]

## The Market for Practical Instruments

Alexander Mackenzie (1755?–1820), embarking on his exploration in North America of what became known as the Mackenzie River, in 1792, wrote:

> In this [first] voyage, I was not only without the necessary books and instruments, but also felt myself deficient in the sciences of astronomy and navigation: I did not hesitate, therefore, to undertake a winter's voyage to this country [i.e. England], in order to procure the one and acquire the other. These objects being accomplished, I returned, to determine the practicability of a commercial communication through the continent of North America, between the Atlantic and Pacific Oceans ... Nor do I hesitate to declare my decided opinion, that very great and essential advantages may be derived by extending our trade from one sea to another.[31]

His purpose was to reach the Pacific Ocean overland, in order to open up and exploit new territories for the fur trade, under the auspices of one of the aggressively commercial Canadian fur companies. From whom he acquired his instruments, and who gave him instruction, is not known; but it is safe to surmise that both were based in London, rather than in his native Stornoway. The market for practical instruments, those used in surveying, navigation or teaching, by those defined by Bryden as 'professional' customers, was the one which grew – for provincial English makers – most substantially throughout the period 1760 to 1850.[32] Teaching will be discussed as a separate category below.

It was in the hands of the large group of practising mathematicians – the surveyor, the navigator and what was to become the precision engineer – that the development of the trade in scientific instruments lay, through technological breakthrough and market growth. Before the Industrial Revolution, the use of instruments encapsulated skills, performed by a few numerate specialists. During the Industrial Revolution, the mathematical practitioner was professionalized:

---

[29]   *Catalogue...* (1862), 27.
[30]   The single exception was the work of Hill (1770), carried out using an Adams 'Variable' microscope: Bradbury (1967), 152.
[31]   Mackenzie (1801), Preface, v. His instruments are not known to have survived; but for a discussion of what he might have used, and the accuracy of his survey, see Swannell (1959).
[32]   Bryden (1972), 10–15.

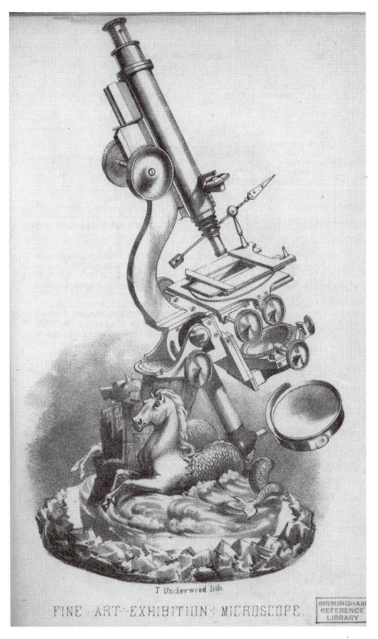

**Figure 9.2   James Parkes & Son's 'Fine Art Exhibition Microscope', offered in 1862**

*Source*: Birmingham Library Services

surveyors were no longer exclusively local men, owning their own instruments. Either they moved in under those great state umbrellas, such as the Ordnance Survey and the Great Trigonometrical Survey of India, or they combined into businesses of their own. These state, or imperial, practitioners, will be looked at below.

Men like James Brindley (1716–72), architect of the Bridgwater Canal between Manchester and Liverpool, who had his portrait painted with his surveyor's level conspicuously visible (Figure 9.3), transformed the face of England from a country where the internal means of transport were slow, dangerous and expensive: first by providing the routes of the canals; latterly, the railways; and finally the roads, while the coastal trade continued to ply between ports, whose harbours were significantly improved during this period. Transport improvements, especially those involving engineering alterations to the landscape, clearly generated an extra demand for surveying instruments. With the rise of the empire and Britain's growing maritime trade, every ship had to have navigation instruments for a safe passage. Usually these were bought in London, although during this period, as we have seen, it became possible to acquire them elsewhere, particularly in the larger ports of Bristol and Liverpool, and subsequently in others such as Kingston-upon-Hull, Newcastle-upon-Tyne and Portsmouth.[33]

In her work on consumerism during the early modern period, Lorna Weatherill listed the probate inventory of William Cartwright of Muxton in Shropshire, who died in 1718, and who was described as a 'mathematician'. Although his possessions were not especially valuable, his eight-roomed house was comfortably furnished. Amongst his belongings were 'one hundred books, [a] three leg staffe, one plaine table [for drawing up a survey], one wood Quadrant, one small brass Quadrant, ... one Brass sights, one pair Brass Compasses, ... one pair Globes and box'. Cartwright was known to have made estate maps, and surveying would appear to have been his means of making a living. This source does not reveal whether his instruments were made locally or in London; but despite living in a somewhat remote part of England, he had acquired the tools of his trade.[34]

Harold Perkin has demonstrated how a fourth category, which he identifies as the professional class, emerged by the early nineteenth century. This was created as a by-product of the social upheaval caused by industrialization, through the interaction between the contending aristocratic, entrepreneurial and working class ideals, 'characterized by expert, esoteric service demanding integrity in the purveyor and trust in the client and community, and by non-competitive reward in the form of a fixed salary or standard and unquestioned fee'.[35] As they gained respectability and self-respect, he noted that 'at the same time the new professions

---

[33]  The Royal Navy was involved in the almost continual wars with France during the latter part of the eighteenth century, and together with the merchant navy, the numbers of ships rose during this period: see Chapter 8 and Mitchell (1988), 535–6.

[34]  Weatherill (1988), 181; see Bendall (1997), II, 87, for Cartwright.

[35]  Perkin (1969), 254.

**Figure 9.3    F. Parsons, portrait of James Brindley, engraving by R. Dunkarton, 1770**

*Source*: © National Museum of Science and Industry

proliferated, and organized themselves to demand the same kind of status as the old [doctors, lawyers, clergy]: the civil engineers in 1818, the architects in 1837, the pharmacists in 1841, the mechanical engineers in 1847, and so on'.[36] It was not until 1868 that the surveyors formed their institution.

In his study of the profession, F.M.L. Thompson shows how the surveyor emerged through the troublesome times in the aftermath of the Restoration: 'from a more secure and reliable mastery over the craft of measuring and plotting, the land surveyor was diversifying into essential supporting roles in matters of valuing, letting, buying, selling, and improving land ... but in all spheres, the commanding heights remained in other hands, in those of attorneys, stewards, scriveners, or architects'.[37] The growing desire for estate improvement and enclosure on the part of landowners assisted the professionalization of the surveyor in the mid-eighteenth century, shown through the appearance of textbooks about surveying, which often described the instrumentation involved and its use. Thompson notes the advent of the improved theodolite of Jonathan Sisson of the Strand, which included a telescopic sight and spirit level grafted on to the original instrument. Other improvements in the tripod stand, the compass needle mounting, and the accuracy of the division of the scale 'converted an interesting gadget into a serviceable and portable field instrument'.[38] Over the next century, as we saw in the case of the microscope, a proliferation of designs and 'improvements' in surveying instrumentation appeared: 'the maker', observes J.A. Bennett, 'could not leave the surveyor in peace'.[39]

Most of these design improvements appear to have taken place in the influential London workshops, although the market for their use came from all over England as improving landowners mapped their increasingly valuable estates: nevertheless, Thompson warns that 'enclosure ... [was not] the be-all and end-all of eighteenth-century surveying'.[40] He quotes an analysis of eighteenth-century manuscript maps in the Bedfordshire Record Office, showing that only 35 per cent were enclosure maps, with a further 46 per cent being made for the owner's other purposes, such as inheritance, for sale or ordinary estate management. However, from 1790 to 1815, the picture is different: 'this was the age of busy, almost feverish, enclosing; in this period 60 per cent of the maps were enclosure maps, and only 34 per cent were estate maps.'[41]

Were English provincial instrument makers responding to this demand? Certainly, in Scotland, the surviving output of the Edinburgh firm run by John Miller and his nephew Alexander Adie appears to have been one created in response to the surveying market, and there is great variety in the design of

---

36   Ibid., 255.
37   Thompson (1968), 26.
38   Ibid., 28.
39   Bennett (1987), 150.
40   Thompson (1968), 33.
41   Ibid.

their surveying instrumentation.[42] In Ireland and America, the demand was for a different type of instrument, based around the compass, to suit the lower, wooded landscapes; in England, as with the rest of Europe, where buildings and church spires often formed local landmarks, the demand grew for the altazimuth theodolite.[43]

In some areas of England, makers of specialist surveying instruments adapted their wares for their customers: in Cornwall, from about 1825, William Wilton of St Day produced special equipment for the tin mines.[44] Also catering for the mining industry was a firm which had its origins in Leeds with a family of immigrant Jewish instrument makers who settled in Derby in 1830.[45] John Davis, nephew to Gabriel Davis and brother of Gabriel's partner Edward Davis, worked for the company, travelling to Liverpool, Cheltenham and Derby with their wares. With the growth of the railway system, Derby came into closer contact with the capital, but it also came into direct contact with the expanding industrial areas of the West Riding, and the Derbyshire, Nottinghamshire and Leicestershire coalfields.

Davis manufactured and marketed two extremely popular mining instruments: Benjamin Biram's anemometer, patented in 1842 (Figure 9.4), a device which measured ventilation air-flow in mines, and John Hedley's improvement of an altitude sight to the standard miner's dial, for surveying inclined underground passages, dating from about 1850 (Figure 9.5).[46] Both these designers worked as mining engineers, with practical experience of particular circumstances, and their local adaptations to instruments were carried out by local instrument makers. This is a reflection of real change within provincial England, as the London instrument makers do not appear to have been suppliers for the mining industry. Elsewhere in England, there were compass makers to be found in Birmingham, from the date of the first street directory in 1767 (and thus probably before), and specialist surveyors' measuring tape manufacturers both there and in Sheffield.[47]

A similar pattern is to be found with marine instruments. Although figures of merchant and coastal shipping volumes are frequently given in tons rather than in numbers of vessels, it is clear that there was substantial growth in the amount of merchant shipping afloat. The rise in numbers has been assessed by Mitchell, and according to McCloskey, rates of tonnage growth ran at about 2.3 per cent per year, rising to 3.3 per cent per year between 1814 and 1860. This had a large

---

[42]   Clarke et al. (1989), 25–31.
[43]   Burnett and Morrison-Low (1989), 24–7; Bennett (1987), 149.
[44]   Wilton died in 1869 and his eldest son William Henry acquired the business, which he sold in 1874, emigrating to Valparaiso: see Wilton (1989), 71.
[45]   The first advertisement for 'G. Davis & Co., Working Opticians' appeared in the *Leeds Intelligencer*, 7 May 1821.
[46]   English patent 9249 of 1842; Anon. (1979).
[47]   Birmingham and Sheffield directories, *passim*.

**Figure 9.4    Biram's anemometer, by Davis, Derby, *c*.1850**

*Source*: Museum of the History of Science, Oxford, inv. no. 51556

**Figure 9.5    Hedley's dial, by Davis, Derby, detail, *c*.1855**

*Source*: National Museums of Scotland, NMS.T.1968.122

cumulative effect over time, allowing freight and passenger fares to fall.[48] One of the great technical problems of the age was that of finding a ship's position at sea when out of sight from the land. After 1707 this became a state-sponsored affair, which will be discussed below, along with state-sponsored surveys.

Meanwhile, even ships hugging the coastline required direction-finding aids, and it appears that these were occasionally produced and sold in the provinces.[49] We have seen in Chapter 2 that the ports of Bristol and Liverpool produced navigation instruments, apparently in some quantity; manufacturers in Birmingham and Sheffield did so too, although by 1866 'in consequence of the inland situation of Birmingham, nautical instruments are not produced to any great extent.'[50] Despite this statement, it is worth pointing out that the Birmingham firm James Parkes & Son's 1848 trade catalogue offered six unpriced 'ship compasses', and a further half-dozen 'best ship compasses, in square oak box, brass cup, agate cap needle', between six and eleven inches in diameter. Smaller 'miners' and mariners' compasses', from 1s 9d to 8s 6d each were also available.[51] The street directories describe a number of 'manufacturers of mathematical instruments, and mariners' and miners' compasses' during this period, and presumably the 1866 comment reflects that octants and sextants were not made there. In Sheffield, the largest of the early nineteenth century producers, Chadburns, described themselves as 'opticians and manufacturers of nautical instruments' from 1833, but the precise type of these instruments was unspecified.[52]

A ship would require at least one sighting instrument for measuring the Sun's altitude at midday (Figure 9.6), and from this, and from knowledge of the Sun's position related to the stars, the ship's latitude could be determined. By the mid-eighteenth century, the backstaff was being replaced by the octant; and subsequently, it, too, was superseded by the sextant.[53] Longitude is much more difficult to determine, but the problem was greatly simplified with the commercial availability of the first precision chronometer in the 1760s.[54] After that, what Alun Davies characterized as 'the very high demand – from ships' officers, from the Admiralty, and from the trading companies – attracted a number of watchmaking firms to concentrate on, or specialize in, the production of the instrument.'[55] Because these were high-value items, and numbered, Davies was able to trace the economic development and decline of the chronometer trade.

---

[48]  Mitchell (1988), 535–6; McCloskey (1981), 251.
[49]  Clifton (2003).
[50]  Timmins (1866), 534.
[51]  Parkes (1848), 18 and 22.
[52]  Birmingham and Sheffield street directories, *passim*.
[53]  The octant was apparently not widely used by English mariners before the 1750s or 1760s, according to Clifton (2005).
[54]  See the essays in Andrewes (1996).
[55]  Davies (1978), 511.

**Figure 9.6    'Our Captain, Our Guide over pathless waters', photograph by B.W.
Kilburn, Littleton, New Hampshire, 1890**

*Source*: Howarth-Loomes Collection, National Museums of Scotland

With one, later two or three, chronometers per vessel (five on a flagship), one
with Greenwich time, and another adjusted daily after local noon was determined,
Davies reckoned that supply matched demand by about 1840. In the longer term
because of the instrument's static technology and extreme durability this meant
that replacement was minimal, so new demand declined.[56] There does seem to have
been a considerable market in second-hand instruments, not solely chronometers,
and this is apparent from advertisements. Partly because the maritime market
was conservative in its purchases, but also because the only real improvement in
sighting instruments during this period was the ever-increasing accuracy of scale

---

[56]   Ibid.

division, many octants and sextants were overhauled and re-sold. Repairing and maintaining must have been the bread-and-butter business for most 'nautical instrument makers' in provincial ports around Britain. This is shown, for example, by an 1808 advertisement by R.& C. Beilby of Bristol:

> R.& C. BEILBY (Successors to *Mr Springer*) respectfully inform the PROPRIETORS and CAPTAINS of SHIPS, that they have a large and well assorted Stock of COMPASSES, QUADRANTS, TELESCOPES, and other Musical [sic] Instruments, which may be depended upon as correct and good.
>
> N.B. Any of the above instruments REPAIRED with accuracy.[57]

Another method for finding the longitude at sea was by the 'lunar distance method' – measuring the distance of certain stars from the ever-changing position of the Moon – and this required more accuracy than was generally obtainable from the octant, which was invariably made of wood. However, good octants of this period had backsights, which allowed obtuse angles to be measured. The sextant, a more compact and better engineered instrument in metal, capable of much great refinement and accuracy, was developed around 1770, and the best were skilfully divided by the most eminent London instrument makers: Bird, Ramsden and Troughton.[58]

Although octants with provincial signatures appear from the late eighteenth century, sextants seem to have been produced only in London until the mid-nineteenth century. This was presumably because the rigid and more durable metal frame of the sextant was only an advantage if it could be made light enough and therefore small enough, for ease of use at sea. It was initially only the best London makers who had access to the dividing engines and sophisticated fabrication methods necessary to achieve this. Often, wealthier naval officers, or members of the East India Company, bought their own instruments: sextants in particular being 'in great request in the naval service'.[59] It does not seem to be possible to gauge the numbers which were required, and although the design did not change much over the next one hundred years, supply does not appear to have outstripped demand.

Better navigation instruments allowed for longer and safer voyages, and once the problem of 'finding the longitude' was solved, were arguably one of the factors which allowed Britannia to rule the waves in the peace that followed Waterloo. As the amount of shipping, both governmental and mercantile, grew to cater for the demands of the Empire, so demand for instrumentation to afford it a safe passage kept pace with it.

---

[57] *Bristol Weekly Intelligencer*, 20 August 1808.
[58] Clifton (forthcoming).
[59] Pearson (1828), 576.

## The Growth of Natural Philosophy and Other Lecturing

The effect of the cultural and social diffusion of a scientific culture during the period of the Industrial Revolution has received considerable attention from historians of science during the last 30 years. Although difficult to quantify, a more widespread understanding of scientific principles, it has been argued, may have been associated with industrial advance. The audience for science grew enormously during the eighteenth century. The early itinerant lecturers, spreading the Newtonian gospel, found eager listeners, first in London, and subsequently in the provinces.[60] 'The community of experimenters, the instrument makers, and self-styled engineers with their varying degrees of dependence on Newton's principles, and the devotees of the public lectures, constructed a broad bottom for natural philosophy', Larry Stewart has written.[61]

These first London-based lecturers, at the start of the eighteenth century, usually involved the collaboration of a university-educated lecturer with an instrument maker: examples cited by Morton and Wess are James Hodgson with Francis Hauksbee the younger (1687–1763), and Benjamin Worster with William Vream.[62] A later generation, which included Benjamin Martin (1704–82) and James Ferguson (1710–76), would combine these roles in the same person. At first, only the syllabuses of the lecture courses were published, but in due course the lecture text, together with illustrations of the demonstration apparatus – much of which had evolved specifically for lecturing purposes – was published in 'textbooks which often gave details that would help someone wanting to replicate the equipment'.[63]

Morton and Wess link the increased mid-century activity of natural philosophy lecturing with the successful establishment of the press, and the ability of the lecturers to attract their audiences through newspaper advertisement; however, this fell away as the audience was diverted by other attractions, including the Society of Arts and other institutions that offered a more stable environment with extensive facilities.[64] The nucleus of George III's collection of instruments was formed by his tutor, Stephen Demainbray (1710–82), who had previously been an itinerant lecturer, but whose career had ended when his audience evaporated, and he obtained his royal appointment in 1769 through the patronage of the Earl of Bute. As Morton and Wess comment, the collection contains 'items acquired on his travels ... several in Edinburgh ... a number in France ... Henry Hindley of York also made a pyrometer for Demainbray, possibly to the latter's design'.[65]

---

[60]  Inkster (1973), 99; Porter (2000), 142–55.
[61]  Stewart (1992), 386.
[62]  Morton and Wess (1993), 52.
[63]  Ibid., 56.
[64]  Ibid., 72–87.
[65]  Ibid., 123; inv. no. NMSI 1927–1184.

Clearly the market demand here was not large, although it was challenged by the younger generation. The later eighteenth century lecture-demonstrators, of whom Benjamin Martin and James Ferguson are the most frequently cited, encouraged the continuing interest in natural philosophy through the spread of literacy by publishing their own populist works, and in Martin's case, as we have seen, by advertising the apparatus in trade catalogues bound with each volume.[66] We have also seen how Martin (together with other London makers and suppliers) was able to equip Harvard College with a suite of instruments after the fire of 1764.[67] John Millburn commented in his 1986 critique that 'it is not even known with any certainty precisely who, or what class of person, attended the scientific lectures which are thought to have played an important part in developing the market for the instrument makers' products'.[68] In fact, much of this has been remedied, in part by the work of Ian Inkster, whose work on the growth of provincial science included the study of just such audiences in relation to their class-consciousness, political and religious affiliations: in particular, audiences in Sheffield, Liverpool and Derby.[69]

In the provinces, Inkster has shown that 'the activities of the itinerant lecturers in Sheffield were fundamental in the formation of an intellectual community.' However, the restructuring of that culture, through the formation of various scientific societies, in particular the Mechanics' Institutes and literary and philosophical societies, meant that eventually the itinerants' independence became unviable.[70] In Sheffield, by the early nineteenth century, 'opticians and instrument makers were particularly active members of the [scientific] community ... such men provided the apparatus around which science in the institutions revolved'.[71] In another essay, Inkster charts the success of these itinerants, who with their apparatus, began moving out from London to provincial England and beyond, from the mid-century onwards, becoming common in 'the growing industrial centres of Manchester, Birmingham, Sheffield, Leeds, Glasgow, Dublin and elsewhere'.[72]

Subsequently, they were unable to compete as science itself was reorganized: indeed, Inkster agrees with E.G.R. Taylor, that 'between the 1820s and the 1840s ... the older style of practitioners "disappeared"'.[73] Although this led to the setting up of a variety of institutions that were dependent on the members of the local scientific community, often their apparatus was not acquired locally. Dr Thomas S. Traill went to London in 1823 to purchase apparatus for the Liverpool

66 Millburn (1976), 104–7; and (1986b).
67 Wheatland (1968); Millburn (1976), 128–48.
68 Millburn (1986c), 84.
69 Inkster (1973), (1976), (1977) and (1980); also Elliott (2000).
70 Inkster (1976), 225.
71 Inkster (1973), 113.
72 Inkster (1980), 85.
73 Ibid., 95, quoting Taylor (1966), 95–107.

Royal Institution, where he 'went to [John] Newmans [Instrument Maker to the Royal Institution] and purchased upwards of £130 worth of Voltaic and chemical apparatus including what I had before ordered ...'.[74] Other London makers were visited, and orders placed with them by Dr Traill, which suggests that by this date the firm of A. Abraham, which had made its first appearance in the 1818 Liverpool directory, did not yet stock the teaching apparatus which it clearly produced by 1851.

In fact, as Inkster sums up, 'the educative public science lecture gave way to specialized educational instruments designed to service the needs of the middle class, both industrial and professional'.[75] A wide variety of provincial audiences, including women and children, were exposed to ideas which they would not otherwise have encountered. This was accomplished through lecture demonstrations at the meetings of societies, such as the Literary and Philosophical Society at Hull, which were formed with the intention of putting together libraries, museum collections, and demonstration apparatus. By 1835, the Sheffield Literary and Philosophical Society had a collection of electrical apparatus, an air pump and associated pneumatic accessories, and other instruments for demonstration or study (including a microscope and a balance).[76] In contrast, the Bristol Institution was 'notably short of instruments ... containing only a lucernal [projection] microscope, an air pump, some meteorological instruments' and an Atwood fall machine (a piece of apparatus devised in 1784 by the mathematician George Atwood to demonstrate the laws of motion).[77]

As we have seen, such societies fostered local exhibitions, which were well attended, and often displayed locally made or designed instruments. As the structure for scientific teaching became more formalized, apparatus which would initially have been brought by an itinerant lecturer was later provided by the societies, which invited the lecturers to be tied to them in a more formal way, and latterly such apparatus was owned by individual schools and colleges. It was this final phase, which came into its own after late nineteenth century legislation made education compulsory, that led to tremendous growth in this area, as more people were educated for longer. Even by the time of the Great Exhibition, local instrument makers were able to supply increasing amounts of educational apparatus to a public thirsty for knowledge: and this is reflected in those instrument makers' trade catalogues that have survived.[78]

---

74   National Library of Scotland, MS 19353, Diary of Thomas S. Traill.
75   Inkster (1980), 106.
76   Brears (1984), 3 and 19.
77   Neve (1983), 188–9.
78   Surviving trade catalogues from outside London dating from 1851 and before include two by Chadburns of Sheffield, and one by James Parkes of Birmingham.

**The Domestic Market**

In her work on consumer behaviour, Lorna Weatherill has shown that the ownership of domestic goods increased between 1675 and 1725. Using probate inventories for a range of English counties, and looking at the luxury end of the market, she demonstrated that in London domestic clocks (among other indicators) were to be found three times more frequently by 1715 than they had been in 1685.[79] By 1715, such clocks were considerably less expensive to make and their technology had improved radically (while high precision clocks and complex timepieces remained pricey), but the trend is there to be marked; they were on their way to becoming an everyday item in the home as the purchasing power of families grew. Unfortunately, her study cannot be extended further in time into the period under discussion here, because the nature of the records alters significantly, with information in the probate inventories changing.

A small domestic demand for certain types of instruments, such as the barometer, appears to have grown out of the teaching category. By being exposed to new scientific ideas through public lectures, or by reading about them in the proliferating local press, people came to desire these objects for their homes. These items came to be considered as 'everyday', in the same sense that domestic clocks and pocket watches had been previously. The demand grew for domestic barometers, which Nicholas Goodison links with the furniture trade (rather than specifically with the instrument trade). With wider distribution of wealth 'the growing middle classes took an interest in furnishing their houses comfortably. The expansion of the furniture trade was therefore assured: and the vast majority of domestic mercurial barometers which survive date from this period [1660–1860]'.[80]

It is the housing of these scientific instruments which is the important fashion element here, so that in the instance of barometer construction, the cabinet-maker clearly had to be aware of trends in furniture design (which incidentally illustrates the division of labour in the construction of this type of instrument). Similarly, other types of equipment can be considered as fashionable: telescopes, globes and microscopes as accoutrements for libraries and studies, or long case clocks in hallways. Yet in spite of this domestication of certain types of scientific instrument, the instrument maker continued to refine, manufacture and adapt instruments to market demand, acknowledging, however, that some of the demand was for more obviously 'scientific' or accurate versions. By the late nineteenth century, the largest barometer makers had adapted to producing the instrument in large numbers from factories in Birmingham and central London: 'Birmingham', stated an account of the trade in 1866, 'produces more barometers and thermometers than any place except London'.[81]

---

[79]  Weatherill (1988), 25.
[80]  Goodison (1977), 83.
[81]  Timmins (1866), 534.

Domestic thermometers were produced in huge numbers, and began to be used in a diversity of household chores, from jam-making to ensuring the survival of indoor plant-life. The most successful version of this instrument from the instrument maker's point-of-view was the clinical thermometer, invented in 1867 (and thus in effect outside our time scale, but included here because something is known about the stimulation of demand through its successful marketing). It was manufactured to great success with patent protection and advertising bombast, so that by the time J.J. Hicks of Hatton Garden, London, retired in 1914 he could claim to have sold 13 million.[82] Unlike the barometer, relatively secure on the wall, the fragility of the mercury-in-glass thermometer allowed a built-in obsolescence and thus further purchases.

The rise of interest in natural history, particularly botany and gardening, during the early nineteenth century, especially amongst middle-class women, meant that increasing numbers of thermometers and barometers were kept in the house, conservatory, or in special shelters outside, to record and forecast weather conditions. Other equipment for these new, widespread and socially acceptable hobbies included microscopes and killing bottles for entomologists, aquaria and dredge-nets for marine biologists, and binoculars and guns for ornithologists. The camera had to wait for the faster gelatine-emulsion films of the late nineteenth century before it, too, could be easily used as an investigative tool.[83]

Items that became 'everyday' included those constructed for amusement, perhaps first encountered through education, but which could be used for fun. G. L'E. Turner explains that books which encouraged improving parlour games became extremely popular from the early eighteenth century onwards, and that three of the most ancient 'toys' known to mankind – the whip-top, the hoop and the yo-yo – demonstrate the principle of conservation of angular momentum.[84] One of the most popular optical toys of the period of the Industrial Revolution was the kaleidoscope, which, as we have already seen in Chapter 8, was manufactured, retailed and sold widely throughout provincial England.

Other optical devices which grew in popularity were those which assisted drawing, one of the sought-after middle-class female accomplishments. These included the camera obscura, a device known since the sixteenth century, and the camera lucida, patented in 1807 and developed through a series of improvements. Both had a profound effect on the early development of photography, although this could not have been foreseen.[85] Similarly, various educational toys, including the magic lantern (which in turn had evolved from the solar microscope), were to influence greatly the genesis of the cinema at the end of the nineteenth century.[86]

---

[82]  McConnell (1998).
[83]  Allen (1976); Barber (1980). For scientific photography see, for example, Thomas (1997). The new popularity of glass-houses is discussed by Hix (1996).
[84]  Turner (1983a), 293–5.
[85]  See Morrison-Low and Simpson (1995).
[86]  Turner (1983a), 301–6; Hecht (1993).

With growth of culture and leisure, demand for opera glasses and small telescopes or field glasses also grew, assisted by canny advertisements by the retailers, as we have seen in Chapter 8.

The greatest domestic demand remained, however, for the one 'instrument' which most people require with age: spectacles. By the mid-nineteenth century, the word 'optician' no longer meant 'optical instrument maker', and instrument makers were no longer making spectacles for their bread-and-butter – spectacle making became a separate enterprise. This development can be seen in Birmingham, where, for instance in 1815, Thomas Askey was described in local directories as an optician, then by 1830 as 'optician and spectacle maker' and finally by 1850 as a 'spectacle maker':

> The manufacture of spectacles appears among the Birmingham trades as early as 1784, and was doubtless carried on some years earlier. The "goggle spectacles" of our grandfathers were made here in large quantities, and the patterns remained unchanged till about fifty years ago. Even as late as 1820, hampers of spectacles were sent away from Dudley Street, like packages of nails or chains, to be distributed throughout the country. The frames were large, thick, and clumsy, mostly of some sort of white metal, varying according to price. Mr Lancaster and Mr Godfrey were the first improvers, and as soon as steel wire became adapted for spectacles, a lighter and more elegant article was produced. At present [in 1866] there are at least ten manufacturers engaged in making spectacles, and about 200 hands are employed, Birmingham being the chief seat for the trade.[87]

Yet these necessities have always been subject to fashion, as shown by a York advertisement of 1754: '… Spectacles of all Sorts, set in Gold and Silver, Tortoiseshell, Horn, and Leather; also Reading-Glasses, Burning Glasses and Concaves for Persons near-sighted…'.[88] If there was a demand, the instrument maker could supply it, and offer permutations often undreamed of by his would be customer. More importantly, as pointed out by David Landes, most people require spectacles for close work after the age of about 40, because of physical changes within the structure of the eye. This necessity provides a constant demand, and clearly rises as the population expands. It remained a staple product of instrument houses in London and the provinces throughout the period. Using spectacles prolonged the working life of a craftsman by twenty years, and moreover, qualitatively, these were his best years; thus investment in an experienced workforce was encouraged. Corrective lenses 'doubled the skilled workforce, and more than doubled it if one takes into account the value of experience'.[89]

---

87  Birmingham directories, *passim.*; Timmins (1866), 533–4.
88  *Yorkshire Courant*, 12 February 1754.
89  Landes (1998), 46–7.

**The 'Scientist' and the State**

The 'scientific' demand for instruments was always a small one, and remained particularly so for makers based in the provinces. Apart from a very few examples – John Dalton (1766–1844) of Manchester was supplied with a microscope by J.B. Dancer (1822–87); his pupil James Prescott Joule (1818–89) ordered instruments from the same maker for his work on the mechanical equivalent of heat; Thomas Cooke's order book contains such eminent scientific customers as the astronomers Charles Piazzi Smyth (1819–1900), David Gill (1843–1914) and the engineer James Nasmyth (1808–90) – most men of science went to London to order their special equipment. [90]

Similarly, aspiring instrument makers in eighteenth-century provincial England moved to London to find their markets: as we have seen in earlier chapters, most of the makers of the 'heroic age' of instrument-making were born outside the metropolis. Once established there, their customers would come to them with their diverse demands. The few London makers who ventured out into the provinces from the 1780s onwards appear to have been less specialized, and were supported by diverse supplies from the metropolis which they were then able to retail. The term 'scientist' was not coined until 1833, and it implies an element of professionalism. For much of the Industrial Revolution, experimental science, demanding special custom-made apparatus, was undertaken by wealthy amateurs, and not – as in the late nineteenth century – in the two English universities.

One of the largest customers during this period was the state itself. Clearly, weights and measures, the basis of all quantification, whether in the market place or the laboratory, had been enshrined in English legislation since at least medieval times. They appear to have been generally accepted as standard throughout the kingdom, with the occasional legal clarification, and a fairly major overhaul in 1824.[91] With the expansion in trade from local to regional, and from national to international, the need to standardize units of measurement was essential. The state had to define the market standards in order to ensure its share. By the eighteenth century there was a demand by the state for increasing exactitude in measurement, this being essential for the correct regulation of markets, for taxation purposes and for ships finding their way across the oceans.[92] Money was put aside by Parliament at various dates to fund a national observatory, to find the longitude at sea, to pay for instruments used by various government departments, including Customs and Excise, the Board of Longitude and the Admiralty. Their efficacy was tested by another quasi-government institution, the Royal Society.

---

[90]   For Dancer, see Wetton (1990–1), 43, 61–2; for Cooke, see McConnell (1993c).
[91]   Connor (1987), 255–61; Ashworth (2003), 282–8.
[92]   See Frängsmyr et al. (1990); Wise (1995), and Connor and Simpson (2004), Chapter 9.

In Chapter 6, we saw how setting up a national observatory with precision equipment proved expensive, but impressed foreign visitors sufficiently to generate orders for the same instruments abroad from the London specialist makers. Similarly, J.A. Bennett has explained that the career paths of the London makers of the 'heroic age' were bound up around the Royal Observatory, the Board of Longitude and the Royal Society.[93] Others, including the popular novelist Dava Sobel, have looked at the *raison d'être* for the Board of Longitude, since, of the works that depended on precision timekeeping, as David Landes has written, 'the most important of these, politically as well as economically [was] finding the longitude at sea'.[94] Here is evidence of direct government intervention, with prizes being awarded for chronometers, lathes and dividing engines that broke through technological frontiers, as we have seen in Chapter 7.[95] In exchange for the prize being awarded to an instrument, the information about it had to be published and instruction in its use given to other craftsmen.[96] Above all, the work had to be replicable, because it was for national advancement.

The Board of Longitude was run by a group of government and Royal Society appointees, together with university professors and admirals; here, the Royal Society acted in an advisory capacity. The Royal Society could also act as arbiter, as it did in the case of new hydrometers authorized by Act of Parliament in 1802, after which the Excise Board advertised, requesting that instrument makers offer accurate and reliable instruments for adoption as standard.[97] As Anita McConnell recounts, nineteen instruments were submitted, of which nine were selected for further examination by a committee formed of Fellows of the Royal Society and Excise representatives: a number of makers from outside London sent instruments, including, as we have seen in Chapter 7, Mary Dicas of Liverpool.

The competition was won by a design devised by Bartholomew Sikes (1731–1803), who had worked in the Excise Department for almost fifty years. He also produced a set of specialized excise tables, which greatly impressed the committee (Figure 9.7). Unfortunately, he died, aged 73, in October 1803. His widow petitioned for the approval of her late husband's hydrometer in May 1805, and in December 1806 suggested she might be awarded £3,000 for the rights to the instrument. The Excise thought this over-valued, and in January 1807, Mary Sikes (now remarried) reduced the sum to £2,000, but proposed that Robert Brettell

---

[93] Bennett (1985).

[94] Landes (1998), 212.

[95] For chronometers, see Randall (1996); for lathes, see Woodbury (1972) and dividing engines, see Brooks (1992).

[96] The history of the tasks of the Board of Longitude, 1714–1828, is discussed by Stimson (1985).

[97] 42 George III c.37. For an account of this, see McConnell (1993a), 9–18; also Ashworth (2001) and (2003), 261–79.

Bate (1782–1847), her nephew and son-in-law, should be granted the sole right to manufacture the instruments.[98]

**Figure 9.7    Tables by Bartholomew Sikes, and hydrometer by R.B. Bate, *c.*1830**

*Source*: National Museums of Scotland Library

As McConnell has shown, between 1824 and 1831 Bate was paid a total of £18,131 18s 2d for the supply and repair of hydrometers and saccharometers to the Excise. He was also 'supplying brewers and distillers who needed to provide themselves with the instruments specified [in the legislation] … £2½ million [tax] came in annually from this source and the allowance of even a small error in the distillers' favour amounted to a sizeable loss of revenue'.[99] Bate also won the contract to verify all the weights and measures supplied under the 1824 legislation: each set cost £105 5s 0d, or about £160 if cased and engraved with the coat-of-arms of the purchasing authority (Figure 9.8). By 1834, 324 full and 149 part sets

[98]    McConnell (1993a).
[99]    Ibid., 17–18.

had been delivered to local authorities all over the United Kingdom.[100] Clearly, winning a government contract could lead to further state business and prove to be immensely lucrative for the successful bidder. Bate went on to become an agent for selling Admiralty charts.[101]

Earlier, during the wars with France, contractors were supplying both the Admiralty and the Board of Ordnance. John Millburn has done extensive work on the papers of the Board of Ordnance, examining invoices of instrument suppliers.[102] As might be expected, he found that: 'the number and value of orders were ... extremely small in comparison with orders for (say) weapons and ammunition'.[103] He shows that the London maker William Deane supplied the Ordnance between 1723 and 1747 (a 24 year period), with a total of 102 invoices for a total of almost £1,200. With the outbreak of war in Europe, Millburn drily remarks, 'the outlook brightened', and for the first five years of the 1740s 'Deane received a total of 34 orders worth in all £453'.[104]

Millburn's work on the Board of Ordnance papers for the mid-eighteenth century investigated the years 1748 to 1772, when George Adams senior was Instrument Maker to the Board of Ordnance: 'during this period Adams supplied over 1500 instruments, ranging from drawing pens to theodolites, detailed in 148 bills amounting to a total value of £2425'.[105] He found that there was little change in the design of the instruments supplied during this particular quarter-century, although more would have been found by comparing the beginning with the end of the eighteenth century. An analysis of Adams's bills 'shows a marked correlation with the state of activity of Britain's armed forces, particularly in the early stages of the Seven Years War'.[106] However, Millburn concludes with a warning: the lack of complete business records makes it impossible to estimate what 'proportion of Adams' total turnover the Ordnance orders represented, nor what profit margin was made on them'.[107] In summary:

> the principal conclusion to be drawn from this exercise is therefore that even a long sequence of records of a major customer, such as a Government Department ... provides only a small contribution to understanding the nature and extent of the trade of an individual business. Bearing in mind the number of scientific instrument makers who were operating simultaneously in London in the mid-eighteenth century, this serves

---

[100] Ibid., 28.
[101] Ibid., 41–6; for weights and measures, see Connor (1987), 256–7; for the Admiralty charts, see Ritchie and David (1995).
[102] Millburn (1988a), (1992a), (1992b), (1992c) and (1995).
[103] Millburn (1992b), 1.
[104] Millburn (1995), 17–18.
[105] Millburn (1988a), 221.
[106] Ibid., 290.
[107] Ibid., 292.

**Figure 9.8　Set of weights and measures by R.B. Bate, sold to the Royal Burgh of Haddington in 1824**

*Source:* National Museums of Scotland

to underline how little is really known at present about the overall manufacturing capacity of the instrument-making trade at this time.[108]

Millburn came to a similar conclusion in his later work on the Adams business: 'the full extent of Adams's output still remains virtually unknown'.[109]

Indeed, Millburn scarcely touched on the subcontracting issue, because 'evidence for the mid-eighteenth century is elusive'. He commented that:

> It seems likely that in practice Adams would have made use of both internal and external sources of labour. Certain types of instrument, for example globes, are known to have been made by specialists whose names are mostly unrecorded. The basic skills of a mathematical instrument maker were metalworking and engraving, so one might expect a wide-ranging business like Adams's to employ other specialists, such as joiners for making the wooden parts of instruments, and turners for making the parts which had to be accurately turned to size. The optical parts of microscopes and telescopes would almost certainly have been bought in from specialist grinders who did nothing else, rather than made on the premises.[110]

Although these would have been London-based, there is evidence that specialist makers of instrument parts could be found in the newer population centres from the time that each became large enough to provide listings for commercial directories.

A later state enterprise, the Survey of India, reveals a little more of the underpinning substructure of the instrument trade. From fairly slow beginnings, but using large and expensive London-made instruments for its primary survey, the Great Trigonometrical Survey is probably identified most closely with the man who galvanized it into becoming a professional body in 1829, George Everest (1790–1866). The Survey spent £5000 on new instruments, and paid for London-based Henry Barrow to go to Madras to set up as full-time instrument maker and repairer . There, he instructed and oversaw an entire workshop.[111] By 1880:

> the stock of instruments in the depot was increased ... about 7540 instruments ... were obtained from England; 500 were purchased locally ... nearly 9950 were manufactured in the workshop ...; nearly 5970 instruments were received by inter-departmental exchange ... The number of instruments issued from stock amounted to 20 158.[112]

Clearly, the instruments discussed here were not those used in primary triangulations, but to undertake the vast tasks of the secondary and detailed infill

---

[108] Ibid.

[109] Millburn (2000), 153.

[110] Ibid., 135.

[111] There is a substantial literature, most recently encompassed by Edney (1997); for Barrow, see Insley (1995).

[112] Walker (1880), 52, quoted by Clarke et al. (1989), 81 n.26, in support of the subcontracting nature of the workshop of the London instrument maker Patrick Adie.

surveys. Already, English provincial sub-contractors were involved – the order book of Thomas Cooke of York shows they were supplying other contractors, including Newman of Calcutta (perhaps with some of the instruments being 'purchased locally'). But as Anita McConnell has shown, Cooke's display at the 1862 Exhibition attracted the attention of officials from the Survey of India, and a first direct order was placed with them in June 1864 for 16 variously sized theodolites for a total of £368.[113] Previously, major instruments had been commissioned for the Survey from the London makers, Troughton & Simms, but Cooke's new factory and willingness to introduce new designs persuaded the Survey to place orders outside London.

Until the mid-nineteenth century, to obtain state patronage the instrument contractor had to be located in London. This, manifestly, was the centre of communications: it was the port from which instruments would be sent – to the battlefront, to naval establishments, to the Empire overseas. It was also the centre of the instrument-contracting network, and the place from where organizers such as George Adams or R.B. Bate were able to subcontract, either within London or without, to obtain instruments or their parts to fulfil those lucrative government contracts. Provincial instrument makers were unable to break into this market, except as subcontractors, until well after the Great Exhibition.

Although the London trade has been examined in this book from the point-of-view of how it supported and interacted with provincial activities, it is not self-evident that the instrument trade followed a similar pattern to the closely allied and better-documented watch-making trade. As described by F.A. Bailey and T.C. Barker, watch-making was developed in the Prescot area of Lancashire from the late seventeenth century, and the many intricate parts were separately manufactured by a highly skilled workforce using specially developed precision machinery.[114] The parts were sent to London for finishing and assembling, as David Landes has shown, and put into cases signed with a London watchmaker's name.[115]

As L.D. Schwarz has written, 'the relationship of the Clerkenwell watchmakers to those of Lancashire and, subsequently, Coventry is unclear. They all seem to have achieved a tolerable *modus vivendi*, with a rapidly expanding market at home and abroad, though London workers seem to have concentrated more on the finishing and assembly end of the process … in retrospect, it is clear that many London trades were vulnerable to provincial competition'. But, writes Schwarz, this 'would not become obvious until the 1860s'.[116] The demands on the instrument trade, as we have seen, were considerably more varied than that on the watch trade – which had a single product, applicable to a number of somewhat limited markets. The instrument trade, as we have seen, may have in

---

[113]  McConnell (1992), 54–6; McConnell (1993c), 437.
[114]  Bailey and Barker (1969). See also Weiss (1982).
[115]  Landes (1983), 230–34.
[116]  Schwarz (1992), 38–9.

some of its elements resembled the watch trade, but it covered a wider variety of products which would appeal to customers from a range of categories, as suggested by Table 9.1.

As we saw earlier, the instrument trade was subject to division of labour, as recounted in John Holland's eyewitness description of a Sheffield shop-floor in about 1800. This was not, however, along the same lines as the Prescot watch trade at a similar date. Holland's description details a 'systematic distribution of work throughout the establishment, one man being mostly employed in a special class of articles, in the making of which he acquired great dexterity',[117] rather than individual elements being manufactured by particular workers. Neither is there any discussion by Holland of the sending of unfinished items to London for finishing, although as we have seen elsewhere, the retailer's name could be added there. Jesper Bidstrup's account of the London shop-floor varies from that of Holland: either parts were subcontracted out, or, as in the special and remarkable case of Jesse Ramsden, everything was made *in situ* but with a strict division of labour according to the specific skills of individuals. It remains an open question as to whether parts may have been manufactured elsewhere in the provinces for assembly in London, although brass castings could clearly be produced in Birmingham and delivered to the capital by an early date.

The relationship between supply and demand is, of course, an interdependent one, and the supply of instruments during the Industrial Revolution appears to have remained reasonably elastic. So the workforce of skilled labour grew in the provinces as craftsmen moved out of London for a variety of reasons. There is little evidence of any technological bottlenecks in supply (as can be found in, for instance, textiles) during this period. As prices appear to have been relatively stable, and no supply blockages were suddenly overcome, creating an immediate demand, the slow growth of a gradually enlarging pool of skilled labour must have meant that supply and demand did not outstrip each other.

The size of the market categories as outlined in Table 9.1 can be judged proportionally to each other. The dilettante market, however serious in its intentions, remained a small and mainly London-based demand sector throughout this period. Its significance lay in keeping up the momentum of novelty in design and topicality of application, thus keeping the skills of the makers in constant use: if these were not practised, they would be lost, just as horological skills are under threat today. Not all wealthy patrons were interested in science: others put their efforts towards conspicuous consumption into art, furniture, acquisitions on the Grand Tour, architecture, landscape gardening and other expensive pastimes.[118] Only an influential handful of dilettantes could ever have been interested in instrumentation and its development. A much larger – if not the largest component – of demand came from the practical instrumentation used in jobs which were becoming professionalized at this period: surveying, navigation, architecture.

---

[117] Holland (1867).
[118] Brewer (1997), 206–10.

A recent assessment of surveying practice in Great Britain and Ireland from 1530 to 1850 has demonstrated 'how the number of new surveyors, by the date at which they are first documented or the time when they started to practise (taken as the age of 20), grew steadily and especially markedly from the late eighteenth century',[119] and gives the numbers of new surveyors between 1784 and 1850 as 7,886, or 119 a year, compared with the figure between 1725 and 1783 as 3,276, or 56 a year. The inference has to be that as numbers of surveyors in the field rose, so did their demand for the instruments of their trade.

As we have seen, both the merchant and Royal navies grew in size, according to the number of British-registered ships during this period: 12,464 in 1778 compared with 26,043 in 1851, each requiring a suite of instruments to ensure safe and accurate navigation. Both the expanding navigation and architectural trades required drawing instruments for chart-work and plans, which ranged from special writing implements to the engineer's rolling parallel rule. As the population grew, there was an increased demand for more houses with better drainage, indirectly leading to increased demand for the tools of these occupations.

The size of the lecture-demonstration audience is more difficult to calculate. On the one hand this movement has been characterized, notably by Roy Porter, as an emulation of metropolitan values by the provinces; and on the other, as a growth area demonstrating significant cultural evolution as a concomitant of the rise of industrialization, for instance by Ian Inkster. Inkster has pointed out that it was through this area of the market that the new audiences of women and children were encouraged; and indeed, this can be inferred from the compositions of the well-known paintings of Joseph Wright of Derby. From witnessing a demonstration, it is a logical move to acquire the apparatus to undertake one's own experiments, and by the end of the period the chemical promoter and supplier J.J. Griffin had successfully developed a range of new kits, which were being bought in sufficiently large numbers to ensure the survival of the firm well into the twentieth century.[120]

The growth of a domestic market in scientific instruments for an assortment of everyday items rests largely on the economic historians' thesis of the rise of a consumer society at this time, and the evidence to support it can be found with the increasing amount of surviving contemporary artefacts. Although there are not the household inventories to support this theory, it is very clear from the amount of middle-class survivals that go through the auction houses each year that a considerable quantity of household objects were bought new from instrument suppliers and used in a domestic capacity. In particular, clocks, optical instruments and barometers became part of the domestic scene: the largest of these instrument categories, spectacles, are less likely to have survived, because they were made for individuals and were less intrinsically 'precious'.

---

[119]  Bendall (1997), 10.
[120]  Gee and Brock (1991).

From these arguments we may deduce that the instrument trade was largely a demand-led industry, where astute makers were able to stimulate demand for new items through careful marketing. During this period, they were assisted by a prevailing intellectual curiosity from the aspiring middle classes, and market growth through new groups of consumers: women, students and younger people generally. A broader-based literacy, demonstrated by the growth of publishing and the spread of newspapers, enabled a much wider audience to understand how instrumentation could extend the senses. Farmers wanted to predict the weather: they were encouraged to buy barometers; medical students needed to examine tissues and fluids: especially inexpensive microscopes were aimed at the student market; women enthusiastically took up botanizing: portable 'field' microscopes were advertised for their needs; and children could be indulged with special toys which used scientific or dynamical principles.

The growing purchasing power of middle-class women meant that their attention to fashion in the home could be channelled into acquiring quasi-scientific items, such as drawing instruments or globes, along with the pianoforte of the drawing room. There could be sundials in the garden, and thermometers in the greenhouse. The general growth in all market sectors during the Industrial Revolution, in the traditional areas as well as these newer markets, meant that instrument makers in the provinces were creating markets closer to their points of production, rather than merely supplying the main one to be found in London, and through London, abroad. From 20 instrument-making firms located in six provincial centres in 1775, the number had grown to 155 in many more centres by 1851.[121] From this, it can be reasonably deduced that both the volume of output for traditional items had expanded, and the variety of 'new' products had grown to fulfil increasing demand.

---

[121] See Graph 1.2.

# Chapter 10

# Conclusions

Much of this book has been descriptive, rather than quantitative, because of the dispersed nature of the evidence, and because it is covering new ground. However, some indication of the numbers of businesses outside London which were concerned with the production of scientific instruments, either fully or part time, has been gleaned from the local and national street directories. These numbers rose significantly between about 1760 and 1851, and are borne out by Census information at an individual level. In contrast, the material evidence that survives – old instrumentation – has indicated very few items with a provincial signature. This has led unwary instrument historians to conclude that almost nothing was produced outside London. As Lorna Weatherill has written:

> surviving artefacts are cared for in museums or collected privately, and this influences the works about them, for their main intention is to provide detailed guides, descriptions, attributions. This fact, together with the nature of surviving objects themselves, gives a quite different view of consumption … [yet] on the other hand, economic and social historians tend to regard the objects as illustrative material for their studies and show a surprising disregard for the physical remains of the past.[1]

Looking at the material evidence alone, she says, gives a picture showing the upper end of the market, not a true cross-section. It can produce as biased a picture as if one had ignored it entirely. With instrumentation, proportionally more later nineteenth-century items demonstrably originating outside London have survived, but there was no adequate explanation of how provincial manufacturers managed to compete with the apparently longer-established London makers, nor how or why some of them were apparently were able to break into the international market without acting through a London middleman.

## Millburn's Agenda: What has been Covered?

This research has looked to a criticism of instrument history, written by a universally respected instrument historian in 1986, as a framework or agenda for conducting research into instrument history in a virtually uncharted area.[2] This investigative programme covered essential business components such as

---

1   Weatherill (1988), 21.
2   Millburn (1986c).

financing, marketing, organization, employee skills and industrial relations, and the research has uncovered more about some aspects than others. The instrument trade in the provinces appears to have been more extensive, in that there were many more producers, than had previously been believed. The dearth of business (and official) records from this period precludes any detailed discussion about finances, particularly profit or loss, inputs or outputs.

There are financial indicators, however, concerning some individual firms: for instance, bankruptcies, although the reasons for particular firms failing are often clouded by lack of evidence. Official papers demonstrate that state contracts could be lucrative for the holder, and in at least one case there was a scramble amongst competitors when a contract was to be renewed.[3] However, these papers do not show how the provincial trade was involved, and it was not until after the mid-nineteenth century that contracts were made directly with provincial wholesalers, who advertised these in their trade literature.[4] Bearing in mind the range of products covered by the term 'scientific instruments' – from 'ornaments of consumption ... [to] tools of engineering'[5] – there is some evidence of how financing was linked with marketing. This linkage appears to have been two-tier: bread-and-butter retailing and specialist construction.

There is little information on pricing, particularly outside London, although there is the evidence of trade prices being offered by G. & W. Proctor of Sheffield in 1814, which has been compared with London retail prices given by W. & S. Jones at almost the same date.[6] This demonstrates the considerably cheaper rate per item of the Sheffield products. Some manuscript annotations in the Proctor pattern book give an indication of piece-work rates for various brass or wooden components. Such information is quite limited in its scope, however. There is no information about pricing, for instance, in the form of a price series for a 'standard' instrument between 1760 and 1851 – even identifying such an item seems almost impossible, given the variety and consumer delight in novelty, with the makers' corresponding response to accommodate this.

However, the retail prices gleaned from a series of London price lists dating between 1784 and 1855 shows that prices remained relatively stable throughout the period. How can this stability be explained? If productivity was increasing, then the price should have fallen; if demand was elastic – responding to pricing – then its share in the economy should grow with time. Today's contemporary example of the ubiquitous personal computer demonstrates that market growth, responding to demand, should bring the unit price down for the consumer. Yet for instrumentation during the Industrial Revolution, prices remained stable, and although the industry grew – with the addition of more firms – it was not through

---

[3]    Tate and Gabb (1930).
[4]    For example, Parkes (1857): 'Instrument Makers to the Board of Trade, and Government Schools of Design'.
[5]    Berg (1998), 154.
[6]    See Table 6.4, p. 173.

rising productivity. Methods of production did not dramatically change, and by and large the instrument industry remained a craft industry. Perhaps the answer is that the bulk of the demand came from the professional user, and although numbers of these certainly grew, the rate of the increase was moderate and fairly steady. Many suppliers had protected their share of the market, so there was little scope for the unit price to drop.

There was no sudden move into factories, although this was gradually beginning to happen by the mid-nineteenth century. The London firm Troughton & Simms of Fleet Street, set up purpose-built premises in a greenfield site in Woolwich, which was in operation by 1866. By 1871, it employed 61 men and 18 boys, increasing to 78 men and 20 boys ten years later.[7] Outside London, as early as 1855, Thomas Cooke of York was the first to erect customized premises, a factory in which all the processes of instrument production were undertaken, with a loan from a family friend.[8] Elsewhere, the Grubbs in Dublin manufactured a variety of light engineering products – cast-iron billiard tables, engraving machines, glass working machinery, with telescope construction as a sideline – but with the growing international reputation of their large reflecting telescopes, they became more specialized, and built new premises in the Dublin suburb of Rathmines, in about 1875.[9] In Glasgow, Lord Kelvin's firm James White appears to have moved into factory premises by 1884:

> the growth of the workshop represents the transition from craft-based manufacture to factory-based production, although in the absence of adequate evidence for the period 1849 to 1870 it is difficult to say when this occurred. Certainly the size of the workforce in 1881 suggests that specialisation on separate components of particular instruments within the shop was occurring.[10]

This was clearly an industry that remained in transition until the late nineteenth century.[11] The manufactories uncovered in my research for this volume in Sheffield – Proctors, Cutts and Chadburns – provide little supporting evidence as to size, numbers, or date of establishment. That they existed at all can only be inferred from the firms' advertising, and a single contemporary description.

The instrument trade outside London was clearly prepared to expand into new markets, demonstrated by its willingness, for instance, to participate in the 1855 Society of Arts competition to promote a cheap, and newly designed microscope with significant market potential. Where did the capital come from to invest in this enterprise? As with most investment before limited liability was enforced by statute in 1862, this was provided by the family through common law partnerships. The family acted as a supporting network, not solely for financial

---

[7]  McConnell (1992), 42.
[8]  Ibid., 51.
[9]  Glass (1997), 2–3; 82–4, where a photograph and plan of the new works are shown.
[10]  Clarke et al. (1989), 258.
[11]  Meliconi (2000), 267–72.

capital, but also for reasons of trust in an uncertain and hazardous business climate. As Mary Rose has shown, the family business operated in some measure as a self-regulating entity:

> whilst the family represented an internal market of skilled and managerial labour and a source of funds for establishment and expansion, family connections could also be reliable sources of market information. Such involvement of family and connections could be especially helpful in transactions between provincial centres and London or in overseas trade.[12]

Several examples of exactly these sorts of networks occur in the instrument trade, where brothers, for instance, set up in different provincial centres. Three instrument-making sons of Alexander Adie of Edinburgh did just that: John remained in Edinburgh, eventually taking over his father's business; Richard went to Liverpool, where he set up as an 'optician, philosophical and mathematical instrument maker' in 1835, subsequently running the Edinburgh and Liverpool businesses in tandem after both Alexander and John died in the 1850s, until his own death in 1881; while the youngest son, Patrick, sailed for London in 1844, where he ran a successful enterprise which continued well after his death in 1886. The latter developed useful commercial links into Kew Observatory, which at that time verified the accuracy of certain classes of instrument, initially for the British Association.[13]

In a review of the literature on the financing of business, Pat Hudson explains that the nature of the family firm – the model which prevailed in metalwares, including instrument making – had further ramifications:

> Partnerships were usually family or extended family concerns with partners having close links through birth, marriage, community or religious affiliation ... High failure rates, coupled with high risk, uncertainty and continuous change in the business environment, encouraged the predominance of family concerns.[14]

This, she explains, meant that there were implications for the financing of such enterprises. The very nature of the family and its networks meant that 'the ownership and finance of most firms tended to be local or regional'. Furthermore, the family connections which allowed for consolidation, respectability and continuity also meant that provision for offspring could eventually necessitate withdrawal of capital and lead to fragmentation of the operation.[15] François Crouzet, in an illuminating review article on 'Capital formation in Great Britain during the Industrial Revolution' suggests that despite the economic history

---

[12]   Rose (1994), 63–9.
[13]   Clarke et al. (1989), 25–84.
[14]   Hudson (1994), 90.
[15]   Ibid., 91

literature concerning 'takeoff' and heated discussions about rates of change, whether slower or more rapid than previously thought:

> many firms ... had quite modest beginnings, and then gradually increased the scale of their operations, enlarging their buildings and buying new machinery ... All in all, during the first stages of the Industrial Revolution, the need for investment in fixed capital was modest, the threshold for entry in industry – factory industry included – was low ... The total sums of money which provided 'the material envelope' for the new technology were thus relatively small.[16]

As Hudson has observed, 'urban and rural workshop industries ... flourished during industrialization. These required more overhead finance, but, using mainly hand skills and labour-intensive methods, their fixed capital needs remained modest'.[17] Later, as these workshops tried to establish markets outside their own localities, the financial demands on them grew. This is where it is difficult to understand just how, for instance, Abraham of Liverpool (run at this stage by Charles West and George Smart Wood) managed to afford to display a range of apparatus at the Great Exhibition, or how, in 1854, the Sheffield firm J.P. Cutts, Sutton & Son managed to retain an agent in New York.[18]

The state had a long-term interest in seeing the instrument industry developed – for instance, in ensuring that both the merchant marine and the Royal Navy did not encounter another disaster of the magnitude of the one that befell Sir Cloudesley Shovel in 1707. It was, the current view would have it, famously hampered by its inability to allocate funds. However, this perception was not entirely correct, and, as we have seen, the government provided substantial capital, for instance, in setting up a national observatory, which subsequently produced increasingly accurate star maps for the safety of its navigators. It also provided injections of capital to the instrument industry through the Board of Longitude and other purchasing government departments, with the Royal Society on occasion acting as an arbiter.

Yet none of this valuable patronage appears to have gone outside a charmed circle of London makers, who were still known on a personal level by those making the crucial financial decisions. Only with changes in the organization of science in the early years of the nineteenth century, as described by J.A. Bennett, did this situation alter.[19] Despite this, instrument makers in the provinces appear to have survived, by inference subcontracting – as described by John Holland in 1834 – to those in London who needed to fulfil large contracts.[20] There is no evidence

---

[16]  Crouzet (1990), 161.
[17]  Hudson (1994), 92.
[18]  *1851. Gore's Directory for Liverpool and its Environs* (Liverpool: J. Mawdsley, n.d.); *Post Office Directory of Sheffield, with the neighbouring Towns and Villages* (London: printed and published by Kelly and Co, 1854).
[19]  Bennett (1985).
[20]  Holland (1834), 261.

– apart from one or two early examples in Sheffield – that they diversified into other trades, such as pubs, brewing or armaments, all of which metalworkers traditionally took up in hard times – indeed, they often combined two occupations simultaneously.[21] From the evidence of the local directories, instrument makers described themselves as making instruments or other pieces of metalware, or they moved into light engineering.

To fully answer Millburn's questions about the financing of the industry, it is necessary to obtain more information. How much did it take to set up in business in the provinces? Why would one do so, there, then? Why would one not – to use a twentieth-century political metaphor anachronistically – 'get on one's bike' and find an instrument-making job in London? It may well have been the inhibiting factor of family enterprise and local forms of capital investment that prevented this, but more supportive evidence to confirm this needs to be found.

Millburn suggested that 'marketing techniques' should be investigated, and these appear to have been developed throughout this period, and many were adopted by the instrument industry. At a time when the local press was expanding, in step with rising literacy levels and keeping pace with demand for news from London and overseas, instrument makers who had newly moved out of London were able to use the local papers to publicize their range of wares and expertise. As discussed in Chapter 8, provincial instrument businesses grasped every new method of promoting their wares as soon as they could: establishing attractive shop windows in fashionable spas; issuing literature which drew attention to patronage by the nobility and gentry; advertising the availability of a wide variety of items, whether described in famous textbooks or made to order; selling by lottery; adding price lists to the back of textbooks; participating in exhibitions of an educational nature; and undertaking lecture tours using demonstration apparatus.

Even articles in encyclopaedias blatantly advertised instruments made by particular makers – anything to place the objects in front of a public thirsty for new scientific knowledge in the hope of an impulse buy. However, despite all of these ploys – many of which were successful for both London makers and those based outside – it appears that there was little or no direct export market for the English provincial trade until after the establishment of the international exhibitions. Unlike the situation in 1760, by 1850 it was no drawback to be located outside London; transport networks were developed sufficiently to allow material to be moved much more rapidly into London. But also, by 1850, the Industrial Revolution had produced a broader range of activities in the provinces, so that London as a market was less important: the trade had generated its own external economies, and this can be seen particularly in the cases of Sheffield and Birmingham.[22]

---

[21] Berg (1994), 54.
[22] Berg (1993).

Outside London, the growth of instrument-making generally mirrored population growth, but as an industry it is too small to be mentioned in the statistics. N.F.R. Crafts's magisterial work demonstrates that during the Industrial Revolution, rates of growth in iron and cotton went down, while everything else went up: however, all measurements at this date are partial. The instrument trade was an area of steady growth during this period, and there were no dramatic price falls or significant changes in techniques, but instead an overall expansion in economic activity. The new methods of marketing were an important component of this. On the supply side, industries supplying the raw materials – the brass and optical glass – experienced growth and some considerable technological change, as outlined in Chapter 7. From being fairly localized industries with products of a somewhat uneven quality in about 1760, these industries became, with some injection of European know-how, more than sufficient to meet the increased demand of the instrument trade, whether based in the provinces or in London.

'Almost nothing is known for certain about the size of individual instrument makers' workshops', wrote Millburn, 'or how many different specialist workmen were involved in the construction of different types of instrument.'[23] Anita McConnell has made a determined attempt to ascertain the size of Jesse Ramsden's workshop, and has managed to name 36 workmen who worked for him at some point.[24] Before official Census returns are available, particularly those after 1851, it is difficult to discover this sort of information.

Outside London, new evidence has been uncovered, particularly for Sheffield, where there was some specialization in the Proctor workshop, yet still a considerable amount of autonomy for individual skilled hands. They appeared to have been at liberty to engage in the rural aspects of their working lives as the seasons demanded, something which was not to be found in the later York factory of Thomas Cooke. Although Holland's account gives an unambiguous account of the division of labour within the Proctor workshop, we cannot tell whether his description of individuals being devoted to making particular instruments was peculiar to that particular workshop, or whether others elsewhere were also constrained to particular components, materials or operations.[25] The evidence from Thomas Cooke's 1856–68 orderbook shows that the scale of incoming orders was increasing. However, the size of this workshop remains unknown: no definite figures were revealed before the 1861 Census, and from this it can be deduced that most enterprises must have remained small-scale craft workshops.[26]

What do we know about the employees? We know that 'foreigners', whether incomers from a different region or from abroad, or groups of similar dissenting religious persuasion, tended to live and work together. By 1850, the instrument workforce may have had a greater division of labour than that of 1760, but most

---

[23]  Millburn (1986c), 84.
[24]  McConnell (forthcoming).
[25]  Holland (1867), reprinted in Morrison-Low (1994b).
[26]  This is supported by other 1861 Census figures.

of the skills were still learned 'on the job' as there was no form of education for the younger men other than an apprenticeship, formal or otherwise.[27] The work of Inkster and others has demonstrated that in provincial England, instrument makers were prominent amongst those actively promoting scientific education through lecturing, the formation of societies, and the holding of exhibitions.[28] Employees may well have become more numerate than their counterparts in 1760 – thus forming part of the national 'human capital' – on their way to becoming skilled artisans. Eventually, some seem to have been able to set up in business for themselves in a small way.

Outside London, there were no effective guild restrictions to make setting up on one's own more expensive for an individual. Unlike other industries hit with economic convulsion through rapid industrialization, employees in the scientific instrument trade did not become deskilled through depressed wages as a consequence of technological changes in their industry. There is no direct evidence for actual figures for wages, apart from John Smeaton's brief daily accounts for a six-month period in 1751–52, where the amount paid varied according to the competence of the workman.[29] We know next to nothing about industrial relations generally, which is unsurprising given the paucity of evidence about individuals who ran even relatively successful businesses. It can be inferred, though, in a small, craft-based workshop, where masters and men worked side-by-side throughout this period, that relations remained paternalistic; and in some cases, as we have seen, former apprentices married the boss's daughter, thus extending and reinforcing the family network already discussed.

### What was the Effect of the Industrial Revolution on Instrument Production?

The Industrial Revolution produced cheaper and better quality brass and glass, new methods of engineering and machine tools of considerable sophistication, which were specially developed or brought in from allied trades. The industry had to wait for the implementation of Whitworth's standards, though, before being able to move on to interchangeable parts and the possibility of 'mass-production'.[30] The most that was achievable prior to this was large batch production, but in this the individual components were fine-tuned by hand and eye to each individual instrument.

Was there cheaper power? Although power could be applied to hand tools, especially in areas like Sheffield, where there was readily available waterpower, there does not appear to be much evidence for steam-power being applied to instrument-making machinery, which would have entailed a move into the factory.

---

[27]   Meliconi (2000), 86–102.
[28]   Inkster (1973), (1976) and (1980).
[29]   See Chapter 7.
[30]   Meliconi (2000), 186–9.

However, there is evidence that by the end of the period, power was being applied to various repetitive tasks in Birmingham works that produced a range of goods including instruments.

By 1850, the workforce may have experienced a greater division of labour, but all employees appeared to continue to learn by doing: beyond apprenticeship, whether formal or otherwise, there was no other way to obtain the skills, which remained mainly hand skills. Even if the workforce had become more numerate – and instrument makers, by the very nature of their job would have to be among the more literate and numerate of the British workforce – their formal education remained what it had been, supplemented by what could be self-taught or learned through experience. The state was not to intervene here until the later nineteenth century.[31]

Unlike workers in other sectors of the economy which experienced dramatic economic upheaval through technological change during the Industrial Revolution, the skilled artisans of the scientific instrument trade did not become deskilled through sudden changes in technology – as did, for instance, the handloom weavers.[32] The instrument trade thus forms part of the 'slow growth' model of industry during the Industrial Revolution. This is unsurprising, as most of the products were still hand-made, so productivity was always going to remain slow.

The changes that took place occurred at the margins of the industry; crucial, for instance, was the introduction of the dividing engine, in London in the late eighteenth century. As we have seen, so far there is no evidence for the existence of a dividing engine in the provincial trade until Thomas Cooke constructed one from first principles in 1864–66.[33] This is supported by the oft-quoted remark made by Edward Troughton in his article on 'Graduation', written (about 1812) for David Brewster's *Edinburgh Encyclopaedia*, where he stated that there were ten or 12 dividing engines in London at that time, implying that these were the only ones available to the trade. Yet, there was a dividing engine in Edinburgh as early as 1793. It is possible that evidence for one in England outside London will emerge in due course.[34]

Did the quality of the finished products of the instrument industry change during the Industrial Revolution? There is no way of measuring this, in terms of output per man, or costing of a particular instrument, but it would appear that prices remained relatively stable. Instruments did not get cheaper, and although they were produced (apparently) in greater quantities, the customers

---

[31]  Ibid., 86–102.
[32]  Bythell (1969).
[33]  McConnell (1992), 54–5.
[34]  For instance, in Stimson (1985), 112; Chapman (1995), 134. For the Edinburgh dividing engine, see Clarke et al. (1989), 30.

appeared – mostly – to be satisfied.[35] Was there any increase in the numbers of instruments being produced in the provinces at this time? Again, although there is no direct evidence for this in terms of output per annum, the present research has demonstrated that numbers of businesses increased during this period, began to produce trade literature, and began to offer a wider variety of items directly to customers who had previously been seen as exclusively metropolitan: the conclusion must be that more instruments were supplied.

### What was the Effect of Instrument Production on the Industrial Revolution?

Rather than answer this query directly, it helps to turn it round and pose a counter-factual question: what would have been missing if there had been no instruments produced during the Industrial Revolution? Firstly, there would have been no Empire: Britannia would have been unable to rule the waves. Her navies would have remained coast-hugging, unable to command the oceans with the various (hard-won through war and diplomacy) strategically important islands used as fuelling stations. She would have been unable to map efficiently – and therefore tax and administer comprehensively – her substantial dominions overseas: namely, India, South Africa, Canada and Australia.

At home, the transport revolution, a necessary concomitant to the Industrial Revolution, would not have taken place with the same efficiency and productivity gains: plotting canal routes would have been a hit-and-miss affair; the grading of railway track would have been similarly difficult to achieve; the new road system, replacing that of the Romans, might have been wastefully constructed, coping with contours in a way that horse-drawn vehicles would be unable to negotiate.

In industry, standards could not have been maintained without using thermometers, pyrometers (for measuring heat above temperatures where conventional glass thermometer would melt), saccharometers (for measuring sugar content), microscopic thread-counters, and the other instruments which were introduced during this period to keep up the beginnings of quality control, particularly in the chemical industry. The state itself, as we have seen, would have lost out in taxation, in particular in the brewing and distilling industries, without the use of the hydrometer, for measuring the specific gravity of a liquid.

Without an instrument trade, there would have been little investigative science, with all the implications that has for the human understanding of the environment, the universe, or the development of preventative medicine. The customers identified in Chapter 9 – from the wealthy amateur through to the new markets of women and students – would have gone unenlightened and uneducated. Ships would have been lost at sea; people would have been lost on land. Electricity, the study of which developed from an observed phenomenon demonstrated by

---

[35] Dissatisfied customers of London suppliers can be found in the letter books of government departments; and Bugge (1777), 191.

travelling lecturers, might never have become the domestic commodity we take for granted today.

The instrument trade was crucial to the Industrial Revolution in this country at a number of levels. Within industry itself, instruments allowed the extension of the senses. Using spectacles allowed an ageing workforce to enable their sight to last a further decade or so of close work, as David Landes has shown.[36] Good eyesight was essential for the production of the gauging tools that were necessary to measure components of any sort of machinery at all, from pithead winding-gear to shoe-maker's lasts. The coal industry developed new instruments to make mine surveys possible, and to measure the flows of air within mines; thermometry was required in most production of food and beverages. Subsequent testing for purity might require the knowledge of the government chemist using analytical equipment, but that would have been derived from already-existing instrumentation.

As scientific knowledge grew in the second half of the nineteenth century, instrumentation was applied more frequently to industrial processes and in a less haphazard way, and came to be seen as part of the process of quality control and standardization. This practice grew from small beginnings, and instruments individually commissioned from the maker. In summary: the growing availability of instruments during this period allowed the development of knowledge, assisted in the growth of empire, and contributed to the transformation of the landscape through the transport revolution. Is it too much to identify such an industry as one of cutting edge technology?

**Conclusions**

John Millburn's questions were posed as long ago as 1986 to focus attention on how little was known about the more prominent London makers operating at the end of the eighteenth century. His questions have proved fruitful grounds for the study, carried out in this work, of the English trade through a wider time span than a single century and for a larger geographical area beyond metropolitan city limits. The investigations reported here have demonstrated that, as Gloria Clifton suspected, the instrument-making trade in the English regions was much more dynamic than previously thought. By the 1850s, the provincial trade was able to compete with London on many fronts, but the most important unanswered question posed by Millburn remains that of how these enterprises were financed.

It is clear from the surviving papers of Thomas Cooke of York that financing an instrument-making business from scratch, as he did, must have been a risky endeavour. Capital investments – plant, shop premises and advertising meant that the initial outlay was large, resulting in an immediate cash-flow problem.

---

[36] Landes (1998), 46–7.

Day-to-day expenses – labour and materials – would have been a continued drain before he ever saw even a fraction of return on his initial outlay. It is not entirely clear how this problem was resolved, either in this individual case or in general for new entrants to the industry.

From the evidence uncovered, it would appear that the way forward was through good personal contacts, and borrowing from wealthy friends or family, although it is possible that by this date customers were being asked for stage payments. The contents of Cooke's order book seems to suggest that there was a balance between the large and expensive orders, which would take time to complete, and the smaller and cheaper items, which could be produced relatively quickly. It is probable (although not provable with the available evidence) that, as he became better established and won a greater international reputation, more effort was put into the larger orders, and it was less necessary to fund that side of the business with cheaper items.

Although not all of Millburn's questions have found a ready answer, much of his agenda has provided a framework for understanding how the development of the regional instrument trade came to underpin the British instrument trade between the time of the Great Exhibition and the outbreak of the First World War. In the latter part of the nineteenth century, important firms were to be found throughout England – many still in London – but several also in locations as far apart as Birmingham, Cambridge and York, as well as the other centres described here. This book has, I hope, taken a first positive step towards providing Millburn's 'reliable and comprehensive synthesis of the trade', especially in the areas of marketing, materials and structure. However, more of his 'painstaking [extraction] piece by piece from a variety of sources' will have to be undertaken to advance this synthesis, by adding more of the maddeningly elusive information that lies just below the surface of the available historic evidence.[37]

---

[37]  Millburn (1986c), 84.

# Appendix

**Directory of the Instrument Trade in the English Provinces, by Location to 1851**

For directory sources, see Bibliography.

*Birmingham*

**ALLEN, Thomas (late ALLEN & ROWE), 1850–1851+**
Manufacturer of English and foreign box and ivory box rules
1850–1851+    12 St Mary's Row

Previously Allen & Rowe.

**ALLEN, William, 1788–1798**
Philosophical, mathematical instrument maker and optician
1788            37 High Street
1791–1798    Bull Ring

**ALLEN & ROWE, 1847–1849**
Box and ivory rule makers
1847            59 Duke Street
1849            12 St Mary's Street

Succeeded by Thomas Allen

**ANDERTON & CALLEY, 1785–1811**
Button, toy and mathematical instrument makers
1785–1798    Weaman Street
1800–1811    31 Weaman Street

By 1800, description no longer contains instruments: in 1800, described as 'button, toy makers and factors'; by 1808, 'button, toy makers, cock-founders and factors'.

Previously Anderton, Son & Calley.

**ANDERTON, SON & CALLEY, 1783**
Manufacturers of watch keys, seals and toys, gilt, plated, and fancy buttons, brass compasses, mathematical instruments, tin cases, tin buckles etc.
1783            31 Weaman Street

Succeeded by Anderton & Calley.

**ASKEY, Thomas, 1808–1833**
Optician and brace-maker
1808–1822    77 Lichfield Street
1823–1833    80 Lichfield Street

By 1830, described as 'optician and spectacle maker'; by 1835 a 'spectacle maker'.

**ASTON & DAWSON, 1815–1818**
Rule makers
1815–1818    Hill Street

**ASTON, Joseph, 1805–1833**
Compass maker, plate silverer, gilder, silver plater
1805–1808    Bradford Street, Deritend
1811–1822    Coleshill Street
1823–1833    16 Coleshill Street

By 1830, described as 'compass and pincer maker'.

**ASTON, Sampson, 1833–1851+**
Box and ivory rule maker, and bacon warehouse
1833            Jennen's Row
1835–1839    1 Jennen's Row
1842            Masshouse Lane
1845–1851+    24 Masshouse Lane

**ASTON, Samuel, 1800–1822**
Box and ivory rule maker
1800–1801    5 Water Street
1803–1818    Birchole Street, Deritend
1821–1822    Cheapside

**ASTON, Samuel, 1850**
Box and ivory rule maker
1850        Willis Street

**ASTON, T., 1845**
Rule maker
1845        94 Great Brook Street

Probably Thomas Aston of 3 Brook Street.

**ASTON, Thomas, 1849**
Box and ivory rule manufacturer
1849        3 Brook Street

**ASTON, Thomas, 1818–1851+**
Rule maker
1818–1822        Coleshill Street
1822        Bartholomew Square
1823–1833        20 Bartholomew Row
1835–1851+        17 Jennen's Row

By 1829, described as 'box and ivory box rule maker'.

**ASTON, Thomas, 1845–1851+**
Box and ivory rule maker
1845        25 Brewery Street, and
        3 court, Upper Windsor
        Street
1849–1851+        25½ Willis Street

**AULT, John, 1770–1777**
Compass maker
1770–1775        62 Moor Street
1777        42 and 43 Park Street

**AULT, Samuel, 1767–1781**
Compass maker
1767–1781        Deritend

A Samuel Ault was listed in the 1785 directory as a 'victualler and compass maker' in Alcester Street, and continued at this address as a 'victualler' only until 1801.

**AULT, Widow, 1780–1781**
Compass maker
1780        8 Wood Street
1781        60 Park Street

**AULT, William, 1785–1798**
Victualler and compass maker; pincer maker
1785–1798        Bradford Street

**AVERN, Edward, 1785**
Compass and pincer maker
1785        77 Park Street

**BAGNALL, Robert, 1774–1775**
Compass maker
1774–1775        63 Moor Street

Previously and subsequently William Bagnall.

**BAGNALL, William, 1770, 1777–1798**
Compass maker
1770        63 Moor Street
1777–1781        63 Moor Street
1788–1798        Lancaster Street

Between 1774 and 1775, Robert Bagnall heading the firm.

**BAKER, Henry, 1839–1851+**
Box and ivory rule maker
1839–1842        court, Cecil Street
1845        Phillips Buildings, Cecil
        Street
1846        62 Cecil Street
1849–1850        court 61, Cecil Street
1851+        41 Newtown Row

**BAKER & WILKES, 1822**
Rule maker
1822        Dale End

**BAKEWELL, Isabella, 1828–1830**
Mathematical instrument maker, rule maker (and surveyors' measuring tapes)
1828–1830        42 Loveday Street

Previously run by Isabella Bakewell's husband, Richard Bakewell.

Succeeded by Isaac Trow.

**BAKEWELL, Richard, 1791–1825**
Mathematical instrument, rule, dog-collar
        and watch key maker
1791–1822        Loveday Street

1823–1825    49 Loveday Street

By 1823 described as a 'manufacturer of mathematical instruments, brass and miners' compasses, plated and brass dog-collars, ivory and box rules, land surveyors' measuring tapes, etc.'

Succeeded by Isabella Bakewell.

**BALTON, T. & H., 1839**
Mathematical instrument makers
1839          62 Loveday Street

**BARNETT, Asher, 1777–1781**
Optician
1777–1781    25 Froggery

Described as a 'spectacle grinder' at 25 Colemore Street from 1770 to 1775.

**BARRINGTON, Philip, 1845–1851+**
Box and ivory rule maker
1845–1847    3 court, Smith Street, St
             George's
1849–1851+   court 176, Unett Street

**BARTON, John, 1831–1835**
Optician and spectacle maker
1831          7 court, Barr Street
1835          55 Barr Street

Described as a 'spectacle maker' from 1828 to 1830, and from 1835 to 1842.

**BEDDOE, William, 1845–1847**
Mathematical instrument maker
1845–1846    18 court, Lionel Street
1847          109 Lionel Street

**BEDINGTON, George, 1845–1847**
Measuring tape maker
1845–1846    10 court, Snow Hill
1847          Back of 95 Snow Hill

**BEDINGTON, James, 1845–1851+**
Manufacturer of mathematical instruments, box and ivory rules, surveyors' chains, compasses etc.
1845–1851+   10 Russell Street

**BEDINGTON, John, 1842–1851+**
Mathematical instrument maker, measuring tape manufacturer and box and ivory rule maker
1842          107 Lancaster Street
1845–1851+   40 Digbeth, St Martin's
             Lane

**BEDINGTON, Robert & Sons, 1842**
Leather and brass box measuring tape manufacturers, and manufacturers of the improved measuring tape on the multiplying principle
1842          107 Lancaster Street

**BELCHER & HASSALL, 1793–1797**
Rule makers
1793–1797    Bull Street

**BELLAMY, Obadiah, 1777–1781**
Instrument case maker
1777–1781    17 Exeter Street

**BENTON, John, 1818–1825**
Manufacturer of plated and brass telescopes, fancy hearth brushes, toasting forks, plated and brass tubes for umbrellas &c. plated and brass tubes of every description, umbrella and parasol frames complete &c. &c. &c.
1818–1825    8 Livery Street

**BERRICK, Ralph, 1770**
Rule maker
1770          Queen Street,
             Wolverhampton

**BETTS, Edwin, 1849–1851+**
Box and ivory rule maker
1849–1851+   3 Marshall Street

**BETTS, James, 1823–1842**
Box and ivory rule maker
1823–1825    31 Horse Fair
1828–1830    228 Bristol Street
1829–1831    32 Duke Street
1839          32 Ashted Row
1842          7 court, Ashted Row

**BETTS, John, 1823–1849**
Box and ivory rule maker
1823–1825    9 Blucher Street, Exeter
             Row
1835         Vauxhall Road
1845         5 court, St James's Place,
             Vauxhall Road
1849         46 St James's Place

**BETTS, Thomas, 1816–1835**
Rule maker
1816         top of Bromgrove Street
1818–1821    Inge Street
1822         Bromsgrove Street
1835         Great Brooke Street
1839         42 Great Brook Street
1842         128 Great Brooke Street
1845–1851+   125 Great Brook Street

In 1845, described as 'rule manufacturer and beer retailer'; in 1849 'beerhouse and rule maker'.

**BETTS, William, 1828–1837**
Rule maker
1828–1831    102 Bromsgrove Street
1835         2 Exeter Row
1837         1 court, Exeter Row

**BILBY** [sic] **& PROCTOR, 1805–1808**
Opticians
1805–1808    Newhall Street

See Proctor & Beilby.

**BILLING, Joseph, 1835**
Optician
1835         14 Moland Street

**BINGHAM, Charles, 1808–1818;
  1829–1839**
Sundial and church chimes maker
1808–1818    Ann Street
1829–1831    52 Congreve Street
1835–1839    53 Great Charles Street

Succeeded by Charles Bingham & Son, 1821–1825; and by Thomas Bingham 1842–1851+.

**BINGHAM, Thomas, 1842–1851+**
Church and turret clock and chime and sundial maker
1842–1851+   21 Meriden Street

**BINGHAM & Son, Charles, 1821–1825**
Sundial makers, and church clock makers
1821         Ann Street
1823         6 Ann Street

Succeeded by Charles Bingham

**BLYTH, Thomas, 1777–1781**
Compass maker
1777–1781    34 Deritend

**BOLTON, Frederick, 1835**
Rule and mathematical instrument maker
1835         55 Summer Lane

Previously Thomas Bolton.

Succeeded by Frederick and Henry Bolton.

**BOLTON, Frederick and Henry, 1837–
  1851+**
Mathematical instrument makers and rule makers
1837–1851+   61 and 62 Loveday Street

Previously Frederick Bolton.

**BOLTON, Thomas, 1808–1835**
Mathematical instrument and rule maker
1808–1818    Colmore Row
1828–1835    61 and 62 Loveday Street

Not in directories from 1818 to 1825.

Succeeded by Frederick, and Frederick and Henry Bolton.

**BORINI, Peter, 1815–1842**
Carver and gilder, picture frame, looking glass, barometer and thermometer maker
1815–1816    Bull Street
1818         Snowhill
1821         Bull Street
1823–1842    40 Bull Street

Previously P. Borini & Co.

**BORINI, P. & Co., 1808–1812**
Opticians and carvers and gilders
1808–1811      14 Edgbaston Street
1812            Bull Street

Succeeded by Peter Borini.

**BOURN, P., 1839**
Carver and gilder, manufacturer of picture frames, chimney and pier glasses, etc., barometers and thermometers, etc.
1839 40 Bull Street

**BOURNE, Joseph jun., 1845–1846**
Optician
1845–1846      7 Digby Street, Aston Road

**BRADBURN, Thomas, 1835**
Rule maker
1835            7 court, Digbeth

Probably succeeded by George and Thomas Bradburn.

**BRADBURN, George and Thomas, 1842–1851+**
Brassfounders, coppersmiths and rule makers
1842–1851+      18 Alcester Street

**BRADLEY, John, 1829–1851+**
Box and ivory rule maker
1829            8 Hurst Street
1833            Worcester Street
1835–1837      10 Hurst Street
1839            19 Hurst Street
1842–1847      5 Hurst Street

**BRIDGEN, George, 1808–1811**
Compass and pincer–maker
1808–1811      Wheeley's court, Hurst
                Street

**BRITTLE, Joseph, 1835–1839**
Rule maker
1835–1839      Palmer Street

**BROWN, William Henry, 1835–1851+**
Box and ivory rule maker
1835            1 Vittoria Street
1835–1851+      11 Caroline Street

**BRUNNER, Ignatius, 1849–1851+**
Barometer and thermometer maker
1849–1851+      66 Edgbaston Street

**BURGESS, John, 1846**
Rule maker
1846            129 Great Charles Street

**BUTLER, Benjamin, 1828–1851+**
Box and ivory rule maker
1828–1830      4 court, Lionel Street
1829–1831      65 Brearley Street
1835–1837      Snowhill Grinding Mill
1839            Snowhill
1842            9 court, Snowhill
1845            Circular sawmills, Cecil
                Street; Newtown Row and
                86 Brearly Street
1846            86 Cecil Street
1847            152 Brearly Street West
1849–1851+      New Summer Street

**BUTLER, John, 1829**
Rule maker
1829            51 Great Hampton Street

**BUTLER & Co., 1812–1815**
Rule makers
1812–1815      Lionel Street

Succeeded by Butler & Powell.

**BUTLER & POWELL, 1816–1822**
Rule makers
1816–1822      Lionel Street

Succeeded by Benjamin Butler, and Robert Powell.

**CADDICK, Benjamin, 1797–1803**
Spectacle maker
1797            Brick Kiln Lane
1800–1803      13 Bristol Street

**CADDICK, Charles, 1839–1842**
Optician and fine steel spectacle maker
1839            30 Great Hampton Street
1842            110 Constitution Hill

**CALLOW, James, 1816**
Mathematical instrument, compass and
dog-collar maker
1816　　　　　Ashted Row

Succeeded by Mary Ann Callow.

**CALLOW, James, jun. (late John Callow),
　1812–1815**
Mathematical instrument, compass and
dog-collar maker
1812–1815　　Ashted Row

Succeeded by James Callow.

**CALLOW, John, 1800–1811**
Mathematical instrument, compass and
dog-collar maker
1800–1811　　31 Ashted Row

Succeeded by James Callow, junior.

**CALLOW, Mary Ann, 1818**
Mathematical instrument, compass and
dog-collar maker
1818　　　　　Steelhouse Lane

Successor to James Callow.

**CANDY, Peter, 1805–1811**
Wood clock and weather glass maker
1805–1811　　Queen Street

**CAPELLA, Michael, 1850–1851+**
Barometer and thermometer maker
1850–1851+　104 Digbeth and 53
　　　　　　　Edgbaston Street

**CARPENTER, Mrs Catherine, 1845**
Mathematical instrument case maker
1845　　　　　New John Street, Newtown
　　　　　　　Row

Successor to Joseph Carpenter.

**CARPENTER, Joseph, 1835–1842**
Cabinet and mathematical instrument case
manufacturer
1835　　　　　6 York Street
1839　　　　　York Street
1842　　　　　62 Cecil Street

In 1842, described as a 'mathematical
instrument maker'.

Succeeded by Mrs Catherine Carpenter.

**CARPENTER, Philip, 1808–1833**
Optician
1808–1812　　Inge Street
1815–1822　　Bath Row
1823–1825　　111 New Street and Bath
　　　　　　　Row
1828　　　　　111 New Street
1829　　　　　111 New Street and 33
　　　　　　　Navigation Street
1830–1833　　111 New Street

Succeeded by Carpenter & Westley.

**CARPENTER, Thomas, 1821–1835**
Compass and heavy steel toy maker
1821　　　　　Lombard Street
1823–1825　　Vauxhall Lane
1835　　　　　New Canal Street

**CARPENTER & WESTLEY, 1835**
Opticians
1835　　　　　111 New Street

Previously Philip Carpenter.

**CASS, John, 1808–1831**
Compass maker
1808–1818　　Essex Street
1821–1822　　Hill Street
1823–1831　　court 18, Hill Street

**CLARK, William, 1829–1842**
Rule maker
1829　　　　　7 Hospital Street
1835–1837　　9 Hospital Street
1842　　　　　122 Hospital Street

**CLARKE, William, 1850–1851+**
Box and ivory box rule maker
1850–1851+　No 7 court, Henrietta
　　　　　　　Street

**CLIFF, WASTEL & Co., 1803–1808**
Opticians
1803–1808　　Mount Street

**COLLINS, Samuel, 1770**
Gilt and silver box and instrument case
maker
1770          28 St John's Street

**COOK & BARTON, 1825**
Manufacturers of mathematical
instruments, surveyors' measuring tapes,
miners' and mariners' compasses, sun
dials, brass and plated dog-collars etc.
1825          69 Moland Street

**COOKE, John, 1767**
Shagreen case maker
1767          High Street

**CORBETT, Thomas, 1849–1851+**
Mathematical instrument, surveyors'
measuring tape, and box and ivory rule
manufacturer
1849–1850     Edmund Street
1851+          Spencer Street

**CORFIELD, Richard, 1849–1851+**
Surveyors' measuring tape manufacturer
and dealer in coffin furniture
1849–1851+    17 Newton Street

Previously Corfield & Co., and Corfield &
Russell.

**CORFIELD & Co., 1847**
Coffin furniture and measuring tape
manufacturers
1847          Newton Street

Succeeded by Richard Corfield.

**CORFIELD & RUSSELL, 1845–1846**
Manufacturers of measuring tapes and
coffin furniture makers
1845–1846     17 Newton Street

Succeeded by Corfield & Co.

**COX, Ann, 1800–1803**
Rule maker
1800–1801     70 Hill Street
1803          Suffolk Street

Succeeded By Ann and George Cox.

**COX, Francis Blakemore, 1822–1851+**
Box and ivory rule maker
1822          Coleshill Street
1828–1831     Camden Street
1833–1851+    50 Camden Street

In 1829, and from 1845, described as
'(successor to George Cox & Co.)'.

**COX, George, 1812–1831**
Box and ivory rule manufacturer of all
descriptions
1812–1818     Navigation Street
1821          Regent Place
1822          Graham Street
1823–1825     Regent's Place
1828–1831     1 Vittoria Street

Previously Thomas Cox & Co., and Ann
and George Cox.

**COX, Thomas, 1777–1798**
Box and ivory rule maker
1777–1781     28 Bull Street
1783–1784     New Hall Street
1785–1788     22 New Hall Street
1791–1793     Newhall Street
1797          Hill Street
1798          Newhall Street

Succeeded by Ann Cox.

**COX, Ann and George, 1808–1811**
Rule makers
1808–1811     Suffolk Street

Succeeded by Thomas Cox & Co.

**COX, Thomas & Co., 1812**
Rule makers
1812          Suffolk Street

Succeeded by George Cox.

**DAVIS, George John, 1845–1851+**
Box and ivory rule maker
1845–1850     2 Key Hill
1851+          29 Ashted Row

**DAWSON, William, 1818–1821**
Rule and bed-screw maker
1818–1821     Hill Street

**DAYKIN, Francis, 1770**
Instrument case maker
1770          4 Upper Priory

Possibly Francis Deakin.

**DEAKIN, Francis, 1774–1781**
Cutler and instrument maker
1774–1781     4 Upper Priory

**DICKINS, Richard, 1803–1815**
Glass grinder
1803–1809     Bordesley Street
1812–1815     Freemen Street

**DUGMORE, John, 1835–1842**
Painter and manufacturer of surveyors'
measuring tapes
1835–1842     17 Newton Street

**EASTHORPE, James, 1808–1811**
Compass and pincer maker
1808–1811     Cambridge Street, Crescent

**EDWARDS, Joseph, 1767–1781**
Rule maker
1767          Bull Street
1770–1777     46 Worcester Street
1780–1781     46 Needless Alley

**EGGINGTON, George, 1829–1831**
Steam engine model manufacturer and
philosophical instrument maker
1829          10 Little Hampton Street
1830–1831     18 Livery Street

Described in the 1833 directory in his
final appearance as a 'steam engine model
maker' at 33 Little Hampton Street.

**ELKINGTON, George Richards, 1835–
          1837**
Optician
1835–1837     44 St Paul's Square

**ELKINGTON, James, 1818–1831**
Optician and spectacle maker
1818–1821     St Paul's Square
1823–1825     60 St Paul's Square
1828          76 Bishopsgate Street
1829          43 St Paul's Square

1830–1831     76 Bishopsgate Street

Previously in the directories from 1812 as
a 'tortoise shell, spectacle and toy maker'.

Succeeded by George Richards Elkington.

**FALCIOLA, Barnard, 1830–1835**
Barometer and thermometer manufacturer
1830–1831     Hill Street
1833–1835     51 Edgbaston Street

Succeeded by B. Falciola & Co.

**FALCIOLA, Bernard, 1850**
Carver and gilder
1850          168 High Street, Deritend

**FALCIOLA, B. & Co., 1839**
Carvers and gilders, barometer and
          looking glassmakers
1839          35 Edgbaston Street

Succeeded by Falciola & Casartelli.

**FALCIOLA & CASARTELLI, 1842–1847**
Carver and gilders, barometer and looking
glass makers
1842–1847     53 Edgbaston Street

Succeeded by Bernard Falciola.

**FARMER, William, 1839–1851+**
Optician
1839          Bridge Street, Broad Street
1842          removed to Heyseech Mills

From 1852 described as an 'optical glass
manufacturer, Smethwick'.

**FARROLL, John, 1818–1846**
Box and ivory rule maker
1818–1822     Constitution Hill
1823–1825     1 Northwood Street
1828–1831     111 Constitution Hill
1833–1839     2 court, Snowhill
1845–1846     11 court, Summer Lane

From 1828 described as 'John Farnol'.

**FIELD, Robert, 1830–1842**
Spectacle maker and optician
1830–1837     33 Navigation Street

1839–1842  33 Navigation Street and
           111 New Street

Succeeded by Robert Field & Son.

**FIELD, Robert & Son, 1845–1851+**
Opticians
1845–1851+  113 New Street

**FLOYD, William, 1839–1845**
Box and ivory rule maker
1839       32 Milk Street
1845       141 Adderley Street

**FREETH, B. & Co., 1818**
Compass and pincer maker
1818       High Street, Bordesely

**FROST, –, 1777–1781**
Rule maker
1777–1781  Great Charles Street

**FROST & WITHNOLL, 1767–1777**
Rule makers
1767       Lichfield Street
1770–1777  14 Lichfield Street

Succeeded by Frost, and William Withnol.

**GABRIEL, William, 1845–1851+**
General parallel rule maker
1845–1851+  78 Barr Street

**GARGORY, James, 1833–1851+**
Optician and mathematical instrument
maker
1833–1847  4 Bull Street
1849–1851+  5 Bull Street

**GERREDD, James, 1835**
Rule maker
1835       83 Weaman Street

**GERRETT & Co., 1850**
Box and ivory rule makers
1850       147 Bath Street

**GODFREY, John, 1828–1842**
Optician and spectacle maker
1828–1842  93 Coleshill Street

Succeeded by Mrs Mary Godfrey & Co.

**GODFREY, Mary A., 1847**
Optician
1847       93 Coleshill Street

Succeeded by Mary and Mary Ann
Godfrey.

**GODFREY, Mary Ann, 1850–1851+**
Optician
1850–1851+  93 Coleshill Street

Previously Mary and Mary Ann Godfrey.

**GODFREY, Mary and Mary Ann, 1849**
Opticians etc.
1849       93 Coleshill Street

Succeeded by Mary Ann Godfrey.

**GODFREY, Mrs Mary & Co., 1845**
Working opticians, gold, silver and general
spectacle makers
1845       93 Coleshill Street

Succeeded by Mary Godfrey & Co.

**GODFREY, Mary & Co., 1846**
Opticians
1846       93 Coleshill Street

Succeeded by Mary A. Godfrey.

**GREATREX, John, 1842**
Brass measuring tape box maker and
librarian
1842       65 Belmont Row

**GREAVES, Thomas, 1777–1798**
Optician and spectacle maker
1777–1781  40 Old Hinkleys
1785–1798  Old Hinkleys

**GREEN, William, 1815–1816**
Spectacle and glass grinder
1815–1816  Fazeley Street

**GREENFIELD & GREENFIELD, 1839**
Globemakers
1839       Cleveland Street

**GREGORY, Thomas, 1845–1851+**
Optician
| 1845 | 35 Suffolk Street, Smallbrook Street |
| 1846–1851+ | 35 Suffolk Street |

**GREW, William, 1785–1788**
Rule maker
| 1785–1788 | Bradford Street |

**GRIFFITHS, Thomas, 1842–1851+**
Rule maker
| 1842–1851+ | 33 Kenion Street |

**GUGGIARI, Charles, 1846**
Barometer and thermometer maker
| 1846 | 4 Bath passage |

**HANSON, George, 1797–1811**
Spectacle maker, optician
| 1797 | Worcester Street |
| 1803–1811 | Ann Street |

**HANSON, William, 1839–1851+**
Optician and wholesale spectacle manufacturer
| 1839–1842 | 76 Newhall Street |
| 1845–1846 | 26 Digbeth Street |
| 1847 | George Street |
| 1851+ | 40 Great Colmore Street |

**HARPER, Nathan, 1849**
Box and ivory rule maker
| 1849 | Brighton Place |

**HARRIMAN, John, 1829–1851+**
Box and ivory rule, thermometer and barometer maker
| 1829 | 1 court, New Summer Street |
| 1835–1837 | New John Street |
| 1839–1846 | 58 Church Street |
| 1847 | Church Street |
| 1849–1851+ | 58 Church Street |

**HARRIMAN, Thomas, 1800–1850+**
Box and ivory rule maker
| 1800–1801 | Aston Road |
| 1805–1808 | Ashted Row |
| 1809–1822 | Loveday Street |

| 1823–1829 | 24 Loveday Street |
| 1830–1831 | 40 Loveday Street |
| 1833–1851+ | 24 Loveday Street |

**HARRISON, John, 1788**
Spectacle maker
| 1788 | Moat Lane |

**HARRISON, John, 1846**
Rule maker
| 1846 | 58 Church Street |

**HARRISON, Joseph, 1842**
Box and ivory rule maker
| 1842 | 394 Summer Lane |

See William Harrison.

**HARRISON, Josh., 1839**
Box and ivory rule maker
| 1839 | Gopsall Street |

**HARRISON, Mary, 1823–1825**
Optician
| 1823–1825 | 7 Ann Street |

**HARRISON, William, 1788–1801**
Spectacle maker
| 1788–1798 | Back of 128 Digbeth |
| 1800–1801 | Ladywell Walk |

**HARRISON, William, 1839–1849**
Box and ivory rule maker
| 1839–1849 | 394 Summer Lane |

**HART, Joseph, 1788–1812**
Optician, spectacle maker, optical, mathematical and philosophical instrument maker
| 1788 | 5 Digbeth |
| 1791–1798 | Digbeth |
| 1800–1801 | 5 Digbeth |
| 1803–1808 | 65 Dale End |
| 1808–1812 | Dale End |

**HAYCOCK, Samuel, 1808–1821**
Mathematical instrument and brass compass maker etc.
| 1808–1812 | Lench Street |
| 1816 | Price Street |
| 1818–1821 | Bagot Street |

1822 2 Bagot Street

Succeeded by Samuel Haycock junior.

**HAYCOCK, Samuel, jun., 1821–1847**
Manufacturer of mathematical drawing instruments, and land surveyor's measuring tapes, brass compasses, plated and brass dog collars
| 1821–1822 | 5 Cock Street, near St Paul's |
| 1828 | Aston Road |
| 1829 | 26 Aston Road |
| 1830–1831 | 42 Loveday Street |
| 1833–1839 | Woodcock Street |
| 1842–1847 | 40 Woodcock Street |
| 1845 | 40 Woodcock Street, Ashted Row and at Erdington |

Succeeded by Edward Samuel Haycock & Co.

**HAYCOCK, Edward Samuel & Co., 1849–1850**
Manufacturers of mathematical instruments, measuring tapes, box and ivory rules
| 1849 | 40 Woodcock Street |
| 1850 | 46 Woodcock Street |

Succeeded in 1852 by Edward Samuel Haycock, rule maker at 46 Woodcock Street, and Samuel Haycock, mathematical instrument maker, at 40 Woodcock Street.

**HEATH, James, 1849**
Brass founder and manufacturer of inkstands, lustres, flower glasses, thermometers, watchstands, etc.
| 1849 | court 7, Essex Street |

**HEMMING, Edwin, 1847–1849**
Box and ivory rule maker
| 1847 | 76 Cardigan Street |
| 1849 | 49 Vauxhall Road |

**HIGGISON, John, 1833–1851+**
Box and ivory rule maker and retail brewer
| 1833 | 23 court and 186 Bromsgrove Street |
| 1835 | 23 court, Bromsgrove Street |
| 1837–1842 | Bristol Street |
| 1845–1851+ | 226½ Bristol Street |

**HILL, Abraham, 1830–1831**
Rule maker and victualler
| 1830–1831 | 13 Smallbrook Street |

**HITCHIN, Thomas, 1847–1851+**
Box and ivory rule maker
| 1847–1849 | 37 Horsefair |
| 1850 | 47 Horsefair |
| 1851+ | 52 New John Street, west |

**HODGES, William, 1801–1818**
Victualler, compass and pincher maker
| 1801 | Deritend Street |
| 1803–1818 | Alcester Street, Deritend |

**HODGETTS, William, 1829–1835**
Box and ivory rule maker
| 1829 | 23 Little Hampton Street |
| 1835 | 92 Upper Tower Street |

**HOLLICK, Joseph, 1822**
Optician
| 1822 | Digbeth |

**HOLT, H., 1849**
Thermometer maker
| 1849 | 15 Cardigan Street |

**HORN, William, 1777–1781**
Instrument maker
| 1777–1781 | 148 Moor Street |

**HORTON, George, Melville & Co., 1835–1842**
Opticians
| 1835 | 126 Great Hampton Street and at 17 Thaives Inn, Holborn |
| 1837 | 136 Great Hampton Street and at 32 Hatton Garden, London |

1842    126 Great Hampton Street, 1 Hall Street and Hatton Garden, Holborn

Listed in 1842 as 'goldsmiths, silversmiths, and jewellers'.

**HUG, Lawrence, 1850–1851+**
Mathematical instrument maker
1850–1851+    44 Constitution Hill

**HUGHES, John, 1850–1851+**
Rule maker
1850–1851+    Cambridge Street

**HUGHES, Thomas, 1785–1798**
Manufacturer of rules, steel toys, and paper cases
1785–1788    26 Duke Street
1791–1798    Aston Road

**HURD, Thomas, 1815–1816**
Compass maker
1815–1816    Whittal Street

**INMAN, Charles, 1849–1851+**
Box and ivory rule maker
1849    11 Newton Street
1850    113 Great Hampton Street
1851+    40 Lowe Street

**INMAN, William, 1835–1837**
Rule maker
1835    Market Street
1837    13 court, Coleshill Street

Succeeded by Inman & Son.

**INMAN & Son, 1839**
Box and ivory rule makers
1837    13 court, Coleshill Street

Succeeded by William Inman & Son.

**INMAN, William & Son, 1842**
Rule makers
1842    36 Ashted Row

Succeeded by Charles Inman.

**INSHAW, HINCKSMAN & BAKEWELL, 1783–1788**
Manufacturers of watch keys, seals, steel and metal toys, brass dog collars, compasses, etc.
1783    Catharine Street

From 1785 to 1788 they were listed as 'toymakers' in Whittall Street.

See Richard Bakewell.

Succeeded by Inshaw & Rushton.

**INSHAW & RUSHTON, 1791–1801**
Toy and mathematical instrument makers
1791–1801    Whittall Street

In 1800 and 1801, they were listed as 'gilt toy–makers'.

**JACOB, Christopher, 1767–1777**
Rule and snuff maker
1767    Smallbrook Street
1770    Chapel Row
1774–1777    Gosty Green

**JACOB, William, 1770**
Rule maker
1770    29 Smallbrook Street

**JARVIS, Charles, 1774–1788**
Pincer and compass maker
1774–1777    30 Smallbroke Street
1777–1781    Windmill Street
1785–1788    Windmill Hill

Succeeded by Susan Jarvis.

**JARVIS, Daniel, 1767–1770**
Compass and pincer maker
1767    Windmill Hill
1770    30 Smallbrook Street

Succeeded by Charles Jarvis.

**JARVIS, Susan, 1793–1798**
Compass and steel toy maker
1793–1798    Windmill Hill

Succeeded by Susan and John Jarvis.

**JARVIS, Susan and John, 1800–1803**
Steel toys and compass makers
1800–1803     Windmill Hill

Previously Susan Jarvis.

**JINKS, William, 1818–1842**
Working optician and spectacle maker
1818–1842     33 court, Livery Street

Not in directories for 1822 to 1825, or
1835 to 1837.

**JONES, James, 1785–1798**
Optician and mathematical instrument
maker
1785     79 Bull Street
1788     92 Snowhill
1791–1798     Newton Street

Previously William Jones.

**JONES, William, 1783–1784**
Optician
1783–1784     Bull Street

Succeeded by James Jones.

**KELSALL, Thomas, 1842**
Mathematical instrument and measuring
tape maker
1842     75 Woodcock Street

**LANCASTER, James, 1849–1851+**
Optician
1849–1850     7 Summer Lane
1851+     5 Colmore Row

**LANCASTER, Patrick, 1800–1809**
Spectacle maker
1800–1803     63 Snowhill
1809     Nova Scotia Street

**LANGFORD, Richard Thomas, 1845**
Rule maker
1845     13 court, Great Hampton
    Row

Previously Thomas Langford.

**LANGFORD, Thomas, 1839**
Rule maker
1839     137 Great Hampton Street

Succeeded by Richard Thomas Langford.

**LAWLEY, George, 1833–1842**
Box and ivory rule maker
1833–1837     51 Summer Lane
1839     22 court, Lower Tower
    Street
1842     44 Newtown Row

**LEA, Thomas, 1767**
Compass maker
1767     Moor Street

**LEE, Samuel, 1839–1847**
Optician and cigar manufacturer
1839–1842     100 New Street
1845–1846     43 New Street
1847 New Street

Previously Solomon Lee.

**LEE, Solomon, 1837**
Optician
1837     100 New Street

Succeeded by Samuel Lee.

**LLOYD, James, 1788–1809**
Spectacle maker
1788     50 Dudley Street
1791–1809     Hurst Street

**LOWE, John, 1788–1798**
Bookseller, stationer, print and music
seller also all kinds of stamps, optical
and mathematical instruments, London
newspapers, and an extensive circulating
library of upwards of 3,000 vols.
1788–1793     14 High Street
1797     Cherry Street
1798     High Street

**LUCAS, William, 1842–1850**
Brass founder and brass rule cutter
1842     Constitution Hill
1845–1850     36 Constitution Street

**LUDLOW, Sarah, 1850**
Rule maker
1850                2 Bartholomew Street

Succeeded by William Ludlow, rule maker,
11 George Street, Parade, from 1851+.

Previously Thomas Ludlow.

**LUDLOW, Thomas, 1822–1849**
Box and ivory rule maker
1822                Allison Street
1823–1825          81 Allison Street
1829–1842          32 Park Street
1845–1846          22 Bartholomew Street
1847–1849          2 Bartholomew Street

Succeeded by Sarah Ludlow.

**LUNT, Joseph, 1835–1849**
Box and ivory rule maker and victualler
1835–1837          22 Camden Street
1842–1849          20 Camden Street

From 1842 running 'The Golden Cup' at
20 Camden Street; after 1850 only 'The
Golden Cup'.

**MACKLOW, Charles and George,
                1842–1847**
Optical glass manufacturers
1842                255 Bradford Street
1845–1847          Pershore Mill, Sherlock
                   Street

Succeeded by John and George Macklow.

**MACKLOW, John and George,
                1849–1850+**
Optical glass manufacturers
1849–1851+         214 Sherlock Street

Previously Charles and George Macklow.

**MALLIN, Abraham, 1845–1851+**
Box and ivory rule manufacturer
1845                5 Chapel Street, St
                   Bartholomew Square
1847                Gopsall Street
1849–1851+         5 Chapel Street

**MALLIN, William, 1845–1851+**
Box and ivory rule maker
1845–1846          52 Hatchet Street,
                   Newtown Row
1849–1851+         50 Newtown Row

**MALLIN & Co., 1842**
Rule manufacturers
1842                12 Hampton Street

Succeeded by Abraham Mallin, and
William Mallin.

**MAN, Thomas Harry, 1849**
Box and ivory rule maker
1849                24 Loveday Street

**MANN, John, 1835**
Optician
1835                200 New Street

**MANSELL, John, 1770–1781**
Rule maker
1770–1781          Queen Street,
                   Wolverhampton

**MARSH, Benjamin, 1846**
Barometer and thermometer maker
1846                83 Coleshill Street

**MELLER, Joseph, 1823–1825**
Mathematical instrument maker
1823–1825          28 Princep Street

Succeeded by Norris & Meller.

**MORRIS, William, 1800–1833**
Box and ivory rule maker
1800–1801          Great Charles Street
1803–1821          Summer Row
1822                Newhall Row
1828                17 court, Great Charles
                   Street
1829                Northwood Street
1830–1833          17 court, Great Charles
                   Street

**MUCKLOW, Benjamin, 1835–1839**
Spectacle and optical glass manufacturer
1835                St James's Place
1837                Rea Mill, Lawley Street

1839            St James's Place, Lawley
                Street

**MUMFORD, Robert, 1800–1803**
Spectacle maker
1800–1803      Loveday Street

**NELSON, Joseph, 1839–1845**
Ivory and box rule maker
1839            7 court, Nelson Street
1845            court, Cottage Lane

**NEWEY, James, 1822**
Electrical machine maker
1822            Summer Lane

**NICHOLLS, Thomas Merrit, 1850–1851+**
Measuring tape manufacturer and dealer
in box and ivory rules etc.
1850–1851+      21 St Mary's Row

**NISBETT, Joseph, 1845–1849**
Box and ivory rule manufacturer
1845–1849       209 Lawley Street, Ashted
                Row

**NORRIS & MELLER, 1839–1851+**
Mathematical instrument and measuring
tape manufacturers
1839–1850       1 court, Ward Street, Lower
                Tower Street
1851+           78 Lichfield Street

**OAKLEY, Joseph, 1767–1781**
Spectacle and other optical instrument
maker
1767            Upper Priory
1770–1781       79 Bull Street

**ONIONS, Benjamin, 1823–1851+**
Rule maker
1823–1825       2 Northwood Street
1829            92 Northwood Street
1833            Haywood's Building, Livery
                Street
1839–1849       29 court, Livery Street
1850–1851+      137 Livery Street

**ONIONS, Thomas, 1767–1808**
Box and ivory rule maker
1767–1770       Brick-kiln Lane,
                Wolverhampton
1780–1781       Brick-kiln Lane,
                Wolverhampton
1783–1784       Cherry Street
1785            Walmer Lane
1788–1793       Lancaster Street
1797            Great Hampton Street
1798            Lancaster Street
1800–1808       Great Hampton Street

**OSBORNE, Thomas, 1800–1801**
Astronomical and musical clock maker
and watch repairer; also all sorts of
experimental and philosophical apparatus,
etc.
1800–1801       Vauxhall Street

**PARKES, Henry, 1829–1835**
Rule maker
1829            Little Hampton Street
1835            Vauxhall Road

Not listed in the directories between 1830
and 1835.

**PARKES, Isaac, 1821–1825**
Optician
1821            Barford Street
1823–1825       23 Barford Street

**PARKES, J., 1842**
Optician
1842            20 Lower Terrace

**PARKES, James, 1839–1842**
Gilt toy, compass and measuring tape
                maker
1839–1842       5 St Mary's Row

Succeeded by James Parkes & Son.

**PARKES, John, 1815–1835**
Optician and manufacturer of all kinds
of spectacles in silver, tortoise-shell, gilt,
plated or steel frames, etc.
1815–1835       Sand Pits

Succeeded by John Parkes & Son.

**PARKES, John, 1842–1849**
Spectacle maker and dealer in marine
stores
1842–1849      89 Livery Street

**PARKES, Samuel, 1777–1801**
Compass maker and mathematical
instrument maker
1777–1781      8 Sand Street
1788           St Mary's Row
1797–1801      Legge Street

Succeeded by Samuel Parkes & Son.

**PARKES, Samuel, 1821–1831**
Mathematical instrument, box and ivory
rule maker
1821           Little Hampton Street
1822–1831      16 Little Hampton Street

Previously Samuel Parkes & Son.

**PARKES, William, 1845–1846**
Optician
1845–1846      4 court, Digbeth

**PARKES, William, 1842–1851+**
Optician and mathematical instrument
maker
1842 21 Sand pits
1845–1846      20 Sandpits, Summer Hill
1847–1851+     28 Paradise Street

Previously John Parkes & Sons.

**PARKES & Son, 1805–1808**
Rule makers
1805–1808      Snowhill

**PARKES, James & Son, 1845–1851+**
Mathematical instrument, measuring tape
and gilt toy makers
1845–1851+     5 St Mary's Row

By 1850, the proprietor was named as
Samuel Hicklin Parkes.

Previously James Parkes.

**PARKES, John & Son, 1837**
Opticians
1837           Sand Pits

Succeeded by John Parkes & Sons.

**PARKES, John & Sons, 1839**
Opticians
1839           Sand–pits

Succeeded by William Parkes.

**PARKES, Samuel & Son, 1801–1818**
Mathematical instrument, box and ivory
rule makers
1801           Legge Street, Workhouse
               Field
1803–1815      Bull Street
1808           Bull Street and Coleshill
               Street
1816–1818      66 Bull Street

Succeeded by Samuel Parkes.

**PARKES, Susannah & Sons, 1842**
Gilt toy and compass makers
1842           7 Bath Street

**PARSON, Henry, 1812–1825**
Pincer and compass maker
1812           Lower Temple Street
1815           Windmill Hill
1816–1822      Hill Street
1823–1825      court 10, Hill Street

**PARSONS, Ann, 1830–1831**
Compass, pincer and hammer maker
1830–1831      13 court, Inge Street

Previously John Parsons.

**PARSONS, John, 1816–1825**
Compass and pincer maker
1816–1822      Inge Street
1823–1825      13 Inge Street

Succeeded by Ann Parsons.

**PARTRIDGE, Ephraim, 1845–1846**
Mathematical instrument makerr
1845–1846      83 Henry Street, Great
               Brook Street

**PEARSON, Joseph, 1791–1816**
Optician, spectacle maker, glass stainer, quicker, gilder, and lapidary
| | |
|---|---|
| 1791 | Castle Street |
| 1797 | Moor Street |
| 1798 | Castle Street |
| 1800–1816 | 129 Moor Street |

**PEARSON, Joseph junior, 1811–1818**
Optician, spectacle maker
| | |
|---|---|
| 1811–1818 | Steelhouse Lane |
| 1823–1825 | 100 Great Charles Street |
| 1828 | 43 Moor Street |
| 1830 | 53 and 114 Moor Street |
| 1831 | 43 Moor Street |
| 1833–1842 | 114 Moor Street |

**PEVERELLE, John Bernard, 1849–1851+**
Picture frame and thermometer maker
1849–1851+     16 Pershore Street

**PHILLIPS, George, 1829**
Rule maker
1829     14 court, Brearley Street

**PHILLIPS, Samuel, 1777**
Glass grinder
1777     11 Freeman Street

**PIERCY, Joseph, 1816–1822**
Compass and pincer maker
1816–1822     Newhall Street

**POWELL, – , 1823–1825**
Ivory and box, and measuring tape maker
1823–1825     court 4, Lionel Street

**POWELL, Robert, 1823–1825**
Box and ivory rule, and joiner's tool maker
1823–1825     20 King Edward's Place

**POWELL, Thomas C., 1846**
Optician
1846     91 Pershore Street

**POWERS, Samuel, 1767–1781**
Spectacle and case maker
| | |
|---|---|
| 1767 | Colemore Street |
| 1780–1781 | 3 and 4 Colemore Street |

**PRATT, Joseph, 1850**
Rule maker
1850     20 Heneagest

**PROBIN, William, 1845–1849**
Shopkeeper and rule maker
1845–1849     62 New Summer Street

**PROCTOR, George, 1818**
Optician
1818     Newhall Street

Previously George and William Proctor.

**PROCTOR, George and William, 1815–1816**
Opticians
1815–1816     Newhall Street

Succeeded by George Proctor.

**PROCTOR & BEILBY, 1800–1808**
Opticians
1800–1808     Newhall Street

Succeeded by Proctor, Beilby & Co.

**PROCTORS & BEILBY, 1788–1798**
Opticians
| | |
|---|---|
| 1788 | Price Street |
| 1791–1798 | Newhall Street |

Succeeded by Proctor & Beilby.

**PROCTOR, BEILBY & Co., 1809–1816**
Opticians
| | |
|---|---|
| 1809–1811 | Newhall Street and Market Street, Sheffield |
| 1812 | Newhall Street |
| 1816 | Newhall Street |

Not in directory for 1815, but see George & William Proctor.

Succeeded by George and William Proctor.

**PURSALL, John, 1785–1788**
Glass grinder and victualler
1785–1788     Hill Street

**RABALLIO, Peter, 1788**
Weather-glass maker
1788          Edgbaston Street

**RABONE, Elizabeth, 1812–1845**
Rule maker
1812–1821    Water Street
1822          13 Water Street
1823–1830    33 Water Street
1830–1833    Ludgate Hill
1835–1837    Summer Street Place
1839          172 Hockley Place
1839          171 Hockley Hill
1845          172 Hockley Hill

**RABONE, Ephraim, 1816–1818**
Rule maker
1816          14 Water Street
1818          Water Street

**RABONE, John, 1822–1851+**
Barometer maker and box and ivory rule
maker
1822          Ludgate Hill
1823          61 St Paul's Square
1828–1830    33 Ludgate Hill
1830–1851+   61 St Paul's Square

In partnership as Rabone & Mason in
1835.

**RABONE, Michael, 1800–1803**
Rule maker and wood turner
1800–1801    Bull Street
1803          8 Snowhill

Succeeded by Elizabeth Rabone & Son.

**RABONE, Thomas, 1829–1851+**
Manufacturer of thermometers,
barometers, levels, bronzed egg glasses,
rules etc.
1829          8 court, Water Street
1833–1835    12 court, Bread Street
1837          Frederick Street, Great
               Hampton Street
1839–1842    171 Hockley Hill
1845–1851+   172 Hockley Hill

**RABONE & MASON, 1835**
Barometer and thermometer makers
1835          61 St Paul's Square
– not in 1839 [W] or [R] –

**RABONE, Elizabeth & Son, 1808–1811**
Ivory and box rule makers
1808–1811    Water Street

Succeeded by Elizabeth Rabone.

**RABY, Edward, 1835**
Optician
1835          Great Brook Street

**RAETOR, John, 1800–1801**
Optical, mathematical and philosophical
instrument maker
1800–1801    49 Cheapside, Deritend

**RAXTER, John, 1815–1829**
Mathematical and surveying instrument
maker and repairer
1815–1822    6 John Street
1823–1825    32 John Street
1829          20 court, Lichfield Street

Succeeded by Robert Raxter.

**RAXTER, Robert, 1829–1839**
Mathematical instrument maker
1829          89 Livery Street
1830–1831    144 Livery Street
1833          137 Livery Street
1835          Livery Street
1839          137 Livery Street

Previously John Raxter.

**REDFERN, Joseph, 1842–1851+**
Optician and spectacle maker
1842–1846    85 Smallbrook Street
1845–1851+   37 Exeter Row

**REVENEY, Charles, 1800–1812**
Military feather and barometer maker
1800–1808    30 Edgbaston Street
1809–1811    Dudley Street
1812          Edgbaston Street

**RICHARDS, Alfred, 1850–1851+**
Mathematical instrument maker and
optician
| | |
|---|---|
| 1850 | Lea Bank Road |
| 1851+ | 3 Bull Street |

**RICHARDS, Daniel, 1835–1847**
Optician and spectacle maker
| | |
|---|---|
| 1835–1837 | 27 Church Street |
| 1839–1842 | 26 Church Street |
| 1847 | 36 Church Street |

**RICHARDS, Esther, 1800–1812**
Box and ivory rule maker
| | |
|---|---|
| 1800–1801 | 94 Lichfield Street |
| 1803 | 95 Lichfield Street |
| 1805–1812 | Lichfield Street |

Previously William Richards.

Succeeded by John Richards.

**RICHARDS, John, 1815–1825**
Rule maker
| | |
|---|---|
| 1815–1821 | Lichfield Street |
| 1822 | 95 Lichfield Street |
| 1823–1825 | 98 Lichfield Street |

Previously Esther Richards.

Succeeded by Richards & Lockyer.

**RICHARDS, William, 1785–1798**
Box and ivory rule maker
| | |
|---|---|
| 1785–1788 | 14 Lichfield Street |
| 1791–1798 | Lichfield Street |

Succeeded by William Richards.

**RICHARDS & LOCKYER, 1828–1831**
Rule makers
| | |
|---|---|
| 1828–1831 | 20 Jamaica Row |

**ROBERTS, Henry, 1835–1837**
Optician
| | |
|---|---|
| 1835–1837 | 48 Inge Street |

**ROBINSON, Thomas Baker, 1812–1825**
Carver, gilder, glass grinder, polisher and
picture frame maker
| | |
|---|---|
| 1812–1815 | Carved Greyhound, Bull Street |
| 1818–1821 | Bull Street |

| | |
|---|---|
| 1823–1825 | 64 Bull Street |

**ROTE, Candy, 1800–1803**
Barometer maker
| | |
|---|---|
| 1800–1803 | Spiceal Street |

**ROTTON, Ambrose, 1829–1842**
Rule maker (and surveyors' measuring
tapes)
| | |
|---|---|
| 1829 | 1 court, Price Street |
| 1833–1835 | 2 court, Price Street |
| 1839–1842 | 12 Price Street |

**ROWLEY, Thomas, 1808–1831**
Optician and tortoise–shell spectacle
frame manufacturer
| | |
|---|---|
| 1808–1812 | Bromsgrove Street |
| 1815 | Horse Fair |
| 1828–1831 | 54 Constitution Hill |

**RUDHALL, William Henry, 1845–1851+**
Optician and spectacle maker
| | |
|---|---|
| 1845–1846 | 36 Bath Street |
| 1850–1851+ | no 7 court, Cox Street |

**RUSHTON, William, 1800–1825**
Gilt toy, mathematical instrument maker
and bell founder
| | |
|---|---|
| 1800–1823 | 8 Whittal Street |
| 1825 | 10 Whittall Street |

**RUSSELL, Edward, 1850–1851+**
Manufacturers of measuring tapes, box and
ivory rules and mathematical instruments
| | |
|---|---|
| 1850–1851+ | 29 Whittall Street |

Previously Edward Russell & Co.

**RUSSELL, Edward & Co., 1849–1850**
Manufacturers of land surveyors'
measuring tapes, box and ivory rules and
mathematical instruments
| | |
|---|---|
| 1849–1850 | 29 Whittall Street |

Succeeded by Edward Russell.

**RYLAND, Thomas, 1800–1811**
Button–maker, optician, manufacturer of
gilt toys
| | |
|---|---|
| 1800–1803 | Great Charles Street |
| 1808–1811 | Mary-ann Street, St Paul's |

**SALT, Abraham, 1803–1815**
Rule maker and cutler
1803–1815     Worcester Street

Succeeded by Abraham Salt & Son.

**SALT, Isaac, 1825–1835**
Rule maker, cutler and ironmonger
1825–1835     19 Worcester Street

Previously Abraham Salt & Son.

**SALT, Abraham & Son, 1816–1823**
Rule makers, cutlers and ironmongers
1816–1822     Worcester Street
1823          19 Worcester Street and
              Bristol Street

Succeeded by Isaac Salt.

**SALT, Joseph and Abraham, 1797–1801**
Rule makers
1797          Smallbrook Street
1800–1801 Windmill Street, Bristol Street

Succeeded by Abraham Salt.

**SAMUELS & Co., 1846**
Opticians
1846          108 New Street

**SCATTERGOOD, Mary, 1849–1850**
Manufacturer of improved measuring tapes
1849 –1850     32½ Livery Street

Previously Samuel Scattergood.

**SCATTERGOOD, Samuel, 1845–1847**
Manufacturer of mathematical
instruments and surveyors' measuring
tapes etc.
1845–1847     32½ Livery Street

Succeeded by Mary Scattergood.

**SHAW, William, 1823–1825**
Rule maker
1823–1825     18 Smallbrook Street

**SHERWOOD, Samuel, 1815–1818**
Compass and pincer maker
1815–1816     Hurst Street
1818          Smallbrooke Street

**SHUTTLEWORTH, Joseph, 1828–1849**
Mathematical instrument, and surveyors'
measuring tape and miners' and mariners'
compass maker
1828–1830     63 Lichfield Street
1829–1835     73 Lichfield Street
1837–1842     133 Broad Street, Islington
1845–1849     2 Newhall Street

Succeeded by Joseph Peace Shuttleworth.

**SHUTTLEWORTH, Joseph Peace,
   1850–1851+**
Mathematical instruments and measuring
tapes manufacturer
1850          2 Newhall Street
1851+         73 Newhall Street

Previously Joseph Shuttleworth.

**SMITH, B., 1822**
Compass and pincer maker
1822          St Paul's Square

Previously Benjamin Smith & Co.

**SMITH, Samuel Albert, 1845–1851+**
Box and ivory rule manufacturer for
gauging, navigation, surveying, drawing,
and all kinds of foreign rules for
exportation
1845–1846     Davis's Buildings, Upper
              Trinity Street, Bordesley
1849–1851+    368 Coventry Road

**SMITH, William, 1835–1851+**
Mathematical instrument, dog collar and
sundial maker
1835–1839     6 court, Loveday Street
1842–1851+    29 Loveday Street,
              Steelhouse Lane

**SMITH, Benjamin & Co., 1816–1818**
Compass and pincer makers
1816–1818     Constitution Hill

Succeeded by B. Smith.

**SNELSON, Joseph, 1829**
Rule maker
1829          8 Shadwell Street

**SOLOMON, Aaron, 1800–1801**
Optician
1800–1801     Bell Street

**SOLOMON, Wolfe, 1829–1851+**
Optician and dealer in watch materials
1829              15 Smallbrook Street
1835–1839     Smallbrook Street
1842–1851+   15 Smallbrook Street

Not in directories for 1830 to 1833, 1837
or 1849.

**STANLEY, John, 1822**
Compass and pincer maker
1822              22 Great Charles Street

**STANLEY, Thomas, 1800–1831**
Mathematical instruments, brass dog-
collar, and compass maker
1800–1801     St Mary's Row
1803–1808     Aston Street
1809–1812     Ashted Row
1816–1822     10 Bath Street
1823–1825     73 Bath Street
1828–1831     Ashted

**TIMMINS, Richard, 1797–1818, 1822**
Compass and pincer maker
1797–1818     Hurst Street
1822              Hurst Street

Succeeded by Richard Timmins & Sons.

**TIMMINS, Richard & Sons, 1821–1825**
Compass, pincer and heavy steel toy
                  manufacturers
1821              Hurst Street
1823–1825     56 Hurst Street

**TIMMINS, Thomas, 1777–1801**
Optician, spectacle maker and victualler
1777              1 Old Hinkleys
1780–1781     Pinfold Street
1785              Brick Kiln Lane
1800–1801     19 Fleet Street

**TIMMINS, Thomas, 1815–1818**
Optician
1815–1818     Bromsgrove Street

**TOMBS, William, 1822**
Rule maker
1822              Steelhouse Lane

**TOMPON, Samuel, 1770–1777**
Optician
1770              in a yard between 18 and 19
                  Dudley Street
1774–1777     19 Dudley Street

**TROW, Isaac (late Richard Bakewell),
      1829–1851+**
Manufacturer of mathematical
instruments, surveyors' measuring
tapes, dog collars, mariners' and miners'
compasses, sun dials etc.
1829 39 Loveday Street and 65 Worcester
                  Street
1830–1833     40 Loveday Street
1835–1839     8 court, Loveday Street
1839–1851+   40 Loveday Street

**TURNER, Daniel, 1822–1825**
Optician, brass founder, philosophical and
astronomical instrument maker
1822              Suffolk Street
1823–1825     39 Suffolk Street

**TURNER, John, 1845–1847**
Box and ivory rule maker
1845–1847     17 court, Wharf Street,
                  Suffolk Street

**TURNER, Joseph, 1839–1850**
Box and ivory rule maker
1839              Livery Street
1845              court, Great Lister Street,
                  Aston Road
1850              no 8 court, William Street
                  north; no 1 court, Adam
                  Street

**VEISEY & BEST, 1833–1839**
Manufacturers of telescopes, hearth
brushes, toasting forks, thermometers and
stands
1833–1839     111 Upper Tower Street

**WAINWRIGHT, THOMPSON & Co., 1849**
Opticians and spectacle manufacturers
1849          10 Union Passage

**WALTON, Edward, 1845**
Rule maker
1845          Lozells

**WARDEN, William, 1770**
Instrument case maker
1770          Market Place, Walsall

**WARNER, Thomas, 1830–1833**
Compass and pincer maker
1830–1833    15 court, Queen Street

**WEARDON, William, 1767**
Instrument maker
1767          High Street, Walsall

**WHARTON, Thomas, 1830–1833**
Glass cutter, japanner, and mariners' and miners' compass maker, also paper snuff box, picture and miniature frame manufacturer
1830–1831    90 New Street
1833–1835    4 Great Charles Street

**WILLETTS, William, 1847**
Rule maker
1847          Henry Street

**WILLSON, William, 1845–1851+**
Box and ivory rule maker
1845–1846    136 Hampton road, St George's
1847          137 Hampton Street
1849–1851+   9 Mott Street

Name sometimes given as 'Wilson'.

**WILSON & Co., 1791–1798**
Opticians
1791–1798    Warehouse, Castle Street

**WITHNOL, William, 1777**
Rule maker
1777          20 Ann Street or Mount Place

**WITHNOL & Co., 1777**
Mathematical instrument makers
1777          Great Charles Street

Succeeded by Wood & Withnol.

**WOLLER, Charles, 1835–1851+**
Barometer and thermometer maker, watch and clock maker
1835–1851+   63 Edgbaston Street

**WOLLER, Matthew, 1800–1831**
Clock and barometer maker
1800–1821    51 Edgbaston Street
1823–1831    63 Edgbaston Street

Succeeded by Woller & Brunner.

**WOLLER & BRUNNER, 1833**
Clock and watch, barometer and thermometer makers
1833          62 Edgbaston Street

Succeeded by Charles Brunner.

**WORRALL, John, 1839–1851+**
Mathematical and surgical instrument case maker
1839          79 Weaman Street
1845–1851+   7 Newton Street, Lichfield Street

**WOOD, Henry, 1777**
Rule maker
1777          29 Great Charles Street

Succeeded by Wood & Withnol.

**WOOD, John, 1777**
Rule maker
1777          16 London–'prentice Street

**WOOD, Thomas, 1767–1770**
Rule maker
1767–1770    Brick Kiln Lane, Wolverhampton

**WOOD & WITHNOL, 1780–1781**
Rule makers
1780–1781    29 Great Charles Street

Previously Henry Wood and William Withnol.

**WRIGHT, Thomas, 1800–1803**
Spectacle maker
1800–1803    Great Hampton Street

**WRIGHT, William, 1785–1805**
Box and ivory rule maker
1785–1788    46 Worcester Street
1791–1798    Philip Street
1800–1803    14 Philip Street
1805         Queen Street

**WYNN, William and Cornelius, 1816–1839**
Compass and pincer makers
1816–1822    Suffolk Street
1830–1839    142 Suffolk Street

**YOULE, John, 1812–1825**
Tortoise-shell spectacle and optic glass
mounter
1812–1825    Barford Street

*Bristol*

**BALE, Thomas, 1844–1851+**
Working jeweller and optician
1844–1851    11 Broad Mead
1852 +       36 Wine Street, two doors
             from the top of Union
             Street

**BARTON, S. & J., 1819–1835**
Coach builders and odometer makers
1819–1826    Hotwells
1827–1828    Hotwells
1829–1831    Milk Street
1832–1835    Milk Street and Bedminster
             Bridge

Previously 'Coach builders Hotwells',
from 1814, and again from 1836.

Between 1827 and 1833, listed as 'Barton,
J. & S.'

**BEILBY, Richard and Charles, 1809–1820**
Optical, mathematical and philosophical
instrument makers
1809–1820    2 Clare Street

R. & C. Beilby 1809–13; C. Beilby 1814–15;
Charles Beilby 1816–1819; Richard Beilby
1820. Succeeded by John King.

**BENNETT, Thomas, 1775–1803**
Hour glass maker
1775    49 Wade Street
1793–1803    Bridewell Lane

Not in directories for 1785 or 1787.

**BIRD, Thomas, 1839–1842**
Leather hose manufacturer, optical and
mathematical instrument maker
1839–1842    20 St Augustine's Place

**BLAINEY, William, 1847–1853**
Rule and gauge maker
1847–1853    5 Lower Maudlin Street

**BRAHAM, John, 1828–1838**
Optician, mathematical instrument
warehouse
1828         12 Clare Street
1829         42 College Green
1830–1838    10 St Augustine's Parade,
             nearly opposite the
             Drawbridge

By 1833, described as 'optician,
mathematical, philosophical and nautical
instrument maker; agent for the sale of the
charts and plans published by the Lords
Commissioners of the Admiralty'.

Succeeded in 1839 by John Braham & Co.

**BRAHAM, John, 1840–51**
Optician; mathematical, philosophical
and nautical instrument maker; agent for
the sale of the charts and plans published
by the Lords Commissioners of the
Admiralty
1840–1844    10 St Augustine's Parade
1845–1851    17 St Augustine's Parade,
             opposite the Drawbridge

From 1845, 'patentee and manufacturer
of the patent pantoscopic spectacle and
eye preserver'; succeeded in 1852–53 by

Braham Brothers (late John Braham), reverting to John Braham between 1854 and 1860. By 1866, the firm was being run by Joseph Braham at 24 College Green.

### BRAHAM (late Jackson), 1842–1844
Watch, clock and chronometer maker, goldsmith and jeweller
1842–1844     17 St Augustine's Parade

Succeeded by John Braham.

### BRAHAM, John & Co., 1839
Opticians; mathematical, philosophical and nautical instrument makers; agents for the sale of the charts and plans published by the Lords Commissioners of the Admiralty
1839     17 St Augustine's Parade, near the Drawbridge

Succeeded in 1840 by John Braham.

### BROWNE, Benjamin, 1792–1831
Mathematical instrument maker
1792–1813     Quay
1814–1815     Quay and Wilson Street
1816–1819     Quay and 14 Wilson Street
1820–1824     Quay
1825–1826     2 Old Park Hill and opposite the Crane, no 7 Quay
1827–1831     Opposite the Crane, no 7 Quay

### DAVIS, James, 1830–1851+
Miniature glass blower and maker of all kinds of tubes for chemical experiments, thermometers, barometers etc.
1830–1851+     8 Lewin's Mead

In 1854, the description changes to 'thermometer and barometer makers – all kinds of tubes for chemical experiments etc.'.

### EDGEWORTH, Henry, 1775–1787
Mathematical, philosophical and optical instrument maker
1775     51 on the Key [sic]
1783–1787     Quay

Described as 'optician' in directories in 1783 and 1784, and as 'mathematical instrument maker' in 1785 and 1787.

### FAULDER, John, 1841–1842
Philosophical instrument maker and general machinist
1841     3 Peter Street
1842     75 Castle Street

In 1842, described as 'mathematical instrument maker etc.'

### FOWLER, William, 1825
Rule and gauging instrument maker
1825     at the Bell, Hillgrove Street

### GWYLLYM, Joshua (late Webb), 1832–1851+
Mathematical instrument maker and rule maker
1832–1833     3 doors from the Infirmary, Earl Street
1834–1851+     Earl Street

From 1852 described as 'rule maker' only. Succeeded Thomas Webb.

### HYDE, John Moor, 1841–1851+
Mathematical and philosophical instrument maker
1841–1846     1 Broad Quay
1847–1852     1 Broad Quay and 11 Grenville Street
1853–1854     1 Broad Quay

From 1847 to 1851, 'and nautical academy'; reverts to original description. Hill & Price (late Hyde) at this address from 1855.

### KING, J., 1819
Mathematical instrument maker
1819     Redcliff Hill

Not in 1820 directory. Moves to Clare Street.

### KING, John, 1821–1822
Optical, mathematical and philosophical instrument maker
1821–1822     2 Clare Street

Succeeded by John King & Son.

**KING, John, 1836–1846**
Optical, mathematical and philosophical
instrument manufacturer
1836–1846     at the Post Captain, 2 Clare
               Street

From 1841 to 1843 at '37 Wind Street,
Swansea'; from 1844 'agent for the
sale of warranted marine and pocket
chronometers'.

Succeeded by Thomas D. King.

**KING, Thomas D., 1847–1850**
Optician, mathematical and philosophical
instrument manufacturer, agent for the
sale of warranted marine and pocket
chronometers, and for Dring & Fage's
hydrometers, saccharometers, etc.
1847–1850     2 Clare Street

Succeeded by King & Coombs.

**KING, John & Son, 1823–1835**
Optical, mathematical and philosophical
instrument makers
1823–1835     2 Clare Street

From 1831 'agents for the sale of marine
and pocket chronometers'; from 1830,
address 'at the Post Captain, 2 Clare
Street'.

Succeeded by John King at this address.

**KING & COOMBS, 1851+**
Opticians, mathematical and philosophical
instrument manufacturers, agents for
the sale of warranted marine and pocket
chronometers, and for Long's hydrometers,
saccharometers, etc.
1851–1853     Clare Street

Succeeded by Thomas D. King, 1854–1856
at 1 Denmark Street, St Augustine's
Parade and John King, 1855–1860+ at 2
Clare Street.

**KNIGHT, Henry & Co., 1845–1847**
Chemists and druggists, manufacturers
and dealers in every kind of chemical and
philosophical apparatus, chemicals, tests
and specimens
1845–1847     25 College Green

**LEVI, Jacob, 1775–1785**
Spectacle maker
1775          14 Temple Street
1785          Temple Street

Succeeded by H. & L. Levi in 1792.

**LEVY, Levy, 1805–1818**
Opticians and glass warehouse
1805–1811     Temple Street
1812          138 Thomas Street;
               warehouse, Temple Street
1813–1815     138 Thomas Street
1816–1818     10 Bath Street

Succeeded by J. Levy & Co.

**LEVI, H. & L., 1792–1803**
Opticians
1792–1803     Temple Street

Their name became H. & L. Levy in 1798;
from 1801 they were described as 'and
glass warehouse'.

Succeeded by L. Levy in 1805.

**LEVY, J. & Co., 1819–1822**
Opticians
1819–1821     1 Sims's Alley, St James's
1822          9 Canon Street, St James's

Succeeded by Levy Levy, glass dealer
and engraver, 1825–28; then Levy & Co.'s
Bazaar as importers and dealers, 1837–40;
Levy & Co., ran Levy's Bristol Bazaar
from 1841 at 39 College Green, including
the description 'opticians'; it continued
well beyond 1851.

**LOVELL, Elias, 1827–1844**
Optician
1827–1844     34 Lower Arcade

Described as 'toy manufacturer' in 1827,
a glass dealer from 1828–1833, although
'optician' in trades directory.

**LYONS, G., 1807–1811**
Optician and broker
1807–1811     133 and 134 Thomas Street

From 1812 to 1817, 'broker' at the same
address.

**MATTHIAS, James, 1830–1831**
Rule and gauging instrument maker
1830–1831     6 Stoney Hill

In directories at this address with no trade from 1827.

**PASSEY, Daniel, 1801**
Mathematical, optical and philosophical instrument maker
1801          Old Market

**ROWLAND, Edward, 1842–1851**
Mathematical instrument maker
1842–1851    50 Quay

Edward Rowland declared bankrupt in 1851.

Previously Thomas and Edward Rowland.

**ROWLAND, Richard, 1793–1811**
Mathematical instrument maker
1793–1803    Quay
1805–1811    50 Quay

At 34 Quay in 1793 and 1797.

Succeeded by Richard Rowland & Sons.

**ROWLAND, Richard & Sons, 1812–1819**
Mathematical instrument makers
1812–1815    50 Quay
1816–1817    53 Quay
1818–1819    50 Broad Quay

Succeeded by Edward and Thomas Rowland in 1820.

**ROWLAND, Thomas and Edward, 1820–1841**
Mathematical instrument makers
1820–1830    50 Broad Quay
1831–1841    50 Quay

Described as 'Edward & Thomas Rowland' 1820–1821.

Succeeded by Edward Rowland.

**ROWLEY, Thomas, 1831–1832**
Optician and spectacle maker
1831–1832    31 Back

**SOLOMON, John, 1836–1851+**
Optician
1836          Chatterton Square
1837–1847    Bath Parade, Temple Gate
1848–1851+   17 Cathay

Described as 'optician and spectacle manufacturer' between 1840 and 1845.

**SPRINGER, Joshua, 1775–1809**
Mathematical instrument maker
1775–1809    2 Clare Street

Varied descriptions: 'mathematical, philosophical, optical and musical instrument maker' in 1775; 'optician' in 1783 and 1784; and addition of 'electrician' between 1797 and 1803.

**SPRINGER, William, 1775–1811**
Mathematical instrument maker
1775          24 Charles Street
1783–1784    Quay
1785–1811    Charles Street

Also described as 'optician' between 1783–1784, 1793–1811; and at John Street in 1787, and St John's Bridge 1793–1795.

**STRACHAN, J., 1818–1821**
Electrician
1818–1821    Lower Maudlin Street

**TARONE, P., 1806–1812**
Weatherglass and thermometer maker
1806–1812    Tucker Street

**TIMMINS, Thomas, 1819–1833**
Optician
1818          1 Trenchard Street
1820–1822    6 Bridewell Lane
1823–1824    6 Bridewell Lane and
             Lower Castle Street
1825–1826    6 Bridewell Lane and
             Broad Weir
1828–1833    33 Lower Arcade

In 1828 and 1829, listed as 'The Original Optician'.

**TOOLE, James, 1821–1823**
Mathematical instrument maker
1821         9 Somerset Place
1823         Bell Avenue, Cathay

Toole appeared with no trade at Pruin Street Cathay in 1825.

**WATKINS, William, 1805–1832**
Mathematical instrument maker
1805–1811    St Michael's Hill
1814–1832    16 St Augustine's Back

From 1816 his description is 'manufacturer of mathematical, philosophical optical and nautical instruments'; from 1829 the address is '16 St Augustine's Parade'.

**WEBB, Thomas, 1793–1851**
Rule maker
1793–1816    Earl Street
1817–1822    3 doors from the Infirmary, Earl Street
1823–1830    2 doors from the Infirmary, Earl Street
1831–1832    3 doors from the Infirmary, Earl Street

1835–1851    Earl Street

Described as 'rule maker and gauging instrument maker' between 1827 and 1833; as 'T. Webb (see Gwyllym)' from 1835–1846; and 'T. Webb (now Gwyllym)', 1847–1851. Gone by 1852.

**WILLIAMS, R., 1825**
Astronomical clock and orrery maker, teacher of astronomy and its occult properties
1825         2 Portland Terrace, Wilder street

Between 1821 and 1824, described as 'clock and umbrella maker, teacher of astronomy and its occult properties' at 56 Broad Mead.

**WOOD, John, 1822–1825**
Rule maker
1822–1825    Sign of the Bell, Hillgrove Street

Described as 'rule and gauging instrument maker' in 1822, and with no trade in 1825.

*Liverpool*

**ABRAHAM, Abraham, 1818–1849**
Optician
1818         8 Lord Street
1821–1822    10 Lord Street
1822         8 Lord Street
1824–1825    7 Lord Street
1825         6 Lord Street
1828         9 Lord Street
1828         7 Lord Street
1832–1833    9 Lord Street
1835         76 Lord Street
1837         78 Lord Street
1839–1849    20 Lord Street

From 1843 described as 'and mathematical instrument maker'. Succeeded by Abraham Abraham & Co., with partners Charles West and George Smart Wood.

**ABRAHAM, Abraham & Co., 1851+**
Opticians and mathematical instrument makers
1851+         20 Lord Street

**ADIE, Richard, 1835–1851+**
Optician
1835         26 Bold Street
1837         28 Bold Street
1839–1851+   55 Bold Street

From 1837 described as 'and philosophical instrument maker'.

**ADLINGTON, Thomas, 1824–1827**
Mathematical instrument maker
1824–1825    55 South Side, Old Dock
1827         1 Ironmonger Lane

**ARSTALL, Ellen (Widow A. & Son), 1835–1849**
Scale-beam and improved weighing machines manufacturers
1835          3 Juvenal Street
1837          37 Moorfields
1839–1849     26 and 28 Cable Street

Succeeded in 1851 by Frederick Arstall, scale-beam and improved weighing machine manufacturer, 5A Thomas Street.

**ARSTALL, George, 1807–1821**
Scale beam and mathematical instrument maker
1807          7 North Side Old Dock
1809          Temple court
1810–1811     29 Pembroke Place; manufactory 1 Temple court
1814          32 Pembroke Place; manufactory 1 Temple court
1816          43 Pembroke Place; manufactory 1 Temple court
1821          Bank Buildings, 50 Castle Street

Described as 'maker of Dicas' hydrometer' between 1811 and 1816.

Not in directories between 1822, and 1827.

**ARSTALL, Widow, 1829**
Scale beam manufacturer
1829          33 Moorfields

Not in directory for 1830.

**ARSTALL, Widow & Son, 1832**
Scale beam manufacturers
1832          37 Moorfields

Not in directory for 1834.

**BACON, John, 1825**
Optician
1825          53 Trueman Street

**BASNETT, James, 1834–1851+**
Optician
1834          13 Robert Street North

1835          16 Robert Street North
1837          19 Robert Street North
1839–1851+    1 Robert Street North

Described as 'and mathematical instrument maker' in 1846, and 'and chronometer maker' from 1847 onwards.

**BAYLIS, William, 1837–1851+**
Rule maker
1837          56 Dale Street
1839          67 Dale Street and 27 Park Lane
1843          27 Park Lane
1845–1849     27 South John Lane
1851+         2 Prices Street

From 1841 to 1843, described as 'rule and mathematical instrument maker'; from 1845 to 1849 'brass founder and rule manufacturer'; and from 1851 'optician and mathematical instrument maker'.

**BELL, George, 1835–1849**
Mathematical instrument maker
1835          3 Cow Lane, Primrose Hill
1839–1841     7 Cow Lane, Fontenoy Street
1843–1849     38 Fontenoy Street

Not in directories for 1837, 1843, 1846, or 1851 and beyond.

**BELL, James, 1835**
Optician
1835          15 Glover Street, Harrington

**BELL, John, 1824**
Mathematical instrument maker
1824          Brook's Alley, Post Office Place

**BLINKHORN, Horatio, 1839–1851+**
Mathematical instrument maker
1839–1848     45 Great Crosshall Street
1849–1851+    17 Sun Street

Described as 'optician and mathematical instrument maker' in 1846 and 'optician' in 1848.

**BURGESS, Henry, 1790–1816**
Mathematical instrument maker
1790         24 Thomas Street
1816         2 Burgess Street

Does not appear in directories between 1794 and 1814; described as 'gentleman, 61 London Road' in 1818.

**BYWATER, John, 1814–1835**
Optician
1814         9 Mount Pleasant
1816         49 Gloucester Street
1818–1824    52 Gloucester Street
1825–1829    42 Seymour Street
1832–1835    44 Seymour Street

Described as 'optician and stationer' from 1825 to 1835; not in directories for 1814, 1822, 1830, 1834 and 1837, for which see Bywater & Co., and Bywater, Dawson & Co.

**BYWATER, John & Co., 1822–1830**
Mathematical instrument makers and navigation warehouse
1822–1823    20 Pool Lane
1824         13 Pool Lane
1825–1827    19 Pool Lane
1829–1830    20 Pool Lane

Succeeded by Bywater, Dawson & Co.

**BYWATER & Co., 1821**
Opticians, stationers, map and chart sellers
1821         20 Pool Lane

Succeeded by John Bywater & Co.

**BYWATER, DAWSON & Co., 1832–1835**
Opticians and stationers
1832–1835    20 Pool Lane

Succeeded by Dawson & Melling.

**CAMERON, Alexander, 1848–1849**
Chronometer and nautical instrument maker
1848–1849    54 South Castle Street

Succeeded by John Cameron.

**CAMERON, John, 1851+**
Chronometer and nautical instrument maker
1851+        54 South Castle Street

**CARTLICH, Henry, 1810–1811**
Mathematical instrument maker
1810–1811    54 Upper Frederick Street

**CASARTELLI, Anthony, 1848–1851+**
Optician and glassblower
1848–1851+  20 Duke Street

A successor to Anthony and Lewis Casartelli.

**CASARTELLI, L., 1821–1843**
Barometer maker
1821         39 King Street
1823         37 and 38 King Street
1824–1825    39 King Street
1827–1829    36 King Street
1830         39 King Street
1832         30 King Street
1835–1837    133 Duke Street
1839–1843    20 Duke Street

Not in directories for 1822 or 1834. Succeeded by Anthony & Lewis Casartelli, and then by Anthony Casartelli and Lewis Casartelli on their own accounts.

**CASARTELLI, Lewis, 1848–1851**
Optician
1848–1849    6 South John Street
1851         20 Duke Street

Not in directories beyond 1852.

**CASARTELLI, Anthony and Lewis, 1845–1848**
Barometer and thermometer makers, opticians and mathematical instrument makers
1845–1847    20 Duke Street

Successors to L. Casartelli.

**CATTERALL, James, 1841**
Rule manufacturer
1841         1 Threfall Street, Toxteth Park

**CHADBURN, Charles Henry, 1845–1851+**
Optician
1845–1851+   71 Lord Street

Described as 'manufacturing optician' in 1846 and 1851.

**CHADWICK, William, 1827–1830**
Optician
1827          8 Duke's Place
1829          Shop, 46 Wapping
1830          8 Duke's Place

**CHRISTIAN, George, 1825–1851+**
Mathematical instrument maker
1825          16 Regent Street
1827–1829     16 Strand Street
1832          31 Strand Street
1834–1851+    11 Strand Street

**CHRISTIAN, Hannah, 1843**
Optician
1843          110 Pitt Street

**CLARKE, John, 1832–1851+**
Engraver and mathematical instrument maker
1832          21 King Street
1834          25 King Street
1835          21 King Street
1839–1843     57 Atherton Street
1847–1849     67 Paradise Street
1851+         25 Duke Street

Not in directories for 1837, 1845, 1846 or 1853; described in 1834 as 'optician', in 1839 as 'barometer maker' and from 1841 to 1851 as 'philosophical instrument maker'.

**COHEN, Morice, 1848–1849**
Optician
1848–1849     59 Pitt Street

Not in the directory for 1851.

**CRITCHLEY, Henry, 1822–1829**
Optician
1822          3 North Side, Old Dock Gates
1825          3 Barnes court, Livesley Place

Not in directories for 1823, 1824, 1825, 1827 and 1830: see Critchley & Mather.

**CRITCHLEY & MATHER, 1816–1830**
Opticians
1816          2 Old Dock Gates
1821–1825     3 North Side, Old Dock Gates
1827–1830     5 Oldhall Street

Previously Jones, Critchley & Mather, subsequently John Mather.

**DALY, Garrett, 1814**
Optician
1814          41 Redcross Street

**DANCER, John, 1837–1841**
Optician
1837          11 Pleasant Street
1839–1841     21 Pleasant Street

Son and successor to Josiah Dancer; moved to Manchester in 1843.

**DANCER, Josiah, 1821–1835**
Optician
1821–1829     20 Grafton Street
1832          22 Wolfe Street
1834          4 Chapel Walks
1835          13 Pleasant Street

Succeeded by John B. Dancer in 1837.

**DAVIS, Edward, 1839–1843**
Optician and instrument repository
1839–1843     65 Bold Street

See John Davis below.

**DAVIS, James, 1824–1841**
Marine store dealer
1824          12 Lever Street
1841          51 Paradise Street

May be two men of the same name: the second description is for a 'thermometer maker'.

**DAVIS, John, 1839**
Optician and instrument repository
1839          5 Bold Street

See Edward Davis, above.

**DAVIS, Saul & Co., 1839–1841**
Chronometer, watch and nautical
instrument makers
1839–1841     36 Robert Street North

**DAWSON & MELLING, 1837–1839**
Opticians, stationers etc.
1837          20 South Castle Street
1839          39 South Castle Street

Succeeded by Dawson, Melling and Payne.

**DAWSON, MELLING & PAYNE, 1841**
Optical, mathematical and navigation
warehouse
1841          39 South Castle Street

Succeeded by Melling & Payne, see below.

**DESILVA, William, 1851+**
1851          250 Great Howard Street
1853+         40 Regent Road

Not in the directory for 1852.

**DICAS, Ann, 1818–1822**
Patent hydrometer maker
1818          20 Trowbridge
1821–1822     83 Brownlow Hill

Succeeded by Benjamin Gamage.

**DICAS, John, 1790–1799**
Mathematical instrument maker and
navigation shop
1790–1799     27 Pool Lane

John Dicas first appears in the directories
as a merchant from 1774 to 1777, and a
liquor, wine or brandy merchant from
1781 to 1787. In 1796 he is described as
'patent hydrometer and mathematical
instrument maker'.

Succeeded by Mary Dicas.

**DICAS, Mary, 1800–1808**
Patent hydrometer and mathematical
instrument maker
1800          27 Pool Lane
1803–1808     7 North Side Old Dock

Succeeded by Dicas & Arstall

**DICAS & ARSTALL, 1807–1811**
Patent hydrometer makers
1807–1811     8 North Side Old Dock

Succeeded by George Arstall.

**DICAS PATENT HYDROMETER
MANUFACTORY, 1832–1837**
1832          17 Clarence Street
1835–1837     133 Brownlow Hill

Not in directories for 1834, or 1839.

**DITTON, Henry John, 1841–1847**
Mathematical instrument maker
1841          33 School Lane
1847          46 Gerard Street

Succeeded by James Ditton.

**DITTON, James, 1848–1851**
Mathematical instrument maker and brass
finisher
1848–1851     46 Gerard Street

Succeeded by Henry Ditton at this address
in 1853.

**DRURY, William, 1769–1773**
Mathematical instrument maker
1769          Dale Street
1772–1773     North Side Old Dock

**ELLIS, Hugh, 1841–1845**
Mathematical instrument maker
1841          13 Gilbert Street
1843          35 Gilbert Street
1845          68 Gilbert Street

**EWING, Walter, 1849–1851+**
Looking–glass and barometer maker
1849–1851     50A Renshaw Street
1853          54 Renshaw Street

Not in directory for 1852.

**EYRES, Jessica, 1807–1810**
Navigation shop
1807–1810     12 Old Church Yard

**FAZAKERLEY, Thomas, 1839**
Optician, grocer and flour dealer
1839          45 Upper Milk Street

**FOSTER, John, 1823, 1832–1837**
Mathematical instrument maker
1823            21 Wapping
1832–1837    33 Strand Street

Not in directories for 1830, 1839 and 1841.

Succeeded by John Foster & Co.1824–1829, and by Jonathan Foster in 1843.

**FOSTER, Jonathan, 1843–1851+**
1843–1845    7 Redcross Street
1846–1848    52 South Castle Street
1848–1849    18A South John Street
1853+         1 Sydney Road, Queen
               Street, Tranmere

Not in directories for 1851 or 1852.

Successor to John Foster.

**FOSTER, John & Co., 1824–1829**
Mathematical instrument maker and
               stationer
1824–1829    21 Wapping

Successor to John Foster, succeeded by John Foster.

**FOSTER & JONES, 1822**
Opticians
1822            7 Wapping

Succeeded by John Foster.

**FRODSHAM, Henry, 1835–1851+**
Chronometer and nautical instrument maker
1835–1837    38 Castle Street
1839–1843    40 Castle Street
1845–1851+   17 South Castle Street

Previously Parkinson & Frodsham.

**GALLETTI, A., 1834–1851+**
Carver, gilder, print seller, optician and fishing tackle manufacturer
1834–1837    10 Castle Street
1839–1841    19 Castle Street
1843            33 Castle Street
1845–1851+   17 Castle Street

Previously William and Anthony Galletti.

**GALLETTI, William and Anthony, 1823–1832**
Carver and gilders, and opticians
1823–1832    10 Castle Street

Succeeded by A. Galletti.

**GAMAGE, Benjamin, 1823–1851+**
Hydrometer maker and stationer
1823–1829    11 Clarence Street
1832            17 Clarence Street
1835            133 Brownlow Hill
1837–1839    129 Brownlow Hill
1841            35 Pleasant Street
1843–1845    32 Great Orford Street
1846–1851+   57 Brownlow Street

Husband and successor to Ann Dicas.

**GIBBS, Charles, 1851+**
Mathematical instrument maker
1851+         30 Manchester Street

Not in directory for 1852.

**GOULD, John, 1790**
Mathematical instrument maker
1790            1 Drury Lane

**GRAY, John, 1805–1810, 1814–1829**
Mathematical instrument maker
1805–1810    10 East Side Dry Dock
1814–1818    10 East Side Dry Dock
1821–1822    11 East Side Dry Dock
1829            25 Bridgewater Street

Not in directories for 1807 and 1809.

Succeeded by Gray & Lessels, 1811. Apparently succeeded in business at the same address by Charles Jones 1823–1827, when Gray does not appear in the directories. Does not appear in directories for 1830, 1832, 1834, 1835 and 1837.

**GRAY, John, 1839–1851+**
Optician
1839            3 Chester Street, Toxteth
               Park
1841–1845    25 Strand Street
1847            2 Stanley House, New Ferry
1849–1851    St Clemet's Terrace, Upper
               Park Street

Apart from 1841 to 1845, these appear to be Gray's home addresses, as all the entries have in brackets Jones & Co., for 1839, Jones, Gray & Keen for 1841 to 1845, and Gray & Keen for 1846 to 1851+.

## GRAY & KEEN, 1846–1851+
Opticians, mathematical and nautical
        instrument makers
1846–1851+    25 Strand Street

Described as 'opticians and mathematical instrument makers and correctors of iron vessels' in 1847, and 'opticians and chronometer makers' in 1849 and 1851.

## GRINDROD, John, 1766–1767
Mathematical instrument maker
1766        Wolstenholme's Square
1767        Ansdell's Wient

## HARPER, Robert, 1790–1807
Mathematical instrument maker
1790–1803    68 Peter Street
1804        20 Peter Street
1805–1807    61 Peter Street

Described in 1796 directory as 'cotton machine maker'.

## HART, Saul, 1837–1841
Box and ivory rule maker
1837        112 Dale Street
1839–1841    114 Dale Street

## HASLEDEN, George, 1800
Bookseller, stationer, and mathematical instrument maker
1800        34 Paradise Street

## HAYES, James, 1790–1821
Mathematical instrument maker
1790        63 Old Dock
1794        South Side Old Dock
1796        63 Old Dock
1799        South Side Old Dock
1800–1804    24 Norfolk Street; shop, 51
              Old Dock
1805–1811    53 South Side Old Dock
1821        21 Manstey's Lane

Not in directories between 1814 and 1818: described in 1821 as 'dealer in marine stores'.

## HAYES, John, 1794–1799
Quadrant maker
1794–1799    South Side Old Dock

Described in 1796 as 'mathematical instrument maker'.

## HAZELL, Benjamin, 1837
Optician and flag maker
1837        10 Lower Sparling Street

## HEWITT, Samuel, 1816–1827
Rule maker
1816        48 Dale Street
1818        51 Duke Street
1821–1823    123 Dale Street
1824–1827    43 Dale Street

## HOLLIWELL, William, 1804–1832
Mathematical instrument maker
1804–1816    5 Bromfield Street,
              Salthouse Dock
1818–1825    West End, Old Dock
1827        31 Stanhope Street and 1
              Hurst Street
1829        31 Stanhope Street
1830        Mersey Street
1832        34 Stanhope Street

Not in the directory for 1834.

Succeeded by William Holliwell & Son.

## HOLLIWELL, Thomas and William, 1848–1851+
Mathematical and nautical instrument makers and opticians
1848–1849    9 Salthouse Dock
1851+       64 Park Lane

Successors to William Holliwell & Son, and joined by a third brother, Charles in 1851. Also listed as Holliwell Brothers.

## HOLLIWELL, William & Son, 1829–1847
Mathematical and nautical instrument makers and opticians
1829–1832    1 Hurst Street

1834        7 Darwen Street
1835–1837   7 East Side Salthouse Dock
1839–1847   9 East Side Salthouse Dock

Successors to William Holliwell, and succeeded by Holliwell Brothers.

**HOUGHTON, John, 1835–1841**
Mathematical instrument maker
1835        2 Comus Terrace, Common
1841        14 Beresford Street

Not in directories for 1837, 1839 or 1843.

**HOULDIN, John, 1834–1841**
Optician and printers' joiner
1834        22 Pellew Street
1835        20 Pellew Street
1837        21 Pellew Street
1839–1841   41 Pellew Street

**HOWARD, James, 1841**
Optician
1841        38 Leeds Street

**HOWARD, Thomas, 1767–1784**
Mathematical instrument maker
1767–1773   Temple Bar
1774–1781   2 Temple Bar
1784        3 Temple Bar

Not in the directory for 1783.

**HOWELL, John, 1810**
Mathematical instrument maker
1810        9 Pembroke Place

But see John Powell, below.

**INTROVINO, Anthony, 1821–1825**
Carver, gilder, optician etc.
1821–1824   138 Duke Street
1825        140 Duke Street

**JOHNSON, Adam, 1816–1829**
Mathematical instrument maker,
navigation and astronomical school
1816–1825   4 Salthouse Lane
1827        27 Wolfe Street
1829        90 Park Lane

**JONES, Charles, 1818–1837**
Mathematical instrument maker
1818        58 Stanley Street
1821–1822   57 Stanley Street
1823–1824   11 East Side Dry Dock
1825        10 East Side Old Dock
1827        11 East Side Old Dock
1829–1830   28 Strand Street
1832–1837   25 Strand Street

Described as 'optician' from 1823

Succeeded by Jones & Gray, and subsequently Jones, Gray & Keen.

**JONES, David, 1827–1843**
Optician
1827        53 Pool Lane
1829        68 Hanover Street
1832        103 Richmond Row
1834        120 Richmond Row
1835        125 Richmond Row
1837        63 Great George Street
1839–1843   26 Great George Street

**JONES, Isaac, 1846–1847**
Optician and mathematical instrument
maker
1846–1847   2 Bath Street

**JONES, John, 1804–1810**
Navigation and stationery warehouse
1804 Bottom of Pool Lane, Old Dock
1805        27 Pool Lane
1807–1810   29 Pool Lane

Succeeded by Jones & Rust.

**JONES, Thomas, 1816–1830**
Mathematical instrument maker, optician
            and navigation warehouse
1816–1818   5 Harrington Street
1821–1830   4 Harrington Street

**JONES & GRAY, 1839**
Opticians
1839        26 Strand Street

Previously Charles Jones and John Gray; succeeded by Jones, Gray & Keen.

**JONES & ROOSE, 1816**
Mathematical instrument makers, and
navigation warehouse
1816        27 near the bottom of Pool
            Lane

Previously Jones & Rust; succeeded by
Thomas Roose.

**JONES & RUST, 1811–1814**
Navigation and stationery warehouse
1811        29 Pool Lane
1814        31 Pool Lane

Previously John Jones; succeeded by Jones
& Roose.

**JONES, CRITCHLEY & MATHER,
   1816–1818**
Opticians and mathematical instrument
makers
1816–1818   Old Dock Gates

Succeeded by Critchley & Mather.

**JONES, GRAY & KEEN, 1841–1845**
Opticians
1841–1845   25 and 26 Strand Street

Previously Jones & Gray; succeeded by
Gray & Keen.

**KIBBLE, John, 1821–1837**
Mathematical instrument maker
1821        46 Cheapside
1823–1824   81 Highfield Street
1825–1832   24 Great Crosshall Street
1835–1837   21 Great Crosshall Street

Not in directory for 1834.

**KNEEN, Thomas, 1851**
Mathematical instrument maker
1851        9 Wood Street

Not in directories for 1852 or 1853.

**LATHAM, Thomas, 1843–1847**
Watchmaker, working jeweller and
optician
1843–1847   81 Hanover Street

**LAVERACK, Henry, 1834**
Optician
1834        31 Sussex Street,
            Harrington

**LEVERTON, John, 1766–1784**
Mathematical, philosophical and optical
instrument maker
1766–1769   Water Street
1772–1773   Pool Lane
1774        30 Pool Lane
1777–1784   31 Pool Lane

Succeeded by Susannah Leverton.

**LEVERTON, Susannah, 1787–1790**
Mathematical instrument maker
1787        Pool Lane
1790        31 Pool Lane

**MANN, John, 1781–1810**
Mathematical instrument maker, quadrant
and compass maker
1781        3 Mann Island
1787        Water Street
1790        19 Water Street
1794–1800   20 Water Street
1804        Church Alley, Water Street
1805        1 Church Alley and 17
            Water Street
1807–1810   1 Church Alley and 16
            Water Street

By 1803, alternative occupation as
'victualler', becoming 'mariner's tavern
and mathematical shop' by 1805. By 1811,
'mariner's tavern' only.

**MANN, William, 1774–1781**
1774        56 Cable Street
1777        57 Cable Street
1781        3 east side George's Dock
            Passage

**MASSEY, Edward, 1835–1851+**
Watch and chronometer maker
1835–1837   37 Warren Street
1839–1851+  41 Russell Street

**MATHER, John, 1832–1848**
Optician and medicinal baths
1832–1848     St Paul's Square

From 1849, occupation described
as 'medicinal baths' only. Previously
Critchley & Mather.

**McGINNES, Francis, 1830–32**
Optician and mathematical instrument
maker
1830          68 Vauxhall Road
1832          4 Aldemay Street

**MELLING & Co., Edward, 1847–1851+**
Opticians and chronometer makers
1847–1851+   39 South Castle Street

Previously Melling & Payne.

**MELLING & PAYNE, 1843–1845**
Optical, mathematical and navigation
warehouse
1843–1845     39 South Castle Street

Previously Dawson, Melling & Payne;
succeeded by Edward Melling & Co.

**MORRIS, John, 1830**
Measuring tape maker
1830          World's End Tavern, Upper
              Pitt street

**NEWCOMB, James, 1841–1845; 1851+**
Mathematical instrument maker
1841          7 Gerard Street
1843          1 Fleet Street
1845          35 Wapping
1851          3 Orford Street

Partnership 1846 to 1849 with James
Mansell as Newcomb & Mansell.

**NEWCOMB & MANSELL, 1846–1849**
Nautical instrument makers and opticians
1846–1849     35 Wapping

Succeeded by James Newcomb and James
Mansell independently.

**NICHO, Paul, 1835–1841**
Weather glass maker
1835          5 Freemasons Row
1837          4 Freemasons Row
1839–1841     9 Freemasons Row

**O'NEILL, Michael, 1841–1847**
Mathematical instrument maker
1841          Chester Place, 5
              Chesterfield Street, Toxteth
              Park
1845–1847     110 Chester Street, Toxteth
              Park

Not in directory for 1843.

**ORFORD, Jonathan, 1804–1814**
Mathematical instrument maker and
stationery warehouse
1804          Wapping
1805–1809     27 Wapping
1811          Wapping
1814          74 Park Lane

**OSBORNE, David, 1823–1841**
Optician
1823–1824     2 Cropper Street
1825          132 Park Lane
1827          131 Park lane
1829          22 Park Lane
1832          21 Park Lane
1834–1837     18 Park Lane
1839          37 Park Lane
1841          25 Bridgewater Street

**OWEN, William, 1829**
Mathematical instrument maker and
furniture broker
1829          44 Dale Street

**OWENS, Peter, 1794–1803**
Mathematical instrument maker
1794–1803     31 Pool Lane
1796          11 Pool Lane

**PALMER, STEELE & Co., 1814–1818**
Mathematical instrument makers and
stationery warehouse
1814–1818     6 Duke's Place

Succeeded by John Steele.

**PARKINSON & FRODSHAM, 1832–1834**
Chronometer makers and opticians
1832–1834      38 Castle Street

**PARLASCA, Biagio, 1834–1845**
Optician
1834      46 Vernon Street
1835      40 Vernon Street
1837      45 Sparling Street
1839–1845      91 Sparling Street

In 1834 his first name is given as 'Buzes', from 1835–1839 as 'Biaglo', and from 1841–1845 as 'Biagio'.

**PASTORELLI, John, 1834–1851+**
Barometer maker and optician
1834–1837      28 Cable Street
1839–1847      55 Cable Street
1848–1851+      61 Cable Street

**PAYNE, George Patmore, 1846–1849**
Optician, chronometer and mathematical instrument maker
1846–1848      39 South Castle Street
1849      129 Mill Street, Toxteth Park

Second name given as 'Pitmore' in 1846.

Previously Melling & Payne.

**PEDRONE, Louis, 1835–1851+**
Jeweller, optician, silversmith and watch manufacturer
1835–1837      27 Lord Street
1839–1851+      57 Lord Street

**PIERS, Charles, 1848–1851+**
Chronometer maker and optician
1848–1851+      34 Strand Street

**POWELL, John, 1811**
Mathematical instrument maker
1811      16 Pembroke Place

But see John Howell, above.

**PRINCE, Abraham, 1829**
Jeweller and optician
1829      43 Whitechapel

**ROBERTSON, Robert, 1837–1841**
Optician
1837      9 Dexter Street, Toxteth Park
1839      8 Dexter Street, Toxteth Park
1841      7 Dexter Street, Toxteth Park

**ROBINSON, John, 1800–1803**
Mathematical instrument maker
1800–1803      20 Old Frederick Street

**ROBINSON, John, 1846–1851+**
Optician and mathematical instrument maker
1846–1851+      48 Scotland Street

**RODGERSON, William, 1837–1851+**
Optician and nautical instrument maker
1837–1841      Chatham Buildings, 19 South John Street
1843–1851+      10 St James Street

Previously William Rodgerson & Co., from 1849 also druggist in partnership as Cannon & Rodgerson.

**RODGERSON, William & Co., 1837**
Nautical instrument makers
1837      11 South John Street

Previously Rodgerson & McGaa; succeeded by William Rodgerson.

**RODGERSON & McGAA, 1835**
Opticians, printers, stationers and bookbinders
1835      26 St James Street and 11 South John Street

Succeeded by William Rodgerson & Co.

**ROOKER, Edward, 1845**
Mathematical divider and barometer and thermometer maker
1845      12 Williamson Street

**ROOSE, Thomas, 1816–1825**
Mathematical instrument maker,
stationery, navigation and optician's
warehouse

| | |
|---|---|
| 1816–1818 | 27 Pool Lane |
| 1821–1825 | 8 Moore Place |
| 1821–1822 | 16 North Side Old Dock |

Previously Jones & Roose.

**SAMPSON, Lyon, 1823–1843**
Optician

| | |
|---|---|
| 1823–1824 | 74 Brownlow Hill |
| 1825 | 86 Brownlow Hill |
| 1827 | 2 Gildart Street |
| 1829–1834 | 4 Roden Place, Ilford Street |
| 1835 | 12 Bridport Place |
| 1839–1841 | 18 Upper Pitt Street |
| 1843 | 10 Gildart street |

Name given as 'Samson' from 1839.

**SAMUEL, Edwin, L., 1849–1851+**
Optician, watchmaker and bullion office

| | |
|---|---|
| 1849–1851+ | 9 South Castle Street |

Previously Louis Samuel.

**SAMUEL, Louis, 1845–1848**
Watchmaker, silversmith and optician

| | |
|---|---|
| 1845–1848 | 46 Paradise Street and 9 South Castle Street |

Succeeded by Edwin L. Samuel.

**SCHIAVI, Antonio, 1823–1827**
Looking glass manufacturer, carver and
gilder

| | |
|---|---|
| 1823 | 17 Pellew Street |
| 1824–1827 | 67 Stanley street |

**SIMPSON, John, 1823–1825**
Optician

| | |
|---|---|
| 1823–1825 | 38 Wapping |

**SMITH, Ann, 1790–1796**
Navigation shop

| | |
|---|---|
| 1790–1796 | 18 Pool Lane |

Previously Egerton Smith

Succeeded by Ann & Egerton Smith.

**SMITH, Egerton [senior], 1774–1787**
Mathematical instrument maker, lecturer
on philosophy, printer, stationer and
navigation shop

| | |
|---|---|
| 1774–1777 | Newton's Head, 17 Pool Lane |
| 1781–1787 | 18 Pool Lane |

Previously schoolmaster and printer at
Redcross Street, Cable street and Church
Street.

Succeeded by Ann Smith.

**SMITH, William, 1843–1849**
Mathematical instrument maker

| | |
|---|---|
| 1843 | 17 Dean Street |
| 1847 | 20 Pleasant Street, Kirkdale |
| 1849 | 54 Barlow Street, Kirkdale |

**SMITH, Ann & Egerton, 1800**
Navigation shop

| | |
|---|---|
| 1800 | 18 Pool Lane |

Previously Ann Smith

Succeeded by Egerton & William Smith.

**SMITH, Egerton & William, 1803–1808**
Stationers, printers, mathematical
instrument makers and navigation shop

| | |
|---|---|
| 1803–1805 | 18 Pool Lane |
| 1804–1808 | 19 Pool Lane |

Previously Ann & Egerton Smith

Succeeded by Egerton Smith [junior] &
Co.

**SMITH, Egerton [junior] & Co., 1810–1818**
Printers and navigation shop

| | |
|---|---|
| 1810–1811 | 19 Pool Lane |
| 1814–1818 | 20 Pool Lane |

By 1821, main business is publishing the
*Liverpool Mercury.*

**SMITH & BRADSHAW, 1832**
Ivory and box rule makers

| | |
|---|---|
| 1832 | 2 Leigh Street |

**STEELE, John, 1822–1825**
Mathematical instrument maker and
navigation warehouse
1822–1825     6 Duke's Place

Previously Palmer, Steele & Co., and
subsequently John Steele & Son.

**STEELE, John & Son, 1827–1851+**
Stationers, opticians and mathematical
instrument makers
1827–1829     10 Duke's Place
1830–1837     9 Duke's Place
1839–1851     21 Duke's Place

Previously John Steele.

**SWAN, Thomas, 1790–1837**
Quadrant and mathematical instrument
maker
1790          14 Strand Street
1796          5 Murray Square, Atherton
              Street
1800–1803     10 Gibraltar Row, Canal
1810          8 Freemason's Row
1811          31 Freemason's Row
1814          37 Freemason's Row
1816–1818     43 Banastre Street
1821–1827     54 Banastre Street
1832          2 Bridgewater Place,
              Bridgewater Street
1837          3 Bridgewater Place

Not in directories for 1794, 1804–1808,
1829, 1830, 1834, 1835 or 1839.

**TAYLOR, Samuel, 1807–1811**
Optician
1807–1811     28 Parliament Street

**THISTLEWOOD, William, 1830–1845**
Optician and mathematical instrument
maker
1830          15 Plumb Street
1841          216 Vauxhall Road
1843–1845     218 Vauxhall Road

Not in directories 1832–1839; by 1845
described also as 'sexton of St Martin's
cemetery'.

**TURCONI, Gasparo, 1835–1848**
Optician and barometer maker
1835          62 Christian Street
1846–1848     54 London Road

Not in directories between 1837–1845, or
1847; name given as 'Gaspero' in earlier
directories.

**UNDERHILL, Thomas, 1824–1827**
Mathematical instrument and rule maker
1824          124 Whitechapel
1825          6 Cooper's Row
1827          32 Mersey Street

**WALKER, John & Alexander, 1823–1851**
Navigation and stationery warehouse,
mathematical instrument makers,
opticians and chart sellers
1823–1835     33 Pool Lane
1837          34 South Castle Street
1839–1851     72 South Castle Street

Succeeded by Alexander Walker.

**WEST, Charles, 1839–1851+**
Optician
1839–1851     20 Lord Street

In partnership with A. Abraham, and with
George Smart Wood as A. Abraham &
Co., from 1851.

**WILDING, James, 1790–1816**
Mathematical instrument maker and
victualler
1790          Plumb Street
1794          26 Prussia Street
1796          14 Prussia Street
1799          26 Prussia Street
1800–1805     12 Prussia Street
1807–1811     13 Prussia Street
1816          17 Prussia Street

**WILLIAMS, George, 1832**
Optician and jeweller
1832          39 Whitechapel

**WILSON, Charles, 1837**
Nautical instrument maker
1837          30 Harper Street, Toxteth
              Park

**WOOD, Alfred Josiah, 1843–1847**
Optician and mathematical instrument maker

| | |
|---|---|
| 1843–1845 | 30 Wappping |
| 1846 | 29 Wapping |

**WOOD, Benjamin, 1810–1841**
Mathematical instrument maker and optician

| | |
|---|---|
| 1810 | 41 Wapping |
| 1811 | 52 Wapping |
| 1814–1822 | 50 Wapping |
| 1823 | 49 Wapping |
| 1824–1829 | 50 Wapping |
| 1829 | 50 Wapping and 6 Bath Street |
| 1830 | 49 Wapping |
| 1832 | 50 Wapping and 12 Bath Street |
| 1834 | 46 Wapping and 21 Bath Street |
| 1835 | 46 Wapping and 28 Bath Street |
| 1837 | 45 Wapping |
| 1839–1841 | 30 Wapping |

Succeeded by Benjamin Jasper Wood, junior.

**WOOD, Benjamin Jasper, junior, 1837–1851+**
Optician and teacher of navigation

| | |
|---|---|
| 1837 | 21 Bath Street |
| 1839–1851+ | 7 Bath Street |

**WOOD, George Smart, 1848–1851+**
Optician

| | |
|---|---|
| 1848–1851+ | 20 Lord Street |

With A. Abraham, and in partnership there with Charles West as A. Abraham & Co., from 1851.

*Manchester*

**ABRAHAM & DANCER, 1843**
Mathematical and philosophical instrument makers

| | |
|---|---|
| 1843 | 13 Cross Street, King Street |

Succeeded by John Benjamin Dancer from 1845.

**AGNEW, Thomas, 1837–1851+**
Optician, barometer, looking glass maker and repository for fine arts

| | |
|---|---|
| 1837–1851+ | 14 Exchange Street |

Previously Agnew & Zanetti.

**AGNEW & ZANETTI, 1828–1836**
Carvers, gilders, looking glass and picture frame manufacturers, print sellers, publishers, barometer, thermometer and hydrometer makers

| | |
|---|---|
| 1828–1830 | 10 Exchange Street |
| 1832–1834 | 18 Exchange Street |
| 1836 | 14 Exchange Street |

Succeeded by Thomas Agnew

**AITKEN, Henry, 1848–1851+**
Manufacturer of surgical instruments, trusses etc., cutler and optician

| | |
|---|---|
| 1848 | 8 King Street |

From 1850 a 'surgical instrument maker' at 3 Ducie Street, Exchange.

**ARSTALL, Frederick Dicas, 1836–1845**
Scale beam etc. maker

| | |
|---|---|
| 1836 | 1 Bradshaw Street |
| 1838–1841 | 5 Bradshaw Street |
| 1843–1845 | 7 Bradshaw Street |

Previously Widow Arstall & Son.

**ARSTALL, Thomas, 1817–1819**
Scale beam–maker

| | |
|---|---|
| 1817 | 25 Market Place; manufactory Rainhill, near Prescot (late at Brookbank, near St Helens) |
| 1818–1819 | 25 Market Place |

**ARSTALL, Widow & Son, 1833**
Scale beam manufacturers

| | |
|---|---|
| 1833 | 1 Bradshaw Street, Shudehill |

Succeeded by Frederick Dicas Arstall.

**BLACKBURNE, Thomas, 1800**
Mathematical instrument maker
1800          Blossom Street

**BOLONGARO, Dominic 1817–1846**
Carver, gilder, barometer and
mathematical instrument maker,
printseller, and ladies' repository for fancy
painting
1817–1830     2 Old Millgate
1832–1833     14 Market Street
1834–1841     32 Market Street
1843–1846     65 Market Street

Succeeded by Bolongaro & Son.

**BOLONGARO & SON, 1848–1851+**
Carvers, gilders, printsellers, looking–
glass, barometer etc. makers
1848–1851+    32 Market Street

**BOLTON, Robert, 1834**
Magnet manufacturer
1834          34 Back Turner Street

**BOWEN, Thomas Michael, 1825–1851+**
Optician and mathematical instrument
maker
1825–1836     12 Market Place
1834–1851+    27 Market Place

**BROWN, George, 1846**
Optician
1846          1 Old Millgate and 8 King
              Street

**CAMINADA, Louis, 1840–1841**
Optician
1840–1841     1 Scholes Street

**CAPPRANI, Anthony,1836–1851+**
Barometer maker and picture frame maker
1836–1843     110 Tib Street
1845–1846     98 Tibb Street
1848          9 Carpenter's Lane, Tib
              Street
1850–1851+    26 Thomas Street,
              Shudehill

**CHADWICK, William Henry, 1836–
1851+**
Barometer maker and carver and gilder
1836–1838     21 Ridgefield
1840–1848     9 King Street
1850–1851+    23 Lower King Street

**COLLAR, George, 1814–1830**
Optician
1814–1830     101 Market Street
1816          101 Market Street and 135
              Chapel Street, Salford
1817          New Market
1825          42 Market Street

Not in directories for 1828, 1829 or 1832

**COOPER, Sarah, 1845–1851+**
Rule maker
1845–1846     16 Miller Street, Shudehill
1848–1850     6 Miller Street
1852          16 Miller Street

Succeeded Stephen Norris Cooper.

**COOPER, Stephen Norris, 1818–1843**
Ivory and box rule maker
1818–1830     25 Miller Street
1832–1843     16 Miller Street

Succeeded by Sarah Cooper.

**DANCER, John Benjamin, 1845–1851+**
Optician, barometer, thermometer,
mathematical and philosophical
instrument maker
1845–1846     13 Cross Street, King Street
1848–1851+    43 Cross Street

Previously Abraham & Dancer.

**FISHER, William, 1848–1850**
Rule maker and cutler
1848          65 Shudehill
1850          23 Dean Street, Great
              Ancoats Street

**FOX & GRUNDY, 1830**
Opticians, barometer and looking glass
makers
1830          St Ann's Square

See Grundy & Fox.

**FRANCKS, Isaac, 1840–1841**
Optician
1840–1841    3 Barton Street, Bridgwater
Street

Previously Aubrey and Isaac Francks.

**FRANCKS, Jacob, 1817–1846**
Optician, clothes dealer
1817–1819    283 Oldham Street
1821–1825    378 Oldham Road
1829         9 Withy Grove
1832–1833    8 Withy Grove
1836–1837    19 Withy Grove and 25 St
Mary's Gate
1838         25 St Mary's Gate
1840–1846    114 Deansgate

Described in 1817 as 'hawker'; name
changes to 'Franks' from 1840.

Succeeded by Abraham Franks.

**FRANCKS, Aubrey and Isaac, 1838**
Opticians
1838         114 Deansgate

Succeeded by Isaac Francks.

**FRANKS, Abraham, 1848–1851+**
Optician and lecturer on the anatomy and
physiology of the human eye
1848–1851+   Next door to the Star
Hotel, opposite the Bazaar,
114 Deansgate and 44
Market Street

**FRANKLIN, Abraham, 1832–1836**
Watch maker, jeweller, silver–smith,
optician, importer of foreign
manufactures and exchanger broker
1832–1836    1 St Ann's Place

**FRANKLIN, Abraham, 1846**
Optician
1846         6 Old Millgate

**FRANKLIN, Jacob Abraham, 1832–1840**
Optician, philosophical and mathematical
instrument maker
1832–1840    1A St Ann's Place

Succeeded by Franklin & Co.

**FRANKLIN & Co., 1841**
Opticians, barometer and looking glass
makers
1841         1A St Ann's Place

Succeeded by Abraham Franklin & Co.

**FRANKLIN & Co., 1846**
Mathematical and philosophical
instrument makers
1846         Old Millgate

**FRANKLIN, Abraham & Co., 1843–1845**
Watchmakers, jewellers and opticians
1843–1845    20 St Ann's Square

**GALE, Joseph, 1828–1845**
Carver, gilder, printseller, barometer
maker and optician
1828–1830    98 Market Street
1832–1833    32 Market Street
1834–1843    46 King Street
1845         4 Princess Street

Described in 1845 as 'auctioneer and
appraiser'.

**GALLY, John, 1794–1797**
Print seller and weatherglass and picture
frame maker
1794         45 Fountain Street
1797         3 Spring Gardens

**GREGORY, Thomas, 1834**
Optician
1834         3 Quay Street

**GRUNDY, John Clowes, 1832–1834, 1840–1851+**
Barometer maker, carver, gilder, printseller
and optician, artist's colourman, and
fancy repository
1832–1851+   4 Exchange Street

Succeeded by, and successor to Grundy &
Goadsby.

**GRUNDY & FOX, 1829**
Carvers, gilders, printsellers, opticians,
colourmen to artists, and fancy repository
1829         25 St Ann's Square

Succeeded by Fox & Grundy, and then John Clowes Grundy.

**GRUNDY & GOADSBY, 1836–1838**
Barometer makers, carvers, gilders, printsellers, artist's colourmen, opticians, and dealers in lamps, bronzes, etc.
1836–1838      4 Exchange Street

**HANCOCK, James, 1838–1851+**
Optician
1838      2 Arthur Street, Hulme
1845      36 St John's Street, Salford
1848–1851+      1 Old Millgate

**HARPER, Nathaniel, 1838–1851+**
Optician
1838–1841      34 Portland Street
1843      12 Tasle Street
1845      11 Sounding Alley
1846      14 Oxford Street, Chorlton on Medlock
1848      3 Chester Street, Chorlton on Medlock
1850+      32 Clarendon Street, Chorlton on Medlock

**HEWITT, Joseph, 1836**
Rule maker
1836      31 Withy Grove
1838      10 Makin Street, Chorley on Medlock

No occupation given in 1838.

**HOLMES, John, 1804**
Electrician etc.
1804      9 Fountain Street

**INTROVINI, Gaspar, 1818–1845**
Barometer and looking glass maker
1818–1825      43 Thomas's Street
1828–1829      96 St George's Road
1832–1833      16 Rook Street
1838      Foundry Street
1840–1845      88 St George's Road

Not in directories for 1830, 1846; possibly succeeded by John Introvini, tinplate worker at 35 Roger Street Redbank, 1848–1850 who was then succeeded by

Gasper Introvini, barometer maker, at the same address in 1852.

**INTROVINI, Anthony and Gaspar, 1816**
Barometer and looking-glass makers
1816      39 Bridge Street and 43 Thomas Street

Succeeded by Gaspar Introvini (or 'Introvino').

**LEVY, Abraham, 1794–1799**
Optician
1794–1799      Miller's Street

In the directory for 1800, given as 'gentleman, 68 Oldham Street'.

**LEWIS, Richard, 1837–1841**
Optician and glassblower
1837      38 Oldham Street
1840–1841      19 Stott Street, Hulme

Succeeded by John Lewis, glass blower.

**MALACRIDA, Charles, 1843–1851+**
Optician and barometer maker
1843      47 Camp Street, Deansgate
1845–1848      4 Withy Grove
1851+      67 Long Millgate

**MERONE, Joseph, 1800–1846**
Barometer maker, carver, gilder, printseller
1800–1808      3 Market Street Lane
1811      98 Market Street Lane
1813–1824      98 Market Street
1825–1830      100 Market Street
1832–1846      28 Market Street

**MYERS, Philip, 1821**
Optician
1821      Piccadilly

**NATHAN, Asher, 1841**
Optician
1841      1 Old Millgate

Presumably in business with Elias Nathan at the same address.

**NATHAN, Elias, 1834–1852+**
Optician and jeweller

| | |
|---|---|
| 1836–1837 | 1 Old Millgate |
| 1838–1841 | 8 King Street and 1 Old Millgate |
| 1845 | 10 Victoria Street |
| 1846 | 6 Victoria Street |
| 1848 | 3 Chester Street, Chorlton on Medlock |
| 1850–1851+ | 6 Victoria Street, Market Street |

**NEGRETTI, Gaetan, 1841–1843**
Barometer and looking glass maker (and thermometers, hydrometers and glass apparatus for experiments), working optician and mathematical instrument maker

| | |
|---|---|
| 1841 | 3 Thomas Street |
| 1843 | 4 Withy Grove |

**ODBER, Joseph Thomas, 1850**
Engraver, brass turner and optician

| | |
|---|---|
| 1850 | Angel yard, Market Place |

**PEDUZZI, Anthony, 1817–1846**
Barometer maker, carver, gilder, looking glass and picture frame maker

| | |
|---|---|
| 1817 | 19 Tib Street |
| 1818–1819 | 31 Oldham Street |
| 1821–1824 | 31 Oldham Street and 44 Deansgate |
| 1828–1830 | 31 Oldham Street |
| 1832–1837 | 33 Piccadilly |
| 1838 | 35 Piccadilly |
| 1840–1841 | 33 Piccadilly |
| 1843–1846 | 41 Piccadilly |

**PEDUZZI, James, 1821–1848**
Picture dealer, barometer and looking glass maker

| | |
|---|---|
| 1821–1833 | 49 Oldham Street |
| 1834–1846 | 97 Oldham Street |
| 1848 | 8 Foundry Street, Oldham Road |

**PERCIVAL, William, 1850–1851+**
Rule maker

| | |
|---|---|
| 1850 | 38 Lower Moseley Street |

| | |
|---|---|
| 1852 | 34 Lower Moseley Street and 8 Old Millgate |

**PIZZOTTI, John, 1841–1851+**
Barometer and looking glass maker

| | |
|---|---|
| 1841–1851+ | 36 Spear Street |

In 1841 directory 'Pezzotti'.

**PREDARY, James, 1817–1851+**
Barometer maker, picture frame and looking glass manufacturer

| | |
|---|---|
| 1817–1824 | 24 Church Street |
| 1828–1836 | 13 Oak Street |
| 1838–1851+ | 17 Oak Street, Thomas Street |

**PRINCE, Mary, 1848**
Optician & looking-glass frame manufacturer

| | |
|---|---|
| 1848 | 101 Shudehill |

In the directory for 1850, listed as 'widow, 29 Grindle Street, Young Street'.

Previously Thomas Prince.

**PRINCE, Thomas, 1843–1846**
Carver, gilder and optician

| | |
|---|---|
| 1843–1846 | 101 Shudehill |

Succeeded by Mary Prince.

**RONCHETTI, Baptist, 1800–1804**
Weather glass manufacturer

| | |
|---|---|
| 1800 | Warwick Street, Oldham Street |
| 1804 | 51 Spear Street |

Succeeded by Joshua Rochetti.

**RONCHETTI, Joshua, 1808–1836, 1838–1840, 1850**
Weather-glass manufacturer, optician and mathematical instrument maker

| | |
|---|---|
| 1808 | 51 Spear Street |
| 1817–1824 | 29 Balloon Street |
| 1828–1829 | 4 Cateaton Street |
| 1830 | 1 St Ann's Place |
| 1833–1836 | 43 Market Street |
| 1838–1840 | 43 Market Street |
| 1850 | 43 Market Street |

Succeeded by Joshua Ronchetti & Son, then by John B. & Joshua Rochetti, and subsequently by Joseph Casartelli (successor to J. Ronchetti) in 1852.

## RONCHETTI, Baptist and Co., 1794
Weather glass makers
1794          15 High Street

Not in directory for 1797.

Succeeded by Baptist Ronchetti.

## RONCHETTI, Joshua & Son, 1837
Opticians, barometer and looking glass, hydrometer, saccharometer and alkalimeter makers
1837          43 Market Street

Successors to Joshua Ronchetti; succeeded by Joshua Ronchetti.

## RONCHETTI, John B. & Joshua, 1841–1848
Opticians, mims., barometer and looking glass makers (and chymical instruments)
1841–1848    43 Market Street

Successors to Joshua Ronchetti; succeeded by Joshua Ronchetti.

## ROTHWELL, William, 1821–1822
Optical, mathematical and philosophical instrument maker
1821–1822    13 Bridge Street

## SANDERS, George, 1850–1851+
Optician
1850–1851+   5 Half Street

## SEDDON, John, 1813–1825
Optician
1813–1825    2 New Bailey Street, Salford

## SIDDONS, E.O., 1814
Optician
1814          Market Place

## SIMMONS, Isaac, 1840–1850
Silversmith, watchmaker, jeweller and optician
1840–1848    9 St Ann's Square
1850          7 St Ann's Square

## TELFORD, William, 1850
Optician
1850          5A Bridge Street, Deansgate

Not in directory for 1852.

## UNDERHILL, Thomas, 1828–1850+
Rule and mathematical instrument maker
1828          15 Withy Grove
1832–1838    40 Water Street, Bridge Street
1840–1841    70 Bridge Street, Deansgate
1843          5 Old Millgate, and 49 Brook Street, David Street
1845          5 Old Millgate
1846–1848    4 Old Millgate
1850          8 Old Millgate, Market Place
1851+         1 St Mary's Gate

## VITTORE, I. and V., 1800
Carvers, gilders, looking-glass and weather-glass manufacturers
1800          93 Market Street Lane

Previously Vittore & Marone.

## VITTORE & MARONE, 1797
Carvers, gilders, looking-glass and weather-glass manufacturers
1797          93 Market Street Lane

Succeeded by Joseph Merone and I. & V. Vittore.

## ZANETTI, Ann, 1843–1850
Carver and gilder, printseller, publisher, and barometer maker and dealer in artists' colours, etc.
1843–1850    16 St Ann's Street

Not in directory for 1852.

Previously Joseph Zanetti.

**ZANETTI, Joseph, 1832–1841**
Carver, gilder, barometer and looking
glass maker
1832–1836     no occupation address
1838–1841     100 King Street

Succeeded by Ann Zanetti.

**ZANETTI, Vincent, 1804–1833**
Barometer and looking glass maker
1804          59 Fountain Street
1811–1824     5 Wright's close, Market
              Street Lane
1828–1833     10 Blackfriars Street,
              Deansgate

**ZANETTI, Vittore, 1804–1817**
Carver and gilder and barometer maker
1804–1808     37 Market Street Lane
1811–1813     89 Market Street Lane

1814–1817     94 Market Street

Described as 'Vittorie Zannette & Co.' in
1808, and 'Zannetti, Bolongaro & Agnew'
in 1816'.

Succeeded by Zannetti & Agnew; see
Agnew & Zannetti.

**ZANETTI & AGNEW, 1818–1825**
Barometer and looking glass makers,
carvers, gilders, etc. and opticians
1818–1824     94 Market Street
1825          10 Exchange Street

By 1825, described as 'carvers &
gilders, mathematical and philosophical
instrument makers, print sellers and
publishers'.

Succeeded by Agnew & Zanetti.

*Sheffield*

**ABRAHAM, G. & C., 1825**
Manufacturers of spectacles and glasses
for all kinds of optical instruments, rag
merchants and trunk makers
1825          17 Snig Hill

Previously Gerson Abraham, trunk maker,
at this address 1797 to 1822.

**ALBERTI, Angelo, 1817–1828**
Barometer maker
1817          Church Street
1822–1825     Fargate
1828          8 Waingate

Described as 'japanner and gilder' in
1817; and in 1828 as 'dealer in Sheffield,
Birmingham and London goods, also
manufacturer of weather glasses'.

**ASHMORE, William, 1837–1846**
Optical works, spectacle, telescope, and all
kinds of optical instrument maker
1837          1 Burgess Street and Duke
              Street
1839–1841     103 Fargate
1845–1846     104 Fargate

Succeeded by the Executors of William
Ashmore, and Mrs Frances Ashmore.

**ASHMORE, Executors of William;
    ASHMORE, Mrs Frances 1849**
Opticians and spectacle manufacturers
1849          104 Pool Square

Succeeded at this address by Leedham &
Robinson.

**ASHMORE & OSBORNE, 1825–1837**
Opticians, manufacturers of spectacles
and optical instruments
1825          Pinstone Street
1828–1837     42 Burgess Street

Succeeded by William Ashmore, and
Thomas Paine Gerald Osborne.

**BARBER, Isaac, 1846–1849**
Optician
1846–1849     173 Eyre Street

**BARNASCONE, Lewis, 1833–1841**
Optician, cutler and hardwareman
1833–1837     23 Waingate
1841          19 Waingate

Described in 1841 as 'wholesale dealer in Birmingham and Sheffield goods'; continues in business after this date but not as an optical or mathematical instrument maker.

**BARTON, Jabez, 1845–1851+**
Optician
1845            82 Talbot Street
1849–1851+    71 Charles Street

**BARTON & WOODCOCK, 1845–1846**
Opticians
1845–1846    court, 71 Charles Street

Succeeded by Jabez Barton.

**BARTRAM, James, 1816–1822**
Magnet maker
1816–1818    Paradise Street
1822            2 Workhouse Croft

**BEAL, Richard, 1845**
Optician
1845            76 Rockingham Lane

**BELCHER, John, 1834–1837**
Rule maker
1834–1837    2 Bright Street

Probably part of Zachariah Belcher & Sons.

**BELCHER, Zachariah, 1797–1822**
Rule maker
1797            Sheffield Moor
1816–1818    Bright Street
1822            4 Bright Street

Appears as 'Zachary Belcher' in 1797.

Succeeded by Zachariah Belcher & Sons.

**BELCHER, Zachariah & Sons, 1828–1851+**
Box and ivory rule makers
1828–1830    4 Bright Street, Sheffield Moor
1833–1837    1 Bright Street
1839–1851+    270 Bright Street

Previously Zachariah Belcher.

**BELL, Alexander, 1849–1852**
Glass grinder
1849–1852    Crookes Moor Side

**BIRD, Thomas, 1818–1828**
Optician
1818–1822    High Street
1828            3 Hawksworth's Yard, High Street

**BUSH, William, 1841–1851+**
Optician
1841–1851+    115 Devonshire Street

**CAM, James, 1784–1821+**
Optician, scythe and edge tool manufacturer
1814–1817    Norfolk Street

In directories for 1784 and 1798 as 'file smith' Spring Street; in 1805, 1808 and 1811, a 'file, edge-tool & wool-shear manufacturer' at 52 Norfolk Street; then part of Rodger & Cam 1809–1811; Cam & Cutt from 1816 to 1818; from 1821 continues as James Cam 'edge-tool, scythe, hay-knife, file and steel manufacturer'.

**CAM & CUTT, 1816–1818**
Opticians
1816–1818    Norfolk Street

**CHADBURN, John, 1821–1834**
Optician
1821–1834    3 Mulberry Street

**CHADBURN, William, 1816–1828**
Optician
1816            81 Wicker
1817–1821    Wicker
1828            Johnson Street, Stanley Street

Succeeded by William Chadburn & Co.

**CHADBURN, William & Co., 1833–1834**
Opticians and manufacturers of nautical instruments, optical glasses, spectacles etc.
1833            23 Nursery Street

| 1834 | Albion Works, 27 Nursery Street, Lady's Bridge |
|---|---|

Succeeded by Chadburn Brothers.

**CHADBURN BROTHERS, 1837–1851+**
Optical, philosophical, mathematical and nautical instrument makers

| 1837 | Albion Works, 27 Nursery Street, Lady's Bridge |
|---|---|
| 1839 | 26 Nursery Street; manufactory, 46 Johnson Street |
| 1841–1851+ | Albion Works, 26 Nursery Street; Steam wheel, Johnson Street |

**CHADBURN & Co. [John Chadburn], 1830–1833**
Opticians

| 1830 | 40 Lady's Bridge, Nursery Street |
|---|---|
| 1833 | 3 Mulberry Street |

**CHADBURN & WRIGHT, 1818–1825**
Opticians

| 1818 | 81 Ladies' Bridge |
|---|---|
| 1821–1822 | 85 Wicker |
| 1825 | 40 Nursery Street |

In 1825 directory described as 'opticians and manufacturers of spectacles, reading and opera glasses, telescopes etc., also dealers in all kinds of hardware'.

Succeeded by Wright & Sykes.

**CHESTERMAN, James, 1822–1841**
Patentee of the spring tape measures, and inventor and manufacturer of improved self-acting map and window blind rollers

| 1822 | Harvest lane |
|---|---|
| 1833 | Porter Street |
| 1834–1841 | at Mr Cutts', Division Street |

Described in the 1822 directory as 'patent gunpowder flask & shot belt manufacturer'.

**CLARK, James, 1816–1822**
Optician

| 1816 | 36 High Street |
|---|---|
| 1821 | Eyre Street |
| 1822 | 13 South Street |

Not in directory for 1818; described in 1817 as 'optician and victualler'.

**CRESWICK, Edward, 1845**
Optician

| 1845 | 122 Thomas Street |
|---|---|

Described in the 1849 directory as a 'spectacle frame maker'.

**CUTTS, John Preston, 1822–1841**
Optician, manufacturer of telescopes, microscopes, spectacles, etc.

| 1822 | 58 Norfolk Street |
|---|---|
| 1825 | near St Paul's Church, 58 Arundel Street |
| 1828–1837 | Division Street |
| 1839 | 43 Division Street; & 265 Glossop Road |
| 1841 | 39 Division Street |

Succeeded by I.P. Cutts, Sons & Sutton.

**CUTTS, I.P. Sons & Sutton, 1845–1851+**
Opticians to Her Majesty, mathematical instrument makers etc.

| 1845–1846 | 39 Division Street |
|---|---|
| 1849–1851+ | 43 Division Street |

**CUTTS, CHESTERMAN & BEDINGTON, 1849–1852**
Patentees and manufacturers of spring tape measures, blind and map rollers, door hinges, roasting jacks etc.

| 1849–1852 | 43 Division Street |
|---|---|

Became Cutts, Chesterman & Co. in 1854.

**DARBYSHERE, John, 1845–1851+**
Optician and spectacle manufacturer

| 1845–1851+ | 38 Nursery Street |
|---|---|

**FANSHAW, John, 1839–1851+**
Optician

| 1839 | 54 Trafalgar Street |
|---|---|
| 1845–1851+ | 16 Siddall Street |

**FANSHAW, Robert, 1839–1846**
Optician
1839–1846    232 Moorfields

**FRITH, James, 1849–1851+**
Optician and powder flask, shot pouch,
liquor bottle etc. manufacturer
1849–1851+    105 Arundel Street

Previously Frith Brothers.

**FRITH, J.& H., 1839**
Opticians and powder flask manufacturers
1839    105 Arundel Street

**FRITH, Peter & Co., 1814–1851+**
Optician and powder flask manufacturers
1814–1822    Arundel Street
1825–1837    37 Arundel Street
1841–1851+    81 Arundel Street
1841    81 Arundel Street, and 4
    Bolt court, Fleet Street,
    London
1845    105 Arundel Street

**FRITH BROTHERS, 1841–1846**
Opticians, and manufacturers of patent
fire proof powder flasks, lever shot
pouches, liquor bottles, etc.
1841–1846    105 Arundel Street

**FRITH & ROBINSON, 1805–1811**
Opticians & powder flask makers
1805–1811    7 West Bar

**FROGGATT, Samuel, 1814–1817**
Optical glass grinder, optician
1814–1817    Walk Mill

Succeeded by Thomas Froggatt.

**FROGGATT, Thomas, 1818–1851+**
Optician
1818–1825    Walk Mill, Wicker
1825–1841    Saville Street, Walk Mill
1845–1846    New Inn, 119 Saville Street
1849–1851+    Saville Street East

In 1833, 1837 and 1841, described as
'optician and New Inn (beerhouse)', and
'optician and victualler' in 1845; in 1849
and 1852 as 'optician and glass grinder'.

**FROGGATT, Thomas, 1845**
Optician (journeyman)
1845    121 Bath Street

**FROGGATT, R.T., 1822–1828**
Optician, manufacturer
1822–1828    Twelve O'clock

**GUGGIARI, Charles, 1828–1830**
Manufacturer of picture frames,
barometers, thermometers, hydrometers,
etc.
1828–1830    32 Church Street

**HANCOCK, Hannah (late William),
    1828–1837**
Optician and beer machine manufacturer,
maker of rollers for cotton, and all sorts
of brasswork
1828    24 Waingate
1830–1837    7 Waingate

**HANCOCK, John, 1841**
Optician
1841    Waingate

Possibly successor to Hannah Hancock.

**HANCOCK, William, 1822–1825**
Optician and beer machine manufacturer
1822    6 Park Hill
1825    24 Waingate

Succeeded by Hannah (late William)
Hancock.

**HANDCOCK, John, 1774**
Ring sun-dial, and buckle-maker
1774    Fargate

**HARPER, Edwin, 1846**
Optician
1846    4 Hawley Croft

**HATFIELD, George, 1821**
Optician
1821    61 Spring Street

**HILL, Joseph, 1821**
Optician
1821    Arundel Street

**HOBSON, William Henry, 1845–1846**
Optician, surgical and optical instrument
maker
1845–1846    Dronfield Mill and 86
                Scotland Street

**HOUGHTON, William, 1821**
Optician
1821         Ward's square

**HOUNSFIELD, Bartholomew, 1833**
Merchant and manufacturer of Patent
spring tape measures, etc.
1833         14 Little Pond Street

**JARVIS, Caroline, 1839**
Optician
1839         28 Broad Lane

**LEE, John, 1845–1851+**
Optician
1845         27 Chester Street
1849–1851+    Cherrytree Yard, Gibraltar
                Street

**LENTON, John, 1828–1851+**
Optician
1828         15 Pond Street
1830–1837     14 Waingate
1839–1851+    8 Waingate

**LEVICK, Joseph & Son, 1816–1822**
Magnet makers
1816         111 Pond Street
1818         Pond Street
1822         83 and 84 Great Pond
                Street

**LIDDALL, George, 1845–1851+**
Optician and jeweller
1845–1846    63 South Street
1849–1851+    23 Division Street

**MARRIOTT, William, 1818–1822**
Optician
1818–1822    12 Market Street

**MITCHELL, George, 1833–1851+**
Optician
1833         East Street Park

1837         East Street
1841         59 South Street
1845         53 South Street
1849–1851+    53 South Street, Park

Not in 1834, 1839, 1846 directories.

**MYCOCK, John, 1816–1822**
Magnet maker
1816–1822    Burgess Street

Not in directories for 1817 or 1821.

**OSBORNE, Thomas, 1821**
Optician
1821         Bank Street
1825         (see Ashmore & Osborne)
                23 Bank Street

**OSBORNE, Thomas Paine Gerald,
   1839–1851+**
Optician
1839         57 Scotland Street and
                Netherthorpe Place
1841–1851+    57 Scotland Street

**PRANDI, Francis, 1825**
Carver and gilder, wheel barometer,
thermometer, hydrometer, looking glass
and picture frame manufacturer, and
Catholic book agent
1825         32 Church Street

Previously Francis Prandi & Co.

**PRANDI, F. & Co., 1822**
Carvers, gilders and barometer etc.
manufacturers
1822         11 High Street

Succeeded by Francis Prandi.

**PROCTOR, William, 1822–1834**
Optician
1822         Townhead Street
1822         Bell's Square, Trippet Lane
1825         Kelham Wheel and Bell
                Square, Trippet Lane
1830–1834    Bell Square

Previously George and William Proctor.

**PROCTOR, George and William, 1814–1817**
Opticians
1814          Market Street
1816          11 Market Street
1817          Market Street

Succeeded by William Proctor.

**PROCTOR & Co., 1805–1808**
Opticians
1805–1808     Market Street

Succeeded by Proctor, Beilby & Co.

**PROCTOR & BEILBY, 1781–1798**
Opticians, telescope, microscope,
perspective, reading glass and spectacle
makers
1781–1787     Milk Street
1797–1798     11 Market Street

Succeeded by Proctor & Co.

**PROCTOR, BEILBY & Co., 1809–1811**
Opticians
1809–1811     Market Street, and New
              Hall Street, Birmingham

Succeeded by George and William
Proctor.

**RIVA, Ferdinand, 1833–1834**
Frame and weather glass manufacturer
1833          court 3, High Street
1834          7 Watson Walk

**ROBERTS, Mrs Fanny, 1849–1851+**
Rule maker
1849–1851+    15 Westbar Green

Successor to William Roberts.

**ROBERTS, Richard, 1849–1851+**
Rule maker
1849–1851+    14 Steelhouse Lane

Previously William Roberts.

**ROBERTS, William, 1822–1841**
Box and ivory rule maker
1822          1 Sportsman's Inn Yard,
              West Bar

1828          Sportsman's Yard, 21 West
              Bar
1830          Gibraltar Street
1833          court 23 Gibraltar Street
1834          15 Westbar Green
1837          22 Gibraltar Street
1839          31 Westbar Green
1841          15 Westbar Green

Succeeded by Mrs Fanny Roberts.

**ROBERTS, William, 1839–1845**
Rule maker
1839–1845     14 Steelhouse Lane

Succeeded by Richard Roberts.

**ROGER & CAM, 1809–1811**
Opticians
1809–1811     Sheaf Bridge

**SHARP, Samuel, 1845–1851+**
Optician (journeyman) and preparer of
microscopic objects
1845          35 Wellington Street
1849–1851+    New George Street

**SHAW, Hannah, 1839**
Magnet maker
1839          68 Burgess Street

Succeeded by Thomas Shaw.

**SHAW, John, 1825–1837**
Magnet and instantaneous light box
manufacturers
1825          Burgess Street
1833–1837     34 Burgess Street

Succeeded by Hannah and Thomas Shaw.

**SHAW, Robert, 1821**
Optic maker
1821          Charles Street

**SHAW, Thomas, 1841, 1851+**
Magnet manufacturer
1841          68 Burgess Street
1851+         68 Burgess Street

Succeeded by Mrs Hannah Shaw & Sons
in 1845.

**SHAW, Hannah and Thomas, 1837**
Magnet manufacturers
1837            34 Burgess Street

Succeeded by Hannah Shaw, then Thomas Shaw.

**SHAW, Mrs Hannah & Sons, 1845–1849**
Magnet manufacturers
1845–1849       68 Burgess Street

Succeeded by Thomas Shaw.

**SILVESTER, Edmund, 1821**
Optician
1821            Barker Pool

**SKIDMORE, Charles, 1818**
Optician (and mathematical instrument case maker)
1818            35 Silver Street

**SMITH, Arthur, 1845–1851+**
Optician and surgeon's instrument maker
1845–1846       13 Norfolk Lane
1849–1851+      6 Howard Street

**SMITH, William, 1821, 1833**
Optic maker, optician
1821            Arundel Lane
1833            New George Street

**STOAKES, George, 1821**
Optician
1821            New Street, Little Sheffield

**STOCKS, James, 1845**
Optician
1845            34 Regent Street

**STOPANI, John, 1833–1851+**
Barometer maker
1833            Castle Green
1837            10 Castle Green
1839            25 Castle Green
1852            Castlegreen

Does not appear in directories between 1841 and 1852.

Successor to Nicholas Stopani.

**STOPANI, Nicholas, 1822–1825**
Barometer maker
1822–1825       Orchard Street

Succeeded by John Stopani.

**TAYLOR, James, 1834–1841**
Magnet manufacturer
1834–1837       Division lane
1839–1841       5 Burgess Street

Described in 1839 as 'dealer in horns etc.', and in 1841 as 'horn, buck stag &c. cutter and presser, and magnet manufacturer'.

**THORPE, James, 1828–1851+**
Optician
1828            Westbar Green
1830–1834       17 Westbar Green
1837            42 Westbar Green
1839            55 Westbar Green
1841            35 Westbar Green
1845–1851+      21 Westbar Green

**WALKER, William, 1821**
Optician
1821            Rockingham Street

**WARRIS, Thomas, 1814**
Optician
1814            Church Street

Previously Warris & Son.

**WARRIS & Son, 1797–1811**
Opticians and merchants
1797            6 Church Lane
1798–1811       Church Street

Succeeded by Thomas Warris.

**WHITE, Stephen Rowland, 1845–1851+**
Optician
1845            21 Monmouth Street
1846            Trafalgar Street
1849–1851+      42 Trafalgar Square

**WILLSON, Benjamin, 1821**
Optician
1821            Snowhill

**WILSON, Benjamin, 1833, 1841**
Optician
1833        23 Division Street
1841        78 Division Street

**WILSON, George, 1821**
Glass grinder
1821        Charles Street

**WILSON, John, 1841**
Optician, glass
1841        86 Pond Street

**WILSON, Joseph, 1774–1787**
Optician, mathematical instrument maker
and spectacle maker
1774–1787    Norfolk Street

**WRIGHT, David, 1821–1822, 1830–1849**
Optician
1821–1822    Corn Hill
1830         58 Campo Lane
1833–1837    94 Fargate
1839–1841    30 Fargate
1845–1846    72 Fargate
1849         90 Norfolk road

In 1825, see Chadburn & Wright; in 1828
see Wright & Sykes; not in the directory
for 1852.

**WRIGHT & SYKES, 1828**
Opticians
1828        Nursery Street

Previously and successively David Wright.

# Bibliography

## I    Manuscript sources

Birmingham: Birmingham Reference Library, Archives Department
    Boulton & Watt Papers
Bristol: Bristol Record Office
    Apprenticeship records
    Correspondence concerning the King family
Cambridge, MA,: Harvard University Archives
    Harvard University College Papers
Copenhagen: Royal Library
    Ny Kongelig Samling
Edinburgh: National Library of Scotland
    Diary of Thomas S. Traill
Liverpool: National Museums and Galleries on Merseyside
    Instrument makers files
London: British Library
    Add Mss. 8097
London: British Museum
    Ambrose Heal Collection
London: Institute of Civil Engineers
    Smeaton Mss.
London: The National Archives
    Colonial Office Papers
    Probate papers, Wills
London: Royal Astronomical Society
    Herschel Letters
London: Royal Society of Arts
    Mss Minutes of Council
    Mss Minutes of Committees
    Correspondence
London: Science Museum Library
    Trade Card Collection
Manchester: Museum of Science and Industry
    Instrument makers files
Philadelphia: American Philosophical Society
    Society Archives
Rochester: GEC
    Elliott Archive
St Andrews: University of St Andrews Library
    William Carmichael McIntosh Papers
Sheffield: Sheffield City Libraries and Archives
    Special Collections

York: York City Archives
    Register of Freemen, 1680–1986
York: University of York, Borthwick Institute
    Vickers Archive


## II   Newspapers

**Birmingham:**
*Aris's Gazette*
*Birmingham Journal*
*Birmingham Weekly Post*
**Bristol:**
*Felix Farley's Bristol Journal*
*Bristol Weekly Intelligencer*
*Bristol Journal*
**Cornwall:**
*West Briton*
**Leeds:**
*Leeds Intelligencer*
**Liverpool:**
*The Albion*
*Gore's Liverpool General Advertiser*
**Manchester:**
*Manchester Courier*
*Manchester Guardian*
**Newcastle-upon-Tyne:**
*Newcastle Chronicle*
**Sheffield:**
*Sheffield and Rotherham Independent*
*Sheffield Independent*
*Sheffield Telegraph*
*Sheffield Mercury*
**York:**
*York Chronicle*
*Yorkshire Courant*
*Yorkshire Gazette*


## III   Directories

Listed by place, then by date, giving the reference number in Norton (1950), or date if after 1855.

*Bath*

7       [Tunicliffe's] *A Topographical Survey of the Counties of Somerset, Gloucester, Worcester, Stafford, Chester & Lancashire* ... by William Tunicliffe (Bath, 1789).

635   *The Bath Directory* ... (Bath, 1837).
      1854  *A Directory for the City and Borough of Bath, the City of Wells and the Towns of* ... (London and Bath, 1854).


## Birmingham

699   *Sketchley's Birmingham, Wolverhampton and Walsall Directory* ... 3rd edition ([Birmingham], 1767).
700   *Sketchley's and Adams's Tradesman's True Guide; or, an Universal Directory, for the Towns of Birmingham, Wolverhampton, Walsal [sic], Dudley, and the manufacturing villages in the Neighbourhood of Birmingham* ... 4th edition (Birmingham, 1770).
701   *The New Birmingham Directory,* ... (Birmingham,[1774]).
702   Swinney's *Birmingham Directory* [Birmingham, 1775].
703   Swinney's *Birmingham Directory* ... (Birmingham, n.d. [1775–6])
705   *The Birmingham, Wolverhampton, Walsall and Willenhall Directory* ... (Birmingham, 1780).
706   *The Birmingham, Wolverhampton, Walsall and Willenhall Directory* ... (Birmingham, 1780).
1     *Bailey's Northern Directory for the Year 1781* (Warrington, n.d. [1781]).
2     *Bailey's Western and Midland Directory; or Merchant's and Tradesman's useful companion of the year 1783* ... (Birmingham, 1783).
3     *Bailey's British Directory ... for the year 1784 in 4 vols. Vol I, First edition* (London, 1784).
708   Charles Pye, *A New Directory for the Town of Birmingham, and Hamlet of Deritend* ... (Birmingham, 1785).
710   Charles Pye, *The Birmingham Directory for the Year 1788* (Birmingham, n.d. [1788]).
711   [title page absent] Charles Pye, *The Birmingham Directory for the Year 1791* (Birmingham, n.d. [1791]).
13    *The Universal British Directory of Trade and Commerce ... London, Westminster and ... all the cities, towns and principal villages in England and Wales ... vol. II* [London, 1793].
713   [title page absent] Charles Pye, *The Birmingham Directory for the Year 1797* (Birmingham, [1797]).
14    *The Universal British Directory of Trade and Commerce ... London, Westminster and ... all the cities, towns and principal villages in England and Wales ... vol. II* [2nd/3rd edition] [London, 1797].
714   *The New Birmingham Directory, for the Year 1798* ... (Birmingham, n.d.[1798]).
717   Chapman's *Birmingham Directory* ... (Birmingham, [1800]).
718   Chapman's *Birmingham Directory* ... (Birmingham, 1801).
719   Chapman's *Birmingham Directory* ... (Birmingham, 1803).
21    *Holden's Triennial Directory (Fifth Edition) for 1805, 1806 and 1807* ... 2 vols (London, n.d. [1805]).
22    *Holden's Triennial Directory (Fourth Edition) Including the year 1808* ... (London, n.d. [1808]).
721   Chapman's *Annual Directory ... of Birmingham* (Birmingham, 1808).
723   *New Triennial Directory of Birmingham* ... (Birmingham, 1808).

23    *Holden's Triennial Directory (Fifth Edition,) for 1809, 1810, 1811* vol. II (London, n.d. [1809]).

24    *Holden's Annual London and County Directory ... in three volumes, for the year 1811* ... (London, n.d. [1811]).

724   *New Triennial Directory of Birmingham* ... (Birmingham, 1812).

725   *Wrightson's New Triennial Directory of Birmingham* ... (Birmingham, 1815).

30    *The Commercial Directory for 1816–1817* (Manchester, 1816).

26    [Underhill's, late Holden] *Biennial Directory. Class Third, comprising the addresses of ... mathematical instrument makers ... opticians ... residing in London, and 480 separate towns ...* 1st edition for the years 1816 & 1817 (London, n.d. [1816]).

31    [Pigot's]*Commercial Directory for 1818–19-20* ... (Manchester, 1818).

726   *Wrightson's New Triennial Directory of Birmingham* ... (Birmingham, 1818).

727   *Wrightson's New Triennial Directory of Birmingham* ... (Birmingham, 1821).

35    *Pigot's Commercial Directory for London and Provinces* ... (London, 1822–23).

728   *Wrightson's Triennial Directory of Birmingham* ... (Birmingham, 1823).

729   *Wrightson's Triennial Directory of Birmingham* ... (Birmingham, 1825).

47    *Pigot and Co.'s National Commercial Directory for 1829* ... (London & Manchester, n.d. [1829]).

737   *Pigot and Co.'s Commercial Directory of Birmingham, and its Environs;* ... (London & Manchester, 1829).

693   William West, *History, Topography and Directory of Warwickshire* ... (Birmingham and London, 1830), containing Wrightson's *Annual Directory of Birmingham...* (Birmingham, 1830).

50    *Pigot & Co.'s National Commercial Directory* ... [Cheshire, Cumberland, Derbyshire, Durham, Lancs., Leics., Lincs., Northumberland, Notts., Rutland, Salop., Staffs., Warks., Westmorland, Worcs., Yorks., & N. Wales] (London & Manchester, 1830–31).

730a  *Wrightson's Annual Directory of Birmingham* ... (Birmingham, 1831).

731   [Wrightson's] *The Directory of Birmingham* ... (Birmingham, 1833).

732   [Wrightson's] *The Directory of Birmingham* ... (Birmingham, 1835).

62    *Pigot and Co.'s National Commercial Directory ... [for] the Counties of Derby, Hereford, Leicester, Lincoln, Monmouth, Nottingham, Rutland, Salop, Stafford, Warwick and Worcester* ... (London and Manchester, 1835).

64    *Pigot's Directory of Scotland, Isle of Man, Manchester, Liverpool, Leeds, Hull, Birmingham, Sheffield, Carlisle and Newcastle upon Tyne* (Manchester, 1837).

733   [Wrightson's] *The Directory of Birmingham* ... (Birmingham, 1839).

739   *Robson's Birmingham and Sheffield Directory* ... (London, n.d. [1839]).

740   *Pigot and Co.'s ... Directory of Birmingham and its Environs* ... (Birmingham and London, n.d. [1841]).

734   *The Directory of Birmingham* ... (Birmingham, n.d. [1842]).

109   [Kelly's] *Post Office Directory of Birmingham, Warwickshire and part of Staffordshire* (London, n.d. [1845]).

81    *I. Slater's National Commercial Directory of Ireland ... to which are added Classified Directories of the Important English Towns of Manchester, Liverpool, Birmingham, West Bromwich, Leeds, Sheffield and Bristol* ... (Manchester and London, 1846).

735   *The Directory of Birmingham;* ... (Birmingham, n.d. [1847]).

741   [Francis White & Co.] *History and General Directory of the Borough of Birmingham* ... (Sheffield, 1849).

694     *History and Gazetteer and Directory of Warwickshire* ... by Francis White & Co. (Sheffield, 1850).

86     [Slater's] Directory of Warwickshire [Manchester, 1850].

95     *Slater's (late Pigot & Co.) Royal National Commercial Directory & Topography of Scotland ... to which are added classified directories for the important English towns of Manchester, Liverpool, Birmingham, Leeds, Hull, Sheffield, Carlisle & Newcastle upon Tyne* (Manchester and London, 1852).

742     *Slater's General and Classified Directory of Birmingham, and its Vicinities, for 1852–3 ...* (Manchester, n.d. [1852]).

       1858   General and Commercial Directory of the Borough of Birmingham ... by W.H. Dix & Co. (Birmingham, 1858).

       1860   Post Office Directory of Birmingham, with Warwickshire, Worcestershire and Staffordshire (London, 1860).

       1865   The Post Office Directory of Birmingham and ... the Hardware District, edited by E.R. Kelly (London, 1865).

*Bristol*

251     Sketchley's *Bristol Directory 1775* (Bath, 1971).

2a     *Bailey's Western and Midland Directory; or Merchant's and Tradesman's useful companion of the year 1783 ...* (Birmingham, 1783).

3     *Bailey's British Directory ... for the year 1784 in 4 vols. Vol. I, First edition* (London, 1784).

252     *The Bristol Directory ...* (Bristol, 1785).

253     1787 dedication from William Bailey: *The Bristol & Bath Directory ... being the Third Number of the General Directory of England, Wales &c* (Bristol, 1787).

254     John Reed, *The New Bristol Directory, for the Year 1792 ...* (Bristol, n.d. [1792]).

13     *The Universal British Directory of Trade and Commerce ... London, Westminster and ... all the cities, towns and principal villages in England and Wales ... vol. II* [London, 1793].

255     *Matthews's New Bristol Directory for the Year 1793–4* [1st edition] (Bristol, n.d. [1793]).

256     *Matthews's New Bristol Directory for the Year 1795* [2nd edition] (Bristol, n.d. [1795]).

257     *Matthews's New Bristol Directory for the Year 1797* [3rd edition] (Bristol, n.d. [1797]).

14     *The Universal British Directory of Trade and Commerce ... London, Westminster and ... all the cities, towns and principal villages in England and Wales ... vol. II* [2nd/3rd edition: London, 1794].

258     *Matthews's Complete Bristol Directory for the Year 1798* [4th edition] (Bristol, n.d. [1798]).

259     *Matthews's Complete Bristol Directory for the Year 1799 and 1800* [5th edition] (Bristol, n.d. [1799]).

260     *Matthews's Complete Bristol Directory, corrected to May 1801 ...* [6th edition] (Bristol, n.d. [1801]).

261     *Matthews's Complete Bristol Directory, corrected to May 1803 ...* [7th edition] (Bristol, n.d. [1803]).

262  *Mathews's Complete Bristol Directory, continued to February 1805* ... [8th edition] (Bristol, n.d. [1805]).

21  *Holden's Triennial Directory (Fifth Edition) for 1805, 1806 and 1807* ... 2 vols. (London, n.d. [1805]).

263  *Mathews's Complete Bristol Directory, continued to January 1806* ... [9th edition] (Bristol, n.d. [1806]).

264  *Mathews's Complete Bristol Directory, continued to January 1807* ... [10th edition] (Bristol, n.d. [1807]).

22  *Holden's Triennial Directory (Fourth Edition,) Including the year 1808* ... (London, n.d. [1808]).

265  *Mathews's Complete Bristol Directory, continued to February 1808* ... 11th edition (Bristol, n.d. [1808]).

266  *Mathews's Complete Bristol Directory, continued to February 1809* ... 12th edition (Bristol, n.d. [1809]).

23  *Holden's Triennial Directory (Fifth Edition,) for 1809, 1810, 1811* vol. II (London, n.d. [1809]).

267  *Mathews's Complete Bristol Directory, corrected to February 1810* ... 13th edition (Bristol, n.d. [1810]).

24  *Holden's Annual London and County Directory ... in three volumes, for the year 1811* ... (London, n.d. [1811]).

268  *Mathews's Complete Bristol Directory, corrected to February 1810, with a corrected supplement to February 1811* ... 13th edition (Bristol, n.d .[1811]).

269  *Mathews's Complete Bristol Directory, corrected to February 1812* ... 14th edition (Bristol, n.d. [1812]).

270  *Mathews's Annual Bristol Directory for the Year 1813* ... 15th edition (Bristol, n.d. [1813]).

271  *Mathews's Annual Bristol Directory for the Year 1814* ... 16th edition (Bristol, n.d. [1814]).

272  *Mathews's Annual Bristol Directory for the Year 1815* ... 17th edition (Bristol, n.d. [1815]).

273  *Mathews's Annual Bristol Directory for the Year 1816* ... 18th edition (Bristol, n.d. [1816]).

26  [Underhill's, late Holden] *Biennial Directory. Class Third, comprising the addresses of ... mathematical instrument makers ... opticians ... residing in London, and 480 separate towns* ... 1st edition for the years 1816 & 1817 (London, n.d. [1816]).

274  *Mathews's Annual Bristol Directory for the Year 1817* ... 19th edition (Bristol, n.d. [1817]).

275  *Mathews's Annual Bristol Directory for the Year 1818* ... 20th edition (Bristol, n.d. [1818]).

276  *Mathews's Annual Bristol Directory for the Year 1819* ... 21st edition (Bristol, n.d. [1819]).

277  *Mathews's Annual Bristol Directory for the Year 1820* ... 22nd edition (Bristol, n.d. [1820]).

278  *Mathews's Annual Bristol Directory for the Year 1821* ... 23rd edition (Bristol, n.d. [1821]).

35  *Pigot's Commercial Directory for London and Provinces* ... (London, 1822–23).

279  *Mathews's Annual Bristol Directory for the Year 1822* ... 24th edition (Bristol, n.d. [1822]).

280     *Mathews's Annual Bristol Directory for the Year 1823* ... 25th edition (Bristol, n.d. [1823]).

281     *Mathews's Annual Bristol Directory ... for ... 1824* ... 26th edition (Bristol, n.d. [1824]).

282     *Mathews's Annual Bristol Directory ... for 1825* ... 27th edition (Bristol, n.d. [1825]).

283     *Mathews's Annual Bristol Directory ... for 1826* ... 28th edition (Bristol, n.d. [1826]).

284     *Mathews's Annual Bristol Directory ... for 1827* ... 29th edition (Bristol, n.d. [1827]).

285     *Mathews's Annual Bristol Directory ... for 1828* ... 30th edition (Bristol, n.d. [1828]).

286     *Mathews's Annual Bristol Directory ... for 1829* ... 31st edition (Bristol, n.d. [1829]).

53     *Pigot & Co.'s Provincial Directory 1830* [London: 1830].

287     *Mathews's Annual Bristol Directory ... for 1830* ... 32nd edition (Bristol, n.d. [1830]).

288     *Mathews's Annual Bristol Directory ... for 1831* ... 33rd edition (Bristol, n.d. [1831]).

289     *Mathews's Annual Bristol Directory ... for 1832* ... 34th edition (Bristol, n.d. [1832]).

290     *Mathews's Annual Bristol Directory ... for 1833* ... 35th edition (Bristol, n.d. [1833]).

291     *Mathews's Annual Bristol Directory ... for 1834* ... 36th edition (Bristol, n.d. [1834]).

292     *Mathews's Annual Bristol Directory ... for 1835* ... 37th edition (Bristol, n.d. [1835]).

293     *Mathews's Annual Bristol Directory ... for 1836* ... 38th edition (Bristol, n.d. [1836]).

294     *Mathews's Annual Bristol Directory ... for 1837* ... 39th edition (Bristol, n.d. [1837]).

295     *Mathews's Annual Bristol Directory ... for 1838* ... 40th edition (Bristol, n.d. [1838]).

296     *Mathews's Annual Bristol Directory ... for 1839* ... 41st edition (Bristol, n.d. [1839]).

297     *Mathews's Annual Bristol Directory ... for 1840* ... 42nd edition (Bristol, n.d. [1840]).

298     *Mathews's Annual Bristol Directory ... for 1841* ... 43rd edition (Bristol, n.d. [1841]).

299     *Mathews's Annual Bristol Directory ... for 1842* ... 44th edition (Bristol, n.d. [1842]).

300     *Mathews's Annual Bristol Directory ... for 1843* ... 45th edition (Bristol, n.d. [1843]).

301     *Mathews's Annual Bristol Directory ... for 1844* ... 46th edition (Bristol, n.d. [1844]).

302     *Mathews's Annual Bristol Directory ... for 1845* ... 47th edition (Bristol, n.d. [1845]).

303    *Mathews's Annual Bristol Directory and Almanack: 1846* 48th edition (Bristol, n.d. [1846]).

81     *I. Slater's National Commercial Directory of Ireland ... to which are added Classified Directories of the Important English Towns of Manchester, Liverpool, Birmingham, West Bromwich, Leeds, Sheffield and Bristol ...* (Manchester and London, 1846).

304    *Mathews's Annual Bristol Directory and Almanack: 1847* 49th edition (Bristol, n.d. [1847]).

305    *Mathews's Annual Bristol Directory and Almanack: 1848* 50th edition (Bristol, n.d. [1848]).

306    *Mathews's Annual Bristol Directory and Almanack: 1849* 51st edition (Bristol, n.d. [1849]).

307    *Mathews's Annual Bristol Directory and Almanack: 1850* 52nd edition (Bristol, n.d. [1850]).

308    *Mathews's Annual Bristol Directory and Almanack: 1851* 53rd edition (Bristol, n.d. [1851]).

309    *Mathews's Annual Bristol Directory ... for 1852 ...* 54th edition (Bristol, n.d. [1852]).

310    *Mathews's Annual Bristol & Clifton Directory & Almanack: 1853* 55th edition (Bristol, n.d. [1853]).

311    *Mathews's Annual Bristol Directory ... for 1854 ...* 56th edition (Bristol, n.d. [1854]).

312    *Mathews's Annual Bristol Directory ... for 1855 ...* 57th edition (Bristol, n.d. [1855]).

       1856  *M*athews's Annual Bristol Directory ... for 1856 ... 58th edition (Bristol, n.d. [1856]).

       1857  Mathews's Annual Directory ... for Bristol: 1857 59th edition (Bristol, n.d. [1857]).

       1858  Mathews's Annual Bristol Directory ... for 1858 ... 60th edition (Bristol, n.d. [1858]).

       1860  Mathews's Annual Directory ... for the City and County of Bristol ... 1860 62nd edition (Bristol, n.d. [1860]).

       1866  Mathews's Annual Directory ... for the City and County of Bristol ... 1866 68th edition (Bristol, n.d. [1866]).

## Cheltenham

327    *The Cheltenham Annuaire and Directory ... for the year 1843 ...* (Cheltenham, [1843]).

338    *1854. The Cheltenham Annuaire and Directory ...* (Cheltenham, [1854]).

## Derby

166    *The Directory of the County of Derby ... accurately taken during the years 1827, '8 and '9,* by Stephen Glover (Derby, 1829).

62     *Pigot and Co.'s National Commercial Directory ... [for] the Counties of Derby, Hereford, Leicester, Lincoln, Monmouth, Nottingham, Rutland, Salop, Stafford, Warwick and Worcester ...* (London and Manchester, 1835).

167   Samuel Bagshaw, *History, Gazetteer and Directory of Derbyshire* ... (Sheffield, 1846).

126   *Post Office Directory of Derbyshire, Leicestershire, Nottinghamshire and Rutlandshire* ... (London, 1855).
      1857  Francis White & Co., *History, Gazetteer and Directory of the County of Derby ... to which is added a Directory of the Borough of Sheffield* (Leeds, 1857).

## Hull

786   *History, Directory and Gazetteer of the County of York* ..., by Edward Baines, vol. 2, North and East Ridings, the directory department by W. Parson (London, 1823).

50    *Pigot & Co.'s National Commercial Directory* ... (London & Manchester, 1830–31).

64    *Pigot's Directory of Scotland, Isle of Man, Manchester, Liverpool, Leeds, Hull, Birmingham, Sheffield, Carlisle and Newcastle upon Tyne* (Manchester, 1837).

791   *History, Gazetteer and Directory of the West-Riding of Yorkshire ... in two volumes*, by William White (Sheffield, 1837 and 1838).

862   Messrs. Williams & Co., *City of York Directory* ... (Hull, 1843).

799   F. White & Co., *General Directory of Kingston-on-Hull and the City of York* ... (Sheffield, 1846).

801   Francis White & Co., *General Directory and Topography of Kingston-upon-Hull and the City of York* ... (Sheffield, 1851).

95    *Slater's (late Pigot & Co.) Royal National Commercial Directory & Topography of Scotland ... to which are added classified directories for the important English towns of Manchester, Liverpool, Birmingham, Leeds, Hull, Sheffield, Carlisle & Newcastle upon Tyne* (Manchester and London, 1852).
      1858  Francis White & Co., *General Directory and Topography of Kingston-upon-Hull and the City of York* ... (Sheffield, 1858).

## Liverpool

436   *The Liverpool Directory for the Year 1766* ... (Liverpool, 1766).

437   *Gore's Liverpool Directory for the Year 1767* ... (Liverpool, n.d.).

438   *Gore's Liverpool Directory for the Year 1769* ... (Liverpool, n.d.).

439   *Gore's Liverpool Directory for the Year 1772* ... (Liverpool, n.d.).

440   *Gore's Liverpool Directory for the Year 1774* ... (Liverpool, n.d.).

441   *Gore's Liverpool Directory for the Year 1777* ... (Liverpool, n.d.).

442   *Gore's Liverpool Directory for the Year 1781* ... (Liverpool, n.d.).

2     *Bailey's Western and Midland Directory; or Merchant's and Tradesman's useful companion of the year 1783* ... (Birmingham, 1783).

445   *Gore's Liverpool Directory for the Year 1790* ... (Liverpool, n.d.).

15    *The Universal British Directory of Trade and Commerce ... London, Westminster and ... all the cities, towns and principal villages in England and Wales ... vol. III* [London, 1794].

447   *Gore's Liverpool Directory for the Year 1796* ... (Liverpool, n.d.).

448   *Gore's Liverpool Directory for the Year 1800* ... (Liverpool, n.d.).

450   *Gore's Liverpool Directory for the Year 1803* ... (Liverpool, n.d.).
451   *Woodward's New Liverpool Directory* ... (Liverpool: J. Lang, n.d. [1804]).
453   *Gore's Liverpool Directory for the Year 1805* ... (Liverpool, n.d.).
21    *Holden's Triennial Directory (Fifth Edition) for 1805, 1806 and 1807* ... 2 vols. (London, n.d. [1805]).
454   *Gore's Liverpool Directory for the Year 1807* ... (Liverpool, n.d.).
23    *Holden's Triennial Directory (Fifth Edition,) for 1809, 1810, 1811* vol. II (London, n.d. [1809]).
455   *Gore's Liverpool Directory for the Year 1810* ... (Liverpool, n.d.).
456   *Gore's Directory for Liverpool and its Environs for the Year 1811* ... (Liverpool, n.d.).
457   *Gore's Directory for Liverpool and its Environs for the Year 1814* ... (Liverpool, n.d.).
29    *The Commercial Directory for 1814–15* ... (Manchester, n.d. [1814]).
459   *1816. Gore's Liverpool Directory and its Environs for the Year 1816* ... (Liverpool, n.d.).
26    [Underhill's, late Holden] *Biennial Directory. Class Third, comprising the addresses of ... mathematical instrument makers ... opticians ... residing in London, and 480 separate towns* ... 1st edition for the years 1816 & 1817 (London, n.d. [1816]).
31    [Pigot's] *Commercial Directory for 1818–19-20* ... (Manchester, 1818).
460   *1818. Gore's Liverpool Directory and its Environs for the Year 1818* ... (Liverpool, n.d.).
461   *Gore's Liverpool Directory* ... (Liverpool, 1821).
786   Edward Baines, *History, Directory and Gazetteer of the County of York* ... Vol. I. West Riding (Leeds, 1822).
35    *Pigot's Commercial Directory for London and Provinces* ... (London, 1822–23).
462   *Gore's Directory for Liverpool and its Environs for the Year 1823* ... (Liverpool, n.d.).
422   Edward Baines, *History, Directory and Gazetteer of the County Palatine of Lancaster* ... 2 vols. (Liverpool, 1824–25).
463   *Gore's Directory for Liverpool and its Environs for the Year 1825* ... (Liverpool, n.d.).
464   *1827. Gore's Directory for Liverpool and its Environs* (Liverpool, n.d.).
466   *Gore's Directory for Liverpool and its Environs for 1829* (Liverpool, n.d.).
50    *Pigot & Co.'s National Commercial Directory* ... [Cheshire, Cumberland, Derbyshire, Durham, Lancs., Leics., Lincs., Northumberland, Notts., Rutland, Salop., Staffs., Warks., Westmorland, Worcs., Yorks., & N. Wales] (London & Manchester, 1830–31).
468   *Gore's Directory for Liverpool and its Environs for 1832* (Liverpool, n.d.).
61    *National Commercial Directory of the merchants...in the counties of Chester, Cumberland, Durham, Lancaster, Northumberland, Westmorland and York* ... (London, 1834).
469   *1834. Gore's Directory for Liverpool and its Environs* (Liverpool, n.d.).
64    *Pigot's Directory of Scotland, Isle of Man, Manchester, Liverpool, Leeds, Hull, Birmingham, Sheffield, Carlisle and Newcastle upon Tyne* (Manchester, 1837).
471   *1837. Gore's Directory for Liverpool and its Environs* (Liverpool, n.d.).
472   *1839. Gore's Directory for Liverpool and its Environs* (Liverpool, n.d.).
473   *1841. Gore's Directory for Liverpool and its Environs* (Liverpool, n.d.).

474    *1843. Gore's Directory for Liverpool and its Environs* (Liverpool, n.d.).

484    [no title page] *Pigot and Slater's Directory of Liverpool and its suburbs ...* (Manchester, 1843).

475    *1845. Gore's Directory for Liverpool and its Environs* (Liverpool, n.d.).

81     *I. Slater's National Commercial Directory of Ireland ... to which are added Classified Directories of the Important English Towns of Manchester, Liverpool, Birmingham, West Bromwich, Leeds, Sheffield and Bristol ...* (Manchester and London, 1846).

476    *1847. Gore's Directory for Liverpool and its Environs* (Liverpool, n.d.).

486    *McCorquodale's Annual Liverpool Directory...* (Liverpool, November 1848).

523    *Slater's General and Classified Directory of Manchester and Salford, and the whole of Lancashire and Cheshire ...* (Manchester, 1848).

477    *1849. Gore's Directory for Liverpool and its Environs* (Liverpool, n.d.).

478    *1851. Gore's Directory for Liverpool and its Environs* (Liverpool, n.d.).

95     *Slater's (late Pigot & Co.) Royal National Commercial Directory & Topography of Scotland ... to which are added classified directories for the important English towns of Manchester, Liverpool, Birmingham, Leeds, Hull, Sheffield, Carlisle & Newcastle upon Tyne* (Manchester and London, 1852).

479    *1853. Gore's Directory for Liverpool and its Environs* (Liverpool, n.d.).

*Manchester*

487    *The Manchester Directory for the Year 1772* by Elizabeth Raffald (reprinted 1889; and *c*.1990).

488    *The Manchester Directory for the Year 1773* by Elizabeth Raffald (reprinted 1889).

489    *The Manchester and Salford Directory for the Year 1781* by Elizabeth Raffald (Manchester, n.d. [1781]).

490    *Lewis's Manchester Directory for 1788* (reprinted 1888 and 1984).

491    *Scholes's Manchester and Salford Directory ...* (Manchester, 1794).

15     *The Universal British Directory of Trade and Commerce ... London, Westminster and ... all the cities, towns and principal villages in England and Wales ... vol. III* First edition ([London, 1794]).

492    *Scholes's Manchester and Salford Directory ...* (Manchester, 1797).

492    *Scholes's Manchester and Salford Directory...* second edition (Manchester, 1797).

17     *The Universal British Directory of Trade and Commerce ... London, Westminster and ... all the cities, towns and principal villages in England and Wales ... vol. III* [3rd edition: London, 1799].

493    *Bancks's Manchester and Salford Directory...* (Manchester, 1800).

495    *Deans & Co.'s Manchester and Salford Directory...* (Manchester, 1804).

21     *Holden's Triennial Directory (Fifth Edition) for 1805, 1806 and 1807 ...* 2 vols. (London, n.d. [1805]).

496    *Deans' Manchester & Salford Directory for 1808 & 1809 ...* (Manchester, n.d. [1808]).

23     *Holden's Triennial Directory (Fifth Edition,) for 1809, 1810, 1811.* vol II (London, n.d.[1809]).

498    *Pigot's Manchester & Salford Directory for 1811 ...* (Manchester, n.d. [1811]).

499    *Pigot's Manchester & Salford Directory for 1813 ...* (Manchester, n.d. [1813]).

29    *The Commercial Directory for 1814–15* ... (Manchester, n.d. [1814]).

30    *The Commercial Directory for 1816–1817* (Manchester, 1816).

26    [Underhill's] *Biennial Directory. Class Third, comprising the addresses of ... mathematical instrument makers ... opticians ... residing in London, and 480 separate towns ...* 1st edition for the years 1816 & 1817 (London, n.d. [1816]).

501   *Pigot and Deans' Manchester & Salford Directory for 1817* ... (Manchester, [1817]).

31    [Pigot's] *Commercial Directory for 1818–19-20* ... (Manchester, 1818).

502   *Pigot and Deans' Manchester & Salford Directory for 1819–20* ... (Manchester, n.d. [1819]).

503   *Pigot and Deans' Manchester, Salford, &c. Directory for 1821–22* ... (Manchester, n.d. [1821]).

35    *Pigot's Commercial Directory for London and Provinces* ... (London, 1822–23).

504   *Pigot and Deans' Manchester, Salford, &c. Directory for 1824–5* ... (Manchester, n.d. [1824]).

422   Edward Baines, *History, Directory and Gazetteer of the County Palatine of Lancaster* ... 2 vols. (Liverpool, 1824–28).

505   *The Manchester and Salford Directory and Memorandum Book for 1828* (Manchester, n.d. [1828]).

507   *Pigot and Son's General Directory of Manchester, Salford, &c. for 1829;* ... (Manchester, n.d. [1829]).

506   *The Manchester and Salford Director for 1829* ... (Manchester, n.d. [1829]).

50    *Pigot & Co.'s National Commercial Directory* ... (London & Manchester, 1830–31).

508   *Pigot and Son's General Directory of Manchester, Salford, &c. for 1830;* ... (Manchester, n.d. [1830]).

509   *Pigot and Son's General and Classified Directory of Manchester, Salford, &c. for 1832;* ... (Manchester, n.d. [1832]).

510   *Pigot and Son's General and Classified Directory of Manchester, Salford, &c. for 1832; with an addenda for 1833:* ... (Manchester, n.d. [1833]).

61    *Pigot & Co.'s National Commercial Directory for [Northern Counties] ... Durham, Lancaster, Northumberland, Westmorland and York* ... (London and Manchester, 1834).

512   *Pigot and Son's General and Classified Directory of Manchester and Salford* ... (Manchester, 1836).

64    *Pigot's Directory of Scotland, Isle of Man, Manchester, Liverpool, Leeds, Hull, Birmingham, Sheffield, Carlisle and Newcastle upon Tyne* (Manchester, 1837).

513   *Pigot & Son's ... Directory of Manchester and Salford:* ... (Manchester, 1838).

514   *Pigot & Slater's General, Classified and Street Directory of Manchester and Salford,* ... (Manchester, 1840).

515   *Pigot & Slater's General, Classified and Street Directory of Manchester and Salford,* ... (Manchester, 1841).

70    *Pigot & Co.'s Royal National & Commercial Directory ... York, Leicester & Rutland, Lincoln, Northampton & Nottingham; ... Manchester and Salford* (London & Manchester, 1841).

517   *Pigot & Slater's General and Classified Directory ... of Manchester and Salford,* ... (Manchester, 1843).

518   *Pigot & Slater's General and Classified Directory ... of Manchester and Liverpool* ... (Manchester, 1843).

521   I. Slater's *General and Classified Directory ... of Manchester and Salford ...* (Manchester, 1845).

81    *I. Slater's National Commercial Directory of Ireland ... to which are added Classified Directories of the Important English Towns of Manchester, Liverpool, Birmingham, West Bromwich, Leeds, Sheffield and Bristol* ... (Manchester and London, 1846).

523   *Slater's General and Classified Directory of Manchester and Salford, and the whole of Lancashire and Cheshire* ... (Manchester, 1848).

524   *Slater's General and Classified Directory ... of Manchester and Salford, and their vicinities* ... (Manchester, 1850).

525   *Slater's Alphabetical and Classified Directory of Manchester and Salford, and their vicinities* ... (Manchester, 1851).

95    *Slater's (late Pigot & Co.) Royal National Commercial Directory & Topography of Scotland ... to which are added classified directories for the important English towns of Manchester, Liverpool, Birmingham, Leeds, Hull, Sheffield, Carlisle & Newcastle upon Tyne* (Manchester and London, 1852).

527   *Slater's General and Classified Directory ... of Manchester and Salford, with their vicinities* ... (Manchester, 1852).

*Newcastle-upon-Tyne*

584   *The First Newcastle Directory 1778, reprinted in facsimile with an introduction by J.R. Boyle* (Newcastle-upon-Tyne, 1889).

587   *Whitehead's Newcastle and Gateshead Directory for 1790* ... (Newcastle, n.d. [1790]; reprinted 1902).

234   *William Parson and William White, History, Directory and Gazetteer of the Counties of Durham and Northumberland ... in 2 volumes* vol. 1 (Leeds, 1827).

51    *Pigot's Directory for Northumberland* (London, 1829; reprinted 1978).

592   Alexander Ihler, *A Directory of ... Newcastle and Gateshead ...* (Newcastle, 1833).

61    *Pigot & Co.'s National Commercial Directory for [Northern Counties] ... Durham, Lancaster, Northumberland, Westmorland and York ...* (London and Manchester, 1834).

593   M.A. Richardson, *Directory of the Towns of Newcastle upon Tyne and Gateshead for the year 1838* (Newcastle, n.d. [1838]).

594   *Supplement to Richardson's Directory for the Town of Newcastle and Gateshead* (Newcastle, 1839) [bound with 1838 directory].

106   *Robson's Commercial Directory of Durham* (London, 1840).

577   *Ward's North of England Directory ... 1851* (Newcastle on Tyne, 1851).

*Sheffield*

848   *Sketchley's Sheffield Directory* (Bristol, n.d. [1774]).

1     *Bailey's Northern Directory ... for the year 1781* (Warrington, n.d. [1781]).

3     *Bailey's British Directory ... for the year 1784 in 4 vols. Vol. I, First edition* (London, 1784).

849    *A Directory of Sheffield ... compiled and printed by [Joseph] Gales and [David Martin]* (London, 1787).

850    *A Directory of Sheffield ...* (Sheffield, 1797).

18     *Universal British Directory of Trade, Commerce and manufacturer: comprising Lists of Inhabitants of London, Westminster and Southwark, and of all the [Cities?], Towns, and Principal Villages in England and Wales* (London, n.d. [1798]).

21     *Holden's Triennial Directory (Fifth Edition) for 1805, 1806 and 1807 ...* 2 vols. (London, n.d. [1805]).

22     *Holden's Triennial Directory (Fourth Edition,) Including the year 1808 ...* (London, n.d. [1808]).

23     *Holden's Triennial Directory (Fifth Edition,) for 1809, 1810, 1811.* vol II (London, n.d. [1809]).

24     *Holden's Annual London and County Directory ... in three volumes, for the year 1811 ...* (London, n.d.[1811]).

29     *The Commercial Directory for 1814–15 ...* (Manchester, n.d. [1814]).

30     *The Commercial Directory for 1816–17 ...* (Manchester, 1816).

851    *Sheffield General Directory ... by W Brownell* (Sheffield, 1817).

31     [Pigot's] *Commercial Directory for 1818–19-20 ...* (Manchester, 1818).

852    *Sheffield General and Commercial Directory ...* compiled by R. Gell and R. Bennett (Sheffield, 1821).

35     *Pigot's Commercial Directory for London and Provinces ...* (London, 1822–23).

786    Edward Baines, *History, Directory and Gazetteer of the County of York ...* Vol. I. West Riding (Leeds, 1822).

853    *A new general and commercial Directory of Sheffield and its vicinity ... Compiled by R Gell* (Manchester, 1825).

854    *Sheffield Directory and Guide ...* (Sheffield, 1828).

738    *Commercial Directory of Birmingham, Sheffield and their environs ...* (London, 1830).

50     *Pigot & Co.'s National Commercial Directory ...* (London & Manchester, 1830–31).

855    *History and General Directory of the Borough of Sheffield ... By William White* (Sheffield, 1833).

61     *National Commercial Directory of the merchants...in the counties of Chester, Cumberland, Durham, Lancaster, Northumberland, Westmorland and York ...* (London, 1834).

64     *Pigot's Directory of Scotland, Isle of Man, Manchester, Liverpool, Leeds, Hull, Birmingham, Sheffield, Carlisle and Newcastle upon Tyne* (Manchester, 1837).

791    *History, Gazetteer and Directory of the West-Riding of Yorkshire ... in two volumes,* by William White (Sheffield, 1837 and 1838).

793    *Robson's Birmingham and Sheffield Directory ...* (London, n.d. [1839]).

857    *The Sheffield and Rotherham Directory ...,* by Henry A. and Thomas Rodgers (Sheffield, 1841).

856    *White's General Directory of the Town and Borough of Sheffield ...* (Sheffield, 1841).

70     *Pigot & Co.'s Royal National & Commercial Directory ... York, Leicester & Rutland, Lincoln, Northampton & Nottingham; ... Manchester and Salford* (London & Manchester, 1841).

858     *General Directory of the Town and Borough of Sheffield ... By William White.* (Sheffield, 1845).

81     *I. Slater's National Commercial Directory of Ireland ... to which are added Classified Directories of the Important English Towns of Manchester, Liverpool, Birmingham, West Bromwich, Leeds, Sheffield and Bristol ...* (Manchester and London, 1846).

859     *General Directory of the Town and Borough of Sheffield ... By William White.* (Sheffield, 1849).

95     *Slater's (late Pigot & Co.) Royal National Commercial Directory & Topography of Scotland ... to which are added classified directories for the important English towns of Manchester, Liverpool, Birmingham, Leeds, Hull, Sheffield, Carlisle & Newcastle upon Tyne* (Manchester and London, 1852).

803     *Gazetteer and General Directory of the Town and Borough of Sheffield ... By William White.* (Sheffield, 1852).

860     *Post Office Directory of Sheffield, with the neighbouring Towns and Villages* (London, 1854).

       1856   *General Directory of ... Sheffield ...,* by William White (Sheffield, 1856).

       1857   Francis White & Co., *History, Gazetteer and Directory of the County of Derby ... to which is added a Directory of the Borough of Sheffield* (Leeds, 1857).

       1859   Melville & Co.'s *Commercial Directory of Sheffield, Rotherham and the Neighbourhood* (Sheffield, 1859).

       1860   *General Directory of the Town, Borough, and Parish of Sheffield ...* by Wm. White (Sheffield, 1860).

       1861   *General and Commercial Directory and Topography of the Borough of Sheffield ...* by Francis White & Co. (Sheffield, 1861).

       1862   *Business Directory of Sheffield* (Sheffield, 1862).

       1871   *White's General and Commercial Directory of Sheffield ...* by William White (Sheffield, 1871).

       1879   *White's General and Commercial Directory of Sheffield ...* by William White (Sheffield, 1879).

       1895   *The Sheffield City Directory 1895* (Sheffield, [1895]).

## York

1     *Bailey's Northern Directory for the Year 1781* (Warrington, n.d. [1781]).

3     *Bailey's British Directory ... for the year 1784 in 4 vols. Vol. III, First edition* (London, 1784).

15     *The Universal British Directory of Trade and Commerce ... London, Westminster and ... all the cities, towns and principal villages in England and Wales ... vol. III* First edition [London, 1794].

18     *The Universal British Directory of Trade and Commerce ... London, Westminster and ... all the cities, towns and principal villages in England and Wales ... vol. IV* (London, n.d. [1798]).

17     *The Universal British Directory of Trade and Commerce ... London, Westminster and ... all the cities, towns and principal villages in England and Wales ... vol. III* [3rd edition; London, 1799].

21     *Holden's Triennial Directory (Fifth Edition) for 1805, 1806 and 1807 ... 2 vols.* (London, n.d. [1805]).

22    *Holden's Triennial Directory (Fourth Edition,) Including the year 1808 ...* (London, n.d. [1808]).

23    *Holden's Triennial Directory (Fifth Edition,) for 1809, 1810, 1811* vol. II (London, n.d.[1809]).

24    *Holden's Annual London and County Directory ... in three volumes, for the year 1811* ... (London, n.d. [1811]).

29    *The Commercial Directory for 1814–15 ...* (Manchester, n.d. [1814]).

26    [Underhill's, late Holden] *Biennial Directory. Class Third, comprising the addresses of ... mathematical instrument makers ... opticians ... residing in London, and 480 separate towns ...* 1st edition for the years 1816 & 1817 (London, n.d. [1816]).

30    *The Commercial Directory for 1816–1817* (Manchester, 1816).

31    [Pigot's] *Commercial Directory for 1818-19-20 ...* (Manchester, 1818).

35    *Pigot's Commercial Directory for London and Provinces ...* (London, 1822–23).

786    Edward Baines, *History, Directory and Gazetteer of the County of York ...* Vol. I. West Riding (Leeds, 1822).

786    *History, Directory and Gazetteer of the County of York ...,* by Edward Baines, vol 2, North and East Ridings, the directory department by W. Parson (London, 1823).

788    *Directory of Borough of Leeds, the City of York ...,* by William Parsons and William White (Leeds, 1830).

50    *Pigot & Co.'s National Commercial Directory ...* (London & Manchester, 1830–31).

61    *Pigot & Co.'s National Commercial Directory for [Northern Counties] ... Durham, Lancaster, Northumberland, Westmorland and York ...* (London and Manchester, 1834).

64    *Pigot's Directory of Scotland, Isle of Man, Manchester, Liverpool, Leeds, Hull, Birmingham, Sheffield, Carlisle and Newcastle upon Tyne* (Manchester, 1837).

791    *History, Gazetteer and Directory of the West-Riding of Yorkshire ... in two volumes,* by William White (Sheffield, 1837 and 1838).

70    *Pigot & Co.'s Royal National & Commercial Directory ... York, Leicester & Rutland, Lincoln, Northampton & Nottingham; ... Manchester and Salford* (London & Manchester, August 1841).

862    Messrs. Williams & Co., *City of York Directory ...* (Hull, 1843).

81    *I. Slater's National Commercial Directory of Ireland ... to which are added Classified Directories of the Important English Towns of Manchester, Liverpool, Birmingham, West Bromwich, Leeds, Sheffield and Bristol ...* (Manchester and London, 1846).

799    F. White & Co., *General Directory of Kingston-on-Hull and the City of York ...* (Sheffield, 1846).

84    *Slater's (late Pigot & Co.) Royal National Commercial Directory ... of Yorkshire and Lincolnshire ...* (Manchester and London, 1849).

801    Francis White & Co., *General Directory and Topography of Kingston-upon-Hull and the City of York ...* (Sheffield, 1851).

95    *Slater's (late Pigot & Co.) Royal National Commercial Directory & Topography of Scotland ... to which are added classified directories for the important English towns of Manchester, Liverpool, Birmingham, Leeds, Hull, Sheffield, Carlisle & Newcastle upon Tyne* (Manchester and London, 1852).
    1858        Francis White & Co., *General Directory and Topography of Kingston-upon-Hull and the City of York ...* (Sheffield, 1858).

## IV Printed Primary Sources

Abraham (1853). [Trade catalogue] *Descriptive and illustrated catalogue of optical, mathematical and philosophical instruments, manufactured by A. Abraham and Co., 20 Lord Street, Liverpool. 1853.* 80pp.

Abraham (1855). [Trade catalogue] *Descriptive and illustrated catalogue of optical, mathematical and philosophical instruments, manufactured by A. Abraham and Co., 20 Lord Street, Liverpool. 1855.* 60pp.

Adams (1746). [Trade catalogue] *A catalogue of mathematical, philosophical, and optical instruments, as made and sold by George Adams* ... (London, 1746), in George Adams, *Micrographia Illustrata,* first edition (London, 1746), 243–63.

Adams (1771). George Adams, *Micrographia Illustrata,* fourth edition (London, 1771).

Anon. (1789). Anon., *An Alphabetical List of all the Bankrupts from the 1st January 1774 to the 30th June 1786* (London, 1789).

Anon. (1831). Anon., [Obituary for William Jones], *Gentlemen's Magazine,* 101, part 1 (1831), 275.

Baker (1855). [Trade catalogue] C. Baker *A catalogue of achromatic microscopes and photographic apparatus* ... in Jabez Hogg, *The Microscope: its History, Construction and Applications* second edition (London, 1855). 16pp.

Bidstrup (1792). [Trade catalogue] *A catalogue of optical, mathematical & philosophical instruments, made and sold by J. Bidstrup (No. 36.) St Martin's Street, Leicester Square, London* (London, n.d.[1792]). 8pp.

Billing (1858). [M. Billing], *New Illustrated Directory entitled Men & Things of Modern England, being a Direct Guide to the Highest Class of Commercial Houses, Manufacturing Establishments, Hotels, &c. &c.* (Birmingham, n.d. [1858]).

Bugge (1777). Transcript of Thomas Bugge's Diary of his 1777 visit to the Netherlands and England, translated [into English] and edited by Karl Møller Pedersen of Aarhus University, 1997.

Carpenter (1834). [Trade catalogue] *A catalogue of optical and mathematical instruments manufactured and sold by P. Carpenter, Microcosm, No. 24 Regent Street (four doors below Piccadilly,) London. 1834.* 16pp.

Catalogue ... (1838). *Catalogue of the Philosophical Instruments, Models of Invention, Products of National Industry, &c. &c. contained in the First Exhibition of the British Association for the Advancement of Science* (Newcastle-upon-Tyne, 1838).

Catalogue ... (1851). *Illustrated Catalogue of the Exhibition of all Nations* ... (London, 1851).

Catalogue ... (1855). *Paris Universal Exhibition 1855: Catalogue of the Works exhibited in the British Section of the Exhibition* ... (London, 1855).

Chadburn [1851]. [Trade catalogue] *Chadburn Brothers (Opticians to H.R.H. Prince Albert,) Catalogue with prices of optical, mathematical, philosophical, and other instruments, manufactured and sold by them at their exhibition & sale rooms, Albion Works, Nursery Street, Sheffield* ... (Sheffield, n.d. [1851]), 28pp.

Cooke [1863]. [Trade catalogue] *Catalogue of Astronomical, Surveying, and Mathematical Instruments, &c., manufactured by T. Cooke & Sons, 31 Southampton Street, Strand, W.C. Manufactory, Buckingham Works, York...* (Liverpool, n.d. [1863]), 16pp.

Cooke (1868). [Trade catalogue] *1868. Catalogue. T. Cooke & Sons, 31 Southampton Street, Strand, London, and Buckingham Works, York.* (York, [1868]), 48pp.

Crosland (1969). Maurice Crosland (ed.), *Science in France in the Revolutionary Era, Described by Thomas Bugge, Danish Astronomer Royal and Member of the International Commission on the Metric System (1798–1799)* (Cambridge, MA, and London, 1969).

Dancer [1855]. [Trade catalogue] *Achromatic microscopes & apparatus made by J.B. Dancer, optician, 43, Cross Street, Manchester* in John Quekett, *A Practical Treatise on the Use of the Microscope,* third edition (London, 1855), endpapers: 1p.

Dancer (1873). [Trade catalogue] *Catalogue of microscopes and apparatus, barometers, thermometers, hygrometers, urinometers, hydrometers, etc., etc., manufactured by John B. Dancer, optician, 43 Cross Street, Manchester. 1873.* 24pp.

De Saint Fond (1907). B. Faujas de Saint Fond, *A Journey through England and Scotland to the Hebrides in 1784*, a revised edition of the English translation ... by Archibald Geikie, vol. I (Glasgow, 1907).

Field (1855). [Trade catalogue] *Society of Arts Prize Microscopes. R. Field & Son, New Street, Birmingham,* in Jabez Hogg, *The Microscope,* second edition (London, 1855), endpapers, quarter page.

Field (1859). [Trade catalogue] in [H. Woodward], *The Prize Microscopes of the Society of Arts; with Plain Directions for Working with them* (London and Birmingham, 1859); with a *Condensed catalogue of optical and philosophical instruments manufactured by R. Field and Son, New Street, Birmingham* (n.p., n.d. [Birmingham, 1859]). 13pp.

Field (1863). [Trade catalogue] in H. Woodward, *The Prize Microscopes of the Society of Arts; with Plain Directions for Working with them* (Birmingham, 1863); with a *Condensed catalogue of optical and philosophical instruments manufactured by R. Field and Son, New Street, Birmingham* (n.p., n.d. [Birmingham, 1863]). 13pp.

Griffin (1894). [Trade catalogue] John J. Griffin & Sons Ltd., *Chemical Handicraft: Illustrated and Descriptive Catalogue of Chemical Apparatus* ... (London, 1894). 440pp.

'H.B.' (1895). 'H.B.', 'Magic Lanterns and Slides: Notes & Queries No. 3463', *Birmingham Weekly Post,* 16 March 1895.

Hammond (1860). W.F. Hammond, *A Catalogue of the Mathematical and Philosophical Instruments, the Property of the late W. & S. Jones, for Sale by Auction, by Mr W.F. Hammond* ... (London, 1860).

Hill (1770). John Hill, *The Construction of Timber* (London, 1770).

Holland (1834). [John Holland], *The Cabinet Cyclopaedia conducted by the Rev. Dionysius Lardner* ... *A Treatise on the Progressive Improvement and Present State of the Manufactures in Metal, vol. III Tin, Lead, Copper and Other Metals* (London, 1834).

Holland (1867). [John Holland], 'Reminiscences of an Old Sheffield Workshop', *Sheffield Telegraph,* 23, 24, 26 and 27 December 1867.

Jones [1784]. [Trade catalogue] John Jones and Son, *A Catalogue of Optical, mathematical, and Philosophical Instruments made and sold by John Jones, and Son* ... (London, [1784]), bound with W. Jones, *Description and use of a New Portable Orrery* second edition (London, 1784).

Jones [1793]. [Trade catalogue] W. & S. Jones, *A Catalogue of Optical, Mathematical, and Philosophical Instruments, made and sold by Willm. and Saml. Jones* ... (London, [1793]), bound with B. Martin, revised by W. Jones, *Description and Use of the Pocket Case of Mathematical Instruments* (London, 1793).

Jones [1794]. [Trade catalogue] W. & S. Jones, *A Catalogue of Optical, Mathematical, and Philosophical Instruments, made and sold by Willm. and Saml. Jones* ... (London,

[1794]), bound with W. Jones, *Description and Use of a New Portable Orrery* fourth edition (London, 1794).

Jones [1797a]. [Trade catalogue] W. & S. Jones, *A Catalogue of Optical, Mathematical, and Philosophical Instruments, made and sold by W. and S. Jones* ... (London, [1797]), bound with G. Adams, *Geometrical and Graphical Essays* ... second edition (London, 1797).

Jones [1797b]. [Trade catalogue] W. & S. Jones, *A Catalogue of Optical, Mathematical, and Philosophical Instruments, made and sold by W. and S. Jones* ... (London, [1797]), bound with G. Adams, *Astronomical and Geographical Essays* ... third edition (London, 1795).

Jones [1797c]. [Trade catalogue] W. & S. Jones, *A Catalogue of Optical, Mathematical, and Philosophical Instruments, made and sold by W. and S. Jones* ... (London, [1797]), bound with B. Martin, revised by W. Jones, *Description and Use of the Pocket Case of Mathematical Instruments* (London, 1797).

Jones [1797d]. [Trade catalogue] W. & S. Jones, *A Catalogue of Optical, Mathematical, and Philosophical Instruments, made and sold by W. and S. Jones* ... (London, [1797]), bound with G. Adams, *Lectures on Natural and Experimental Philosophy* second edition, ed. W. Jones (London, 1799), vol. V.

Jones [1800?]. [Trade catalogue] W. & S. Jones, *A Catalogue of Optical, Mathematical, and Philosophical Instruments, made and sold by W. and S. Jones* ... (London, [1800?]), bound with William Jones, *Methods of Finding a Time Meridian Line* ... (London, 1795).

Jones (1801). [Trade catalogue] W. & S. Jones, *A Catalogue of Optical, Mathematical, and Philosophical Instruments, made and sold by W. and S. Jones* ... (London, 1801), bound with G. Adams, *Astronomical and Geographical Essays* ... fifth edition (London, 1803); also bound with G. Adams, *Essay on Electricity* fifth edition (London, 1799).

Jones (1804). [Trade catalogue] W. & S. Jones, *A Catalogue of Optical, Mathematical, and Philosophical Instruments, made and sold by W. and S. Jones* ... (London, 1804), bound with G. Adams, *Essays on the Microscope* second edition (London, 1798); also bound in G. Adams, *Astronomical and Geographical Essays* ... fifth edition (London, 1803).

Jones (1805). [Trade catalogue] W. & S. Jones, *A Catalogue of Optical, Mathematical, and Philosophical Instruments, made and sold by W. and S. Jones* ... (London, 1805), unlocated xeroxes.

Jones (1810). [Trade catalogue] W. & S. Jones, *A Catalogue of Optical, Mathematical, and Philosophical Instruments, made and sold by W. and S. Jones* ... (London, 1810), bound with G. Adams, *An Essay on Electricity* ... third edition (London, 1787).

Jones (1811). [Trade catalogue] W. & S. Jones, *A Catalogue of Optical, Mathematical, and Philosophical Instruments, made and sold by W. and S. Jones* ... (London, 1811), bound with G. Adams, *Astronomical and Geographical Essays* ... sixth edition (London, 1812).

Jones (1814a). [Trade catalogue] W. & S. Jones, *A Catalogue of Optical, Mathematical, and Philosophical Instruments, made and sold by W. and S. Jones* ... (London, 1814), bound with J. Cuthbertson, *Practical Electricity and Galvanism* (London, 1807); also in G. Adams, *Astronomical and Geographical Essays* ... sixth edition (London, 1812).

Jones (1814b). [Trade catalogue] W. & S. Jones, *A Catalogue of Optical, Mathematical, and Philosophical Instruments, made and sold by W. and S. Jones* ... (London, 1814), bound with G. Adams, *Essay on the Microscope* 2nd edition (London, 1798).

Jones (1817). [Trade catalogue] W. & S. Jones, *A Catalogue of Optical, Mathematical, and Philosophical Instruments, made and sold by W. and S. Jones* ... (London, Nov. 1817), bound with Henry James Brooke, *A Familiar to Crystallography* ... (London, 1823).

Jones (1818). [Trade catalogue] W. & S. Jones, *A Catalogue of Optical, Mathematical, and Philosophical Instruments, made and sold by W. and S. Jones* ... (London, Jan. 1818), separate pamphlet.

Jones (1825). [Trade catalogue] W. & S. Jones, *A Catalogue of Optical, Mathematical, and Philosophical Instruments, made and sold by W. and S. Jones* ... (London, October, 1825), separate pamphlet.

Jones (1827). [Trade catalogue] W. & S. Jones, *A Catalogue of Optical, Mathematical, and Philosophical Instruments, made and sold by W. and S. Jones* ... (London, August, 1827), separate pamphlet.

Jones (1830). [Trade catalogue] W. & S. Jones, *A Catalogue of Optical, Mathematical, and Philosophical Instruments, made and sold by W. and S. Jones* ... (London, 1830), separate pamphlet.

Jones (1835). [Trade catalogue] W. & S. Jones, *A Catalogue of Optical, Mathematical, and Philosophical Instruments, made and sold by W. and S. Jones* ... (London, 1835); bound in the back of G. Adams, *Geometrical and Graphical Essays* ... second edition (London, 1797).

Jones (1836). [Trade catalogue] W. & S. Jones, *A Catalogue of Optical, Mathematical, and Philosophical Instruments, made and sold by W. and S. Jones* ... (London, 1836), separate pamphlet.

Jones (1838). [Trade catalogue] W. & S. Jones, *A Catalogue of Optical, Mathematical, and Philosophical Instruments, made and sold by W. and S. Jones* ... (London, 1838), separate pamphlet.

Jones (1843). [Trade catalogue] W. & S. Jones, *A Catalogue of Optical, Mathematical, and Philosophical Instruments, made and sold by W. and S. Jones* ... (London, 1843), separate pamphlet.

Jones (1850). [Trade catalogue] W. & S. Jones, *A Catalogue of Optical, Mathematical, and Philosophical Instruments, made and sold by W. and S. Jones* ... (London, 1850), separate pamphlet.

Jones (1855). [Trade catalogue] W. & S. Jones, *A Catalogue of Optical, Mathematical, and Philosophical Instruments, made and sold by W. and S. Jones* ... (London, 1855), separate pamphlet.

Lankester(1859) Edwin Lankester, 'The President's Address', *Transactions of the Microscopical Society of London*, n.s. 7 (1859), 77.

Liverpool: St Nicholas Parish Registers: Marriages.

Mackenzie (1801). Alexander Mackenzie, *Voyages from Montreal, on the River St. Laurence, through the Continent of North America, to the Frozen and Pacific oceans; in the years 1789 and 1793. With a Preliminary Account of the Rise, progress, and Present State of the Fur Trade of that Country* (London, 1801).

Matthews (1895). Arthur Bache Matthews, 'The Manufacture of Magic Lanterns in Birmingham: Notes & Queries No. 3423', *Birmingham Weekly Post*, 5 January 1895.

Mayhew (1861). Henry Mayhew, *London Labour and the London Poor* Vol.I (New York, 1861; reprinted, London, 1968).

'Memoranda' (1855). 'Memoranda: Cheap Microscopes', *Quarterly Journal of Microscopical Science*, 3 (1855), 234–5.

Mudge (1777). John Mudge, 'Directions for making the best Composition for the Metals of reflecting Telescopes; together with a Description of the Process of grinding, polishing, and giving the great Speculum the true parabolic Curve', *Philosophical Transactions*, 67 (1777), 296–349.

Parkes (1848). [Trade catalogue] *James Parkes & Son, No. 5, St. Mary's Row, Birmingham, Manufacturers of Improved Measuring Tapes, Land Chains, Mathematical Instruments, Miners' & Mariners' Compasses, Watch Keys, Seals, &c., &c.* (Birmingham, 1848). 24pp.

Parkes (1857). [Trade catalogue] *Wholesale catalogue of optical, mathematical and philosophical instruments manufactured by James Parkes & Son (patentees,) Instrument makers to the Board of Trade, and Government Schools of Design, 5 St. Mary's Row, Birmingham* (London, 1857). 32pp.

Parkes (1862). [Trade catalogue] *Wholesale catalogue of simple and compound microscopes and microscopic apparatus, manufactured by James Parkes & Son (Patentees), No 5 St. Mary's Row, Birmingham...* (London, 1862). 20pp.

Parkes (1867). [Trade catalogue] *Wholesale catalogue of optical, mathematical and philosophical instruments ... manufactured by James Parkes & Son, ... 5 St. Mary's Row, Birmingham* (n.d.[1867]). 56pp.

Parkes (1886). [Trade catalogue] *Wholesale catalogue of microscopes and microscopic apparatus manufactured by James Parkes & Son, patentees, 5 & 6 St. Mary's Row, Birmingham*, second edition (n.d.[1886]). 34pp.

'Premiums' (1855). 'Premiums Awarded: Session 1854–55', *Journal of the Society of Arts*, 3 (1855), 590.

*Reports ...*(1852). *Exhibition of the Works of Industry of All Nations, 1851: Reports of the Juries of the Subjects in the Thirty Classes into which the Exhibition was Divided* (London, 1852).

*Reports ...* (1863). *International Exhibition 1862: Reports by the Juries on the Subjects in the Thirty-six Classes into which the Exhibition was divided* (London, 1863).

Smith (1738). Robert Smith, *A Compleat System of Opticks* (Cambridge, 1738).

'Special Prizes' (1855). 'Special Prizes', *Journal of the Society of Arts*, 3 (1855), 167.

Strauss et al.(1864). G.L.M. Strauss et al., *England's Workshops* (London, 1864).

Timmins (1866). S. Timmins (ed.), *The Resources, Products, and Industrial History of Birmingham and the Midland Hardware District ...* (London, 1866).

Thompson and Yeo (1973). E.P. Thompson and Eileen Yeo (eds), *The Unknown Mayhew: Selections from the Morning Chronicle 1849–1850* (London, 1973).

Woodcroft (1854). Bennet Woodcroft, *Alphabetical Index of Patentees of Invention* (London, 1854, reprinted 1969).

## V   Unpublished Theses

Averley (1989). Gwendoline Averley, 'English Scientific Societies of the Eighteenth and Early Nineteenth Centuries', unpublished PhD thesis, Teesside Polytechnic, December 1989.

Barry (1985). Jonathan Barry, 'The Cultural Life of Bristol, 1640–1775', unpublished DPhil thesis, University of Oxford, 1985.

Brooks (1989). Randall C. Brooks, 'The Precision Screw in Scientific Instruments of the 17th to 19th Centuries, with particular reference to Astronomical, Nautical and Surveying Instruments', unpublished PhD thesis, Leicester University, 1989.

Cookson (1994). Gillian Cookson, 'The West Yorkshire Textile Engineering Industry, 1780–1850', unpublished DPhil thesis, University of York, 1994.

Fairclough (1975). Oliver Fairclough, 'Joseph Finney and the clock and watchmakers of 18th century Liverpool', unpublished MA thesis, University of Keele, 1975.

Gee (1989). Brian Gee, 'The Place and Contribution of the Instrument Maker in Scientific Development, 1820–1850, with special reference to Electromagnetism and the Diffusion of Science', unpublished PhD thesis, University of Leicester, 1989.

Ginn (1993). William Thomas Ginn, 'Philosophers and Artisans: the Relationship between Men of Science and Instrument Makers in London 1820–1860', unpublished PhD thesis, University of Kent, 1993.

Inkster (1977). Ian Inkster, 'Studies in the Social History of Science in England during the Industrial Revolution', unpublished PhD thesis, University of Sheffield, 1977.

Meliconi (2000). Ilaria Meliconi, 'Aspects of the Development of British Scientific Instrument Making in the Second half of the Nineteenth Century', unpublished DPhil thesis, University of Oxford, 2000.

Robischon (1983). M.M. Robischon, 'Scientific Instrument Makers in London during the Seventeenth and Eighteenth Centuries', unpublished PhD thesis, University of Michigan, 1983.

Setchell (1971). J.R.M. Setchell, 'Henry Hindley and Son: Instrument and Clockmakers of York', unpublished BLitt thesis, University of Oxford, 1971.

Simpson (1981). A.D.C. Simpson, 'The Early Development of the Reflecting Telescope in Britain', unpublished PhD thesis, University of Edinburgh, 1981.

Sorrenson (1993). Richard John Sorrenson, 'Scientific Instrument Makers at the Royal Society of London, 1720–1780', unpublished PhD thesis, Princeton University, 1993.

Walters (1992). Alice Nell Walters, 'Tools of Enlightenment: the Material Culture of Science in 18th century England', unpublished PhD thesis, University of California at Berkeley, 1992.

## VI   Unpublished Articles

Anon. (1979). Anon., 'Changing the Image of Industry: John Davis & Son (Derby)', unpublished business history, 1979.

Barry (1983). Jonathan Barry, 'An Analysis of Bristol Probate Inventories 1640–1775', unpublished article 1983.

Christensen (1998). Dan Ch. Christensen, 'English Instrument Makers Observed by Predacious Danes', unpublished paper presented at the XVIIth Scientific Instrument Symposium, Søro, Denmark, July 1998.

McConnell (1996). Anita McConnell, 'A Survey of Networks bringing a Knowledge of Optical Glass-working to the London Trade, 1500–1800', unpublished typescript, 1996.

Millburn (1992b). John R. Millburn, 'The Ordnance Records as a Source for Studies of Instruments and their Makers in the Eighteenth Century', unpublished booklet, 1992.

Millburn (1992c). John R. Millburn, 'Instrument-Makers' Ordnance Bills, transcribed from Ordnance Bill Books (Classes WO51, 52) at the Public Record Office, Kew', unpublished booklet, 1992.

Wess (1998). Jane Wess, 'Mathematical instruments and the building of the British state', paper read at the XVII International Scientific Instrument Symposium, Denmark, July 1998.

## VII Books and Articles

Ackermann (1998). Silke Ackermann (ed.), *Humphrey Cole: Mint, Measurement and Maps in Elizabethan England* (London, 1998).

Ackermann and Wess (2003). Silke Ackermann and Jane Wess, 'Between Antiquarianism and Experiment: Hans Sloane, George III and collecting science', in Kim Sloane and Andrew Burnett (eds), *Enlightenment: Discovering the World in the Eighteenth Century* (London, 2003), 150–57.

Alger (1982). K.R. Alger, *Mrs Janet Taylor 'Authoress and Instructress in Navigation and Nautical Academy' (1804–1870)* (London, 1982).

Allen (1976). D.E. Allen, *The Naturalist in Britain: a Social History* (London, 1976).

Amelin (1994). Olov Amelin, 'Daniel Ekström: Maker of Scientific Instruments in 18th century Sweden', in G. Dragoni, A. McConnell and G. L'E. Turner (eds), *Proceedings of the Eleventh International Scientific Instrument Symposium* (Bologna, 1994), 81–3.

Andersen (1993). Hemming Andersen, 'Jeppe Smith (1759–1821): a Danish Instrument-Maker', in R.G.W. Anderson, J.A. Bennett and W.F. Ryan (eds), *Making Instruments Count: Essays on Historical Scientific Instruments presented to Gerard L'Estrange Turner* (Aldershot, 1993), 403–17.

Andersen (1995). Hemming Andersen, *Historic Scientific Instruments in Denmark* (Copenhagen, 1995).

Anderson (1985). R.G.W. Anderson, 'Were Scientific Instruments in the Nineteenth Century Different? Some Initial Considerations', in P.R. de Clercq (ed.), *Nineteenth-Century Scientific Instruments and Their Makers* (Amsterdam and Leiden, 1985), 1–12.

Anderson (1993). R.G.W. Anderson, 'Introduction', to R.G.W. Anderson and G.L'E. Turner (eds), *An Apparatus of Instruments: the Role of the Scientific Instrument Commission* (London, 1993), 1–3.

Anderson (2003). R.G.W. Anderson, 'The Status of Instruments in Eighteenth-century Cabinets', in R.G.W. Anderson (ed.), *Enlightening the British: Knowledge, Discovery and the Museum in the Eighteenth Century* (London, 2003), 55–60.

Anderson (2005). R.G.W. Anderson, 'To Thrive or Survive? The State and Status of Research in Museums', *Museum Management and Curatorship*, 20 (2005), 297–311.

Anderson and Lawrence (1987). R.G.W. Anderson and Christopher Lawrence (eds), *Science, Medicine, and Dissent: Joseph Priestley (1733–1804)* (London, 1987).

Anderson et al. (1990). R.G.W. Anderson, J. Burnett and B. Gee, *Handlist of Scientific Instrument-makers' Trade Catalogues 1600–1914* (Edinburgh and London, 1990).

Andrewes (1996). William J.H. Andrewes (ed.), *The Quest for Longitude* (Cambridge, MA, 1996).

Angus-Butterworth (1958). L.M. Angus-Butterworth, 'Glass', in C. Singer et al. (eds), *A History of Technology: Volume IV The Industrial Revolution c.1750–c.1850* (Oxford, 1958), 358–78.

Anon (1893). Anon., *The Century's Progress: Yorkshire* (London, 1893).

Anon. (1898). Anon., 'Where Lord Kelvin's Instruments are made,' *The Ludgate*, 7 (1898), 148–54.

Ashton (1968). T.S. Ashton, *The Industrial Revolution 1760–1830*, 2nd edition (Oxford, 1968).

Ashworth (2001). William J. Ashworth, '"Between the Trade and the Public": British Alcohol Standards and the Proof of Good Governance', *Technology and Culture*, 41 (2001), 27–50.

Ashworth (2003). William J. Ashworth, *Customs and Excise: Trade, Production and Consumption in England 1640–1845* (Oxford, 2003).

Baddeley (1986). Jon Baddeley, *The Gentleman Collector: A catalogue published to accompany a special exhibition at Burghley House, Stamford* (Stamford, 1986).

Bailey and Barker (1969). F.A. Bailey and T.C. Barker, 'The Seventeenth-century Origins of Watchmaking in South-West Lancashire', in J.R. Harris (ed.), *Liverpool and Merseyside: Essays in the Economic and Social History of the Port and its Hinterland* (London, 1969), 1–15.

Baker (1995). Malcolm Baker, 'A Rage for Exhibitions: the Display and Viewing of Wedgwood's Frog Service', in Hilary Young (ed.), *The Genius of Wedgwood* (London, 1995), 118–27.

Banfield (1991). Edwin Banfield, *Barometer Makers and Retailers 1660–1900* (Trowbridge, Wiltshire, 1991).

Banfield (1993). Edwin Banfield, *The Italian Influence on English barometers from 1780* (Trowbridge, Wiltshire, 1993).

Barber (1980). Lynn Barber, *The Heyday of Natural History 1820–1870* (London, 1980).

Barclay (1993). R.L. Barclay, 'The Metals of the Scientific Instrument Maker, Part I: Brass', *Bulletin of the Scientific Instrument Society*, No. 39 (1993), 32–6.

Barker (2003). Nicolas Barker (ed.), *The Devonshire Inheritance: Five Centuries of Collecting at Chatsworth* (Alexandria, VA, 2003).

Barnes (2005). Colin Barnes, 'John Davis & Son (Derby) Ltd', *Journal of the Oughtred Society*, 14 (2005), 22–31.

Barnes (1992). Janet Barnes (ed.), *The Cutting Edge: an Exhibition of Sheffield Tools* (Sheffield, 1992).

Barraclough (1976). K.C. Barraclough, *Sheffield Steel* (Sheffield, 1976).

Beauchamp (1997). K.G. Beauchamp, *Exhibiting Electricity* (London, 1997).

Bechler (1975). Z. Bechler, '"A less agreeable matter": the Disagreeable Case of Newton and Achromatic Refraction', *British Journal for the History of Science*, 8 (1975), 101–26.

Bedini (1964). Silvio Bedini, *Early American Scientific Instruments and their Makers* (Washington DC, 1964).

Bedini (1993). Silvio Bedini, 'Of "Science and Liberty": the Scientific Instruments of King's College and Eighteenth Century Columbia College in New York', *Annals of Science*, 50 (1993), 201–27.

Bendall (1997). Sarah Bendall, *Dictionary of Land Surveyors and Local Map-makers of Great Britain and Ireland 1530–1850*, 2 vols (London, 1997).

Bennett (1983). J.A. Bennett, *Science at the Great Exhibition* (Cambridge, 1983).

Bennett (1985). J.A. Bennett, 'Instrument Makers and the "Decline of Science in England": the Effects of Institutional Change on the élite Makers of the early Nineteenth Century', in P.R. de Clercq (ed.), *Nineteenth-Century Scientific Instruments and Their Makers* (Amsterdam and Leiden, 1985), 13–28.

Bennett (1987). J.A. Bennett, *The Divided Circle: a History of Instruments for Astronomy, Navigation and Surveying* (Oxford, 1987).

Bennett (1992). J.A. Bennett, 'The English Quadrant in Europe: Instruments and the Growth of Consensus in Practical Astronomy', *Journal for the History of Astronomy*, 23 (1992), 1–14.

Bennett (1993). J.A. Bennett, 'Science Museums and Science History', in R.G.W. Anderson and G.L'E. Turner (eds), *An Apparatus of Instruments: the Role of the Scientific Instrument Commission* (London, 1993), 15–17.

Bennett (1995). J.A. Bennett, 'Book review [of Gloria Clifton, *Directory of British Scientific Instrument Makers 1550–1851* (London, 1995)], *Bulletin of the Scientific Instrument Society*, No. 47 (1995), 34.

Bennett (2002). James A. Bennett, 'Shopping for Instruments in Paris and London', in Pamela H. Smith and Paula Findlen (eds), *Merchants and Marvels: Commerce, Science and Art in Early Modern Europe* (New York and London, 2002), 370–95.

Berg (1991). Maxine Berg (ed.), *Markets and Manufacture in Early Industrial Europe* (London and New York, 1991).

Berg (1993). Maxine Berg, 'Small Producer Capitalism in Eighteenth Century England', *Business History*, 35 (1993), 17–39.

Berg (1994). Maxine Berg, *The Age of Manufactures 1700–1820*, 2nd edition (London, 1994).

Berg (1998). M. Berg, 'Product Innovation in Core Consumer Industries in Eighteenth Century Britain', in M. Berg and K. Bruland (eds), *Technological Revolutions in Europe: Historical Perspectives* (Cheltenham, 1998), 138–57.

Berg et al. (1983). M. Berg, P. Hudson and M. Sonenscher (eds), *Manufacture in Town and Country Before the Factory* (Cambridge, 1983).

Berg and Hudson (1992). M. Berg and P. Hudson, 'Rehabilitating the Industrial Revolution', *Economic History Review*, 45 (1992), 24–50.

Betts (1996). Jonathan Betts, 'Arnold and Earnshaw: the Practicable Solution', in William J.H. Andrewes (ed.), *The Quest for Longitude* (Cambridge, MA, 1996), 311–28.

Boase and Courtney (1878). G.C. Boase and W.P. Courtney, *Bibliotheca Cornubiensis*, 3 vols (London, 1874–1882).

Booth (1963). Andrew D. Booth, 'A drum Microscope Made by John Davis', *Journal of the Royal Microscopical Society*, 82 (1963), 293–5.

Boss (1972). V. Boss, *Newton and Russia. The Early Influence, 1698–1796* (Cambridge, MA, 1972).

Bracegirdle (1996). Brian Bracegirdle, *Notes on Modern Microscope Manufacturers* (Oxford, 1996).

Bracegirdle and McCormick (1993). Brian Bracegirdle and James B. McCormick, *The Microscopic Photographs of J.B. Dancer* (Chicago, 1993).

Bradbury (1967). S. Bradbury, 'The Quality of the Image produced by the Compound Microscope: 1700–1840', in S. Bradbury and G.L'E. Turner (eds), *Historical Aspects of Microscopy* (Cambridge, 1967), 151–73.

Brears (1984). Peter Brears, 'Temples of the Muses: the Yorkshire Philosophical Museums, 1820–50', *Museums Journal*, 84 (1984), 3–19.

Brech and Matthew (1997). Alison Brech and Jim Matthew, 'Thomas Cooke and the Yorkshire Philosophical Society: from Artisan to Honorary Member', *Yorkshire Philosophical Society Annual Report 1996* (York, 1997), 45–55.

Brewer (1997). John Brewer, *The Pleasures of the Imagination: English Culture in the Eighteenth Century* (London, 1997).

Briggs (1975). Asa Briggs, *Victorian People* (London, 1975).

Bristow (1992). H.R. Bristow, 'The Society's Visit to Liverpool, Prescot and Manchester. Part III: Liverpool Instrument Makers', *Bulletin of the Scientific Instrument Society*, No. 33 (1992), 18.

Bristow (1993). H.R. Bristow, 'Elliott, Instrument Makers of London: Products, Customers and Development in the 19th Century', *Bulletin of the Scientific Instrument Society*, No. 36 (1993), 8–11

Brooks (1992). John Brooks, 'The Circular Dividing Engine: Development in England 1739–1843', *Annals of Science*, 49 (1992), 101–35.

Brooks (1989a). Randall C. Brooks, 'Gleaning Information from Screw Threads', *Bulletin of the Scientific Instrument Society*, No. 22 (1989), 7–11.

Brown (1978). Joyce Brown, *Mathematical Instrument-Makers in the Grocers' Company, 1688–1830* (London, 1978).

Brown (1979). Joyce Brown, 'Guild Organization and the Instrument-Making Trade 1550–1830: the Grocers' and Clockmakers' Companies', *Annals of Science*, 36 (1979), 1–34.

Brown (1986). Olivia Brown, *Whipple Museum of the History of Science Catalogue 7: Microscopes* (Cambridge, 1986).

Brown and Samuel (1982–86). M. Brown and J. Samuel, 'The Jews of Bath', *Jewish Historical Studies*, 29 (1982–86), 135–64.

Bryant (1994). T.J. Bryant, 'John Handsford of Birmingham and Bristol', *Bulletin of the Scientific Instrument Society*, No. 40 (1994), 11–12.

Bryant (1999). Terry J. Bryant, 'Henry Edgeworth', *Bulletin of the Scientific Instrument Society*, No. 61 (1999), 18–19.

Bryden (1968). D.J. Bryden, *James Short and his Telescopes* (Edinburgh, 1968)

Bryden (1972). D.J. Bryden, *Scottish Scientific Instrument Makers 1600–1900* (Edinburgh, 1972).

Bryden (1984). D.J. Bryden, 'Provincial Scientific Instrument Making', *Bulletin of the Scientific Instrument Society*, No. 2 (1984), 4.

Bryden (1992). D.J. Bryden, 'Evidence from Advertising for Mathematical Instrument Making in London 1556–1714', *Annals of Science*, 49 (1992), 301–36.

Bryden (1993). D.J. Bryden, 'Made in Oxford: John Prujean's 1701 Catalogue of Mathematical Instruments', *Oxoniensia*, 58 (1993), 263–85.

Burnett (1986). John Burnett, 'The Use of New Materials in the Manufacture of Scientific Instruments c.1880–c.1920', in John T. Stock and Mary Virginia Orna (eds), *The History and Preservation of Chemical Instrumentation* (Dordrecht, Boston, Lancaster, Tokyo, 1986), 217–38.

Burnett and Morrison-Low (1989). J.E. Burnett and A.D. Morrison-Low, *'Vulgar & Mechanick': the Scientific Instrument Trade in Ireland 1650–1921* (Dublin and Edinburgh, 1989).

Butler (1987). Stella Butler, 'Microscopes in Manchester', *Microscopy*, 35 (1987), 570–72.

Bythell (1969). Duncan Bythell, *The Handloom Weavers: a Study in the English Cotton Industry during the Industrial Revolution* (Cambridge, 1969).

Calvert (1971). H.R. Calvert, *Scientific Trade Cards in the Science Museum Collection* (London, 1971).

Cannadine (1984). David Cannadine, 'The Past and the Present in the English Industrial Revolution', *Past and Present*, 103 (1984), 149–58.

Cardwell (1994). Donald Cardwell, *The Fontana History of Technology* (London, 1994).

Carpenter (1856). W.B. Carpenter, *The Microscope and Its Revelations* (London, 1856).

Carpenter (1862). W.B. Carpenter, *The Microscope and Its Revelations* third edition (London, 1862).

Carpenter (1888). W.B. Carpenter, *Nature and Man: Essays, Scientific and Philosophical* (London, 1888).

Cattermole and Wolfe (1987). M.J.G. Cattermole and A.F. Wolfe, *Horace Darwin's Shop: A History of the Cambridge Scientific Instrument Company 1878–1968* (Bristol, 1987).

Chance (1919). James Frederick Chance, *A History of the Firm of Chance Brothers & Co., Glass and Alkali Manufacturers* (London, 1919).

Chapman (1995). Allan Chapman, *Dividing the Circle: the Development of Critical Angular Measurement in Astronomy 1500–1850*, 2nd edition (Chichester, 1995).

Chenakal (1972). Valentin L. Chenakal, *Watchmakers and Clockmakers in Russia 1400 to 1850* (London, 1972).

Cherry (1994). John Cherry, 'Medieval and Later Antiquities: Sir Hans Sloane and the Collecting of History', in Arthur MacGregor (ed.), *Sir Hans Sloane: Collector, Scientist, Antiquary, Founding Father of the British Museum* (London, 1994), 198–221.

Chesworth (1984). Mary Chesworth, *'Bought of': 19th century Sheffield through its Billheads and Related Documents* (Sheffield, 1984).

Christensen (1993). Dan Ch. Christensen, 'Spying on Scientific Instruments: the Career of Jesper Bidstrup', *Centaurus*, 36 (1993), 209–44.

Clark (1982). Alice Clark, *Working Life of Women in the Seventeenth Century*, 2nd edition (London, 1982).

Clarke et al. (1989). T.N. Clarke, A.D. Morrison-Low and A.D.C. Simpson, *Brass and Glass: Scientific Instrument Making Workshops in Scotland* (Edinburgh, 1989).

Clifton (1993a). Gloria C. Clifton, 'The Spectaclemakers' Company and the Origins of the Optical Instrument-Making Trade in London', in R.G.W. Anderson, J.A. Bennett and W.F. Ryan (eds), *Making Instruments Count: Essays on Historical Scientific Instruments presented to Gerard L'Estrange Turner* (Aldershot, 1993), 341–64.

Clifton (1993b). Gloria C. Clifton, 'An Introduction to the History of Elliott Brothers up to 1900', *Bulletin of the Scientific Instrument Society*, No. 36 (1993), 2–7.

Clifton (1994). Gloria Clifton, 'The Growth of the British Scientific Instrument Trade, 1600–1850', in G. Dragoni, G. L'E. Turner and A. McConnell (eds), *Proceedings of the Eleventh Scientific Instrument Symposium, Bologna, 1991* (Bologna, 1994), 61–70.

Clifton (1995). Gloria Clifton, *Directory of British Scientific Instrument Makers 1550–1851* (London, 1995).

Clifton (2003). Gloria Clifton, 'The London Mathematical Instrument Makers and the British Navy, 1700–1850', in Pieter van der Merwe (ed.), *Science and the French and British Navies, 1700–1850* (London, 2003), 24–33.

Clifton (2005). Gloria Clifton, 'The Adoption of the Octant in the British Isles', in Remmelt Daalder, Frits Loomeijer and Diederick Wildeman (eds), *Koersvast: Vijf eeuwen navigatie op zee* (Zaltbommel, 2005), 85–94.

Clifton (forthcoming). Gloria Clifton, 'The Sextant and the Longitude Problem: the Bigger Picture', in Jan Parmentier (ed.), *Navigating the Northern Seas* (forthcoming).

Coleman (1983). D.C. Coleman, 'Proto-Industrialization: A Concept Too Many', *Economic History Review*, 36 (1983), 435–48.

Colvin (1995). Howard Colvin, *A Biographical Dictionary of British Architects 1600–1840*, 3rd edition (New Haven and London, 1995).

Connor (1987). R.D. Connor, *The Weights and Measures of England* (London, 1987).

Connor and Simpson (2004). R.D. Connor and A.D.C. Simpson, edited by A.D. Morrison-Low, *Weights and Measures in Scotland: A European Perspective* (Edinburgh, 2004).

Cookson (1996). Gillian Cookson, 'Millwrights, Clockmakers and the Origins of Textile Machine-Making in Yorkshire', *Textile History*, 27 (1996), 43–57.

Corfield (1982). P. Corfield, *The Impact of English Towns during the Eighteenth Century* (Oxford, 1982).

Cosh (1969). Mary Cosh, 'Clockmaker Extraordinary: the Career of Alexander Cumming', *Country Life* (12 June 1969), 1528, 1531 and 1535.

Crafts (1985). N.F.R. Crafts, *British Economic Growth During the Industrial Revolution* (Oxford, 1985).

Craven (1996). Maxwell Craven, *John Whitehurst of Derby: Clockmaker and Scientist 1713–88* (Ashbourne, Derbyshire, 1996).

Crawforth (1985). MA Crawforth, 'Evidence from Trade Cards for the Scientific Instrument Industry', *Annals of Science*, 42 (1985), 453–554.

Crawforth (1987a). MA Crawforth, 'Makers and Dates', *Bulletin of the Scientific Instrument Society*, No. 13 (1987), 2–8.

Crawforth (1987b). MA Crawforth, 'Instrument Makers in the London Guilds', *Annals of Science*, 44 (1987), 319–77.

Crom (1989). Theodore R. Crom, *Trade Catalogues 1542 to 1842* (Melrose, FLA, 1989).

Cross (1979). A.G. Cross, *Great Britain and Russia in the Eighteenth Century: Contacts and Comparisons* (Newtonville, MA, 1979).

Cross (1980). A.G. Cross, *"By the Banks of the Thames": Russians in Eighteenth Century Britain* (Newtonville, MA, 1980).

Crossley et al. (1989). David Crossley, et al. (eds), *Water Power on the Sheffield Rivers* (Sheffield, 1989).

Crouzet (1967). François Crouzet, 'England and France in the Eighteenth Century: a Comparative Analysis of Two Economic Growths', in R.M. Hartwell (ed.), *The Causes of the Industrial Revolution in England* (London, 1967), 139–74.

Crouzet (1990). François Crouzet, 'Capital Formation in Great Britain during the Industrial Revolution', in François Crouzet, *Britain Ascendant: Comparative Studies in Franco-British Economic History* (Cambridge, 1990), 149–212.

Daumas (1958). Maurice Daumas, 'Precision Mechanics', in Charles Singer et al. (eds), *A History of Technology: Volume IV The Industrial Revolution c.1750–c.1850* (Oxford, 1958), 379–416.

Daumas (1972). Maurice Daumas, *Les instruments scientifiques aux xvii et xviii siècles* (Paris, 1953); trans. Mary Holbrook, *Scientific Instruments of the Seventeenth and Eighteenth Centuries and their Makers* (London, 1972).

Daunton (1995). M.J. Daunton, *Progress and Poverty: an Economic and Social History of Britain 1700–1850* (Oxford, 1995).

Davidoff and Hall (1987). Leonore Davidoff and Catherine Hall, *Family Fortunes: Men and Women of the English Middle Class 1780–1860* (London, 1987).

Davies (1978). Alun C. Davies, 'The Life and Death of a Scientific Instrument: the Marine Chronometer, 1770–1920', *Annals of Science*, 35 (1978), 509–25.

Davis (1966). Dorothy Davis, *A History of Shopping* (London, 1966).

Davis (1973). Ralph Davis, *The Rise of the Atlantic Economies* (London, 1973).

Davis and Dreyfuss (1986). Audrey B. Davis and Mark S. Dreyfuss, *The Finest Instruments Ever Made: A Bibliography of Medical, Dental, Optical and Pharmaceutical Company Trade Literature 1700–1939* (Arlington, MA, 1986).

Dawes (1996). H.A.L. Dawes, 'John Frederick Newman 1784–1860: "The ingenious instrument maker, Mr Newman of Lisle Str."', *Bulletin of the Scientific Instrument Society*, No. 50 (1996), 11–14.

Day (1984). Joan Day, 'The Continental Origins of Bristol Brass', *Industrial Archaeology Review*, 7 (1984), 32–56.

Deane and Cole (1967). P. Deane and W.A. Cole, *British Economic Growth, 1688–1959* (Cambridge, 1967).

De Clercq (1985). P.R. de Clercq (ed.), *Nineteenth-Century Scientific Instruments and Their Makers* (Amsterdam and Leiden, 1985).

De Clercq (1997). Peter de Clercq, *At the Sign of the Oriental Lamp: the Musschenbroek Workshop in Leiden 1660–1750* (Rotterdam, 1997).

De Clercq (2005a). Peter de Clercq, 'Second-hand Instruments in a W. & S. Jones Catalogue of 1795', *Bulletin of the Scientific Instrument Society*, No. 85 (2005), 38–9.

De Clercq (2005b). Peter de Clercq, 'Een Deense astronoom op bezoek in Nederland en Engeland. Het reisjournaal van Thomas Bugge uit 1777', in Remmelt Daalder, Frits Loomeijer and Diederick Wildeman (eds), *Koersvast: Vijf eeuwen navigatie op zee* (Zaltbommel, 2005), 74–84.

Defoe (1971). Daniel Defoe, *A Tour through the Whole Island of Great Britain* [first published 1724–26], Penguin edition (London, 1971).

Delehar (1989). Peter Delehar, 'Drawings by George Scharf', *Bulletin of the Scientific Instrument Society*, No. 23 (1989), 21–2.

Derry and Williams (1960). T.K. Derry and Trevor I. Williams, *A Short History of Technology* (Oxford, 1960).

Dickens (1970). Charles Dickens, *Dombey and Son* [first published 1848], Penguin edition (London, 1970).

Downing (1984). Hayden J. Downing, *Scientific Instrument Makers of Victorian London* (Victoria, Australia, 1984).

Dragoni et al. (1994). G. Dragoni, A. McConnell and G. L'E. Turner (eds), *Proceedings of the Eleventh International Scientific Instrument Symposium* (Bologna, 1994).

Dutton (1984). H.I. Dutton, *The Patent System and Inventions Activity during the Industrial Revolution 1750–1852* (Manchester, 1984).

Edney (1997). Matthew H. Edney, *Mapping an Empire: the Geographical Construction of British India, 1765–1843* (Chicago and London, 1997).

Elliott (2000). Paul Elliott, 'The Birth Place of Public Science in the English Provinces: Natural Philosophy at Derby', *Annals of Science*, 57 (2000), 61–100.

Emerson (2002). R.L. Emerson, 'The Scientific Interests of Archibald Campbell, 1st Earl of Ilay and 3rd Duke of Argyll, 1682–1761', *Annals of Science*, 59 (2002), 21–56.

Everitt (1979). Alan Everitt, 'Country, County and Town: Patterns of Regional Evolution in England', republished in Peter Borsay (ed.), *The Eighteenth Century Town: a Reader in English Urban History 1688–1820* (London, 1990), 83–115

Fairclough (1976–78). Oliver Fairclough, 'Joseph Finney of Liverpool', *Antiquarian Horology*, 10 (1976–78), 32–40; 294–307.

Field (1988). Field, J.V. 1988) 'What is Scientific about a Scientific Instrument?', *Nuncius: Annali dell'Istituto e Museo di Storia della Scienza*, 3 (1988), 3–26.

Fine and Leopold (1993). Ben Fine and Ellen Leopold, *The World of Consumption* (London, 1993).

Fisher (2001). Susanna Fisher, *The Makers of the Blueback Charts: a History of Imray Laurie Norie & Wilson Ltd* (St Ives, Cambridgeshire, 2001).

Fitzgerald (1896). W.G. Fitzgerald, 'Sir Howard Grubb, FRS, FRAS, etc. etc.', *Strand Magazine*, 7 (1896), 396–81.

Floud (1976). Roderick Floud, *The British Machine Tool Industry 1850–1914* (Cambridge 1976).

Floud (1997). Roderick Floud, *The People and the British Economy 1830–1914* (Oxford, 1997).

Ford (1985). B.J. Ford, *Single Lens: the Story of the Simple Microscope* (London, 1985).

Fournier (1996). Marian Fournier, *The Fabric of Life: Microscopy in the Seventeenth Century* (Baltimore, MD, 1996).

Fournier (2003). Marian Fournier, *Early Microscopes: a Descriptive Catalogue* (Leiden, 2003).

Fox (1993). Robert Fox, 'Collections and Research in the History of Science', in R.G.W. Anderson and G.L'E. Turner (eds), *An Apparatus of Instruments: the Role of the Scientific Instrument Commission* (London, 1993), 19–22.

Fox and Turner (1998). Robert Fox and Anthony Turner (eds), *Luxury Trades and Consumerism in* Ancien Régime *Paris: Studies in the History of the Skilled Workforce* (Aldershot, 1998).

Frängsmyr et al. (1990). T. Frängsmyr, J.L. Heilbron and R.E. Rider (eds), *The Quantifying Spirit in the Eighteenth Century* (Berkeley, CA, 1990).

Fraser (1990). David Fraser, 'Joseph Wright of Derby and the Lunar Society', in Judy Egerton (ed.), *Wright of Derby* (London, 1990), 15–24.

Froggatt (1991). Clive R. Froggatt, 'Sheffield Froggatts – The Opticians', *Froggatt Genealogy Research*, 9, No. 5 (Sept/Oct 1991), 22–3.

Gee (1992). Brian Gee, 'The Newtons of Chancery Lane and Fleet Street Revisited. Part I: A Question of Establishment', *Bulletin of the Scientific Instrument Society*, No. 35 (1992), 3–6.

Gee (1993). Brian Gee, 'The Newtons of Chancery Lane and Fleet Street Revisited. Part II: The Fleet Street Business and Other Genealogy', *Bulletin of the Scientific Instrument Society*, No. 36 (1993), 12–14.

Gee (1996). Brian Gee, 'John Newman: A Second Look', *Bulletin of the Scientific Instrument Society*, No. 51 (1996), 22–25.

Gee (1998a). Brian Gee, 'The Spectacle of Science and Engineering in the Metropolis Part I: E.M. Clarke and the Early West End Exhibitions', *Bulletin of the Scientific Instrument Society*, No. 58 (1998), 11–18.

Gee (1998b). Brian Gee, 'The Spectacle of Science and Engineering in the Metropolis Part II: E.M. Clarke and the Royal Panopticon of Science and Art', *Bulletin of the Scientific Instrument Society*, No. 59 (1998), 6–13.

Gee and Brock (1991). Brian Gee and William H. Brock, 'The Case of John Joseph Griffin, from Artisan-Instructor to Business-Leader', *Ambix*, 38 (1991), 29–62.

Glass (1997). I.S. Glass, *Victorian Telescope Makers: The Lives and Letters of Thomas and Howard Grubb* (Bristol and Philadelphia, 1997).

Glennie (1995). Paul Glennie, 'Consumption within Historical Studies', in Daniel Miller (ed.), *Acknowledging Consumption: a Review of New Studies* (London and New York, 1995), 164–203.

Golinski (1992). Jan Golinski, *Science as Public Culture: Chemistry and Enlightenment in Britain, 1760–1820* (Cambridge, 1992).

Goodison (1969). Nicholas Goodison, 'The Foreign Origins of Domestic Barometers', *Connoisseur*, 170 (1969), 76–83.

Goodison (1977). Nicholas Goodison, *English Barometers 1680–1860*, 2nd edition (Woodbridge, Suffolk, 1977).

Gordon (1869). M.M. Gordon, *The Home Life of Sir David Brewster* (Edinburgh, 1869).

Goss (1932). C.W.F. Goss, *The London Directories 1677–1855* (London, 1932).

Greenacre (1973). Francis Greenacre, *The Bristol School of Artists: Francis Danby and Painting in Bristol 1810–1840* (Bristol, 1973).

Greenhalgh (1988). Paul Greenhalgh, *Ephemeral Vistas: the Expositions Universelles, Great Exhibitions and World's Fairs, 1851–1939* (Manchester, 1988)

Gunther (1920–68). R.T. Gunther, *Early Science in Oxford*, 14 vols (Oxford, 1920–68).

Hackmann (1985). W.D. Hackmann, 'The Nineteenth-Century Trade in Natural Philosophy Instruments in Britain', in P.R. de Clercq (ed.), *Nineteenth-Century Scientific Instruments and Their Makers* (Amsterdam and Leiden, 1985), 53–92.

Hakluyt (1886). Richard Hakluyt, *The Principal Navigations, voyages, Traffiques and Discoveries of the English Nation*, 4 vols (Edinburgh, 1885–90), III.

Hall (1984). Marie Boas Hall, *All Scientists Now: the Royal Society in the Nineteenth Century* (Cambridge, 1984).

Hall (1991a). Elizabeth Hall et al., *Catalogue of Scientific Instruments from Burton Constable Hall* (n.p., n.d. [Hull, 1991]).

Hall (1991b). Ivan and Elizabeth Hall, *Burton Constable Hall* (Hull, 1991).

Hallam (1984). Douglas J. Hallam, *The First Hundred Years. A Short History of Rabone Chesterman Limited* (Birmingham, 1984).

Hallett (1979). Michael Hallett (ed.), *John Benjamin Dancer 1812–1887: Selected Documents and Essays* (Birmingham, 1979).

Hallett (1986). Michael Hallett, 'John Benjamin Dancer 1812–1887: A Perspective', *History of Photography*, 10 (1986), 237–55.

Hamilton (1967). Hamilton, H. (1967), *The English Brass and Copper Industries to 1800*, 2nd edition (London, 1967).

Hammond and Austin (1987). John Hammond and Jill Austin, *The Camera Lucida in Art and Science* (Bristol, 1987).

Hankins and Silverman (1995) . Thomas L. Hankins and Robert J. Silverman, *Instruments and the Imagination* (Princeton, NJ, 1995).

Harkness (2002). Deborah E. Harkness, '"Strange" Ideas and "English" Knowledge: Natural Science Exchange in Elizabethan London' in Pamela H. Smith and Paula Findlen (eds), *Merchants and Marvels: Commerce, Science and Art in Early Modern Europe* (New York and London, 2002), 137–60.

Harris (1964). J.R. Harris, *The Copper King: A Biography of Thomas Williams of Llanidan* (Liverpool, 1964).

Harris (1969). J.R. Harris (ed.), *Liverpool and Merseyside: Essays in the Economic Histories of the Port and its Hinterland* (London, 1969).

Harris (1976). J.R. Harris, 'Skills, Coal and British Industry in the Eighteenth Century', *History*, 61 (1976), 18–33.

Harris (1998). J.R. Harris, *Industrial Espionage and Technology Transfer: Britain and France in the Eighteenth Century* (Aldershot, 1998).

Harrison (1957). J.A. Harrison, 'Blind Henry Moyes, "An Excellent Lecturer in Philosophy"', *Annals of Science*, 13 (1957), 109–25.

Harrison (1971). Brian Harrison, *Drink and the Victorians* (London, 1971).

Hecht (1993). Hermann Hecht, *Pre-Cinema History: an Encyclopaedia and Annotated Bibliography of the Moving Image before 1896* (London, 1993).

Heal (1925). Ambrose Heal, *London Tradesmen's Cards of the XVIII Century: An Account of their Origin and Use* (London, 1925; reprinted, New York, 1968).

Hey (1972). David G. Hey, *The Rural Metalworkers of the Sheffield Region* (Leicester, 1972).

Hey (1991). David Hey, *The Fiery Blades of Hallamshire: Sheffield and Its Neighbourhood, 1660–1740* (Leicester, 1991).

Higton (2002). Hester Higton, *Sundials at Greenwich: a Catalogue of the Sundials, Nocturnals and Hororary Quadrants in the National Maritime Museum, Greenwich* (Oxford, 2002).

Hills (2002). R.L. Hills, *James Watt Volume I: His Time in Scotland 1736–1774* (Ashbourne, 2002).

Hind (1999). David J. Hind, 'Davis Derby – a History of Engineering', *Mining History*, 14 (1999), 1–8.

Hix (1996). John Hix, *The Glasshouse* (London, 1996).

Hogg (1856). Jabez Hogg, *The Microscope: its History, Construction and Applications*, 2nd edition (London, 1856).

Hogg (1858). Jabez Hogg, *The Microscope: its History, Construction and Applications*, 3rd edition (London, 1858).

Holbrook et al. (1992). Mary Holbrook, R.G.W. Anderson and D.J. Bryden, *Science Preserved: A Directory of Scientific Instruments in Collections in the United Kingdom and Eire* (London, 1992).

Holland (1993). Julian Holland, 'Relations between Scientific Instrument Manufacturers', *Bulletin of the Scientific Instrument Society*, No. 36 (1993), 15–16.

Honeyman and Goodman (1998). Katrina Honeyman and Jordan Goodman, 'Women's Work, Gender Conflict and Labour Markets in Europe 1500–1900' [first published in the *Economic History Review*, 44 (1991)], in Robert Shoemaker and Mary Vincent (eds), *Gender and History in Western Europe* (London, 1998), 353–76.

Hopkins (1989). Eric Hopkins, *Birmingham: the First Manufacturing Town in the World, 1760–1840* (London, 1989).

Hoppit (1990). J. Hoppit, 'Counting the Industrial Revolution', *Economic History Review*, 43 (1990), 173–93.

Howse (1975). Derek Howse, *Greenwich Observatory Volume 3: the Buildings and Instruments* (London, 1975).

Howse (1989). Derek Howse, 'Prices of Lalande's Astronomical Instruments in 1791', *Bulletin of the Scientific Instrument Society*, No. 21 (1989), 9–10.

Hudson (1992). Pat Hudson, *The Industrial Revolution* (London, 1992).

Hudson (1994). Pat Hudson, 'Financing Firms, 1700–1850', in Maurice W. Kirby and Mary B. Rose (eds), *Business Enterprise in Modern Britain from the Eighteenth to the Twentieth Century* (London and New York, 1994), 88–112.

Hudson and Luckhurst (1954). D. Hudson and K.W. Luckhurst, *The Royal Society of Arts 1754–1954* (London, 1954).

Impey and MacGregor (1983). Oliver Impey and Arthur MacGregor (eds), *The Origins of Museums: the Cabinet of Curiosities in Sixteenth- and Seventeenth-Century Europe* (Oxford, 1983 and London, 2001).

Inkster (1973). Ian Inkster, 'The Development of a Scientific Community in Sheffield 1790–1850: a Network of People and Interests', *Transactions of the Hunter Archaeological Society*, 10 (1973), 99–131.

Inkster (1976). Ian Inkster, 'Culture, Institutions and Urbanity: the Itinerant Science Lecturer in Sheffield 1790–1850', in Sidney Pollard and Colin Holmes (eds), *Essays in the Economic and Social History of South Yorkshire* (Barnsley, 1976), 218–32.

Inkster (1980). Ian Inkster, 'The Public Lecture as an Instrument for Science Education for Adults – the Case of Great Britain, c.1750–1850', *Paedagogica Historica*, 20 (1980), 80–107.

Inkster (1991). Ian Inkster, *Science and Technology in History: an Approach to Industrial Development* (London, 1991).

Inkster and Morrell (1983)

Ian Inkster and Jack Morrell (eds), *Metropolis and Province: Science in British Culture, 1780–1850* (London, 1983).

Insley (1995). Jane Insley, 'Making Mountains out of Molehills? George Everest and Henry Barrow, 1830–39', *Indian Journal of History of Science*, 30 (1995), 47–55.

Jackson (1992). R.V. Jackson, 'Rates of Industrial Growth during the Industrial Revolution', *Economic History Review*, 45 (1992), 1–23.

Jacyna (1997). S. Jacyna, 'John Hughes Bennett and the Origins of Medical Microscopy in Edinburgh: Lilliputian Wonders', in G.J. Piller (ed.), *John Hughes Bennett and the Discovery of Leukaemia: Proceedings of the Royal College of Physicians of Edinburgh Supplement No. 3*, 27 (1997), 12–21.

Jeremy (1977). David Jeremy, 'Damming the Flood: British Government Efforts to Check the Outflow of Technicians and Machinery, 1780–1843', *Business History Review*, 51 (1977), 1–34.

Jones and Taylor (1984). Michael Jones and Jean Taylor, *A Handlist of Trade Catalogues and Associated Literature in the Wellcome Museum of the History of Medicine* (London, 1984).

King (1955). Henry C. King, *The History of the Telescope* (London, 1955).

Kingzett (1998). Dick Kingzett, 'From a Dealer's Viewpoint', in Michael Foster (ed.), *Art Treasures of England: the Regional Collections* (London, 1998), 60–65.

Kusamitsu (1980). Toshio Kusamitsu, 'Great Exhibitions before 1851', *History Workshop*, 9 (1980), 70–89.

Kusamitsu (1985) Toshio Kusamitsu, 'Mechanics' Institutes and Working Class Culture: Exhibition Movements, 1830–1840s', in Ian Inkster (ed.), *The Steam Intellect Societies: Essays on Culture, Education and Industry circa 1820–1914* (Nottingham, 1985), 33–43.

Landes (1969). David S. Landes, *The Unbound Prometheus: Technological Change and Industrial Development in Western Europe from 1750 to the Present* (Cambridge, 1969).

Landes (1983). David S. Landes, *Revolution in Time: Clocks and the Making of the Modern World* (Cambridge, MA and London, 1983).

Landes (1993). David S. Landes, 'The Fable of the Dead Horse; or, The Industrial Revolution Revisited', in Joel Mokyr (ed.), *The British Industrial Revolution: An Economic Perspective* (Boulder, CO, and Oxford, 1993), 132–70.

Landes (1998). David S. Landes, *The Wealth and Poverty of Nations: Why Some Are So Rich and Some So Poor* (London, 1998).

Law (1971). R.J. Law, 'Henry Hindley of York 1701–1771: Part I', *Antiquarian Horology*, 7 (1971), 205–21 and 'Part II', ibid., 682–99.

Leader (1875). Robert Eador Leader (ed.), *Reminiscences of Old Sheffield, its Streets and its People* (Sheffield, 1875).

Leader (1905). Robert Eador Leader, *Sheffield in the Eighteenth Century* (Sheffield, 1905).

Logan (1989). Gerrard Logan, *John Benjamin Dancer FRAS 1812 to 1887: Microscopist, Optician, Instrument Maker, Inventor and Photographic Pioneer* ([Blackpool], 1989).

Loomes (1981). Brian Loomes, *The Early Clockmakers of Great Britain* (London, 1981).

Luther (1992). Frederic Luther, 'John Benjamin Dancer (1812–87): A Family History', *History of Photography*, 16 (1992), 123–34.

Macleod (1988). Christine Macleod, *Inventing the Industrial Revolution* (Cambridge, 1988).

Macleod (1998). Christine Macleod, 'James Watt, Heroic Invention and the Idea of the Industrial Revolution', in M. Berg and K. Bruland (eds), *Technological Revolutions in Europe: Historical Perspectives* (Cheltenham, 1998), 96–116.

McCann (1983). Alison McCann, 'A Private Laboratory at Petworth House, Sussex, in the late Eighteenth Century', *Annals of Science*, 40 (1983), 638–55.

McCloskey (1981). D. McCloskey, 'The Industrial Revolution, 1780–1860: a Survey', in R. Floud and D. McCloskey (eds), *The Economic History of Britain since 1700* (Cambridge, 1981), 103–27.

McConnell (1985). Anita McConnell, 'Nineteenth Century Geomagnetic Instruments and their Makers', in P.R. de Clercq (ed.), *Nineteenth-Century Scientific Instruments and Their Makers* (Amsterdam and Leiden, 1985), 29–52.

McConnell (1989). Anita McConnell, 'Aluminium and its Alloys for Scientific Instruments, 1855–1900', *Annals of Science*, 46 (1989), 611–620.

McConnell (1992). Anita McConnell, *Instrument Makers to the World: a History of Cooke, Troughton & Simms* (York, 1992).

McConnell (1993a). Anita McConnell, *R.B. Bate of the Poultry 1782–1847: the Life and Times of a Scientific Instrument Maker* (London, 1993).

McConnell (1993b). Anita McConnell, 'W. Harris & Co., London and Hamburg', *Bulletin of the Scientific Instrument Society*, No. 36 (1993), 16.

McConnell (1993c). Anita McConnell, 'Thomas Cooke's Order Book: Analysis of an Optical Business, 1856–1868', in R.G.W. Anderson, J.A. Bennett and W.F. Ryan (eds), *Making Instruments Count: Essays on Historical Scientific Instruments presented to Gerard L'Estrange Turner* (Aldershot, 1993), 431–42.

McConnell (1994a). Anita McConnell, 'Bankruptcy Proceedings against William Harris, Optician, of Cornhill, 1830', *Annals of Science*, 51 (1994), 273–79.

McConnell (1994b). Anita McConnell, 'From Craft Workshop to Big Business - the London Scientific Instrument Trade's Response to Increasing Demand', *London Journal*, 19 (1994), 36–53.

McConnell (1998). Anita McConnell, *King of the Clinicals: the Life and Times of J.J. Hicks (1837–1916)* (York, 1998).

McConnell (2004). McConnell, Anita (2004) 'Industrial Spies', *Oxford Dictionary of National Biography* (Oxford, 2004).

McConnell (forthcoming). Anita McConnell, *The Gentleman of Piccadilly: Jesse Ramsden* (forthcoming).

McKendrick (1960). Neil McKendrick, 'Josiah Wedgwood: an Eighteenth Century Entrepreneur in Salesmanship and Marketing Techniques', *Economic History Review*, 12 (1960), 408–33.

McKendrick (1982). Neil McKendrick, 'The Commercialization of Fashion', in Neil McKendrick, John Brewer and J.H. Plumb, *The Birth of a Consumer Society: the Commercialization of Eighteenth-century England* (London, 1982), 34–99.

Maddison (1963). F.R. Maddison, 'Early Astronomical and Mathematical Instruments: A Brief Survey of Sources and Modern Studies', *History of Science,* 2 (1963), 17–50.

Makepeace (1984). Chris E. Makepeace, *Science and Technology in Manchester: Two Hundred Years of the Lit. and Phil.* (Manchester, 1984).

Marriner (1980). Sheila Marriner, 'English Bankruptcy Records and Statistics before 1850', *Economic History Review*, 33 (1980), 351–66.

Marriner (1982). Sheila Marriner, *The Economic and Social Development of Merseyside* (London, 1982).

Marsden (2004). Jonathan Marsden, 'Patronage and Collecting', in Jane Roberts (ed.), *George III and Queen Charlotte: Patronage, Collecting and Court Taste* (London, 2004), 152–67; 287–302.

Mathias (1979). Peter Mathias, *The Transformation of England: Essays in the Economic and Social History of England in the Eighteenth Century* (London, 1979).

Mathias (1983). Peter Mathias, *The First Industrial Nation: an Economic History of Britain, 1700–1914*, 2nd edition (London, 1983).

Maurer (1998). Andreas Maurer, 'A Compendium of All Known William Herschel Telescopes', *Journal of the Antique Telescope Society*, 14 (1998), 4–15.

Mercer (1981). Vaudrey Mercer, *The Frodshams: the Story of a Family of Chronometer Makers* (London, 1981).

Millar (1969). Oliver Millar, *The Later Georgian Pictures in the Collection of Her Majesty the Queen* 2 vols (London, 1969).

Millburn (1976). John R. Millburn, *Benjamin Martin – Author, Instrument-Maker and 'Country Showman'* (Leiden, 1976).

Millburn (1986a). John R. Millburn, *Benjamin Martin: Supplement* (London, 1986).

Millburn (1986b). John R. Millburn, *Retailer of the Sciences: Benjamin Martin's Scientific Instrument Catalogues* (London, 1986).

Millburn (1986c). John R. Millburn, 'Essay Review [of Porter, 1985]: Trade in Scientific Instruments', *Annals of Science*, 43 (1986), 81–6.

Millburn (1988a). John R. Millburn, 'The Office of Ordnance and the Instrument Making Trade', *Annals of Science*, 45 (1988), 221–93.

Millburn (1988b). John R. Millburn, *Wheelwright of the Heavens: the Life and Work of James Ferguson FRS* (London, 1988).

Millburn (1989). John R. Millburn, 'British Archives for the History of Instruments', *Bulletin of the Scientific Instrument Society*, No. 21 (1989), 3–7.

Millburn (1991). John R. Millburn, 'Instrument Makers and the Royal Arms', *Bulletin of the Scientific Instrument Society*, No. 28 (1991), 2–7.

Millburn (1992a). John R. Millburn, 'John Rowley's Gunnery Instruments', *Bulletin of the Scientific Instrument Society*, No. 32 (1992), 4–6.

Millburn (1992d). John R. Millburn, 'The Bardin Family, Globe-makers in London, and their Associate, Gabriel Wright', *Der Globusfreund*, No. 40/41 (1992), 21–57.

Millburn (1995). John R. Millburn, 'William Deane and his Ordnance Bills', *Bulletin of the Scientific Instrument Society*, No. 45 (1995), 12–18.

Millburn (2000). John R. Millburn, *Adams of Fleet Street, Instrument Makers to King George III* (Aldershot, 2000).

Millburn and Rossaak (1993) . John R. Millburn and Tor E. Rossaak, 'Bardin Globes and Their Makers', *Bulletin of the Scientific Instrument Society*, No. 36 (1993), 20–21.

Mills (1990). Allan Mills, 'The Manufacture of Precision Brass Tubing', *Bulletin of the Scientific Instrument Society*, No. 27 (1990), 10–15.

Mitchell (1988). B.R. Mitchell, *British Historical Statistics* (Cambridge, 1988).

Mitchell (1995). David Mitchell (ed.), *Goldsmiths, Silversmiths and Bankers: Innovation and the Transfer of Skill 1550–1750* (Stroud, 1995).

Mokyr (1977). Joel Mokyr, 'Demand vs. Supply in the Industrial Revolution', *Journal of Economic History*, 37 (1977), 981–1008.

Mokyr (1990). Joel Mokyr, *The Lever of Riches: Technological Creativity and Economic Progress* (Oxford, 1990).

Mokyr (1993). Joel Mokyr, 'Editor's Introduction: The New Economic History and the Industrial Revolution', in Joel Mokyr (ed.), *The British Industrial Revolution: an Economic Perspective* (Boulder, CO, and Oxford, 1993), 1–131.

Mollan (1995). Charles Mollan, *Irish National Inventory of Historic Scientific Instruments* (Dublin, 1995).

Morrison-Low (1984). A.D. Morrison-Low, 'Brewster and Scientific Instruments', in A.D. Morrison-Low and J.R.R. Christie (eds), *'Martyr of Science': Sir David Brewster, 1781–1868* (Edinburgh, 1984), 58–65.

Morrison-Low (1990). A.D. Morrison-Low, 'Women in the Nineteenth-Century Scientific Instrument Trade', in Marina Benjamin (ed.), *Science and Sensibility: Gender and Scientific Enquiry, 1780–1945* (Oxford, 1990), 89–117.

Morrison-Low (1992). A.D. Morrison-Low, 'William Nicol FRSE c1771–1851: Lecturer, Scientist and Collector', *Book of the Old Edinburgh Club*, NS 2 (1992), 123–31.

Morrison-Low (1994a). A.D. Morrison-Low, 'The Road to Ruin? Bankruptcy and Some Legal Consequences for the Instrument Maker in 19th-century Britain', in G. Dragoni, G. L'E. Turner and A. McConnell (eds), *Proceedings of the Eleventh Scientific Instrument Symposium, Bologna, 1991* (Bologna, 1994), 53–9.

Morrison-Low (1994b). A.D. Morrison-Low, 'Proctor & Beilby, Part I: Early Scientific Instrument Making in the English Midlands', *Bulletin of the Scientific Instrument Society*, No. 41 (1994), 9–15; 'Proctor & Beilby, Part II: Proctor & Beilby's Sheffield', ibid., No. 42 (1994), 17–21.

Morrison-Low (1995a). A.D. Morrison-Low, 'Sold at Sotheby's: Sir John Findlay's Cabinet and the Scottish Antiquarian Tradition', *Journal of the History of Collections*, 7 (1995), 197–209.

Morrison-Low (1995b). A.D. Morrison-Low, 'The Role of the Subcontractor in the Manufacture of Precision Instruments in Provincial England during the Industrial Revolution', in I. Blanchard (ed.), *New Directions in Economic and Social History* (Avonbridge, 1995), 13–19.

Morrison-Low (1996). A.D. Morrison-Low, 'George Arstall and Scale-beam "Manufacture" in Early Nineteenth-century Liverpool', *Equilibrium* (1996) No. 2, 2003–14.

Morrison-Low (1997a). A.D. Morrison-Low, 'John Hughes Bennett: a Catalogue of Some Surviving Artefacts', *Proceedings of the Royal College of Physicians of Edinburgh*, 27 (1997), 183–93.

Morrison-Low (1997b). A.D. Morrison-Low, '"Spirit of Place": some geographical implications of the English provincial instrument trade, 1760–1850', *Bulletin of the Scientific Instrument Society*, No. 53 (1997), 19–24.

Morrison-Low (2002). A.D. Morrison-Low, '"Feasting my Eyes with the View of Fine Instruments": Scientific Instruments in Enlightenment Scotland, 1680–1820', in Charles W.J. Withers and Paul Wood (eds), *Science and Medicine in the Scottish Enlightenment* (East Linton, 2002), 17–53.

Morrison-Low and Simpson (1995). A.D. Morrison-Low and A.D.C. Simpson, 'A New Dimension: a Context for Photography before 1860', in Sara Stevenson (ed.), *Light from the Dark Room: a Celebration of Scottish Photography* (Edinburgh, 1995), 15–28.

Morrison-Low and Nuttall (2003). A.D. Morrison-Low and R.H. Nuttall, 'Hugh Miller in an Age of Microscopy', in Lester Boreley (ed.), *Celebrating the Life and Times of Hugh Miller: Scotland in the Early 19th Century* (Cromarty and Aberdeen, 2003), 214–26.

Morton and Wess (1993). A.Q. Morton and J.A. Wess, *Public and Private Science: the King George III Collection at the Science Museum* (London and Oxford, 1993).

Musson (1975). A.E. Musson, 'Continental Influences on the Industrial Revolution in Great Britain', in Barrie M. Ratcliffe (ed.), *Great Britain and Her World 1750–1914: Essays in Honour of W.O. Henderson* (Manchester, 1975), 71–85.

Musson (1978). A.E. Musson, *The Growth of British Industry* (London, 1978).

Musson and Robinson (1969). A.E. Musson and E. Robinson, *Science and Technology in the Industrial Revolution* (London, 1969).

Neve (1983). Michael Neve, 'Science in a Commercial City: Bristol 1820–60', in Jack Morrell and Ian Inkster (eds), *Metropolis and Culture: Science in British Culture, 1780–1850* (London, 1983), 177–204.

Norton (1950). J.E. Norton, *Guide to the National and Provincial Directories of England and Wales, excluding London, published before 1856* (London, 1950).

Nuttall (1976). R.H. Nuttall, 'Philip Carpenter and the "Microcosm" Exhibition', *Microscopy*, 33 (1976), 62–5.

Nuttall (1977). R.H. Nuttall, 'Andrew Pritchard, Optician and Microscope Maker', *The Microscope*, 25 (1977), 65–81.

Nuttall (1979). R.H. Nuttall, *Improving the Image: Microscopes from the Frank Collection 1800–1860* (Jersey, 1979).

Nuttall (1980). R.H. Nuttall, 'Microscopes for Manchester', *Chemistry in Britain*, 16 (1980), 132–136.

Nuttall (2004). R.H. Nuttall, '"An Outdoor Man": Charles Peach and the Luminosity of the Sea', *Microscopy*, 39 (2004), 783–91.

Nuttall (2004a). R.H. Nuttall, 'Dancer, John Benjamin', *Oxford Dictionary of National Biography* (Oxford, 2004).

Otto (1970). Ludwig Otto, 'Microscopes of Georges Oberhaeuser (1798–1868) from the Collection of the Optical Museum in Jena', *Supplement to the Jena Review* (1970), 1–8.

Pearson (1828). William Pearson, *Practical Astronomy* (London, 1828).

Pedersen (2001). K. M. Pedersen, 'Thomas Bugge's Journal of a Voyage through Germany, Holland and England, 1777', in Jesper Lützen (ed.), *Around Caspar Wessel and the Geometric Representation of Complex Numbers* (Copenhagen, 2001), 29–46.

Perkin (1969). Harold Perkin, *Origins of Modern English Society* (London, 1969).

Perkin (1990). Michael Perkin, 'Egerton Smith and the Early Nineteenth Century Book Trade in Liverpool', in *Spreading the Word: the Distribution Networks of Print* (Winchester, 1990), 151–64.

Phillips (1990). Patricia Phillips, *The Scientific Lady: a Social History of Woman's Scientific Interests 1520–1918* (London, 1990).

Pinchbeck (1981). Ivy Pinchbeck, *Women Workers and the Industrial Revolution 1750–1850*, 2nd edition (London, 1981).

Pipping (1977). Gunnar Pipping, *The Chamber of Physics* (Stockholm, 1977).

Pollard (1959). Sidney Pollard, *A History of Labour in Sheffield* (Liverpool, 1959).

Pollard (1992). Sidney Pollard, 'The Concept of the Industrial Revolution', in G. Dosi, R. Giannetti and P.A. Toninelli (eds), *Technology and Enterprise in a Historical Perspective* (Oxford, 1992), 29–62.

Pope (1997). Peter E. Pope, *The Many Landfalls of John Cabot* (Toronto, 1997).

Porter (2000). Roy Porter, *Enlightenment: Britain and the Creation of the Modern World* (London, 2000).

Porter et al. (1985). Roy Porter, Simon Schaffer, Jim Bennett and Olivia Brown, *Science and Profit in 18th-Century London* (Cambridge, 1985).

Raistrick (1950). Arthur Raistrick, *Quakers in Science and Industry* (Newton Abbott, 1968), first published 1950.

Randall (1996). Anthony G. Randall, 'The Timekeeper that Won the Longitude Prize', in William J.H. Andrewes (ed.), *The Quest for Longitude* (Cambridge, MA, 1996), 236–54.

Ritchie and David (1995). G.S. Ritchie and Andrew David, *The Admiralty Chart: British Naval Hydrography in the Nineteenth Century*, 2nd edition (Edinburgh, 1995).

Robinson (1963). E. Robinson, 'Eighteenth Century Commerce and Fashion: Matthew Boulton's Marketing Techniques', *Economic History Review*, 14 (1963), 39–60.

Rolt (1965). L.T.C. Rolt, *Tools for the Job: a Short History of Machine Tools* (London, 1965).

Ronan et al. (1993). Colin Ronan, G.L'E. Turner, Jon Darius, Joachim Rienitz, Derek Howse and S.D. Ringwood, 'Was there an Elizabethan Telescope?', *Bulletin of the Scientific Instrument Society*, 37 (1993), 2–10.

Ronchetti (1990). Barbara Ronchetti, 'The Earliest Italian Immigrants in Manchester', in Anthony Ria, *Italians in Manchester* (Aosta, 1990), 51–5.

Rose (1994). Mary B. Rose, 'The Family Firm in British Business, 1780–1914', in Maurice W. Kirby and Mary B. Rose (eds), *Business Enterprise in Modern Britain from the Eighteenth to the Twentieth Century* (London and New York, 1994), 61–87.

Rosenberg (1976). Nathan Rosenberg, *Perspectives on Technology* (Cambridge, 1976).

Rosenberg (1982). Nathan Rosenberg, *Inside the Black Box: Technology and Economics* (Cambridge, 1982).

Rosenberg (1994). Nathan Rosenberg, *Exploring the Black Box: Technology, Economics, and History* (Cambridge, 1994).

Rowlands (1975). M.B. Rowlands, *Masters and Men in the West Midland Metalware Trades before the Industrial Revolution* (Manchester, 1975).

Rubens (1955–59). A. Rubens, 'Portrait of Anglo-Jewry 1656–1836', *Transactions of the Jewish Historical Society of England,* 19 (1955–59), 13–52.

Ryan (1966). W.F. Ryan, 'John Russell, R.A., and Early Lunar Mapping', *Smithsonian Journal of History*, 1 (1966), 27–48.

Samuel (1977). Raphael Samuel, 'Workshop of the World: Steam Power and Hand Technology in Mid-Victorian Britain', *History Workshop*, 3 (1977), 6–72.

Schaaf (2004). Larry J. Schaaf, '"Do not burn my history": the Physical Evidence of W.H.F. Talbot's Creative Mind', in Bernard Finn (ed.), *Presenting Pictures* (London, 2004), 29–45.

Schechner (1982). Sara J. Schechner, 'John Prince and Early American Scientific Instrument Making', in Frederick S. Allis, and Philip C.F. Smith (eds), *Sibley's Heir: a Volume in Memory of Clifford Kenyon Shipton*, Publications of the Colonial Society of Massachusetts, No. 59 (Boston, MA, 1982), 431–503.

Schechner Genuth (1996). Sara Schechner Genuth, 'Tools for Teaching and Research: John Prince, the Deerfield Academy, and Educational Reform in the Early Republic', *Rittenhouse*, 10 (1996), 97–120.

Schofield (1963). Robert E. Schofield, *The Lunar Society of Birmingham: A Social History of Provincial Science and Industry in Eighteenth Century England* (Oxford, 1963).

Schwarz (1992). L.D. Schwarz, *London in the Age of Industrialisation: Entrepreneurs, Labour Force and Living Conditions, 1760–1850* (Cambridge, 1992).

Schweizer (1988). Karl W. Schweizer (ed.), *Lord Bute: Essays in Re-interpretation* (Leicester, 1988).

Setchell (1970a). J.R.M. Setchell, 'The Friendship of John Smeaton, F.R.S., with Henry Hindley, Instrument and Clockmaker of York and the Development of Equatorial Mounting Telescopes', *Notes and Records of the Royal Society of London*, 25 (1970), 79–86.

Setchell (1970b). J.R.M. Setchell, 'Further Information on the Telescopes of Hindley of York', *Notes and Records of the Royal Society of London*, 25 (1970), 189–92.

Setchell (1973). J.R.M. Setchell, 'Henry Hindley & Son, Clock and Instrument Makers and Engineers of York', *Yorkshire Philosophical Society Annual Report for the Year 1972* (York, 1973), 39–67.

Shapin (1996). Steven Shapin, *The Scientific Revolution* (Chicago, 1996).

Shapin and Schaffer (1985). Steven Shapin and Simon Schaffer, *Leviathan and the Air-Pump: Hobbes, Boyle, and the Experimental Life* (Princeton, 1985).

Shaw (1982). Gareth Shaw, 'British Directories as Sources in Historical Geography', *Historical Geography Research Series* No. 8 (April 1982).

Shaw and Tipper (1988). Gareth Shaw and Allison Tipper, *British Directories: A Bibliography and Guide to Directories published in England and Wales (1850–1950) and Scotland (1773–1950)* (Leicester, 1988).

Shoemaker and Vincent (1998). Robert Shoemaker and Mary Vincent (eds), *Gender & History in Western Europe* (London, 1998).

Simpson (1985). A.D.C. Simpson, 'Richard Reeves – the "English Campani" – and the Origins of the London Telescope-Making Tradition', *Vistas in Astronomy*, 28 (1985), 357–65.

Simpson (1993). A.D.C. Simpson, 'A Sub-contractor of W. & S. Jones Identified', *Bulletin of the Scientific Instrument Society*, No. 39 (1993), 23–27.

Simpson (1993a). A.D.C. Simpson, 'The Pendulum as the British Length Standard: a Nineteenth-century Legal Aberration', in R.G.W. Anderson, J.A. Bennett and

W.F. Ryan (eds), *Making Instruments Count: Essays on Historical Scientific Instruments presented to Gerard L'Estrange Turner* (Aldershot, 1993), 174–90.

Simpson (1995). A.D.C. Simpson, '"Le plus brilliant collection qui existe au monde": a Lost American Collection of the Nineteenth Century', *Journal of the History of Collections*, 7 (1995), 187–96.

Simpson (1996). A.D.C. Simpson, 'Talbot's Photometer: or, Developments before Photography', *Studies in Photography: 1996* (Edinburgh, 1996), 8–10.

Simpson and Connor (2004). A.D.C. Simpson and R.D. Connor, 'The Mass of the English Troy Pound in the Eighteenth Century', *Annals of Science*, 61 (2004), 321–49.

Skempton (1981). A.W. Skempton (ed.), *John Smeaton FRS* (London, 1981).

Smiles (1865). Samuel Smiles, *Lives of Boulton and Watt* (London, 1865).

Smiles (1878). Samuel Smiles, *Robert Dick, Baker of Thurso, Geologist and Botanist* (London, 1878).

Smiles (1884). Samuel Smiles, *Men of Invention and Industry* (London, 1884).

Smith (1977). Alan Smith, *A Catalogue of Tools for Watch- and Clockmakers by John Wyke of Liverpool* (Winterthur, DE, 1977).

Smith (1987). D.J. Smith, 'The Birth of Photography in Sheffield, 1840–1870', *Transactions of the Hunter Archaeological Society*, 14 (1987), 64–74.

Sorrenson (1995). Richard Sorrenson, 'The State's Demand for Accurate Astronomical and Navigational Instruments in Eighteenth Century Britain', in Ann Bermingham and John Brewer (eds), *The Consumption of Culture: Image, Object, Text* (London, 1995), 263–71.

Sorrenson (1999). Richard Sorrenson, 'George Graham, Visible Technician', *British Journal of the History of Science*, 32 (1999), 203–21.

Sorrenson (2001). Richard Sorrenson, 'Dollond & Son's Pursuit of Achromaticity, 1758–1789', *History of Science*, 39 (2001), 31–55.

Sponza (1988). Lucio Sponza, *Italian Immigrants in Nineteenth Century Britain: Realities and Images* (Leicester, 1988).

Stedman Jones (1976). Gareth Stedman Jones, *Outcast London: a Study in the Relationship between Classes in Victorian Society* (Harmondsworth, 1976).

Stewart (1992). Larry Stewart, *The Rise of Public Science: Rhetoric, Technology and Natural Philosophy in Newtonian Britain, 1660–1750* (Cambridge, 1992).

Stimson (1985). A.N. Stimson, 'Some Board of Longitude Instruments in the Nineteenth Century', in P.R. de Clercq (ed.), *Nineteenth-Century Scientific Instruments and Their Makers* (Leiden and Amsterdam, 1985), 93–115.

Stimson (1996). Alan Stimson, 'The Longitude Problem: the Navigator's Story', in William J.H. Andrewes (ed.), *The Quest for Longitude* (Cambridge, MA, 1996), 72–84.

Strong et al. (1977). Roy Strong et al., *The Victoria and Albert Museum Souvenir Guide* (London, 1977).

Surtees (1823). Robert Surtees, *History and Antiquities of the County Palatine of Durham*, vol. 3 (London, 1823).

Swannell (1959). F.C. Swannell, 'Alexander Mackenzie as Surveyor', *The Beaver: Magazine of the North*, 290 (1959), 20–25.

Tann (1970). Jennifer Tann, *The Development of the Factory* (London, 1970).

Tate and Gabb (1930). Francis G.H. Tate and George H. Gabb, *Alcoholometry. An Account of the British Method of Alcoholic Strength Determination* (London, 1930).

Taylor (1954). E.G.R. Taylor, *The Mathematical Practitioners of Tudor and Stuart England, 1485–1714* (Cambridge, 1954).

Taylor (1966). E.G.R. Taylor, *The Mathematical Practitioners of Hanoverian England, 1714–1840* (Cambridge, 1966; reprinted, Redondo Beach, CA, 1989).

Thomas (1997). Ann Thomas (ed.), *Beauty of Another Order: Photography in Science* (New Haven and London, 1997).

E.P. Thompson (1968). E.P. Thompson, *The Making of the English Working Class* (London, 1968).

Thompson (1968). F.M.L. Thompson, *Chartered Surveyors: the Growth of a Profession* (London, 1968).

Thompson (1988). F.M.L. Thompson, *The Rise of the Respectable Society: A Social History of Victorian Britain 1830–1900* (London, 1988).

Thoren (1990). V.E. Thoren, *The Lord of Uraniborg: a Biography of Tycho Brahe* (Cambridge, 1990).

Thorpe (1929). W.A. Thorpe, *A History of English and Irish Glass*, 2 vols (London, 1929).

Thykier (1990). Claus Thykier (ed.), *Dansk Astronomi gennem firehundrede ar* (Copenhagen, 1990).

Timmins (1998). Geoffrey Timmins, *Made in Lancashire: a History of Regional Industrialisation* (Manchester, 1998).

Torrens (2003). H.S. Torrens, 'Natural History in Eighteenth-century Museums in Britain', in R.G.W. Anderson (ed.), *Enlightening the British: Knowledge, Discovery and the Museum in the Eighteenth Century* (London, 2003), 81–9.

Treherne (1977). Alan Treherne, *The Massey Family: Clock, Watch, Chronometer and Nautical Instrument Makers* (Newcastle-under-Lyme, 1977).

Turner (1977). Anthony Turner, *Science and Music in Eighteenth Century Bath* (Bath, 1977).

Turner (1987). Anthony Turner, *Early Scientific Instruments: Europe 1400–1800* (London, 1987).

Turner (1989). A.J. Turner, *From Pleasure and Profit to Science and Security: Etienne Lenoir and the Transformation of Precision Instrument-making in France 1760–1830* (Cambridge, 1989).

Turner (1993). A.J. Turner, 'Interpreting the History of Scientific Instruments', in R.G.W. Anderson, J.A. Bennett and W.F. Ryan (eds), *Making Instruments Count: Essays on Historical Scientific Instruments presented to Gerard L'Estrange Turner* (Aldershot, 1993), 17–26.

Turner (1998). Anthony Turner, 'Mathematical Instrument-Making in Early Modern Paris', in Robert Fox and Anthony Turner (eds), *Luxury Trades and Consumerism in* Ancien Régime *Paris: Studies in the History of the Skilled Workforce* (Aldershot, 1998), 63–96.

Turner (2003). Anthony Turner, 'John Dee, Louvain and the Origins of English Instrument Making', in M. Beretta, P. Galluzzi and C. Triavico (eds), *Musa Musaei: Studies in Scientific Instruments in Honour of Mara Miniati* (Florence, 2003), 63–78.

Turner (1967). G.L'E. Turner, 'The Auction Sales of the Earl of Bute's Instruments, 1793', *Annals of Science*, 23 (1967), 213–42.

Turner (1969a). G.L'E. Turner, 'The History of Optical Instruments: A Brief Survey of Sources and Modern Studies', *History of Science*, 8 (1969), 53–93.

Turner (1969b). G.L'E. Turner, 'James Short FRS, and his Contribution to the Construction of Reflecting Telescopes', *Notes and Records of the Royal Society*, 24 (1969), 91–108.

Turner (1969c). G.L'E. Turner, 'Hugh Powell, Andrew Ross and James Smith: Makers of Microscopes', in J.D. North (ed.), *Mid-Nineteenth-Century Scientists* (Oxford, 1969), 104–38.

Turner (1979a). G.L'E. Turner, 'The London Trade in Scientific Instrument-Making in the Eighteenth Century', *Vistas in Astronomy*, 20 (1979), 173–82.

Turner (1979b). G.L'E. Turner, 'The Number Code on Reflecting Telescopes by Nairne & Blunt', *Journal for the History of Astronomy*, 10 (1979), 177–84.

Turner (1981). G.L'E. Turner, *Collecting Microscopes* (London, 1981).

Turner (1983a). G.L'E. Turner, *Nineteenth-Century Scientific Instruments* (London and Berkeley, California, 1983).

Turner (1983b). G.L'E. Turner, 'Scientific Instruments', in P. Corsi and P. Weindling (eds), *Information Sciences in the History of Science and Medicine* (London, 1983), 243–58.

Turner (2000). G. L'E. Turner, 'The Government and the English Optical Glass Industry, 1650–1850', *Annals of Science*, 57 (2000), 399–414.

Turner and Bryden (1997). G.L'E. Turner and D.J. Bryden, *A Classified Bibliography on the History of Scientific Instruments* (Oxford, 1997).

Uglow (2002). Jenny Uglow, *The Lunar Men: the Friends who made the Future* (London, 2002).

Uvarov et al. (1971). E.B. Uvarov, D.R. Chapman and Alan Isaacs, *The Penguin Dictionary of Science*, 4th edition (Harmondsworth, 1971).

Van Helden (1977). A. van Helden, 'The Invention of the Telescope', *Transactions of the American Philosophical Society*, 67 (1977), part 4.

Van Helden and Hankins (1994). Albert van Helden and Thomas L. Hankins (eds), *Instruments: Osiris second series*, 9 (1993).

Walker (1880). J.T. Walker (ed.), *General Report of the Operations of the Survey of India comprising the Great Trigonometrical, the Topographical and the Revenue Surveys under the Government of India during 1880–81* (Dehra Dun, 1880).

Walsh (1995). Claire Walsh, 'The Design of London Goldsmiths' Shops in the Early Eighteenth Century', in David Mitchell (ed.), *Goldsmiths, Silversmiths and Bankers: Innovation and the Transfer of Skill* (London, 1995), 96–111.

Walters (2002). Alice Walters, 'Importing Science in the Early Republic: Union College's "First Purchase" of Instruments and Books', *Rittenhouse*, 16 (2002), 85–107.

Warner (1990). D.J. Warner, 'What is a Scientific Instrument, When Did it Become One, and Why?', *British Journal for the History of Science*, 23 (1990), 83–93.

Warner (1991). D.J. Warner, 'American Hydrometers, 1753–1876', *Rittenhouse*, 5 (1991), 33–45.

Warner (1998a). Deborah Jean Warner, 'John Bird and the Origins of the Sextant', *Rittenhouse*, 12 (1998), 1–11.

Warner (1998b). Deborah Jean Warner, 'Telescopes for Land and Sea', *Rittenhouse*, 12 (1998), 33–54.

Warner (1998c). Deborah Jean Warner, 'Edward Nairne, Scientist and Instrument Maker', *Rittenhouse*, 12 (1998), 65–93.

Weatherill (1988). Lorna Weatherill, *Consumer Behaviour and Material Culture in Britain 1660–1760* (London, 1988).

Webster (1976). Mary Webster, *Johan Zoffany 1733–1810* (London, 1976).

Weiss (1982). Leonard Weiss, *Watch-making in England, 1760–1820* (London, 1982).

Werner (forthcoming). Alex Werner, 'Jonathan and Jeremiah Sisson, and London's Eighteenth-century Mathematical Instrument Trade', in Jan Parmentier (ed.), *Navigating the Northern Seas* (forthcoming).

Westall (1984). Oliver M. Westall, *The Historian and the Business of Insurance* (Manchester, 1984).

Wetton (1990–91). Jenny Wetton, 'Scientific Instrument Making in Manchester 1790–1870', *Memoirs and Proceedings of the Manchester Literary and Philosophical Society*, 130 (1990–91), 37–68.

Wetton (1991). Jenny Wetton, 'John Benjamin Dancer: Manchester Instrument Maker', *Bulletin of the Scientific Instrument Society*, No. 23 (1991), 4–8.

Wetton (1994). Jenny Wetton, 'Scientific Instrument Making in Manchester 1790–1870', in G. Dragoni, A. McConnell and G.L'E. Turner (eds), *Proceedings of the Eleventh International Scientific Instrument Symposium* (Bologna, 1994), 71–9.

Wetton (1996). Jenny Wetton, 'Scientific Instrument Making in Manchester 1870–1940. I: Setting the Scene', *Bulletin of the Scientific Instrument Society*, No. 51 (1996), 26–30.

Wetton (2004). Jenny Wetton, 'Casartelli, Joseph Lewis', in *Oxford Dictionary of National Biography* (Oxford, 2004).

Wheatland (1968). David P. Wheatland, *The Apparatus of Science at Harvard 1765–1800* (Cambridge, MA, 1968).

Williams (1985). Bill Williams, *The Making of Manchester Jewry* (Manchester, 1985).

Williams (1994). Mari Williams, *The Precision Makers: a History of the Instruments Industry in Britain and France, 1870–1939* (London, 1994).

Wilson (1995). Catherine Wilson, *The Invisible World: Early Modern Philosophy and the Invention of the Microscope* (Princeton, NJ, 1995).

Wilton (1989). Robert Wilton, *The Wiltons of Cornwall* (Chichester, 1989).

Wise (1995). M. Norton Wise (ed.), *The Values of Precision* (Princeton, 1995).

Wolfman (1995). Joseph Wolfman, 'Joseph Sewill & Co., Nautical Instrument Makers', *Liverpool Nautical Research Society*, 38 (1995), 89–93.

Wood (1913). Henry Trueman Wood, *A History of the Royal Society of Arts* (London, 1913).

Woodbury (1972). Robert S. Woodbury, *Studies in the History of Machine Tools: History of the Gear-Cutting Machine; History of the Grinding Machine; History of the Milling Machine; History of the Lathe to 1850* (Cambridge, MA, 1972).

Woolrich (1988). A.P. Woolrich, *Mechanical Arts & Merchandise: Industrial Espionage and Travellers' Accounts as a Source for Technical Historians* (Eindhoven, n.d. [1988]).

# Index